Instructor's Manual
with Test Item File and Video Guide

ESSENTIALS OF ORGANIZATIONAL BEHAVIOR

Eighth Edition

Stephen P. Robbins

Stephen Farner
Bellevue University

Patricia Buhler
Goldey-Beacom College

Upper Saddle River, New Jersey 07458

VP/Editorial Director: Jeff Shelstad
Acquisitions Editor: Michael Ablassmeir
Assistant Editor: Melissa Yu
Manager, Print Production: Christy Mahon
Production Editor & Buyer: Carol O'Rourke
Printer/Binder: Technical Communication Services

Pearson Prentice Hall™ is a trademark of Pearson Education, Inc.

10 9 8 7 6 5 4 3 2
ISBN 0-13-144572-3

Essentials of Organizational Behavior, 8/e
Stephen P. Robbins

Suggested Course Outlines

Course outlines for a 75-minute, 30-session class and a 200-minute, 12-session class are described below. The activities and discussion modules are suitable for lecturing, videos, or the Analyzing Your Organization module found at the end of each chapter. Lectures on the chapters are split because each chapter offers a lot of information, and it is important to allow for class discussion of the content after students have read each chapter.

Course Outline 1: 30 Class Meetings of 75–80 Minutes

Session	Course Outline
1	Introduction to Course/Analyzing Your Organization
2	Lecture Chapter 1
3	Lecture Chapter 2
4	Lecture Chapter 2
5	Chapter 2 Activities, Discussion, or Analyzing Your Organization
6	Lecture Chapter 3
7	Lecture Chapter 4
8	Chapter 3-4 Activities, Discussion, or Analyzing Your Organization
9	Exam 1
10	Lecture Chapter 5
11	Chapter 5 Activities, Discussion, or Analyzing Your Organization
12	Lecture Chapter 7
13	Chapter 7 Activities, Discussion, or Analyzing Your Organization
14	Group Dynamics & Teambuilding Exercises
15	Lecture Chapter 8
16	Chapter 8 Activities, Discussion, or Analyzing Your Organization
17	Lecture Chapter 9
18	Chapter 9 Activities, Discussion, or Analyzing Your Organization
19	Exam 2
20	Lecture Chapter 10
21	Chapter 11
22	Chapter's 10 & 11 Activities, Discussion, or Analyzing Your Organization
23	Lecture Chapter 12
24	Chapter 12 Activities, Discussion, or Analyzing Your Organization
25	Lecture Chapter 13
26	Lecture Chapter 14
27	Chapter's 13 & 14 Activities, Discussion, or Analyzing Your Organization
28	Lecture Chapter 15
29	Lecture Chapter 16
30	Exam 3

Course Outline 2: 12 Class Meetings of 200 Minutes

Session	Course Outline
1	Introduction to course
	Chapter 1
2	Chapter 2
	Chapter 3
3	Chapter 4
	Chapter 5
4	Chapter 6
5	Chapter 7
6	Exam 1
	Chapter 8
7	Chapter 9
8	Chapter 10
	Chapter 11
9	Chapter 12
	Chapter 13
10	Chapter 14
11	Chapter 15
12	Exam 2
	Chapter 16

CHAPTER 1 - INTRODUCTION TO ORGANIZATIONAL BEHAVIOR

CHAPTER OBJECTIVES
After reading this chapter students should be able to:
1. Define organizational behavior (OB).
2. Identify the primary behavioral disciplines contributing to OB.
3. Describe the three goals of OB.
4. List the major challenges and opportunities for managers to use OB concepts.
5. Describe how OB concepts can help make organizations more productive.
6. Discuss why work force diversity has become an important issue in management.
7. Explain how managers and organizations are responding to the problem of employee ethical dilemmas.
8. Discuss how knowledge of OB can help managers stimulate organizational innovation and change.

LECTURE OUTLINE
I. THE FIELD OF ORGANIZATIONAL BEHAVIOR
   A. Definition
      1. Organizational behavior is the systematic study of the actions and attitudes that people exhibit within organizations. (ppt 4)
      2. Key parts of the definition
         a) Systematic study (ppt 5)
            (1) The use of scientific evidence gathered under controlled conditions and measured and interpreted in a reasonably rigorous manner to attribute cause and effect. (ppt 6)
            (2) OB—its theories and conclusions—is based on a large number of systematically designed research studies.
         b) Systematic study of actions (or behaviors) and attitudes include three areas: productivity, absenteeism, and turnover. (ppt 7)
            (1) Managers clearly are concerned with the quantity and quality of output that each employee generates.
            (2) Absence and turnover—particularly excessively high rates—can adversely affect this output.
            (3) Organizational citizenship—discretionary behavior that is not part of an employee's formal job requirements but promotes effective organizational functioning—is a fourth type of behavior that has recently been found to be important in determining employee performance. (ppt 8-9)
            (4) Organizational behavior is also concerned with employee job satisfaction, which is an attitude. (ppt 10)
            (5) Job satisfaction is a concern for three reasons.
               (a) There may be a link between satisfaction and productivity.
               (b) Satisfaction appears to be negatively related to absenteeism and turnover.
               (c) It can be argued that managers have a humanistic responsibility to provide their employees with jobs that are challenging, intrinsically rewarding, and satisfying.
         c) Systematic study of people within an organization
            (1) OB is specifically concerned with work-related behavior.

(2) An organization is a consciously coordinated social unit, which comprises two or more people and functions on a relatively continuous basis to achieve a common goal or set of goals. (ppt 11)

(3) OB is characterized by formal roles that define and shape the behavior of its members.

B. Contributing Disciplines (ppt 12)

1. Organizational behavior is applied behavioral science.
   a) The predominant contributing disciplines are psychology, sociology, social psychology, anthropology, and political science.
   b) Psychology contributes mainly at the individual/micro level of analysis, whereas the latter disciplines contribute on the group/macro level of analysis.

2. Psychology is the science that seeks to measure, explain, and sometimes change the behavior of humans and other animals.
   a) Psychologists concern themselves with studying and attempting to understand individual behavior.
   b) Contributors are learning theorists, personality theorists, counseling psychologists, and, most important, industrial and organizational psychologists.
   c) Early industrial psychologists concerned themselves with problems of fatigue, boredom, and any other factor relevant to working conditions that could impede efficient work performance.
   d) More recently, their contributions have been expanded to include learning, perception, personality, emotions, training, leadership effectiveness, needs and motivational forces, job satisfaction, decision-making processes, performance appraisals, attitude measurement, employee-selection techniques, job design, and work stress.

3. Sociology studies people in relation to their fellow human beings.
   a) Greatest contribution has resulted from their study of group behavior in organizations, particularly formal and complex organizations.
   b) Areas of valuable input include group dynamics, design of work teams, organizational culture, formal organization theory and structure, bureaucracy, communications, status, power, conflict, and work/life balance.

4. Social psychology is an area within psychology, blending concepts from psychology and sociology.
   a) It focuses on the influence of people on one another.
   b) A major area of concern—change—how to implement it and how to reduce barriers to its acceptance.
   c) Areas of significant contributions are in measuring, understanding, and changing attitudes, communication patterns, the ways in which group activities can satisfy individual needs, and group decision-making processes.

5. Anthropology is the study of societies to learn about human beings and their activities.
   a) It includes human physical character, evolutionary history, geographic distribution, group relationships, and cultural history and practices.
   b) This has helped us understand differences in fundamental values, attitudes, and behavior between people in different countries and within organizations.

6. Political science, the study of the behavior of individuals and groups within a political environment, is frequently overlooked.

a) Specific topics of concern to political scientists include structuring of conflict, allocation of power, and how people manipulate power for individual self-interest.

II. GOALS OF ORGANIZATIONAL BEHAVIOR
    A. What three goals does OB seek (ppt 13)

    B. Explanation
        1. Seek to answer why an individual or a group of individuals did something.
        2. Explanation is the least important of the three goals, from a management perspective, because it occurs after the fact.

    C. Prediction
        1. The goal of prediction focuses on future events to determine what outcomes will result from a given action.
        2. There are various ways to implement a major change, so the manager is likely to assess employee responses to several change interventions. Such information can be used in making the decision as to which change effort to use.

    D. Control
        1. The most controversial goal is to control behavior because most of us live in democratic societies, which are built upon the concept of personal freedom.
        2. OB does offer technologies that facilitate the control of people.
            a) Whether those technologies should be used in organizations becomes an ethical question.

III. CHALLENGES AND OPPORTUNITIES FOR OB: A MANAGERIAL PERSPECTIVE
    A. The ability to explain, predict, and control organizational behavior has never been more important to managers because of changing workforce demographics; global competition which require flexibility, rapid change and innovation; and organizational commitment and loyalty changes. (ppt 14-15)

    B. Increased Foreign Assignments
        1. Organizations are no longer constrained by national borders, which means as a manager, you're increasingly likely to find yourself in a foreign assignment.

    C. Working with People from Different Cultures
        1. Globalization also means that you will be working with bosses, peers, and other employees that were raised in different cultures.

    D. Coping with Anti-Capitalism Backlash
        1. Capitalism's focus on efficiency and growth is not accepted worldwide.

    E. Overseeing Movement of Jobs to Countries with Low-Cost Labor
        1. Management is under pressure to keep labor costs down, yet moving jobs to lower labor cost countries also gets criticized.
        2. Workforce diversity means that organizations are becoming a more heterogeneous mix of people.
        3. Workforce diversity means that organizations are becoming more heterogeneous in terms of gender, race, and ethnicity.

      a) Encompasses anyone who varies from the norm. In addition to the more obvious groups—women, African Americans, Hispanic Americans, and Asian Americans—it also includes the physically disabled, homosexuals, and the elderly.

F. Embracing Diversity (ppt 16-17)
1. Traditional melting pot approach to differences in organizations assumed that people who were different would somehow automatically want to assimilate.
2. Now the challenge for organizations is to make themselves more accommodating to diverse groups.

G. Changing U.S. Demographics
1. Diverse groups were such a small percentage of the U.S. workforce.
    a) The bulk of the pre-1980s workforce was male Caucasians working full time to support a non-employed wife and school-aged children.
    b) Currently, 46.6 percent of the U.S. labor force are women. Minorities and immigrants make up 23 percent.
2. Workforce diversity has important implications for management practice.
    a) Managers need to recognize differences and respond to them.
        (1) Diversity, if positively managed, can increase creativity and innovation in organizations as well as improve decision making by providing different perspectives on problems.

H. Improving Quality and Productivity (ppt 18)
1. Managers are facing constant challenges to improve quality and productivity. To do this, they are implementing programs such as quality management and process reengineering, which require extensive employee involvement. (ppt 19-20)
    a) See Exhibit 1-3, What Is Total Quality Management?
2. Process reengineering asks managers to reconsider how work would be done and how would their organization be structured if they were to start over.

I. Improving People Skills (ppt 21-22)
1. People skills are critical to managerial effectiveness.
2. There are specific people skills that managers can use on the job.
    a) The text will raise this as you read.

J. Improving Customer Service
1. The majority of employees in developed countries work in service jobs, which requires substantial interaction with an organization's customers.
2. OB can contribute to performance by showing how employee attitudes and behavior are associated with customer satisfaction.

K. Empowering People
1. The reshaping of the relationship between managers and those they are supposedly responsible for managing.
    a) Decision-making is being pushed down to the operating level.
    b) Managers are allowing employees full control of their work.
    c) An increasing number of organizations are using self-managed teams.
2. Managers are empowering employees.
3. Managers are having to learn how to give up control, and employees are having to learn how to take responsibility for their work and make appropriate decisions.

L. Working in Networked Organizations
   1. Technology has allowed people to communicate and work together even though they may be thousands of miles apart.

M. Stimulating Innovation and Change
   1. Today's successful organizations must foster innovation and master the art of change or they will become candidates for extinction.
   2. Victory will go to those organizations that maintain their flexibility, continually improve their quality, and beat their competition to the marketplace with a constant stream of innovative products and services.
   3. The challenge for managers is to stimulate employee creativity and tolerance for change.
      a) The field of OB provides a wealth of ideas and techniques to aid in realizing these goals.

N. Coping with "Temporariness"
   1. Managers have always been concerned with change. What is different is the amount of time between change implementations.
   2. Today, change is an ongoing activity for most managers. The concept of continuous improvement, for instance, implies constant change.
   3. Managing used to be characterized by long periods of stability interrupted occasionally by short periods of change.
      a) That is reversed today.
   4. Managers and employees face a world of permanent "temporariness."
      a) Workers need to continually update their knowledge and skills to perform new job requirements.
      b) Work groups are also increasingly in a state of flux. In the past employees were assigned to a specific department, and that assignment was relatively permanent.
      c) Organizations themselves are in a state of flux. They continually reorganize their various divisions, sell off poorly performing businesses, downsize operations, and replace permanent employees with temporaries.
   5. Today's managers and employees must learn to learn to live with flexibility, spontaneity, and unpredictability.

I. Helping Employees Balance Work/Life Conflicts
   1. The typical employee no longer shows up Monday through Friday for an eight- or nine-hour shift.
   2. A number of forces have contributed to the blurring of the line between work and nonwork time, thus, creating personal conflicts and stress.
      a) The creation of global organizations means the work world never sleeps.
      b) Communication technology allows employees to do their work anywhere—at home, in their car, or on the beach.
      c) Organizations are asking employees to put in longer hours.
      d) Few families have only a single breadwinner.
   3. Employees are not happy about work squeezing out personal lives.
   4. Organizations that do not help their people achieve work/life balance will find it increasingly hard to attach and retain employees.

J. Declining Employee Loyalty

1. Corporate employees used to believe that their employers would reward loyalty and good work with job security, generous benefits, and steady pay increases.
2. That changed beginning in the mid-1980s as corporations sought to become "lean and mean" by closing factories, moving operations to lower-cost countries, selling off or closing down less-profitable businesses, eliminating entire levels of management, replacing permanent employees with temporaries, and substituting performance-based pay systems for seniority-based programs.
3. European companies are also doing this.
4. These changes have resulted in a sharp decline in employee loyalty.

K. Improving Ethical Behavior
1. In today's organizational world it is not surprising that many employees feel pressured to cut corners, break rules, and engage in other forms of questionable practices.
2. Members of organizations are increasingly finding themselves facing ethical dilemmas, situations in which they are required to define right and wrong conduct.
3. Good ethical behavior has never been clearly defined.
   a) In recent years the line differentiating right from wrong has become even more blurred.
   b) All around them employees see people—elected officials, successful executives, and employees in other companies—engaging in unethical practices.
4. There are a variety of responses to this problem.
   a) Write and distribute codes of ethics to guide employees through ethical dilemmas.
   b) Offer seminars, workshops, and similar training programs to try to improve ethical behaviors.
   c) Provide in-house advisors, who can be contacted, in many cases anonymously, for assistance in dealing with ethical issues.
   d) Create protection mechanisms for employees who reveal internal unethical practices.
5. Today's manager needs to create an ethically healthful climate in which his or her employees can do their work productively and confront a minimal degree of ambiguity regarding what constitutes right and wrong behaviors.

IV. THE PLAN OF THIS BOOK
A. The book uses a building block approach. (ppt 23)
1. See Exhibit 1-4.
2. Chapters 2 through 6 deal with the individual in the organization.
   a) The foundations of individual behavior—values, attitudes, perception, and learning.
   b) The role of personality and emotions in individual behavior.
   c) Conclude with motivation issues and individual decision making.
3. Chapters 7 through 12 address group behavior.
   a) Introduce a group behavior model.
   b) Discuss ways to make teams more effective.
   c) Consider communication issues and group decision-making.
   d) Investigate leadership and the issues of trust, power, politics, and conflict and negotiation.

4. Organizational behavior reaches its highest level of sophistication when we add the formal organization system to our knowledge of individual and group behavior. Chapters 13 through 16, discuss:
    a) How an organization's structure, work design, and technology affect behavior.
    b) The effect that an organization's human resource policies and practices have on people.
    c) How each organization has its own culture that acts to shape the behavior of its members.
    d) The various organizational change and development techniques that managers can use to affect behavior for the organization's benefit.

SUMMARY (ppt 24-25)

1. Organizational behavior (OB) is the systematic study of the actions and attitudes that people exhibit within organizations.
2. Organizational behavior is applied behavioral science. The predominant contributing disciplines are psychology, sociology, social psychology, anthropology, and political science.
3. The three primary goals of OB are to explain why an individual or a group of individuals do something; to predict future events—to determine what outcomes will result from a given action; and to control behavior, the most controversial goal of the three. OB does offer technologies that facilitate the control of people. Whether those technologies should be used in organizations becomes an ethical question.
4. The major challenges and opportunities for managers to use OB concepts occur in the areas of customer service, improving quality and productivity through the use of quality management, reengineering and other techniques; improving people skills; managing workforce diversity—a key challenge since organizations are becoming more heterogeneous in terms of gender, race, and ethnicity; responding to globalization; empowering people by the reshaping of the relationship between managers and those they're supposedly responsible for managing; stimulating innovation and change; coping with temporariness as the workforce becomes more part time and contingency based; dealing with declining employee loyalty; and improving ethical behavior.
5. The plan of the book is built on a building-block approach. Chapters 2 through 6 deal with the individual in the organization. Chapters 7 through 12 address group behavior. Chapters 13 through 16, discuss how an organization's structure, work design, and technology affect behavior, the effect that an organization's human resource management policies and practices have on people, how each organization has its own culture that acts to shape the behavior of its members, and the various organizational change and development techniques that managers can use to affect behavior for the organization's benefit.

DISCUSSION QUESTIONS

1. Define organizational behavior (OB).
    Answer - Organizational behavior is the systematic study of the actions and attitudes that people exhibit within organizations. There are three key parts. Systematic study is the use of scientific evidence gathered under controlled conditions and measured and interpreted in a reasonably rigorous manner to attribute cause and effect. Systematic study of actions (or behaviors) and attitudes occurs in three areas: productivity, absenteeism, and turnover. Systematic study within an organization—OB is specifically concerned with work-related behavior—and that takes place in organizations. A fourth type of behavior, organizational citizenship, has been added as a determiner of organizational effectiveness.

2. Identify the primary behavioral disciplines contributing to OB.
    Answer - Organizational behavior is applied behavioral science. Psychology is the science that seeks to measure, explain, and sometimes change the behavior of humans and other animals. Sociology studies people in relation to their fellow human beings. Greatest contribution was through their study of group behavior in organizations, particularly formal and complex organizations. Social Psychology is an area within psychology, blending concepts from psychology and sociology. It focuses on the influence of people on one another. Anthropology is the study of societies to learn about human beings and their activities. This has helped us understand differences in fundamental values, attitudes, and behavior between people in different countries and within organizations. Political science, the study of the behavior of individuals and groups within a political environment, is frequently overlooked.

3. Describe the three goals of OB.
    Answer – Explanation, which seeks to answer why an individual or a group of individuals did something. It is the least important of the three goals, from a management perspective, because it occurs after the fact. Prediction focuses on future events to determine what outcomes will result from a given action. Control is the most controversial goal because most of us live in democratic societies, which are built upon the concept of personal freedom. OB does offer technologies that facilitate the control of people. Whether those technologies should be used in organizations becomes an ethical question.

4. List the major challenges and opportunities for managers to use OB concepts.
    Answer - Improving quality, customer service, and productivity through the use of quality management, reengineering and other techniques; improving people skills; managing workforce diversity—a key challenge since organizations are becoming more heterogeneous in terms of gender, race, and ethnicity; responding to globalization; empowering people by the reshaping of the relationship between managers and those they are supposedly responsible for managing; stimulating innovation and change; coping with temporariness as the workforce becomes more part time and contingency based; dealing with declining employee loyalty; and improving ethical behavior.

5. Explain the key elements in quality management.
    Answer - See Exhibit 1-3, What Is Quality Management?

6. Discuss why workforce diversity has become an important issue in management.
    Answer - Workforce diversity means that organizations are becoming more heterogeneous in terms of gender, race, and ethnicity. It encompasses anyone who varies from the norm. In addition to the more obvious groups—women, African Americans, Hispanic Americans, and Asian Americans—it also includes the physically disabled, the elderly, and so on. Traditional melting pot approach to differences in organizations assumed that people who were different would somehow automatically want to assimilate. Traditionally, diverse groups were such a small percentage of the U.S. workforce. Currently, 46 percent of the U.S. labor force are women. Minorities and immigrants make up 23 percent.

7. Discuss two ways in which globalization affects a manager's people skills.
    Answer – First, a manager will likely find himself in a foreign assignment in which he will be managing a workforce, which is likely to be very different in needs, aspirations, and attitudes from the ones "back home." Second, even in their own countries, managers could likely find themselves working with bosses, peers, and employees who were born and raised in different cultures.

8. A number of forces have contributed to blurring the lines between employees' work and personal lives. Discuss four of these forces.
    Answer – First, the creation of global organizations means the work world never sleeps. Second, communication technology allows employees to do their work anywhere—at home, in their cars, on the beach. Third, organizations are asking employees to put in longer hours. Fourth, few families have only a single breadwinner, requiring married employees to find the time to fulfill commitments to home, spouse, children, parents, and friends.

9. Explain how managers and organizations are responding to the problem of employee ethical dilemmas.
    Answer – Managers and organizations write and distribute codes of ethics to guide employees through ethical dilemmas. They offer seminars, workshops, and similar training programs to try to improve ethical behaviors and provide in-house advisors, who can be contacted, in many cases anonymously, for assistance in dealing with ethical issues. They create protection mechanisms for employees who reveal internal unethical practices. Today's managers need to create an ethically healthful climate in which their employees can do their work productively and confront a minimal degree of ambiguity regarding what constitutes right and wrong behaviors.

EXERCISES

A. Have students introduce themselves by giving their name, and any other information you deem appropriate, and by offering one short one- to three-minute story about an experience they had with an organization. Give students several minutes to think about their story, keep time, and stop students who go too long. Use the stories to introduce the importance of OB to them.

B. Divide the class into groups of three to five students each. Have each group identify a current news story from the popular press such as newscasts, newspapers, journals, and so on, which involve management and/or organizational behavior. These stories/situations can be local, domestic, or international. Give the groups several minutes to discuss the story details, and have each group evaluate how the current managers handled the situation. Then have each group orally provide a brief (three to four minute) critique of the current managers' response. Suggested topics might be a current business merger, the implementation of the euro, a local plant closing or relocation, an article or story about a diversity issue or work/family balance.

C. Divide the class into groups of three, and have them discuss their experiences with managers. They may discuss items such as their last performance appraisal, a job interview, or a customer service issue. Use this as a starting point to discuss the importance of "people" in an organizational context.

D. If you have older adult students, have them share their experiences regarding how the workplace used to look. Examine such issues as the demographic make-up of the organization, and the attitudes of workers towards management. Emphasize how new the field of OB is, based upon these anecdotes.

Analyzing Your Organization (additional exercise not in the textbook)

The end of each chapter will have a hands-on activity in which students will apply the material to the organization in which they work. If they don't currently work, they could pick an organization to use as a model, such as their local grocer. You also could adapt this assignment to an organization that they research in the library or on the web, although it will lose its "real world" feel. The point is to take the theories and concepts and apply them to real organizations.

There are a number of ways you can use this in your class. For example, it could serve as homework to be turned in each week, or a project to be built upon each week and turned in at the end of the class as a term paper/project. You could also use the exercise as a class discussion item, selecting students to do short discussion starter presentations several times per term. Still another use is to have them summarize their findings in small groups, and have each group report a summary to the class.

Most of these activities will involve interviewing someone who has knowledge of the topic. For example, when covering the human resource issues in chapter 15, they will most likely want to discuss the assignment with someone in HR.

Use the questions provided as a guideline, but be sure to adapt them to the student's needs. I would also suggest that the student's get approval from their manager or supervisor early on in the semester. Because we are dealing with "people issues" all semester they should detail the project to the relevant parties early on.

For the first assignment, have them take this course syllabus and a description of the project to their supervisor. This will allow the supervisor to see the scope of topics discussed, and possibly spark some ideas for conversation points in the future. In week 2 of the course, have the student's briefly describe their chosen organization, discussing what goods or services they produce, how many employees it has, what the structure looks like, and a general overview of how the organization is managed.

CHAPTER 2 - FOUNDATIONS OF INDIVIDUAL BEHAVIOR

CHAPTER OBJECTIVES
After reading this chapter, students should be able to:
1. List the dominant values in today's workforce.
2. Describe the relationship between satisfaction and productivity.
3. Explain the theory of cognitive dissonance.
4. Summarize the relationship between attitudes and behavior.
5. Explain how two people can see the same thing and interpret it differently.
6. Summarize attribution theory.
7. Outline the learning process.

LECTURE OUTLINE
I. VALUES
   A. Introduction (ppt 4)
   B. Values represent basic convictions that a specific mode of conduct or end-state of existence is personally or socially preferable to an opposite or converse mode of conduct or end-state of existence (ppt 5).
      1. Value systems contain a moral flavor in that they carry an individual's ideas as to what is right, good, or desirable.
   C. Value systems represent a prioritizing of individual values (ppt 6).
      1. Values are identified by the relative importance an individual assigns to them, such as freedom, pleasure, self-respect, honesty, obedience, and equality.

   D. Types of Values
      1. Rokeach Value Survey (ppt 7)
         a) Milton Rokeach created the Rokeach Value Survey.
         b) The RVS consists of two sets of values, with each set containing eighteen individual value items.
         c) One set, terminal values, refers to desirable end-states of existence. These are the goals that a person would like to achieve during his or her lifetime. (ppt 8)
         d) The other set, instrumental values, refers to preferable modes of behavior or means of achieving the terminal value. (ppt 9)
           (1) Exhibit 2-1 gives common examples for each of these sets.
         e) RVS values vary among groups.
           (1) People in the same occupations or categories (e.g., corporate managers, union members, parents, and students) tend to hold similar values. (ppt 10)
      2. Contemporary Work Cohorts (ppt 11)
         a) A four-group model that attempts to capture the unique values of different cohorts or generations in the U.S. workforce.
           (1) Exhibit 2-2 proposes that employees can be segmented by the era in which they entered the workforce.
           (2) Because most people start work between the ages of 18 and 23, the eras also correlate closely with the chronological age of employees.
         b) "Veterans" are workers who grew up influenced by the Great Depression, and so on, who entered the workforce from the through the 1950s and early 1960s. (ppt 12)
           (1) They believe in hard work, the status quo, and authority figures.

          (2) Once hired, they tend to be loyal to their employer.

          (3) They are likely to place the greatest importance on a comfortable life and family security.

    c) "Boomers" entered the workforce during the mid-1960s through the mid-1980s and were influenced heavily by the civil rights movement, the Beatles, the Vietnam War, and baby-boom competition. (ppt 13)

          (1) They brought with them the "hippie ethic" and distrust of authority.

          (2) They place a great deal of emphasis on achievements and material success, believing that ends can justify means.

          (3) A desire for autonomy, directs their loyalty toward themselves, and a view that organizations that employ them are merely vehicles for their careers.

          (4) Terminal values such as a sense of accomplishment and social recognition rank high with Boomers.

    d) Generation X—"Xers"—have been shaped by globalization, two-career parents, MTV, AIDS, and computers (ppt 14):

          (1) They value flexibility, life options, and job satisfaction.

          (2) Family and relationships are very important to this cohort.

          (3) Team-oriented work is important.

          (4) Money is important as an indicator of career performance.

          (5) They are willing to trade off salary increases, titles, security, and promotions for increased leisure time and expanded lifestyle options.

          (6) On the RVS, they rate high on friendship, happiness, and pleasure.

    e) The most recent entrants to the workforce, the "Nexters" have grown up during prosperous times, and tend to be optimistic about the economy (ppt 15):

          (1) They tend to believe in themselves and be confident about their ability to succeed.

          (2) They are at ease with diversity and are the first generation to take technology for granted.

          (3) Nexters are very money-oriented and desirous of the things that money can buy, seeking financial success.

          (4) Teamwork is enjoyed but self-reliance is important.

          (5) Terminal values such as freedom and a comfortable life rank high with Nexters.

  3. An understanding that individuals' values differ but tend to reflect the societal values of the period in which they grew up can be a valuable aid in explaining and predicting behavior.

E. Values, Loyalty, and Ethical Behavior (ppt 16)

  1. If ethical standards have fallen, perhaps we should look to our four-stage model of work cohort values for a possible explanation.

    a) See Exhibit 2-2.

  2. Through the mid-1970s, the managerial ranks were dominated by Veterans whose loyalties were to their employer. When faced with ethical dilemmas, their decisions were made in terms of what was best for their organization.

  3. Beginning in the mid-to-late 1970s, Boomers began to rise into the upper levels of management. They were soon followed by pragmatic types.

  4. By the early 1990s, a large portion of middle and top management positions in business organizations were held by Boomers.

a) The loyalty of Boomers is to their careers. Their focus is inward, and their primary concern is with looking out for number one.

b) Such self-centered values would be consistent with a decline in ethical standards.

5. The potential good news in this analysis is that Xers are now in the process of moving into middle-management slots and soon will be rising into top management.

6. Since their loyalty is to relationships, they are more likely to consider the ethical implications of their actions on others around them.

7. We might look forward to higher ethical standards in business over the next decade or two merely as a result of changing values within the managerial ranks.

F. Values Across Cultures
1. Hofstede's Framework for Assessing Cultures (ppt 17)
   a) A widely referenced approach for analyzing variations among cultures has been done by Geert Hofstede.
      (1) He found that managers and employees vary on the following five value dimensions of national culture:
   b) Power distance
      (1) The degree to which people in a country accept that power in institutions and organizations is distributed unequally.
   c) Individualism vs. collectivism
      (1) Individualism is the degree to which people in a country prefer to act as individuals rather than as members of groups.
      (2) Collectivism is the opposite or the equivalent of low individualism.
   d) Quantity of life vs. quality of life
      (1) Quantity of life is the degree to which values like assertiveness, the acquisition of money and material goods, and competition prevail.
      (2) Quality of life is the degree to which people value relationships and show sensitivity and concern for the welfare of others.
   e) Uncertainty avoidance
      (1) The degree to which people in a country prefer structured over unstructured situations.
      (2) In countries that score high on uncertainty avoidance, people have an increased level of anxiety that manifests itself in great nervousness, stress, and aggressiveness.
   f) Long-term vs. short-term orientation
      (1) People in long-term orientation countries look to the future and value thrift and persistence.
      (2) A short-term orientation values the past and present and emphasizes respect for tradition and social obligations.
2. The Globe Framework for Assessing Cultures (ppt 18)
   a) The GLOBE team identified nine dimensions on which national cultures differ. This extends the work of Hofstede.
   b) Assertiveness- The extent to which a society encourages people to be tough and assertive.
   c) Future orientation- The extent to which a society rewards future oriented behaviors such as planning and investing.
   d) Gender differentiation- The extent to which a society maximizes gender role differences.
   e) Uncertainty avoidance- Same as Hofstede's definition

                f) Power distance- Same as Hofstede's definition

                g) Individualism/Collectivism- Same as Hofstede's definition

                h) In-group collectivism- The extent t which members of a society take pride in membership in small groups, such as family.

                i) Performance orientation- The degree to which a society rewards group members for performance improvement.

       3. Implications for OB

           a) Most of the concepts that currently make up OB have been developed by Americans using American subjects within domestic contexts.

                (1) Therefore not all OB theories and concepts are universally applicable to managing people around the world.

II. ATTITUDES

    A. Introduction (ppt 19)

       1. Attitudes are evaluative statements—either favorable or unfavorable—concerning objects, people, or events.

       2. They reflect how one feels about something.

       3. OB focuses on a very limited number of job-related attitudes—job satisfaction, job involvement (the degree to which a person identifies with his or her job and actively participates in it), and organizational commitment (an indicator of loyalty to, and identification with, the organization). (ppt 21)

           a) Job satisfaction has received the bulk of attention.

    B. Job Satisfaction

       1. Job satisfaction refers to an individual's general attitude toward his or her job.

           a) A person with a high level of job satisfaction holds positive attitudes toward the job.

           b) A person who is dissatisfied with his or her job holds negative attitudes about that job and has a low level of satisfaction.

       2. What Determines Job Satisfaction? (ppt 22)

           a) The most important factors conducive to job satisfaction are mentally challenging work, equitable rewards, supportive working conditions and supportive colleagues.

           b) Employees tend to prefer jobs that give them opportunities to use their skills and abilities and that offer a variety of tasks, freedom, and feedback on how well they are doing.

           c) Employees want pay systems and promotion policies that they perceive as just, unambiguous, and in line with their expectations.

           d) Employees are concerned with their work environment for both personal comfort and job facilitation.

                (1) They prefer physical surroundings that are safe, comfortable, clean, and have a minimum degree of distractions.

           e) For most employees, work also fills the need for social interaction; therefore, friendly and supportive co-workers lead to increased job satisfaction.

       3. Satisfaction and Productivity (ppt 23)

           a) This topic has attracted a lot of attention and interest.

           b) The early views were "a happy worker is a productive worker."

           c) A more careful analysis indicates that if satisfaction does have a positive effect on productivity, that effect is fairly small.

                (1) The introduction of moderating variables, however, has improved the relationship.

d)   Currently, on the basis of a comprehensive review of the evidence, it appears that productivity is more likely to lead to satisfaction rather than the other way around.

4.   Satisfaction and Organizational Citizenship Behavior (OCB) (ppt 24)

a)   Early discussions of OCB assumed that it was closely linked with satisfaction.

b)   More recent evidence, however, suggests that satisfaction influences OCB, but through perceptions of fairness.

c)   There is a modest overall relationship between job satisfaction and OCB; satisfaction is unrelated to OCB when fairness is controlled for.

d)   Job satisfaction comes down to conceptions of fair outcomes, treatment, and procedures.

(1)   If employees perceive organizational processes and outcomes to be fair, trust develops.

(2)   When employees trust the employer, they are more willing to voluntarily engage in behaviors that go beyond formal job requirements.

C.   Reducing Dissonance (ppt 25)

1.   Cognitive dissonance occurs when there are inconsistencies between two or more of a person's attitudes or between a person's behavior and attitudes.

a)   The theory of cognitive dissonance suggests that people seek to minimize dissonance and the discomfort it causes.

2.   A person's desire to reduce dissonance is determined by the importance of the elements creating the dissonance, the degree of influence the individual believes he or she has over the elements, and the rewards that may be involved in dissonance.

a)   If the elements creating the dissonance are relatively unimportant, the pressure to correct this imbalance will be low.

b)   The degree of influence that individuals believe they have over the elements involved will have an impact on how they will react to the dissonance.

c)   If they perceive the dissonance to be an uncontrollable result—something that they can't change—they are not likely to be receptive to attitude change.

3.   Rewards also influence the degree to which individuals are motivated to reduce dissonance.

a)   The tension inherent in high dissonance may be reduced if accompanied by a high reward.

4.   Organizational Implications

a)   It can help to predict the propensity to engage in both attitudinal and behavioral change.

b)   The greater the dissonance—after it has been moderated by importance, choice, and reward factors—the greater the pressure to reduce it.

D.   The Attitude-Behavior Relationship (ppt 26-27)

1.   The early research on the relationship between attitudes (A) and behavior (B) assumed a causal relationship; that is, the attitudes people hold determine what they do.

2.   In the late 1960s, however, this assumed relationship between attitudes and behavior (A-B) was challenged by a review of the research.

a)   A reviewer of a number of studies concluded that attitudes were either unrelated to behavior or, at best, only slightly related.

        b) More recent research has demonstrated that there is indeed a measurable relationship if moderating contingency variables are taken into consideration.

3. Concentration on both specific attitudes and specific behaviors improves our chances of finding significant A-B relationships.
    a) The more specific the attitude we are measuring and the more specific we are in identifying a related behavior, the greater the probability that we can show a relationship between A and B.

4. Social constraints also moderate behavior.
    a) Discrepancies between attitudes and behavior may occur because the social pressures on the individual to behave in a certain way are exceptionally powerful.

5. Of course, A and B may be at odds for other reasons.
    a) Individuals can and do hold contradictory attitudes at a given time.

III. PERCEPTION

A. Introduction (ppt 28-30)
1. Perception is a process by which individuals organize and interpret their sensory impressions in order to give meaning to their environment.
2. Research consistently demonstrates that different individuals may look at the same thing yet perceive it differently.

B. Factors Influencing Perception (ppt 31)
1. A number of factors operate to shape and sometimes distort perception.
2. These factors can reside in the perceiver, in the object or target being perceived, or in the context of the situation in which the perception is made.
3. Personal characteristics affecting perception include attitudes, personality, motives, interests, past experiences, and expectations.
4. Characteristics of the target being observed can affect what is perceived.
5. Because targets are not looked at in isolation, the relationship of a target to its background influences perception as does our tendency to group close things and similar things together.

C. Attribution Theory (ppt 32)
1. Much of the research on perception is directed at inanimate objects.
    a) OB is concerned with human perception.
    b) Our perception and judgment of a person's actions will be significantly influenced by the assumptions we make about that person's internal state.
2. Attribution theory develops explanations of how we judge people differently depending on what meaning we attribute to a given behavior.
3. The theory suggests that when we observe an individual's behavior, we attempt to determine whether it was internally or externally caused.
    a) That determination depends on three factors: (1) distinctiveness, (2) consensus, and (3) consistency. (ppt 33)
    b) Internally caused behaviors are believed to be under the personal control of the individual.
    c) Externally caused behavior results from outside causes; that is, the person is seen as forced into the behavior by the situation.
4. Distinctiveness refers to whether an individual displays different behaviors in different situations.
    a) What we want to know is whether this behavior is unusual.
    b) If it is, the observer is likely to give the behavior an external attribution.

c) If this action is not unique, it will probably be judged as internal.
5. If everyone who is faced with a similar situation responds in the same way, we can say the behavior shows consensus.
   a) From an attribution perspective, if consensus is high, you would be expected to give an external attribution to the employee's tardiness.
   b) If other employees who took the same route made it to work on time, you would conclude the tardiness had an internal cause.
6. Consistency. Does the person respond the same way over time?
   a) The more consistent the behavior, the more the observer is inclined to attribute it to internal causes.
7. We look at actions and judge them within their situational context.
   a) If you have a reputation as a good student yet fail one test in a course, the instructor is likely to disregard the poor exam.
   b) Why? He or she will attribute the cause of this unusual performance to external conditions.
8. Another important finding from attribution theory is that errors or biases distort attributions. (ppt 34)
   a) There is substantial evidence that when we judge the behavior of other people, we tend to underestimate the influence of external factors and overestimate the influence of internal or personal factors.
      (1) This is called the fundamental attribution error.
   b) Individuals also tend to attribute their own successes to internal factors such as ability or effort while putting the blame for failure on external factors such as luck.
      (1) This is called the self-serving bias and suggests that feedback provided to employees in performance reviews will be predictably distorted by recipients depending on whether it is positive or negative.

D. Shortcuts to Judging Others
1. People in organizations do make judgments about others all the time.
   a) To make the task easier, individuals take shortcuts.
2. Individuals cannot assimilate all they observe, so they use selectivity. (ppt 35)
   a) Selective perception allows us to "speed read" others but not without the risk of drawing an inaccurate picture.
3. Assumed similarity, or the "like me" effect, results in an individual's perception of others being influenced more by what the observer is like than by what the person being observed is actually like.
4. When we judge someone on the basis of our perception of the group to which he or she belongs, we are using the shortcut called stereotyping. (ppt 36)
5. When we draw a general impression about an individual on the basis of a single characteristic such as intelligence, sociability, or appearance, a halo effect is operating.

IV. LEARNING
A. Introduction (ppt 37)
1. Almost all complex human behavior is learned. If we want to explain, predict, or control behavior, we need to understand how people learn.
2. A more accurate definition of learning is any relatively permanent change in behavior that occurs as a result of experience.
   a) Exhibit 2-4 summarizes the learning process.
3. First, learning helps us adapt to, and master, our environment.

        a)   By changing our behavior to accommodate changing conditions, we become responsible citizens and productive employees.

4. Learning is built upon the law of effect, which says that behavior is a function of its consequences. (ppt 38)
   a) Behavior that is followed by a favorable consequence tends to be repeated; behavior followed by an unfavorable consequence tends not to be repeated.
   b) *Consequence*, in this terminology, refers to anything a person considers rewarding (i.e., money, praise, promotions, a smile).
5. Two theories, or explanations, of how we learn.
   a) Shaping
   b) Modeling
6. When learning takes place in graduated steps, it is shaped.
   a) Much of our learning has been done by shaping.
   b) When we speak of "learning by mistakes," we are referring to shaping. We try, we fail, and we try again.
7. In addition, much of what we have learned is the result of observing others and modeling our behavior after them.
   a) Modeling can produce complex behavioral changes quite rapidly.

V. IMPLICATIONS FOR MANAGERS

  A. Introduction
1. Exhibit 2-5 summarizes the discussion of individual behavior.
   a) Although they are not permanently fixed, an employee's values, attitudes, and personality are essentially givens at the time he or she enters an organization.
   b) Ability has also been added to our model to acknowledge that an individual's behavior is influenced by the talents and skills that person holds when he or she joins the organization.

  B. Values (ppt 39)
1. Knowledge of an individual's value system can provide insight into his or her attitudes.
2. Given that people's values differ, managers can use the Rokeach Value Survey to evaluate job applicants and determine if their values align with the dominant values of the organization.
   a) An employee's performance and satisfaction are likely to be higher if his or her values fit well with the organization.
3. Managers are more likely to appreciate, evaluate positively, and allocate rewards to employees who "fit in," and employees are more likely to be satisfied if they perceive that they do "fit in."

  C. Attitudes
1. Managers should be interested in their employees' attitudes because attitudes influence behavior.
2. Research on the satisfaction-productivity relationship suggests that the goal of making employees happy on the assumption that doing so will lead to high productivity is probably misdirected.
   a) Managers would get better results by directing their attention primarily to what will help employees become more productive.
3. Managers should also be aware that employees will try to reduce cognitive dissonance.

a) If employees are required to engage in activities that appear inconsistent to them or are at odds with their attitudes, the pressures to reduce the resulting dissonance are lessened when the employee perceives the dissonance as externally imposed and thus beyond his or her control or if the rewards are significant enough to offset the dissonance.

D. Perception
   1. Managers need to recognize that their employees react to perceptions, not to reality.
   2. Employees naturally organize and interpret what they see; inherent in this process is the potential for perceptual distortion.
   3. Managers need to pay close attention to how employees perceive both their jobs and management practices.

E. Learning
   1. The issue is whether managers are going to let employee learning occur randomly or whether they are going to manage learning—through the rewards they allocate and the examples they set.
   2. If marginal employees are rewarded with pay raises and promotions, they will have little reason to change their behavior.
   3. Similarly, managers should realize that employees will look to them as models.

SUMMARY (ppt 40-41)

1. The dominant values in today's workforce vary with the work cohort the individual belongs to: Veterans, Boomers, Xers, or Nexters. Exhibit 2-2 outlines the values for each group.
2. The Hofstede & GLOBE studies are frameworks used to analyze variations among cultures.
3. Job satisfaction refers to an individual's general attitude toward his or her job. There has been a lot of discussion about job satisfaction and productivity. The early views were "a happy worker is a productive worker." A more careful analysis indicates that if satisfaction does have a positive effect on productivity, that effect is fairly small. Currently, on the basis of a comprehensive review of the evidence, it appears that productivity is more likely to lead to satisfaction rather than the other way around.
4. Cognitive dissonance occurs when there are inconsistencies between two or more of a person's attitudes or between a person's behavior and attitudes. The theory of cognitive dissonance suggests that people seek to minimize dissonance and the discomfort it causes. A person's desire to reduce dissonance is determined by the importance of the elements creating the dissonance, the degree of influence the individual believes he or she has over the elements, and the rewards that may be involved in dissonance.
5. Early research on the relationship between attitudes and behavior assumed a causal relationship; that is, the attitudes people hold determine what they do. In the late 1960s a reviewer of a number of studies concluded that attitudes were either unrelated to behavior or, at best, only slightly related. More recent research has demonstrated that there is indeed a measurable relationship if moderating contingency variables are taken into consideration.
6. Two people can see the same thing and interpret it differently because a number of factors operate to shape and sometimes distort perception. These factors can reside in the perceiver, in the object or target being perceived, or in the context of the situation in which the perception is made. Personal characteristics affecting perception include attitudes, personality, motives, interests, past experiences, and expectations. Characteristics of the target being observed can also affect what is perceived.
7. Attribution theory develops explanations of how we judge people differently depending on what meaning we attribute to a given behavior. The theory suggests that when we observe an

individual's behavior, we attempt to determine whether it was internally or externally caused and that determination depends on three factors: (1) distinctiveness, (2) consensus, and (3) consistency. Another important finding from attribution theory is that errors or biases distort attributions. This is called the fundamental attribution error.

8. Almost all complex human behavior is learned. If we want to explain, predict, or control behavior, we need to understand how people learn. An accurate definition of learning is any relatively permanent change in behavior that occurs as a result of experience. Exhibit 2-4 summarizes the learning process.

DISCUSSION QUESTIONS

1. What is the Rokeach Value Survey?

   Answer - The Rokeach Value Survey (RVS) was developed by Milton Rokeach. The RVS consists of two sets of values, with each set containing eighteen individual value items. One set, terminal values, refers to desirable end-states of existence. These are the goals that a person would like to achieve during his or her lifetime. The other set, instrumental values, refers to preferable modes of behavior or means of achieving the terminal value. Exhibit 2-1 gives common examples for each of these sets.

2. What are the dominant values in today's workforce as segmented by work cohort, and why is understanding them important for managers?

   Answer - A four-group model can be used to show the unique values of the different "workforces." Exhibit 2-2 shows how employees can be segmented by the era in which they entered the work force. Workers who grew up influenced by the Great Depression, and so on, who entered the workforce through the 1950s and early 1960s believe in hard work, the status quo, and authority figures. Once hired, "Veterans" tended to be loyal to their employer, were likely to place the greatest importance on a comfortable life and family security. "Boomers" entered the workforce from the mid-1960s through the mid-1980s and were influenced heavily by the civil rights movement, the Beatles, the Vietnam war, and baby-boom competition. They brought with them the "hippie ethic" and distrust of authority. But they place a great deal of emphasis on achievement and material success, believing that ends can justify means. Boomers see the organizations that employ them merely as vehicles for their careers. Terminal values like a sense of accomplishment and social recognition rank high with them. Xers have been shaped by globalization, two-career parents, MTV, AIDS, and computers. They value flexibility, life options, and job satisfaction. Family and relationships are very important to this cohort. Money is important as an indicator of career performance, and they are willing to trade off salary increases, titles, security, and promotions for increased leisure time and expanded lifestyle options. Xers are less willing to make personal sacrifices for the sake of their employers, and on the RVS they rate high on true friendship, happiness, and pleasure. The most recent entrants to the workforce, the Nexters, have grown up during prosperous times, so they tend to be optimistic about the economy, to believe in themselves, and to be confident about their ability to succeed. Nexters are at ease with diversity and the first generation to take technology for granted. This generation is very money-oriented and desirous of the things that money can buy. They seek financial success. They tend to emphasize terminal values such as freedom and a comfortable life. An understanding that individuals' values differ but tend to reflect the societal values of the period in which they grew up can be a valuable aid in explaining and predicting behavior.

3. Discuss the five value dimensions of national culture identified by Geert Hofstede, which can be used to analyze variations among cultures.

   Answer – Power distance is the degree to which people in a country accept that power in institutions and organizations is distributed unequally. Individualism vs. collectivism—

Individualism is the degree to which people in a country prefer to act as individuals rather than as members of groups. Collectivism is the opposite. Quantity of life vs. quality of life—Quantity of life is the degree to which values such as assertiveness, the acquisition of money and material foods, and competition prevail. Quality of life is the degree to which people value relationships, and show sensitivity and concern for the welfare of others. Uncertainty avoidance is the degree to which people in a country prefer structured over unstructured situations. Long-term vs. short-term orientation—People in long-term-orientation countries look to the future and value thrift and persistence. A short-term orientation values the past and present, and emphasizes respect for tradition and fulfilling social obligations. Exhibit 2-3 provides a summary of how a number of countries rate on these five dimensions.

4. Discuss whether the research on Hofstede is still valuable given that the study was conducted in one company, and it was done in the late 1970's.
    Answer- The fact that the study was completed in one organization actually enhances the results, because fewer outside variables can interfere with the results. As far as the age of the study, it is true that countries have shifted on the dimensions since the original study, but the dimensions are still valid.

5. Discuss the relationship between the GLOBE framework and the Hofstede study.
    Answer- They both compliment each other well. The GLOBE framework is more current, but uses many of the same variables as Hofstede did.

6. Describe the relationship between satisfaction and productivity.
    Answer - The relationship between job satisfaction and productivity has attracted a lot of attention and interest. The early view was "a happy worker is a productive worker." A more careful analysis indicates that if satisfaction does have a positive effect on productivity, that effect is fairly small. The introduction of moderating variables, however, has improved the relationship. Currently, on the basis of a comprehensive review of the evidence, it appears that productivity is more likely to lead to satisfaction rather than the other way around.

7. Explain the theory of cognitive dissonance and its implications for organizations.
    Answer - Cognitive dissonance occurs when there are inconsistencies between two or more of a person's attitudes or between a person's behavior and attitudes. The theory of cognitive dissonance suggests that people seek to minimize dissonance and the discomfort it causes. A person's desire to reduce dissonance is determined by the importance of the elements creating the dissonance, the degree of influence the individual believes he or she has over the elements, and the rewards that may be involved in dissonance. If the elements creating the dissonance are relatively unimportant, the pressure to correct this imbalance will be low. The degree of influence that individuals believe they have over the elements involved will have an impact on how they will react to the dissonance. If they perceive the dissonance to be an uncontrollable result—something that they can't change—they are not likely to be receptive to attitude change. Rewards also influence the degree to which individuals are motivated to reduce dissonance. The tension inherent in high dissonance may be reduced if accompanied by a high reward. The organizational implication is that it can help to predict the propensity to engage in both attitudinal and behavioral change. The greater the dissonance after it has been moderated by importance, choice, and reward factors, the greater the pressure to reduce it.

8. Summarize the relationship between attitudes and behavior.
    Answer - Early research on the relationship between attitudes and behavior assumed a casual relationship; that is, the attitudes people hold determine what they do. In the late 1960s, however, this assumed relationship between attitudes and behavior (A-B) was challenged by a review of the research. More recent research has demonstrated that there is indeed a measurable relationship if moderating contingency variables are taken into consideration. Concentration on both specific attitudes and specific behaviors improves our chances of finding significant A-B relationships. The more specific the attitude we are measuring and the more specific we are in identifying a related behavior, the greater the probability that we can show a relationship between A and B. Social constraints also moderate behavior. Discrepancies between attitudes and behavior may occur because the social pressures on the individual to behave in a certain way are exceptionally powerful.

9. Explain how two people can see the same thing and interpret it differently.
    Answer - Perception is a process by which individuals organize and interpret their sensory impressions in order to give meaning to their environment. Research consistently demonstrates that different individuals may look at the same thing yet perceive it differently. There are a number of factors that influence perception and sometimes distort perception. These factors can reside in the perceiver, in the object or target being perceived, or in the context of the situation in which the perception is made. Personal characteristics affecting perception include attitudes, personality, motives, interests, past experiences, and expectations. Characteristics of the target being observed can affect what is perceived. Because targets are not looked at in isolation, the relationship of a target to its background influences perception as does our tendency to group similar or nearby objects together.

10. Summarize attribution theory.
    Answer - Attribution theory develops explanations of how we judge people differently depending on what meaning we attribute to a given behavior. The theory suggests that when we observe an individual's behavior, we attempt to determine whether it was internally or externally caused. That determination depends on three factors: (1) distinctiveness, (2) consensus, and (3) consistency.

11. Summarize the difference between the fundamental attribution error and the self-serving bias.
    Answer – The fundamental attribution error is the tendency to underestimate the influence of external factors and overestimate the influence of internal or personal factors which making judgments about the behavior of other people. The self-serving bias is a tendency for individuals to attribute their own successes to internal factors such as ability or effort while putting the blame for failure on external factors such as luck when view one's own behavior.

12. Explain the various shortcuts we use to evaluate people and their potential problems.
    Answer - Making judgments about others is done all the time by people in organizations. To make the task easier, individuals take shortcuts. Individuals cannot assimilate all they observe, so they use selectivity. Selective perception allows us to "speed read" others but not without the risk of drawing an inaccurate picture. Assumed similarity, or the "like me" effect, results in an individual's perception of others being influenced more by what the observer is like than by what the person being observed is actually like. When we judge someone on the basis of our perception of the group to which he or she belongs, we are using the shortcut called stereotyping. When we draw a general impression about an individual on the basis of a single characteristic such as intelligence, sociability, or appearance, a halo effect is operating.

13. Explain the learning process.

Answer - Almost all complex human behavior is learned. If we want to explain, predict, or control behavior, we need to understand how people learn. A more accurate definition of learning is any relatively permanent change in behavior that occurs as a result of experience. Exhibit 2-4 summarizes the learning process. First, learning helps us adapt to, and master, our environment. Learning is built upon the law of effect, which says that behavior is a function of its consequences. There are two theories of how we learn; through shaping and through modeling. When learning takes place in graduated steps, it is shaped. When we speak of "learning by mistakes," we refer to shaping. We try, we fail, and we try again. In addition, much of what we have learned is the result of observing others and modeling our behavior after them. Modeling can produce complex behavioral changes quite rapidly.

EXERCISES

A. Interviewing Cohorts

The purpose of this exercise is to show to the students how much work values really vary. The students will develop an interview instrument and use it to interview three to five people who are clearly in different age categories (i.e., work cohorts).

1. Put students into small groups.
2. As separate groups, brainstorm questions for an interview regarding job satisfaction, life goals, and so on.
3. As a class discuss the questions and ideas and narrow them to a list of five to ten questions, something that could be administered in an oral interview in thirty minutes.
4. Each group should assign one member to each cohort.
   - Workers who grew up influenced by the Great Depression, and so on, who entered the workforce from the mid-1940s through the late-1950s.
   - Employees who entered the workforce during the 1960s through the mid-1970s were influenced heavily by John F. Kennedy, and so on.
   - Individuals who entered the workforce from the mid-1970s through the mid-1980s reflect the society's return to more traditional values but with far greater emphasis on achievement and material success.
   - Generation X has been shaped by globalization, the fall of communism, MTV, and so on.
5. The interviewer should identify an individual and conduct an interview using the questionnaire created in class.
   - Students might consider scouting the local McDonald's or Wal-Mart. These types of businesses hire across the age spectrum and would make it easier to find candidates to interview.
6. Groups should meet and consolidate their information into a report, either a ten minute oral or a three to five page written report.
   - As part of their report they should discuss a practical implication for managing an individual from each of the cohorts.
   - How would they manage them differently based on the information they've found?
7. Groups should present and discuss their findings in class.
   - Students will find information that will support and conflict with what the text says.
   - Students will discover that workers have very different views of the nature of work, life goals, etc.

B. Application of Hofstede and the GLOBE Framework

This exercise works best if the class is really diverse. Create groups of student's from different cultures, or student's who have traveled to different cultures. Have them discuss which dimensions really "hit home" with them, and which may seem incorrect based upon their own experiences. Have them discuss how these dimensions impacted their attitudes and behaviors as they traveled to different cultures. Have them discuss specific items that surprised them. For example, what did they experience when moving from a high power distance to a lower power distance culture? After the small group discussion, discuss this with the entire class. Make sure to apply it to management, or it can turn into a very general discussion.

C.   Application of The Law of Effect

This law basically says that people do what they are rewarded to do. Ask student's to provide examples of when this has affected them at work. For example, your manager gets mad when you bring him problems, so you quit talking to him. This same manager then wonders why nobody is "communicating" with him anymore. Look for positive examples too, like when customers compliment your service, and therefore get better service.

D.   Identifying Shortcuts to Judging Others

During class discussion, have students identify (even blurt out) commonly held stereotypes about different groups. The instructor can begin by identify a group of people and having the student indicate the associated short cut, or stereotype. Eventually, have the students themselves identify both the groups and the stereotype. Some groups the instructor might begin with could include blondes (dumb), women drivers (reckless), Jewish business owners (frugal). A suggestion would be to include ethnic short cuts, gender short cuts, national origin short cuts, and even attempt to go global with short cuts about different cultures.

End this exercise by reminding students of the dangers of short cuts or stereotyping. But, that if individuals are aware of commonly-held stereotypes, they are most likely to avoid them, rather than "blindly" believe.

Analyzing Your Organization

For this exercise, you will explore what your organization's terminal and instrumental values are. Interview your manager, and possibly several others. Give them an example of instrumental and terminal values as they are used in this chapter, and have them list for you what they believe the values of the organization are.

For the second part of the assignment, interview various individuals and discuss with them their basic attitudes towards work, organizations, and life in general. How much do they value work versus family? How do they view the organization? What do they think the values of the organization are or should be?

Compare the responses of boomers, xers, nexters, etc. Begin thinking about how the different values will affect the organization. Based upon these responses, how would you manage the different categories of individuals? Be prepared to discuss with the class your responses.

CHAPTER 3 - PERSONALITY AND EMOTIONS

CHAPTER OBJECTIVES
After reading this chapter, students should be able to:
1. Describe the eight categories in the Myers-Briggs Type Indicator (MBTI) personality framework.
2. Identify the Big Five personality variables and their relationship to behavior in organizations.
3. Describe the impact of job typology on the personality/job performance relationship.
4. Differentiate felt from displayed emotions.
5. Identify the six universal emotions.
6. Explain if it is possible for a person to be emotionless.
7. Describe ways in which emotions influence work-related behavior.

LECTURE OUTLINE
I. PERSONALITY
   A. Introduction
      1. When we describe people in terms of characteristics such as quiet, passive, loud, and so on, we categorize them in terms of personality traits.
      2. An individual's personality, therefore, is the combination of psychological traits we use to classify that person. (ppt 4)

   B. The Myers-Briggs Type Indicator (MBTI) (ppt 5)
      1. One of the most widely used personality frameworks.
      2. Essentially a 100-question personality test that asks people how they usually feel or act in particular situations.
      3. Individuals are classified as:
         a) extroverted or introverted (E or I) (ppt 6)
         b) sensing or intuitive (S or N) (ppt 7)
         c) thinking or feeling (T or F) (ppt 8)
         d) perceiving or judging (P or J) (ppt 9)
      4. These classifications are then combined into sixteen personality types.
         a) A study that profiled thirteen contemporary business people who created super-successful firms such as Apple Computer, FedEx, Honda Motors, Microsoft, Price Club, and Sony found all thirteen to be intuitive thinkers (NTs).
         b) This finding is particularly interesting because intuitive thinkers represent only about five percent of the population.
      5. More than two million people a year take the MBTI in the United States alone.
      6. There is no hard evidence that the MBTI is a valid measure of personality. But lack of such evidence does not seem to deter organizations from using it.

   C. The Big-Five Model (ppt 10)
      1. An impressive body of research supports that five basic personality dimensions underlie all others.
      2. Factors in the Big-Five Model are:
         a) Extroversion—one's comfort level with relationships (ppt 11)
         b) Agreeableness—an individual's propensity to defer to others (ppt 12)
         c) Conscientiousness—a measure of reliability
         d) Emotional stability—dimension measuring a person's ability to withstand stress. Positive emotional stability (calm, enthusiastic, secure) as opposed to

negative emotional stability (tense, nervous, depressed, and insecure) (ppt 13).

- e) Openness to experience—an individual's range of interests and fascination with novelty (ppt 14)

3. Research on the Big Five found important relationships between these personality dimensions and job performance.
    - a) A broad spectrum of occupations were examined: professionals (including engineers, architects, accountants, attorneys), police, managers, sales, and semiskilled and skilled employees.
    - b) Job performance was defined in terms of performance ratings, proficiency during training programs, and personnel data such as salary level.
    - c) Conscientiousness predicted job performance for all occupational groups.
    - d) For the other personality dimensions, predictability depended on both the performance criterion and occupational group.

D. Other Key Personality Attributes
1. Six additional personality attributes have been identified that appear to have more direct relevance for explaining and predicting behavior in organizations.
    - a) Locus of control
    - b) Machiavellianism
    - c) Self-esteem
    - d) Self-monitoring
    - e) Risk propensity
    - f) Type A personality
2. Locus of Control (ppt 15)
    - a) Some people believe they are masters of their own fate.
    - b) Other people see themselves as pawns of fate.
    - c) Locus of control in the first case is internal; those who see their life as being controlled by outsiders are externals.
        - (1) Employees who rate high in externality are less satisfied with their jobs, more alienated from the work setting, and less involved in their jobs than are internals.
3. Machiavellianism
    - a) Is named after Niccolo Machiavelli, who wrote in the sixteenth-century on how to gain and use power.
    - b) An individual exhibiting strong Machiavellian tendencies is manipulative, maintains emotional distance, and believes that ends can justify means.
        - (1) "If it works, use it" is consistent with a high-Mach perspective.
    - c) High Machs are more likely to engage in behavior that is ethically questionable than are low Machs.
    - d) In jobs that require bargaining skills or where there are substantial rewards for winning, high Machs will be productive.
4. Self-esteem
    - a) People differ in the degree to which they like or dislike themselves.
    - b) Research finds that self-esteem is directly related to expectations for success; high self-esteem employees believe that they possess the ability need to succeed at work.
    - c) Self-esteem (SE) has also been found to affect susceptibility to outside influences; low SEs are more susceptible to external influences than are high SEs.

        d)   Evidence indicates that high SEs are more satisfied with their jobs than are low SEs.
- 5. Self-monitoring (ppt 16)
  - a) Some people are much better than others at adjusting their behavior to changing situations.
  - b) High self-monitors are sensitive to external cues and can behave differently in different situations.
    - (1) They are chameleons able to change to fit the situation and to hide their true selves.
  - c) On the other hand, low self-monitors are consistent.
    - (1) They display their true dispositions and attitudes in every situation.
  - d) High self-monitors tend to pay closer attention to the behavior of others and are capable of conforming.
  - e) High self-monitors also tend to be better at playing organizational politics.
- 6. Risk Propensity
  - a) Individuals with a high-risk propensity make more rapid decisions and use less information in making their choices than individuals with low risk propensity.
- 7. Type A Personality
  - a) Excessively competitive and always seem to be experiencing a chronic sense of time urgency.
  - b) Type As are characterized by an incessant struggle to achieve more and more in less and less time.
  - c) They are impatient, cope poorly with leisure time, and create a life of self imposed deadlines.
    - (1) In the North American culture such characteristics tend to be highly prized and positively associated with ambition and the successful acquisition of material goods.
  - d) In terms of work behavior Type As are fast workers.
    - (1) They emphasize quantity over quality.
    - (2) Type As are rarely creative.

E. Personality and National Culture
  1. There are certainly no common personality types for a given country.
  2. Yet a country's culture influences the dominant personality characteristics of its population.
     - a) Let's build this case by looking at two personality attributes—locus of control and the Type A personality.
  3. Cultures differ in terms of people's relationship to their environment.
     - a) In North America people believe that they can dominate their environment.
     - b) People in other societies, such as Middle Eastern countries, believe that life is essentially preordained.
       - (1) Notice the close parallel to internal and external locus of control.
  4. The Prevalence of Type A Personalities
     - a) There will be more in capitalistic countries, where achievement and material success are highly valued.
       - (1) It is estimated that about 50 percent of the North American population is Type A.
       - (2) In cultures such as Sweden and France, where materialism is less revered, we would predict a smaller proportion of Type A personalities.

    F. Matching Personalities and Jobs
1. Efforts have been made to match personalities with the proper jobs.
2. The most-researched personality-job-fit theory is the six-personality-types model. (ppt 17)
3. This model states that an employee's satisfaction with and propensity to leave his or her job depend on the degree to which the individual's personality matches his or her occupational environment.
    a) The six major personality types are listed in Exhibit 3-1, along with their compatible occupations. (ppt 18)
4. A Vocational Preference Inventory Questionnaire
    a) There are 160 occupational titles.
    b) Respondents indicate which of these occupations they like or dislike, and their answers are used to form personality profiles.
    c) Research strongly supports the hexagonal diagram in Exhibit 3-2. (ppt 19)
5. The theory argues that satisfaction is highest and turnover lowest where personality and occupation are in agreement. (ppt 20)

II. EMOTIONS

    A. Introduction
1. Example of Tim Lloyd, a network administrator, who put a "software time bomb" in the computer, resulting in $12 million in damages.
2. Emotions are an important factor in employee behavior.
3. Until very recently, the topic of emotions had been given little or no attention within the field of OB.
    a) The myth of rationality was one hindrance.
       (1) Since the late nineteenth century, organizations have been essentially designed with the objective of trying to control emotions.
       (2) It was believed that a well-run organization was one that successfully eliminated frustration, anger, love, hate, joy, grief and similar feelings.
    b) The second factor that acted to keep emotions out of OB was the belief that emotions of any kind were disruptive.
       (1) When emotions were considered, the discussion focused on strong negative emotions—especially anger—that interfered with an employee's ability to do his or her job effectively.
       (2) Emotions were rarely viewed as being constructive or able to stimulate performance-enhancing behaviors.

    B. What Are Emotions?
1. Clarify three terms that are closely intertwined: *affect, emotions,* and *moods.*
2. *Affect* is a generic term that covers a broad range of feelings that people experience. (ppt 21)
    a) It's an umbrella concept that encompasses both emotions and moods.
3. *Emotions* are intense feelings that are directed at someone or something.
4. *Moods* are feelings that tend to be less intense than emotions and they lack a contextual stimulus.
5. Emotions are reactions to an object, not a trait.
    a) They are object specific.
    b) Moods, on the other hand, are not directed at an object.
    c) Emotions can turn into moods when you lose focus on the contextual object.
6. Emotional labor (ppt 22)
    a) Most jobs also require emotional labor.

        b) This is when an employee expresses organizationally desired emotions during interpersonal transactions.

        c) The concept was originally developed in relation to service jobs.

        d) Today, the concept of emotional labor seems relevant to almost every job.

C. Felt vs. Displayed Emotions (ppt 23)
1. Emotional labor creates dilemmas for employees when their job requires them to exhibit emotions that are incongruous with their actual feelings.
2. Emotions can be separated into felt vs. displayed.
    a) Felt emotions are an individual's actual emotions.
    b) In contrast, displayed emotions are those that are organizationally-required and considered appropriate in a given job.
       (1) They're not innate; they're learned.
3. The key point here is that felt and displayed emotions are often different.
    a) Many people have problems working with others simply because they naively assume that the emotions they see others display are what those others actually feel.

D. The Six Universal Emotions (ppt 24)
1. Research has identified six universal emotions: anger, fear, sadness, happiness, disgust, and surprise.
    a) Exhibit 3-3 illustrates that these six emotions can be conceptualized as existing along a continuum.
    b) The closer any two emotions are to each other on this continuum, the more likely people are to confuse them.
2. These six basic emotions surface in the workplace.

E. Gender and Emotions (ppt 25)
1. It's widely assumed that women are more "in touch" with their feelings than men.
    a) The evidence does confirm differences between men and women when it comes to emotional reactions and ability to read others.
2. Women show greater emotional expression than men.
    a) They experience emotions more intensely and they more frequently express both positive and negative emotions, except anger.
    b) They have more comfort in expressing emotions.
    c) They are better at reading nonverbal cues than are men.
3. Three possible answers to explain these differences.
    a) The different ways men and women have been socialized.
    b) Women may have more innate ability to read others and present their emotions than do men.
    c) Women may have a greater need for social approval and, thus, a higher propensity to show positive emotions like happiness.

F. Emotions and National Culture
1. Cultural norms in the United States dictate that employees in service organizations should smile and act friendly when interacting with customers.
2. But this norm does not apply worldwide.
    a) In Israel smiling by supermarket cashiers is seen as a sign of inexperience, so cashiers are encouraged to look somber.

           b) In Moslem cultures smiling is frequently taken as a sign of sexual attraction, so women are socialized not to smile at men.

    3. This illustrates the need to consider cultural factors as influencing what is or is not considered as emotionally appropriate.

           a) There tends to be high agreement on what emotions mean within cultures but not between cultures.

G. OB Applications (ppt 26)

    1. Ability and Selection

           a) People who know their own emotions and are good at reading others' emotions may be more effective in their jobs.

           b) Emotional intelligence (EI) refers to an assortment of noncognitive skills, capabilities, and competencies that influence a person's ability to succeed in coping with environmental demands and pressures. (ppt 27)

           c) It's composed of five dimensions:

               (1) Self-awareness, or the ability to know what you are feeling.

               (2) Self-management, or the ability to manage one's own emotions and impulses.

               (3) Self-motivation, or the ability to persist in the face of setbacksand failures.

               (4) Empathy, or the ability to sense how others are feeling.

               (5) Social skills, or the ability to handle the emotions of others.

    2. EI may play an important role in job performance.

           a) The implications from the initial evidence on EI is that employers should consider it as a factor in selection, especially in jobs that demand a high degree of social interaction.

    3. Decision Making

           a) Traditional approaches to the study of decision making in organizations have emphasized rationality.

           b) It is naive to assume that decision choices aren't influenced by one's feelings at a particular moment.

           c) You can improve your understanding of decision making by considering "the heart" as well as "the head." People use emotions as well as rational and intuitive processes in making decisions.

    4. Motivation

           a) Like decision making, the dominant approaches to the study of motivation reflect an over rationalized view of individuals.

           b) Motivation theories basically propose that individuals are motivated to the extent that their behavior is expected to receive desired outcomes.

           c) People's perceptions and calculations of situations are filled with emotional content that significantly influences how much effort they exert.

    5. Leadership

           a) The ability to lead others is a fundamental quality sought by organizations.

           b) Almost all effective leaders rely on the expression of feelings to help convey their messages.

           c) Corporate executives know that emotional content is critical if employees are to buy into their vision of their company's future and accept change.

               (1) By arousing emotions and linking them to an appealing vision, leaders increase the likelihood that managers and employees alike will accept change.

    6. Interpersonal Conflict

        a) Whenever conflicts arise, you can be fairly certain that emotions are also surfacing.

        b) A manager's success in trying to resolve conflicts, in fact, is often largely due to his or her ability to identify the emotional elements in the conflict and to get the conflicting parties to work through their emotions.

7. Deviant Workplace Behaviors

        a) Negative emotions can lead to a number of deviant workplace behaviors.

        b) Employee deviance, or voluntary actions that violate established norms and threaten the organization, its members, or both, falls into several categories:

           (1) Production—leaving early, intentionally working slowly

           (2) Property—stealing, sabotage

           (3) Political—gossiping, blaming co-workers

           (4) Personal aggression—sexual harassment, verbal abuse

III. IMPLICATIONS FOR MANAGERS

  A. Personality

    1. The importance of a manager's understanding of personality differences probably lies in selection.

    2. You are likely to have higher-performing and more-satisfied employees if consideration is given to matching personality types with compatible jobs.

    3. In addition managers can expect that individuals with an external locus of control may be less satisfied with their jobs than internals, and also that they may be less willing to accept responsibility for their actions.

  B. Emotions

    1. Emotions are a natural part of an individual's make-up.

    2. Managers often err by ignoring the emotional elements in OB and assessing individual behavior as if it were completely rational.

    3. As one consultant aptly put it, "You can not divorce emotions from the workplace because you can not divorce emotions from people."

    4. Managers who understand the role of emotions will significantly improve their ability to explain and predict individual behavior.

    5. Emotions affect job performance.

        a) They can hinder performance, especially negative emotions.

        b) Emotions can also enhance performance in two ways.

           (1) Emotions can increase arousal levels, thus acting as motivators to higher performance.

           (2) Emotional labor recognizes that feelings can be part of a job's required behavior. For instance, the ability to effectively manage emotions in leadership and sales positions may be critical to success in those positions.

SUMMARY (ppt 28-29)

1. The MBTI personality framework is one of the most widely used personality frameworks. It is essentially a 100-question personality test that asks people how they usually feel or act in particular situations. The results classify people into sixteen personality types.

2. An impressive body of research supports that five basic personality dimensions underlie all others. This Big Five Model has five key factors: extroversion—one's comfort level with relationships; agreeableness—an individual's propensity to defer to others; conscientiousness—a measure of reliability; emotional stability—dimension measuring a person's ability to withstand stress. Positive emotional stability (calm, enthusiastic, secure) as

opposed to negative emotional stability (tense, nervous, depressed, and insecure); openness to experience—an individual's range of interests and fascination with novelty.

3. Six additional personality attributes have been identified that appear to have more direct relevance for explaining and predicting behavior in organizations: locus of control, Machiavellianism, self-esteem, self-monitoring, risk propensity, and type A personality.

4. Research shows that national culture does have some impact on personality. While there are no common personality types for a given country, a country's culture should influence the dominant personality characteristics of its population.

5. Efforts have been made to match personalities with the proper jobs. The most researched personality-job-fit theory is the six-personality-types model. This model states that an employee's satisfaction with and propensity to leave his or her job depend on the degree to which the individual's personality matches his or her occupational environment. The six major personality types are listed in Exhibit 3-1, along with their compatible occupations.

6. Until very recently, the topic of emotions had been given little or no attention within the field of OB. The myth of rationality was one hindrance. The second factor that acted to keep emotions out of OB was the belief that emotions of any kind were disruptive. To understand emotions we need to understand three terms that are closely intertwined: *affect, emotions,* and *moods.* Emotions are reactions to an object, not a trait. Research has identified six universal emotions: anger, fear, sadness, happiness, disgust, and surprise.

7. It is widely assumed that women are more "in touch" with their feelings than men. The evidence does confirm differences between men and women when it comes to emotional reactions and ability to read others. Women show greater emotional expression than men.

8. Cultural norms as to the appropriate expression of emotion vary across cultures. There tends to be high agreement on what emotions mean within cultures but not between cultures.

9. These various findings regarding emotions can be applied in a number of organizational behavioral contexts: selection, decision-making, motivation, leadership, and in managing interpersonal conflict.

DISCUSSION QUESTIONS

1. Describe the eight categories in the MBTI personality framework.
   Answer - The MBTI is essentially a 100-question personality test that asks people how they usually feel or act in particular situations. Individuals are classified as: extroverted or introverted (E or I), sensing or intuitive (S or N), thinking or feeling (T or F), perceiving or judging (P or J). These classifications are then combined into sixteen personality types.

2. What is the value of the "Big Five" personality model for organizations?
   Answer - The Big-Five model has five key factors: extroversion—sociable, talkative, assertive; agreeableness—good-natured, cooperative, and trusting; conscientiousness— responsible, dependable, persistent, and achievement oriented; emotional stability—calm, enthusiastic, secure (positive) as opposed to tense, nervous, depressed, and insecure (negative); and openness to experience—imaginative, artistically sensitive, and intellectual. Research on the Big Five found important relationships between these personality dimensions and job performance. Five categories of occupations were examined: professionals (including engineers, architects, accountants, attorneys), police, managers, sales, and semiskilled and skilled employees. Job performance was defined in terms of performance ratings, training proficiency (performance during training programs), and personnel data such as salary level. Conscientiousness predicted job performance for all five occupational groups. For the other personality dimensions, predictability depended on both the performance criterion and occupational group.

3. Identify and describe the six additional personality attributes that appear to have more direct relevance for explaining and predicting behavior in organizations than other measures.
    Answer - Locus of control—Some people believe they are masters of their own fate. Other people see themselves as pawns of fate. Locus of control in the first case is internal, those who see their life as being controlled by outsiders are externals. Machiavellianism is close to authoritarianism. An individual exhibiting strong Machiavellian tendencies is manipulative, maintains emotional distance, and believes that ends can justify means. Self-esteem, or the degree to which employees like or dislike themselves. Those with high self-esteem believe that they possess the ability need to succeed at work. Self-esteem (SE) has also been found to affect susceptibility to outside influences. Low SEs are more susceptible to external influences than are high SEs. Evidence indicates that high SEs are more satisfied with their jobs than are low SEs. Self-monitoring: some people are much better than others at adjusting their behavior to changing situations. High self-monitors are sensitive to external cues and can behave differently in different situations. On the other hand, low self-monitors are consistent. They display their true dispositions and attitudes in every situation. Risk propensity—individuals with high risk propensity make more rapid decisions and use less information in making their choices than individuals with low risk propensity. Type A personality: excessively competitive and always seem to be experiencing a chronic sense of urgency. Type As are characterized by an incessant struggle to achieve more and more in less and less time.

4. What is the relationship between national culture and individual personality?
    Answer - Research shows that national culture does have some impact on personality. While there are no common personality types for a given country, a country's culture should influence the dominant personality characteristics of its population.

5. What is the value of matching personality with vocation?
    Answer - Efforts have been made to match personalities with the proper jobs. The most re-searched personality-job-fit theory is the six-personality-types model. This model states that an employee's satisfaction with and propensity to leave his or her job depend on the degree to which the individual's personality matches his or her occupational environment. The six major personality types are listed in Exhibit 3-1, along with their compatible occupations.

6. Differentiate between *affect*, *emotions*, and *moods*.
    Answer – *Affect* is a generic term that covers a broad range of feelings that people experience. It's an umbrella concept that encompasses both emotions and moods. *Emotions* are intense feelings that are directed at someone or something. *Moods* are feelings that tend to be less intense than emotions—and they lack a contextual stimulus. They are not directed at an object.

7. Describe what is meant by an increasingly important organizational behavior known as emotional labor.
    Answer – Emotional labor is when employees express organizationally desired emotions during interpersonal transactions. The concept of emotional labor originally developed in relation to service jobs. But today the concept seems relevant to almost every job.

8. Differentiate felt from displayed emotions.
    Answer - Emotions can be separated into felt vs. displayed. Felt emotions are an individual's actual emotions. In contrast, displayed emotions are those that are organizationally required and considered appropriate in a given job. They are not innate; they are learned. The key point here is that felt and displayed emotions are often different. Many people have problems

working with others simply because they naively assume that the emotions they see others display are what those others actually feel.

9. Identify the six universal emotions.
    Answer - Research has identified six universal emotions: anger, fear, sadness, happiness, disgust, and surprise. Exhibit 3-3 illustrates that these six emotions can be conceptualized as existing along a continuum. The closer any two emotions are to each other on this continuum, the more likely people are to confuse them.

10. What is the relationship of national culture and the expression of emotions?
    Answer - Cultural norms in the United States dictate that employees in service organizations should smile and act friendly when interacting with customers. But this norm does not apply worldwide. In Israel, smiling by supermarket cashiers is seen as a sign of inexperience, so cashiers are encouraged to look somber. This illustrates the need to consider cultural factors as influencing what is or is not considered as emotionally appropriate. There tends to be high agreement on what emotions mean within cultures but not between cultures.

11. Describe ways in which emotions influence work-related behavior.
    Answer - There are a number of OB applications of the research on emotions. Selection: people who know their own emotions and are good at reading others' emotions may be more effective in their jobs. Emotional intelligence (EI) refers to an assortment of noncognitive skills, capabilities, and competencies that influence a person's ability to succeed in coping with environmental demands and pressures. Decision-making: traditional approaches to the study of decision making in organizations have emphasized rationality. You can improve your understanding of decision making by considering the heart as well as the head. People use emotions as well as rational and intuitive processes in making decisions. Motivation: motivation theories basically propose that individuals are motivated to the degree they expect to receive desired outcomes. People's perceptions and calculations of situations are filled with emotional content that significantly influences how much effort they exert. Leadership: The ability to lead others is a fundamental quality sought by organizations. Effective leaders almost all rely on the expression of feelings to help convey their messages. By arousing emotions and linking them to an appealing vision, leaders increase the likelihood that managers and employees alike will accept change. Interpersonal Conflict: whenever conflicts arise, you can be fairly certain that emotions are also surfacing. A manager's success in trying to resolve conflicts is often largely due to his or her ability to identify the emotional elements in the conflict.

EXERCISES
A.   Dyadic Discussion
The purpose of this exercise is to facilitate understanding between male and female students through the discussion of emotions. This can be done in pairs, in a group of four, half women and half men, or in a "fish bowl," a mixed pair discussing in the center of the class with fellow students watching.
1. Select the partners.
2. Individually they should complete the following questions:
    a. When I graduate I will _____.
    b. When I'm out with my friends having a pizza we talk about _____.
    c. The things that make me happy or joyful are _____.
    d. Things that make me angry or sad are _____.
    e. When a professor treats me unfairly I _____.
    f. When my parents are unjustly angry with me I _____.

g.   When my girlfriend(boyfriend) is upset I _____.

h.   When I'm happy or joyful I _____.

i.   When I'm sad or angry I _____.

3.   Once the questions are answered students should come together in their pairs or groups and discuss their answers to the questions.

4.   Once they've discussed all the previous questions, using questions h and i. students should discuss how they show these feelings.

5.   The students or observers should note how congruent their previous behavior was with what they said about how they manage feelings of joy, sadness, or anger.

6.   Coming back together as a class, have volunteers share what they learned. Discuss how what they've learned, especially in terms of gender, matches or disagrees with course content.

B.   Application of Myers-Briggs

Ask students to raise their hands if they have taken the Myers-Briggs, and would be willing to share the results with the class. Discuss with the students which types of jobs would be most suited to their personality type. You might also discuss if they have had the opportunity to be in a job that matches their personality. This is a good lead in to the exercise below on matching personalities and jobs.

C.   Matching Personalities and Jobs

This exercise could be used as a group or individual exercise, and could be used as an in-class activity, or an out-of-class assignment.

Have each student identify a previously held job, full- or part-time, that he or she truly enjoyed (great job), and a previously held job that he or she truly disliked (crummy job). When these jobs have been identified, have the student make of a list of the job activities or duties that caused him or her to like the great job, and make a list of the job activities or duties that caused him or her to dislike the crummy job. Then, using the text information about personalities and personality typologies, have the student identify the matches and mismatches between his or her personality and the great job activities/duties, and the crummy job activities/duties.

If using this activity as an in-class exercise, the lists could be discussed in a small group manner. Or, even have students trade lists with a partner, and have the partner "analyze" the job requirement lists in terms of personality match, and act as an "OB consultant."

D.   Application of Emotional Intelligence

Based upon the five dimensions of emotional intelligence, have the class discuss situations in which they have worked or interacted with people of either really low or really high EQ. You might want to do this in small groups first. What were the outcomes of these interactions? Ask them if based upon what we know, they consider EQ to be valuable predictor of behavior.

Analyzing Your Organization

This exercise involves observing your co-workers in action, and taking notes. Your objective is to observe how the concepts in this chapter actually manifest themselves in your workplace. You are to keep a journal for one week observing how both emotions and personality impact work. There are no right or wrong answers to this, but keep the following questions in mind as you observe.

1. Can you see the difference between the introverts and extroverts on the Myers-Briggs scale? Remember this variable encompasses much more than just "quiet" versus "outgoing."
2. What traits on the Big Five scale can you see evidence of in your observations? Consider, for example ones level of agreeableness. What types of workers are these. Are they more effective than individuals who don't exhibit these characteristics?
3. Consider the impacts of the other variables discussed also (locus of control. Machiavellianism, self-esteem, self-monitoring, risk propensity, Type A). What did you find?
4. What types of workers would you rather manage? For example, what are the management implications of a low versus high locus of control?

Be ready to discuss with the class your observations, recognizing that it is not an exact science trying to determine one's personality. For example, you can't assume one is an extrovert just because they appear to be "loud" at work. Nevertheless, record your observations, and come to class ready to discuss your findings.

CHAPTER 4 - BASIC MOTIVATION CONCEPTS

CHAPTER OBJECTIVES
After reading this chapter, students should be able to:
1. Outline the basic motivation process.
2. Describe Maslow's hierarchy of needs theory.
3. Contrast Theory X and Theory Y.
4. Differentiate motivators from hygiene factors.
5. List the characteristics that high achievers prefer in a job.
6. Summarize the types of goals that increase performance.
7. Contrast reinforcement and goal-setting theories.
8. Explain the job characteristics model.
9. Describe equity theory.
10. Clarify the key relationships in expectancy theory.

LECTURE OUTLINE
I. WHAT IS MOTIVATION?
   A. Definition (ppt 4)
      1. May be defined in terms of some outward behavior.
         a) People who are motivated exert a greater effort to perform than those who are not motivated.
      2. A more descriptive but less substantive definition.
         a) Motivation is the willingness to do something and is conditioned by this action's ability to satisfy some need for the individual.
         b) A need, in our terminology, means a physiological or psychological deficiency that makes certain outcomes appear attractive.
         c) The motivation process is shown in Exhibit 4-1.

   B. Needs and Drives (ppt 5)
      1. An unsatisfied need creates tension, which stimulates drives within the individual. (ppt 6)
      2. These drives generate a search for particular goals that, if attained, will satisfy the need and lead to the reduction of tension.
      3. Motivated employees are in a state of tension.
         a) To relieve this tension, they engage in activity.
         b) The greater the tension, the more activity will be needed to bring about relief.

II. EARLY THEORIES OF MOTIVATION
   A. Hierarchy of Needs Theory (ppt 7)
      1. The best-known approach to motivation is Abraham Maslow's hierarchy of needs theory.
      2. He hypothesized that every human being has an internal hierarchy of five needs.
         a) Physiological needs—hunger, thirst, shelter, sex, and other bodily needs
         b) Safety needs—security and protection from physical and emotional harm
         c) Social needs—affection, a sense of belonging, acceptance, and friendship
         d) Esteem need—internal factors such as self-respect, autonomy, and achievement and external factors such as status, recognition, and attention
         e) Self-actualization needs—the drive to become what one is capable of becoming; includes growth, achieving one's potential, and self-fulfillment
      3. As each is satisfied, the next need becomes dominant.

a) See Exhibit 4-2 for the hierarchy.
b) A substantially satisfied need no longer motivates.
4. Maslow separated the five needs into higher and lower orders.
a) Physiological and safety needs were lower order and were predominately satisfied externally.
b) Social, esteem, and self-actualization were categorized as higher-order needs and are satisfied internally.
c) The natural conclusion is that, in times of economic plenty, almost all permanently employed workers will have their lower-order needs substantially met.
5. Maslow's need theory has received wide recognition, particularly among practicing managers.
a) This acceptance is due to the logic and ease with which the theory is intuitively understood.
b) However, research does not generally validate the theory.
(1) There is little support for the prediction that need structures are organized along the dimensions proposed.
(2) Nor does the prediction that the substantial satisfaction of a given need leads to the activation of the next higher need seem true.

B. Theory X and Theory Y (ppt 8)
1. Douglas McGregor proposed two distinct views of human beings.
a) One basically negative, labeled Theory X.
b) The other basically positive, labeled Theory Y.
2. Theory X has four assumptions.
a) Employees inherently dislike work and, whenever possible, will attempt to avoid it.
b) Since employees dislike work, they must be coerced, controlled, or threatened with punishment to achieve desired goals.
c) Employees will avoid responsibilities and seek formal direction whenever possible.
d) Most workers place security above all other factors associated with work and will display little ambition.
3. Theory Y has four contrasting assumptions.
a) Employees can view work as being as natural as rest or play.
b) A person who is committed to the objectives will exercise self-direction and self-control.
c) The average person can learn to accept, and even seek responsibility.
d) The ability to make innovative decisions is widely dispersed throughout the population and is not necessarily the sole province of those in management positions.
4. Implications if you accept McGregor's analysis.
a) Theory X assumes that lower-order needs dominate individuals.
b) Theory Y assumes that higher-order needs dominate individuals.
5. Unfortunately, no evidence confirms that either set of assumptions is valid.

C. Two-Factor Theory (ppt 10)
1. The two-factor theory, or the motivation-hygiene theory, was proposed by psychologist Frederick Herzberg.
2. Herzberg investigated the question, "What do people want from their jobs?"

3. Research showed people replied significantly differently based on whether they felt good or bad about their jobs.
4. He isolated certain characteristics.
   a) Exhibit 4-3
   b) Some internal factors such as advancement, recognition, responsibility, and achievement are consistently related to job satisfaction.
   c) Extrinsic factors such as supervision, pay, company policies, and working conditions relate to job dissatisfaction.
5. The opposite of satisfaction is not dissatisfaction, as removing dissatisfying characteristics from a job does not necessarily make the job satisfying.
   a) Managers who seek to eliminate factors that can create job dissatisfaction may bring about peace but not necessarily motivation—they will be placating their work force rather than motivating them.
   b) Conditions surrounding the job such as quality of supervision, pay, company policies, and so on, were characterized as hygiene factors.
   c) When they are adequate, people will not be dissatisfied; neither will they be satisfied.
   d) To motivate people, Herzberg suggested emphasizing factors associated with the work itself or to outcomes directly derived from it, such as promotional opportunities, personal growth opportunities, and so on.
   e) These are the characteristics that people find intrinsically rewarding.
6. Criticisms of the Theory
   a) The procedure that Herzberg used is limited by its methodology.
   b) The reliability of Herzberg's methodology is questionable.
   c) No overall measure of satisfaction was utilized.
   d) The theory is inconsistent with previous research; it ignores situational variables.
   e) Herzberg assumed a relationship between satisfaction and productivity, but his research methodology looked only at satisfaction, not at productivity.
7. Regardless of criticisms, Herzberg's theory has been widely popularized, and few managers are unfamiliar with his recommendations.

III. CONTEMPORARY THEORIES OF MOTIVATION
A. McClelland's Theory of Needs (ppt 11)
   1. David McClelland and others have proposed three major relevant motives or needs in the workplace, McClelland's Theory of Needs.
      a) The need for achievement (nAch) is the drive to excel, to achieve in relation to a set of standards, to strive to succeed.
      b) The need for power (nPow) is the need to make others behave in a way they would not have behaved otherwise.
      c) The need for affiliation (nAff) is the desire for friendly and close interpersonal relationships.
   2. Some people have a compelling drive to succeed, but they are striving for personal achievement rather than the rewards of success. (ppt 12)
      a) This drive is the need for achievement.
      b) McClelland found that high achievers differentiate themselves from others by their desire to do things better.
      c) They seek situations in which they can attain personal responsibility for finding solutions to problems, receive rapid and unambiguous feedback on their performance, and set moderately challenging goals.

      d) They prefer working at a challenging problem and accepting the personal responsibility for success or failure rather than leaving the outcome to chance or the actions of others.

      e) High achievers perform best when they perceive their probability of success as 50-50.

      f) They like to set realistic but difficult goals that require stretching themselves a little.

3. The need for power is the desire to have an impact, to be influential, and to control others.

      a) Individuals high in nPow enjoy being in charge, strive for influence over others, prefer competitive and status-oriented situations, and tend to be more concerned with gaining prestige and influence over others than with effective performance.

4. The third need is the need for affiliation.

      a) This need has received the least attention of researchers.

      b) Individuals with a high nAff strive for friendship, prefer cooperative situations rather than competitive ones, and desire relationships involving a high degree of mutual understanding.

5. All three motives are typically measured through a projective test in which subjects respond to a set of pictures.

6. Predictions can be made on the basis of the relationship between achievement need and job performance.

      a) Individuals with a high need to achieve prefer job situations with personal responsibility, feedback, and an intermediate degree of risk.

          (1) High achievers are successful in entrepreneurial activities such as running their own business, managing a self-contained unit within a large organization, and many sales positions.

      b) A high need to achieve does not necessarily lead to being a good manager.

      c) The needs for affiliation and power tend to be closely related to managerial success.

          (1) The best managers are high in the need for power and low in their need for affiliation.

      d) Employees have been successfully trained to stimulate their achievement need.

B. Goal-Setting Theory (ppt 13)

1. Considerable evidence supports goal-setting theory.

2. Intentions that are expressed as goals can be a major source of work motivation.

3. Specific, difficult-to-achieve goals produce a higher level of output than a generalized goal of "do your best."

4. The specificity of the goal itself acts as an internal stimulus.

5. If factors such as ability and acceptance of the goals are held constant, we can also state that the more difficult the goals, the higher the level of performance.

6. If employees have the opportunity to participate in the setting of their own goals, will they try harder?

      a) The evidence is mixed.

      b) A major advantage of participation may be in increasing acceptance of the goal itself as a desirable one.

      c) Participative goals may have no superiority over assigned goals when acceptance is taken as a given; participation does increase the probability that more difficult goals will be agreed to and acted upon.

7. Studies testing goal-setting theory have demonstrated the superiority of specific and challenging goals as motivating forces. (ppt 14)
8. There appears to be a contradiction between the findings on achievement motivation and goal setting.
   a) It is not actually a contradiction.
   b) First, goal-setting theory deals with people in general.
   c) The conclusions on achievement motivation are based only on people who have a high nAch, and probably fewer than 10 to 20 percent of any country's workforce are naturally high achievers.
   d) Second, goal setting's conclusions apply to those who accept, and are committed to, the goals. Difficult goals will lead to higher performance only if they are accepted.

C. Reinforcement Theory (ppt 15)
   1. A counterpoint to goal-setting theory is reinforcement theory.
      a) The former is a cognitive approach, proposing that an individual's purposes direct his or her actions.
      b) Reinforcement theory uses a behavioristic approach, which argues that reinforcement conditions behavior.
   2. The two theories are clearly at odds philosophically.
      a) Reinforcement theorists see behavior as environmentally caused. What controls behavior are reinforcers—any consequences that, when immediately following a response, increase the probability that the behavior will be repeated.
   3. Reinforcement theory ignores the inner state of the individual and concentrates solely on what happens to a person when he or she takes some action. (ppt 16)
      a) Because it does not concern itself with what initiates behavior, it is not, strictly speaking, a theory of motivation.
   4. Chapter 2 introduced the law of effect (behavior is a function of its consequences) and showed that reinforcers (consequences) condition behavior and explains how people learn.
      a) Research indicates that people will exert more effort on tasks that are reinforced than on tasks that are not.
      b) But reinforcement is not the single explanation for differences in employee motivation.
      c) Goals, for instance, have an impact on motivation; so, too, do levels of achievement motivation, inequities in rewards, and expectations.

D. Job Design Theory (ppt 17)
   1. Based upon the notion that the work itself is a source of motivation. The two most important theories are the job characteristics model, and the social information-processing model.
   2. The Job Characteristics Model (ppt 18)
      a) In the JCM any job can be described in terms of five core job dimensions.
         (1) Skill variety—The degree to which the job requires a variety of different activities so the worker can use a number of different skills and talents.
         (2) Task identity—The degree to which the job requires completion of a whole and identifiable piece of work.
         (3) Task significance—The degree to which the job has a substantial impact on the lives or work of other people.

                (4) Autonomy—The degree to which the job provides substantial freedom, independence, and discretion to the individual in scheduling the work and in determining the procedures to be used in carrying it out.

                (5) Feedback—The degree to which carrying out the work activities required by the job results in the individual's obtaining direct and clear information about the effectiveness of his or her performance.

      b) Exhibit 4-4 presents the model.

                (1) The first three dimensions—skill variety, task identity, and task significance—combine to create meaningful work.

                (2) Jobs that possess autonomy give the job incumbent a feeling of personal responsibility for the results and that, if a job provides feedback, the employee will know how effectively he or she is performing.

                (3) From a motivational standpoint, the model says that internal rewards are obtained by an individual when she learns (knowledge of results) that she personally (experienced responsibility) has performed well on a task that she cares about (experienced meaningfulness).

      c) The more that these three psychological states are present, the greater the employee's motivation, performance, and satisfaction and the lower his or her absenteeism and likelihood of leaving the organization will be.

      d) Individuals with a high growth need are more likely to experience the psychological states when their jobs are enriched than are their counterparts with a low growth need.

      e) The core dimensions can be combined into a single variable, called the motivating potential score (MPS).

      f) The job characteristics model has been well researched and the evidence supports the general framework of the theory.

                (1) There is still considerable debate around the five specific core dimensions in the JCM and the validity of growth need strength as a moderating variable.

      g) Probable conclusions

                (1) People who work on jobs with high-core job dimensions are generally more motivated, satisfied, and productive than are those who do not.

                (2) Job dimensions operate through the psychological states in influencing personal and work outcome variables rather than influencing the outcomes directly.

   3. Social Information-Processing Model (ppt 19)

      a) People respond to their jobs as they perceive them rather than to the objective jobs themselves.

      b) The SIP model argues that employees adopt attitudes and behaviors in response to the social cues provided by others with whom they have contact.

                (1) These others can be co-workers, supervisors, friends, family members, or customers.

      c) A number of studies generally confirm the validity of the SIP model.

                (1) It has been shown that employee motivation and satisfaction can be manipulated by such subtle actions as a co-worker or boss commenting on the existence or absence of job features like difficulty, challenge, and autonomy.

E. Equity Theory (ppt 20)

   1. Employees make comparisons.

      a) The issue centers around relative rewards and what you believe is fair.

    b) Employees compare their own job inputs and outcomes with those of others and those inequities can influence the degree of effort that employees exert.

2. Equity theory says that employees weigh what they put into a job situation (input) against what they get from it (outcome) and then compare their input-outcome ratio with the input-outcome ratio of relevant others.
    a) If they perceive equity, they feel that their situation is fair, that justice prevails. (ppt 21)
    b) If the ratios are unequal, inequity exists; that is, the employees tend to view themselves as underrewarded or overrewarded. (ppt 22)

3. When inequities occur, employees will attempt to correct them.
    a) The referent that employees choose to compare themselves against is an important variable in equity theory.

4. The three referent categories have been classified as "other," "system," and "self."
    a) The other category includes other individuals with similar jobs in the same organization and also includes friends, neighbors, or professional associates.
    b) The system category considers organizational pay policies and procedures as well as the administration of this system.
    c) The self category refers to input-outcome ratios that are unique to the individual. This category is influenced by such criteria as past jobs or family commitments.

5. The choice of a particular set of referents is related to the information available about referents as well as to their perceived relevance.

6. When employees envision an inequity, they may make one or more of five choices (ppt 23):
    a) Distort either their own or others' inputs or outcomes.
    b) Behave so as to induce others to change their inputs or outcomes.
    c) Behave so as to change their own inputs or outcomes.
    d) Choose a different comparison referent.
    e) Quit their job.

7. Equity theory recognizes that individuals are concerned with both the absolute amount of rewards and the relationship of that amount to what others receive.

8. Inputs, such as effort, experience, education, and competence, are compared with outcomes such as salary levels, raises, recognition, and other factors.

9. Specifically, the theory establishes four propositions relating to inequitable pay:
    a) Given payment by time, overrewarded employees will produce more than equitably paid employees.
    b) Given payment by quantity of production, overrewarded employees will produce fewer but higher-quality units than equitably paid employees.
    c) Given payment by time, underrewarded employees will produce less or a poorer quality of output.
    d) Given payment by quantity of production, underrewarded employees will produce a large number of low-quality units in comparison with equitably paid employees.

10. A review of the recent research tends to consistently confirm the equity thesis:
    a) Employee motivation is influenced significantly by relative rewards as well as by absolute rewards.
    b) When employees perceive inequity, they will act to correct the situation.

11. Problems with the theory.
    a) Some key issues unclear.

                (1) How do employees decide who is included in the "other" referent category?

                (2) How do they define inputs and outcomes?

                (3) How do they combine and weigh their inputs and outcomes to arrive at totals?

                (4) When and how do the factors change over time?

    12. Regardless of these problems, equity theory has an impressive amount of research support and offers us some important insights into employee motivation.

F. Expectancy Theory (ppt 24)

    1. The most comprehensive explanation of motivation is expectancy theory.

    2. Expectancy theory argues that the strength of a tendency to act in a certain way depends on the strength of an expectation that the act will be followed by a given outcome and on the attractiveness of that outcome to the individual.

    3. Three variables (ppt 25):

        a) Attractiveness—the importance the individual places on the potential outcome or reward that can be achieved on the job.

        b) Performance/reward linkage—the degree to which the individual believes that performing at a particular level will lead to the attainment of a desired outcome.

        c) Effort/performance linkage—the probability perceived by the individual that exerting a given amount of effort will lead to performance.

        d) Exhibit 4-5 simplifies expectancy theory into its major contentions (ppt 26).

    4. The strength of a person's motivation to perform (effort) depends on how strongly she believes she can achieve what she attempts.

    5. Four steps are inherent in the theory.

        a) What perceived outcomes does the job offer the employee, positive or negative?

        b) How attractive do employees consider these outcomes? Are they valued positively, negatively, or neutrally?

        c) What kind of behavior must the employee exhibit in order to achieve these outcomes? The outcomes are not likely to have any effect on the individual employee's performance unless the employee knows, clearly and unambiguously, what she must do in order to achieve them.

        d) How does the employee view her chances of doing what is asked of her?

    6. Issues

        a) It emphasizes payoffs or rewards. As a result, rewards need to align with what the employee wants.

            (1) This requires an understanding and knowledge of what value the individual puts on organizational payoffs.

        b) Second, expectancy theory emphasizes expected behaviors.

        c) Finally, the theory is concerned with the individual's expectations.

IV. DON'T FORGET: MOTIVATION THEORIES ARE CULTURE BOUND

    A. Most current motivation theories were developed in the United States by Americans and about Americans.

        1. The pro-American characteristic in these theories is the strong emphasis on individualism and quantity-of-life factors.

        2. Maslow's hierarchy of needs theory argues that people start at the physiological level and then move progressively up the hierarchy in this order: physiological, safety, social, esteem, and self-actualization.

      a) This hierarchy aligns with American culture.
3. Another motivation concept with a U.S. bias is the achievement need.
4. Goal-setting theory is also certainly culture bound.
      a) It assumes that subordinates will be reasonably independent (not too high a score on power distance), managers and subordinates will seek challenging goals (low in uncertainty avoidance), and performance is considered important by both (high in quantity of life).
      b) Goal-setting theory's recommendations are not likely to increase motivation in countries in which the opposite conditions exist, such as France, Portugal, and Chile.

V. IMPLICATIONS FOR MANAGERS (ppt 27)

1. Many of the theories presented in this chapter have demonstrated reasonably strong predictive value.
2. How does a manager concerned with motivating employees apply these theories?
3. Certain general suggestions can be extracted for application, at least for managers in North America. For instance, the following recommendations are consistent with the findings in this chapter:
      a) Recognize individual differences.
      b) Match people to jobs.
      c) Use goals.
      d) Ensure that goals are perceived as attainable.
      e) Individualize rewards.
      f) Link rewards to performance.
      g) Check the system for equity.
4. These suggestions, of course, would need to be modified to reflect cultural differences outside of North America.
5. The importance of motivating employees today justifies more specifics than the concepts we have just offered.
6. The next chapter builds on the concepts we have presented here, providing a review of the more popular motivation techniques and programs.

SUMMARY (ppt 28-29)

1. Motivation may be defined in terms of some outward behavior. It is the willingness to do something and is conditioned by this action's ability to satisfy some need for the individual.
2. An unsatisfied need creates tension, which stimulates drives within the individual. These drives generate a search for particular goals that, if attained, will satisfy the need and lead to the reduction of tension.
3. The best-known approach to motivation is Abraham Maslow's hierarchy of needs theory. He hypothesized that every human being has an internal hierarchy of five needs: physiological needs, safety needs, social needs, esteem needs, and self-actualization needs. Maslow separated the five needs into higher and lower orders. Maslow's need theory has received wide recognition, particularly among practicing managers. Research does not generally validate the theory.
4. Douglas McGregor proposed two distinct views of human beings. One basically negative, labeled Theory X and the other basically positive, labeled Theory Y. If you accept McGregor's analysis, Theory X assumes that lower-order needs dominate individuals and Theory Y assumes that higher-order needs dominate individuals. Unfortunately, no evidence confirms that either set of assumptions is valid.
5. The two-factor theory, motivation-hygiene theory, was proposed by psychologist Frederick Herzberg. He isolated certain characteristics, some consistently related to job satisfaction—

internal factors—such as advancement, recognition, responsibility, and achievement. Others related to job dissatisfaction—extrinsic factors—such as supervision, pay, company policies, and working conditions. His theory has been criticized for its methodology and reliability. Regardless of criticisms, Herzberg's theory has been widely popularized, and few managers are unfamiliar with his recommendations.

6. David McClelland and others have proposed three major relevant motives or needs in the workplace—McClelland's Theory of Needs. The need for achievement (hAch)—the drive to excel, to achieve in relation to a set of standards, to strive to succeed. The need for power (nPow)—the need to make others behave in a way they would not have behaved otherwise. The need for affiliation (nAff)—the desire for friendly and close interpersonal relationships.

7. Goal-setting theory is well supported by research. Intentions—expressed as goals—can be a major source of work motivation. The specificity of the goal itself acts as an internal stimulus. Studies testing goal-setting theory have demonstrated the superiority of specific and challenging goals as motivating forces.

8. A counterpoint to goal-setting theory is reinforcement theory. Reinforcement theory uses a behavioristic approach, which argues that reinforcement conditions behavior. Reinforcement theory ignores the inner state of the individual and concentrates solely on what happens to a person when he or she takes some action.

9. In Hackman and Oldham's job characteristics model (JCM), any job can be described in terms of five core job dimensions: skill variety, task identity, task significance, autonomy, and feedback. The job characteristics model has been well researched and the evidence supports the general framework of the theory.

10. The social information-processing model (SIP) argues that people respond to their jobs, as they perceive them rather than to the objective jobs themselves. The SIP model argues that employees adopt attitudes and behaviors in response to the social cues provided by others with whom they have contact. A number of studies generally confirm the validity of the SIP model.

11. Equity theory proposes that employees make comparisons. Employees compare their own job inputs and outcomes with those of others and any inequities can influence the degree of effort that employees exert. Equity theory says that employees weigh what they put into a job situation (input) against what they get from it (outcome) and then compare their input-outcome ratio with the input-outcome ratio of relevant others. If they perceive equity, they feel that their situation is fair, and that justice prevails. If the ratios are unequal, inequity exists; that is, the employees tend to view themselves as underrewarded or overrewarded. Equity theory recognizes that individuals are concerned with both the absolute amount of rewards and the relationship of that amount to what others receive. A review of the recent research tends to consistently confirm the equity thesis.

12. The most comprehensive explanation of motivation is expectancy theory. Expectancy theory argues that the strength of a tendency to act in a certain way depends on the strength of an expectation that the act will be followed by a given outcome and on the attractiveness of that outcome to the individual. There are three variables: attractiveness, the importance the individual places on the potential outcome or reward that can be achieved on the job; performance-reward linkage, or the degree to which the individual believes that performing at a particular level will lead to the attainment of a desired outcome; and effort-performance linkage, or the probability perceived by the individual that exerting a given amount of effort will lead to performance.

DISCUSSION QUESTIONS

1. Outline the basic motivation process.
    Answer - See Exhibit 4-1.

2. Describe Maslow's hierarchy of needs theory.

   Answer - Maslow's hierarchy of needs theory is the best-known approach to motivation. He hypothesized that every human being has an internal hierarchy of five needs. As each is satisfied, the next need becomes dominant. A substantially satisfied need no longer motivates. Maslow separated the five needs into higher and lower orders. Physiological and safety needs were lower order and were predominately satisfied externally. Social, esteem, and self-actualization were categorized as higher-order needs and are satisfied internally. The natural conclusion is that, in times of economic plenty, almost all permanently employed workers will have their lower-order needs substantially met. Maslow's need theory has received wide recognition, particularly among practicing managers. This acceptance is due to the logic and ease with which the theory is intuitively understood. However, research does not generally validate the theory. There is little support found for the prediction that need structures are organized along the dimensions proposed.

3. Contrast Theory X and Theory Y.

   Answer - Douglas McGregor proposed two distinct views of human beings, one basically negative, labeled Theory X, and the other basically positive, labeled Theory Y. Each has four assumptions which tend to be the opposite of each other. Theory X assumptions: 1) Employees inherently dislike work and, whenever possible, will attempt to avoid it. 2) Since employees dislike work, they must be coerced, controlled, or threatened with punishment to achieve desired goals. 3) Employees will avoid responsibilities and seek formal direction whenever possible. 4) Most workers place security above all other factors associated with work and will display little ambition. Theory Y contrasting assumptions: 1) Employees can view work as being as natural as rest or play. 2) A person who is committed to the objectives will exercise self-direction and self-control. 3) The average person can learn to accept, even seek, responsibility. 4) The ability to make innovative decisions is widely dispersed throughout the population and not necessarily the sole province of those in management. Theory X assumes that lower-order needs dominate individuals. Theory Y assumes that higher-order needs dominate individuals.

4. Differentiate motivators from hygiene factors.

   Answer - The two-factor theory, motivation-hygiene theory, was proposed by psychologist Frederick Herzberg. He investigated the question, "What do people want from their jobs?" Research showed people replied significantly differently based on whether they felt good or bad about their jobs Internal factors such as advancement, recognition, responsibility, and achievement seem to be related to job satisfaction. Extrinsic factors such as supervision, pay, company policies, and working conditions relate to job dissatisfaction. The opposite of satisfaction is not dissatisfaction. Removing dissatisfying characteristics from a job does not necessarily make the job satisfying. Managers who seek to eliminate factors that can create job dissatisfaction will be placating their workforce rather than motivating them. Conditions surrounding the job such as quality of supervision, pay, company policies, and so on, were characterized as hygiene factors. When they are adequate, people will not be dissatisfied; neither will they be satisfied. To motivate people, Herzberg suggested emphasizing factors associated with the work itself or to outcomes directly derived from it, such as promotional opportunities, personal growth opportunities, and so on.

5. While the three early theories of motivation have been heavily attacked and their validity called into question, why should you know these early theories?

   Answer – Because (1) these early theories represent a foundation from which contemporary theories have grown, and (2) practicing managers regularly use these theories and their terminologies in explaining employee motivation.

6. List and define the three major relevant motives or needs in the workplace as identified by David McClelland and others.
    Answer – The need for achievement (nAch) is the drive to excel, to achieve in relation to a set of standards, to strive to succeed. The need for power (nPow) is the need to make others behave in a way they would not have behaved otherwise. The need for affiliation (nAff) is the desire for friendly and close interpersonal relationships.

7. List the characteristics that high achievers prefer in a job.
    Answer - Some people have a compelling drive to succeed, but they are striving for personal achievement rather than the rewards of success. This drive is the need for achievement. McClelland found that high achievers differentiate themselves from others by their desire to do things better. They seek situations in which they can attain personal responsibility for finding solutions to problems, receive rapid and unambiguous feedback on their performance, and set moderately challenging goals. They prefer working at a challenging problem and accepting the personal responsibility for success or failure rather than leaving the outcome to chance or the actions of others. High achievers perform best when they perceive their probability of success as being 50-50. They like to set realistic but difficult goals that require stretching themselves a little.

8. Summarize the types of goals that increase performance.
    Answer – Intentions expressed as goals can be a major source of work motivation. Difficult-to-achieve goals produce a higher level of output than a generalized goal of "do your best." The specificity of the goal itself acts as an internal stimulus. If factors such as ability and acceptance of the goals are held constant, we can also state that the more difficult the goals, the higher the level of performance. Participative goals may have no superiority over assigned goals when acceptance is taken as a given. Participation does increase the probability that more difficult goals will be agreed to and acted upon. Studies testing goal-setting theory have demonstrated the superiority of specific and challenging goals as motivating forces.

9. Contrast reinforcement and goal-setting theories.
    Answer - A counterpoint to goal-setting theory is reinforcement theory. The former is a cognitive approach, proposing that an individual's purposes direct his or her actions. Reinforcement theory uses a behavioristic approach, which argues that reinforcement conditions behavior. The two theories are clearly at odds philosophically. Reinforcement theorists see behavior as environmentally caused. What controls behavior are reinforcers— any consequences that, when immediately following a response, increase the probability that the behavior will be repeated. Reinforcement theory ignores the inner state of the individual and concentrates solely on what happens to a person when he or she takes some action. Because it does not concern itself with what initiates behavior, it is not, strictly speaking, a theory of motivation. But reinforcement is not the single explanation for differences in employee motivation. Goals, for instance, have an impact on motivation; so, too, do levels of achievement, inequities in rewards, and expectations.

10. Discuss the 5 variables in the job characteristics model. Which one(s) are most important from a motivational standpoint?
    Answer- Although all variables are important, if you look at the MPS equation, autonomy and feedback are the most important in that a job has no motivating potential if either of these variables don't exist in the job. You might want to discuss, however, that it is virtually impossible to have a job with zero autonomy or zero feedback.

11. You are responsible for a customer service telemarketing unit with fifty employees. They tend to do the same tasks each day, answer the phones, answering questions, finding answers from other sources if they don't know the answer, and so on. You are the sole supervisor of this large group. Using the job characteristics model, describe how you might improve their jobs in order to improve motivation, performance, and job satisfaction.

    Answer - Students' answer will show significant variety depending on how much they assume. The "minicase" is deliberately written to leave room for making assumptions. Students should cover most elements of the model. In the JCM, any job can be described in terms of five core job dimensions.

    - Skill variety—The degree to which the job requires a variety of different activities so the worker can use a number of different skills and talents.
    - Task identity—The degree to which the job requires completion of a whole and identifiable piece of work.
    - Task significance—The degree to which the job has a substantial impact on the lives or work of other people.
    - Autonomy—The degree to which the job provides substantial freedom, independence, and discretion to the individual in scheduling the work and in determining the procedures to be used in carrying it out.
    - Feedback—The degree to which carrying out the work activities required by the job results in the individual's obtaining direct and clear information about the effectiveness of his or her performance.

12. What is the value of the social information-processing model for managers?

    Answer - According to the social information-processing model people respond to their jobs as they perceive them rather than to the objective jobs themselves. The SIP model argues that employees adopt attitudes and behaviors in response to the social cues provided by others with whom they have contact. These others can be co-workers, supervisors, friends, family members, or customers. It has been shown that employee motivation and satisfaction can be manipulated by such subtle actions as a co-worker or boss commenting on the existence or absence of job features like difficulty, challenge, and autonomy.

13. Explain equity theory.

    Answer - Equity theory says that employees weigh what they put into a job situation (input) against what they get from it (outcome) and then compare their input-outcome ratio with the input-outcome ratio of relevant others. If they perceive equity, they feel that their situation is fair, that justice prevails. If the ratios are unequal, inequity exists; that is, the employees tend to view themselves as underrewarded or overrewarded. When inequities occur, employees will attempt to correct them. The referent that employees choose to compare themselves against is an important variable in equity theory. The three-referent categories have been classified as "other," "system," and "self."

    - Other includes other individuals with similar jobs in the same organization and also includes friends, neighbors, or professional associates.
    - System considers organizational pay policies and procedures as well as the administration of this system.
    - Self refers to input-outcome ratios that are unique to the individual. This category is influenced by such criteria as past jobs or family commitments.

    Equity theory recognizes that individuals are concerned with both the absolute amount of rewards and the relationship of that amount to what others receive. Inputs, such as effort, experience, education, and competence, are compared with outcomes such as salary levels, raises, recognition, and other factors. Specifically, the theory establishes four propositions relating to inequitable pay:

- Given payment by time, overrewarded employees will produce more than equitably paid employees.
- Given payment by quantity of production, overrewarded employees will produce fewer but higher-quality units than equitably paid employees.
- Given payment by time, underrewarded employees will produce less or a poorer quality of output.
- Given payment by quantity of production, underrewarded employees will produce a large number of low-quality units in comparison with equitably paid employees.

14. Clarify the key relationships in expectancy theory.

Answer - The most comprehensive explanation of motivation is expectancy theory. Expectancy theory argues that the strength of a tendency to act in a certain way depends on the strength of an expectation that the act will be followed by a given outcome and on the attractiveness of that outcome to the individual. Expectancy theory has three variables: attractiveness, which is the importance the individual places on the potential outcome or reward that can be achieved on the job; performance-reward linkage, which is the degree to which the individual believes that performing at a particular level will lead to the attainment of a desired outcome; and effort-performance linkage, which is the probability perceived by the individual that exerting a given amount of effort will lead to performance. Exhibit 4-4 simplifies expectancy theory into its major contentions. Four steps are inherent in the theory.

- First, what perceived outcomes does the job offer the employee—positive or negative?
- Second, how attractive do employees consider these outcomes? Are they valued positively, negatively, or neutrally?
- Third, what kind of behavior must the employee exhibit in order to achieve these outcomes? The outcomes are not likely to have any effect on the individual employee's performance unless the employee knows, clearly and unambiguously, what she must do in order to achieve them.
- Fourth, how does the employee view her chances of doing what is asked of her?

EXERCISES

A.   What Motivates Me?

The goal of this exercise is to have students realize the complexity of motivation and how as managers they will probably use several different approaches. It should also give students insight into the different styles of their professors.

1. Ask students to take five minutes and to individually write down how they would motivate students to study, turn in assignments on time, and treat each other with respect in class.
2. Begin a class discussion, noting on the board the suggestions.
3. Next have the students individually categorize the suggestions by theory.
4. Lead a class discussion, noting on the board the general consensus as to which ideas belong to which theoretical approaches.
5. Finally, as a class, discuss how motivating each suggestion would be to them individually. Help students note that what some students think is motivational would not be to others. [Also, you will probably discover that some students will want to "motivate" others in ways they themselves would not like to be motivated.]

B.   Hygiene or Motivator? That is the question.

This exercise will help students differentiate between what really motivates, and what simply creates dissatisfaction, i.e. motivator versus hygiene factors. Have the students identify what they expect to find waiting for them at the site of their first "real" job after they graduate. The instructor can write this list on the board, or just simply have students verbally make suggestions. Be sure they name things as simple as pens, pencils, paper, a desk, a chair, a computer, a telephone (do they want a shared line or a private line?), a light, heating and cooling/ climate control, OSHA standards (or would they mind sharing the work space with a few small mice and gas fumes?), and so on.

Then guide the students to identify what they truly would like to receive if they were rewarded for doing an outstanding job on a particular project that resulted in organizational profits. These should be the true motivators.

Finish the discussion by relating the motivators and hygiene factors back to Hofstede's quantity of life versus quality of life in a discussion of global motivation methods. The worker from Sweden might not be as motivated by a new computer on a desk in a corner office with a view.

C.   Is that Job Motivating or Not?

Assign students to identify a job they either currently hold or have previously held that they really liked and enjoyed going to, and a job they either currently hold or have previously held that they truly disliked and couldn't wait to quit. Then assign the students to assess both of those jobs using the job characteristics model. Encourage the students to use the information provided about the five core job dimensions, and the SIP model. Ask for volunteers to discuss the poorest design job in the class, versus the best designed job. Use this as a springboard to discuss how much of motivation is contained in the job itself

D.   Equity Theory in Action

Have students discuss times that they felt like they were being treated unfair at work. Have them describe the emotions, and follow up with what specific behavior they engaged in because of the emotions. For example, did they work less hours or quit the job?

Another effective technique is to role play being treated unfair. The instructor can be the manager who pays students different amounts for the same job. Have the students then describe their emotions, and what they would do about this in the real world.

Analyzing Your Organization

Pass out an index card or a half-sheet of paper with the following question typed on it:

"List the two things at work that motivate you the most. These can be things that already exist in your job, or things that you wish that you had."

If they ask for examples, one might be "the flexible scheduling that I have," or "the opportunity to socialize with nice people." Don't give too many examples, because you don't want to prompt them into ideas that they did not come up with themselves.

Pass out the sheets to as many people as you can get to participate. Collect the sheets anonymously at the end of the day, and re-type them. What you should find is a large variance in the types of things that motivate people. This illustrates one point of this chapter, that we are all motivated by different things.

For the next step, discuss this with your manager. Ask him or her what they think motivates "most" workers. Then, show him your sheet with the tallied results. Was your manager surprised? Is there anything that they can do to motivate workers better based upon your results? Bring your list and a summary of your discussion to the class, and be ready to discuss your findings.

CHAPTER 5 - MOTIVATION: FROM CONCEPTS TO APPLICATIONS

CHAPTER OBJECTIVES
After reading this chapter, students should be able to:
1. Identify the four ingredients common to management by objectives (MBO) programs.
2. Outline the five-step problem-solving model in OB Mod.
3. Explain why managers might want to use employee involvement programs.
4. Contrast participative management with employee involvement.
5. Explain how employee stock ownership plans (ESOPs) can increase employee motivation.
6. Describe how a job can be enriched.
7. Compare the benefits and drawbacks from telecommuting from the employee's point of view.
8. Describe the link between skill-based pay plans and motivation theories.

LECTURE OUTLINE
I. MANAGEMENT BY OBJECTIVES
   A. Goal-setting Theory
     1. An impressive base of research support
     2. How do you make goal setting operational?
       a) Install an MBO program.

   B. What is MBO?
     1. Management by objectives (MBO) emphasizes participatively set goals that are tangible, verifiable, and measurable. (ppt 4)
       a) MBO was originally proposed by Peter Drucker forty-five years ago as a means of using goals to motivate people rather than to control them.
     2. MBO appeal is the emphasis on converting overall organizational objectives into specific objectives for organizational units and individual members.
       a) See Exhibit 5-1 for the process by which objectives cascade down through the organization. (ppt 5)
     3. MBO works from the bottom up as well as from the top down.
       a) The hierarchy of objectives link objectives at one level to those at the next level.
       b) If all the individuals achieve their goals, then their unit's goals will be attained and the organization's overall objectives will become a reality.
     4. Four ingredients are common to MBO programs: goal specificity, participative decision making, an explicit time period, and performance feedback. (ppt 6-8)
       a) The objectives in MBO should be concise statements of expected accomplishments.
       b) MBO replaces imposed goals with participatively determined goals.
       c) Each objective has a specific time period in which it is to be completed. Typically, the time period is three months, six months, or a year.
       d) MBO seeks to give continuous feedback on progress toward goals so that individuals can monitor and correct their own actions.
         (1) Continuous feedback, supplemented by more formal periodic managerial evaluations, takes place at the top of the organization as well as at the bottom.

   C. Linking MBO and Goal-Setting Theory
     1. Goal-setting theory demonstrates:
       a) Hard goals result in a higher level of individual performance.

                b) Feedback on one's performance leads to higher performance.
        2. MBO directly advocates:
                a) Specific goals and feedback.
                b) MBO implies, rather than explicitly states, that goals must be perceived as feasible.
                c) Consistent with goal setting theory, MBO would be most effective when the goals are difficult enough to require the person to do some stretching.
        3. The only area of possible disagreement between MBO and goal-setting theory is related to the issue of participation.
                a) MBO strongly advocates it.
                b) Goal-setting theory demonstrates that assigning goals to subordinates frequently works just as well.
                c) The major benefit to using participation, however, is that is appears to induce individuals to establish more difficult goals.

    D. MBO in Practice
        1. Reviews of studies suggest that it is a popular technique.
                a) MBO programs are in business, health care, educational, government, and nonprofit organizations.
        2. MBO's popularity should not be construed to mean that it always works.
                a) There are a number of documented cases in which MBO was implemented but failed to meet management's expectations.
                b) The problems rarely lie with MBO's basic components.
                c) The causes tend to be unrealistic expectations, lack of top-management commitment, and an inability or unwillingness by management to allocate rewards based on goal accomplishment.

II. BEHAVIOR MODIFICATION
    A. Emery Air Freight Study
        1. Occurred more than thirty years ago with freight packers at Emery Air Freight (now part of FedEx)
                a) Management wanted packers to aggregate shipments into freight containers rather than handle many separate items.
                b) Packers claimed 90 percent of shipments were put in containers.
                c) Analysis showed container use rate was only 45 percent.
                d) In order to encourage employees to use containers, management established a program of feedback and positive reinforcement.
                e) Container use jumped to more than 90 percent on the first day of the program and held to that level.
                f) This simple program saved the company millions of dollars.
        2. The Emery Air Freight study illustrates the use of organizational behavior modification (OB Mod). (ppt 9)

    B. What is OB Mod?
        1. See Exhibit 5-2. (ppt 10)
        2. A five-step problem-solving model:
                a) Identify performance-related behaviors.
                b) Measure the behaviors.
                c) Identify behavioral contingencies.
                d) Develop and implement an intervention strategy.
                e) Evaluate performance improvement.

    3. Identify the behaviors that have a significant impact on the employee's job performance.

        a) These are those 5 to 10 percent of behaviors that may account for up to 70 or 80 percent of each employee's performance.

    4. The manager then develops some baseline performance information.

        a) The number of times the identified behavior is occurring under present conditions.

    5. The third step is to perform a functional analysis to identify the behavioral contingencies or consequences of performance.

        a) This tells the manager which cues emit the behavior and which consequences are currently maintaining it.

    6. Now the manager is ready to develop and implement an intervention strategy to strengthen desirable performance behaviors and weaken undesirable behaviors.

        a) The appropriate strategy will entail changing some element of the performance-reward linkage—structure, processes, technology, groups, or the task—with the goal of making high-level performance more rewarding.

    7. The final step in OB Mod is to evaluate performance improvement.

C. Linking OB Mod and Reinforcement Theory

    1. Reinforcement theory relies on positive reinforcement, shaping, and recognizing the impact of different schedules of reinforcement on behavior.

    2. OB Mod uses these concepts to provide managers with a powerful/proven means for changing employee behavior.

D. OB Mod in Practice

    1. OB Mod has been used to improve employee productivity and to reduce errors, absenteeism, tardiness, and accident rates.

    2. A general review of OB programs found an average 17 percent improvement in performance.

III. EMPLOYEE RECOGNITION PROGRAMS (ppt 11)

A. The Laura Schendell Example

    1. Organizations are increasingly recognizing what Laura Schendell is acknowledging: recognition can be a potent motivator.

B. What Are Employee Recognition Programs?

    1. Numerous forms

    2. The best use multiple sources and recognize both individual and group accomplishments.

C. Linking Recognition Programs and Reinforcement Theory

    1. A survey of 1,500 employees regarding the most powerful workplace motivator.

        a) Their response was recognition, recognition, and more recognition.

    2. Consistent with reinforcement theory, rewarding a behavior with recognition immediately following that behavior is likely to encourage its repetition. (ppt 12)

    3. And that recognition can take many forms.

        a) Personally congratulate an employee in private for a good job.

        b) Send a handwritten note or an e-mail message.

        c) Publicly recognize accomplishments.

        d) And to enhance group cohesiveness and motivation, you can celebrate team successes.

D. Employee Recognition Programs in Practice
   1. Today's cost pressures make recognition programs particularly attractive.
      a) Recognizing an employee's superior performance often costs little or no money.
      b) A survey of 291 companies found that 84 percent had some program to recognize worker achievement.
      c) Critics argue that these programs are susceptible to political manipulation by management. (ppt 13)

IV. EMPLOYEE INVOLVEMENT PROGRAMS
   A. Example
      1. Teams perform many tasks and assume many of the responsibilities once handled by their supervisors.

   B. What is Employee Involvement?
      1. *Employee involvement* has become a convenient catchall term to cover a variety of techniques.
         a) Employee participation or participative management
         b) Workplace democracy
         c) Empowerment
         d) Employee ownership
      2. Employee involvement is a participative process that uses the entire capacity of employees and is designed to encourage increased commitment to the organization's success. (ppt 14)
         a) The underlying logic involves workers in decisions that will affect them and increases their autonomy and control, which will result in higher motivation, greater commitment, more productivity, and more satisfaction. (ppt 15-16)
      3. Participation and employee involvement are not synonyms.
         a) Participation is a more limited term.
         b) It is a subset within the larger framework of employee involvement.

   C. Examples of Employee Involvement Programs
      1. Three forms of employee involvement: participative management, representative participation, and employee stock ownership plans.
      2. Participative Management (ppt 17)
         a) Characteristic of all participative management programs is joint decision making.
         b) Has been promoted as a panacea for poor morale and low productivity.
         c) Not always appropriate. For it to work:
            (1) There must be adequate time to participate. (ppt 18)
            (2) The issues must be relevant to the employees.
            (3) Employees must have the ability to participate.
            (4) The organization's culture must support employee involvement.
         d) Dozens of studies have been conducted on the participation-performance relationship.
            (1) Mixed findings
      3. Representative Participation (ppt 19)
         a) Rather than participating directly in decisions, workers are represented by a small group of employees who actually participate.

            (1) The most widely legislated form of employee involvement around the world.

4. The goal of representative participation is to redistribute power within an organization.
5. The two most common forms that representative participation takes are works councils and board representatives. (ppt 20)
    a) Works councils link employees with management. They are groups of nominated or elected employees who must be consulted when management makes decisions involving personnel.
    b) Board representatives are employees who sit on a company's board of directors and represent the interests of the firm's employees. In some countries, large companies may be legally required to make sure that employee representatives have the same number of board seats as stockholder representatives.
6. The overall influence of representative participation on working employees seems to be minimal.
    a) Works councils are dominated by management and have little impact on employees or the organization.
    b) The greatest value of representative participation is symbolic.
7. Employee Stock Ownership Plans (ESOPs) (ppt 21)
    a) Company-established benefit plans in which employees acquire stock as part of their benefits.
        (1) United Airlines, Publix Supermarkets, Graybar Electric, and Anderson Corporation are four examples of companies that are more than 50 percent owned by employees.
    b) In the typical ESOP an employee stock ownership trust is created.
    c) Companies contribute either stock or cash to buy stock for the trust and allocate the stock to employees.
    d) Employees usually cannot take physical possession of their shares or sell them as long as they're still employed at the company.
    e) ESOPs increase employee satisfaction and frequently result in higher performance.

D. Linking Employee Involvement Program and Motivation Theories
    1. Employee involvement draws on several motivation theories.
        a) Theory Y is consistent with participative management.
        b) Theory X aligns with the more traditional autocratic style of managing people.
        c) Two-factor theory relates to employee involvement programs that provide employees with intrinsic motivation by increasing opportunities for growth, responsibility, and involvement in the work itself.

E. Employee Involvement Programs in Practice
    1. Germany, France, the Netherlands, and the Scandinavian countries have firmly established the principle of industrial democracy in Europe, and other nations, including Japan and Israel, have traditionally practiced some form of representative participation for decades.
    2. Participative management and representative participation were much slower to gain ground in North American organizations.
        a) Now, employee involvement programs stressing participation are the norm.
    3. ESOPs

a) They are becoming a popular employee involvement program-having grown to around 10,000, covering more than 10 million employees.

V.   JOB REDESIGN AND SCHEDULING PROGRAMS
   A. Work Redesign (ppt 22)
      1. Job Rotation (ppt 23)
         a) If employees suffer from overroutinization of their work, one alternative is to use job rotation (or what many now call cross-training).
         b) The strengths of job rotation are that it reduces boredom and increases motivation through diversifying the employee's activities.
         c) It can also have indirect benefits for the organization since employees with a wider range of skills give management more flexibility in scheduling work, adapting to changes, and filling vacancies.
         d) Drawbacks
            (1) Training costs increase.
            (2) Productivity is reduced.
            (3) It creates disruptions—members of the work group have to adjust to the new employee.
            (4) It can demotivate intelligent and ambitious trainees who seek specific responsibilities in their chosen specialty.
      2. Job Enlargement (ppt 24)
         a) Increasing the number and variety of tasks that an individual performed resulted in jobs with more diversity.
         b) Efforts at job enlargement met with less than enthusiastic results.
            (1) "Before I had one lousy job. Now, through enlargement, I have three."
         c) There have been some successful applications of job enlargement.
            (1) U.S. Shoe Co. created modular work areas to replace production lines in over half of its factories. The result has been footwear produced more efficiently and with greater attention to quality.
      3. Job Enrichment
         a) Job enrichment refers to the vertical expansion of jobs.
         b) It increases the degree to which the worker controls the planning, execution, and evaluation of his or her work.
         c) An enriched job organizes tasks so as to allow the worker to do a complete activity, increases the employee's freedom and independence, increases responsibility, and provides feedback, so an individual will be able to assess and correct his or her own performance.
         d) How to enrich an employee's job (See Exhibit 5-3). (ppt 25)
            (1) Combine tasks. This measure increases skill variety and task identity.
            (2) Create natural work units. This increases employee "ownership" of the work.
            (3) Establish client relationships. Managers should try to establish direct relationships between workers and their clients to increase skill variety, autonomy, and feedback for the employee.
            (4) Expand jobs vertically. Vertical expansion gives employees responsibilities and control that were formerly reserved for management.
            (5) Open feedback channels. Ideally, feedback about performance should be received directly as the employee does the job, rather than from management on an occasional basis.
         e) Example of effect—Job enrichment program for the international-trade banking department at First Chicago Corporation.

(1) Productivity has more than tripled, employee satisfaction has soared, and transaction volume has risen more than 10 percent a year.

(2) Increased skills have translated into higher pay for the employees who are performing the enriched jobs.

    f) The overall evidence generally shows that job enrichment reduces absenteeism and turnover costs and increases satisfaction, but on the critical issue of productivity the evidence is inconclusive.

B. Popular Work Schedule Options

   1. Flextime (ppt 26)

    a) Short for "flexible work hours"

    b) Scheduling option that allows employees some discretion over when they arrive at and leave work.

    c) Employees have to work a specific number of hours a week, but they are free to vary the hours of work within certain limits.

    d) See Exhibit 5-4.

    e) Flextime has become an extremely popular scheduling option, with about 28 percent of the U.S. full-time workforce having flexibility in their daily arrival and departure time.

    f) Benefits

      (1) Reduced absenteeism

      (2) Increased productivity

      (3) Reduced overtime expenses

      (4) A lessening in hostility toward management

      (5) Reduced traffic congestion

      (6) Elimination of tardiness

      (7) Increased autonomy and responsibility that may increase employee job satisfaction

    g) Drawback

      (1) Not applicable to every job

   2. Job Sharing (ppt 27)

    a) Two or more individuals share the same job.

    b) Allows the organization to draw upon the talents of more than one individual.

    c) Allows skilled-workers to work when they otherwise could not due to schedules.

   3. Telecommuting (ppt 28-29)

    a) Employees who do their work at home at least two days a week on a computer that is linked to the office telecommute.

    b) A closely related term, *virtual office,* is being increasingly used to describe employees who work out of their home on a relatively permanent basis.

    c) Three categories of jobs lend themselves to telecommuting

      (1) Routine information-handling tasks

      (2) Mobile activities

      (3) Professional and other knowledge-related tasks

    d) As the cost of traditional office space has escalated and the cost of telecommunications equipment has plummeted, managers are increasingly motivated to introduce the virtual office.

    e) The long-term future of telecommuting depends on answers we don't yet know.

      (1) Will employees who do their work at home be at a disadvantage in office politics?

    (2) Might these employees be less likely to be considered for salary
        increases and promotions?
    (3) Is being out of sight equivalent to being out of mind?
    (4) Will nonwork-related distractions such as children, neighbors, and the
        close proximity of the refrigerator significantly reduce productivity?

4. Linking Job Redesign and Scheduling to Motivation Theories
    a) Exhibit 5-3 relates to the jobs characteristics model.
    b) The scheduling options all allow flexibility, which impacts motivation

5. Job Redesign and Scheduling in Practice
    a) Job rotation has been popular in manufacturing firms because it adds
        flexibility and reduces layoffs.
    b) Job enlargement is not used as a motivational device, primarily because it
        does not challenge workers or make jobs more meaningful.
    c) Job enrichment has been widely applied in organizations
    d) Flextime, job sharing, and telecommuting continue to increase in popularity.

VI. VARIABLE-PAY PROGRAMS (ppt 31)
A. What Are Variable-Pay Programs?
    1. Piece-rate plans, wage incentives, profit sharing, bonuses, and gain sharing are
        all forms of variable-pay programs. (ppt 32)
    2. Differ from traditional programs in that a person is paid not only for time on the
        job or seniority but for some individual or organizational measure of
        performance or both.
    3. Variable pay is not an annuity.
        a) With variable pay, earnings fluctuate with the measure of performance.
    4. This fluctuation makes these programs attractive to management.
        a) Part of an organization's fixed labor costs become a variable cost.
        b) In addition, when pay is tied to performance, earnings recognize contribution
            rather than being a form of entitlement.
    5. Four of the more widely used of the variable-pay programs follow.
        a) Piece-rate wages have been around for nearly a century.
            (1) Popular as a means for compensating production workers.
            (2) Workers are paid a fixed sum for each unit of production completed.
            (3) A system in which an employee gets no base salary and is paid only for
                what he or she produces is a pure piece-rate plan.
            (4) Many organizations use a modified piece-rate plan, in which employees
                earn a base hourly wage plus a piece-rate differential.
        b) Bonuses can be paid exclusively to executives or to all employees.
            (1) Increasingly, bonus plans are taking on a larger net within organizations
                to include lower-ranking employees.
        c) Profit-sharing plans are organization-wide programs that distribute
            compensation based on some established formula designed around a
            company's profitability.
            (1) These can be direct cash outlays or, particularly in the case of top
                managers, allocated as stock options.
        d) The variable-pay program that has gotten the most attention in recent years is
            undoubtedly gainsharing.

(1) A formula-based group incentive plan. Improvements in group productivity—from one period to another—determine the total amount of money to be allocated.

(2) The productivity savings can be split between the company and employees in any number of ways, but 50-50 is pretty typical.

(3) Gainsharing is similar to profit sharing, not the same.

    (a) By focusing on productivity gains rather than on profits, gainsharing rewards specific behaviors that are less influenced by external factors than profits are.

    (b) Employees in a gainsharing plan can receive incentive awards even when the organization isn't profitable.

  6. Variable-pay programs increase motivation and productivity.

    a) Gain sharing has been found to improve productivity in most cases and often has a positive impact on employee attitudes.

B. Linking Variable-Pay Programs and Expectancy Theory

  1. Variable pay is compatible with expectancy theory predictions.

  2. Group and organization-wide incentives encourage employees to sublimate personal goals in the best interests of their department or the organization.

  3. Group-based performance incentives help build a strong team ethic.

C. Variable-Pay Programs in Practice

  1. Variable pay is rapidly replacing the annual cost-of-living raise because of:

    a) its motivational power.

    b) the cost implications.

    c) the need to avoid the fixed expense of permanent salary boosts.

  2. Pay-for-performance has been important for compensating managers for more than a decade.

  3. The new trend has been to expand this practice to nonmanagerial employees.

    a) Seventy-two percent of all U.S. companies had some form of variable-pay plan for nonexecutives in the year 2000.

  4. Gainsharing's popularity seems to be restricted to large, unionized manufacturing companies.

VII. SKILL-BASED PAY PLANS

A. What Are Skill-Based Pay Plans? (ppt 33)

  1. Skill-based pay is an alternative to job-based pay.

  2. Skill-based pay (also called competency-based pay) sets pay levels on the basis of how many skills employees have or how many jobs they can do.

  3. The appeal of skill-based pay plans is flexibility.

    a) Filling staffing needs is easier when employee skills are interchangeable.

    b) It facilitates communication throughout the organization because people gain a better understanding of others' jobs.

    c) It lessens dysfunctional "protection of territory" behavior.

    d) Skill-based pay also helps meet the needs of ambitious employees who confront minimal advancement opportunities.

  4. There are downsides of skill-based pay.

    a) People can "top out" relearning all the skills the program calls for them to learn.

    b) Skills can also become obsolete.

        c) Skill-based plans do not address level of performance, only whether someone can perform the skill.

  B. Linking Skill-Based Pay Plans to Motivation Theories
     1. Skill-based pay plans are consistent with several motivation theories.
     2. Because they encourage employees to learn, expand their skills, and grow, they are consistent with Maslow's hierarchy of needs theory.
     3. Paying people to expand their skill levels is also consistent with research on the achievement need.
        a) High achievers have a compelling drive to do things better or more efficiently.
     4. There is also a link between reinforcement theory and skill-based pay.
        a) Skill-based pay encourages employees to develop their flexibility, to continue to learn, to cross train, to be generalists rather than specialists, and to work cooperatively with others in the organization.
        b) To the degree that management wants employees to demonstrate such behaviors, skill-based pay acts as a reinforcer.
     5. Skill-based pay may also have equity implications.
        a) When employees make their input-outcome comparisons, skills may provide a fairer input criterion for determining pay.

  C. Skill-Based Pay in Practice
     1. The overall conclusion of studies is that the use of skill-based pay is expanding and that it generally leads to higher employee performance and satisfaction.

VIII.   A FINAL THOUGHT: MOTIVATING THE DIVERSIFIED WORKFORCE
  A. All of the techniques discussed in this chapter vary in effectiveness based upon the individual. Managers must recognize that in order to maximize employee motivation, they must be flexible and take into account individual employee needs. (ppt 34)

IX. IMPLICATIONS FOR MANAGERS
     1. Organizations have introduced a number of programs designed to increase employee motivation, productivity, and satisfaction. Importantly, these programs are grounded on basic motivation theories.
     2. It is easy to criticize educators and researchers for their focus on building theories. Students and practitioners often consider these theories unrealistic or irrelevant to solving real-life problems. This chapter makes a good rebuttal to those critics. It illustrates how tens of thousands of organizations and millions of managers in countries around the globe are using motivation theories to build practical incentive programs.
     3. The six motivation programs we discussed in this chapter are not applicable to every organization or every manager's needs. But an understanding of these programs will help you design internal systems that can increase employee productivity and satisfaction.

SUMMARY (ppt 35-36)

1. Management by objectives (MBO) emphasizes participatively set goals that are tangible, verifiable, and measurable. Its appeal is its ability to convert overall organizational objectives into specific objectives for organizational units and individual members. MBO works from the bottom up as well as from the top down. There are four ingredients common to MBO

programs: goal specificity, participative decision making, an explicit time period, and performance feedback.

2. MBO and goal-setting theory are complementary. Goal-setting theory demonstrates that hard goals result in a higher level of individual performance and that feedback on one's performance leads to higher performance. MBO advocates specific goals and feedback. Consistent with goal setting theory, MBO would be most effective when the goals are difficult enough to require the person to do some stretching. MBO and goal-setting theory differ in terms of participation; MBO strongly advocates it, while goal-setting theory demonstrates that assigning goals to subordinates frequently works just as well.

3. The five-step problem-solving model in OB modification model includes identifying performance-related behaviors, measuring the behaviors, identifying behavioral contingencies, developing and implementing an intervention strategy, and evaluating performance improvement. It requires the identification of the behaviors that have a significant impact on the employee's job performance.

4. Employee involvement has become a convenient catchall term to cover a variety of techniques: employee participation, or participative management; workplace democracy; empowerment; and employee ownership. Employee involvement is a participative process that uses the entire capacity of employees and is designed to encourage increased commitment to the organization's success. The underlying logic involves workers in decisions that will affect them and increase their autonomy and control, which will result in higher motivation, greater commitment, more productivity, and more satisfaction.

5. There are three primary types of employee involvement programs. Participative management involves joint decision making and is often promoted as a panacea for poor morale and low productivity. Representative participation, involves workers being represented by a small group of employees who actually participate. And ESOPs or employee stock ownership plans, company-established benefit plans in which employees acquire stock as part of their benefits.

6. Employee involvement programs are practiced around the world. Germany, France, the Netherlands, and the Scandinavian countries have firmly established the principle of industrial democracy in Europe, and other nations, including Japan and Israel, have traditionally practiced some form of representative participation for decades.

7. ESOPs can increase employee motivation. They tend to increase employee satisfaction and frequently result in higher performance. They are company-established benefit plans in which employees acquire stock as part of their benefits. Employees usually cannot take physical possession of their shares or sell them as long as they're still employed at the company.

8. Work redesign has several techniques within it that managers can use to increase worker motivation. If employees suffer from overroutinization of their work, one alternative is to use job rotation (or what many now call cross-training). Job enlargement, increasing the number and variety of tasks that an individual performed resulted in jobs with more diversity. Job enrichment refers to the vertical expansion of jobs. It increases the degree to which the worker controls the planning, execution, and evaluation of his or her work.

9. In a work world where employees are increasingly complaining about being pressed for time and the difficulty of balancing personal and work lives, work schedule options such as flextime and telecommuting can be a way to improve employee motivation, productivity, and satisfaction

10. Variable-pay programs are another way to motivate employees through piece-rate plans, wage incentives, profit sharing, bonuses, and gain sharing are all forms of variable-pay programs. These differ from traditional programs in that a person is paid not only for time on the job or seniority but for some individual or organizational measure of performance or both.

11. Variable pay is compatible with expectancy theory predictions. The evidence supports the importance of this linkage, especially for operative employees working under piece-rate

systems. Group and organization-wide incentives encourage employees to sublimate personal goals in the best interests of their department or the organization.

12. Skill-based pay is an alternative to job-based pay. Its sets pay levels on the basis of how many skills employees have or how many jobs they can do. The appeal of skill-based pay plans is flexibility. There are some downsides however. People can "top out" relearning all the skills the program calls for them to learn, skills can also become obsolete, and so on.

DISCUSSION QUESTIONS

1. How does management by objectives work?
   Answer - MBO emphasizes participatively set goals that are tangible, verifiable, and measurable. Its appeal is in the emphasis on converting overall organizational objectives into specific objectives for organizational units and individual members. Exhibit 5-1 shows the process by which objectives cascade down through the organization. MBO works from the bottom up as well as from the top down. The hierarchy of objectives link objectives at one level to those at the next level.

2. Describe the characteristics of an effective MBO program.
   Answer - There are four common characteristics: goal specificity, participative decision making, an explicit time period, and performance feedback. The objectives in MBO should be concise statements of expected accomplishments. MBO replaces imposed goals with participatively determined goals. Each objective has a specific time period in which it is to be completed. Typically, the time period is three months, six months, or a year. MBO seeks to give continuous feedback on progress toward goals so that individuals can monitor and correct their own actions. Continuous feedback, supplemented by more formal periodic managerial evaluations, takes place at the top of the organization as well as at the bottom.

3. Design a behavior modification program for training bank tellers in customer service.
   Answer - Students answers will vary, but they should cover the basic steps. 1) Identify the behaviors that have a significant impact on the employee's job performance. 2) Develop baseline performance information by observing the number of times the identified behavior is occurring under present conditions. 3) Perform a functional analysis to identify the behavioral contingencies or consequences of performance. 4) Develop and implement an intervention strategy to strengthen desirable performance behaviors and weaken undesirable behaviors. 5) The final step in OB Mod is to evaluate performance improvement.

4. Why would a company use job rotation as a work redesign strategy?
   Answer - If employees suffer from overroutinization of their work, one alternative is to use job rotation (or what many now call cross-training). The strengths of job rotation are that it reduces boredom and increases motivation through diversifying the employee's activities. It can also have indirect benefits for the organization since employees with a wider range of skills give management more flexibility in scheduling work, adapting to changes, and filling vacancies.

5. In what ways can a job be enriched?
   Answer - Job enrichment refers to the vertical expansion of jobs. It increases the degree to which the worker controls the planning, execution, and evaluation of his or her work. An enriched job organizes tasks so as to allow the worker to do a complete activity, increases the employee's freedom and independence, increases responsibility, and provides feedback, so an individual will be able to assess and correct his or her own performance.
   - See Exhibit 14-3.
   - Combine tasks. This measure increases skill variety and task identity.

- Create natural work units. This increases employee "ownership" of the work.
- Establish client relationships. Managers should try to establish direct relationships between workers and their clients to increase skill variety, autonomy, and feedback for the employee.
- Expand jobs vertically. Vertical expansion gives employees responsibilities and control that were formerly reserved to management.
- Open feedback channels. Ideally, feedback about performance should be received directly as the employee does the job, rather than from management on an occasional basis.

6. Why might managers want to use employee recognition programs?
   Answer – Recognition can be a potent motivator. The best programs use multiple courses and recognize both individual and group accomplishments. Consistent with reinforcement theory, rewarding a behavior with recognition immediately following that behavior is likely to encourage its repetition. In contrast to most other motivators, recognizing an employee's superior performance often costs little or not money, and is therefore attractive in today's highly competitive global economy.

7. Why might managers want to use employee involvement programs?
   Answer - Employee involvement is a participative process that uses the entire capacity of employees and is designed to encourage increased commitment to the organization's success. The underlying logic involves workers in decisions that will affect them and increases their autonomy and control, which will result in higher motivation, greater commitment, more productivity, and more satisfaction. Employee involvement draws on several motivation theories—Theory Y is consistent with participative management, Theory X aligns with the more traditional autocratic style of managing people, and two-factor theory relates to employee involvement programs that provide employees with intrinsic motivation by increasing opportunities for growth, responsibility, and involvement in the work itself.

8. If a manager decided to implement an employee involvement program what choices would he or she have? Why would he use one rather than another?
   Answer – Use participative management. Characteristic of all participative management programs is joint decision making. Use representative participation. Workers are represented by a small group of employees who actually participate. It is the most widely legislated form of employee involvement around the world. The goal of representative participation is to redistribute power within an organization. The two most common forms that representative participation takes are works councils and board representatives. Employee stock ownership plans are company-established benefit plans in which employees acquire stock as part of their benefits.

9. Explain how ESOPs can increase employee motivation.
   Answer - Employee stock ownership plans are company-established benefit plans in which employees acquire stock as part of their benefits. In the typical ESOP an employee stock ownership trust is created. Companies contribute either stock or cash to buy stock for the trust and allocate the stock to employees. Employees usually cannot take physical possession of their shares or sell them as long as they're still employed at the company. ESOPs increase employee satisfaction and frequently result in higher performance.

10. What is the difference between gain sharing and profit sharing as a variable-pay program?
    Answer – They are similar but not the same. By focusing on productivity gains rather than on profits, gain sharing rewards specific behaviors that are less influenced by external factors

than profits are. Employees in a gain sharing plan can receive incentive awards even when the organization isn't profitable.

11. What is the relationship between skill-based pay plans and motivation theories?
    Answer - Skill-based pay plans are consistent with several motivation theories. Because they encourage employees to learn, expand their skills, and grow, they are consistent with Maslow's hierarchy of needs theory. Paying people to expand their skill levels is also consistent with research on the achievement need. High achievers have a compelling drive to do things better or more efficiently. There is also a link between reinforcement theory and skill-based pay. Skill-based pay encourages employees to develop their flexibility, to continue to learn, to cross train, to be generalists rather than specialists, and to work cooperatively with others in the organization. Skill-based pay may also have equity implications. When employees make their input-outcome comparisons, skills may provide a fairer input criterion for determining pay.

EXERCISES
A.   An Application of Motivation—MBO

The goal here is to help students apply MBO as they will most likely have to deal with it in their first jobs. The emphasis should be on creating measurable realistic objectives. We will apply the MBO process to the classroom. Consider using this as an exercise to organize students' effort for the semester. You can use this as part of your grading for the course by holding the students accountable for their objectives at the end of the semester.
1. Review the principles of MBO with the class.
2. Assign them the task of individually creating five MBOs for themselves for this class for the semester.
   - By now the students have been in class long enough to have a sense of course content, your style, and so on.
   - Students should have a clear idea of your objectives for the class.
   - Students should have a syllabus or an idea of the assignments or projects that will be due.
3. Have students write one MBO in class.
   - Ask volunteers to share their objective.
   - You will get a number of, "Get an A in the course." Be gentle as you point out why this is not an effective objective.
   - Critique the objective stressing both the principles of an effective objective and how well it relates to the course objectives.
4. Have students complete their assignment and bring written objectives into the next class.
5. Place students in pairs or small groups of five or fewer and have them share their objectives with each other.
6. Have each group share the three to five best objectives with the class either orally or by copying them on the board.
7. Discuss the objectives, collect the written copies.

B.   An Application of Motivation—ESOP

The goal is to help students better understand Employee Stock Ownership Plans, as many of them will be employed (currently or in the future) by organization which use ESOPs as a motivational tool. In fact, many organizations even use the ESOP as a recruitment tool, and students need to understand how this benefit/program can work for them, and if this is a plan has enough value to them to be considered in the job choosing/accepting phase of being employed.

1. Review the principles of ESOPs with the class.
2. Have students, using various research methods (Internet, primary research, library research) identify several organizations, a minimum of three, which utilize an ESOP. Have students gather as much detailed information as possible about the particulars of each ESOP.
3. Have each student which a brief synopsis, or summary, or the three ESOPs they researched, and bring these synopses to class.
4. In class have the students share details about their research either as a whole class, or in small groups, with these small groups reporting the most interesting facts to the whole class.
5. If the local area supports enough organizations, the students could be encouraged/required to contact only local organizations for ESOP information. However, the exercise could be expanded to include any type of organization or industry. A comparison ESOPs across industries would be an interesting option also.

C.   An Application of Job Enrichment

Discuss with the class the various ways that they would react to a job rotation program, and enrichment program, or an enlargement program. Discuss this in the context of how it relates to the motivation theories discussed previously in the course, such as Maslow or Herzberg.

D.   Flexible Scheduling

One drawback of the flexible scheduling options is that it is more difficult to monitor employees when they are not physically present. Start a class discussion about how a manager might monitor and assess employee performance if the various scheduling options are in use.

Analyzing Your Organization

Discuss with your manager the possibility of implementing one or more of the concepts in this chapter. For example, you could try the OB Mod model using positive reinforcement on a particular department in your organization. Another idea would be to take a department or a project and try and implement a MBO program. Keep the scope of the intervention small, so that you can analyze the results, look for problems, and tweak the program to suit your organization's needs. If it works, discuss with your boss the possibility of expanding the program beyond your department. Be prepared to discuss with your class the results.

CHAPTER 6 - INDIVIDUAL DECISION MAKING

CHAPTER OBJECTIVES
After reading this chapter, students should be able to:
1. Explain the six-step rational decision-making model and its assumptions.
2. Identify the key components in the three-component model of creativity.
3. Describe actions of the boundedly rational decision maker.
4. Identify six common decision errors or biases.
5. Explain when intuition can enhance the quality of a decision
6. Identify four decision-making styles.
7. Describe how organizational constraints affect decision making.
8. Explain the implications of stages of moral development to decision making.

LECTURE OUTLINE
I. INTRODUCTION
   A. Individuals in organizations make decisions. (ppt 4)
       1. Top managers determine their organization's goals, what products or services to offer, how best to organize corporate headquarters, and so on.
       2. Middle- and lower-level managers determine production schedules, select new employees, and decide how pay raises are to be allocated.
       3. Non-managerial employees also make decisions that affect their jobs and the organizations for which they work.
       4. All individuals in every organization regularly engage in decision making—they make choices from among two or more alternatives.

II. HOW SHOULD DECISIONS BE MADE?
   A. The Rational Model
       1. The optimizing decision maker is rational.
           a) He or she makes consistent, value-maximizing choices within specified constraints.
       2. The Rational Model
           a) See Exhibit 6-1 for the six steps in the rational decision-making model. (ppt 5)
       3. The model begins by defining the problem.
           a) A problem exists when there is a discrepancy between an existing and a desired state of affairs.
       4. Next, the decision maker needs to identify the decision criteria that will be important in solving the problem.
           a) Determining what is relevant to making the decision.
           b) The decision maker's interests, values, and personal preferences are brought into the process.
       5. The third step requires the decision maker to weigh the previously identified criteria in order to give them correct priority in the decision.
       6. The fourth step requires the generation of possible alternatives that could succeed in resolving the problem.
           a) Alternatives are not yet appraised, just listed.
       7. Once the alternatives have been generated, the decision maker must critically analyze and evaluate each one.
           a) This is done by rating each alternative on each criterion.
       8. The final step in this model requires computing the optimal decision.

a) This is done by evaluating each alternative against the weighted criteria and selecting the alternative with the highest total score.

9. Assumptions of the Model (ppt 6)

a) Problem clarity: the problem is clear, unambiguous, and the decision maker has complete information.

b) Known options: The decision maker can identify all the relevant criteria, can list all the viable alternatives, and is aware of all the possible consequences.

c) Clear preferences: rationality assumes that the criteria and alternatives can be ranked and weighted to reflect their importance.

d) Constant preferences: specific decision criteria are constant and that the weights assigned to them are stable over time.

e) No time or cost constraints: the rational decision maker can obtain full information about criteria and alternatives because it is assumed that there are no time or cost constraints.

f) Maximum payoff: the rational decision maker will choose the alternative that yields the highest perceived value.

B. Improving Creativity in Decision Making

1. Creativity is the ability to produce novel and useful ideas. (ppt 7)

2. Creativity allows the decision maker to more fully appraise and understand the problem, including seeing problems others cannot see.

3. The most obvious value is in helping the decision maker identify all viable alternatives.

4. Creative Potential

a) To tap creative potential, most people have to climb out of their psychological ruts.

b) Need to learn how to think about a problem in divergent ways.

5. People differ in their inherent creativity.

a) A study of lifetime creativity of 461 men and women found that fewer than 1 percent were exceptionally creative. But 10 percent were highly creative, and about 60 percent were somewhat creative.

6. Three-Component Model of Creativity

a) Based on considerable research, this model proposed that individual creativity requires: expertise, creative-thinking skills, and intrinsic task motivation.

(1) See Exhibit 6-2. (ppt 8)

(2) Studies confirm that the higher the level of each of these three components, the higher the creativity is.

(3) Expertise is the foundation of all creative work. The potential for creativity is enhanced when individuals have abilities, knowledge, proficiencies, and similar expertise in their fields of endeavor.

(4) Creative-thinking skills encompass personality characteristics associated with creativity, the ability to use analogies, and a talent for seeing the familiar in a different light.

(5) Intrinsic task motivation is the desire to work on something because it is interesting, involving, exciting, satisfying, or personally challenging. This component turns creativity potential into actual creative ideas.

b) Organizational factors that impede creativity include expected evaluation, surveillance, external motivators, competition, and constrained choice. (ppt 9)

III. HOW DECISIONS ARE ACTUALLY MADE IN ORGANIZATIONS
   A. Are decision makers in organizations rational?
      1. When decision makers are faced with a simple problem having few alternative courses of action, and when the cost of searching out and evaluating alternatives is low, the rational model provides a fairly accurate description of the decision-making process.
      2. But such situations are the exception. Most decisions in the real world do not follow the rational model.

   B. Bounded Rationality (ppt 11)
      1. College search example
      2. When faced with a complex problem, most people respond by reducing the problem to a level at which it can be readily understood.
         a) People "satisfice." That is, they seek solutions that are satisfactory and sufficient.
      3. Because of the limitations of the human mind most individuals operate within the confines of bounded rationality.
         a) They construct simplified models that extract the essential features from problems without capturing all of their complexity.
      4. How does it work?
         a) A problem is identified; then the search for criteria and alternatives begins.
         b) The decision maker limits alternatives to the more conspicuous choices.
            (1) Such choices are easy to find and tend to be highly visible.
            (2) They represent familiar criteria and tried-and-true solutions.
         c) The limited set of alternatives is reviewed.
            (1) Review is limited.
            (2) It begins with alternatives that differ only in a relatively small degree from the choice currently in effect.
            (3) The decision maker proceeds to review alternatives only until he or she identifies an alternative that is good enough—one that meets an acceptable level of performance.
         d) The first alternative that meets the "good enough" criterion ends the search.
         e) So the final solution represents a "satisficing" choice rather than an optimal one.
      5. The order in which alternatives are considered is critical in determining which alternative is selected because the "satisficing" choice will be the first acceptable one the decision maker encounters.
         a) Solutions that depart least from the status quo and meet the decision criteria are most likely to be selected.

   C. Common Biases and errors (ppt 12-13)
      1. Research shows that decision makers allow biases and errors to creep into their judgments. The following highlights the most common distortions.
         a) Overconfidence Bias- we think we know more than we actually do.
         b) Anchoring Bias- the tendency to fixate on the first piece of information we receive.
         c) Confirmation Bias- selectively gathering information that supports our existing views.
         d) Availability Bias- basing judgments on information that is readily available.
         e) Representative Bias- assessing the likelihood of an occurrence by matching it with a preexisting category.

f) Escalation of Commitment- staying with a decision despite clear evidence that it is wrong.

g) Randomness error- trying to create meaning out of random events.

h) Hindsight Bias- to believe we'd have accurately predicted the outcome of an event, after that outcome is actually known.

D. Intuition (ppt 14)

1. Managers regularly use their intuition, and this may actually help improve decision making.

2. Intuitive decision making is an unconscious process created out of distilled experience.

   a) It complements the rational approach.

   b) Research on chess playing provides an excellent illustration of how intuition works.

      (1) Experience allows the expert to recognize a situation and draw upon previously learned information associated with that situation in order to quickly arrive at a decision.

      (2) The result is that the intuitive decision maker can decide rapidly with what appears to be very limited information.

      (3) There is growing recognition that rational analysis has been overemphasized, and that in certain instances, relying on intuition can improve decision making. Intuitive decision making is useful under the following conditions. (ppt 15-16)

         (a) When a high level of uncertainty exists.

         (b) When there is little precedent to draw on.

         (c) When variables are less scientifically predictable.

         (d) When "facts" are limited.

         (e) When facts don't clearly point the way.

         (f) When analytical data are of little use.

         (g) When there are several plausible alternative solutions from which to choose.

         (h) When time is limited.

E. Individual Differences

1. Two individual differences seem particularly relevant to decision making in organizations—decision-making styles and level of moral development.

2. Decision-Making Styles

   a) The foundation of the model is the recognition that people differ along two dimensions.

      (1) The first is their way of thinking.

      (2) The other dimension addresses a person's tolerance for ambiguity.

   b) When these two dimensions are diagrammed, they form four styles of decision making.

      (1) See Exhibit 6-3. Four styles are directive, analytical, conceptual, and behavioral. (ppt 17)

   c) Directive style

      (1) Low tolerance for ambiguity and seek rationality.

      (2) Efficient and logical. Decisions are based on minimal information after the consideration of few alternatives.

      (3) Directive types make decisions fast, and they focus on the short run.

   d) Analytical style

     (1) Greater tolerance for ambiguity than do directive decision makers.

     (2) They desire more information and consider more alternatives than do directives.

     (3) Characterized as careful decision makers with the ability to adapt or cope with new situations.

   e) Conceptual style

     (1) Very broad in their outlook and consider many alternatives.

     (2) Focus is long range, and they are very good at finding creative solutions to problems.

   f) Behavioral style

     (1) Characterizes decision makers who work well with others.

     (2) They are concerned with the achievement of peers and subordinates.

     (3) They are receptive to suggestions from others and rely heavily on meetings for communicating.

     (4) This type of manager tries to avoid conflict and seeks acceptance.

   g) Most managers have characteristics that fall into more than one.

     (1) But they have a dominant style and a backup style.

     (2) Business students, lower-level managers, and top executives tend to score highest in the analytic style.

   h) Focusing on decision styles can be useful for helping you understand how two equally intelligent people, with access to the same information, can differ in their decision making and their final choices.

 3. Gender (ppt 18)

   a) Women analyze decisions more than men.

   b) Women are more likely than men to "ruminate," or overthink problems.

   c) This can lead to more careful consideration of problems or choices, or it can make problems harder to solve.

 4. Level of Moral Development

   a) Many decisions have an ethical dimension.

   b) Research confirms the existence of three levels of moral development, each comprises two stages.

     (1) See Exhibit 6-4. (ppt 19)

     (2) At each successive stage, an individual's moral judgment grows less and less dependent on outside influences.

   c) Preconventional. Individuals respond to notions of right or wrong only when personal consequences are involved.

   d) Conventional. Reasoning at this level indicates that moral value resides in maintaining the conventional order and the expectations of others.

   e) Principled. Individuals make a clear effort to define moral principles apart from the authority of the groups to which they belong or society in general.

 5. Conclusions

   a) People proceed through the six stages in a lock-step fashion. They gradually move up a ladder, stage by stage.

   b) There is no guarantee of continued development. Development can terminate at any stage.

   c) Most adults are at stage four. They are limited to obeying the rules and laws of society.

   d) The higher the stage a manager reaches, the more he or she will be predisposed to make ethical decisions.

F. Organizational Constraints (ppt 20)
    1. The organization itself constrains decision makers.
    2. Performance evaluation
        a) Managers are strongly influenced by the criteria by which they are evaluated.
    3. Reward systems
        a) The organization's reward system influences decision makers by suggesting to them what choices are preferable in terms of personal payoff.
    4. Formal Regulations
        a) Formally implementing rules and procedures speeds up decision making, but limits the decision maker's choices.
    5. System-imposed time constraints
        a) Organizations impose deadlines on decisions.
    6. Historical precedents
        a) Decisions have a context; individual decisions are more accurately characterized as points in a stream of decisions.
        b) Decisions made in the past are ghosts that continually haunt current choices.

G. Cultural Differences (ppt 21)
    1. The rational model does not acknowledge cultural differences.
    2. The cultural background of the decision maker can significantly influence his or her selection of problems, depth of analysis, the importance placed on logic and rationality, or whether organizational decisions should be made autocratically by an individual manager or collectively in groups.
    3. Cultures, for example, differ in terms of time orientation, the importance of rationality, their belief in the ability of people to solve problems, and preference for collective decision making.

IV. ETHICS IN DECISION MAKING
    A. Three different ways to frame decisions (ppt 22)
        1. Utilitarian criterion
            a) Decisions are made solely on the basis of their outcomes or consequences.
            b) The goal is to provide the greatest good for the greatest number.
            c) This view tends to dominate business decision making.
        2. Focus on rights
            a) This calls on individuals to make decisions consistent with fundamental liberties and privileges as set forth in documents such as the Bill of Rights.
            b) An emphasis on rights in decision making means respecting and protecting the basic rights of individuals, such as the right to privacy, to free speech, and to due process.
        3. Focus on justice
            a) This requires individuals to impose and enforce rules fairly and impartially so there is an equitable distribution of benefits and costs.
            b) Union members typically favor this view.
        4. Advantages and liabilities
            a) Utilitarianism
                (1) Promotes efficiency and productivity, but it can result in ignoring the rights of some individuals, particularly those with minority representation in the organization.
            b) Rights

73

(1) Protects individuals from injury, and is consistent with freedom and privacy, but it can create an overly legalistic workplace that hinders productivity and efficiency.

   c) Justice

(1) Protects the interests of the underrepresented and less powerful, but it can encourage a sense of entitlement that reduces risk taking, innovation, and productivity.

5. Decision makers, particularly in for-profit organizations, tend to feel safe and comfortable when they use utilitarianism.
6. Increased concerns in society about individual rights and social justice suggest the need for managers to develop ethical standards based on nonutilitarian criteria.

V. IMPLICATIONS FOR MANAGERS (ppt 23)

1. Individuals think and reason before they act. Thus, an understanding of how people make decisions can be helpful if we are to explain and predict their behavior.
2. Under some decision situations, people follow the rational model. Most people and most nonroutine decisions do not use this model. Few important decisions are simple or unambiguous enough for the rational model's assumptions to apply. So individuals look for solutions that "satisfice" rather than optimize, inject biases and prejudices into the decision process, and rely on intuition.
3. Given the evidence described on how decisions are actually made in organizations, what can managers do to improve their decision making? Here are five suggestions.

- Analyze the situation. Adjust your decision-making style to the national culture in which you are operating and to criteria your organization evaluates and rewards. Similarly, organizations differ in terms of the importance they place on risk, the use of groups, and the like. Adjust your decision-making style to the organization's culture.
- Be aware of biases and errors. We all bring biases to the decisions we make. If you understand the biases influencing your judgment, you can begin to change the way you make decisions to reduce those biases.
- Combine rational analysis with intuition. These are not conflicting approaches to decision making. By using both, you can actually improve your decision-making effectiveness.
- Don't assume that your specific decision-making style is appropriate for every job. Just as organizations differ, so, too, do jobs within organizations. And your effectiveness as a decision maker will increase if you match your decision style to the requirements of the job. For instance, if you have a directive style of decision making, you'll be more effective working with people whose jobs require quick action. This style, for example, would match up well with managing stockbrokers. An analytic style, on the other hand, would work well managing accountants, market researchers, or financial analysts.
- Try to enhance your creativity. Overtly look for novel solutions to problems, attempt to see problems in new ways, and use analogies. In addition try to remove work and organizational barriers that might impede your creativity.

SUMMARY (ppt 24-25)

1. Top managers determine their organization's goals, what products or services to offer, how best to organize corporate headquarters, and so on. Middle- and lower-level managers determine production schedules, select new employees, and decide how pay raises are to be allocated. Nonmanagerial employees also make decisions that affect their jobs and the organizations for which they work.

2. The rational decision-making process uses six steps. It begins by defining the problem. Then the decision maker needs to identify the decision criteria that will be important in solving the problem. Next, the decision maker weighs and prioritizes the criteria. Next comes the generation of possible alternatives, which must be critically analyzed and evaluated. The final step in this model requires computing the optimal decision.

3. Creativity is the ability to combine ideas in a unique way or to make unusual associations between ideas. Creativity allows the decision maker to more fully appraise and understand the problem, including seeing problems others cannot see. People differ in their inherent creativity but everyone can stimulate their individual creativity.

4. When decision makers are faced with a simple problem having few alternative courses of action and when the cost of searching out and evaluating alternatives is low, the rational model provides a fairly accurate description of the decision-making process. When faced with a complex problem, most people respond by reducing the problem to a level at which it can be readily understood. People "satisfice," that is, they seek solutions that are satisfactory and sufficient.

5. Managers regularly use their intuition, and this may actually help improve decision making. Intuitive decision making is an unconscious process created out of distilled experience.

6. Decision makers identify and select problems based on their visibility and the decision maker's self-interest. Since decision makers seek a "satisficing" solution, they tend to show a minimal use of creativity.

7. All decision makers allow systematic biases and errors to creep into their judgments, primarily out of their attempts to short-cut the decision making process.

8. Two individual differences seem particularly relevant to decision making in organizations—decision-making styles and level of moral development. When these two dimensions are diagrammed, they form four styles of decision making—directive, analytical, conceptual, and behavioral.

9. The cultural background of the decision maker can significantly influence his or her selection of problems, depth of analysis, the importance placed on logic and rationality, or whether organizational decisions should be made autocratically by an individual manager or collectively in groups.

10. There are three different ways to frame decisions. Utilitarian criteria focus decisions solely on the basis of their outcomes or consequences. A focus on rights calls on individuals to make decisions consistent with fundamental liberties and privileges as set forth in documents such as the Bill of Rights.

11. A justice perspective requires individuals to impose and enforce rules fairly and impartially so there is an equitable distribution of benefits and costs.

DISCUSSION QUESTIONS

1. As a manager you need to decide between two different vendors for your computer needs. Use the six-step rational model to think through this decision.
   Answer - Students' answers will vary but they should clearly apply all six steps of the model. See Exhibit 6-1 for the six steps in the rational decision-making model.
   - The model begins by defining the problem. A problem exists when there is a discrepancy between an existing and a desired state of affairs.

- Next, identify the decision criteria that will be important in solving the problem. Determine what is relevant to making the decision.
- Third, weigh the criteria (i.e., prioritize the criteria).
- The fourth step requires the generation of possible alternatives that could succeed in resolving the problem.
- Fifth, critically analyze each alternative by rating each alternative on each criterion.
- Finally, compute the optimal decision by evaluating each alternative against the weighted criteria and selecting the alternative with the highest total score.

2. How can you stimulate your creativity in decision making?
   Answer – Most people have creative potential that they can use. But to unleash that potential, they have to get out of the psychological ruts most of us get into and learn how to think about a problem in divergent ways. Based on the three-component model of creativity, individual creativity essentially requires expertise, creative-thinking skills, and intrinsic task motivation (See Exhibit 6-2). The higher the level of each of these components, the higher the creativity is. Additionally, organizational factors that impede creativity—expected evaluation, surveillance, external motivators, competition, constrained choice—need to be eliminated or reduced.

3. The rational process may seem unrealistic. A more "real" way of making decisions is bounded rationality. Explain how this is different than the rational model.
   Answer - When faced with a complex problem, most people respond by reducing the problem to a level at which it can be readily understood. People satisfice—they seek solutions that are satisfactory and sufficient. Because of the limitations of the human mind most individuals operate within the confines of bounded rationality. They construct simplified models that extract the essential features from problems without capturing all of their complexity. As with the rational model the process begins when a problem is identified and the search for criteria and alternatives is started. The difference is that the decision maker limits alternatives to the more conspicuous choices - choices that are easy to find and that tend to be highly visible. The limited set of alternatives is reviewed. The review is limited; it begins with alternatives that differ only in a relatively small degree from the choice currently in place. The decision maker proceeds to review alternatives only until he or she identifies an alternative that is good enough—one that meets an acceptable level of performance. The order in which alternatives are considered is critical in determining which alternative is selected because the "satisficing" choice will be the first acceptable one the decision maker encounters. Solutions that depart least from the status quo and meet the decision criteria are most likely to be selected.

4. Give an example of "anchoring bias."
   Answer- There are many, but one example might be purchasing a new car. There are various anchors, or starting points, but one often used is the sticker price. Another example might be deciding whether to take a new job. Individuals might use as an anchor for determining pay what they make on their previous job, even though it may have little relevance.

5. "Sometimes you've just got to go with your gut feeling." Is this a wrong way for a manager to make a decision?
   Answer – No. Managers regularly use their intuition, and doing so may actually help improve decision making. Intuitive decision making is an unconscious process created out of distilled experience. It does not necessarily operate independently of rational analysis; rather the two complement each other. Studies show that experience allows the "seasoned" decision-maker to recognize a situation and draw on previously learned information

associated with the situation to arrive quickly at a decision. The result is that the intuitive decision-maker can decide rapidly with what appears to be very limited information.

6. What is the mental process most managers use to handle the immense amount of information involved in decision making, and how does the technique work?
Answer - In order to avoid information overload, decision makers rely on heuristics, or judgmental shortcuts, in decision making. An availability heuristic is the tendency for people to base their judgments on information that is readily available to them. A representative heuristic assesses the likelihood of an occurrence by trying to match it with a preexisting category.

7. What causes managers, CEOs, and other leaders to pursue a course of action that is failing rather than abandon it?
Answer - This is known as an escalation of commitment. It is an increased commitment to a previous decision, often in spite of negative information. It has been well documented that individuals escalate commitment to a failing course of action when they view themselves as responsible for the failure. They "throw good money after bad" to demonstrate that their initial decision was not wrong and to avoid having to admit they made a mistake. Many an organization have suffered large losses because a manager was determined to prove that his or her original decision was right by continuing to commit resources to what was a lost cause from the beginning.

8. Identify four decision-making styles.
Answer - Two individual differences seem particularly relevant to decision making in organizations—decision-making styles and level of moral development. The foundation of the four-style model is the recognition that people differ along two dimensions. The first is their way of thinking. The other dimension addresses a person's tolerance for ambiguity. When these two dimensions are diagrammed, they form four styles of decision making. See Exhibit 6-2. Four styles are directive, analytical, conceptual, and behavioral.

- Directive style
  - Low tolerance for ambiguity and seek rationality.
  - Efficient and logical. Decisions are based on minimal information after the consideration of few alternatives.
  - Directive types make decisions fast, and they focus on the short run.
- Analytical style
  - Greater tolerance for ambiguity than do directive decision makers.
  - They desire more information and consider more alternatives than do directives.
  - Characterized as careful decision makers with the ability to adapt or cope with new situations.
- Conceptual style
  - Very broad in their outlook and consider many alternatives.
  - Focus is long range, and they are very good at finding creative solutions to problems.
- Behavioral style
  - Characterizes decision makers who work well with others.
  - They are concerned with the achievement of peers and subordinates.
  - They are receptive to suggestions from others and rely heavily on meetings for communicating.
  - This type of manager tries to avoid conflict and seeks acceptance.

- Focusing on decision styles can be useful for helping you understand how two equally intelligent people can differ in their decisions.

9. Explain the implications of stages of moral development to decision making.
   Answer - This is the second of the individual differences that are particularly relevant to decision making in organizations. Many decisions have an ethical dimension. Research confirms the existence of three levels of moral development, each comprising two stages. (See Exhibit 6-3.) At each successive stage, an individual's moral judgment grows less and less dependent on outside influences.
   - Preconventional. Individuals respond to notions of right or wrong only when personal consequences are involved.
   - Conventional. Reasoning at this level indicates that moral value resides in maintaining the conventional order and the expectations of others.
   - Principled. Individuals make a clear effort to define moral principles apart from the authority of the groups to which they belong or society in general.

   Conclusions. First, people proceed through the six stages in a lock-step fashion. They gradually move up a ladder, stage by stage. Second, there is no guarantee of continued development. Development can terminate at any stage. Third, most adults are at stage four. They are limited to obeying the rules and laws of society. Finally, the higher the stage a manager reaches, the more he or she will be predisposed to make ethical decisions.

10. How do organizations shape both the alternatives considered and the final decisions made by managers?
    Answer - The organization itself constrains decision makers. 1) Performance evaluation—Managers are strongly influenced by the criteria by which they are evaluated. 2) Reward systems—The organization's reward system influences decision makers by suggesting to them what choices are preferable in terms of personal payoff. 3) System-imposed time constraints—Organizations impose deadlines on decisions. 4) Historical precedent—Decisions have a context, individual decisions are more accurately characterized as points in a stream of decisions. Decisions made in the past are ghosts that continually haunt current choices.

11. How can dedicated, well-educated and trained, experienced managers have different ethical perspectives? What are the three primary approaches to framing an ethical issue?
    Answer – There are three different ways to frame decisions.
    - Utilitarian criterion
      - Decisions are made solely on the basis of their outcomes or consequences.
      - The goal is to provide the greatest good for the greatest number.
      - This view tends to dominate business decision making.
    - Focus on rights
      - This calls on individuals to make decisions consistent with fundamental liberties and privileges as set forth in documents such as the Bill of Rights.
      - An emphasis on rights in decision making means respecting and protecting the basic rights of individuals, such as the right to privacy, to free speech, and to due process.
    - Focus on justice
      - This requires individuals to impose and enforce rules fairly and impartially so there is an equitable distribution of benefits and costs.
      - Union members typically favor this view.

    Advantages and liabilities. Utilitarianism promotes efficiency and productivity, but it can result in ignoring the rights of some individuals, particularly those with minority representation in the organization. Rights protect individuals from injury and are consistent with freedom and privacy, but they can create an overly legalistic workplace that hinders productivity and efficiency. Justice protects the interests of the underrepresented and less powerful, but it can encourage a sense of entitlement that reduces risk taking, innovation, and productivity.

EXERCISES
A. You Decide
The following case can be used as an individual or group exercise. It is written in such a way a number of arguments can be made. The important factor is that the students experience a decision-making process and see how different each strategy is in effort, process, and quality of decision. The Scroggs case on which the decision is to be made follows these instructions:

1. As an individual exercise: Give instructions in one class, have students report results in the next.
2. Prior to passing out the case, divide the class into three large groups without telling them how or why they are being divided.
    - Those who will use a rational model.
    - Those who will use bounded rationality.
    - Those who will make their decision intuitively.
3. Go to each group and quietly tell them the model they are to use to make their decision. Each large group should not know how the other groups are making their decisions.
    - Those using the rational model must be prepared to outline how they came to their decision.
    - Those using bounded rationality must be prepared to explain why they stopped where they did.
    - Those using intuition are to read the case and make a decision based on their reaction without rereading the case or studying the details.
    - Each group is to track how long it took them to come to their decision.
    - Refer students to the appropriate section of their text for their process.
4. During the next class, have students note on the board or orally present what their decisions were. Simply tabulate their decisions, responsible or not.
    - Begin with those using the rational model, those using bounded rationality, and end with the intuitive.
    - Note if there is any pattern to the decisions. Did one style lead to a particular decision?
5. Now ask for volunteers to offer their reasons for their decision. Draw from each group and keep track of their reasons.
6. Now ask for times; how long did it take to make the decision?
7. Ask the students, after hearing the decisions and reasons, would anyone change their mind?
    - Who would change to guilty?
    - Who would change to not guilty?
    - Who wouldn't change?
8. Discuss the quality of the decisions, the influence of reasons, and so on.

State vs. *Scroggs*

In the fall of 1875 Hiram Smith filed a claim on a very fertile piece of land in South Dakota with the land office. Before he could put any improvements on the land, he died. A young Swede, newly immigrated, filed a counterclaim to the land at once, and by late spring of the following year had built a home and had begun to cultivate the land.

In the meantime the widow of the original claimant was on her way west with her two daughters and her son. She built a house on the land, across a ravine from the Swede's home, and cultivated that half of the claim. Both parties sent their claims to the Department of the Interior, but ten years went by without a decision. Both the Swede and Mrs. Smith built barns and cultivated the land intensively each on their own side of the ravine.

A distant relative of Mrs. Smith, a minister named Scroggs lived in a small town about two miles from the rival farms. He had been an advisor for the Swede on all matters of religion and politics since the fellow had first taken up farming in Dakota.

He had often complimented the Swede on his land and had expressed his opinion at the general store that it was the best land in the west.

Scroggs had acted as arbiter for the disputants and had corresponded with the Secretary of the Interior in regard to the land. One day at the general store he told the Swede that he thought the Swede's claim would be supported. The Swede swore that no one was going to put him off the land. The next day Scroggs went to the Smith farm and showed Mrs. Smith a paper from Washington, D.C., ratifying her claim to the land. He said it would be all right for them to take possession. Young Smith hitched a team to the plow and went over on to the Swede's side of the farm. Scroggs, Mrs. Smith, and the two daughters went along, Scroggs on his horse. Young Smith had just started plowing when the Swede ran out of his house with a gun and shot him.

Two more shots killed the horses at the plow. Scroggs galloped off and shouted that he was going after the marshal. When the marshal and a posse arrived, they found the Swede had killed the three women and had then committed suicide. Scroggs, being the only relative of the dead woman, inherited both pieces of land.

Should Scroggs be held responsible for the killings?

B.   Biases and Errors in Decision Making

Ask for a show of hands of those that have interviewed others for a job. Discuss with them the biases that they may have had during the interview process, especially considering how short many interviews are., or how quickly interviewers make a decision. Point out that we all make the errors, the key is creating an environment in which one has the best chance of selecting the right candidate. You can also discuss this from the perspective of the interviewee. Did they have biases in determining whether or not they wanted to work at a particular case. Can they think of circumstances in which they were a victim of these biases?
This same discussion works with the performance appraisal process also.

C.   Which Decision is the Ethical One?

Identify a current even in the community or world, and have the students make decisions using the three different criteria: utilitarian criterion, rights criterion, and justice criterion. Their decisions can even then be presented in a debate form in class as an exercise. This assignment could be done on an individual basis where each student is assigned to generate a decision based on using one or all three criteria. Or, the assignment could be done as an in-class activity with the class being divided into small groups, and the groups being assigned a particular decision criterion.

The following is simply an example of one decision situation that could be utilized:

A current local issue in one community is the excessive amount/number of cars "cruising" up and down a major retail district thoroughfare. The interesting issues include: a) the individuals' rights to drive where they want, when they want; b) the perceived, and perhaps true, belief that cruisers are impeding the ingress and egress of actual shoppers of the retail establishments on this particular street; c) the significant relationship between the increased number of cruisers at certain times which corresponds to the increased incidents of vandalism, and disturbance of the peace situations requiring law enforcement intervention.

The City Council decide to impose a "no cruising" ordinance that was already "on the books" of city ordinances. This means that individual cars are recorded as passing a surveillance post on the particular street more than two times within a one-hour period of time, they will be ticketed. Each subsequent recording of that license number during that "no cruising time period" will result in a higher level of fine, until the cruiser is jailed.

Have students/groups evaluate this decision by the City Council using the different ethical criteria: utilitarian, rights, and justice.

Analyzing Your Organization

For this exercise, keep a journal in which you write down every substantial decision that you make during the next two days. These could be simple decisions, such as deciding whether or not to speak up at a meeting, or they could be a complicated management decision, such as whom to lay off.

After the two days, sort your decisions by importance. Analyze for each decision the type of processing that occurred. For example, did you try and use the steps in the rational model? How much did intuition come into play? Did any of your decisions use the three component model of creativity? What types of biases could have potentially caused you to make the wrong decision?

Be ready to discuss these decisions with the class. Note how during the class discussion how the type of job impacts the decision making style.

CHAPTER 7 - FOUNDATIONS OF GROUP BEHAVIOR

CHAPTER OBJECTIVES
After reading this chapter, students should be able to:
1. Differentiate between formal and informal groups.
2. Explain why people join groups.
3. Describe how role requirements change in different situations.
4. Explain the importance of the Hawthorne studies.
5. Describe the importance of the Asch studies.
6. Explain what determines status.
7. Identify the implications of social loafing.
8. Outline the benefits and disadvantages of cohesive groups.
9. Explain the effect of diversity on group performance.

LECTURE OUTLINE
I. DEFINING AND CLASSIFYING GROUPS
    A. Definition (ppt 4)
        1. A group is defined as two or more individuals, interacting and interdependent, who come together to achieve particular objectives. Groups can be either formal or informal.
            a) By formal, we mean a group that is defined by the organization's structure, with designated work assignments establishing tasks and work groups.
            b) In formal groups the behaviors that one should engage in are stipulated by and directed toward organizational goals.
            c) In contrast, informal groups are alliances that are neither structured nor organizationally determined. In the work environment these groups form naturally as responses to the need for social contact.
        2. Subclassify groups into command, task, interest, or friendship categories. (ppt 5)
            a) Command and task groups are dictated by the formal organization, whereas interest and friendship groups are informal alliances.
            b) The command group is determined by the organizational chart.
            c) Task groups, also organizationally determined, represent persons working together to complete a job.
                (1) A task group's boundaries are not limited to its immediate hierarchical superior.
                (2) All command groups are also task groups, but the reverse need not be true.
            d) Groups may affiliate to attain a specific objective. This is an interest group.
            e) Friendship groups often develop because the individual members have one or more common characteristics or social allegiances.
        3. Informal groups provide a very important function by satisfying their members' social needs.
        4. Exhibit 7-1 summarizes the most popular reasons why people join a group. (ppt 6)

II. BASIC GROUP CONCEPTS (ppt 7)
    A. Groups have a structure that shapes the behavior of their members.
    B. Roles (ppt 8-9)

1. Laura Campbell is a buyer with Marks & Spencer, the large British retailer. Her job requires her to play a number of roles; that is, to engage in a set of expected behavior patterns that are attributed to occupying a given position in a social unit.
2. Like Laura Campbell, we all are required to play a number of roles, and our behavior varies with the role we're playing.
3. The understanding of role behavior would be dramatically simplified if each of us chose one role and played it regularly and consistently.
   a) We are required to play diverse roles, both on and off our jobs.
   b) Different groups impose different role requirements on people.
4. Psychological contracts are unwritten agreements between employees and employers that sets out the mutual expectations.
5. Role research conclusions:
   a) People play multiple roles.
   b) People learn roles from the stimuli around them: friends, books, movies, television.
   c) People have the ability to shift roles rapidly when they recognize that the situation and its demands clearly require major changes.
   d) People often experience role conflict when compliance with one role requirement is at odds with another.
6. What is the value of a knowledge of roles?
   a) It helps to think in terms of what group they're predominantly identifying with at the time and what behaviors would be expected of them in that role.
   b) It allows the manager to more accurately predict the employee's behavior.

C. Norms (ppt 10)
   1. Norms are acceptable standards of behavior within a group that are shared by the group's members.
   2. Each group will establish its own set of norms.
   3. Probably the most widespread norms—and the ones with which managers tend to be most concerned—deal with performance-related processes.
      a) Work groups typically provide their members with explicit cues on how hard they should work, how to get the job done, their level of output, appropriate communication channels, and the like.
      b) These norms are extremely powerful in affecting an individual employee's performance.
   4. A key point about norms is that groups exert pressure to bring members' behavior into conformity with the group's standards.
   5. The Hawthorne studies (ppt 11-13)
      a) Full-scale appreciation of the importance norms play in influencing worker behavior did not occur until the early 1930s.
      b) This enlightenment grew out of a series of studies undertaken at Western Electric Company's Hawthorne Works in Chicago between 1924 and 1932.
         (1) Initiated by Western Electric officials.
         (2) Later overseen by Harvard professor Elton Mayo.
      c) The Hawthorne studies concluded that a worker's behavior and sentiments were closely related. Group influences were significant in affecting individual behavior. Group standards were highly effective in establishing individual worker output, and money was less of a factor in determining worker output than were group standards, sentiments, and security.
      d) The Hawthorne researchers began by examining the relation between the physical environment and productivity.

          (1) Illumination and other aspects of working conditions were manipulated.

          (2) Initial findings contradicted anticipated results.

  e) Results varied but in no case were the increase or decrease in output in proportion to the increase or decrease in illumination.

          (1) Researchers introduced a control group. An experimental group was presented with varying intensity of illumination, while the controlled unit worked under a constant illumination intensity.

  f) Again, the results were bewildering. Output rose for both the control and the experimental groups whether light was raised or lowered.

          (1) The Hawthorne researchers concluded that illumination intensity was only a minor influence among the many influences on an employee's productivity.

  g) A second set of experiments was performed in the relay assembly test room at Western Electric.

          (1) A small group of women was isolated from the main work group so that their behavior could be more carefully observed.

          (2) They went about their job of assembling telephones, the only significant difference was the placement in the room of a research assistant who acted as an observer keeping records of output, rejects, working conditions, and describing everything that happened in a daily log.

          (3) Observations over a multiyear period found that this small group's output increased steadily.

          (4) The number of personal absences and those due to sickness were approximately one third of those recorded by women in the regular production department.

          (5) What became evident was that this group's performance was significantly influenced by its status of being a "special" group.

  h) A third study in the bank wiring observation room was introduced to ascertain the effect of a sophisticated wage incentive plan.

          (1) The assumption was that individual workers would maximize their productivity when they saw that it was directly related to economic rewards.

          (2) The most important finding of this study was that employees did not individually maximize their outputs.

          (3) Output became controlled by a group norm that determined what was a proper day's work.

             (a) Output was not only restricted, but individual workers gave erroneous reports.

  i) The group was operating well below its capability.

          (1) Members were afraid that if they significantly increased their output, the unit incentive rate would be cut, the expected daily output would be increased, layoffs might occur, or slower workers would be reprimanded.

          (2) The group established its idea of a fair output—neither too much nor too little.

  j) The norms the group established included a number of "don'ts."

          (1) Don't be a rate-buster, turning out too much work.

          (2) Don't be a chiseler, turning out too little work.

          (3) Don't be a squealer on any of your peers.

  k) How did the group enforce these norms? Their methods were neither gentle nor subtle.

(1) They included sarcasm, name-calling, ridicule, and even physical punches on the upper arms of members who violated the group's norms.

(2) Members would also ostracize individuals whose behavior was against the group's interest.

D. Conformity and the Asch Studies (ppt 14)

1. Group members want acceptance by the group.

　a) Evidence from the now-classic studies undertaken by Solomon Asch, shows that groups can place strong pressures on individual members to change their attitudes and behaviors to conform to the group's standard.

2. Study design

　a) Asch made up groups of seven or eight people who sat in a classroom and were asked to compare two cards held by the experimenter.

　b) One card had one line, the other had three lines of varying length.

　　(1) See Exhibit 7-2. (ppt 15)

　c) The object was to announce aloud which of the three lines matched the single line.

　　(1) The difference in line length was quite obvious; under ordinary conditions, subjects made less than one percent errors.

　d) But what happens if all the members in the group begin to give incorrect answers?

　e) The experiment began with several sets of matching exercises. All the subjects gave the right answers. On the third set, however, the first subject gave an obviously wrong answer.

　f) Asch demonstrated that over many experiments and many trials, subjects conformed in about 35 percent of the trials; that is, the subjects gave answers they knew were wrong but were consistent with the replies of other group members.

　g) The results suggest that there are group norms that press us toward conformity.

E. Status (ppt 16)

1. Status is a socially defined position or rank within a group.

　a) It may be formally imposed by a group.

　b) More often, we deal with status in an informal sense.

　c) Informal status is not necessarily less important than the formal variety.

2. Status is derived from one of three sources: (ppt 17)

　a) The power a person wields over others.

　b) A person's ability to contribute to a group's goals.

　c) An individual's personal characteristics.

3. Status and Norms

　a) Status has been shown to have some interesting effects on the power of norms and pressure to conform.

　b) High-status members often are given more freedom to deviate from norms than are other group members.

　c) High-status people also are better able to resist conformity pressures than their lower-status peers.

　d) These findings explain why many star athletes, famous actors, top-performing salespeople, and outstanding academics seem oblivious to appearance or to the social norms that constrain others.

4. Status and Group Interaction

a) High status people tend to be more assertive.

b) Lower status participants are less active, which can inhibit group creativity.

5. Status Equity

a) It's important for group members to believe that the status hierarchy is equitable.

b) Any perceived inequity creates disequilibrium resulting in various types of corrective behavior.

6. The trappings that go with formal positions are also important elements in maintaining equity.

a) Inequity between the perceived ranking of an individual and the status accouterments generates status incongruence.

7. Even though members of groups generally agree among themselves on status criteria and hence tend to rank individuals fairly closely, conflict can arise when individuals move between groups whose status criteria are different or when groups are formed of individuals with heterogeneous backgrounds.

8. The importance of status varies between cultures. (ppt 18)

F. Cohesiveness (ppt 19)

1. Groups differ in their cohesiveness; that is, the degree to which members are attracted to each other and are motivated to stay in the group.

a) Cohesiveness is important because it has been found to be related to the group's productivity.

2. The relationship of cohesiveness and productivity depends on the performance-related norms established by the group.

a) The more cohesive the group, the more its members will follow its goals.

b) See summary of results in Exhibit 7-3. (ppt 20)

3. What can you do as a manager if you want to encourage group cohesiveness? (ppt 21-22)

a) Make the group smaller.

b) Encourage agreement with group goals.

c) Increase the time members spend together.

d) Increase the status of the group and the perceived difficulty of attaining membership in the group.

e) Stimulate competition with other groups.

f) Give rewards to the group rather than to members.

g) Physically isolate the group.

G. Size (ppt 23)

1. Size affects group behavior.

a) Smaller groups complete tasks faster than larger ones.

b) If the group is engaged in problem solving, however, large groups consistently get better marks than their smaller counterparts.

c) Large groups—with a dozen or more members—are good for gaining diverse input.

(1) If the goal of the group is fact finding, larger groups should be more effective.

d) Smaller groups are better at doing something productive with that input.

(1) Groups of approximately seven members tend to be more effective for taking action.

2. Social loafing is the tendency for individuals to expend less effort when working collectively than when working individually. (ppt 24)

3. A common stereotype about groups is that the sense of team spirit spurs individual effort and enhances the group's overall productivity.
4. But in the late 1920s, a German psychologist named Ringelmann discovered that groups of three people exerted a force only two-and-a-half times the average individual performance.
   a) Groups of eight collectively achieved less than four times the solo rate.
5. Social loafing may be due to a belief that others in the group are not carrying their fair share.

H. Composition (ppt 25-26)
1. Most group activities require a variety of skills and knowledge.
2. Heterogeneous groups—those composed of dissimilar individuals—are more likely to have diverse abilities and information and are more effective than homogeneous groups.
3. When a group is heterogeneous in terms of gender, personalities, opinions, abilities, skills, and perspectives, there is an increased probability that the group will possess the needed characteristics to complete its tasks effectively.
   a) There may be more conflict.
4. The evidence indicates that racial or national differences interfere with group processes, at least in the short term.
   a) These difficulties seem to dissipate with time.
   b) The differences disappear after about three months.
5. Group demography occurs when members of a group share a common demographic attribute such as age, sex, race, educational level.
   a) Groups and organizations are composed of cohorts—a group of individuals who hold a common attribute.
   b) Group demography suggests that attributes such as age or the date that someone joins a specific work group or organization should help predict turnover.
      (1) The logic states that turnover will be greater among those with dissimilar experiences because communication is more difficult, conflict and power struggles are more likely—and severe when they occur, and this in turns leads to less-attractive group membership and voluntary turnover.

III. GROUP DECISION MAKING
A. The belief that two heads are better than one has long been accepted as a basic component of North American and many other countries' legal systems.
1. It has expanded to the point that today many decisions in organizations are made by groups, teams, or committees.

B. The Individual versus the Group (ppt 27)
1. A major plus of individual decision making is speed.
2. Individual decisions have clear accountability.
3. Individual decisions tend to convey consistent values.
   a) Although individuals are not perfectly consistent in their decision making, they do tend to be more consistent than groups.
4. Groups generate more complete information and knowledge.
5. Groups can bring heterogeneity to the decision process.
6. A group will almost always outperform even the best individual with higher-quality decisions.
7. Groups lead to increased acceptance of a solution.

a) Many decisions fail after the final choice is made because people don't accept the solution.
   8. Which is better? It depends.
      a) Individuals are preferred when the decision is relatively unimportant and does not require subordinate commitment to its success.
      b) Similarly, individuals should make the decision when they have sufficient information and when subordinates will be committed to the outcome.
   9. The choice comes down to weighing effectiveness against efficiency.
      a) In terms of effectiveness, groups are superior.
      b) Individuals are more efficient than groups.

C. Groupthink and Groupshift are byproducts of group decision making
   1. Groupthink
      a) Groupthink is the phenomenon that occurs when group members become so enamored of seeking concurrence that the norm for consensus overrides the realistic appraisal of alternative courses of action and the full expression of deviant, minority, or unpopular views.
      b) It describes a deterioration in an individual's mental efficiency, reality testing, and moral judgment as a result of group pressures.
   2. Symptoms of groupthink (ppt 28-29)
      a) Group members rationalize any resistance to the assumptions they've made.
      b) Members pressure any doubters to support the alternative favored by the majority.
      c) To give the appearance of group consensus, doubters keep silent about misgivings and even minimize to themselves the importance of their doubts.
      d) The group interprets members' silence as a "yes" vote for the majority.
   3. The above symptoms lead to a number of decision-making deficiencies, which follow:
      a) Incomplete assessment of the problem
      b) Poor information search
      c) Selective bias in processing information
      d) Limited development of alternatives
      e) Incomplete assessment of alternatives
      f) Failure to examine risks of preferred choice
      g) Failure to reappraise initially rejected alternatives
   4. Studies of decision making in U.S. government agencies have found deficient outcomes were frequently preceded by symptoms of groupthink.
   5. Evidence suggests that not all groups are equally vulnerable to groupthink. (ppt 30)
      a) Researchers have focused on five variables:
         (1) The group's cohesiveness
         (2) Its leader's behavior
         (3) Its insulation from outsiders
         (4) Time pressures
         (5) Failure to follow methodical decision-making procedures
   6. To minimize the influence of groupthink, note the following:
      a) Highly cohesive groups have more discussion and bring out more information than do loose groups but also discourage dissent.
      b) An open leadership style: include encouraging member participation, refraining from stating one's opinion at the beginning of the meeting.

Encourage divergent opinions from all group members, and emphasize the importance of reaching a wise decision.
- c) Do not allow the group to detach itself from external sources.
- d) Downplay time constraints.
- e) Encourage the use of methodical decision-making procedures.
7. Groupshift (ppt 31)
   - a) A shift is toward an extreme position.
     - (1) In the direction of a predisposition of a team member.
     - (2) Most frequently toward greater risk.
   - b) Discussion leads to a significant shift in the positions of members toward a more extreme position in the direction toward which they were already leaning before the discussion.
   - c) The groupshift can be viewed as a special case of groupthink.
     - (1) The decision of the group reflects the dominant decision-making norm.
8. Explanations for the phenomenon follow:
   - a) Discussion creates familiarization among the members, increasing boldness and daring.
   - b) The group diffuses responsibility, freeing any single member from accountability.
9. How does one use the findings on groupshift?
   - a) Recognize that group decisions exaggerate the initial position of the individual members.
   - b) The shift is more often to be toward greater risk.
   - c) The shift is a function of the members' prediscussion inclinations.

D. Selecting the Best Group Decision-Making Technique (ppt 32)
   1. The most common form of group decision making takes place in face-to-face interacting groups.
   2. Brainstorming, the nominal group technique, and electronic meetings have been proposed as ways to reduce many of the problems inherent in the traditional interacting group.
      - a) Brainstorming is meant to overcome pressures for conformity.
      - b) It does so by utilizing an idea-generation process that specifically encourages any and all alternatives while withholding any criticism of those alternatives.
      - c) Typical brainstorming session
        - (1) A half-dozen to a dozen people sit around a table.
        - (2) The group leader states the problem clearly.
        - (3) Members then "freewheel" as many alternatives as they can in a given length of time.
        - (4) No criticism is allowed, and all the alternatives are recorded for later discussion and analysis.
        - (5) Group members are encouraged to "think the unusual."
      - d) Brainstorming, however, is merely a process for generating ideas.
   3. Nominal Group Technique
      - a) The nominal group restricts discussion or interpersonal communication during the decision-making process.
      - b) Group members are all physically present, but operate independently.
      - c) Members meet as a group, but, before any discussion takes place, each member independently writes down his or her ideas on the problem.
      - d) This silent period is followed by each member presenting one idea to the group.

89

(1) No discussion takes place until all ideas have been recorded.
e) The group then discusses the ideas for clarity and evaluates them.
f) Each group member silently and independently ranks the ideas. The final decision is determined by the idea with the highest aggregate ranking.
g) Chief advantage: permits the group to meet formally but does not restrict independent thinking.

4. Electronic Meeting
   a) This is the most recent approach to group decision making.
      (1) Blends the nominal group technique with sophisticated computer technology.
   b) Up to fifty people sit around a horseshoe-shaped table, empty except for a series of computer terminals.
   c) Issues are presented to participants, and they type their responses onto their computer screen.
   d) Individual comments, as well as aggregate votes, are displayed on a projection screen in the room.
   e) The major advantages of electronic meetings are anonymity, honesty, and speed.
      (1) Participants can anonymously type any message they want, and it flashes on the screen for all to see.
      (2) It also allows people to be brutally honest without penalty.
      (3) It is fast.

IV. IMPLICATIONS FOR MANAGERS

1. In order to accomplish work tasks, the individuals who make up an organization are typically united into various work groups.
   a) Group behavior is not merely the summation of the individual behavior of its members. The group itself adds an additional dimension to its members' behavior.
2. Knowledge of the role that a person is attempting to enact can make it easier for us to deal with the person, for we have insight into her expected behavior patterns.
   a) Knowledge of a job incumbent's role makes it easier for others to work with her, for she should behave in ways consistent with others' expectations.
3. Norms control group member behavior by establishing standards of right or wrong.
   a) Knowing the norms of a given group can help us explain the attitudes and behaviors of its members.
4. Should managers seek cohesive groups? Our answer is a qualified "Yes."
   a) The qualification lies in the degree of alignment between the group and the organization's goals.
5. The implications of the social loafing effect on work groups are significant.
   a) When managers use collective work situations to enhance morale and teamwork, they must also provide means by which individual efforts can be identified.
   b) This conclusion is consistent with individualistic cultures, such as the United States and Canada, which are dominated by self-interest.
      (1) It is not consistent with collective societies in which individuals are motivated by in-group goals.

6. To increase the performance of work groups, you should try to choose individuals as members who can bring a diverse perspective to problems and issues.
    a) This may cause conflict in the short term.
    b) As members learn to work with their differences, group performance will improve.
7. Status inequities within a group divert activity away from goal accomplishment and direct it toward resolving the inequities.
    a) When inequities exist, group members reduce their work effort, attempt to undermine the activities of those members with higher status, or pursue similar dysfunctional behaviors.
8. Finally, if managers use group decision making, they should particularly try to minimize groupthink.

SUMMARY (ppt 33-34)

1. A group is defined as two or more individuals, interacting and interdependent, who come together to achieve particular objectives. Groups can be either formal or informal. By formal, we mean a group that is defined by the organization's structure, with designated work assignments establishing tasks and work groups. In contrast, informal groups are alliances that are neither structured nor organizationally determined. In the work environment these groups form naturally as a response to the need for social contact. Groups can also be subclassifed into command, task, interest, or friendship categories.
2. The reasons people join groups is summarized in Exhibit 7-1.
3. We all play different roles in groups and those role requirements change in different situations. Research shows that people play multiple roles, people learn roles from the stimuli around them, and that people have the ability to shift roles rapidly when they recognize that the situation and its demands clearly require major changes.
4. The Hawthorne studies revealed the importance of norms. Norms are acceptable standards of behavior within a group that are shared by the group's members. Each group will establish its own set of norms. A key about norms is that groups exert pressure to bring members' behavior into conformity with the group's standards. Full-scale appreciation of the importance norms play in influencing worker behavior did not occur until the early 1930s. This enlightenment grew out of a series of studies undertaken at Western Electric Company's Hawthorne Works in Chicago between 1924 and 1932.
5. Studies by Solomon Asch showed that group members want acceptance by the group, and just how powerful that need is. Evidence from the now-classic studies undertaken by Asch, shows that groups can place strong pressures on individual members to change their attitudes and behaviors to conform to the group's standard.
6. Social loafing is the tendency for individuals to expend less effort when working collectively than when working individually. A common stereotype about groups is that the sense of team spirit spurs individual effort and enhances the group's overall productivity. But in the late 1920s, a German psychologist named Ringelmann discovered that groups of three people exerted a force only two-and-a-half times the average individual performance. Groups of eight collectively achieved less than four times the solo rate.
7. Groups differ in their cohesiveness; that is, the degree to which members are attracted to each other and are motivated to stay in the group. The relationship of cohesiveness and productiv-ity depends on the performance-related norms established by the group. The more cohesive the group, the more its members will follow its goals. See summary of results in Exhibit 7-3.
8. The composition of the group has an effect on its performance, specifically the diversity of the group. Heterogeneous groups are more likely to have diverse abilities and information and are more effective than homogeneous groups. When a group is heterogeneous in terms of

gender, personalities, opinions, abilities, skills, and perspectives, there is an increased probability that the group will possess the needed characteristics to complete its tasks effectively.

9. Groupthink occurs when group members become so enamored of seeking concurrence that the norm for consensus overrides the realistic appraisal of alternative courses of action and the full expression of deviant, minority, or unpopular views. The groupshift can be viewed as a special case of groupthink. The decision of the group reflects the dominant decision-making norm. It is often a shift toward an extreme position.

10. Managers have a variety of group decision-making techniques at their disposal. The most common form of group decision making takes place in face-to-face interacting groups. Brainstorming, the nominal group technique, and electronic meetings have been proposed as ways to reduce many of the problems inherent in the traditional interacting group. The nominal group technique is similar to brainstorming but it restricts discussion or interpersonal communication during the decision-making process. Electronic meetings are a recent approach to group decision making and is a non face-to-face technique. It blends the nominal group technique with sophisticated computer technology.

DISCUSSION QUESTIONS

1. Organizations are made up of different types of groups. Explain what these are and why they are formed.

   Answer - A group is defined as two or more individuals, interacting and interdependent, who come together to achieve particular objectives. Groups can be either formal or informal. By formal, we mean a group that is defined by the organization's structure, with designated work assignments establishing tasks and work groups. Informal groups are alliances that are neither structured nor organizationally determined. In the work environment these groups form naturally as responses to the need for social contact. Groups may also be classified by their purpose: command, task, interest, or friendship categories. Command and task groups are dictated by the formal organization, whereas interest and friendship groups are informal alliances. Task groups, also organizationally determined, represent persons working together to complete a job. An interest group is composed of people who affiliate to attain a specific objective. Friendship groups often develop because the individual members have one or more common characteristics or social allegiances.

2. Why do people join groups?

   Answer - Exhibit 7-1 summarizes the most popular reasons why people join a group.

3. What are group roles and why is it important for a manager to understand them?

   Answer - We all play different roles in groups and those role requirements change in different situations. Research shows that people play multiple roles, people learn roles from the stimuli around them, and that people have the ability to shift roles rapidly when they recognize that the situation and its demands clearly require major changes. People often experience role conflict when compliance with one role requirement is at odds with another. The knowledge of roles helps managers to think in terms of what group they're predominantly identifying with at the time and what behaviors would be expected of them in that role. It allows the manager to more accurately predict the employee's behavior.

4. What are group norms, and what role do they play in organizational behavior?

   Answer- Norms are acceptable standards of behavior with a group that are shared by the group's members. Each group will establish its own set of norms, and these norms are extremely powerful in affecting an individual employee's performance. When agreed to and accepted by the group, norms act as a means of influencing the behavior of group members with a minimum of external controls. Groups exert pressure on members to bring members' behavior into conformity with the group's standards or norms. If people in the group violate its norms, expect group members to act to correct or even punish the violation.

5. The Hawthorne studies were pivotal both in organizational behavior research and for their impact on future management practices. What were they, how were they conducted, and what were the results?
    Answer - Full-scale appreciation of the importance norms play in influencing worker behavior came from a series of studies undertaken at Western Electric Company's Hawthorne Works in Chicago between 1924 and 1932. They were initiated by Western Electric officials and later overseen by Harvard professor Elton Mayo. The Hawthorne studies concluded that a worker's behavior and sentiments were closely related. Group influences were significant in affecting individual behavior. Group standards were highly effective in establishing individual worker output, and money was less of a factor in determining worker output than were group standards, sentiments, and security. The Hawthorne researchers began by examining the relation between the physical environment and productivity. Results varied but in no case were the increase or decrease in output proportionate to the increase or decrease in illumination. Researchers introduced a control group. An experimental group was presented with varying intensity of illumination, while the controlled unit worked under constant illumination intensity. Again, the results were bewildering. Output rose for both the control and the experimental groups whether light was raised or lowered. A second set of experiments were conducted in the relay assembly test room at Western Electric. A small group of women was isolated from the main work group so that their behavior could be more carefully observed. What became evident was that this group's performance was significantly influenced by its status of being a "special" group. A third study in the bank wiring observation room was introduced to ascertain the effect of a sophisticated wage incentive plan. The assumption was that individual workers would maximize their productivity when they saw that it was directly related to economic rewards. The most important finding of this study was that employees did not individually maximize their outputs. The norms the group established included a number of "don'ts."

6. What is the importance of the Asch studies to understanding the power of a group to shape individual behavior?
    Answer - Evidence from the now-classic studies undertaken by Solomon Asch, shows that groups can place strong pressures on individual members to change their attitudes and behaviors to conform to the group's standard. Asch demonstrated that over many experiments and many trials, subjects conformed in about 35 percent of the trials; that is, the subjects gave answers they knew were wrong but were consistent with the replies of other group members. The results suggest that there are group norms that press us toward conformity.

7. What are the implications of social loafing for group productivity?
    Answer - Social loafing is the tendency for individuals to expend less effort when working collectively than when working individually. In the late 1920s a German psychologist named Ringelmann discovered that groups of three people exerted a force only two-and-a-half times the average individual performance. Groups of eight collectively achieved less than four times the solo rate. Increases in group size are inversely related to individual performance. Social loafing may be due to a belief that others in the group are not carrying their fair share. Another explanation is the dispersion of responsibility in that the relationship between an individual's input and the group's output is clouded.

8. As a manager you want your work teams to work together more effectively and you've decided to help them increase their cohesiveness to that end. What practical steps can you take to increase your work teams' group cohesion?
    Answer -
    - Make the group smaller.
    - Encourage agreement with group goals.
    - Increase the time members spend together.
    - Increase the status of the group and the perceived difficulty of attaining membership in the group.
    - Stimulate competition with other groups.
    - Give rewards to the group rather than to members.
    - Physically isolate the group.

9. How does the diversity of a group affect its performance?
    Answer - Most group activities require a variety of skills and knowledge, so the more diversity, the better. Heterogeneous groups, those composed of dissimilar individuals, are be more likely to have diverse abilities and information and are more effective than homogeneous groups. But they also experience more conflict. The evidence indicates that racial or national differences interfere with group processes, at least in the short term. These difficulties seem to dissipate with time and the differences disappear after about three months.

10. An offshoot of the composition issue is group demography. What are group demography and cohorts?
    Answer – Group demography is the degree to which members of a group share a common demographic attribute such as age, sex, race, educational level, or length of service in the organization, and the impact of this attribute on turnover. Groups and organizations are composed of cohorts, which is defined as a group of individuals who hold a common attribute. The evidence from a number of studies is quite encouraging that identification of cohorts and the attributes of the cohorts can lead to prediction of turnover.

11. You need a quick decision that is consistent with past decisions and you are willing to sacrifice the variety of alternatives considered in order to meet these parameters. Which would be better for making this decision, an individual or group and why?
    Answer - The individual. A major plus of individual decision making is speed. Individual decisions have clear accountability. Individual decisions tend to convey consistent values. Individuals are preferred when the decision is relatively unimportant and doesn't require subordinate commitment to its success. While a group would generate more complete information and knowledge, it will take longer. The choice comes down to weighing effectiveness against efficiency.

12. As a manager what should you know about groupthink and groupshift?
    Answer – Groupthink is the phenomenon that occurs when group members become so enamored of concurrence that the norm for consensus overrides the realistic appraisal of alternative courses of action and the full expression of deviant, minority, or unpopular views. The symptoms of groupthink are:
    - Group members rationalize any resistance to the assumptions they've made.
    - Members pressure any doubters to support the alternative favored by the majority.
    - To give the appearance of group consensus, doubters keep silent about misgivings and even minimize to themselves the importance of their doubts.
    - The group interprets members' silence as a "yes" vote for the majority.

These symptoms lead to a number of decision-making deficiencies.

- Incomplete assessment of the problem
- Poor information search
- Selective bias in processing information
- Limited development of alternatives
- Incomplete assessment of alternatives
- Failure to examine risks of preferred choice
- Failure to reappraise initially rejected alternatives

Managers can minimize the influence of groupthink by emphasizing the following:

- Highly cohesive groups have more discussion and bring out more information than do loose groups but also discourage dissent.
- An open leadership style—including encouraging member participation, refraining from stating one's opinion at the beginning of the meeting, encouraging divergent opinions from all group members, and emphasizing the importance of reaching a wise decision.
- Do not allow the group to detach itself from external sources.
- Downplay time constraints.
- Encourage the use of methodical decision-making procedures.

Groupshift is a shift toward an extreme position generally in the direction of a predisposition of a team member and most frequently toward greater risk. The groupshift can be viewed as a special case of groupthink. This happens for several reasons. Discussion creates familiarization among the members, increasing boldness and daring. The group diffuses responsibility—freeing any single member from accountability. Managers need to recognize that group decisions exaggerate the initial position of the individual members.

13. You need a group to make a decision that is creative, and looks at a number of alternatives, but you have some members who are intimidated by other members and therefore do not tend to speak up in meetings. What technique will work best?
    Answer - Students' choices will vary, but the best choice is a nominal group technique. The nominal group restricts discussion or interpersonal communication during the decision-making process. Group members are all physically present, but operate independently. Members meet as a group, but, before any discussion takes place, each member independently writes down his or her ideas on the problem. This silent period is followed by each member presenting one idea to the group. Chief advantage: permits the group to meet formally but does not restrict independent thinking.

EXERCISES

A.   Win as Much as You Can

This exercise shows the power of cooperation and the damage of competition within a group. You may have seen this exercise as the "Red/Green" matrix or under any of a number of names. It is a forced choice exercise where cooperation leads to rewards, and competition to disaster.

1. You will need a helper to record the decisions, and you will need a set of 3x5 cards marked X and Y for each team. Add a 1, 2, 3, and so on, to correspond to the number of the team.
2. Divide the class in half and move them to opposite sides of the room.
3. On each side form small groups of 3-5 students and have them choose a captain and recorder. (A variation is to form same gender groups, mix gender equally, divide athletes from nonathletes, and so on.)
4. Number the teams so there are two team 1, two team 2, etc., one on each side of the room.
5. Refer to the pair of teams as being "counterparts." Be careful to use this term.
6. Pass out the X and Y cards to the correspondingly numbered team.
7. Pass out the instructions. (Copy follows.)

8. Read through the instructions. Always answer any questions with "The goal is to win as much as you can," without elaboration.
9. Begin the round.
   ▪ Keep time, do not let them have more than two minutes.
   ▪ Be sure to have all teams show their decision cards at the same time.
   ▪ Teams should use the form to track their choices.
   ▪ Only the captain reveals the choice and only when asked.
10. Keep the exercise moving, count and record decisions quickly, score them, and move on.
11. Have your helper count the number of Xs and Ys and then calculate the score as the teams are making their next decision. It keeps the process moving.

	Payoff Schedule
4Xs	-$1 each
3Xs	+$1 each
1Y	-$3 each
2Xs	+$2 each
2Ys	-$2 each
1X	+$3 each
3Ys	-$1 each
4Ys	+$1 each

12. At the beginning of rounds five, eight, and ten let the team captains meet with their "counterpart team captains." (You need a separate room so they meet out of sight and hearing of the teams.) Give them up to five minutes.
13. When they return, the teams have one minute to confer and show their answer.
14. Teams can refuse to meet with their "counterparts."
15. At the end of all ten rounds you will have some teams with very large negative scores.
16. Occasionally one or two teams will catch on and begin cooperating.

Discuss the exercise and the students' interpretation of "win as much as you can," and their strategy. Note that they tend to see it competitively—they win more if someone loses. In reality they can only win if they let their "counterpart team" win as well. Note that if teams cooperated from the beginning their scores could have been a +100. Discuss if they trusted each other, and why or why not. What effort did they make to build trust?

Win as Much As You Can
Instructions

	Payoff Schedule
4Xs	-$1 each
3Xs	+$1 each
1Y	-$3 each
2Xs	+$2 each
2Ys	-$2 each
1X	+$3 each
3Ys	-$1 each
4Ys	+$1 each

Scorecard

Round	Choice Balance	Pattern	Payoff
1	X Y	____ X ____ Y	_____
	_____		

2	X Y	___ X ___ Y	_____
			_____
3	X Y	___ X ___ Y	_____
			_____
4	X Y	___ X ___ Y	_____
			_____
5	X Y	___ X ___ Y x 3	_____
			_____
6	X Y	___ X ___ Y	_____
			_____
7	X Y	___ X ___ Y	_____
			_____
8	X Y	___ X ___ Y x 5	_____
			_____
9	X Y	___ X ___ Y	_____
			_____
10	X Y	___ X ___ Y x 10	_____
			_____

Rules:
1. Win as much as you can.
2. Pick a captain who will count and report your vote.
3. Pick a recorder who will track your vote on this form.
4. Confer only with your group. Group must decide on a single choice. Captain breaks ties.
    *   You will have two minutes to confer.
5. Only the captain reveals the choice and only when asked.
6. For rounds five, eight, and ten your captain may meet with other team captains for a negotiation session.
    *   Your captain will have five minutes to confer.
    *   Your team will have one minute to confer from round five on.

B.   Group Size and Composition

Take any group activity that you do in class, such as the one above, and create a group that is way too large for the task at hand. For example, if you have a large class, split the class into groups of 15 or 20. Have an observer examine and record the such things as how long it takes the group to elect a leader, how decision making occurs, and who has the status in the group. See how far the group can go in 30 minutes or so. If they get very far, discuss that although the group was large, it functioned as small because many probably did not participate. This brings up a host of organizational issues such as how many people to invite to meetings. You might also discuss this in the context of social loafing.

97

Part III   Groups in the Organization

C.   Groups, Roles, and Norms

This exercise could be a written outside-of-class assignment, or could be used as an in-class group discussion type of exercise.

Have each student individually identify three or more groups of which he/she is a member. The student should write down the role played in each group, the specific norms they recognize that impact their behavior in each different group, and identify sources of role conflict and/or "overlap." The attached "grid" could be used as a template for students.

These lists can then be used as a small group discussion or have each student write a short analysis of the groups, roles, norms, and role conflicts that "govern" his/her life. These lists could also be used to start a discussion on how organizations can be responsive to helping employees eliminate or manage role conflicts in their lives, and thus be a more productive and happier employee.

Personal Analysis of Groups and Roles

Name of Group	Role in Group	Group Norms Known	Sources of Conflict
Ex: Immediate Family	Wife	Supportive of husband and his activities; in charge of certain responsibilities as spouse and homemaker; listens without interrupting and is a good partner.	Other roles such as mom, daughter, professional employee
Immediate Family	Mom		
Extended Family	Daughter		
Workplace	Assistant Professor		
Church	Sunday School Teacher		
Church	Choir Member		
Church	Handbell Ringer		
Church	Administrative Board Member		
Girl Scouts	Cookie Manager		

Analyzing Your Organization

Choose one group activity that occurs in your organization this week, such as a meeting, social event, or brainstorming session. During the event, observe the group dynamics in their organization. Analyze variables from this chapter, such as group composition, size, loafing, or norms and roles. The purpose is to report to the class what works and what doesn't work about the group they are observing, and try to analyze why. For example, is the group too small? Too large? Did you observe any social loafing?

Be prepared to discuss your observations with the class. Make sure the focus is on group dynamics, and not your general opinion of the organization.

Note: If you don't regularly work in groups, you can do the same activity with your church group, your circle of friends, or even your family. In fact, this makes another point that the OB principles discussed in this course apply to all types of organizations, not just the workplace.

CHAPTER 8 - UNDERSTANDING WORK TEAMS

CHAPTER OBJECTIVES
After reading this chapter, students should be able to:
1. Explain the growing popularity of teams in organizations.
2. Contrast teams with groups.
3. Describe three types of teams.
4. Identify resources and other contextual influences that make teams effective.
5. Explain composition variables that determine team effectiveness.
6. Describe the role of work design in making effective teams.
7. Identify process variables that affect team performance.
8. Explain how organizations can create team players.
9. Identify the role that teams play in quality management.
10. Describe conditions when teams are preferred over individuals.

LECTURE OUTLINE
I.   WHY HAVE TEAMS BECOME SO POPULAR?
    A. Introduction
        1. Thirty years ago the introduction of teams into production processes made news because no one was doing it. Now the organization that doesn't use teams has become newsworthy.
        2. How do we explain the current popularity of teams? (ppt 4-5)
           a) Teams typically out-perform individuals when the tasks being done require multiple skills, judgment, and experience.
           b) Restructuring to compete more effectively and efficiently, companies have turned to teams as a way to better utilize employee talents.
           c) Teams have the capability to quickly assemble, deploy, refocus, and disband.
           d) Teams facilitate employee participation in operating decisions.
           e) Teams are an effective means for management to democratize their organizations and increase employee motivation.

II. TEAMS VERSUS GROUPS: WHAT'S THE DIFFERENCE?
    A. Definitions (ppt 6-7)
        1. A work group is a group that interacts primarily to share information and to make decisions to help one another perform within each member's area of responsibility.
           a) Work groups have no need or opportunity to engage in collective work that requires joint effort.
           b) Their performance is merely the sum of all the group members' individual contributions.
        2. A work team generates positive synergy through coordinated effort.
           a) The individual efforts result in a level of performance that is greater than the sum of those individual inputs.
        3. See Exhibit 8-1. (ppt 8)
        4. Many organizations have recently restructured work processes around teams looking for that positive synergy that will increase performance.
        5. There is potential but nothing inherently magical in the creation of teams that assures the achievement of this positive synergy.

III. TYPES OF TEAMS

A. Classified According to Their Objective (Exhibit 8-2) (ppt 9)

B. Problem-Solving Teams (ppt 10-11)
   1. Twenty years ago teams were typically were composed of five to twelve hourly employees from the same department who met for a few hours each week to discuss ways of improving quality, efficiency, and the work environment.
      a) These are problem-solving teams.
      b) Members share ideas or offer suggestions on how work processes and methods can be improved.
      c) The teams weren't given the authority to unilaterally implement their suggested actions.
   2. One of the most widely practiced applications of problem-solving teams during the 1980s was quality circles.
      a) Work teams of eight to ten employees and supervisors who had a shared area of responsibility and met regularly to discuss their quality problems, investigate causes of the problems, and recommend solutions.

C. Self-Managed Work Teams (ppt 12-13)
   1. Problem-solving teams didn't go far enough in getting employees involved in work-related decisions and processes.
   2. This led to experimentation with truly autonomous teams that could not only solve problems but also could implement solutions and take full responsibility for outcomes: self-managed work teams.
      a) They are usually composed of ten to fifteen people who take on the responsibilities of their former supervisors.
      b) Responsibilities include collective control over the pace of work, determination of work assignments, organization of breaks, and collective choice of inspection procedures.
      c) Fully self-managed work teams select their own members, and the members evaluate each other's performance.
   3. Eaton-Aeroquip plant in Arkansas example.
   4. A caution
      a) Research on the effectiveness of self-managed teams has not been uniformly positive.
         (1) Employees on self-managed teams seem to have higher absenteeism and turnover rates than do employees in traditional work structures.

D. Cross-Functional Teams (ppt 14-15)
   1. The Boeing example illustrates the use of the team concept—cross-functional teams made up of employees at about the same hierarchical level, but from different work areas, who come together to accomplish a task.
   2. Many organizations have used horizontal, boundary-spanning groups for decades.
      a) A task force is really nothing other than a temporary cross-functional team.
      b) Similarly, committees composed of members from across departmental lines are another example of cross-functional teams.
   3. The popularity of cross-discipline work teams exploded in the late 1980s.
      a) All the major automobile companies went to using this form of team to coordinate complex projects—Toyota, Honda, Nissan, BMW, GM, Ford, and DaimlerChrysler.

(1) Example, Harley-Davidson uses specific cross-functional teams to manage each line of its motorcycles.

b) These teams include Harley employees from design, manufacturing, and purchasing, as well as representatives from key outside suppliers.

4. Cross-functional teams are an effective means of allowing people from diverse areas within an organization (or even between organizations) to exchange information, develop new ideas and solve problems, and coordinate complex projects.

5. Cross-functional teams are difficult to manage.

a) It takes time to build trust and teamwork, especially among people from different backgrounds, with different experiences and perspectives.

E. Virtual Teams (ppt 16-17)

1. Virtual teams use computer technology to tie together physically dispersed members in order to achieve a common goal. They allow people to collaborate online, whether they're only a room apart or separated by continents.

a) Virtual teams can do all the things that other teams do—share information, make decisions, and complete tasks.

b) They can include all members from the same organization or link an organization's members with employees from other organizations (i.e., suppliers and joint partners).

2. The three primary factors that differentiate virtual teams from face-to-face teams are:

a) the absence of paraverbal and nonverbal cues

b) limited social context

c) the ability to overcome time and space constraints

3. In face-to-face conversation people use paraverbal (tone of voice, inflection, voice volume) and nonverbal (eye movement, facial expression, hand gestures, and other body language) cues. These help clarify communication, but they aren't available in online interactions.

4. Virtual teams often suffer from less social rapport and less direct interaction among members.

a) They aren't able to duplicate the normal give-and-take of face-to-face discussion.

b) Virtual team members report less satisfaction with the group interaction process than face-to-face teams.

c) But virtual teams allow people who might otherwise never be able to collaborate to work together.

5. Companies like Hewlett-Packard, Boeing, Ford, VeriFone, and Royal Dutch-Shell have become heavy users of virtual teams.

IV. CREATING EFFECTIVE TEAMS

A. Four general categories of key components have been identified—See Exhibit 8-3. (ppt 19)

1. Contextual
2. Composition
3. Work design
4. Process

B. Team effectiveness is the objective measures of the team's productivity, managers' ratings of the team's performance, and aggregate measure of member satisfaction. (ppt 18)

C. Context (ppt 20)
1. Four contextual factors appear to be most significant to team performance are the presence of adequate resources, effective leadership, a climate of trust, and a performance evaluation and reward system that reflects team contributions.
2. Adequate Resources
   a) A scarcity of resources directly reduces the ability of the team to perform its job effectively.
   b) Resources include support such as timely information, technology, adequate staffing, encouragement, and administrative assistance.
3. Leadership and Structure
   a) Team members must agree on who is to do what and ensure that all members contribute equally in sharing the workload.
   b) Agreeing on the specifics of work and how they fit together to integrate individual skills requires team leadership and structure.
   c) Evidence does indicate that self-managed work teams often perform better than teams with formally appointed leaders who can obstruct high performance whey they interfere.
4. Climate of Trust
   a) Interpersonal trust among team members facilitates cooperation, reduces the need to monitor each other, and bonds members.
5. Performance Evaluation and Reward Systems.
   a) Individual performance evaluations, fixed hourly wages, and individual incentives are not consistent with the development of high-performance teams.
   b) Group-based appraisals, profit sharing, gainsharing, small-group incentives, and other system modifications that reinforce team effort and commitment should be considered.

D. Composition (ppt 21)
1. Abilities of Members—to perform effectively, a team requires three different types of skills.
   a) Technical expertise
   b) Problem-solving and decision-making skills to be able to identify problems, generate alternatives, evaluate those alternatives, and make competent choices
   c) Good listening, feedback, conflict-resolution, and other interpersonal skills
   d) The right mix is crucial.
      (1) It's not uncommon for one or more members to learn the skills in which the group is deficient, thereby allowing the team to reach its full potential.
2. Personality
   a) Many of the dimensions identified in the Big Five personality model have proved to be relevant to team effectiveness—especially extroversion, agreeableness, conscientiousness, and emotional stability.
   b) The evidence indicates that the variance in personality characteristics may be more important than the mean.

        c) Another interesting finding is that "one bad apple can spoil the barrel" in teams of team performance.

  3. Allocating Roles

      a) Teams have different needs, and people should be selected for a team to ensure that there is diversity and that all various roles are filled.

      b) Nine potential team roles can be identified.

         (1) See Exhibit 8-4.

            (a) Creator-Innovators initiate creative ideas.

            (b) Explorer-Promoters champion ideas after they're initiated.

            (c) Assessor-Developers analyze decision options.

            (d) Thruster-Organizers provide structure.

            (e) Concluder-Producers provide direction and follow-through.

            (f) Controller-Inspectors check for details.

            (g) Upholders-Maintainers fight external battles.

            (h) Reporter-Advisers seek full information.

            (i) Linkers coordinate and integrate.

      c) On many teams, individuals will play multiple roles.

      d) By matching individual preferences with team role demands, managers increase the likelihood that the team members will work well together.

  4. Diversity

      a) Diverse teams increase the probability that the team will possess the characteristics needed to complete its tasks.

      b) Diversity does promote conflict, but this stimulates creativity.

  5. Size of Teams

      a) Teams should be neither very small (fewer than four or five) or very large (more than ten).

      b) Very small teams are likely to lack a diversity of views.

      c) Large teams become difficult to get much done because member have trouble interacting constructively and agreeing on much, or can't develop the cohesiveness, commitment, and mutual accountability necessary.

  6. Member Flexibility

      a) Individuals can complete each other's tasks, an obvious plus to a team.

      b) Cross-training should lead to higher team performance over time.

  7. Member Preferences

      a) Not every employee is a team player.

      b) When selecting team members, individual preferences should be considered as well as abilities, personalities, and skills.

      c) High-performing teams are likely to be composed of people who prefer working as part of a group.

E. Work Design (ppt 22)

  1. Freedom and autonomy, the opportunity to utilize different skills and talents, the ability to complete a whole and identifiable task or product, and working on a task or project that has a substantial impact on others.

  2. Evidence indicates that these characteristics enhance member motivation and increase team effectiveness because they increase members' sense of responsibility and ownership over the work and because they make the work more interesting to perform.

F. Process (ppt 23)

1. The process variables include member commitment to a common purpose, establishment of specific team goals, team efficacy, a managed level of conflict, and the reduction of social loafing.
2. A Common Purpose
    a) Effective teams have a common and meaningful purpose that provides direction, momentum, and commitment for members—a vision.
    b) Members of successful teams put a tremendous amount of time and effort into discussing, shaping, and agreeing upon a purpose that belongs to them both collectively and individually.
    c) This common purpose, when accepted by the team, becomes the equivalent of what celestial navigation is to a ship captain—it provides direction and guidance under any and all conditions.
3. Specific Goals
    a) Successful teams translate their common purpose into specific, measurable, and realistic performance goals.
    b) These specific goals facilitate clear communication.
    c) They also help teams maintain their focus on results.
    d) Teams goals should be challenging; difficult goals have been found to raise team performance on those criteria for which they are set.
4. Team Efficacy—the belief by team members that the team can succeed.
    a) Success breeds success.
    b) Management options
        (1) Help teams achieve small successes that build confidence.
        (2) Provide training to improve members' technical and interpersonal skills.
5. Conflict Levels
    a) Conflict on a team isn't necessarily bad. Teams that are completely void of conflict are likely to become apathetic and stagnant.
    b) Types of conflict
        (1) Relationship conflicts are based on interpersonal incompatibilities, tension, and animosity toward others—are almost always dysfunctional.
        (2) Task conflicts—based on task content—are often beneficial because they lessen the likelihood of groupthink, stimulate discussion, promote critical assessment of problems options, and can lead to better team decisions.
6. Social Loafing
    a) Coast on the group's effort because their individual contributions can't be identified.
    b) Effective teams undermine this tendency by holding themselves accountable at both the individual and team level.
    c) Successful teams' members are clear on both their individual and joint responsibilities.

V. TURNING INDIVIDUALS INTO TEAM PLAYERS
    A. The Challenge
        1. One substantial barrier to using work teams is individual resistance.
        2. To perform well as team members, individuals must be able to communicate openly and honestly, confront differences and resolve conflicts, and sublimate personal goals for the good of the team.
        3. The challenge is greatest where:
            a) the national culture is highly individualistic.
            b) the teams are being introduced into an established organization that has historically valued individual achievement.

       c) Examples: AT&T, Ford, Motorola, and other large U.S.-based companies.

   4. On the other hand, the challenge for management is less demanding when teams are introduced:

       a) Where employees have strong collectivist values such as in Japan or Mexico.

       b) Or in new organizations that use teams as their initial form for structuring work.

  B. Shaping Team Players (ppt 24)

   1. The primary options for turning individuals into team players are selection, training, and rewards.

   2. Selection

       a) Some people already possess the interpersonal skills to be effective team players.

       b) When faced with candidates lacking team skills/orientation there are three options.

          (1) Train the candidate.

          (2) Place the candidate in a unit within the organization that doesn't have teams.

          (3) Don't hire the candidate.

   3. Training

       a) People raised on the importance of individual accomplishment can be trained to become team players.

       b) Training improves problem-solving, communication, negotiation, conflict-management, coaching, and group-development skills.

   4. Rewards

       a) The reward system needs to be reworked to encourage cooperative efforts rather than competitive ones.

       b) Promotions, pay raises, and other forms of recognition should be given to individuals for how effective they are as a collaborative team member.

       c) Behaviors that should be rewarded include training new colleagues, sharing information with teammates, helping resolve team conflicts, and mastering new skills that your team needs.

       d) Don't forget the intrinsic rewards that employees can receive from teamwork. Teams provide camaraderie. It's exciting and satisfying to be an integral part of a successful team.

   5. The Ethics of Forced Team Participation

       a) It is debatable as to whether individuals should be forced to join teams when they were not hired under those conditions.

VI.   TEAMS AND QUALITY MANAGEMENT (ppt 25-27)

  A. Quality management is in essence, process improvement.

  B. Employee involvement is the linchpin of process improvement.

  C. Superior work teams are required for employee involvement.

VII.   BEWARE! TEAMS AREN'T ALWAYS THE ANSWER

  A. Teamwork has disadvantages that need to be considered.

   1. Teamwork takes more time.

   2. Teams have increased communication demands.

   3. Teams increase conflict.

    B. Management needs to analyze whether or not the work can be completed by an individual more efficiently than with a team. (ppt 28)
        1. Is the work simple enough that one person can do it more effectively?
        2. Does the work create a common purpose or set of goals for the group?
        3. Are the members of the group interdependent?

VIII. IMPLICATIONS FOR MANAGERS

1. Few trends have influenced jobs as much as the introduction of teams into the workplace. Teams require employees to cooperate with others, share information, confront differences, and sublimate personal interests for the greater good of the team.
2. Effective teams have common characteristics. The work should provide freedom and autonomy, the opportunity to utilize different skills and talents, the ability to complete a whole and identifiable task or product, and doing work that has a substantial impact on others. The teams require people with different types of skills: technical, problem-solving and decision-making, and interpersonal skills, and high scores on the personality characteristics of extroversion, agreeableness, conscientiousness, and emotional stability. Effective teams are neither too large nor too small—typically five to twelve people. They have members who fill role demands, are flexible, and who prefer to be a part of a group. They have adequate resources, effective leadership, and a performance evaluation and reward system that reflects team contributions. They have members committed to a common purpose, specific goals, and members who believe in the team's capabilities, a manageable level of conflict, and a minimal degree of social loafing.
3. Because individualistic organizations and societies attract and reward individual accomplishment, it is more difficult to create team players in these enviroments. To change, management should select individuals with effective interpersonal skills, provide training to develop teamwork skills, and reward individuals for cooperative efforts.
4. Teams are not always preferable to individuals.

SUMMARY (ppt 29-30)

1. Teams are growing in popularity because they typically outperform individuals when the tasks being done require multiple skills, judgment, and experience. When restructuring to compete more effectively and efficiently, companies have turned to teams as a way to better utilize employee talents. Teams also facilitate employee participation in operating decisions and help managers democratize their organizations and increase employee motivation.
2. A work group is a group that interacts primarily to share information and to make decisions to help one another perform within each member's area of responsibility. Work groups have no need or opportunity to engage in collective work that requires joint effort. A work team generates positive synergy through coordinated effort. The individual efforts result in a level of performance that is greater than the sum of those individual inputs.
3. The four most common forms are problem-solving teams, self-managed work teams, cross-functional teams, and virtual teams.
4. There are a number of group concepts that link directly to high performance in teams. The best work teams tend to be not too small nor too large—five to ten persons. The key components making up effective teams can be subsumed into four general categories: contextual influences, composition, work design, and process variables. Composition includes variables that related to how teams should be staffed. To perform effectively, a team

requires three different types of skills: technical expertise, problem-solving and decision-making skills, and good interpersonal skills. Teams have different needs, and people should be selected for a team on the basis of their personalities and preferences. Effective teams include people selected to ensure that there is diversity and that all various roles are filled. Effective teams require adequate resources, effective leadership, and a performance evaluation and reward system that reflects team contributions. Effective teams have a common vision that provides direction, momentum, and commitment for members. Successful teams translate their common purpose into specific, measurable, and realistic performance goals. Effective teams have confidence in themselves and believe they can succeed—team efficacy. Effective teams undermine the tendency toward social loafing by holding themselves accountable at both the individual and team level.

5. Organizations have a number of options when creating team players; selection, training, and through rewarding cooperative effort.

DISCUSSION QUESTIONS

1. Why have teams become a popular organizational tool for productivity improvement and empowerment of employees?
   Answer - Teams typically outperform individuals when the tasks being done require multiple skills, judgment, and experience. In their restructuring to compete more effectively and efficiently, companies have turned to teams as a way to better utilize employee talents. Teams have the capability to quickly assemble, deploy, refocus, and disband. Teams facilitate employee participation in operating decisions. Teams are an effective means for management to democratize their organizations and increase employee motivation.

2. Why is it important for managers to understand the difference between teams and groups?
   Answer - A work group is a group that interacts primarily to share information and to make decisions to help one another perform within each member's area of responsibility. Work groups have no need or opportunity to engage in collective work that requires joint effort. Their performance is merely the summation of all the group members' individual contributions. A work team generates positive synergy through coordinated effort. The individual efforts result in a level of performance that is greater than the sum of those individual inputs. Exhibit 8-1 outlines the differences.

3. As a manager you are assigned a short-term project, three to four months, to study your small company's computer and information needs and then recommend a course of action. You need someone who has expertise in computers, someone with knowledge of information systems, a couple of users within your organization, and a software specialist. But your company only has the users. What type of team would be most effective? Why?
   Answer - Students can make an argument for a problem-solving team using some consultants or a virtual team. They might argue for a cross-functional team, seeing the content experts as functional experts even though they aren't employees of the company. A self-managed team clearly won't work. Problem-solving team-members share ideas or offer suggestions on how work processes and methods can be improved. A cross-functional team is made up of employees at about the same hierarchical level—but from different work areas—who come together to accomplish a task. Many organizations have used horizontal, boundary-spanning groups for decades. A task force is really nothing other than a temporary cross-functional team. Similarly, committees composed of members from across departmental lines are another example of cross-functional teams. Cross-functional teams are an effective means of allowing people from diverse areas within an organization (or even between organizations) to exchange information, develop new ideas and solve problems, and coordinate complex projects. A virtual team uses computer technology to tie together physically dispersed

members in order to achieve a common goal. It allows people to collaborate online, whether they're only a room apart or separated by continents. Virtual teams can do all the things that other teams do—share information, make decisions, and complete tasks. They can include all members from the same organization or link an organization's members with employees from other organizations (i.e., suppliers and joint partners).

4. Several key components have been identified that make up effective teams. Identify these components and define "team effectiveness" as described by this text's model.
   Answer – Exhibit 8-3 summarizes what is currently known about what makes teams effective. Team effectiveness includes objective measures of the team's productivity, managers' ratings of the team's performance, and aggregate measures of member satisfaction.

5. Teams have different needs, and people should be selected for a team to ensure diversity and expertise to fill various roles. Identify and define the nine potential team roles.
   Answer - See Exhibit 8-4.

   > (a) Creator-Innovators initiate creative ideas.
   > (b) Explorer-Promoters champion ideas after they're initiated.
   > (c) Assessor-Developers analyze decision options.
   > (d) Thruster-Organizers provide structure.
   > (e) Concluder-Producers provide direction and follow-through.
   > (f) Controller-Inspectors check for details.
   > (g) Upholders-Maintainers fight external battles.
   > (h) Reporter-Advisers seek full information.
   > (i) Linkers coordinate and integrate

6. As a manager, what basic group concepts do you need to consider in forming effective teams?
   Answer – Size. The best work teams tend to be small. When larger than about ten to twelve members, it becomes difficult to get much done; they will have trouble interacting constructively and agreeing on much. Abilities of members—to perform effectively, a team requires three different types of skills; technical expertise, problem-solving and decision-making skills, and interpersonal skills. Allocating roles and promoting diversity—teams have different needs, and people should be selected for a team on the basis of their personalities and preferences. Effective teams select people to fill all the key roles and play those roles on the basis of their skills and preferences. Commitment to a common purpose—effective teams have a common vision that provides direction, momentum, and commitment for members. Establishing specific goals—successful teams translate their common purpose into specific, measurable, and realistic performance goals. Leadership and structure—Effective teams also need leadership and structure to provide focus and direction. Social loafing and accountability—Effective teams undermine this tendency by holding themselves accountable at both the individual and team level. Successful teams' members are clear on both their individual and joint responsibilities. Appropriate performance evaluation and reward systems—The traditional individually oriented evaluation and reward system must be modified.

7. Your company has always rewarded individual effort. Now top management wants to implement teams as part of a reengineering process. As a manager how can you prepare your people to be team players?
   Answer - You face a challenge because the teams are being introduced into an established organization that has historically valued individual achievement. To perform well as team

members, individuals must be able to communicate openly and honestly, confront differences and resolve conflicts, and sublimate personal goals for the good of the team. The primary options for turning individuals into team players are: Selection—some people already possess the interpersonal skills to be effective team players. Training—people raised on the importance of individual accomplishment can be trained to become team players. Training improves problem solving, communication, negotiation, conflict-management, coaching, and group-development skills. Rewards. The reward system needs to be reworked to encourage cooperative efforts rather than competitive ones. Behaviors that should be rewarded include training new colleagues, sharing information with teammates, helping resolve team conflicts, and mastering new skills that your team needs. Don't forget the intrinsic rewards that employees can receive from teamwork. Teams provide camaraderie. It's exciting and satisfying to be an integral part of a successful team.

Your organization was largely built around individuals who have not experienced, nor do they have the desire, to work in teams. What are the ethical implications of this?
Answer- The key is to understand that not all individuals are suited for the team environment. Many were attracted to the organization because of the nature of the work, which was oriented around individuals. Management needs to understand that this could cause a team effort to fail, and must evaluate this prior to implementation.

Under what conditions are teams not effective?
Answer- For simple tasks, work is often best completed by individuals. Management also needs to examine whether the work in teams will create a common purpose or set of goals that is stronger than the individual goals. Finally, management needs to look at whether the members of the group are interdependent.

EXERCISES

A.   International Office Building

Students will learn not only the power of cooperation but also the importance of planning group work prior to beginning a project.

1.   You will need sufficient Legos to make a parts bag for each team.
     - You will need a second room and a helper.
     - You need to build a model. Gluing it together once you build it so it doesn't come apartis recommended.
     - A suggested model design.

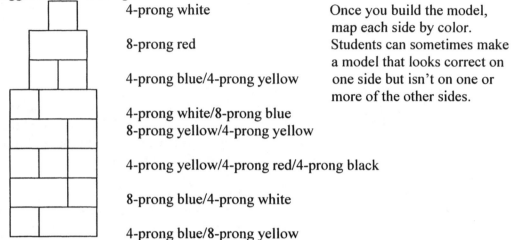

4-prong white

8-prong red

4-prong blue/4-prong yellow

4-prong white/8-prong blue
8-prong yellow/4-prong yellow

4-prong yellow/4-prong red/4-prong black

8-prong blue/4-prong white

4-prong blue/8-prong yellow

Once you build the model, map each side by color. Students can sometimes make a model that looks correct on one side but isn't on one or more of the other sides.

2.   Divide students into teams of six or fewer students.
3.   Pass out the instructions and read through them. ·
     - At this point read the student instructions yourself. They explain the details.
4.   Pass out the bags of Legos. Let students count them to make sure they have the right number of each color. As soon as they do that they must put them on a desk between them and not touch them again until you start the game.
5.   At this point pass out the "international visas," one to a team, and send your helper with the unseen model into another room.
     - The assistant is to collect the visa when students enter and return it when they leave, to control for no more than one student at a time from each team.
     - The assistant is to keep students from touching the model. The students may move around but they may not touch the model.
6.   You made need another assistant in the room with you to keep track of the time when teams report they are moving to construction or when they want to be certified.
     - When a team moves to construction, record the amount of time they spent planning.
     - When a team asks for certification, record the time. If they are certifiable, keep the time. If not, return the model with only the comment, "Not certified," and erase their time, which keeps running.
7.   The first team done wins. You should continue the exercise until at least half of your teams complete their models.
8.   Discuss the results.
     - Ask teams to explain how they decided to go about the task.
     - Ask about leadership and participation.
     - Frequently there is a direct relationship between planning time and construction time. The more time planning the less time constructing.

Student handout

This is a team work exercise. You are to build an overseas headquarters for a multinational America-based corporation. They want their international headquarters to look like their American headquarters. Unfortunately the blueprints for the building have been lost. You must study the American headquarters building and then replicate it. Yours is a competitive company and other project teams have been given the same assignment. The team that accomplishes the task first receives a bonus.

Process

1. You have 45 minutes to build your international office building. Your time is divided into two parts: planning time and building time. You may use as much planning time as you desire before you build, but once you begin to build you MAY NOT return to planning time.

2. Study the American model. Your model American building is located in another room.
   - Only one member of your team may study the model at a time. That team member must return to your circle before the next team member leaves. The "studying" team member must carry his or her international visa to be permitted entry back into the United States.
   - You may take notes, sketches, and so on, but you cannot touch the building.
   - You may send as many or as few of your team as you please.
   - Anyone may visit the site as many times as they please. Each visit, as well as the entire planning process, may take as long as you please.

3. When you finish planning and start to build, you must announce your intention to the Master Builder so he or she may record the transition. Be sure to announce the name of your team and be certain the Master Builder hears you.

4. When you complete your building, call to the Master Builder to certify your construction. Your time stops when you call him/her. If you are certified, you are done. If you are not certified, you may try again but your time begins again from when you first called to the Master Builder.

5. The team with a certified building in the least total time wins. There are significant awards for winning and placing.

Materials

1. Do not open your bag of construction materials until told to do so.
2. When told to open your bag and count your materials make sure that you have the following: (The prong numbers refer to the number of male fittings on the top of the Lego)

5 - Blue 8 prongs	1 - Red 6 prongs	1 - Red 4 prongs
4 - Yellow 8 prongs	1 - White 6 prongs	1 - White 4 prongs
3 - White 8 prongs	3 - Yellow 4 prongs	
2 - Red 8 prongs	1 - Black 4 prongs	

3. Once counted you may not handle your materials any further until we begin.
4. Take the next few minutes and plan your strategy. Remember the restrictions of numbers 1-5 in the process section.
5. Any questions?

Part III   Groups in the Organization

B.   <u>Study Guide</u>

The purpose of this exercise is to indicate to students the relationship between size and team effectiveness. Since all students seem to enjoy, or find comfort in, a study guide, this exercise can result in the development of a good, or a bad, study guide.

Divide the class into different sized teams. Make some teams extremely small and lacking in diversity and skills, and some teams extremely large and cumbersome. Give the teams the instructions that they are to come to consensus on the content of a study guide for Chapter 8. In other words, they are to mutually agree on the items to be included—they cannot vote or otherwise decide some members' contributions are right or wrong—they are to all agree.

You might want to have a quick discussion on team roles, or simply let the teams themselves formally or informally let team roles evolve naturally, and have the teams identify the different role holders after the conclusion of the exercise.

While the teams are developing their study guides, the faculty member should record the team required by each different team to complete its task. Also, the faculty member might choose to walk around the classroom, and listen to the conversations within the different groups—this may provide rich insights as to why some groups completed the task more efficiently than others. After the teams have all developed their study guides, a discussion can be led encouraging the different groups to identify what problems they encountered, and why they think the team had to overcome that particular problem.

The teams might possibly identify (or be led to identify) problems that were caused by (for example):
Size—either to big or too small
Diversity—a lack of, or an overabundance
Team Roles—whether they were fulfilled or void

The following instructions could be verbally given to the teams, or copied and handed out.

<u>Instructions</u>
As a team you are to develop a bulleted study guide for Chapter 8. The items included on the study guide are to fully represent the chapter content. The items are also to be placed in the study guide in descending order of importance. In other words, the most important content item from Chapter 8 is to be listed first, down to the least important content item. The items chosen for inclusion on this study guide, and their order of importance, must be completely agreed upon by ALL members of the team. No use of voting and majority rules can be employed in determining the content of the study guide. Consensus agreement must prevail within the team.

Be sure to include all necessary items. A student should be able to study the items your team includes on this study guide and be fully prepared for an examination on Chapter 8.

Analyzing Your Organization

Analyze the various tasks that you complete at work on a regular basis. Are these tasks best suited for individuals or teamwork? If you were to implement teamwork or teams, how would you do this? Analyze this in the context of all of the variables in this chapter.

If you are currently in an environment of teamwork, interview or discuss with the team leaders some of the variables in this chapter, using the following questions as a guide.
1. How do you determine the size of the team?
2. What types of conflict occur? How do you resolve conflict?
3. Does it take longer to complete tasks in a team environment?
4. Do you have "resistors" to teamwork? If so, how do you manage that?
5. What happened to cause management to look at teams as a more efficient way of doing work?

Be prepared to discuss your findings with the class.

CHAPTER 9 - COMMUNICATION

CHAPTER OBJECTIVES
After reading this chapter, students should be able to:
1. Define communication and list its four functions.
2. Describe the communication process.
3. Contrast the three common types of small-group networks.
4. Identify factors affecting the use of the grapevine.
5. Define knowledge management and explain its importance.
6. Describe common barriers to effective communication.
7. List four rules for improving cross-cultural communication.
8. Outline behaviors associated with providing effective feedback.
9. Identify the behaviors related to effective active listening.

LECTURE OUTLINE
I.   FUNCTIONS OF COMMUNICATION
    A.   Communication's Four Major Functions—control, motivation, emotional expression, and information. (ppt 4)
        1.   Control. Communication controls member behavior in several ways.
           a)   Employees are required to follow authority hierarchies and formal guidelines.
           b)   Informal communication also controls behavior.
              (1) When work groups tease or harass a member who produces too much, they are informally communicating with, and controlling, the member's behavior.
        2.   Motivation. Communication fosters motivation by clarifying for employees what is to be done, how well they are doing, and what can be done to improve performance.
           a)   The formation of specific goals, feedback on progress toward the goals, and reinforcement of desired behavior all stimulate motivation and require communication.
        3.   Emotional expression. For many employees, their work group is a primary source for social interaction.
           a)   Communication within the group is a fundamental mechanism by which members show their frustrations and feelings of satisfaction.
           b)   Communication provides an avenue for expression of emotions and fulfillment of social needs.
        4.   Information. The final function that communication performs is related to its role in facilitating decision making.
           a)   It provides the needed information.
        5.   None of these four functions should be seen as more important than the others.

II.   THE COMMUNICATION PROCESS
    A.   The Model (ppt 5)
        1.   A purpose, expressed as a message to be conveyed, is needed to begin the process.
        2.   It passes between a source (the sender) and a receiver.
        3.   The message is encoded (converted to a symbolic form).
        4.   It is passed by way of some medium (channel) to the receiver.
        5.   The receiver retranslates (decodes) the message initiated by the sender.

6. The result is a transference of meaning from one person to another.
7. See Exhibit 9-1, the communication process.
    a) The sender encodes the message.
    b) The message is the actual physical product from the source encoding.
    c) The channel is the medium through which the message travels. (ppt 6)
        (1) Formal channels are established by the organization and transmit messages that are related to the professional activities of members.
        (2) Other forms of messages, such as personal or social, follow the informal channels in the organization.
    d) The receiver is the object to whom the message is directed.
    e) Before the message can be received, the symbols in it must be translated into a form that can be understood by the receiver—decoding of the message.
    f) The final link is a feedback loop—the check on how successful we have been in transferring our messages as originally intended.

III. DIRECTION OF COMMUNICATION
   A. Direction (ppt 7)
       1. Communication can flow vertically or laterally.
       2. The vertical dimension can be further divided into downward and upward directions.

   B. Downward
       1. Communication that flows from one level of a group or organization to a lower level.
           a) Managers communicating with subordinates.
       2. Used by group leaders and managers to assign goals, provide job instructions, and inform underlings of policies and procedures, point out problems that need attention, and offer feedback about performance.
       3. Not only oral or face-to-face; letters, e-mails, and so on, sent to employees are also downward communication.

   C. Upward
       1. Communication that flows to a higher level in the group or organization.
       2. Used to provide feedback to higher-ups, inform them of progress toward goals, and relay current problems.
       3. Upward communication keeps managers aware.
       4. Examples of upward communication are performance reports prepared by lower management for review by middle and top management, suggestion boxes, employee attitude surveys, grievance procedures, superior-subordinate discussions, and informal gripe sessions in which employees have the opportunity to identify and discuss problems with their boss or representatives of higher management.

   D. Lateral
       1. Communication among members of the same work group, among members of work groups at the same level, among managers at the same level, or among any horizontally equivalent personnel.
           a) Horizontal communications are often necessary to save time and facilitate coordination.
           b) Lateral relationships are formally sanctioned.

        c) Often, they are informally created to short-circuit the vertical hierarchy and expedite action.

        d) Lateral communications can, from management's viewpoint, be good or bad.

IV.   INTERPERSONAL COMMUNICATION (ppt 8)

   A. Oral Communication (ppt 9)

     1. The chief means of conveying messages is oral communication.

       a) Speeches, formal one-on-one and group discussions, and the informal rumor mill or grapevine.

     2. The advantages are speed and feedback.

     3. The major disadvantage is that whenever the message has to be passed through a number of people there is a potential for distortion.

   B. Written Communication (ppt 10)

     1. Written communications include memos, letters, electronic mail, fax transmissions, organizational periodicals, notices placed on bulletin boards, or any other device that is transmitted via written words or symbols.

     2. Advantages

       a) They're tangible and verifiable.

       b) Both the sender and receiver have a record of the communication.

       c) The message can be stored for an indefinite period of time.

       d) Written communications are more likely to be well thought out, logical, and clear.

     3. Drawbacks

       a) Time consuming because it is more precise.

       b) The lack of feedback.

   C. Nonverbal Communication (ppt 11-12)

     1. Verbal messages also impart a nonverbal message.

     2. In some instances, the nonverbal component may stand alone.

     3. Nonverbal communication includes body movements, the intonations or emphasis we give to words, facial expressions, and the physical distance between the sender and receiver.

     4. It can be argued that every body movement has a meaning and no movement is accidental.

       a) We act out our state of being with nonverbal body language.

       b) Body language conveys the extent to which a individuals like one another, and the relative status between the sender and receiver.

     5. We may disagree with the specific meanings of the movements, but we cannot deny that body language adds to, and often complicates, verbal communication.

       a) A body position or movement does not by itself have a precise or universal meaning, but when it is linked with spoken language, it gives fuller meaning to a sender's message.

       b) Intonations can change the meaning of a message.

       c) Facial expression conveys meaning.

       d) Space in terms of physical distance also has meaning.

     6. Look for nonverbal cues as well as listen to the literal meaning of a sender's words.

     7. Particularly be aware of contradictions between the messages.

8. Wc misinform others when we express one emotion verbally, such as trust, but nonverbally communicate a contradictory message that reads, "I don't have confidence in you."
   a) Actions usually speak louder than words in a contradictory situation.

V. ORGANIZATIONAL COMMUNICATION
A. Formal Small-Group Networks
   1. There are three common types of small-group networks.
      a) See Exhibit 9-2. (ppt 13)
      b) The chain rigidly follows the formal chain of command.
      c) The wheel relies on the leader to act as the central conduit for all the group's communication.
      d) The all-channel permits all group members to actively communicate with each other and is most often characterized in practice by the self-managed team.
   2. The effectiveness of each type of network depends on the goals of the group. (ppt 14)
      a) See Exhibit 9-3.
      b) If speed is important, the wheel and all-channel networks are most effective.
      c) For accuracy use the chain or wheel.
      d) The wheel is best for allowing leaders to emerge.
      e) If member satisfaction is important, the all-channel network is best and the wheel worst.

B. The Informal Group Communication Network
   1. In an informal system information flows along the well-known grapevine and rumors can flourish.
   2. A classic study of the grapevine investigated the communication pattern among sixty-seven managerial personnel in a small manufacturing firm.
      a) The grapevine was an important source of information; only 10 percent of the executives acted as liaison individuals. (ppt 15)
      b) Information on events of general interest tended to flow between the major functional groups.
      c) No evidence surfaced to suggest that any one group consistently acted as liaisons; rather, different types of information passed through different liaison persons.
   3. Replication found that only 10 percent act as liaison individuals.
   4. Grapevine accuracy
      a) The grapevine carries information that is 75 percent accurate.
   5. Rumors emerge as a response to situations that are important to us, where there is ambiguity, and under conditions that arouse anxiety.
   6. A rumor will persist either until the wants and expectations creating the uncertainty underlying the rumor are fulfilled or until the anxiety is reduced.
      a) The grapevine is an important part of any group or organization's communication network.
      b) It identifies for managers those confusing issues that employees consider important and that create anxiety.
      c) It acts as both a filter and a feedback mechanism, picking up the issues that employees consider relevant.
      d) For employees, the grapevine is particularly valuable for translating formal communications into their group's own jargon.

C. Computer-Aided Communication (ppt 16)
   1. Includes electronic mail (e-mail), intranet and extranet links, and video-conferencing.
   2. E-mail
      a) Uses the Internet to transmit and receive computer-generated text and documents.
      b) A recent study found that the average U.S. employee receives thirty-one e-mail messages daily.
      c) Benefits
         (1) Message can be quickly written, edited, and stored.
         (2) Messages can be distributed to one person or thousands.
         (3) Messages can be read, in their entirety, at the convenience of the recipient.
         (4) The cost of sending formal e-mail messages is a fraction of the cost to print, duplicate, and distribute a comparable letter or brochure.
      d) Drawbacks
         (1) Information overload.
         (2) Time consuming to read, absorb, and respond to messages daily.
         (3) Messages lack emotional content. The nonverbal cues in a face-to-face message or the tone of voice doesn't come across in e-mail.
         (4) Messages tend to be cold and impersonal.
         (5) Not the best means to convey certain information such as layoffs, plant closings, or other messages that might evoke emotional responses and require empathy or social support.
   3. Instant Messaging (ppt 17)
      a) Instant messaging is essential real-time email.
      b) The advantages over email include no delay, no in-box clutter, and no uncertainty as to whether the message was received.
   4. Intranet and Extranet Links
      a) Intranets are private, organization-wide information networks that look and act like a Web site but to which only people in an organization have access.
      b) Extranet links connect internal employees with selected suppliers, customers, and strategic partners.
   5. Videoconferencing
      a) Permits employees in an organization to have meetings with people at different locations.
      b) Live audio and video images of members allow them to see, hear, and talk with each other.
      c) Unlike previous specially-equipped rooms, cameras and microphones are now being attached to individual computers, allowing people to participate without leaving their desks.
   6. Summary
      a) It is no longer necessary for employees to be at their workstation to be available. Pagers, cellular phones, and personal communicators allow location flexibility for employees.
      b) Organizational boundaries become less relevant as a result of computer-aided communications. Networked computers allow employees to conduct business on a broader basis.
   7. Knowledge Management (ppt 18-22)

a) The process of organizing and distributing an organization's collective wisdom.

b) Important for three reasons.

   (1) Intellectual assets are now as important as other assets.

   (2) As boomers leave the workforce, there will be a wealth of knowledge lost if there are no attempts to capture it.

   (3) A well-designed system will reduce redundancies.

c) Involves developing a database of pertinent information that employees can readily access.

VI. BARRIERS TO EFFECTIVE COMMUNICATION (ppt 23)

A. Filtering

1. Filtering refers to a sender's purposely manipulating information so that the receiver will see it more favorably.

2. The major determinant of filtering is the number of levels in an organization's structure.

   a) The more vertical levels, the more filtering.

   b) Filtering occurs wherever there are status differences.

B. Selective Perception

1. Selective perception occurs when the receiver in the communication process sees and hears things in a selective way based on his needs, motivations, experience/background, and other personal characteristics.

2. The receiver also projects his interests and expectations into communications as he decodes them.

C. Information Overload

1. Individuals have a finite capacity for processing data.

2. When individuals have more information than they can sort and use they tend to weed out, ignore, pass over, or forget information.

D. Gender Styles

1. Men and women use oral communication for different reasons.

2. Men use talk to emphasize status, women use it to create connection.

   a) For many men conversations are primarily a means to preserve independence and maintain status in a hierarchical social order.

   b) For many women conversations are negotiations for closeness in which people try to seek and give confirmation and support.

   c) When men hear a problem, they want to assert their desire for independence and control by providing solutions.

   d) The women present the problem to gain support and connection, not to get the male's advice.

E. Emotions

1. How the receiver feels at the time of receipt of a communication message will influence how he or she interprets it.

2. Extreme emotions are most likely to hinder effective communication.

F. Language

1. Age, education, and cultural background are three of the more obvious variables that influence the language a person uses and the definitions he gives to words.

2. In an organization employees usually come from diverse backgrounds.
3. Grouping employees into departments creates specialists who develop their own jargon or technical language.
4. In large organizations members are also frequently widely dispersed geographically.
5. The existence of vertical levels can also cause language problems.
6. Speaking a common language, English, does not prevent differences in usage of that language.
7. The problem is that members in an organization usually don't know how those with whom they interact have modified the language.

VII. CROSS-CULTURAL COMMUNICATION
   A. Cross-Cultural Factors
      1. The greater the differences in backgrounds between sender and receiver, the greater the differences in meanings attached to particular words or behaviors.

   B. Cultural Context (ppt 24)
      1. High-Context Cultures—China, Vietnam, Saudi Arabia—rely heavily on nonverbal and subtle situational cues when communicating with others.
         a) What is not said may be more significant than what is said.
         b) A person's official status, place in society, and reputation carry considerable weight in communication.
      2. Low-Context Cultures—Europe and North America—rely essentially on words to convey meaning.
         a) Body language or formal titles are secondary to spoken and written words
      3. See Exhibit 9-4.
      4. Communication in high-context cultures implies considerably more trust by parties.
      5. Oral agreements imply strong commitments in high-context cultures.
      6. Enforceable contracts will tend to be in writing, precisely worded, and highly legalistic in low-context cultures.
      7. Low-context cultures value directness; managers are expected to be explicit and precise in conveying intended meaning.

   C. A Cultural Guide (ppt 25)
      1. Four rules to reduce misperceptions, misinterpretations, and misevaluation are:
         a) Assume differences until similarity is proved.
         b) Emphasize description rather than interpretation or evaluation.
            (1) Description is less based on the observer's culture and background than on the interpretation or evaluation.
         c) Practice empathy.
            (1) Before sending a message, put yourself in the receiver's shoes.
         d) Treat your interpretation as a working hypothesis.
            (1) Once you've developed an explanation for a new situation treat your interpretation as a hypothesis that needs further testing.

VIII. ETHICS IN COMMUNICATION: IS IT WRONG TO TELL A LIE?
   A. Most of us differentiate between "real lies" and "little white lies," the latter being an acceptable, even necessary, part of social interaction.

   B. Employee transfer example

IX.   IMPLICATIONS FOR MANAGERS (ppt 26)
    A.   Suggestions for Making Communication More Effective

    B.   Use Multiple Channels.
        1.   You improve the likelihood of clarity if multiple channels are used to convey a message because you stimulate a number of the receiver's senses, and people have different abilities to absorb information.
        2.   Repeating a message by using a different channel acts to reinforce it and decreases the likelihood of distortions.

    C.   Use Feedback.
        1.   Many communication problems can be attributed directly to misunderstandings and inaccuracies.
        2.   These are less likely to occur with effective feedback.
            a)   See Exhibit 9-5.
            b)   The manager can ask a set of questions relating to a message in order to determine whether the message was received as intended.
            c)   Performance appraisals, salary reviews, and promotion decisions represent important but more subtle forms of feedback.
        3.   Feedback does not have to be conveyed in words.
            a)   Actions can speak louder than words.

    D.   Simplify Language.
        1.   Structure messages in ways that will make them clear and understandable.
        2.   Words should be chosen carefully.
        3.   Jargon can facilitate understanding when it is used with other group members who speak that language, but it can cause innumerable problems when used outside that group.

    E.   Listen Actively.
        1.   See Exhibit 9-6.
        2.   Many of us are poor listeners because it is difficult and because it's usually more satisfying to talk.
        3.   Listening, in fact, is often more tiring than talking. It demands intellectual effort.
            a)   The average person speaks at a rate of about 150 words per minute, whereas we have the capacity to listen at the rate of over 1,000 words per minute.
        4.   Active listening is enhanced when the receiver develops empathy with the sender, that is, when the receiver tries to place himself in the sender's position.
        5.   Because senders differ in attitudes, interests, needs, and expectations, empathy makes it easier to understand the actual content of a message.
        6.   An empathetic listener reserves judgment on the message's content and carefully listens to what is being said.

    F.   Constrain Emotions.
        1.   If we're emotionally upset over an issue, we're likely to misconstrue incoming messages.
        2.   The best approach is to defer further communication until composure is regained.

    G.   Use the Grapevine.
        1.   You can't eliminate the grapevine, therefore use it and make it work for you.

2. The grapevine is a valuable source of feedback.
3. The grapevine can carry damaging rumors that reduce the effectiveness of formal communication.
   a) To lessen this destructive force, make good use of formal channels.

SUMMARY (ppt 27-28)

1. Organizations use communication for four primary purposes or functions: control, motivation, emotional expression, and for exchanging information.
2. The communication process model consists of a purpose, expressed as a message that passes between a source (the sender) and a receiver. The message is encoded (converted to a symbolic form). It is passed by way of some medium (channel) to the receiver. The receiver retranslates (decodes) the message initiated by the sender. The result is a transference of meaning from one person to another.
3. Communication can flow in two primary directions in an organization—vertically or laterally. The vertical dimension can be further divided into downward and upward directions.
4. Managers have a number of channels of communication available to them, but each has its own unique strengths and weaknesses. The chief means of conveying messages is oral communication. It is fast and provides feedback. The major disadvantage is that whenever the message has to be passed through a number of people there is a potential for distortion. Written communications are tangible and verifiable. But they are time consuming and often lack in feedback. Verbal messages also impart a nonverbal message.
5. Organizations have both formal small group networks; the chain, wheel, and all-channel networks but also information networks like the grapevine.
6. Communication in today's organizations is enhanced and enriched by computer-aided technologies including electronic mail, instant messaging, intranet and extranet links, videoconferencing, and knowledge-management systems. Each technology has its advantages and its drawbacks.
7. There are six common barriers to effective communication. Filtering refers to a sender's purposely manipulating information so that the receiver will see it more favorably. Filtering occurs wherever there are status differences. Selective perception occurs when the receiver in the communication process sees and hears things in a selective way based on his needs, motivations, experience/background, and other personal characteristics. Information overload is the result of individuals having a finite capacity for processing data, and the information to work with exceeds the processing capacity. Gender styles: men use talk to emphasize status; women use it to create connection. Emotions reflect how the receiver feels at the time of receipt of a communication message and will influence how he or she interprets it. Language—age, education, and cultural background are variables that influence the language a person uses and the definitions he gives to words.
8. Cultures tend to differ in the importance to which context influences the meaning that individuals take from what is actually said or written. High-context cultures—China, Vietnam, and Saudi Arabia—rely heavily on nonverbal and subtle situational cues when communicating with others. Low-context cultures—Europe and North America—rely essentially on words to convey meaning. Body language or formal titles are secondary to spoken and written words. See Exhibit 9-4.
9. There are four rules for improving cross-cultural communication: 1) Assume differences until similarity is proved. 2) Emphasize description rather than interpretation or evaluation. 3) Practice empathy. 4) Treat your interpretation as a working hypothesis.
10. Many communication problems can be attributed directly to misunderstandings and inaccuracies. These are less likely to occur with effective feedback. The steps for effective

feedback are listed in Exhibit 9-5. The manager can ask a set of questions relating to a message in order to determine whether the message was received as intended.

11. Many of us are poor listeners because it's difficult and because it's usually more satisfying to talk. Listening, in fact, is often more tiring than talking. It demands intellectual effort. Active listening is enhanced when the receiver develops empathy with the sender, that is, when the receiver tries to place himself in the sender's position. See Exhibit 9-6.

DISCUSSION QUESTIONS

1. How do managers use communication in an organization?

    Answer - Communication controls member behavior by requiring employees to follow authority hierarchies and formal guidelines. Informal communication also controls behavior. Communication fosters motivation by clarifying for employees what is to be done, how well they are doing, and what can be done to improve performance. Emotional expression as communication within the group is a fundamental mechanism by which members show their frustrations and feelings of satisfaction. Communication provides an avenue for expression of emotions and fulfillment of social needs. The final function that communication performs is related to its role in facilitating decision making. No one of these four functions should be seen as more important than the others.

2. Describe the communication process in terms of a student asking a professor for permission to take an examination later than the rest of his or her class.

    Answer - In their answers have students give special thought to encoding and decoding. What encoding would be especially persuasive, what is the likely decoding of the professor? The student begins with a purpose, expressed as a message to be conveyed, that is needed to begin the process: "I need to take the exam late because I've been ill and unable to keep up on my studies." The message passes between a source (the student) and a receiver (the professor). The message is encoded—converted to a symbolic form (this is the wording chosen by the student). The message then is passed by way of some medium (channel) a note, a face-to-face meeting, to the receiver (the professor). The receiver (professor) retranslates—decodes—phrases into words he or she understands, the message initiated by the sender (student). The result is a transference of meaning from one person to another. The question is did the encoding and decoding match?

3. Describe the three types of communication flows that exist within organizations.

    Answer - Communication can flow vertically or laterally. The vertical dimension can be further divided into downward and upward directions. Downward communication flows from one level of a group or organization to a lower level, as in managers communicating with subordinates. It is used by group leaders and managers to assign goals, provide job instructions, and inform underlings of policies and procedures, point out problems that need attention, and offer feedback about performance. Upward communication flows to a higher level in the group or organization. It is used to provide feedback to higher-ups, inform them of progress toward goals, and relay current problems. Upward communication keeps managers aware. Lateral communication occurs among members of the same work group, among members of work groups at the same level, among managers at the same level, or among any horizontally equivalent personnel.

4. As a manager you have a number of means of communicating to employees. What ways are at your disposal and why would you use one rather than another?

    Answer - The chief means of conveying messages is oral communication. The advantages are speed and feedback. The major disadvantage is that whenever the message has to be passed through a number of people there is a potential for distortion. Written communications include memos, letters, electronic mail, fax transmissions, organizational periodicals, notices placed on bulletin boards, or any other device that is transmitted via written words or symbols. Advantages: they're tangible and verifiable. Written communications are more likely to be well thought out, logical, and clear. The drawbacks are it is time consuming because it is more precise, and it creates a lack of feedback. Nonverbal communication—verbal messages also impart a nonverbal message. Nonverbal communication includes body movements, the intonations or emphasis we give to words, facial expressions, and the physical distance between the sender and receiver.

5. There are a number of common small-group networks. What are the strengths and weaknesses of each?
    Answer - The three common types of small-group networks are shown in Exhibit 9-2. The chain rigidly follows the formal chain of command. The wheel relies on the leader to act as the central conduit for all the group's communication. The all-channel permits all group members to actively communicate with each other and is most often characterized in practice by the problem-solving task force. The effectiveness of each type of network depends on the goals of the group. If speed is important, the wheel and all-channel networks are most effective; for accuracy, the chain or wheel. The wheel is best for allowing leaders to emerge. If member satisfaction is important, the all-channel network is best and the wheel is worst.

6. What is the grapevine, and what important functions does it fulfill for managers and employees?
    Answer – It is an informal system. Information flows along the well-known grapevine and rumors can flourish. A classic study of the grapevine found that the it was an important source of information—only 10 percent of those involved acted as liaison individuals. Information on events of general interest tended to flow between the major functional groups. The grapevine was about 75 percent accurate.

    Rumors emerge as a response to situations that are important to us, where there is ambiguity, and under conditions that arouse anxiety. A rumor will persist either until the wants and expectations creating the uncertainty underlying the rumor are fulfilled or until the anxiety is reduced. The grapevine is an important part of any group or organization's communication network. It identifies for managers those confusing issues that employees consider important and that create anxiety. It acts as both a filter and a feedback mechanism, picking up the issues that employees consider relevant. For employees, the grapevine is particularly valuable for translating formal communications into their group's own jargon.

7. What are the common barriers to effective communication and how do they distort the communication process?
    Answer - Filtering refers to a sender's purposely manipulating information so that the receiver will see it more favorably. The major determinant of filtering is the number of levels in an organization's structure. Selective perception occurs when the receiver, in the communication process, sees and hears things in a selective way based on his needs, motivations, experience/background, and other personal characteristics. The receiver also projects his interests and expectations into communications as he decodes them. Individuals have a finite capacity for processing data, and when the information we have to work with exceeds our processing capacity, the result is information overload. Gender styles: men and women use oral communication for different reasons. Men use talk to emphasize status; women use it to create connection. Emotions reflect how the receiver feels at the time of receipt of a communication message and will influence how he or she interprets it. Extreme emotions are most likely to hinder effective communication. Language—Age, education, and

cultural background are variables that influence the language a person uses and the definitions he gives to words. The problem is that members in an organization usually don't know how those with whom they interact have modified the language.

8. In your organization you are the individual who will be acting as the information contact to the visiting international team from one of your major buyers. The relationship between the buyer organization and your organization is quite important, so you must represent your company as well as possible. This includes your communication style. If the visiting international team is from Saudi Arabia, would your nonverbal and subtle situation cues be more or less important than when you are communicating with a U.S. colleague? (Hint: think in terms of cultural context). Now answer the same scenario, however, the visiting international team is from England. Would your nonverbal and subtle situation cues be more or less important in this situation?
    Answer - The nonverbal and subtle situation cues would be much more important and require more attention when communicating with the visitor from Saudi Arabia because the Saudi Arabian culture is a high-context culture which places more significance on what is not being said than what is being said. In contrast, the visitor from England reflects a low-context culture. The English visitor would rely essentially on words to convey meaning. Body language or formal titles are secondary to the spoken and written words when communicating with the English visitor. (See Exhibit 9-4.)

9. If you were given an overseas assignment with your company, what cross-cultural factors would you need to consider regarding your communication with others in that new culture?
    Answer - The greater the differences in backgrounds between sender and receiver, the greater the differences in meanings attached to particular words or behaviors. Four rules to reduce misperceptions, misinterpretations, and misevaluation follow:
    - Assume differences until similarity is proved.
    - Emphasize description rather than interpretation or evaluation. Description is less based on the observer's culture and background than on the interpretation or evaluation.
    - Practice empathy. Before sending a message, put yourself in the receiver's shoes.
    - Treat your interpretation as a working hypothesis. Once you've developed an explanation for a new situation, treat your interpretation as a hypothesis that needs further testing.

10. You are given the task of conducting communication training for new first line supervisors. What suggestions would you offer them for being more effective communicators?
    Answer - Use feedback. Many communication problems can be attributed directly to misunderstandings and inaccuracies. Simplify language. Structure messages in ways that will make them clear and understandable. Jargon can facilitate understanding when it is used with other group members who speak that language, but it can cause innumerable problems when used outside that group. Listen actively. See Exhibit 9-4 for the steps. Constrain emotions. If we're emotionally upset over an issue, we're likely to misconstrue incoming messages. The best approach is to defer further communication until composure is regained. Watch your nonverbal cues. Assume that actions speak louder than words. Use the grapevine—You can't eliminate the grapevine, therefore use it and make it work for you. The grapevine is a valuable source of feedback.

11. If most of us agree that telling lies is wrong, how do we justify continuing to do it?
    Answer – Most of us differentiate between "real lies" and "little white lies," the latter being an acceptable, even necessary, part of social interaction. You might also discuss the ethical implications of lying for the "common good." For example, is it OK to tell your manager that

a project is going well, when in fact, there are problems? You may lie because you feel it is easier to fix the problems yourself, rather than involve your manager. Is this ethically OK?

12. Outline behaviors associated with providing effective feedback.
   Answer - See Exhibit 9-3.

13. Identify the behaviors related to effective active listening.
   Answer - See Exhibit 9-4.

EXERCISES

A.   Are You Listening?
The purpose of this exercise is to give students the opportunity to both practice and experience active listening.
1. Conduct a mini-lecture on active listening emphasizing the key elements and then demonstrate it with a student in front of the class. Have the student talk about something he or she is comfortable with— family, roommate, food service at the school, and so on. The listener should exhibit the following active listening behavior:
   - Make eye contact.
   - Exhibit affirmative facial expressions.
   - Ask questions.
   - Paraphrase.
   - Avoid interrupting.
2. Using birth month, pair the students.
   - Ask everyone who was born in January and July to hold up their hands. Pair them. Everyone born in February and August, etc. It's simply a different way to make pairs.
3. Have students sit facing each other with their backs to the left and right walls of the room.
4. Tell the students with their backs to the left wall that they are the speakers. The students with their backs to the right wall are the listeners.
5. Tell the speakers to think for a minute about their topic. They can choose anything appropriate [caution them to not discuss anything too personal, illegal, and so on, even as a joke].
6. Tell the listeners they are to actively listen and facilitate the conversation through their active listening.
7. Tell them they have five minutes and have them begin.
8. Call time have them reverse roles. Have the new speakers talk for five minutes.
9. Call time.
10. Now ask them to prepare to answer two questions.
    - As the speaker, how did it feel to be listened to?
    - As a listener, what was the hardest thing about being an active listener?
11. Facilitate a discussion of their experiences. You will probably discover that:
    - Students are surprised at how good it felt to be listened to.
    - Students had a hard time not interjecting their own thoughts and ideas when listening.

B.   Nonverbal Communication

Ask for several student volunteers to participate in a role-playing exercise to demonstrate the value and important that nonverbal communication plays in the decoding of messages. Have different scenarios and roles written on notecards that can be easily given to each "actor." The following scenarios and roles are some examples, but could be easily adapted and expanded.

Scenario 1:
Supervisor—You are a supervisor for an accounting department with a mid-sized manufacturing company. You have an employee, Roger, who is a good employee overall. However, Roger has one bad habit that has continually gotten worse—he is late for work regularly. The lateness has gotten to the level that Roger will be late—fifteen minutes or more—at least three days every week. However, Roger has worked for you for four years, and his work is quite high quality and completed in a timely manner. In general Roger is a good employee, and you would like to keep him. However, but his lateness is beginning to affect office morale, as other employees are beginning and wonder (and talk about) why Roger is given the preferential treatment of being able to come in late and yet still leave on time. You have called Roger into your office to have a visit with him and indicate that he must to work on time, or you will be forced to let him go. Your overall nonverbal messages need to convey a professional attitude of concern, but authority; you need to convey the message that Roger's behavior is not acceptable, and must be changed. So how is he to change it?

Roger—You have worked for Acme for four years, and you are a good employee (at least you think you are, and your past evaluations have reinforced this opinion), but you have a problem getting to work on time. You are truly trying to be an exemplary employee, but your wife has recently left you (you did not tell anyone at work because you don't believe in bringing your home problems into the workplace), and you are now a single parent responsible for getting your 7 year old to school. You must be a work by 8 a.m., but the school where your son attends will not allow him to be in the building until 8 a.m. He cannot ride the bus because you live too close to the school, and he is not eligible to be a bus rider. You have a high school student who is available to pick your son up from school in the afternoon, but she cannot take him in the morning, and you have not found a babysitter who could. Now, your boss is angry because you are late, and has called you into her office. You certainly don't want to lose your job, so you must communicate very openly with her about your changed home status.

The nonverbal messages that you need to convey are a sense of embarrassment about having your wife leave you; a sense of remorse for being late, but you don't know any other way to get your son to school; a sense of urgency because you do not want to lose your job. Suggestions: be very polite to the boss, sit up straight, sit on the forward part of your chair with your hands folded neatly; be sure that your appearance is as "spit and polished" as possible.

Scenario 2:

Supervisor--Same as above.

Roger--You have worked for Acme for four years, and you are a good employee (at least you think you are, and your past evaluations have reinforced this opinion), but you have a problem getting to work on time. You are truly trying to be an exemplary employee; in fact you are good enough that another company has approached you with a potential job offer. This would be a nice step up for your career, and you were getting tired of Acme anyway—time to move on to bigger and better. And, anyway, what's the big deal about being fifteen minutes late? You give Acme enough output, so get off the issue. Pick about something really important. And, now your boss has called you into his office, and you know he's going to chew you out about being late.

The nonverbal messages that you need to convey are basic apathy for the job and the importance of being on time. Suggestions: you may even want to be a big "sloppy" by untucking a shirt or turning a hat around backwards; slouch down in the chair and look down—not at the supervisor while he is talking.

Other scenario suggestions:
- Introduce an international issue such as personal space—have one of the "actors" stand too close to the other.
- Use language that includes jargon that a person of another culture or age group would not understand correctly.
- Have the actors role play different facial expressions and/or intonations.

Analyzing Your Organization

Discuss with various members of your organization where they think the communication breakdowns occur, either in their department or organization-wide. Analyze their answers in the context of Exhibit 9-1 to try and diagnose the details on where the breakdowns occur.

Second, in your organization, examine how technology has changed the communication systems in your organization. Do you use email or instant messaging on a regular basis? If so, has this made things more efficient due to less meetings or phone calls? Keep a log of various communication breakdowns or misinterpretations that occur during the coming week. This may be a simple as an email that was mis-interpreted, or as complex as a meeting that totally got out of hand.

Examine the impact that these new forms of communication have on worker perceptions due to the lack of non-verbal communication. For example, have you ever been "mis-interpreted" in an email because the receiver could not see your facial expressions or hear your tone of voice? If so, discuss this with others in your organization and see if they have had the same experience. Be prepared to discuss this with the class.

CHAPTER 10 - LEADERSHIP AND CREATING TRUST

CHAPTER OBJECTIVES
After reading this chapter, students should be able to:
1. Summarize the conclusions of trait theories.
2. Identify the limitations of behavioral theories.
3. Describe Fiedler's contingency model.
4. Summarize the path-goal theory.
5. List the contingency variables in the leader-participation model.
6. Differentiate transformational from transactional leadership.
7. Describe the pros and cons of charismatic leadership.
8. Explain the role of emotional intelligence in leadership effectiveness.
9. Identify situations when leadership may not be relevant.
10. Summarize how leaders can build trust.

LECTURE OUTLINE
I.   WHAT IS LEADERSHIP?
   A. Defined (ppt 4)
      1. Leadership is the ability to influence a group toward the achievement of goals.
         a) This influence may be formal, such as that provided by the possession of managerial rank in an organization.
         b) Nonsanctioned leadership is the ability to influence that arises outside of the formal structure of the organization.
      2. The leadership literature is voluminous, and much of it is confusing and contradictory.

II. TRAIT THEORIES
   A. Introduction
      1. On the basis of the general connotations in today's media, one might list qualities such as intelligence, charisma, decisiveness, enthusiasm, strength, bravery, integrity, self-confidence, and so on.
      2. The search for characteristics (such as those listed) that would differentiate leaders from nonleaders occupied the early psychologists who studied leadership.
      3. Seven traits on which leaders differ from non-leaders: (ppt 5)
         a) Drive and ambition.
         b) The desire to lead.
         c) Honesty and integrity.
         d) Self-confidence.
         e) Intelligence.
         f) High-self monitors.
         g) Job relevant knowledge.
      4. Most of the traits identified with effective leadership can be subsumed under "The Big Five" personality framework (Chapter 3). (ppt 6-7)
         a) Extroversion is the most important trait of effective leaders.
         b) Conscientiousness and openness to experience also are related to effective leadership.
      5. Traits alone are not sufficient for explaining leadership. (ppt 8)
      6. Their primary failing is that they ignore situational factors.

III. BEHAVIORAL THEORIES

A. Introduction (ppt 9)
   1. The inability to find traits led researchers to look at the behaviors that specific leaders exhibited.
   2. Researchers hoped the behavioral approach would provide more definitive answers and have some practical implications quite different from those of the trait approach.
      a) If behavioral studies were to turn up critical behavioral determinants of leadership, we could train people to be leaders.
      b) The difference between trait and behavioral theories, in terms of application, lies in their underlying assumptions.
         (1) If trait theories were valid, then leaders were basically born.
         (2) If there were specific behaviors that identified leaders, then we could teach leadership.
   3. A number of studies looked at behavioral styles. The two most popular studies are the Ohio State group and the University of Michigan group.

B. Ohio State Studies (ppt 10)
   1. The most comprehensive and replicated of the behavioral theories resulted from research that began at Ohio State University in the late 1940s.
      a) Researchers sought to identify independent dimensions of leader behavior.
      b) They narrowed over a thousand dimensions into two categories that substantially accounted for most of the leadership behavior described by sub-ordinates.
         (1) initiating structure
         (2) consideration
   2. Initiating structure refers to the extent to which a leader is likely to define and structure his or her role and those of subordinates in the search for goal attainment.
      a) Organize work, work relationships, and goals
   3. Consideration is described as the extent to which a person is likely to have job relationships characterized by mutual trust, respect for subordinates' ideas, and regard for their feelings.
      a) Showing concern for his followers' comfort, well being, status, and satisfaction
   4. Research found that leaders high in initiating structure and consideration tended to achieve high subordinate performance and satisfaction more frequently than those who rated low on either initiating structure, consideration, or both.
   5. But the high high-style did not always result in positive consequences—it led to greater rates of grievances, absenteeism, and turnover and lower levels of job satisfaction for workers performing routine tasks.
   6. The Ohio State studies suggested that the high high-style generally resulted in positive outcomes, but enough exceptions were found to indicate that situational factors needed to be integrated into the theory.

C. University of Michigan Studies (ppt 11)
   1. University of Michigan's Survey Research Center studies were done at about the same time as those being done at Ohio State with similar research objectives.
   2. The Michigan group came up with two dimensions of leadership behavior:
      a) employee-oriented
      b) production-oriented

3. Leaders who were employee-oriented were described as emphasizing interpersonal relations; they took a personal interest in the needs of their subordinates and accepted individual differences among members.
4. The production-oriented leaders, in contrast, tended to emphasize the technical or task aspects of the job—their main concern was in accomplishing their group's tasks, and the group members were a means to that end.
5. Researchers strongly favored the leaders who were employee-oriented in their behavior.
   a) Employee-oriented leaders were associated with higher group productivity and higher job satisfaction.
   b) Production-oriented leaders tended to be associated with low group productivity and low worker satisfaction.

D. The Managerial Grid (ppt 12)
   1. Robert Blake and Jane Mouton developed a graphic portrayal of a two-dimensional view of leadership styles.
   2. They proposed a managerial grid based on the styles of "concern for people" and "concern for production," which essentially represents the Ohio State dimensions of consideration and initiating structure or the Michigan dimensions of employee-oriented and production-oriented.
   3. The Grid
      a) See Exhibit 10-1.
      b) Nine possible positions along each axis.
      c) Eighty-one different positions.
      d) Shows the factors that dominate a leader's thinking in regard to getting results.
   4. Conclusions
      a) Managers perform best under a 9,9 style.
      b) The grid offers a better framework for conceptualizing leadership style than for presenting any tangible new information.

E. Summary of Behavioral Theories (ppt 12)
   1. There was very little success in identifying consistent relationships between patterns of leadership behavior and group performance.
   2. What was missing was consideration of the situational factors that influence success or failure.

IV. CONTINGENCY THEORIES
   A. Introduction (ppt 14)
      1. It became increasingly clear that predicting leadership success was more complex than isolating a few traits or preferable behaviors.
      2. The failure to obtain consistent results led to a new focus on situational influences.
      3. Three contingency theories have received the bulk of attention: Fiedler, path-goal, and leader-participation.
      4. We also take a look at gender as a contingency variable.

   B. The Fiedler Model (ppt 15)
      1. Fred Fiedler developed the first comprehensive contingency model for leadership.

2. His model proposes that effective group performance depends on the proper match between the leader's style of interacting with his or her subordinates and the degree to which the situation gives control and influence to the leader.
    a) Least-preferred co-worker (LPC) questionnaire purports to measure whether a person is task oriented or relationship oriented.
    b) He isolated three situational criteria—leader-member relations, task structure, and position power—that he believed could be manipulated so as to create the proper match with the behavioral orientation of the leader. (ppt 16)
    c) Fiedler went significantly beyond trait and behavioral approaches by attempting to isolate situations, relating his personality measure to his situational classification, and then predicting leadership effectiveness as a function of the two.
3. Fiedler Model
    a) An individual's basic leadership style is a key factor in leadership success.
    b) To find the basic style Fiedler created the LPC questionnaire.
        (1) It has sixteen contrasting adjectives.
        (2) The questionnaire asks the respondent to think of all the co-workers he or she has ever had and to describe the one person he/she least enjoyed working with by rating that person on a scale of 1 to 8 for each of the sixteen sets of contrasting adjectives.
    c) Fiedler's premise was that what you say about others tells more about you than it tells about the people you're describing.
        (1) If the least-preferred co-worker was described in relatively positive terms (a high LPC score), then the respondent was primarily interested in good personal relations with co-workers.
        (2) In contrast, if the least-preferred co-worker is seen in relatively unfavorable terms (a low LPC score), the respondent is primarily interested in productivity and thus would be labeled task-oriented.
    d) Fiedler assumed that an individual's leadership style is fixed, either relationship-oriented or task-oriented.
    e) This assumption means that if a situation requires a task-oriented leader and the person in that leadership position is relationship-oriented, either the situation has to be modified or the leader replaced.
4. After an individual's basic leadership style has been assessed through the LPC, it is necessary to match the leader with the situation.
5. The three situational factors, or contingency dimensions, were identified by Fiedler:
    a) Leader-member relations are the degree of confidence, trust, and respect subordinates have in their leader.
    b) Task structure is the degree to which the job assignments of subordinates are structured or unstructured.
    c) Position power is the degree of influence a leader has over power variables such as hiring, firing, discipline, promotions, and salary increases.
6. The next step is to evaluate the situation in terms of the three contingency variables.
    a) Leader-member relations are either good or poor.
    b) Task structure either high or low.
    c) Position power either strong or weak.

7. Fiedler stated that the better the leader-member relations, the more highly structured the job, and the stronger the position power, the more control or influence the leader had.
8. By mixing the three contingency variables, there are potentially eight different situations or categories in which a leader could find himself or herself.
   a) With knowledge of an individual's LPC and an assessment of the three contingency variables, the Fiedler model proposes matching them up to achieve maximum leadership effectiveness.
9. Fiedler studied more than 1,200 groups, comparing relationship vs. task-oriented leadership styles in each of the eight situational categories.
   a) Task-oriented leaders tended to perform better than relationship-oriented leaders in situations that were very favorable to them and in situations that are very unfavorable.
   b) See Exhibit 10-2. (ppt 17)
10. In recent years Fiedler has condensed these eight situations down to three.
    a) Task-oriented leaders perform best in situations with high and low control
    b) Relationship-oriented leaders perform best in moderate control situations
11. Research finds conflicting results depending on the type of studies used.
    a) A generally positive conclusion is that there is considerable evidence to support the model.
    b) But additional variables are probably needed.
       (1) There are problems with the LPC and the practical use of the model that need to be addressed.
       (2) Contingency variables are complex and difficult for practitioners to assess.
12. Fiedler has clearly made an important contribution toward understanding leadership effectiveness.
    a) His model has been the object of much controversy and probably will continue to be.

C. Leader-Member Exchange (LMX) Theory (ppt 18)
   1. LMX argues that leaders establish a special relationship with a small group of their followers.
      a) The leader's in-group—people whom the leader trusts, who get a disproportionate amount of his or her time, and who are more likely to receive special privileges.
      b) Out-group—other followers who get less of the leader's time, less of the preferred rewards that the leader controls, and have leader-follower relations based on formal authority interactions.
   2. Early in the history of the leader-member relationship, the leader implicitly categorizes the follower as an "in" or an "out" and that the relationship is relatively stable over time.
      a) How the leaders choose who falls into each category is unclear.
      b) Evidence indicates that leaders tend to choose in-group members because they have attitude and personality characteristics that are similar to the leader's or that they have a higher level of competence than out-group members.
   3. Studies confirm several LMX theory predictions:
      a) Leaders do differentiate among followers.
      b) Disparities are far from random.

      c) Followers with in-group status have higher performance ratings, lower turnover intentions, greater satisfaction with their superiors, and higher overall satisfaction than those in the out-group.

D. Path-Goal Theory
  1. One of the most respected approaches to leadership.
  2. Developed by Robert House, a contingency model of leadership that extracts key elements from the Ohio State leadership research on initiating structure and consideration and the expectancy theory of motivation.
  3. The essence of the theory is that it's the leader's job to assist his or her followers in attaining their goals and to provide the direction or support needed to ensure that their goals are compatible with the overall objectives of the group or organization. (ppt 19)
    a) The term *path-goal* is derived from the belief that effective leaders clarify the path and reduce roadblocks and pitfalls for their followers.
    b) A leader's behavior is acceptable to subordinates to the degree that they view it as an immediate source of satisfaction or as a means of future satisfaction.
    c) A leader's behavior is motivational to the degree that it:
      (1) Makes subordinate need satisfaction contingent on effective performance.
      (2) Provides the coaching, guidance, support, and rewards that are necessary for effective performance.
  4. House-identified Four Leadership Behaviors. (ppt 20)
    a) The directive leader lets subordinates know what is expected of them, schedules work to be done, and gives specific guidance on how to accomplish tasks.
      (1) Parallels the Ohio State studies' initiating structure
    b) The supportive leader is friendly and shows concern for the needs of subordinates.
      (1) Essentially synonymous with the Ohio State studies' consideration
    c) The participative leader consults with subordinates and uses their suggestions before making a decision.
    d) The achievement-oriented leader sets challenging goals and expects subordinates to perform at their highest level.
    e) House assumes that leaders are flexible; path-goal theory implies that the same leader can display any or all of these behaviors depending on the situation.
  5. See Exhibit 10-3. (ppt 21)
    a) Path-goal theory proposes two classes of situational, or contingency variables.
    b) Those in the environment are outside the control of the leader (task structure, formal authority system, and work group).
    c) Factors in the second class are part of the personal characteristics of the subordinate (locus of control, experience, and perceived ability).
  6. The theory proposes that leader behaviors should complement these contingency variables.
  7. Hypotheses evolving out of path-goal theory.
    a) Directive leadership leads to greater satisfaction when tasks are ambiguous or stressful than when they are highly structured and well laid-out.

b) Supportive leadership results in high employee performance and satisfaction when subordinates are performing structured tasks (leadership complements environment).

c) Directive leadership is likely to be redundant among subordinates with high ability or with considerable experience.

d) The clearer and more bureaucratic the formal authority relationships, the more leaders should exhibit supportive behavior and de-emphasize directive behavior.

e) Directive leadership will lead to higher employee satisfaction when there is substantive conflict within a work group.

f) Subordinates with an internal locus of control (those who believe they control their own destiny) will be most satisfied with a participative style.

g) Subordinates with an external locus of control will be most satisfied with a directive style.

h) Achievement-oriented leadership will increase subordinates' expectations that effort will lead to high performance when tasks are ambiguously structured.

8. The evidence supports the logic underlying the theory.

a) Employee performance and satisfaction are likely to be positively influenced when the leader compensates for things lacking in either the employee or the work setting.

b) However, when the leader spends time explaining what is already clear or when the employee has the ability to handle them without help, the leader is seen as redundant or even insulting.

E. Leader-Participation Model (ppt 22)

1. In 1973 Victor Vroom and Phillip Yetton developed a leader-participation model.

2. These researchers argued that leader behavior must adjust to reflect the task structure.

3. Vroom and Yetton's model was normative—it provided a sequential set of rules that should be followed in determining the form and amount of participation in decision making as determined by different types of situations.

4. The model was a decision tree incorporating seven contingencies (whose relevance could be identified by making "yes" or "no" choices) and five alternative leadership styles.

5. Vroom and Jago revised this model.

a) The new model retains the same five alternative leadership styles but expands the contingency variables to twelve.

b) See Exhibit 10-4.

6. Tests of both models have been encouraging.

7. Unfortunately, the model is far too complex for the typical manager.

a) Vroom and Jago have developed a computer program to guide managers through all the decision branches in the revised model.

V. CHARISMATIC LEADERSHIP

A. Transactional Leaders (ppt 23)

1. These people guide or motivate their followers in the direction of established goals by clarifying role and task requirements.

2. There is another type of leader who inspires followers to transcend their own self-interests for the good of the organization and who is capable of having a profound and extraordinary effect on his or her followers.

a) These are charismatic or transformational leaders.
b) Jesse Jackson, Winston Churchill, General Douglas MacArthur, and Franklin D. Roosevelt are of this latter type.
c) By the force of their personal abilities, they transform their followers by raising the sense of the importance and value of their tasks.

B. What is Charismatic Leadership? (ppt 24)
1. Followers make attributions of extraordinary leadership abilities when they observe certain behaviors.
2. Personal characteristics of charismatic leaders include having a vision, being willing to take risks, being sensitive to both environmental constraints and follower needs, and exhibiting behaviors that are out of the ordinary. (ppt 25)
3. How charismatic leaders influence followers (ppt 26)
a) A four-step process
(1) Articulation of an appealing vision.
(2) Communication of high performance expectations, expressing confidence that the expectations will be achieved.
(3) Conveying a new set of values.
(4) Making self-sacrifices and engaging in unconventional behaviors.
4. The case for and against charismatic leadership
a) There is a high correlation between charisma and high performance and satisfaction among followers. (ppt 27)
b) The "dark side" of charisma is that its effects may be situational.
(1) It is generally needed in tasks that have an ideological component (war, politics, etc.)
(2) It is hard to use charisma at lower levels of the organization because it is harder to define the vision and align this vision with the larger goals of the organization.
(3) Sometimes charismatic leaders don't act in the best interest of their organization.

VI. CONTEMPORARY ISSUES IN LEADERSHIP (ppt 28)
A. Emotional Intelligence and Leadership Effectiveness (ppt 29)
1. Detailed in Chapter 3, but EI has shown to be positively related to job performance at all levels.
B. Ethical Leadership
1. Interest has grown due to the attention paid to high visibility leaders that have ethical shortcoming.
2. Leadership is not value-free.
C. Cross-Cultural Leadership
1. Leaders must adapt their style to different national cultures.

VII. IS LEADERSHIP ALWAYS RELEVANT?
A. Leadership May Not Always Be Important (ppt 30-31)
1. Numerous studies demonstrate that, in many situations, whatever behaviors leaders exhibit are irrelevant.
a) Characteristics of subordinates such as their experience, training, professional orientation, or need for independence can neutralize the effect of leadership.
b) People in jobs that are inherently unambiguous and routine or that are intrinsically satisfying may have little need for a leader.

  c) Organizational characteristics such as explicit formalized goals, rigid rules and procedures, or cohesive work groups can act in the place of formal leadership.

 2. Supporters of the leadership concept have tended to place an undue burden on this variable for explaining and predicting behavior.

  a) It's too simplistic to consider subordinates as being guided to goal accomplishment solely on the basis of the behavior of their leader.

  b) It's important, therefore, to recognize explicitly that leadership is merely another independent variable in explaining organizational behavior.

 3. Even charismatic leadership may not be a panacea.

  a) Charismatic leaders may be ideal for pulling a group or organization through a crisis, but they often perform poorly after the crisis subsides and ordinary conditions return.

  b) Charismatic managers are often self-possessed, autocratic, and given to thinking that their opinions have a greater degree of certainty than they merit.

   (1) These behaviors then tend to drive good people away and can lead their organizations down dangerous paths.

VIII. TRUST AND LEADERSHIP

 A. What Is Trust? (ppt 32)

  1. Trust is a positive expectation that another will not through words, actions, or decisions act opportunistically.

  2. The two most important elements of our definition are familiarity and risks.

   a) The phrase *positive expectation* in our definition assumes knowledge and familiarity about the other party.

    (1) Trust is a history-dependent process based on relevant but limited samples of experience.

    (2) It takes time to form, building incrementally and accumulating.

   b) The term opportunistic refers to the inherent risk and vulnerability in any trusting relationship.

    (1) Trust involves making oneself vulnerable.

    (2) But trust is not taking risk per se; rather it is a willingness to take risk.

  3. Key dimensions that underlie the concept of trust. See Exhibit 10-5. (ppt 33)

   a) Integrity refers to honesty and truthfulness. This one seems to be most critical.

   b) Competence encompasses an individual's technical and interpersonal knowledge and skills.

    (1) Does the person know what he or she is talking about?

   c) Consistency relates to an individual's reliability, predictability, and good judgment in handling situations.

   d) Loyalty is the willingness to protect and save face for another person.

    (1) Trust requires that you can depend on someone not to act opportunistically.

   e) The final dimension of trust is openness. Can you rely on the person to give you the full truth?

 B. Trust and Leadership

  1. Trust appears to be a primary attribute associated with leadership.

   a) When followers trust a leader, they are willing to be vulnerable to the leader's actions.

2. Honesty, for instance, consistently ranks at the top of most people's list of characteristics they admire in their leaders.

C. Three Types of Trust (ppt 34)
1. There are three types of trust in organizational relationships: deterrence-based, knowledge-based, and identification-based.
2. The following analysis assumes two parties are entering into a new relationship. They have no previous experiences to overcome; they're uncertain about each other; they believe they're vulnerable if they disclose too much too quickly; and they're uncertain about the future longevity of the relationship.
3. Deterrence-based trust.
   a) The most fragile relationships.
   b) One violation or inconsistency can destroy the relationship.
   c) This form of trust is based on fear of reprisal if the trust is violated.
   d) Deterrence-based trust will work only to the degree that punishment is possible, consequences are clear, and the punishment is actually imposed if the trust is violated.
   e) To be sustained, the potential loss of future interaction with the other party must outweigh the profit potential that comes from violating expectations.
   f) Most new relationships begin on a base of deterrence.
4. Knowledge-Based Trust
   a) Most organizational relationships are rooted in knowledge-based trust.
   b) Trust is based on the behavioral predictability that comes from a history of interaction.
   c) It exists when you have adequate information about someone to understand him or her well enough to be able to accurately predict his or her likely behavior.
   d) It relies on information rather than deterrence—of the other party and predictability of his or her behavior replaces the contracts, penalties, and legal arrangements more typical of deterrence-based trust.
   e) This knowledge develops over time.
   f) Trust is not necessarily broken by inconsistent behavior.
      (1) If you believe you can adequately explain or understand another's apparent violation, you can accept it, forgive the person, and move on in the relationship.
   g) Most manager-employee relationships are knowledge-based.
5. Identification-Based Trust
   a) The highest level of trust is achieved when there is an emotional connection between the parties.
   b) It allows one party to act as an agent for the other and substitute for that person in interpersonal transactions.
   c) Controls are minimal at this level.
   d) The best example of identification-based trust is a long-term, happily married couple.
   e) Identification-based trust is seen occasionally in organizations among people who have worked together for long periods of time and have a depth of experience that allows them to know each other inside and out.
   f) This is also the type of trust that managers ideally seek in teams.

D. How Do You Build Trust? (ppt 35)

1. Practice openness. Mistrust comes as much from what people don't know as from what they do know. Openness leads to confidence and trust.
2. Be fair. Before making decisions or taking actions, consider how others will perceive them in terms of objectivity and fairness.
3. Speak your feelings. Managers who convey only hard facts come across as cold and distant.
4. Tell the truth. If integrity is critical to trust, you must be perceived as someone who tells the truth.
5. Show consistency. People want predictability. Mistrust comes from not knowing what to expect.
6. Fulfill your promises. Trust requires that people believe that you are dependable.
7. Maintain confidences. You trust people who are discreet and upon whom you can rely. So if people make themselves vulnerable by telling you something in confidence, they need to feel assured that you will not discuss it with others or betray that confidence.
8. Demonstrate competence. Develop the admiration and respect of others by demonstrating technical and professional ability.

IX. IMPLICATIONS FOR MANAGERS

1. Leadership plays a central role in understanding group behavior, so a more accurate predictive capability should be valuable in improving group performance.
2. Some traits have shown to be modest predictors of leadership effectiveness, with the Big Five framework having the most encouraging results.
3. The behavioral approach narrowed leadership into task and people oriented styles, but no one style fit all situations.
4. The contingency models helped us define these situations. Relevant situational variables include the task structure of the job, the level of stress, the level of group support, the leader's intelligence and experience, and certain follower characteristics.
5. During times of crisis or high uncertainty, charismatic leadership will positively affect performance.
6. Finally, we discussed the role that trust plays in leadership. Effective managers today must develop trusting relationships with those they seek to lead. Why? Because as organizations have become less stable and predictable, strong bonds of trust are replacing bureaucratic rules in defining expectations and relationships.

SUMMARY (ppt 36-37)

1. Leadership is the ability to influence a group toward the achievement of goals. This influence may be formal, such as that provided by the possession of managerial rank in an organization.
2. The search for characteristics (such as those listed) that would differentiate leaders from nonleaders occupied the early psychologists who studied leadership.
3. The Big Five framework is emerging as a valid model for studying traits and leadership effectiveness.
4. The early lack of success with the trait approach led researchers to look at the behaviors that specific leaders exhibited. The two most popular studies are the Ohio State group and the University of Michigan group. The Ohio State University studies narrowed over a thousand dimensions into two categories: initiating structure and consideration. The University of Michigan's Survey Research Center studies came up with two dimensions of leadership behavior: employee-oriented and production-oriented.

5. Robert Blake and Jane Mouton proposed a managerial grid based on the styles of "concern for people" and "concern for production," which essentially represent the Ohio State dimensions of consideration and initiating structure or the Michigan dimensions of employee-oriented and production-oriented.

6. There was very little success in identifying consistent relationships between patterns of leadership behavior and group performance. What was missing was consideration of the situational factors that influence success or failure.

7. The failure to obtain consistent results led to a new focus on situational influences. Three contingency theories have received the bulk of attention: Fiedler, path-goal, and leader-participation. Fred Fiedler's model proposes that effective group performance depends on the proper match between the leader's style of interacting with his or her subordinates and the degree to which the situation gives control and influence to the leader.

8. The leader-member exchange (LMX) theory argues that leaders establish a special relationship with a small group of their followers (in-group). Studies confirm several LMX theory predictions: Leaders do differentiate among followers; these disparities are far from random; and followers with in-group status have higher performance ratings, lower turnover intentions, greater satisfaction with their superiors, and higher overall satisfaction than those in the out-group.

9. Path-goal theory is one of the most respected approaches to leadership. Developed by Robert House, the essence of the theory is that it's the leader's job to assist his or her followers in attaining their goals and to provide the direction or support needed to ensure that their goals are compatible with the overall objectives of the group or organization.

10. Another contingency model is the leader-participation model developed in 1973 by Victor Vroom and Phillip Yetton. These researchers argued that leader behavior must adjust to reflect the task structure. Unfortunately, the model is far too complex for the typical manager. Vroom and Jago have developed a computer program to guide managers through all the decision branches in the revised model.

11. The transactional leaders guide or motivate their followers in the direction of established goals by clarifying role and task requirements. Transformational leaders inspire followers to transcend their own self-interests for the good of the organization and who is capable of having a profound and extraordinary effect on his or her followers.

12. Charismatic leadership can be effective, but it also can harm the organization if it is used in the wrong situation.

13. While a great deal is written about leadership, it may not always be important. Numerous studies demonstrate that, in many situations, whatever behaviors leaders exhibit are irrelevant.

14. Trust is critical to a manager's effectiveness. It is a positive expectation that another will not—through words, actions, or decisions—act opportunistically. The text outlines the key elements of trust in Exhibit 10-5. Trust appears to be a primary attribute associated with leadership. Trust and trust-worthiness modulate the leader's access to knowledge and cooperation. There are three types of trust in organizational relationships: deterrence-based, knowledge-based, and identification-based.

DISCUSSION QUESTIONS

1. What were the results of researchers' efforts to identify key leadership traits?
    Answer - On the basis of the general connotations in today's media, one might list qualities such as intelligence, charisma, decisiveness, enthusiasm, strength, bravery, integrity, self-confidence, and so on. The search for characteristics (such as those listed) that would differentiate leaders from nonleaders occupied the early psychologists who studied leadership. Research identified traits consistently associated with leadership have been more successful. Six traits on which leaders differ from nonleaders: ambition and energy, the desire

to lead, honesty and integrity, self-confidence, intelligence, high self-monitoring, and job relevant knowledge. Traits alone are not sufficient for explaining leadership. Their primary failing is that they ignore situational factors.

2. How did the studies at Ohio State and University of Michigan contribute to a behavioral understanding of leadership?
   Answer - The inability to find traits led researchers to look at the behaviors that specific leaders exhibited. The difference between trait and behavioral theories, in terms of application, lies in their underlying assumptions. If trait theories were valid, then leaders were basically born. If there were specific behaviors that identified leaders, then we could teach leadership.

   The most comprehensive and replicated of the behavioral theories resulted from research that began at Ohio State University in the late 1940s. Researchers sought to identify independent dimensions of leader behavior. 1) Initiating structure refers to the extent to which a leader is likely to define and structure his or her role and those of subordinates in the search for goal attainment. 2) Consideration is described as the extent to which a person is likely to have job relationships characterized by mutual trust, respect for subordinates' ideas, and regard for their feelings. Research found that leaders high in initiating structure and consideration tended to achieve high subordinate performance and satisfaction more frequently than those who rated low either on initiating structure, consideration, or both.

   University of Michigan's Survey Research Center studies were done at about the same time as those being done at Ohio State with similar research objectives. The Michigan group came up with two dimensions of leadership behavior. 1) Leaders who were employee-oriented were described as emphasizing interpersonal relations; they took a personal interest in the needs of their subordinates and accepted individual differences among members. 2) The production-oriented leaders, in contrast, tended to emphasize the technical or task aspects of the job—their main concern was in accomplishing their group's tasks, and the group members were a means to that end. Researchers strongly favored the leaders who were employee-oriented in their behavior. Employee-oriented leaders were associated with higher group productivity and higher job satisfaction. Production-oriented leaders tended to be associated with low group productivity and low worker satisfaction.

3. Describe Fiedler's contingency model.
   Answer - Fred Fiedler developed the first comprehensive contingency model for leadership. His model proposes that effective group performance depends on the proper match between the leader's style of interacting with his or her subordinates and the degree to which the situation gives control and influence to the leader. Least-preferred co-worker (LPC) questionnaire purports to measure whether a person is task oriented or relationship oriented. He isolated three situational criteria—leader-member relations, task structure, and position power—that he believed could be manipulated so as to create the proper match with the behavioral orientation of the leader. Fiedler went significantly beyond trait and behavioral approaches by attempting to isolate situations, relating his personality measure to his situational classification, and then predicting leadership effectiveness as a function of the two. Fiedler assumed that an individual's leadership style is fixed, either relationship oriented or task oriented. This assumption means that if a situation requires a task-oriented leader and the person in that leadership position is relationship oriented, either the situation has to be modified or the leader replaced. Fiedler studied more than 1,200 groups, comparing relationship- vs. task-oriented leadership styles in each of the eight situational categories.

4. According to the Leader-Member Exchange (LMX) theory, leaders categorize followers into one of two groups. What are the names and characteristics of these two groups?
   Answer – The in-group is a small group of followers with whom the leader establishes a special relationship. These individuals are those that the leader trusts, who get a disproportionate amount of his or her time, and who are more likely to receive special privileges. Other followers fall into the out-group. They get less of the leader's time, fewer of the preferred rewards that the leader controls, and have leader-follower relations based on formal authority interactions.

5. Why is the path-goal theory an improvement over other contingency-based theories of leadership?
   Answer - One of the most respected approaches to leadership, developed by Robert House. The contingency model of leadership extracts key elements from the Ohio State leadership research on initiating structure and consideration and the expectancy theory of motivation. The essence of the theory is that it's the leader's job to assist his or her followers in attaining their goals and to provide the direction or support needed to ensure that their goals are compatible with the overall objectives of the group or organization. The term *path-goal* is derived from the belief that effective leaders clarify the path and reduce roadblocks and pitfalls for their followers. A leader's behavior is acceptable to subordinates to the degree that they view it as an immediate source of satisfaction or as a means of future satisfaction. The evidence supports the logic underlying the theory. Employee performance and satisfaction are likely to be positively influenced when the leader compensates for things lacking in either the employee or the work setting. Path-goal theory's framework has been tested and appears to have moderate to high empirical support.

6. How does the leader-participation model contingency theory of leadership differ from other theories? Why don't managers use it more?
   Answer - In 1973 Victor Vroom and Phillip Yetton developed a leader-participation model. These researchers argued that leader behavior must adjust to reflect the task structure. Vroom and Yetton's model was normative—it provided a sequential set of rules that should be followed in determining the form and amount of participation in decision making as determined by different types of situations. The model was a decision tree incorporating seven contingencies (whose relevance could be identified by making "yes" or "no" choices) and five alternative leadership styles. Vroom and Jago revised this model. The new model retains the same five alternative leadership styles but expands the contingency variables to twelve. The model is far too complex for the typical manager. Vroom and Jago have developed a computer program to guide managers through all the decision branches in the revised model.

7. Differentiate transformational from transactional leadership.
   Answer - Transactional leaders guide or motivate their followers in the direction of established goals by clarifying role and task requirements. Transformational leaders, by the force of their personal abilities, transform their followers by raising the sense of the importance and value of their tasks. They inspire followers to transcend their own self-interests for the good of the organization and are capable of having a profound and extraordinary effect on their followers. There are six characteristics that distinguish transformation/charismatic leaders.
   - self-confidence—they have complete confidence in their judgment and ability.
   - a vision—an idealized goal that proposes a better future than the status quo.
   - extraordinary behavior—engage in behavior that is perceived as novel, unconventional, and counter to norms.

- strong convictions in that vision—perceived as willing to take on high personal risk, incur high costs, and engage in self-sacrifice to achieve their vision.
- image as a change agent—perceived as agents of radical change rather than as caretakers of the status quo.
- charismatic leaders impact their followers' attitudes and behavior.

8. How do charismatic leaders influence their followers?
Answer –The evidence suggests a four-step process that begins when the leader articulates a vision. The leader then communicates high performance expectations and expresses confidence that the followers can attaint them. Next, the leader conveys a new set of values, and sets an example for the followers. Finally the leader engages in both self-sacrifice and unconventional behavior to demonstrate courage and convictions about the vision.

9. Under what conditions could charismatic leadership harm the organization?
Answer- It is most appropriate when the follower's task has an ideological component, or when the environment involves a high degree of stress. This is not always the case in a normally functioning organization. It is also inappropriate in lower levels of the organization if it is harder to align the vision of a specific department with that of the entire organization.

10. In what circumstances is leadership irrelevant?
Answer - Numerous studies demonstrate that, in many situations, whatever behaviors leaders exhibit are irrelevant. 1) Characteristics of subordinates such as their experience, training, professional orientation, or need for independence can neutralize the effect of leadership. 2) Characteristics of jobs, people in jobs that are inherently unambiguous and routine or that are intrinsically satisfying may have little need for a leader. 3) Organizational characteristics such as explicit formalized goals, rigid rules and procedures, or cohesive work groups can act in the place of formal leadership.

11. Why has ethics in leadership emerged as a contemporary management topic?
Answer- Ethics in general is gaining renewed interest in management studies, in part due to the "ethical shortcomings" of many leaders in the news. We are recognizing that leadership is not value free, meaning we need to look at the means used by the leader to achieve the goals, and also look at the moral content of those goals.

12. You are new on the job. You know the importance of trust for effective management. What can you do to build trust with your new employees?
Answer - Trust is a positive expectation that another will not—through words, actions, or decisions—act opportunistically. The two most important elements of our definition are familiarity and risk. Suggestions for building trust.
- Practice openness. Mistrust comes as much from what people don't know as from what they do know. Openness leads to confidence and trust.
- Be fair. Before making decisions or taking actions, consider how others will perceive them in terms of objectivity and fairness.
- Speak your feelings. Managers who convey only hard facts come across as cold and distant.
- Tell the truth. If integrity is critical to trust, you must be perceived as someone who tells the truth.
- Show consistency. People want predictability. Mistrust comes from not knowing what to expect.
- Fulfill your promises. Trust requires that people believe that you are dependable.

- Maintain confidences. You trust people who are discreet and upon whom you can rely. So if people make themselves vulnerable by telling you something in confidence, they need to feel assured that you will not discuss it with others or betray that confidence.
- Demonstrate competence. Develop the admiration and respect of others by demonstrating technical and professional ability.

13. Identify and define the three types of trust in organizational relationships.
    Answer – Deterrence-based trust is the most fragile types of trust. One violation or inconsistency can destroy the relationship. This form of trust is based on fear of reprisal if the trust is violated. Knowledge-based trust is what most organizational relationships are rooted in. This trust is based on the behavioral predictability that comes from a history of interaction. Knowledge-based trust relies on information rather than deterrence. Identification-based trust is the highest level of trust and is achieved when there is an emotional connection between the parties.

EXERCISES

A.   What Characterizes a Leader?

This exercise will show students different leadership styles in a fun way. It requires some significant preparation on your part.

1. Rent one or more of the following movies.
    - *Karate Kid* - Good for contingency leadership.
    - *Lawrence of Arabia* - Good for charismatic/visionary leadership.
    - *Hoosiers* - Good for transactional leadership.
2. Preview the films on the VCR you will use in class and note where the following sections are. (By previewing you will reduce viewing time to fifteen to twenty minutes out of each film.)
    - *Karate Kid* - When Miagi has Daniel washing, sanding, and painting and then shows that he has learned karate—high task low relationship. When they are on the inlet fishing and Daniel is standing on the boat practicing—moderate task, moderate relationship. And the tournament at the end of the film—high relationship, low task direction.
    - *Lawrence of Arabia* - The beginning of the film when Lawrence gets his assignment and declares it is fun, when he is first riding in the desert and won't drink his water except when his guide does, and then when he is talking the tribal leader into riding across the desert to attack the port city and then later when he talks the second tribal leader into joining them. The pattern shows the development, execution, and creation commitment to a vision.
    - *Hoosiers* - Good for transactional leadership. When Gene Hackman is first coaching the players and tells them to leave if they don't want to work. Choose one or two scenes where he is dictating to them how to play, my way or the highway. Be sure to close with the tournament game where the players finally have enough confidence to tell him they want to do something different and he lets them. This last scene is important to show that transactional leadership does work; you just may not like the method.
3. You can use one or all three films, depending on time.
4. Lead a discussion after watching the clips from each film.
5. As an alternative, watch the entire movie(s), stopping the video periodically and discussing the elements of leadership displayed to that point.

B.   Name that Leader

Begin the class period, before even beginning the discussion of leadership, and have students name/identify who they think are or have been leaders. This list can include past, present, and future; male and female; living or deceased leaders of the following categories: business leaders, governmental leaders—domestic and international—ethnic leaders, and religious leaders from any/all denominations.
Try to encourage a wide variety of leaders, even some leaders that would not be considered socially acceptable, such as Hitler, Saddam Hussein, Osama bin Laden, and cult leaders, because they will lead into the discussion. While they were not exactly nice people, they were able to influence the behavior of others to act in a certain manner.

After the class has generated a relatively lengthy list (twenty or more), have the students identify why all of the people on this list are or were leaders, and what characteristics do they all have in common. Obviously, the students will have an impossible task identify a list of traits that fit all of the members of the leaders list. This leads into a nice discussion on trait theory.

C.   Who Said That?

Make an overhead transparency or a PowerPoint slide of the following list of sayings attributed to famous leaders. Have the students identify the speaker if they can.

WHO SAID THAT?
NAME THAT LEADER

1.   "I have a dream."

2.   "The only thing we have to fear is fear itself."

3.   "I have not yet begun to fight."

4.   "The buck stops here."

5.   "Read my lips."

6.   "And you, madam, are ugly. But I shall be sober in the morning."

7.   "No one can make you feel inferior without your consent."

8.   "Ask not what your country can do for you, but ask what you can do for your country."

9.   "Give me liberty or give me death."

10.   "In matters of style, swim with the current; in matters of principle, stand like a rock."

11.   "If you judge people, you have no time to love them."

12.   "Walk softly and carry a big stick."

WHO SAID THAT?
NAME THAT LEADER
Answer Key

1. Martin Luther King, Jr.

2. Franklin D. Roosevelt

3. John Paul Jones

4. Harry S. Truman

5. George H.W. Bush

6. Winston Churchill

7. Eleanor Roosevelt

8. John F. Kennedy

9. Patrick Henry

10. Thomas Jefferson

11. Mother Teresa

12. Theodore Roosevelt

D.   Ethical Leadership

Have the class research news stories of ethical breakdowns by current leaders.
Discuss them in the context of why the breakdowns occurred. Was it due to a wrong
style, such as using charisma when it did not work? Discuss the concept of traits and
behaviors in the context of what makes a great leader. For example, can one behave
unethically in their personal lives, but still be a great leader?

Analyzing Your Organization

This exercise will have you analyze leadership in your organization using the theories
discussed in this chapter as a framework. Pick one or more theories that you think
applies most to your organization, and actually write a case study on it. For example,
if you think that the Fiedler model is what is driving the leadership in your
organization, write a paper discussing why this is the case. For example, you may
have a strong task oriented leader who is very effective because the situational
variables are either very high or very low.

You can also do this for poorly led organizations also. Do you have examples of
charismatic leadership being used when it should not be? Be ready to present your
findings to the class. Were there a wide variety of theories chosen for this exercise?
Why or why not?

CHAPTER 11 - POWER AND POLITICS

CHAPTER OBJECTIVES
After reading this chapter, students should be able to:
1. Define power.
2. Describe the seven bases of power.
3. Explain what creates dependency in power relationships.
4. Describe how power is central to understanding sexual harassment.
5. Define political behavior.
6. Describe the importance of a political perspective.
7. Explain the factors contributing to political behavior in organizations.
8. Identify seven techniques for managing the impression you make on others.

LECTURE OUTLINE
I. A DEFINITION OF POWER
    A. Power (ppt 4)
        1. Power refers to the capacity that A has to influence the behavior of B so that B does something he or she would not otherwise do.
        2. This definition implies: (ppt 5)
            a) A potential that need not be actualized to be effective.
            b) A dependence relationship.
            c) That B has some discretion over his or her own behavior.
        3. Power may exist but not be used. It is, therefore, a capacity or potential.
        4. Probably the most important aspect of power is that it is a function of dependence. The greater B's dependence on A, the greater A's power is in the relationship.
            a) Dependence is based on alternatives that B perceives and the importance that B places on the alternatives that A controls.
        5. For A to get B to do something he or she otherwise would not do means B must have the discretion to make choices.

II. COMPARING AND CONTRASTING LEADERSHIP AND POWER
    A. A comparison: (ppt 6)
        1. The two concepts of power and leadership are closely intertwined. Leaders use power to attain group goals, and power is a means for facilitating their achievement.
        2. Differences
            a) Power does not require goal compatibility, merely dependence.
            b) Leadership requires some congruence between the goals of the leader and those being led.
            c) Leadership research, for the most part, emphasizes style.
            d) The research on power has tended to encompass a broader area and focus on tactics for gaining compliance.

III. BASES OF POWER—See Exhibit 11-1
    A. There are two general categories of power, formal and personal. The categories of formal power are: (ppt 7)
        1. Coercive Power (ppt 8)
            a) The coercive power base is defined by French and Raven as being dependent on fear.

(1) One reacts to this power out of fear of the negative results that might occur if one fails to comply.

   b) It rests on the application, or the threat of application, of physical sanctions such as the infliction of pain, the generation of frustration through restriction of movement, or the controlling by force of basic physiological or safety needs.

   c) "Of all the bases of power available, the power to hurt others is possibly most often used, most often condemned, and most difficult to control..."

   d) At the organizational level, A has coercive power over B if A can dismiss, suspend, or demote B, assuming that B values his or her job.

2. Reward Power (ppt 9)

   a) The opposite of coercive power is reward power.

   b) People comply with the wishes or directives of another because doing so produces positive benefits.

   c) Rewards can be anything that another person values.

   d) Coercive and reward power are actually counterparts.

     (1) If you can remove something of positive value from another or inflict something of negative value upon him or her, you have coercive power over that person.

   e) If you can give someone something of positive value or remove something of negative value, you have reward power over that person.

   f) You don't need to be a manager to be able to exert influence through rewards.

3. Legitimate Power (ppt 9)

   a) In formal groups and organizations probably the most frequent access to one or more of the power bases is one's structural position.

   b) It represents the power a person receives as a result of his or her position in the formal hierarchy of an organization.

   c) Positions of authority include coercive and reward powers.

   d) Legitimate power is broader than the power to coerce and reward.

     (1) It includes acceptance by members of an organization of the authority of a position.

4. Information Power (ppt 10)

   a) People who have data or knowledge that others need can make others dependent on them.

B. The categories of personal power are: (ppt 11)

1. Expert Power (ppt 12)

   a) Expert power is influence wielded as a result of expertise, special skill, or knowledge.

   b) Expertise has become one of the most powerful sources of influence as the world has become more technologically oriented.

2. Referent Power (ppt 12)

   a) Its base is identification with a person who has desirable resources or personal traits. If I admire and identify with you, you can exercise power over me because I want to please you.

   b) Referent power develops out of admiration of another and a desire to be like that person.

   c) Referent power explains why celebrities are paid millions of dollars to endorse products in commercials.

3. Charismatic Power (ppt 13)

a) Extension of referent power.

b) Many members of the organization may have these qualities as detailed in the last chapter, and can influence others even though they are not in leadership positions.

IV. DEPENDENCY: THE KEY TO POWER

A. The General Dependency Postulate (ppt 14)

1. The greater B's dependency on A, the greater power A has over B.

   a) When you possess anything that others require but that you alone control, you make them dependent on you and, therefore, you gain power over them.

   b) Dependency, then, is inversely proportional to the alternative sources of supply.

2. If you can create a monopoly by controlling information, prestige, or anything that others crave, they become dependent on you.

3. Conversely, the more you can expand your options, the less power you place in the hands of others.

   a) This principle explains, for example, why many of us aspire to financial independence. Financial independence reduces the power others can have over us.

B. What Creates Dependency? (ppt 15)

1. Dependency is increased when the resource you control is important and scarce.

2. Importance

   a) To create dependency, therefore, you must control things that are perceived as important.

   b) The ability to reduce uncertainty increases a group's power and enhances its ability to create dependency.

3. Scarcity

   a) A resource needs to be perceived as scarce to create dependency.

   b) The need to obtain a scarce resource—such as, important knowledge—makes the high-ranking member dependent on the low-ranking member.

   c) Individuals in occupations in which the supply of personnel is low relative to demand can negotiate compensation and benefit packages far more attractive than can those in occupations for which there is an abundance of candidates.

4. Nonsubstitutability

   a) The more that a resource has no viable substitutes, the more power that control over that resource provides.

V. POWER IN GROUPS: COALITIONS

A. Introduction (ppt 16)

1. The natural way to gain influence is to become a powerholder.

   a) In many instances doing so may be difficult, risky, costly, or impossible.

2. In such cases efforts will be made to form a coalition of two or more "outs" who, by joining together, can each better themselves at the expense of those outside the coalition.

3. Predictions about the formation of coalitions.

   a) Coalitions in organizations often seek to maximize their size.

      (1) In organizations, the implementation of and commitment to the decision are at least as important as the decision itself.

          (2) It's necessary, therefore, for coalitions in organizations to seek a broad constituency to support the coalition's objectives, so the coalition must be expanded to encompass as many interests as possible.

      b) More coalitions will likely be created if there is a great deal of task and resource interdependence.

          (1) In contrast, there will be less interdependence among subunits and less coalition formation activity when subunits are largely self-contained or resources are abundant.

      c) Coalition formation will be influenced by the actual tasks that workers perform.

          (1) The more routine the task of a group or the work of individual jobs, the greater the likelihood that coalitions will form.

VI. SEXUAL HARASSMENT: UNEQUAL POWER IN THE WORKPLACE

A. Sexual Harassment (ppt 17)

1. Legally, sexual harassment is defined as any unwanted activity of a sexual nature that affects an individual's employment.

2. But there is a great deal of disagreement about what specifically constitutes sexual harassment.

3. Organizations have made considerable progress in the last few years toward limiting overt forms of sexual harassment.

4. The problems today are likely to surface around the more subtle forms of sexual harassment.

5. Most studies confirm that the concept of power is central to understanding sexual harassment.

    a) This seems to be true whether the harassment comes from a supervisor, a co-worker, or even a subordinate.

6. The supervisor-employee dyad best characterizes an unequal power relationship.

    a) Because of power inequities sexual harassment by one's boss creates great difficulty for the person being harassed.

7. Co-workers don't have legitimate power, but they can have influence and use it to sexually harass peers.

    a) In fact, although co-workers appear to engage in somewhat less severe forms of harassment than do supervisors, co-workers are the most frequent perpetrators of sexual harassment in organizations.

8. Harassment by subordinates doesn't get nearly the attention that harassment by a supervisor does, but it does occur.

    a) Usually the subordinate will devalue the superior through highlighting traditional gender stereotypes that reflect negatively on the person in power.

9. The topic of sexual harassment is about power.

    a) It is about one individual controlling or threatening another.

    b) It is wrong. It is illegal.

VII. POLITICS: POWER IN ACTION

A. A Definition of Political Behavior (ppt 18)

1. Definitions for organizational politics have focused on the use of power to affect decision making in the organization or on behaviors by members that are self-serving and organizationally non-sanctioned.

2. We define political behavior in organizations as those activities that are not required as part of one's formal role in the organization but that influence or

attempt to influence the distribution of advantages and disadvantages within the organization.

3. Key elements
    a) Political behavior is outside one's specified job requirements.
    b) The behavior requires some attempt to use one's power bases.
    c) Politics is concerned with the distribution of advantages and disadvantages within the organization.

B. The Importance of a Political Perspective
    1. Those who fail to acknowledge political behavior ignore the reality that organizations are political systems.
    2. A political view can explain much of what may seem to be irrational behavior in organizations.

C. Factors Contributing to Political Behavior
    1. Individual Factors (ppt 19)
        a) Researchers have identified certain personality characteristics, needs, and other individual factors that are likely to be related to political behavior.
        b) Employees who are authoritarian, have a high-risk propensity, or possess an external locus of control act politically with less regard for the consequences to the organization.
        c) A high need for power, autonomy, security, or status is also a major contributor to an employee's tendency to engage in political behavior.
    2. Organizational Factors (ppt 20)
        a) Political activity is probably more a function of the organization's culture than of individual differences.
        b) Evidence strongly indicates that certain cultures promote politics.
            (1) Cultures characterized by low trust, role ambiguity, unclear performance evaluation systems, zero-sum reward allocation practices, democratic decision making, high pressures for performance, and self-serving senior managers will create opportunities for political activities to be nurtured.
        c) The less trust there is within the organization, the higher the level of political behavior.
        d) Role ambiguity means that the prescribed behaviors of the employee are not clear.
        e) The greater the role ambiguity, the more one can engage in political activity with little chance of it being visible.
        f) The more that organizations use subjective criteria in the performance evaluation/appraisal, emphasize a single outcome measure, or allow significant time to pass between an action and its appraisal, the greater the likelihood an employee can get away with politicking.
        g) The more an organization's culture emphasizes the zero-sum or win-lose approach to reward allocations, the more employees will be motivated to engage in politicking.
        h) Many managers sought their positions in order to have legitimate power to make unilateral decisions. They fought hard and often paid high personal costs to achieve their influential positions. Sharing their power with others rubs directly against their desires. The result is that managers may use the required teams, committees, conferences, and group meetings in a superficial way—as arenas for maneuvering and manipulating.

        i)   The more pressure that employees feel to perform well, the more likely they are to engage in politicking.

        j)   When employees see the people on top engaging in political behavior, especially when they do so successfully and are rewarded for it, a climate is created that supports politicking.

D.   How Do People Respond to Organizational Politics? (ppt 21-22)

   1.   Although it is common to complain about politics at work, there are successful outcomes for individuals who successfully engage in politicking.

   2.   Exhibit 11-1 summarizes the extensive research on the relationship between politics and organizational outcomes.

   3.   The politics-performance relationship appears to be moderated by an individual's understanding of the hows and whys of politics.

      a)   An individual who has a clear understanding of who the decision makers are will have a better idea of how and why things happen.

   4.   Individuals are likely to engage in defensive behaviors when the perceive politics to be a threat to them.

      a)   Exhibit 11-2 details some defensive behaviors. (ppt 23)

E.   Impression Management (ppt 24)

   1.   People have an ongoing interest in how others perceive and evaluate them.

      a)   North Americans spend billions of dollars on diets, health club memberships, cosmetics, and plastic surgery.

      b)   Being perceived positively by others should have benefits for people in organizations.

         (1) In a political context it might help sway the distribution of advantages in their favor.

   2.   The process by which individuals attempt to control the impression others form of them is called impression management.

   3.   Techniques

      a)   Self-descriptions—Statements made by a person that describe personal characteristics such as traits, abilities, feelings, opinions, and personal lives.

      b)   Conformity—Agreeing with someone else's opinion in order to gain his or her approval.

      c)   Accounts—Excuses, justifications or other explanations of a predicament-creating event aimed at minimizing the apparent severity of the predicament.

      d)   Apologies—Admitting responsibility for an undesirable event and simultaneously seeking to get a pardon for the action.

      e)   Acclaiming—Explanation of favorable events by someone in order to maximize the desirable implications for that person.

      f)   Flattery—Complimenting others about their virtues in an effort to make oneself appear perceptive and likable.

      g)   Favors—Doing something nice for someone to gain that person's approval.

   4.   Keep in mind that nothing in impression management implies that the impressions people convey are necessarily false.

      a)   Misrepresentation can have a high cost. If the image claimed is false, you may be discredited.

      b)   Individuals are more likely to misrepresent themselves in some situations than in others.

(1) Highly uncertain or ambiguous situations provide relatively little information for challenging a fraudulent claim and reduce the risks associated with misrepresentation.

5. Effectiveness
   a) Only a few studies have been undertaken to test the effectiveness of IM techniques.
   b) The evidence demonstrates that using IM behaviors seems to work.
   c) Interviewing study.

F. The Ethics of Behaving Politically
   1. While there are no clear-cut ways to differentiate ethical from unethical politicking, there are some questions you should consider.
   2. Exhibit 11-3 illustrates a decision tree to guide ethical actions. (ppt 25)
      a) The first question you need to answer addresses self-interest versus organizational goals.
         (1) Ethical actions are consistent with the organization's goals.
      b) The second question concerns the rights of other parties.
      c) The final question that needs to be addressed is related to whether the political activity conforms to standards of equity and justice.
   3. Unfortunately, the answers to the questions in Exhibit 11-2 are often argued in ways to make unethical practices seem ethical.
      a) Powerful people can become very good at explaining self-serving behaviors in terms of the organization's best interest.
      b) If you have a strong power base, recognize the ability of power to corrupt.

VIII. IMPLICATIONS FOR MANAGERS

1. If you want to get things done in a group or organization, it helps to have power. As a manager who wants to maximize your power, you will want to increase others' dependence on you. You can, for instance, increase your power in relation to your boss by developing knowledge or a skill that he or she needs and for which he or she perceives no ready substitute. But power is a two-way street. You will not be alone in attempting to build your power bases. Others, particularly employees and peers, will be seeking to make you dependent on them. The result is a continual battle. While you seek to maximize others' dependence on you, you will be seeking to minimize your dependence on others. And, of course, others you work with will be trying to do the same.
2. The effective manager accepts the political nature of organizations. By assessing behavior in a political framework, you can better predict the actions of others and use this information to formulate political strategies that will gain advantages for you and your work unit.

SUMMARY (ppt 26-27)

1. Power refers to the capacity that A has to influence the behavior of B so that B does something he or she would not otherwise do. Probably the most important aspect of power is that it is a function of dependence. The greater B's dependence on A, the greater A's power is in the relationship.
2. The two concepts of power and leadership are closely intertwined. Leaders use power to attain group goals, and power is a means for facilitating their achievement. There are several key differences.
3. There are seven bases to power. See Exhibit 11-1. The coercive power base is defined by French and Raven as being dependent on fear. The opposite of coercive power is reward

power. People comply with the wishes or directives of another because doing so produces positive benefits. Legitimate power comes from one's structural position. Information power comes from access and control over information. Expert power is influence wielded as a result of expertise, special skill, or knowledge. Referent power's base is identification with a person who has desirable resources or personal traits. Charismatic power comes from an individual's personality and interpersonal style.

4. A key element to power is dependency. When you possess anything that others require but that you alone control, you make them dependent on you and, therefore, you gain power over them. Dependency is increased when the resource you control is important and scarce or nonsubstitutable. A resource needs to be perceived as scarce to create dependency.

5. The natural way to gain influence is to become a powerholder. Forming a coalition is a way two or more "outs" can gain power. Coalitions in organizations often seek to maximize their size. Coalition formation will be influenced by the actual tasks that workers perform. The more routine the task of a group or the work of individual jobs, the greater the likelihood that coalitions will form.

6. Legally, sexual harassment is defined as any unwanted activity of a sexual nature that affects an individual's employment. There is a great deal of disagreement about what specifically constitutes sexual harassment. Most studies confirm that the concept of power is central to understanding sexual harassment. Sexual harassment is about power. It is about one individual's controlling or threatening another. It is wrong. It is illegal.

7. Political behavior in organizations are those activities that are not required as part of one's formal role in the organization but that influence or attempt to influence the distribution of advantages and disadvantages within the organization.

8. The importance of a political perspective in an organization is that a political view can explain much of what may seem to be irrational behavior in organizations. Those who fail to acknowledge political behavior ignore the reality that organizations are political systems.

9. Political behavior occurs in organizations for a number of reasons. Researchers have identified certain personality characteristics, needs, and other individual factors that are likely to be related to political behavior. Political activity is probably more a function of the organization's culture than of individual differences. The greater the role ambiguity, the more one can engage in political activity with little chance of it being visible. The more that organizations use subjective criteria in the appraisal, the greater the likelihood an employee can get away with politicking. When employees see the people on top engaging in political behavior, especially when they do so successfully and are rewarded for it, a climate is created that supports politicking.

10. Although individuals often complain about the politics in their organization, successfully playing politics can have positive outcomes.

11. Impression management has become more important in organizations. It is the process by which individuals attempt to control the impression others form of them. Individuals manage the impressions they make through their self-descriptions, conformity, using justifications or other explanations of a predicament, apologies, and so on.

12. It is important to think about the ethics of political behavior. Although there are no clear-cut ways to differentiate ethical from unethical politicking, there are some questions you should consider. Exhibit 11-3 illustrates a decision tree to guide ethical actions

DISCUSSION QUESTIONS

1. What is power?

    Answer - Power refers to the capacity that one person has to influence the behavior of another so that the second person does something he or she would not otherwise do. Power may exist but not be used. It is, therefore, a capacity or potential. Probably the most important aspect of power is that it is a function of dependence. The greater B's dependence on A, the greater A's power is in the relationship.

2. Contrast power and leadership.
    Answer - Power refers to the capacity to influence the behavior of others. The concepts of power and leadership are closely intertwined. Leaders use power to attain group goals, and power is a means for facilitating their achievement. The differences are:
- Power does not require goal compatibility, merely dependence.
- Leadership requires some congruence between the goals of the leader and those led.
- Leadership research, for the most part, emphasizes style.
- The research on power has tended to encompass a broader area and focus on tactics for gaining compliance.

3. Manager's power can be based in several circumstances. What are the different bases of power and what are the advantages or disadvantages of using power in terms of its base or origin?
    Answer – See Exhibit 11-1. Coercive power is dependent on fear. It rests on the application, or the threat of application, of physical sanctions such as the infliction of pain, the generation of frustration through restriction of movement, or the control by force of basic physiological or safety needs. Reward power is the opposite of coercive power. People comply with the wishes or directives of another because doing so produces positive benefits. You don't need to be a manager to be able to exert influence through rewards. Legitimate power is based upon one's structural position. It represents the power a person receives as a result of his or her position in the formal hierarchy of an organization. Positions of authority include coercive and reward powers. Legitimate power is broader than the power to coerce and reward. Information power comes from access to and control over information. Expert power is influence wielded as a result of expertise, special skill, or knowledge. Expertise has become one of the most powerful sources of influence as the world has become more technologically oriented. Referent power's base is identification with a person who has desirable resources or personal traits. If I admire and identify with you, you can exercise power over me because I want to please you. Referent power develops out of admiration of another and a desire to be like that person. Charismatic power results from an individual's personality and interpersonal style, and is an extension of referent power. Student's responses regarding advantages/disadvantages will be more of a value discussion than a factual discussion.

4. What is the General Dependency Postulate and why is it central to further understanding of power itself?
    Answer – The General Dependency Postulate states: *The greater B's dependency on A, the greater power A has over B.* Therefore, when you possess anything the others require but that you alone control, you make them dependent on you and, therefore, you gain power over them.

5. Power depends on dependency. As a manager how can you legitimately create dependency among your employees, peers, and your organization?
    Answer - If you can create a monopoly by controlling information, prestige, or anything that others crave, they become dependent on you. Conversely, the more you can expand your options, the less power you place in the hands of others. Dependency is increased when the resource you control is important and scarce. To create dependency, therefore, you must control things that are perceived as important. The ability to reduce uncertainty increases a group's importance and, hence, its power but also what's important is

situational. A resource needs to be perceived as scarce to create dependency. The need to obtain a scarce resource—such as important knowledge—makes the high-ranking member dependent on the low-ranking member.

6. What role do coalitions play in the developing of power bases, especially by individuals or groups that do not have a traditional base of power?
   Answer - The natural way to gain influence is to become a powerholder. In such cases, efforts will be made to form a coalition of two or more "outs" who, by joining together, can each better themselves at the expense of those outside the coalition. Coalitions in organizations often seek to maximize their size. In organizations, the implementation of and commitment to the decision are at least as important as the decision itself. It's necessary, therefore, for coalitions in organizations to seek a broad constituency to support the coalition's objectives, so the coalition must be expanded to encompass as many interests as possible. More coalitions will likely be created if there is a great deal of task and resource interdependence. Coalition formation will be influenced by the actual tasks that workers perform. The more routine the task of a group or the work of individual jobs, the greater the likelihood that coalitions will form.

7. Why do researchers say that power, not sex, is central to understanding sexual harassment?
   Answer - Legally, sexual harassment is defined as unwelcome advances, requests for sexual favors, and other verbal or physical conduct, whether overt or subtle, of a sexual nature. Most studies confirm that the concept of power is central to understanding sexual harassment. This seems to be true whether the harassment comes from a supervisor, a co-worker, or even a subordinate. Because of power inequities sexual harassment by one's boss creates great difficulty for the person being harassed. Co-workers don't have position power, but they can have influence and use it to sexually harass peers. In fact, although co-workers appear to engage in somewhat less severe forms of harassment than do supervisors, co-workers are the most frequent perpetrators of sexual harassment in organizations. Harassment by subordinates doesn't get nearly the attention that harassment by a supervisor does, but it does occur. Usually the subordinate will devalue the superior through highlighting traditional gender stereotypes that reflect negatively on the person in power.

8. How can you recognize political behavior in an organization?
   Answer - The text defines political behavior in organizations as those activities that are not required as part of one's formal role in the organization but that influence or attempt to influence the distribution of advantages and disadvantages within the organization. There are three key elements. 1) Political behavior is outside one's specified job requirements. 2) The behavior requires some attempt to use one's power bases. 3) Politics is concerned with the distribution of advantages and disadvantages within the organization.

9. What factors contribute to political behavior in organizations?
   Answer - There are individual and organizational factors that contribute to political behavior. Individual factors. Researchers have identified certain personality characteristics, needs, and other individual factors that are likely to be related to political behavior. Employees who are authoritarian, have a high-risk propensity, or possess an external locus of control act politically with less regard for the consequences to the organization. A high need for power, autonomy, security, or status is also a major contributor to an employee's tendency to engage in political behavior. Organizational factors. Political

activity is probably more a function of the organization's culture than of individual differences. Evidence strongly indicates that certain cultures promote politics. Cultures characterized by low trust, role ambiguity, unclear performance evaluation systems, zero-sum reward allocation practices, democratic decision making, high pressures for performance, and self-serving senior managers will create opportunities for political activities to be nurtured. The greater the role ambiguity, the more one can engage in political activity with little chance of it being visible. The more that organizations use subjective criteria in the appraisal, emphasize a single outcome measure, or allow significant time to pass between an action and its appraisal, the greater the likelihood an employee can get away with politicking. The more an organization's culture emphasizes the zero-sum or win-lose approach to reward allocations, the more employees will be motivated to engage in politicking.

10. Why do managers and employees engage in political behavior in organizations?
    Answer - Many managers sought their positions in order to have legitimate power to make unilateral decisions. They fought hard and often paid high personal costs to achieve their influential positions. Sharing their power with others rubs directly against their desires. The result is that managers may use the required teams, committees, conferences, and group meetings in a superficial way—as arenas for maneuvering and manipulating. The more pressure that employees feel to perform well, the more likely they are to engage in politicking. When employees see the people on top engaging in political behavior, especially when they do so successfully and are rewarded for it, a climate is created that supports politicking.

11. Regardless of the ethics of impression management (IM), what things can a manager do to manage and enhance his or her image within an organization?
    Answer - The process by which individuals attempt to control the impression others form of them is called impression management. There are seven techniques.
- Self-descriptions—Statements made by a person that describe such personal characteristics as traits, abilities, feelings, opinions, and personal lives.
- Conformity—Agreeing with someone else's opinion in order to gain his or her approval.
- Accounts—Excuses, justifications or other explanations of a predicament-creating event aimed at minimizing the apparent severity of the predicament.
- Apologies—Admitting responsibility for an undesirable event and simultaneously seeking to get a pardon for the action.
- Acclaiming—Explanation of favorable events by someone in order to maximize the desirable implications for that person.
- Flattery—Complimenting others about their virtues in an effort to make oneself appear perceptive and likable.
- Favors—Doing something nice for someone to gain that person's approval.
    Keep in mind that nothing in IM implies that the impressions people convey are necessarily false. Misrepresentation can have a high cost. If the image claimed is false, you may be discredited.

12. Are there any ethical considerations to acting in a political manner within an organization of which managers need to be aware?
    Answer - Although there are no clear-cut ways to differentiate ethical from unethical politicking, there are some questions you should consider. Exhibit 11-3 illustrates a decision tree to guide ethical actions. The first question you need to answer addresses self-interest versus organizational goals. Ethical actions are consistent with the organization's goals. The second question concerns the rights of other parties. The final

question that needs to be addressed is related to whether the political activity conforms to standards of equity and justice.

EXERCISES

A.   What Is Your Power Base?

Our goal is for students to realize through practice what different forms of power look like and which ones they tend to gravitate toward using.

1. Have students read the following situation.
2. Choose students to role play the two positions, S.G.A. representative and Administration.
   - You can have two students fishbowl the exercise.
   - You can create two small teams; two S.G.A. representatives and three Administrators.
   - You can assign the role play to five small groups having each one play out one of the power positions.
3. Have the students role play for ten to twelve minutes. Adjust the time as you see fit, sometimes the negotiation runs out more quickly and sometimes you can let it play out for thirty minutes.
4. The rest of the class should observe the role play and note:
   - What power-base was used by each person?
   - What else could they have done to make the position more powerful?
   - What did they do that didn't fit that power perspective?
   - Did they choose the most appropriate power base for this situation? Why?
5. Once the role play is completed, have the class discuss the following:
   - It is important here is to show almost any power base can work.
   - Also, students will tend to have an orientation to one of the approaches.
   - If both sides choose power approaches that lead to confrontation the negotiation will probably fail.

Power Play

You are a member of the Student Government Association's Executive Body at your college or university. You are an elected student representative, an Executive-level officer, but not the president of the S.G.A. You represent students in the business program/school. This program is a cash cow for the school in that it generates more tuition and grants than it consumes. Graduates tend to become wealthy alumni who make generous contributions. The business school/program and S.G.A. have built a close relationship with a number of these alumni. You also have been part of an undergraduate team that has enticed 20 percent more large corporations to interview at your campus through networking and personal contacts with the executives of these organizations.

The administration has implemented a campus-wide policy affecting all undergraduates that you want changed. [You may choose a current issue on campus, or leave the particulars ambiguous.] This policy is a special pain for business students. The policy came out of administration/alumni talks over the last year. Your chief administrator is a strong but reasonable person, who doesn't easily change direction but is willing to hear someone's perspective. The Chief Administrator is a bit feared by students, respected by faculty, and doesn't have the best relationship with alumni.

1. As the S.G.A. representative, choose one of the four power bases and negotiate the elimination of or modification of this policy.
   - Choose the one you think has the most credibility given this situation.
   - Talk, negotiate, and so on, as you think appropriate given this base of power.
   - Do not make overt statements that will give away your power base.
2. Do not reveal the power base you are using.
3. As the chief administrator, choose a power base in response to the S.G.A. representative.

- Choose the one you think has the most credibility given this situation.
- Talk, negotiate, and so on, as you think appropriate given this base of power.
- Do not make overt statements that will give away your power base.

B.   Power, Politics, Coalitions

Assign your students to watch a one-hour (minimum) television show during prime time to watch for and identify the use of power. Have the students keep a journal of examples of different characters on the show using different bases of power, politics, and coalitions. Some television shows that might be good examples would include *West Wing, ER, Law and Order, CSI, Survivor, JAG, Judging Amy, or NYPD Blue.* The television show must have a wide range of characters, in a work-type setting. Watch drama rather than situation comedy.

When the students are recording in their journals, they should identify the character, the action they see taking place, and describe enough of the scene that they can discuss this example in the next class period.

Have an open class discussion of the different examples the students observed.

C.   Types of Power

Create a class discussion around the implications of the various types of power. Ask students if one type is superior to another, and discuss the ethical implications of "using" the various power types. You might also lead this into a discussion of the ethics involved in applying the impression management techniques discussed in this chapter.

Analyzing Your Organization

Have students keep a journal for one week in which they observe political behaviors and impression management strategies of their coworkers. Meetings are an excellent time to observe these behaviors. In a meeting, have them examine the reactions of participants towards those that have the power, versus those that don't. For example, did the participants tend to agree with the members that have the power regardless of the quality of the ideas and comments? Did those that did not have power tend to get interrupted often? Have them type up the journal and turn it in. Or, you can simply have them discuss it in front of the class. You might want to discuss specific examples anonymously due to the ethical implications of the behaviors they will be observing.

CHAPTER 12 - CONFLICT AND NEGOTIATION

CHAPTER OBJECTIVES
After reading this chapter, you should be able to:
1. Define conflict.
2. Differentiate between the traditional, human relations, and interactionist views of conflict.
3. Contrast functional and dysfunctional conflict.
4. Outline the conflict process.
5. Describe the five conflict-handling orientations.
6. Contrast distributive and integrative bargaining.
7. Identify decision biases that hinder effective negotiation.
8. Explain ways for individuals to improve their negotiating skills.

LECTURE OUTLINE
I.   A DEFINITION OF CONFLICT
   A.   Definition (ppt 4)
      1.   Multiple definitions of conflict.
      2.   Several common themes underlie most definitions.
         a)   For there to be a conflict it must be perceived by the parties involved.
         b)   Additional commonalties among most definitions of conflict are the concepts of opposition, scarcity, and blockage and the assumption there are two or more parties whose interests or goals appear to be incompatible.
         c)   Resources—money, jobs, prestige, and power, for example—are not unlimited, and their scarcity encourages blocking behavior.
      3.   Differences between definitions tend to center around intent and whether conflict is limited only to overt acts.
         a)   The intent issue is a debate over whether blockage behavior must be a determined action or whether it could occur as a result of fortuitous circumstances. As to whether conflict can refer only to overt acts, some definitions, for example, require signs of manifest fighting or open struggle as criteria for the existence of conflict.
      4.   Our definition of conflict acknowledges awareness (perception), opposition, scarcity, and blockage.
      5.   Further, we assume it to be a determined action, which can exist at either the latent or overt level.
      6.   We define conflict as a process in which an effort is purposely made by A to offset the efforts of B by some form of blocking that will result in frustrating B in attaining his or her goals or furthering his or her interests.

II.   TRANSITIONS IN CONFLICT THOUGHT (ppt 5)
   A.   The Traditional View (ppt 6)
      1.   It was assumed that conflict was bad—something to be avoided.
      2.   The traditional view was consistent with the attitudes that prevailed about group behavior in the 1930s and 1940s.
      3.   According to studies such as those done at Hawthorne, conflict was a dysfunctional outcome resulting from poor communication, a lack of openness and trust between people, and the failure of managers to be responsive to the needs and aspirations of their employees.
      4.   The view that all conflict is bad is a simple approach and most of us still evaluate conflict situations on the basis of this outmoded standard.

B. The Human Relations View (ppt 7)
1. Conflict was a natural occurrence in all groups and organizations.
2. Conflict should be accepted as it is inevitable.
3. This view dominated conflict theory from the late 1940s through the mid-1970s.

C. The Interactionist View (ppt 8)
1. This is the current perspective on conflict.
2. The interactionist approach encourages conflict on the grounds that a harmonious, peaceful, tranquil, and cooperative group is likely to become static, apathetic, and nonresponsive to needs for change and innovation.
3. The major contribution of the interactionist approach, therefore, is encouraging group leaders to maintain an ongoing minimal level of conflict—enough to keep the group alive, self-critical, and creative.
4. The text takes an interactionist view.
    a) Whether a conflict is good or bad depends on the type of conflict.
    b) It's necessary to differentiate between functional and dysfunctional conflicts.

III. FUNCTIONAL VERSUS DYSFUNCTIONAL CONFLICT
A. Introduction (ppt 9)
1. The interactionist view does not propose that all conflicts are good.
    a) Some conflicts support the goals of the group and improve its performance; these are functional, constructive forms of conflict.
    b) There are also conflicts that hinder group performance; these are dysfunctional, or destructive forms.
2. The evidence indicates that you need to look at the type of conflict to differentiate between functional and dysfunctional conflict.
3. There are three types of conflict: task, relationship, and process. (ppt 10-11)
    a) Task conflict relates to the content and goals of the work
    b) Relationship conflict focuses on interpersonal relationships.
        (1) Studies demonstrate that relationship conflicts are almost always dysfunctional.
        (2) Friction and interpersonal hostilities inherent in relationship conflicts increase personality clashes and decrease mutual understanding.
    c) Process conflict relates to how the work gets done.
    d) Low levels of process and low-to-moderate levels of task conflict are functional.

IV. THE CONFLICT PROCESS (ppt 12)
A. See Exhibit 12-1, the Conflict Process (ppt 13)

B. Stage I: Potential Opposition (ppt 14)
1. The first step in the conflict process is the presence of conditions that create opportunities for conflict to arise.
2. Three general categories are communication, structure, and personal variables.
3. Communication
    a) The communicative source represents those opposing forces that arise from semantic difficulties, misunderstandings, and "noise" in the communication channels.
    b) One major misconception is that poor communication is the reason for conflicts.

      c) Poor communication is certainly not the source of all conflicts, though there is considerable evidence to suggest that problems in the communication process retard collaboration and stimulate misunderstanding.

      d) A review of the research suggests that semantic difficulties, insufficient exchange of information, and noise in the communication channel are all barriers to communication and potential antecedent conditions to conflict.

          (1) Semantic difficulties arise as a result of differences in training, selective perception, and inadequate information about others.

      e) The potential for conflict increases when either too little or too much communication takes place.

          (1) It is possible to overcommunicate, resulting in an increase in the potential for conflict.

          (2) The channel chosen for communicating can have an influence on stimulating opposition. The filtering process that occurs as information is passed between members and the divergence of communications from formal or previously established channels offer potential opportunities for conflict to arise.

   4. Structure

      a) The term *structure* is used, in this context, to include variables such as size; degree of routinization, specialization, and standardization in the tasks assigned to group members; heterogeneity of the group; leadership styles; reward systems; and the degree of dependence between groups.

      b) Size and specialization act as forces to stimulate conflict.

      c) There is some indication that a close style of leadership, that is, tight and continuous observation with restrictive control of the others' behaviors, increases conflict potential, but the evidence is not strong.

      d) Too much reliance on participation may also stimulate conflict.

          (1) Participation and conflict are highly correlated, apparently because participation encourages the promotion of differences.

          (2) Reward systems, too, are found to create conflict when one member's gain is at another's expense.

          (3) If a group is dependent on another group, or if interdependence allows one group to win at another's expense, opposing forces are stimulated.

   5. Personal Variables

      a) The most important personal variables are individual value systems and individual idiosyncrasies and differences.

          (1) The evidence indicates that certain personality types—for example, individuals who are highly authoritarian, dogmatic, and who demonstrate low self-esteem—lead to potential conflict.

      b) Most important, and probably the most overlooked variable in the study of social conflict, is the notion of differing value systems.

          (1) That is, people differ in the importance they give to values such as freedom, pleasure, hard work, self-respect, honesty, obedience, and equality.

          (2) Differences in value systems are important sources of the potential for conflict.

C. Stage II: Cognition and Personalization (ppt 16)

   1. If the conditions cited in stage I generate frustration, then the potential for opposition becomes realized in the second stage.

2. One or more of the parties must be aware of the existence of the antecedent conditions.
3. Because a conflict is perceived does not mean it is personalized.
    a) It is at the personal level where conflict is felt, when individuals become emotionally involved, that parties experience anxiety, tension, frustration, or hostility.

D. Stage III: Behavior (ppt 16)
1. A member engages in action that frustrates the attainment of another's goals or prevents the furthering of the other's interests.
    a) At this juncture, the conflict is out in the open.
2. Overt conflict covers a full range of behaviors——from subtle, indirect, and highly controlled forms of interference to direct, aggressive, violent, and uncontrolled struggle.
3. This is also when most conflict-handling behaviors are initiated.
4. Five conflict-handling approaches: competition, collaboration, avoidance, accommodation, and compromise.
    a) Competition. When one party seeks to achieve certain goals or to further personal interests, regardless of the impact on the parties to the conflict, he or she competes and dominates.
    b) Collaboration. When each of the parties in conflict desires to satisfy fully the concern of all parties, we have cooperation and the search for a mutually beneficial outcome.
        (1) In collaboration the behavior of the parties is aimed at solving the problem and at clarifying the differences rather than accommodating various points of view.
    c) Avoidance. A party may recognize that a conflict exists but react by withdrawing from it or suppressing the conflict.
        (1) Indifference or the desire to evade overt demonstration of a disagreement can result in withdrawal.
    d) Accommodation. When the parties seek to appease their opponents, they may be willing to place their opponents' interests above their own.
        (1) In order to maintain the relationship, one party is willing to be self-sacrificing.
    e) Compromise. When each party to the conflict must give up something, sharing occurs, resulting in a compromised outcome. In compromising there is no clear winner or loser.
        (1) The distinguishing characteristic of compromise, therefore, is the requirement that each party give up something.
5. The Impact of National Culture on Conflict Behavior. (ppt 17)
    a) Your approach to handling conflict will, to some degree, be influenced by your cultural roots.
        (1) Americans, for example, have a reputation for being open, direct, and competitive. These characteristics are consistent with a society marked by relatively low uncertainty avoidance and high quantity-of-life rankings.
        (2) People in countries low in uncertainty avoidance feel secure and relatively free from threats of uncertainty. Their organizations, therefore, tend to be rather open and flexible.

165

(3) Countries high in quality of life emphasize assertiveness. The cultural climate of low uncertainty avoidance and high quantity of life tend to shape a society that is open, direct, and competitive.

   b) This premise suggests that uncertainty avoidance and quantity/quality of life rankings would be fairly good predictors of which conflict styles are preferred in different countries.

E. Stage IV: Outcomes (ppt 18)
1. Functional Outcomes
   a) Low or moderate levels of conflict could improve the effectiveness of a group.
   b) Conflict is constructive when it improves the quality of decisions, stimulates creativity and innovation, encourages interest and curiosity among group members, provides the medium through which problems can be aired and tensions released, and fosters an environment of self-evaluation and improvement.
      (1) Conflict can enhance the quality of decision making by allowing all points particularly the ones that are unusual or held by a minority, to be weighed in important decisions.
      (2) Conflict is an antidote for groupthink.
   c) A company that has suffered because it had too little functional conflict is General Motors.
   d) A more recent example is Yahoo!
   e) A comparison of six major decisions during the administrations of four U.S. presidents found that conflict reduced the chance that groupthink would overpower policy decisions.
   f) There is further evidence that conflict leads to better and more innovative decisions, as well as increased group productivity.
   g) This means that increasing cultural diversity should provide benefits to the organization.
2. Dysfunctional Conflict
   a) Uncontrolled opposition breeds discontent, which acts to dissolve common ties and eventually leads to destruction of the group.
   b) There is a substantial body of literature to document how the dysfunctional varieties of conflict can reduce group effectiveness.
   c) Among the more undesirable consequences are a retarding of communication, reductions in group cohesiveness, and subordination of group goals to the primacy of infighting among members.
   d) Research on conflict has yet to identify those situations in which conflict is more likely to be constructive than destructive.
3. Creating functional conflict (ppt 19)
   a) Actually creating functional conflict is a tough job.
   b) Organizations need to reward dissent and punish "conflict avoiders."

V. NEGOTIATION
A. Definition (ppt 20)
1. For our purposes, we define negotiation as a process in which two or more parties exchange goods or services and attempt to agree on the exchange rate for them.
2. In addition, we use the terms *negotiation* and *bargaining* interchangeably.

B. Bargaining Strategies
    1. There are two general approaches to negotiation: distributive bargaining and integrative bargaining. See Exhibit 12-2. (ppt 21)
    2. Distributive Bargaining (ppt 22)
        a) Car purchase example.
        b) The negotiating process in the example is called distributive bargaining.
        c) Its most identifying feature is that it operates under zero-sum conditions.
            (1) In the used car example, every dollar you can get the seller to cut from the car's price is a dollar you save.
        d) The essence of distributive bargaining is negotiating over who gets what share of a fixed pie.
        e) Probably the most widely cited example of distributive bargaining is in labor-management negotiations over wages.
        f) Exhibit 12-3 depicts the distributive bargaining strategy.
        g) When engaged in distributive bargaining, one's tactics focus on trying to get one's opponent to agree to one's specific target point or to get as close to it as possible.
    3. Integrative Bargaining (ppt 23)
        a) Sales representative for a women's sportswear manufacturer example.
        b) This sales-credit negotiation is an example of integrative bargaining.
            (1) In contrast to distributive bargaining, integrative problem solving operates under the assumption that one or more settlements exist that can create a win-win solution.
        c) All things being equal, integrative bargaining is preferable to distributive bargaining. Because the former builds long-term relationships and facilitates working together in the future.
    4. We don't see more integrative bargaining in organizations because of the conditions necessary for this type of negotiation.
        a) Parties that are open with information and candid about their concerns.
        b) Sensitivity by both parties to the other's needs.
        c) The ability to trust one another.
        d) A willingness by both parties to maintain flexibility.

C. Issues in Negotiation (ppt 24)
    1. Decision-Making Biases that Hinder Effective Negotiation. (ppt 25)
        a) Irrational escalation of commitment. People tend to continue a previously selected course of action beyond what rational analysis would recommend.
        b) The mythical fixed pie. Bargainers assume that their gain must come at the expense of the other party.
        c) Anchoring and adjustments. People often have a tendency to anchor their judgments on irrelevant information, such as an initial offer. Many factors influence the initial positions people take when entering a negotiation.
        d) Framing negotiations. People tend to be overly affected by the way information is presented to them.
        e) Availability of information. Negotiators often rely too much on readily available information while ignoring more relevant data.
        f) The winner's curse. The regret one feels after closing a negotiation. Because your opponent accepted your offer, you become concerned that you offered too much. This postnegotiation reaction is not unusual.
        g) Overconfidence. Many of the previous biases can combine to inflate a person's confidence in his or her judgment and choices. When people hold

certain beliefs and
expectations, they tend to ignore information that contradicts them.

2. The Role of Personality Traits in Negotiation (ppt 26)
   a) You try but can't predict an opponent's negotiating tactics even if you know something about his or her personality.
   b) Personality traits have no significant direct effect on either the bargaining process or negotiation outcomes.
      (1) You should concentrate on the issues and the situational factors in each bargaining episode and not on your opponent and his or her characteristics.

3. Gender Differences in Negotiations (ppt 27)
   a) Evidence does not support the commonly held notion that women are more cooperative and pleasant in negotiations than men.
   b) Men and women's attitudes toward negotiation are quite different.
   c) Women may penalize themselves by failing to engage in negotiations when they should.

4. Cultural Differences in Negotiations (ppt 28)
   a) Negotiating styles clearly vary among national cultures.
   b) The French like conflict. They frequently gain recognition and develop their reputations by thinking and acting against others. As a result, the French tend to take a long time in negotiating agreements, and they aren't overly concerned about whether their opponents like or dislike them.
   c) The Chinese also draw out negotiations but for a different reason. They believe that negotiations never end. Like the Japanese, the Chinese negotiate to develop a relationship and a commitment to work together rather than to tie up every loose end.
   d) Americans are known around the world for their impatience and their desire to be liked. Astute negotiators from other countries often turn these characteristics to their advantage by dragging out negotiations and making friendship conditional on the final settlement.
   e) The cultural context of the negotiation significantly influences the amount and type of preparation for bargaining the relative emphasis on task versus interpersonal relationships; the tactics used, and even where the negotiation should be conducted.
   f) The first study compared North Americans, Arabs, and Russians.
      (1) North Americans tried to persuade by relying on facts and appealing to logic. They countered opponents' arguments with objective facts. They made small concessions early in the negotiation to establish a relation-ship and usually reciprocated opponents' concessions.
      (2) North Americans treated deadlines as very important.
      (3) Arabs tried to persuade by appealing to emotion. They countered opponents' arguments with subjective feelings. They made concessions throughout the bargaining process and almost always reciprocated oppo-nents' concessions. Arabs approached deadlines very casually.
      (4) Russians based their arguments on asserted ideals. They made few, if any, concessions. Any concession offered by an opponent was viewed as a weakness and was almost never reciprocated. Finally, Russians tended to ignore deadlines.
   g) The second study looked at verbal and nonverbal negotiation tactics exhib-ited by North Americans, Japanese, and Brazilians during half-hour bargaining sessions.

(1) Brazilians on average said "No" eighty-three times compared with five times for the Japanese and nine times for the North Americans.

(2) The Japanese displayed more than five periods of silence lasting longer than ten seconds during each thirty-minute session.

(3) North Americans averaged three and a half such periods; the Brazilians had none.

(4) The Japanese and North Americans interrupted their opponent about the same number of times, but the Brazilians interrupted two-and-a-half to three times more often than the North Americans and the Japanese.

(5) While the Japanese and the North Americans had no physical contact with their opponents during negotiations except for hand-shaking, the Brazilians touched each other almost five times every half hour.

5. The Ethics of Lying and Deceiving in Negotiations
   a) The common perception is that one must deceive to succeed.
   b) Debate continues about whether "little lies" or omissions are ethical in a negotiating context.

VI. IMPLICATIONS FOR MANAGERS

A. Managing Conflict (ppt 29)

1. Many people assume that conflict is related to lower group and organizational performance. That assumption is often false. Conflict can be either constructive or destructive to the functioning of a group or unit. When it's too high or too low, it hinders performance. An optimal level is one in which there is enough conflict to prevent stagnation, stimulate creativity, allow tensions to be released, and sow the seeds for change, yet not so much as to be disruptive.

2. Advice to managers faced with excessive conflict: don't assume that there's one conflict-handling approach that will always be best! Select the resolution technique appropriate for each situation. Guidelines for this include:

   a) Use competition when quick, decisive action is vital (in emergencies); on important issues, where unpopular actions need implementing (in cost cutting, enforcing unpopular rules, discipline); on issues vital to the organization's welfare when you know you're right; and against people who take advantage of noncompetitive behavior.

   b) Use collaboration to find an integrative solution when both sets of concerns are too important to be compromised; when your objective is to learn; to merge insights from people with different perspectives; to gain commitment by incorporating concerns into a consensus; and to work through feelings that have interfered with a relationship.

   c) Use avoidance when an issue is trivial or when more important issues are pressing; when you perceive no chance of satisfying your concerns; when potential disruption outweighs the benefits of resolution; to let people cool down and regain perspective; when gathering information supercedes immediate decision; when others can resolve the conflict more effectively; and when issues seem tangential or symptomatic of other issues.

   d) Use accommodation when you find you are wrong and to allow a better position to be heard, to learn, and to show your reasonableness; when issues are more important to others than to yourself and to satisfy others and maintain cooperation; to build social credits for later issues; to minimize loss when you are outmatched and losing; when harmony and stability are especially important; and to allow subordinates to develop by learning from mistakes.

e) Use compromise when goals are important but not worth the effort of potential disruption of more assertive approaches; when opponents with equal power are committed to mutually exclusive goals; to achieve temporary settlements to complex issues; to arrive at expedient solutions under time pressure; and as a backup when collaboration or competition is unsuccessful.

B. Toward Improving Negotiation Skills (ppt 30)
   1. Recommendations for improving your effectiveness at negotiating.
      a) Research Your Opponent. Acquire as much information as you can about your opponent's interests and goals. What constituencies must he or she appease? What is his or her strategy?
      b) Begin with a Positive Overture. Research shows that concessions tend to be reciprocated and lead to agreements. As a result, begin bargaining with a positive overture—perhaps a small concession—and then reciprocate your opponent's concessions.
      c) Address the Problem, Not Personalities. Concentrate on the negotiation issues not on the personal characteristics of your opponent. It's your opponent's ideas or position that you disagree with, not him or her personally. Separate the people from the problem, and don't personalize differences.
      d) Pay Little Attention to Initial Offers. Treat initial offers as merely a point of departure. Everyone has to have an initial position. They tend to be extreme and idealistic. Treat them as such.
      e) Emphasize Win-Win Solutions. If conditions are supportive, look for an integrative solution. Frame options in terms of your opponent's interests and look for solutions that can allow both you and your opponent to declare a victory.
      f) Create an Open and Trusting Climate. Skilled negotiators are good listeners, ask questions, focus their arguments directly, are not defensive, and have learned to avoid words and phrases that can irritate an opponent.

SUMMARY (ppt 31-32)

1. Conflict is a process in which an effort is purposely made by A to object the efforts of B by some form of blocking that will result in frustrating B in attaining his or her goals or furthering his or her interests. This definition of conflict acknowledges awareness (perception), opposition, scarcity, and blockage.
2. The thinking about conflict has gone through a number of changes. The traditional view assumed that conflict was bad, something to be avoided. The human relations view sees conflict as a natural occurrence in all groups and organizations. The current perspective on conflict is the interactionist view. It encourages conflict on the grounds that a harmonious, peaceful, tranquil, and cooperative group is likely to become static, apathetic, and nonresponsive to needs for change and innovation.
3. The interactionist view does not propose that all conflicts are good. Some conflicts support the goals of the group and improve its performance; these are functional, constructive forms of conflict. There are also conflicts that hinder group performance; these are dysfunctional or destructive forms. The demarcation between functional and dysfunctional is neither clear nor precise.
4. There is a conflict process model; the text outlines it in Exhibit 12-1. The first step in the conflict process is the presence of conditions that create opportunities for conflict to arise. Three general categories: communication, structure, and personal variables. If the conditions

170

cited in stage I generate frustration, then the potential for opposition becomes realized in the second stage. A member engages in action that frustrates the attainment of another's goals or prevents the furthering of the other's interests, this is Stage III and at this juncture, the conflict is out in the open. The fourth and final step focuses on functional outcomes of the conflict.

5.   There are two general approaches to negotiation: distributive bargaining and integrative bargaining. The essence of distributive bargaining is negotiating over who gets what share of a fixed pie. In contrast to distributive bargaining, integrative problem solving operates under the assumption that one or more settlements exist that can create a win-win solution.

6.   We become ineffective in negotiation through irrational escalation of commitment, the mythical fixed pie, anchoring and adjustments, framing negotiations, availability of information, the winner's curse, and overconfidence. Both personality traits and cultural differences also play a role in negotiation.

7.   We can improve our negotiation skills through a number of tactical steps, such as research your opponent; begin with a positive overture; addressing the problem, not personalities; paying little attention to initial offers; emphasizing win-win solutions; and creating an open and trusting climate.

DISCUSSION QUESTIONS

1.   How does the definition of conflict used by the author of your text differ from other traditional definitions of conflict?
     Answer - There are multiple definitions of conflict. Several common themes underlie most definitions: conflict must be perceived by the parties to it, there must be opposition, scarcity, and blockage and the assumption that there are two or more parties whose interests or goals appear to be incompatible, and resources must be involved. Your author's definition of conflict acknowledges awareness (perception), opposition, scarcity, and blockage. Further, they assume it to be a determined action, which can exist at either the latent or overt level. They define conflict as a process in which an effort is purposely made by A to object the efforts of B by some form of blocking that will result in frustrating B in attaining his or her goals or furthering his or her interests. The text takes an interactionist view. Whether a conflict is good or bad depends on the type of conflict. It's necessary to differentiate between functional and dysfunctional conflicts.

2.   How has management thinking about conflict changed over the years?
     Answer - It was assumed that conflict was bad—something to be avoided. The traditional view was consistent with the attitudes that prevailed about group behavior in the 1930s and 1940s. According to studies such as those done by Hawthorne, conflict was a dysfunctional outcome resulting from poor communication, a lack of openness and trust between people, and the failure of managers to be responsive to the needs and aspirations of their employees. Then came the human relations view that conflict was a natural occurrence in all groups and organizations. This view dominated conflict theory from the late 1940s through the mid-1970s. The current perspective is the interactionist view, which encourages conflict on the grounds that a harmonious, peaceful, tranquil, and cooperative group is likely to become static, apathetic, and nonresponsive to needs for change and innovation. The major contribution of the interactionist approach, therefore, is encouraging group leaders to maintain an ongoing minimal level of conflict—enough to keep the group alive, self-critical, and creative.

3.   How does functional conflict differ from dysfunctional conflict?
     Answer - Some conflicts support the goals of the group and improve its performance; these are functional, constructive forms of conflict. There are also conflicts that hinder group

performance; these are dysfunctional, or destructive forms. The demarcation between functional and dysfunctional is neither clear nor precise. The important criterion is group performance. Since groups exist to attain a goal or goals, it is the impact of the conflict on the group, rather than on any single individual, that defines functionality. Conflict is constructive when it improves the quality of decisions, stimulates creativity and innovation, encourages interest and curiosity among group members, provides the medium through which problems can be aired and tensions released, and fosters an environment of self-evaluation and improvement. Conflict is an antidote for groupthink. Uncontrolled opposition breeds discontent, which acts to dissolve common ties and eventually leads to the destruction of the group. There is a substantial body of literature to document how the dysfunctional varieties of conflict can reduce group effectiveness.

4. The evidence indicates that you need to look at the type of conflict to differentiate functional from dysfunctional conflict. Identify and describe the three types of conflict.
    Answer – Task conflict relates to the content and goals of the work. Relationship conflict focuses on interpersonal relationships. Process conflict relates to how the work gets done. Studies demonstrate that relationship conflicts are almost always dysfunctional. Low levels of process conflict and low-to-moderate levels of task conflict are functional.

5. Describe the conflict process.
    Answer - This process is outlined in Exhibit 12-1. The first step in the conflict process is the presence of conditions that create opportunities for conflict to arise. If the conditions cited in Stage I generate frustration, then the potential for opposition becomes realized in the second stage. One or more of the parties must be aware of the existence of the antecedent conditions. A member engages in action that frustrates the attainment of another's goals or prevents the furthering of the other's interests. At this juncture, the conflict is out in the open. The fourth and final stage relates to functional outcomes. Low or moderate levels of conflict could improve the effectiveness of a group.

6. What conflict-handling behavior would be best in each of the following situations?
    a. A manager of marketing is in a conflict with another manager in his cross-functional project team. He'd like to resolve the conflict in a way so that he's on good working terms with his peer.
    b. Tom negotiates to win. He doesn't feel like he's really negotiated until he's left "some blood on the floor."
    c. Henry is in a disagreement with his boss' boss, the executive vice president. Henry doesn't really care about the matter and the executive vice president can make things difficult for Henry in his job in the future.
    d. Jane wants to go to Palm Beach for spring break, her parents are saying no. Her dad's pretty worried that she would even ask because "of all the things college kids do down there." Jane wants to make peace because she really wants to go to Europe with a study group this summer.
    e. Althea and Maya both want a secretary for their departments, but HR will only allocate one new personnel slot to their general area. Neither can really employ a full-time secretary but the company has spent its temporary help budget.
    Answer -
    a. Collaboration. When each of the parties in conflict desires to fully satisfy the concern of all parties, we have cooperation and the search for a mutually beneficial outcome.
    b. Competition. When one party seeks to achieve certain goals or to further personal interests, regardless of the impact on the parties to the conflict, he or she competes and dominates.

172

c. Avoidance. A party may recognize that a conflict exists but react by withdrawing from it or suppressing the conflict. Indifference or the desire to evade overt demonstration of a disagreement can result in withdrawal.

d. Accommodation. When the parties seek to appease their opponents, they may be willing to place their opponents' interests above their own. In order to maintain the relationship, one party is willing to be self-sacrificing.

e. Compromise. When each party to the conflict must give up something, sharing occurs, resulting in a compromised outcome. In compromising there is no clear winner or loser.

7. As a manager, how can you go about creating functional conflict in your organization?
   Answer- This is difficult to do, but the organization needs a climate in which dissent is actually rewarded, and conflict avoiders are punished. The challenge is when managers hear news that they don't want to hear. This fosters communication and gets the conflict out in the open, which benefits the entire organization.

8. As a manager in another country, what things do you need to consider when handling conflict?
   Answer - Be aware that your approach to handling conflict will, to some degree, be influenced by your cultural roots. Americans, for example, have a reputation for being open, direct, and competitive. These characteristics are consistent with a society marked by relatively low uncertainty avoidance and high quantity-of-life rankings. People in countries low in uncertainty avoidance feel secure and relatively free from threats of uncertainty. Their organizations, therefore, tend to be rather open and flexible. Countries high in quality of life emphasize assertiveness. The cultural climate of low uncertainty avoidance and high quantity of life tends to shape a society that is open, direct, and competitive. This premise suggests that uncertainty avoidance and quantity/quality of life rankings would be fairly good predictors of which conflict styles are preferred in different countries.

9. Contrast distributive and integrative bargaining.
   Answer - There are two general approaches to negotiation: distributive bargaining and integrative bargaining. The most identifying feature of distributive bargaining is that it operates under zero-sum conditions. The essence of distributive bargaining is negotiating over who gets what share of a fixed pie. When engaged in distributive bargaining, one's tactics focus on trying to get one's opponent to agree to one's specific target point or to get as close to it as possible. In contrast to distributive bargaining, integrative problem solving operates under the assumption that one or more settlements exist that can create a win-win solution. All things being equal, integrative bargaining is preferable to distributive bargaining, because the former builds long-term relationships and facilitates working together in the future. We don't see more integrative bargaining in organizations because of the conditions necessary for this type of negotiation: parties who are open with information and candid about their concerns, a sensitivity by both parties to the other's needs, the ability to trust one another, and a willingness by both parties to maintain flexibility.

10. When entering into a bargaining situation, particularly using the distributive bargaining strategy, what is the importance of a "target point," a "resistance point," and a "settlement range"?
    Answer – Each party has a target point that defines what he or she would like to achieve. Also each party has a resistance point, which marks the lowest outcome that is acceptable— the point below which they would break off negotiations rather than accept a less-favorable settlement. The area between their resistance points is the settlement range. As long as there

173

is some overlap in their aspiration ranges, there exists a settlement area where each one's aspirations can be met.

11. What are the decision biases that can hinder effective negotiation?
    Answer -
    - Irrational escalation of commitment. People tend to continue a previously selected course of action beyond what rational analysis would recommend.
    - The mythical fixed pie. Bargainers assume that their gain must come at the expense of the other party.
    - Anchoring and adjustments. People often have a tendency to anchor their judgments on irrelevant information, such as an initial offer. Many factors influence the initial positions people take when entering a negotiation.
    - Framing negotiations. People tend to be overly affected by the way information is presented to them.
    - Availability of information. Negotiators often rely too much on readily available information while ignoring more relevant data.
    - The winner's curse. The regret one feels after closing a negotiation. Because your opponent accepted your offer, you become concerned that you offered too much. This postnegotiation reaction is not unusual.
    - Overconfidence. Many of the previous biases can combine to inflate a person's confidence in his or her judgment and choices. When people hold certain beliefs and expectations, they tend to ignore information that contradicts them.

12. How do culture differences affect negotiation styles? Offer examples of those differences in specific countries.
    Answer - Negotiating styles clearly vary among national cultures. The French like conflict. They frequently gain recognition and develop their reputations by thinking and acting against others. As a result, the French tend to take a long time in negotiating agreements, and they aren't overly concerned about whether their opponents like or dislike them. The Chinese also draw out negotiations but for a different reason. They believe that negotiations never end. Like the Japanese, the Chinese negotiate to develop a relationship and a commitment to work together rather than to tie up every loose end. Americans are known around the world for their impatience and their desire to be liked. Astute negotiators from other countries often turn these characteristics to their advantage by dragging out negotiations and making friendship conditional on the final settlement. North Americans tried to persuade by relying on facts and appealing to logic. They countered opponents' arguments with objective facts. They made small concessions early in the negotiation to establish a relationship and usually reciprocated opponents' concessions. North Americans treated deadlines as very important. Arabs tried to persuade by appealing to emotion. They countered opponents' arguments with subjective feelings. They made concessions throughout the bargaining process and almost always reciprocated opponents' concessions. Arabs approached deadlines very casually. Russians based their arguments on asserted ideals. They made few, if any, concessions. Any concession offered by an opponent was viewed as a weakness and was almost never reciprocated. Finally, the Russians tended to ignore deadlines.

13. You are preparing to negotiate for your first car purchase. What techniques could you use to improve the outcome of this negotiation?
    Answer - Students' answers will vary. Some tactics, researching your opponent will clearly fit any situation. Other tactics such as address the problem not personality, may be somewhat irrelevant. Student justification is important.

- Research Your Opponent. Acquire as much information as you can about your opponent's interests and goals.
- Begin with a Positive Overture. Research shows that concessions tend to be reciprocated and lead to agreements.
- Address the Problem, Not Personalities. Concentrate on the negotiation issues not on the personal characteristics of your opponent.
- Pay Little Attention to Initial Offers. Treat initial offers as merely a point of departure. Everyone has to have an initial position. They tend to be extreme and idealistic.
- Emphasize Win-Win Solutions. If conditions are supportive, look for an integrative solution. Frame options in terms of your opponent's interests and look for solutions that can allow both you and your opponent to declare a victory.
- Create an Open and Trusting Climate. Skilled negotiators are good listeners, ask questions, focus their arguments directly, are not defensive, and have learned to avoid words and phrases that can irritate an opponent.

14.   Is it ethical to lie during a negotiation?
       Answer- There are many different perspectives on what constitutes a lie during a negotiation session, and when this is unethical. Use this as a class discussion item.

EXERCISES
A.   Conflict-Management Style Survey*

Instructions: Answer the following questions from a single frame of reference—work-related conflicts, family conflicts, or social conflicts. Allocate ten points among the four alternative answers given for each of the fifteen items below.

Example: When the people I supervise become involved in a personal conflict, I usually:

Intervene to settle the dispute.	Call a meeting to talk over the problem.	Offer to help if I can.	Ignore the problem.		
3	6	1	0	=	10

Be certain that your answers add up to 10.

1. When someone I care about is actively hostile toward me—yelling, threatening, abusive—I tend to:

Respond in a hostile manner.	Try to persuade the person to give up the hostile behavior.	Stay and listen as long as possible.	Walk away.
___	___	___	___

2. When someone who is unimportant to me is actively hostile toward me, i.e., yelling, threatening, abusive, and so on, I tend to:

Respond in a hostile manner.	Try to persuade the person to give up the hostile behavior.	Stay and listen as long as possible.	Walk away.
___	___	___	___

175

3. When I observe people in conflicts in which anger, threats, hostility, and strong opinions are present, I tend to:

Become involved and take a position.	Attempt to mediate.	Observe to see what happens.	Leave as quickly as possible.
_____	_____	_____	_____

4. When I perceive another person as meeting his or her needs at my expense, I am apt to:

Work to do anything I can to change that person.	Rely on persuasion and "facts" when attempting to have that person change.	Work hard at changing how I relate to that person.	Accept the situation as it is.
_____	_____	_____	_____

5. When involved in an interpersonal dispute, I generally:

Draw the other person into seeing the problem as I do.	Examine the issues between us as logically as possible.	Look hard for a workable compromise.	Let time take its course and let the problem work itself out.
_____	_____	_____	_____

6. The quality that I value the most in dealing with conflict would be:

Emotional strength and security.	Intelligence.	Love and openness.	Patience.
_____	_____	_____	_____

7. Following a serious altercation with someone I care for deeply, I:

Strongly desire to go back and settle things my way.	Want to go back and work it out—whatever it takes.	Worry about it a lot but not initiate/plan for further contact.	Let it lie and do not plan.
_____	_____	_____	_____

8. When I see a serious conflict developing between two people I care about, I tend to:

Express my disappointment that this had to happen.	Attempt to persuade them to resolve their differences.	Watch to see what develops.	Leave the scene.
_____	_____	_____	_____

9. When I see a serious conflict developing between two people who are <u>unimportant</u> to me, I tend to:

Express my disappointment that this happened.	Attempt to persuade them to resolve their differences.	Watch to see what develops.	Leave the scene.
_____	_____	_____	_____

10. The feedback that I receive from most people about how I behave when faced with conflict and opposition indicates that I:

Try hard to get my way.	Try to work out differences cooperatively.	Am easygoing and take a soft or conciliatory position.	Usually avoid the conflict.
_____	_____	_____	_____

11. When communicating with someone with whom I am having a serious conflict, I:

Try to overpower the other person with my speech.	Talk a little bit more than I listen.	Am an active listener (feeding back words and feelings).	Am a passive listener (agreeing and apologizing).
_____	_____	_____	_____

12. When involved in an unpleasant conflict, I:

Use humor with the other party.	Make an occasional quip or joke about the situation.	Relate humor only to myself.	Suppress all attempts at humor.
_____	_____	_____	_____

13. When someone does something that irritates me (e.g., smokes in a nonsmoking area or crowds in line in front of me), my tendency in communicating with the offending person is to (select an answer from each row):

Insist that the person look me in the eye.	Look the person directly in the eye and maintain eye contact.	Maintain intermittent eye contact.	Avoid looking directly at the person.
_____	_____	_____	_____
Stand close and make physical contact.	Use my hands and body to illustrate my points.	Stand close to the person without touching him or her.	Stand back and keep my hands to myself.
_____	_____	_____	_____

Use strong, direct language and tell the person to stop.	Try to persuade the person to stop.	Talk gently and tell the person what my feelings are.	Say and do nothing.
_____	_____	_____	_____

CONFLICT-MANAGEMENT STYLE SURVEY SCORING AND INTERPRETATION SHEET

Instructions: When you have completed all fifteen items, add your scores vertically, resulting in four column totals. Put these on the blanks below.

Totals: _____   _____   _____   _____

        Column 1   Column 2   Column 3   Column 4

Your highest score is your dominant conflict management strategy. All of us use all four strategies at one time or another. Your dominant style is the one you prefer and will certainly come out in more intense conflict situations. Knowing your style will help you be more effective in dealing with conflict.

Four conflict-handling approaches: competition, collaboration, avoidance, and accommodation.

Column 1. Competition. When one party seeks to achieve certain goals or to further personal interests, regardless of the impact on the parties to the conflict, he or she competes and dominates.

Column 2. Collaboration. When each of the parties in conflict desires to satisfy fully the concern of all parties, we have cooperation and the search for a mutually beneficial outcome. In collaboration, the behavior of the parties is aimed at solving the problem and at clarifying the differences rather than accommodating various points of view.

Column 3. Accommodation. When the parties seek to appease their opponents, they may be willing to place their opponents' interests above their own. In order to maintain the relationship, one party is willing to be self-sacrificing.

Column 4. Avoidance. A party may recognize that a conflict exists but react by withdrawing from it or suppressing the conflict. Indifference or the desire to evade overt demonstration of a disagreement can result in withdrawal.

Now total your scores for Columns 1 and 2 and Columns 3 and 4.

Column 1 + Column 2 _____ = Score A   Column 3 + Column 4 _____ = Score B

If Score A is significantly higher than Score B (25 points or more), it may indicate a tendency toward assertive conflict management. A significantly higher B score signals a more conciliatory approach.

* Adapted from the work of Marc Robert, in the 1987 University Associates, Inc.

B.   Bargaining: Good, Bad, or Ugly?

Have students work in small groups to develop a "script" to role play the following scenarios in front of the class. You can assign a different scenario to each group, or have two groups role play the same scenario to discuss comparisons and contrasts in style. Require each group to first role play the scenario from a distributive bargaining perspective, and then from an integrative bargaining perspective. This should allow for comparison and contrast of the two styles of bargaining, and then encourage students to discuss which style they believed was more effective for achieving a final outcome.

Scenario:
A group of students is wanting the faculty member to postpone the next exam until after Spring Break. Currently the exam is scheduled for the Friday before Spring Break, and you would prefer to have the exam on the Monday, or even Wednesday, after Spring Break. The week before Break is getting quite busy, and you need the time to study over Spring Break in order to do well on the exam.

Scenario:
The company you currently work for does not have any educational reimbursement benefit available. You would like to have your employer offer this benefit, as you and many of your fellow workers would like to go back to school (part-time) and earn your MBA degree. But, the cost of tuition is expensive, and you would like your company to help with the expenses. Many of the other companies in your locale and industry do offer their employees this educational reimbursement, and you would like your company to do so, as well.

Scenario:
The university is considering adding a "computer fee" to all students who are enrolled at your campus. The reason for the computer fee is to be able to generate funds in order to provide better computer instruction and facilities (labs and classrooms). But, fees are already relatively high. You want the computer instruction and facilities, but you and your group want to have the facilities, but you are reluctant to have fees increase.

Scenario:
You would like to have your company allow you to work on a flexible schedule. You would agree to core hours of 10 a.m. and 2 p.m., when every employee is required to be at the workplace, but you would like to choose the other four hours you work each day. Your job is such that it would support this type of schedule, i.e. you do not work on an assembly line. Present a persuasive discussion to encourage your employer to go to a "flextime schedule."

Analyzing Your Organization

Have students create a negotiation scenario where they may not have thought of negotiating. For example, it is common and accepted that in the U.S. culture we will negotiate for automobiles, but not as widely accepted when purchasing furniture, for example. Challenge the class to negotiate their next major purchase, and have them bring to the class the results of their negotiation attempts. For example, was the negotiation integrative or distributive? Did they implement any of the methods discussed in class for improving negotiation skills? What was the outcome? Did gender or other variables affect the outcome? Did they actually save any money? This can also be a written report or an in-class exercise.

CHAPTER 13 - FOUNDATIONS OF ORGANIZATION STRUCTURE

CHAPTER OBJECTIVES
After reading this chapter, students should be able to:
1. Identify the six key elements that define an organization's structure.
2. Describe a simple structure.
3. Explain the characteristics of a bureaucracy.
4. Describe a matrix organization.
5. Explain the characteristics of a "virtual" organization.
6. Summarize why managers want to create boundaryless organizations.
7. List the factors that favor different organization structures.
8. Explain the behavioral implications of different organization structures.

LECTURE OUTLINE
I. WHAT IS ORGANIZATION STRUCTURE?
    A. Defined (ppt 4)
        1. An organization structure defines how job tasks are formally divided, grouped, and coordinated.
        2. Six key elements—work specialization, departmentalization, chain of command, span of control, centralization and decentralization, and formalization.
            a) See Exhibit 13-1. (ppt 5)

    B. Work Specialization (ppt 6)
        1. Early in the twentieth century, Henry Ford became rich and famous by building automobiles on an assembly line.
            a) By breaking jobs up into small standardized tasks, which could be performed over and over again, Ford was able to produce cars at the rate of one every ten seconds, while using employees who had relatively limited skills.
        2. The term work specialization or division of labor describes the degree to which tasks in the organization are subdivided into separate jobs.
        3. By the late 1940s most manufacturing jobs in industrialized countries were being done with high work specialization.
            a) Management saw this as a means to make the most efficient use of employees' skills.
            b) Employee skills at performing a task successfully increase through repetition.
            c) Training for specialization is more efficient from the organization's perspective. It is easier and less costly to find and train workers to do specific and repetitive tasks than to do a broad range of diverse tasks.
        4. For much of the first half of this century, managers viewed work specialization as an unending source of increased productivity but, by the 1960s, there was increasing evidence that a good thing can be carried too far.
            a) The point was reached of human diseconomies—boredom, fatigue, stress, low productivity, poor quality, increased absenteeism, and high turnover—which more than offset the economic advantages.
            b) See Exhibit 13-2.
        5. Managers then began to increase productivity by enlarging the scope of job activities and by giving employees a variety of activities to do, allowing them to do a whole job, and so on.
        6. Today managers recognize the economies work specialization provides as well as the problems it creates when it's carried too far.

C. Departmentalization (ppt 7)
1. Grouping jobs together so that common tasks can be coordinated.
2. One of the most popular ways is by functions performed.
    a) The major advantage—is economies of scale by placing people with common skills and orientations into common units.
3. Tasks can also be departmentalized by the type of product the organization produces.
    a) The major advantage to this type of grouping is increased accountability for product performance, since all activities related to a specific product are under the direction of a single manager.
4. Another departmentalization is on the basis of geography or territory.
    a) If an organization's customers are scattered over a large geographical area, then this form of departmentalization can be valuable.
5. Process departmentalization groups people by the specific phase they perform in the production process.
    a) Because each process requires different skills, this method offers a basis for the homogeneous categorizing of activities.
6. A final category is the particular type of customer.
    a) The assumption underlying customer departmentalization is that customers in each department have a common set of problems and needs that can best be met by having specialists for each.
7. Large organizations may use all of the forms of departmentalization.
8. Two general trends, however, seem to be gaining momentum in the past decade.
    a) Customer departmentalization has grown in popularity. In order to better monitor the needs of customers and serve them.
    b) The second trend is that rigid functional departmentalization is being complemented by teams that cross over traditional departmental lines.

D. Chain of Command (ppt 8-9)
1. In the 1970s, the chain-of-command was a basic cornerstone in organizational design.
2. The chain of command is an unbroken line of authority that extends from the top of the organization to the lowest echelon and clarifies who reports to whom.
3. It answers questions for employees such as, "To whom do I go to if I have a problem?" and "To whom am I responsible?"
4. Two complementary concepts: authority and unity of command.
    a) Authority refers to the rights inherent in a managerial position to give orders and expect the orders to be obeyed.
    b) The unity-of-command principle helps preserve the concept of an unbroken line of authority. It states that a person should have one and only one superior to whom he or she is directly responsible.
5. The concepts of chain of command, authority, and unity of command have substantially less relevance today for several reasons.
    a) Advancements in computer technology and the trend toward empowering employees.
    b) Operating employees are being empowered to make decisions that previously were reserved for management.
    c) The popularity of self-managed and cross-functional teams and the creation of new structural designs that include multiple bosses.

E. Span of Control (ppt 10)
1. All things being equal, the wider or larger the span, the more efficient the organization.
a) See Exhibit 13-3 as an example. (ppt 11)
2. Wider spans are more efficient in terms of cost. But at some point, wider spans reduce effectiveness. (ppt 12)
3. Narrow spans of control of five or six employees permit a manager to maintain close control.
4. Narrow spans have three major drawbacks.
a) They're expensive because they add levels of management.
b) They make vertical communication in the organization more complex.
c) Narrow spans of control encourage overly tight supervision and discourage employee autonomy.
5. The trend in recent years has been toward wider spans of control.
a) To ensure that performance doesn't suffer organizations have been investing heavily in employee training.

F. Centralization and Decentralization (ppt 13)
1. The term *centralization* refers to the degree to which decision making is concentrated at a single point in the organization.
a) The concept includes only formal authority—the rights inherent in one's position.
b) If top management makes the organization's key decisions with little or no input from lower-level personnel, then the organization is centralized.
c) The more that lower-level personnel provide input or are actually given the discretion to make decisions, the more decentralization there is.
2. In a decentralized organization, action can be taken more quickly to solve problems, more people provide input into decisions, and employees are less likely to feel alienated from those who make the decisions that affect their work lives.
3. There has been a marked trend toward decentralizing decision making.

G. Formalization (ppt 14)
1. Formalization refers to the degree to which jobs within the organization are standardized.
a) If a job is highly formalized, then the job incumbent has a minimum amount of discretion over what is to be done, when it is to be done, and how he or she should do it.
(1) Employees can be expected always to handle the same input in exactly the same way, resulting in a consistent and uniform output.
(2) There are explicit job descriptions, lots of organizational rules, and clearly defined procedures covering work processes in organizations that have a high degree of formalization.
b) Where formalization is low, job behaviors are relatively nonprogrammed and employees have a great deal of freedom to exercise discretion in their work.
c) Standardization not only eliminates the possibility of employees' engaging in alternative behaviors, but it removes the need for employees even to consider alternatives.
2. The degree of formalization can vary widely among organizations and within organizations.

II. COMMON ORGANIZATIONAL DESIGNS
   A. Three Common Organizational Designs are simple structure, bureaucracy, and matrix. (ppt 15)

   B. The Simple Structure (ppt 16)
      1. The simple structure is characterized most by what it is not rather than what it is.
         a) Not elaborate.
         b) Low degree of departmentalization.
         c) Wide spans of control.
         d) Little formalization.
      2. The simple structure is a "flat" organization; it usually has only two or three vertical levels, a loose body of employees, and one individual in whom the decision-making authority is centralized.
         a) It's most widely practiced in small businesses in which the manager and the owner are one and the same.
         b) Preferred in time of temporary crisis because it centralizes control.
      3. Strengths
         a) It is simple.
         b) It is fast, flexible, inexpensive to maintain, and accountability is clear.
      4. Weakness
         a) It is difficult to maintain in anything other than small organizations.
         b) As size increases, decision making typically becomes slower.
         c) It's risky—everything depends on one person.

   C. The Bureaucracy (ppt 17-18)
      1. Standardization—the key that underlies all bureaucracies.
      2. The bureaucracy is characterized by:
         a) Highly routine operating tasks achieved through specialization.
         b) Very formalized rules and regulations.
         c) Tasks that are grouped into functional departments.
         d) Centralized authority.
         e) Narrow spans of control.
         f) Decision making that follows the chain of command.
      3. Strengths
         a) Primary strength—the ability to perform standardized activities efficiently.
         b) Bureaucracies can get by nicely with less talented and, hence, less costly— middle- and lower-level managers.
         c) The pervasiveness of rules and regulations substitutes for managerial discretion.
      4. Weaknesses
         a) Specialization creates sub-unit conflicts. Functional unit goals can override the overall goals of the organization.
         b) Having to deal with people who work in these organizations: obsessive concern with following the rules.
      5. The peak of bureaucracy's popularity was probably in the 1950s and 1960s.
         a) The majority of large organizations still take on basic bureaucratic characteristics, particularly specialization and high formalization.
         b) However, spans of control have generally been widened, authority has become more decentralized, and functional departments have been supplemented with an increased use of teams.

          c)   Another trend is toward breaking bureaucracies up into smaller, though fully functioning, minibureaucracies.

   D. The Matrix Structure (ppt 19)
      1. Used in advertising agencies, aerospace firms, research and development laboratories, construction companies, hospitals, and so on.
      2. The matrix combines two forms of departmentalization—functional and product.
      3. The strength of functional departmentalization is that it puts like specialists together.
          a) Its weakness is that it is difficult to coordinate the specialists' tasks so that their diverse projects are completed on time and within budget.
      4. Product departmentalization, on the other hand, has exactly the opposite strengths and weaknesses.
          a) It facilitates coordination of specialists so that they can meet deadlines and budget targets, and further, it provides clear responsibility for all activities related to a product.
          b) But activities and costs are duplicated.
      5. The most obvious structural characteristic of the matrix is that it breaks the unity-of-command concept.
          a) Exhibit 13-4 shows the matrix form as used in a college of business administration. (ppt 20)
      6. Strengths
          a) The ability to facilitate coordination among multiple complex and interdependent activities.
             (1) As an organization gets larger, its information-processing capacity can become overloaded.
             (2) The direct and frequent contact between different specialties in the matrix can make for better communication and more flexibility.
          b) The matrix reduces bureaupathologies. The dual lines of authority reduce tendencies of departmental members to become so busy protecting their little worlds that the organization's overall goals become secondary.
          c) It facilitates the efficient allocation of specialists.
          d) The matrix achieves the advantages of economies of scale by providing the organization with both the best resources and an effective way of ensuring their efficient deployment.
      7. Disadvantages
          a) It creates confusion.
          b) It has propensity to foster power struggles.
          c) It places stress on individuals.
             (1) When you dispense with the unity-of-command concept, ambiguity is significantly increased, and ambiguity often leads to conflict.

III. NEW OPTIONS
   A. Three Structural Designs—team structure, the virtual organization, and the boundaryless organization. (ppt 21)

   B. The Team Structure
      1. An organization that uses teams as its central coordination device has a team structure.

2. The primary characteristics of the team structure are that it breaks down departmental barriers and decentralizes decision making to the level of the work team.
3. In smaller companies the team structure can define the entire organization.
4. More often the team structure complements what is typically a bureaucracy.

C. The Virtual Organization
1. Why own when you can rent? That's the essence of the virtual organization—a small, core organization that outsources major business functions. In structural terms the virtual organization is highly centralized, with little or no departmentalization.
2. This is a quest for maximum flexibility. These "virtual" organizations have created networks of relationships that allow them to contract out manufacturing, distribution, marketing, or any other business function that management feels can be done better or cheaper by others.
3. The virtual organization stands in sharp contrast to the typical bureaucracy.
4. Exhibit 13-5 shows a virtual organization.
    a) The core of the organization is a small group of executives, overseeing in-house activities and coordinating relationships with the other external organizations.
5. The major advantage to the virtual organization is its flexibility.
6. The primary drawback to this structure is that it reduces management's control over key parts of its business.

D. The Boundaryless Organization
1. Former General Electric chairman, Jack Welch, coined the term *boundaryless organization* to describe what he wanted GE to become.
    a) The boundaryless organization seeks to eliminate the chain of command, have limitless spans of control, and replace departments with empowered teams.
2. By removing vertical boundaries, management flattens the hierarchy.
    a) Status and rank are minimized.
    b) And the organization looks more like a silo than a pyramid.
    c) Cross-hierarchical teams, participative decision-making practices, and the use of 360-degree performance appraisals are examples of what GE is doing to break down vertical boundaries.
3. Functional departments create horizontal boundaries.
    a) Reduce these barriers with cross-functional teams and organize activities around processes.
    b) Cut through horizontal barriers using lateral transfers and rotate people into and out of different functional areas. This approach turns specialists into generalists.
4. When fully operational, the boundaryless organization also breaks down barriers to external constituencies and barriers created by geography.
5. Globalization, strategic alliances, customer-organization linkages, and telecommuting are all examples of practices that reduce external boundaries.
6. The one common technological thread that makes the boundaryless organization possible is networked computers.
    a) They allow people to communicate across intraorganizational and interorganizational boundaries.

IV. WHY DO STRUCTURES DIFFER?

A. See Exhibit 13-6. (ppt 22)
    1. There are two extreme models of organization structure.
        a) Mechanistic—generally synonymous with the bureaucracy in that it has extensive departmentalization, high formalization, a limited information network (mostly downward communication), and little participation by low-level members in decision making.
        b) Organic—looks like a boundaryless organization. Flat, uses cross-hierarchical and cross-functional teams, has low formalization, possesses a comprehensive information network, involves high participation in decision making.

B. Strategy (ppt 23)
    1. An organization's structure is a means to help management achieve its objectives.
    2. Strategy and structure should be closely linked—structure should follow strategy.
    3. Strategy frameworks focus on three strategy dimensions—innovation, cost minimization, and imitation.
        a) An innovation strategy does not mean a strategy merely for simple or cosmetic changes from previous offerings, but rather one for meaningful and unique innovations.
        b) An organization that is pursuing a cost-minimization strategy tightly controls costs, refrains from incurring unnecessary innovation or marketing expenses, and cuts prices in selling a basic product.
        c) Organizations following an imitation strategy try to capitalize on the best of both of the previous strategies.
            (1) They seek to minimize risk and maximize opportunity for profit. Their strategy is to move into new products or new markets only after viability has been proved by innovators.
            (2) They take the successful ideas of innovators and copy them.
    4. Linking strategy and structure.
        a) Innovators need the flexibility of the organic structure.
        b) Cost minimizers seek the efficiency and stability of the mechanistic structure.
        c) Imitators combine the two structures. They use a mechanistic structure in order to maintain tight controls and low costs in their current activities, and at the same time they create organic subunits in which to pursue new undertakings.

C. Organization Size (ppt 24)
    1. An organization's size significantly affects its structure.
        a) Large organizations—those typically employing 2,000 or more tend to have more specialization, more departmentalization, more vertical levels, and more rules and regulations than do small organizations.
        b) But the relationship isn't linear.
        c) Size affects structure at a decreasing rate.

D. Technology
    1. The term *technology* refers to how an organization transfers its inputs into outputs.
    2. Every organization has at least one technology for converting financial, human, and physical resources into products or services.

3. The bottom line on numerous studies on the technology-structure relationship.
   a) The common theme that differentiates technologies is their degree of routineness.
   b) Technologies tend toward either routine or nonroutine activities.
      (1) The former is characterized by automated and standardized operations.
      (2) Nonroutine activities are customized. They include such varied operations as furniture restoring, custom shoe making, and genetic research.
4. The relationship between technology and structure.
   a) Routine tasks are associated with taller and more departmentalized structures.
5. The relationship between technology and formalization, however, is stronger.
   a) Studies consistently show routineness to be associated with the presence of rule manuals, job descriptions, and other formalized documentation.

E. Environmental Uncertainty
   1. An organization's environment is composed of those institutions or forces that are outside the organization and potentially affect the organization's performance.
   2. The environment is considered a key determinant of structure.
   3. An organization's structure is affected by its environment because of environmental uncertainty.
   4. Relationship of environmental uncertainty to different structural arrangements.
      a) The more dynamic and uncertain the environment, the greater the need for flexibility.
      b) Organic structure will lead to higher organizational effectiveness.
      c) Conversely, in stable and predictable environments, the mechanistic form will be the structure of choice.

V. ORGANIZATION STRUCTURE AND EMPLOYEE BEHAVIOR
   A. Affects of Structure on Behavior (ppt 25)
      1. The conclusion of a review of the evidence linking organization structures to employee performance and satisfaction shows that you can't generalize.
         a) Not everyone prefers the freedom and flexibility of organic structures.
         b) Some people are most productive and satisfied with mechanistic structures.
      2. The evidence generally indicates that work specialization contributes to higher employee productivity but at the price of reduced job satisfaction.
      3. Work specialization is not an unending source of higher productivity.
         a) Problems start to surface, and productivity begins to suffer, when the human diseconomies of doing repetitive and narrow tasks overtake the economies of specialization.
      4. Some individuals want work that makes minimal intellectual demands and provides the security of routine. For these people, high work specialization is a source of job satisfaction.

   B. Span of Control
      1. There is no evidence to support a relationship between span of control and employee performance.

2. It is intuitively attractive to argue that wide spans lead to higher employee performance because they provide more distant supervision and more opportunity for personal initiative, but the research fails to support this notion.

3. It is impossible to state that any particular span of control is best for producing high performance or high satisfaction among subordinates due to individual differences.

C. Centralization

1. There is strong evidence linking centralization and job satisfaction.
   a) The less centralization, the greater amount of participative decision making.
   b) Evidence suggests that participative decision making is positively related to job satisfaction.
   c) But, again, individual differences surface.

2. The decentralization-satisfaction relationship is strongest with employees who have low self-esteem.

3. To maximize employee performance and satisfaction, take individual differences into account.

VI. IMPLICATIONS FOR MANAGERS

1. An organization's internal structure contributes to explaining and predicting employee behavior. The structural relationships in which people work have an important bearing on their attitudes and behavior.

2. To the degree that an organization's structure reduces ambiguity for employees and clarifies such concerns as "What am I supposed to do?" "How am I supposed to do it?" "To whom do I report?" and "To whom do I go to if I have a problem?" it shapes their attitudes and facilitates and motivates them to higher levels of performance.

3. Of course, structure also constrains employees to the extent that it limits and controls what they do. Organizations structured around high levels of formalization and specialization, the chain of command, etc., give employees little autonomy. In contrast, organizations that are structured around limited specialization, low formalization, wide spans of control, and the like provide employees greater freedom and, thus, will be characterized by greater behavioral diversity.

SUMMARY (ppt 26-27)

1. An organization structure defines how job tasks are formally divided, grouped, and coordinated and is defined itself by six key elements: work specialization, departmentalization, chain of command, span of control, centralization and decentralization, and formalization.

2. The simple structure is characterized most by what it is not rather than what it is: not elaborate, low degree of departmentalization, wide spans of control, and little formalization. The simple structure is a "flat" organization; it usually has only two or three vertical levels, a loose body of employees, and one individual in whom the decision-making authority is centralized.

3. The bureaucracy is marked by standardization. It is also characterized by highly routine operating tasks achieved through specialization, very formalized rules and regulations, tasks that are grouped into functional departments, centralized authority, narrow spans of control, and so on.

4. The matrix combines two forms of departmentalization—functional and product. Used in advertising agencies, aerospace firms, research and development laboratories, construction companies, hospitals, etc.

5. Why own when you can rent? That's the essence of the virtual organization—a small, core organization that outsources major business functions. In structural terms,, the virtual organization is highly centralized, with little or no departmentalization.

6. The boundaryless organization seeks to eliminate the chain of command, have limitless spans of control, and replace departments with empowered teams. By removing vertical boundaries, management flattens the hierarchy. When fully operational, the boundaryless organization also breaks down barriers to external constituencies and barriers created by geography. Globalization, strategic alliances, customer-organization linkages, and telecommuting are all examples of practices that reduce external boundaries.

7. There are two very different models of organization structure. Mechanistic—generally synonymous with the bureaucracy in that it has extensive departmentalization, high formalization, a limited information network (mostly downward communication), and little participation by low-level members in decision making. Organic—looks like a boundaryless organization. It is flat, uses cross-hierarchical and cross-functional teams, has low formalization, possesses a comprehensive information network, involves high participation in decision making.

8. An organization's structure is a means to help management achieve its objectives. Strategy and structure should be closely linked—structure should follow strategy. Strategy frameworks focus on three strategy dimensions—innovation, cost minimization, and imitation and the structural design that works best with each?

9. The conclusion of a review of the evidence linking organization structures to employee performance and satisfaction shows that you can't generalize. The evidence generally indicates that work specialization contributes to higher employee productivity but at the price of reduced job satisfaction. Work specialization is not an unending source of higher productivity. Some individuals want work that makes minimal intellectual demands and provides the security of routine. For these people, high work specialization is a source of job satisfaction.

DISCUSSION QUESTIONS

1. Identify the six key elements that define an organization's structure.
    Answer - An organization structure defines how job tasks are formally divided, grouped, and coordinated. Six key elements—work specialization, departmentalization, chain of command, span of control, centralization and decentralization, and formalization. The term *work specialization,* or division of labor describes the degree to which tasks in the organization are subdivided into separate jobs. Departmentalization is the grouping of jobs together so those common tasks can be coordinated. The chain of command is an unbroken line of authority that extends from the top of the organization to the lowest echelon and clarifies who reports to whom. Span of control. All things being equal, the wider or larger the span, the more efficient the organization. Wider spans are more efficient in terms of cost. But at some point wider spans reduce effectiveness. Narrow spans of control of five or six employees permit a manager to maintain close control. The term *centralization* refers to the degree to which decision making is concentrated at a single point in the organization. In a decentralized organization, action can be taken more quickly to solve problems, more people provide input into decisions, and employees are less likely to feel alienated from those who make the decisions that affect their work lives. Formalization refers to the degree to which jobs within the organization are standardized.

2. Identify the five most common ways to departmentalize an organization, and give a reason why you would select each particular method.
   Answer - One of the most popular ways to group activities is by functions performed. A manufacturing manager might organize his or her plant this way in order to obtain efficiencies from putting like specialists together and seek economies of scale. Organizations can also departmentalize by the product the organization produces. The major advantage of this type of groups is increased accountability for product performance. A third way to departmentalize is on the basis of geography or territory. This form of departmentalization can be valuable if an organization's customers are scattered over a large geographical area. Process departmentalization is grouping the specialists in one specific phase in the production of the product together. Because each process requires different skills, this method offers a basis for the homogeneous categorization of activities. The final category for departmentalization is to use the particular type of customer the organization seeks to reach. The assumption underlying this method is that customers in each department have a common set of problems and needs that can best be met by having specialists for each.

3. What are the implications for an organization that is departmentalized wrong? For example, what happens if you are grouped by function, but should be grouped by customer type?
   Answer- The key is that the organization needs to be structured based upon the design that is the most efficient. To illustrate this point, discuss the chaos that would follow if a restaurant happened to choose departmentalization by product type. This would result in multiple wait staff waiting on each table, and general inefficiencies. This example illustrates how important this concept is.

4. Why are the concepts of chain of command, authority, and unity of command substantially less relevant today than in previous time periods?
   Answer - The concepts of chain of command, authority, and unit of command have substantially less relevance today because of advancements in computer technology, the trend toward empowering operating employees to make decisions that previously were reserved for management, the popularity of self-managed and cross-functional teams and the creation of new structural designs that include multiple bosses.

5. What characterizes a simple organizational structure? What are its strengths and weaknesses?
   Answer - The simple structure is characterized most by what it is not rather than what it is. The simple structure is a "flat" organization; it usually has only two or three vertical levels, a loose body of employees, and one individual in whom the decision-making authority is centralized. It is most widely practiced in small businesses in which the manager and the owner are one and the same. Preferred in time of temporary crisis because it centralizes control. Its strengths—simplicity, speed, flexible, inexpensive to maintain, and accountability are clear. Its weakness is that it is difficult to maintain in anything other than small organizations. As size increases, decision making typically becomes slower. It's risky—everything depends on one person.

6. Explain the characteristics of a bureaucracy.
   Answer - The bureaucracy is characterized by: highly routine operating tasks achieved through specialization, very formalized rules and regulations, tasks that are grouped into functional departments, centralized authority, narrow spans of control, and decision making that follows the chain of command. Its primary strength—the ability to perform standardized activities efficiently. Bureaucracies can get by nicely with less talented and, hence, less costly—middle- and lower-level managers. The pervasiveness of rules and regulations substitutes for managerial discretion. Its weaknesses—it creates subunit conflicts, functional

unit goals can override the overall goals of the organization, and having to deal with people who work in these organizations with an obsessive concern with following the rules.

7. Describe a matrix organization.
    Answer - The matrix structure is used in advertising agencies, aerospace firms, research and development laboratories, construction companies, hospitals, and so on. It combines two forms of departmentalization—functional and product. The strength of functional departmentalization—putting like specialists together. Weaknesses—it is difficult to coordinate the specialists' tasks so that their diverse projects are completed on time and within budget. Product departmentalization, on the other hand, has exactly the opposite strengths and weaknesses.

8. Why would a company decide to use a "virtual" organizational structure?
    Answer - The essence of the virtual organization—a small, core organization that outsources major business functions. In structural terms the virtual organization is highly centralized, with little or no departmentalization. This is a quest for maximum flexibility. These "virtual" organizations have created networks of relationships that allow them to contract out manufacturing, distribution, marketing, or any other business function that management feels can be done better or cheaper by others. The major advantage to the virtual organization is its flexibility. The primary drawback to this structure is that it reduces management's control over key parts of its business.

9. Why would managers want to create boundaryless organizations?
    Answer - The boundaryless organization seeks to eliminate the chain of command, have limitless spans of control, and replace departments with empowered teams. By removing vertical boundaries, management flattens the hierarchy. Status and rank are minimized. And the organization looks more like a silo than a pyramid. Cross-hierarchical teams, participative decision-making practices, and the use of 360-degree performance appraisals are examples of what GE is doing to break down vertical boundaries. When fully operational, the boundaryless organization also breaks down barriers to external constituencies and barriers created by geography. The one common technological thread that makes the boundaryless organization possible is a networked computer. They allow people to communicate across intraorganizational and interorganizational boundaries.

10. Why do organizational structures differ?
    Answer - There are several key elements that shape organizational structure. Strategy—an organization's structure is a means to help management achieve its objectives. Strategy and structure should be closely linked—structure should follow strategy. Strategy frameworks focus on three strategy dimensions—innovation, cost minimization, and imitation and the structural design that works best with each. Size—Organization's size significantly affects its structure. Large organizations—those typically employing 2,000 or more tend to have more specialization, more departmentalization, more vertical levels, and more rules and regulations than do small organizations. Size affects structure at a decreasing rate. Technology—The term *technology* refers to how an organization transfers its inputs into outputs. Every organization has at least one technology for converting financial, human, and physical resources into products or services. Environmental uncertainty—An organization's environment is composed of those institutions or forces that are outside the organization and potentially affect the organization's performance. The environment is considered a key determinant of structure.

11. Of what behavioral implications of different organization structures should managers be aware?

Answer - The conclusion of a review of the evidence linking organization structures to employee performance and satisfaction shows that you can't generalize. Not everyone prefers the freedom and flexibility of organic structures. Some people are most productive and satisfied with mechanistic structures. The evidence generally indicates that work specialization contributes to higher employee productivity but at the price of reduced job satisfaction. Work specialization is not an unending source of higher productivity. Problems start to surface, and productivity begins to suffer, when the human diseconomies of doing repetitive and narrow tasks overtakes the economies of specialization. Some individuals want work that makes minimal intellectual demands and provides the security of routine. For these people, high work specialization is a source of job satisfaction. There is no evidence to support a relationship between span of control and employee performance. It is impossible to state that any particular span of control is best for producing high performance or high satisfaction among subordinates due to individual differences. There is strong evidence linking centralization and job satisfaction. The less centralization, the greater amount of participative decision making. Evidence suggests that participative decision making is positively related to job satisfaction.

EXERCISES
A.　　University Structure

Students will learn how to analyze organizational structure by examining the structure of their current college or university. [If you can find a local business through the Chamber of Commerce or Kiwanis Club, and soon, consider substituting them for the university.]

1. Divide the class into groups of three to five students, six groups in total.
2. As a class, create a form for analysis of your selected organization(s).
   - Use the elements and their corresponding questions as listed on page 179, Figure 13-1, to create the form.
   - Use a scale of 1 (low) to 5 (high) for each category, i.e., 1- low work specialization, 5 - high departmentalization, and so on.
   - Leave space for written comments explaining the rating and giving details of the structural element.
3. If you are analyzing a large organization, give each team one structural element to study.
4. If you are analyzing a small organization, have each team look at the entire organization.
5. Each team should prepare to report orally or in writing on their findings.
   - If written reports are used, students should give a summary to the class upon submission of their reports.
6. The reports should address:
   - How is the organization currently structured?
   - What type of organizational structure is it—organic/mechanistic, simple, bureaucratic, matrix?
   - Could this organization benefit from a new organizational structure—virtual, team, or boundaryless? How would it benefit?
7. As a class, discuss the each group's findings and come to a consensus on the restructuring action, if any, needed to be taken by the organization(s).

B.　　Brick and Mortar vs. Dot.com Structures

Today's retail world is becoming increasingly on-line in terms of consumer buying behavior and habits. In looking at organizational structure, have students research organizations and identify their structures, using the criteria from Exhibit 13-1, page 179. However, assign some groups the traditional "brick and mortar" type of organization, and other groups the dot.com type of organization. Some companies even have both that would make a "tidy" type of comparative analysis. For instance, Barnes and Noble vs. Barnes and Noble.com could be a comparison. Or, compare Talbots to Coldwater Creek.com for women's apparel. Have the students draw an organizational chart, if possible from their research.

C.   Mom and Pop Compared to Conglomerate

Choose a local, well-known, small organization, i.e., the Mom and Pop type of organization, with which most students are familiar. Then, choose a large, corporate type organization in the same industry. Assign students to compare and contrast the organizational structure of these two organizations, and provide a rationale for why each type of organization utilizes its particular style, and why the style of the other organization would not "work."

Examples would include the local restaurant to McDonald's, a local motel or hotel to a Marriott, a local entertainment venue (the skating rink) to Disneyland, and so on.

This comparison could be assigned as either a writing assignment, or it could take place in class as a small group or whole class discussion.

Analyzing Your Organization

Have students discuss with the top managers in their organization the concept of restructuring. When do they make the decision to restructure? In general, restructurings occur as organizations grow, but there are other variables also. Have them discuss how the past changes in structure impacted the people. You might also discuss plans to restructure in the future, and how they determine when to do this, and the scope of the project.

After the interview, have the students relate their notes to the six key elements. Did any one element stand out? As a class, were there patterns with various types of organizations?

CHAPTER 14 - ORGANIZATIONAL CULTURE

CHAPTER OBJECTIVES
After reading this chapter, students should be able to:
1. Define the common characteristics making up organizational culture.
2. Contrast strong and weak cultures.
3. Identify the functional and dysfunctional effects of organizational culture on people.
4. List the factors that maintain an organization's culture.
5. Clarify how culture is transmitted to employees.
6. Characterize a customer-responsive culture.
7. Describe spirituality and characteristics of a spiritual culture.
8. Contrast organizational culture with national culture.
9. Explain the paradox of diversity.

LECTURE OUTLINE
I. DEFINING ORGANIZATIONAL CULTURE
   A. Organizational Culture
      1. Organizational culture refers to a system of shared meaning held by members that distinguishes the organization from other organizations. (ppt 4)
      2. This system of shared meaning is, on closer examination, a set of key characteristics that the organization values.
      3. Seven primary characteristics are: (ppt 5)
         a) Innovation and risk taking. The degree to which employees are encouraged to be innovative and take risks.
         b) Attention to detail. The degree to which employees are expected to exhibit precision, analysis, and attention to detail.
         c) Outcome orientation. The degree to which management focuses on results or outcomes rather than on the techniques and processes used to achieve those outcomes.
         d) People orientation. The degree to which management decisions take into consideration the effect of outcomes on people within the organization.
         e) Team orientation. The degree to which work activities are organized around teams rather than individuals.
         f) Aggressiveness. The degree to which people are aggressive and competitive rather than easy going.
         g) Stability. The degree to which organizational activities emphasize maintaining the status quo in contrast to growth.
      4. Each of these characteristics exists on a continuum from low to high.
      5. Appraising the organization on these characteristics gives a composite picture of the organization's culture.

   B. Culture Is a Descriptive Term
      1. Organizational culture is concerned with how employees perceive the seven characteristics, not whether they like them.
      2. This point differentiates the concept of organizational culture from that of job satisfaction.
      3. Research on organizational culture has sought to measure how employees see their organization. Research on job satisfaction seeks to measure affective responses to the work environment. It is concerned with how employees feel

about the organization's expectations, reward practices, methods for handling conflict, and the like.
4. Organizational culture is descriptive, whereas job satisfaction is evaluative.

C. Do Organizations Have Uniform Cultures? (ppt 7-8)
   1. Organizational culture represents a common perception held by the organization's members.
   2. There can be subcultures within any given culture.
   3. Most large organizations have a dominant culture and numerous sets of subcultures.
      a) A dominant culture expresses the core values that are shared by a majority of the organization's members.
         (1) It is this macro view of culture that gives an organization its distinct personality.
      b) Subcultures tend to develop in large organizations to reflect common problems, situations, or experiences that members face.
         (1) These subcultures are likely to be defined by department designations and geographical separation.
   4. If organizations had no dominant culture and were composed only of numerous subcultures, the value of organizational culture as an independent variable would be significantly lessened.

D. Strong Vs. Weak Cultures (ppt 9)
   1. It has become increasingly popular to differentiate between strong and weak cultures.
   2. The argument is that strong cultures have a greater impact on employee behavior and are more directly related to reduced turnover.
   3. A strong culture is characterized by the organization's core values being both intensely held and widely shared.
      a) The more members who accept the core values and the greater their commitment to those values, the stronger the culture is.
      b) A strong culture will have a greater influence on the behavior.
   4. One specific result of a strong culture should be low employee turnover.
      a) A strong culture demonstrates high agreement among members about what the organization stands for.

II. WHAT DOES CULTURE DO?
   A. Culture's Functions (ppt 10)
      1. It has a boundary-defining role; that is, it creates distinctions between one organization and others.
      2. It conveys a sense of identity for organization members.
      3. Culture facilitates the generation of commitment to something larger than one's individual self-interest.
      4. It enhances social system stability.
      5. Culture is the social glue that helps hold the organization together by providing appropriate standards for what employees should say and do.
      6. Finally, culture serves as a sense-making and control mechanism that guides and shapes the attitudes and behavior of employees.
         a) Culture defines the rules of the game.
      7. Who is offered a job, who is appraised as a high performer, and who gets a promotion are strongly influenced by the individual-organization fit, that is,

whether the applicant's or employee's attitudes and behavior are compatible with the culture.

B. Culture as a Liability (ppt 11)
   1. Culture enhances organizational commitment and increases the consistency of employee behavior.
   2. From an employee's standpoint, culture is valuable because it reduces ambiguity.
   3. Culture is a liability when the shared values do not agree with those that will further the organization's effectiveness.
      a) This is most likely to occur when the organization's environment is dynamic.
      b) When the environment is undergoing rapid change, the organization's entrenched culture may no longer be appropriate.
      c) Consistency of behavior is an asset to an organization in a stable environment.

III. CREATING AND SUSTAINING CULTURE
A. How a Culture Begins (ppt 12)
   1. An organization's current customs, traditions, and general way of doing things are largely due to what it has done before and the degree of success it had with those endeavors.
      a) The ultimate source of an organization's culture is its founders.
   2. The founders of an organization.
      a) They have a vision of what the organization should be.
      b) They are unconstrained by previous customs for doing things or ideologies.
      c) The small size of any new organization further facilitates the founders' imposition of their vision on all organizational members.
      d) The organization's culture results from the interaction between the founders' biases and assumptions and what the original members learn subsequently from their own experiences.
   3. Microsoft's culture is largely a reflection of co-founder and current CEO, Bill Gates.
      a) Gates himself is aggressive, competitive, and highly disciplined.
      b) Those are the same adjectives often used to describe the software giant he heads.
   4. Other contemporary examples—Bill Gates at Microsoft, Ingvar Kamrad iat IKEA, Herb Kelleher at Southwest Airlines, Fred Smith at Federal Express, Mary Kay at Mary Kay Cosmetics, and Richard Branson at the Virgin Group.

B. Keeping a Culture Alive (ppt 13)
   1. Once a culture is in place, practices within the organization act to maintain it by exposing employees to a set of similar experiences.
      a) An organization's human resource practices reinforce its culture.
   2. Three forces play a particularly important part in sustaining a culture—selection practices, the actions of top management, and socialization methods.
   3. Selection
      a) The explicit goal of the selection process is to identify and hire individuals who have the knowledge, skills, and abilities to perform the jobs within the organization successfully.
      b) With multiple candidates, the final decision about who is hired will be significantly influenced by the decision maker's judgment of how well the candidates will fit into the organization.

c)   This results in the hiring of people who have common values.

d)   The selection process also gives applicants information about the organization.

e)   Candidates who perceive a conflict between their values and those of the organization can self-select themselves out of the applicant pool.

f)   Example—W. R. Gore & Association, maker of Gore-Tex fabric.

4.   Top Management

a)   The actions of top management have a major impact on an organization's culture.

b)   What they say and how they behave establish norms that filter down through the organization.

    (a)   Example—Robert Keirlin, the CEO of Fastenal Co. He takes a small salary and lives a relatively frugal lifestyle, demonstrating that organizations should not waste things.

5.   Socialization

a)   No matter how good a job the organization does in recruiting and selection, new employees are not fully indoctrinated in the organization's culture.

b)   New employees are potentially the most likely to disturb the beliefs and customs that are in place.

c)   The organization will, therefore, want to help new employees adapt to its culture. This adaptation process is called socialization.

d)   Example—Marine boot camp.

e)   The most critical socialization stage is at the time of entry into the organization.

    (1)   Employees who fail to learn the essential or pivotal role behaviors risk being labeled nonconformists or rebels and, ultimately, being expelled.

6.   Socialization's three stages—pre-arrival, encounter, and metamorphosis.

a)   The first stage encompasses all the learning that occurs before a new member joins the organization.

b)   In the second stage, the new employee sees what the organization is really like and confronts the likelihood that expectations and reality may diverge.

c)   In the third stage, the relatively long-lasting changes take place. The new employee masters the skills required for his or her job, successfully performs his or her new roles, and makes the adjustments to his or her work group's values and norms.

7.   Exhibit 14-1 depicts this process. (ppt 14)

a)   The pre-arrival stage occurs before the employee joins the organization; he or she arrives with an established set of values, attitudes, and expectations.

    (1)   These cover both the work to be done and the organization from prior socialization in training and in school.

    (2)   The selection process is part of pre-arrival, organizations use it to inform prospective employees about the organization as a whole and to ensure the inclusion of the right type.

b)   Entry into the organization begins the encounter stage.

    (1)   Now the individuals confront the possible dichotomy between their expectations—about their job, co-workers, boss, and the organization in general and reality.

    (2)   If expectations were accurate, the encounter stage is a reaffirmation.

             (3) Often this is not the case. Where expectations and reality differ, new employees must undergo socialization that will detach them from previous assumptions and replace them with an "acceptable" set.

             (4) At the extreme, new members may become totally disillusioned with the actualities of their job and resign.

      c) New members must work out any problems discovered during the encounter stage. They may have to go through changes, or the metamorphosis stage.

             (1) Exhibit 14-2 presents an organization's socialization options for fostering metamorphosis.

             (2) Metamorphosis and the entry socialization process are complete when new members have become comfortable with the organization and their job.

             (3) They have internalized the norms of the organization and their work group, and they understand and accept those norms.

             (4) New members feel accepted by their peers as trusted and valued individuals.

             (5) Exhibit 14-2 shows, successful metamorphosis should have a positive impact on the new employees' productivity and their commitment to the organization and reduce their propensity to leave the organization.

C. Summary: How Cultures Form

    1. Exhibit 14-3 summarizes how an organization's culture is established and sustained. (ppt 15)

      a) The original culture is derived from the founder's philosophy.

      b) This strongly influences the criteria used in hiring.

      c) The actions of the current top management set the general climate of what is acceptable behavior and what is not.

      d) Employee socialization depends on the degree of success achieved in matching new employees' values to those of the organization in the selection process and top management's preference for socialization methods.

IV. HOW EMPLOYEES LEARN CULTURE (ppt 16)

A. Stories

    1. Example—Henry Ford II was chairman of the Ford Motor Co.—remember "It's my name that's on the building." The message was clear: Henry Ford II ran the company.

    2. Example—Nordstrom refunding a customer's money for tires, a product the story didn't sell because, "but we do whatever we need to do to make the customer happy. I mean it when I say we have a no-questions-asked return policy." Nordstrom then picked up the telephone and called a friend in the auto parts business to see how much he could get for the tires.

    3. Stories such as these contain a narrative of events about the organization's founders, rule breaking, rags-to-riches successes, reductions in the workforce, relocation of employees, reactions to past mistakes, and organizational coping. These stories anchor the present in the past and provide explanations and legitimacy for current practices.

B. Rituals

    1. Rituals are repetitive sequences of activities that express and reinforce the key values of the organization, what goals are most important, which people are important and which are expendable.

2. Example—Wal-Mart's company chant.

C. Material Symbols
1. Example—The Alcoa headquarters is essentially made up of cubicles and meeting rooms.
    a) This conveys their values of openness, equality, creativity, and flexibility.
2. Messages can also be conveyed by material symbols bestowed on executives.
    a) Chauffeur-driven limousines and unlimited use of the corporate jet.
    b) Executives at other firms may get a Chevrolet (with no driver) and the plane seat is in the economy section of a commercial airliner.
3. Other examples of material symbols include the size of offices, their furnishings, executive perks, the use of employee lounges or on-site dining facilities, and so on.
4. These material symbols convey to employees who is important, the degree of egalitarianism desired by top management, and the kinds of behavior (for example, risk taking, conservative, authoritarian, participative, individualistic, social) that are appropriate.

D. Language
1. Many organizations and units within organizations use language as a way to identify members of a culture or subculture.
2. Example—Knight-Ridder Information, a California-based data redistributor: accession number (a number assigned each individual record in a data base); KWIC (a set of key-words-in-context); and relational operator (searching a data base for names or key terms in some order).
3. Organizations often develop unique terms to describe common business matters.
4. New employees are frequently overwhelmed with acronyms and jargon that, after six months on the job, have become fully part of their language.

V. MANAGING CULTURAL CHANGE
1. Because an organization's culture is made up of relatively stable characteristics, it's difficult to change. (ppt 17)
    a) It develops over many years and is rooted in deeply held values.
2. A number of forces maintain a given culture.
    a) Written statements about the organization's mission and philosophy.
    b) The design of physical spaces and buildings.
    c) The dominant leadership style.
    d) Historical selection criteria, past promotion practices, entrenched rituals.
    e) Popular stories about key people and events, etc.
3. Changing an organization's culture is difficult, it isn't impossible.
4. Conditions for effective cultural change.
    a) A dramatic crisis exists or is created. This is the shock that undermines the status quo and calls into question the relevance of the current culture.
        (1) A surprising financial setback, the loss of a major customer, or a dramatic technological breakthrough by a competitor.
        (2) Some executives purposely create a crisis in order to stimulate cultural change.
    b) Turnover in leadership. New top leadership, which can provide an alternative set of key values, is usually needed to make cultural change work.
        (1) A new CEO from outside the organization is more likely to introduce new cultural values.

(2) An outside CEO, in contrast to promoting someone from within the organization, also conveys a message to employees that change is in the wind.

    c) Young and small organizations. Cultural change is more likely to take if the organization is both young and small.

       (1) Cultures in younger organizations are less entrenched.

       (2) It's easier to communicate new values.

    d) Weak culture. The more widely held a culture is and the higher the agreement among members on its values, the more difficult it will be to change.

  5. Even when the above conditions are favorable, managers shouldn't look for immediate or dramatic shifts in their organization's culture. Cultural change is a lengthy process which should be measured in years rather than months.

VI. CREATING AN ETHICAL ORGANIZATIONAL CULTURE (ppt 18-19)

  A. The Nature of Cultural Influences an Organization's Ethical Climate

    1. An organizational culture most likely to shape high ethical standards is high in risk tolerance, low to moderate in aggressiveness, and focuses on means as well as outcomes.

    2. If the culture is strong and supports high ethical standards, it should have a very powerful and positive influence on employee behavior.

    3. Example—Johnson & Johnson has a strong culture that has long stressed corporate obligations to customers, employees, the community, and shareholders, in that order.

      a) Poisoned Tylenol case.

    4. Practices for creating a more ethical culture.

      a) Be a visible role model—Employees will look to top-management behavior as a benchmark for appropriate behavior.

      b) Communicate ethical expectations—An organizational code of ethics should state the organization's primary values and the ethical rules that employees are expected to follow.

      c) Provide ethical training—Use training sessions to reinforce the organization's standards of conduct, to clarify what practices are and are not permissible, and to address possible ethical dilemmas.

      d) Visibly reward ethical acts and punish unethical ones—Performance appraisals of managers should include a point-by-point evaluation of how their decisions measured against the organization's code of ethics.

      e) Provide protective mechanisms—The organization needs to provide formal mechanisms so that employees can discuss ethical dilemmas and report unethical behavior without fear of reprimand.

VII. CREATING A CUSTOMER-RESPONSIVE CULTURE (ppt 20-22)

  A. Most organizations are attempting to create a customer-responsive culture because they recognize the value of customer loyalty.

  B. Six Key Variables Shaping Customer-Responsive Cultures

    1. The selection of employees that are outgoing and friendly

    2. Low levels of formalization

    3. Widespread use of empowerment

    4. Employees with good listening skills

    5. High levels of role-clarity

    6. Employees who exhibit organizational citizenship behaviors.

C. Actions Management can take Based upon the Above Characteristics (ppt 23)
1. Selection- Hire people with the personality and attitudes consistent with a high service orientation.
2. Training and socialization- Training existing employees on improving product knowledge, active listening, patience, and displaying emotions.
3. Structural Design- Reduce the number of rules so employees can handle customer requests.
4. Empowerment- Give employees the discretion to make decisions about job-related activities.
5. Performance evaluation- Appraise employees based on how they behave or act.
6. Reward systems- Reward good customer service.

VIII. SPIRITUALITY AND ORGANIZATIONAL CULTURE
A. What Is Spirituality?
1. Recognizes that people have an inner life that nourishes and is nourished by meaningful work that takes place in the context of community. (ppt 24)
2. Organizations that promote a spiritual culture recognize that people have both a mind and spirit, seek to find meaning and purpose in their work, and desire to connect with other human being and be part of a community.

B. Why Spirituality Now?
1. The study of emotions improved our understanding of organizational behavior, an awareness of spirituality can help you to better understand employee behavior in the twentieth century.
2. See Exhibit 14-4 for reasons for the growing interest in Spirituality.

C. Characteristics of a Spiritual Organization (ppt 25-26)
1. Spiritual organizations are concerned with helping people develop and reach their full potential.
2. Characteristics found to be evident in spiritual organizations:
a) A strong sense of purpose
(1) Spiritual organizations build their cultures around a meaningful purpose.
(2) Five cultural characteristics that tend to be evident in spiritual organizations:
(a) Strong sense of purpose
(i) Spiritual organizations build their cultures around a meaningful purpose.
(b) Focus on individual development
(c) Trust and openness—spiritual organizations are characterized by mutual trust, honesty, and openness.
(d) Employee empowerment
(e) Toleration of employee expression—degree to which they allow people to be themselves.

D. Criticisms of Spirituality
1. Two issues:
a) First, the question is of legitimacy. Do organizations have the right to impose spiritual values on their employees?
b) Second is the question of economics. Are spirituality and profits compatible?

IX. ORGANIZATIONAL CULTURE VS. NATIONAL CULTURE
   1. National culture must be taken into account if accurate predictions are to be made about organizational behavior in different countries.
      a) But does national culture override an organization's culture?
   2. The research indicates that national culture has a greater impact on employees than does their organization's culture.
   3. This conclusion has to be qualified to reflect the self-selection that goes on in hiring.
      a) A British multinational corporation, for example, is less likely to be concerned with hiring the "typical Italian" for its Italian operations than in hiring an Italian who fits with the corporation's way of doing things.
      b) The employee selection process will be used by multinationals to find and hire job applicants who are a good fit with their organization's dominant culture even if such applicants are somewhat atypical citizens of their country.

X. ORGANIZATIONAL CULTURE AND THE PARADOX OF DIVERSITY
   A. A Contemporary Challenge for Managers. (ppt 27-28)
      1. Socializing new employees who, because of race, gender, ethnic, or other differences, are not like the majority of the organization's members creates what we call the paradox of diversity.
         a) Management wants new employees to accept the organization's core cultural values. But at the same time, management wants to openly acknowledge and demonstrate support for the differences that these employees bring to the workplace.
      2. Strong cultures put considerable pressure on employees to conform. They limit the range of values and styles that are acceptable.
      3. The dilemma is that organizations hire diverse individuals because of the alternative strengths these people bring to the workplace, yet these diverse behaviors and strengths are likely to diminish in strong cultures as people attempt to fit in.

XI. IMPLICATIONS FOR MANAGERS
   A. Culture has a strong influence on employee behavior. What can management do to design a culture that molds employees in the way management wants?

   B. When an organization is just being established, management has a great deal of influence.
      1) There are no established traditions. The organization is small.
      2) There are few, if any, subcultures.
      3) Everyone knows the founder and is directly touched by his or her vision.
      4) Management has the opportunity to create a culture that will best facilitate the achievement of the organization's goals.

   C. When the organization is well established, so, too, is its dominant culture.
      1) It becomes very resistant to change.
      2) Strong cultures are particularly resistant to change because employees become so committed to them.
      3) If a given culture needs to be changed there may be little management can do.

4) Under the most favorable conditions, cultural changes have to be measured in years, not weeks or months.
5) The "favorable conditions" are the existence of a dramatic crisis, turnover in the organization's top leadership, an organization that is both young and small, and a dominant culture that is weak.

SUMMARY (ppt 29-30)

1. Organizational culture refers to a system of shared meaning held by members that distinguishes the organization from other organizations. Organizational cultures have seven primary characteristics; innovation and risk taking, attention to detail, outcome orientation, people orientation, team orientation, aggressiveness, and stability. Organizational culture represents a common perception held by the organization's members.
2. It has become increasingly popular to differentiate between strong and weak cultures. A strong culture is characterized by the organization's core values being both intensely held and widely shared.
3. Organizational culture has a boundary-defining role; that is, it creates distinctions between one organization and others. It conveys a sense of identity for organization members.
4. Culture enhances organizational commitment and increases the consistency of employee behavior. Culture is a liability when the shared values do not agree with those that will further the organization's effectiveness.
5. An organization's current customs, traditions, and general way of doing things are largely due to what it has done before and the degree of success it had with those endeavors. The ultimate source of an organization's culture is its founders.
6. Once a culture is in place, practices within the organization act to maintain it by exposing employees to a set of similar experiences. Three forces play a particularly important part in sustaining a culture: selection practices, the actions of top management, and socialization methods.
7. Organizations transmit their cultures to their employees in several ways. Stories contain a narrative of events about the organization's founders, and so on, and they anchor the present in the past and provide explanations and legitimacy for current practices. Rituals are repetitive sequences of activities that express and reinforce the key values of the organization, what goals are most important, which people are important and which are expendable. The material symbols convey messages to new employees. Messages can also be conveyed by material symbols bestowed on executives. Many organizations and units within organizations use language as a way to identify members of a culture or subculture. Because an organization's culture is made up of relatively stable characteristics, it's difficult to change. It develops over many years and is rooted in deeply held values. Therefore certain conditions need to exist for there to be effective cultural change. A dramatic crisis exists or is created. A turnover in leadership.
8. An organizational culture most likely to shape high ethical standards is high in risk tolerance, low to moderate in aggressiveness, and focuses on means as well as outcomes. If the culture is strong and supports high ethical standards, it should have a very powerful and positive influence on employee behavior.
9. National culture—must be taken into account if accurate predictions are to be made about organizational behavior in different countries. The research indicates that national culture has a greater impact on employees than does their organization's culture.
10. Most organizations are recognizing the need to create a customer service oriented culture. They recognize the link between customer loyalty and long-term profitability.
11. Workplace spirituality is not about organized religious practices. It recognizes that people have an inner life that nourishes and is nourished by meaningful work that takes place in the context of community. See Exhibit 14-4 for reasons for the growing interest in spirituality.

12. Socializing of new employees who are not like the majority of the organization's members creates the paradox of diversity. Management wants new employees to accept the organization's core cultural values. But at the same time, management wants to openly acknowledge and demonstrate support for the differences that these employees bring to the workplace.

DISCUSSION QUESTIONS

1. What elements define an organization's culture?

   Answer - Organizational culture refers to a system of shared meaning held by members that distinguishes the organization from other organizations. There are seven primary characteristics. 1) Innovation and risk taking. The degree to which employees are encouraged to be innovative and take risks. 2) Attention to detail. The degree to which employees are expected to exhibit precision, analysis, and attention to detail. 3) Outcome orientation. The degree to which management focuses on results or outcomes rather than on the techniques and processes used to achieve those outcomes. 4) People orientation. The degree to which management decisions take into consideration the effect of outcomes on people within the organization. 5) Team orientation. The degree to which work activities are organized around teams rather than individuals. 6) Aggressiveness. The degree to which people are aggressive and competitive rather than easy going. 7) Stability. The degree to which organizational activities emphasize maintaining the status quo in contrast to growth.

2. How many cultures and what type of cultures can an organization have?

   Answer - Organizational culture represents a common perception held by the organization's members. There can be subcultures within any given culture. Most large organizations have a dominant culture and numerous sets of subcultures. A dominant culture expresses the core values that are shared by a majority of the organization's members. Subcultures tend to develop in large organizations to reflect common problems, situations, or experiences that members face. If organizations had no dominant culture and were composed only of numerous subcultures, the value of organizational culture as an independent variable would be significantly lessened.

   It has become increasingly popular to differentiate between strong and weak cultures. The argument is that strong cultures have a greater impact on employee behavior and are more directly related to reduced turnover. A strong culture is characterized by the organization's core values being both intensely held and widely shared. The more members who accept the core values and the greater their commitment to those values, the stronger the culture is. A strong culture demonstrates high agreement among members about what the organization stands for.

3. What value does an organization's culture bring to the organization? How can its culture hinder organizational effectiveness?

   Answer - Organizational culture has a boundary-defining role; that is, it creates distinctions between one organization and others. It conveys a sense of identity for organization members. Culture facilitates the generation of commitment to something larger than one's individual self-interest. Culture is the social glue that helps hold the organization together by providing appropriate standards for what employees should say and do. Finally, culture serves as a sense-making and control mechanism that guides and shapes the attitudes and behavior of employees.

   Culture is a liability when the shared values do not agree with those that will further the organization's effectiveness. This is most likely to occur when the organization's environment is dynamic. When the environment is undergoing rapid change, the organization's entrenched culture may no longer be appropriate.

4. What are the possible origins of an organization's culture?
    Answer - An organization's current customs, traditions, and general way of doing things are largely due to what it has done before and the degree of success it had with those endeavors. The ultimate source of an organization's culture is its founders. The organization's culture results from the interaction between the founders' biases and assumptions and what the original members learn subsequently from their own experiences.

5. When is organizational culture, especially a strong culture, a liability rather than an asset.
    Answer - Culture is a liability when the shared values do not agree with those that will further the organization's effectiveness. This situation is most likely to occur when the organization's environment is dynamic.

6. As the president of a medium-sized but growing company, you have become concerned that your existing organizational culture be maintained during the growth. What could you direct your managers to do that would help maintain the current culture?
    Answer - Once a culture is in place, practices within the organization act to maintain it by exposing employees to a set of similar experiences. An organization's human resource practices reinforce its culture. Three forces play a particularly important part in sustaining a culture—selection practices, the actions of top management, and socialization methods. The explicit goal of the selection process is to identify and hire individuals who have the knowledge, skills, and abilities to perform the jobs within the organization successfully. The actions of top management have a major impact on an organization's culture. What they say and how they behave establish norms that filter down through the organization. No matter how good a job the organization does in recruiting and selection, new employees are not fully indoctrinated in the organization's culture. The most critical socialization stage is at the time of entry into the organization. Socialization has three stages—pre-arrival, encounter, and metamorphosis. Exhibit 16-2 depicts this process.

7. What could you do to transmit your organizational culture to your new employees?
    Answer - Students can offer several tools but should address some of the following. Stories contain a narrative of events about the organization's founders, rule breaking, rags-to-riches successes, reductions in the workforce, relocation of employees, reactions to past mistakes, and organizational coping. These stories anchor the present in the past and provide explanations and legitimacy for current practices. Rituals are repetitive sequences of activities that express and reinforce the key values of the organization, what goals are most important, which people are important and which are expendable. Material symbols convey messages to new employees. Messages can also be conveyed by material symbols bestowed on executives. Many organizations and units within organizations use language as a way to identify members of a culture or subculture.

8. If a company wanted to reshape its culture what factors might hinder the change? What might assist the change?
    Answer - Because an organization's culture is made up of relatively stable characteristics, it's difficult to change. It develops over many years and is rooted in deeply held values. A number of forces maintain a given culture.
    - Written statements about the organization's mission and philosophy
    - The design of physical spaces and buildings
    - The dominant leadership style

- Historical selection criteria, past promotion practices, entrenched rituals
- Popular stories about key people and events, and so on.

Conditions for effective cultural change.

- A dramatic crisis exists or is created. This is the shock that undermines the status quo and calls into question the relevance of the current culture.
- A surprising financial setback, the loss of a major customer, or a dramatic technological breakthrough by a competitor.
- Turnover in leadership. New top leadership, which can provide an alternative set of key values, is usually needed to make cultural change work.
- Young and small organization. Cultural change is more likely to take if the organization is both young and small.
- Weak culture. The more widely held a culture is and the higher the agreement among members on its values, the more difficult it will be to change.

9. As the leader of your organization, what steps might you encourage that would foster an ethical climate?

Answer - An organizational culture most likely to shape high ethical standards is high in risk tolerance, low to moderate in aggressiveness, and focuses on means as well as outcomes. If the culture is strong and supports high ethical standards, it should have a very powerful and positive influence on employee behavior. There are a number of practices for creating a more ethical culture.

- Be a visible role model. Employees will look to top-management behavior as a benchmark for appropriate behavior.
- Communicate ethical expectations. An organizational code of ethics should state the organization's primary values and the ethical rules that employees are expected to follow.
- Provide ethical training. Use training sessions to reinforce the organization's standards of conduct, to clarify what practices are and are not permissible, and to address possible ethical dilemmas.
- Visibly reward ethical acts and punish unethical ones. Performance appraisals of managers should include a point-by-point evaluation of how their decisions measured against the organization's code of ethics.
- Provide protective mechanisms. The organization needs to provide formal mechanisms so that employees can discuss ethical dilemmas and report unethical behavior without fear of reprimand.

10. What steps can managers take to try and create more of a customer service oriented culture?

Answer- There are a number of actions that management can take, including selecting and training for customer service, having few rules combined with empowered employees, and having performance evaluations and reward systems that emphasize customer service.

11. Is spirituality in the workplace just another name for prayer at work? Provide reasons for growing the growing interest in spirituality.

Answer – Workplace spirituality recognizes that people have an inner life that nourishes and is nourished by meaningful work that takes place in the context of community. Organizations that promote a spiritual culture recognize the people have both a mind and a spirit, seeking to find meaning and purpose in their work, and desire to connect with other human beings and be part of a community. See Exhibit 16-5 for a listing of reasons for the growing interest in spirituality.

12. What is the relationship between organizational culture and national culture?
Answer - National culture must be taken into account if accurate predictions are to be made about organizational behavior in different countries. The research indicates that national culture has a greater impact on employees than does their organization's culture. This conclusion has to be qualified to reflect the self-selection that goes on in hiring.

13. In what way(s) does an organization's culture create a diversity paradox for managers?
Answer - Socializing new employees who, because of race, gender, ethnic, or other differences, are not like the majority of the organization's members. This creates what we call the paradox of diversity. Management wants new employees to accept the organization's core cultural values. But at the same time, management wants to openly acknowledge and demonstrate support for the differences that these employees bring to the workplace. The dilemma is that organizations hire diverse individuals because of the alternative strengths these people bring to the workplace, yet these diverse behaviors and strengths are likely to diminish in strong cultures as people attempt to fit in. Management's challenge in this paradox of diversity is to balance two conflicting goals.

EXERCISES
A.   What Does Our Culture Reveal About Us?
The purpose of this exercise is to increase students' awareness of organizational culture and enhance their ability to read the signs of organizational culture as they enter new organizations.
1.   This may be done individually or in pairs.
2.   Do in class. Create a list of fifteen signs that reveal an organization's culture.
   ▪   Refer students to the text or give a mini review lecture.
   ▪   Have students brainstorm a list of these signs.
   ▪   Create a common set of fifteen signs that will help students identify:
      •   the strength of the organizational culture
      •   norms and expectations
      •   what events, activities, or people sustain the existing culture
      •   key stories, rituals, material symbols, and language specific to an organizational culture
      •   the degree of ethicality of an organization's culture
3.   Outside of class students should pick an organization to examine—social group, the college or university, a workplace, and so on.
   ▪   Students are to evaluate that organization's culture in terms of the list of signs and draw a conclusion as to the nature of its culture.
4.   Students should report their findings and conclusions in class either in written or oral form. If oral, limit each presentation to ten minutes.
5.   Conclude with a general class discussion about organizational culture and how what they learned will help them in their job searches and careers and in choosing where to work.

B.   Customer Service Cultures

As a class, discuss both good and bad customer service encounters recently. You might want to do this in small groups first, then have the groups relate the best stories to the class. As they tell stories, try and make them diagnose the reasons for the encounters in the context of the elements that determine the degree to which a customer service culture exist. For example, a story about a clerk at a video store who charges me a late fee when my video was returned 5-minutes late may not have a choice due to a lack of empowerment or high levels of formalization. Make sure you discuss both good and bad service encounters.

C.   <u>Workplace Spirituality Quest</u>

In class have students develop a strong definition they are comfortable with for "workplace spirituality." Then "armed" with this definition, have students interview 5 full-time employees about their workplaces. Have the student rate each interviewee's workplace on a scale of 1-10, with 1 being no workplace spirituality, and 10 being the greatest amount of workplace spirituality. Then have students write a comparative analysis piece about the different interviewee organizations' level of workplace spirituality.

Tell the students to be prepared to share they written ideas to the class, and get "free" consulting.

Analyzing Your Organization

Have the students meet with some of the "old-timers" in their organization. Have them discuss the various stories that shaped the organization's culture throughout the years. You might ask them what the founder was like, and what his or her values and belief system were or are. Relate these findings to what the current organizational culture is. Is it the same? If not, what has changed over the years, and why? Relate this to the existing materials, symbols, or language that define the culture of the organization.

CHAPTER 15 – HUMAN RESOURCE POLICIES AND PRACTICES

CHAPTER OBJECTIVES
After reading this chapter, students should be able to:
1. Describe jobs for which interviews are effective selection devices.
2. List the advantages of performance-simulation tests over written tests.
3. Identify four types of employee training.
4. Contrast the organization's responsibilities today for career development with the employees responsibilities.
5. Identify the advantages of using behaviors rather than traits in appraising performance.
6. Explain the most popular performance appraisal criteria.
7. Identify who, in addition to the boss, can do performance evaluations.
8. Explain actions that can improve the performance appraisal process.

LECTURE OUTLINE
I.   EMPLOYEE SELECTION (ppt 4)
   A. The three most important selection devices are interviews, written tests, and performance simulation tests.

   B. Interviews
     1. Of all the selection devices that organizations use to differentiate job candidates, the interview continues to be the one most frequently used.
     2. It also seems to carry a great deal of weight; the results tend to have a disproportionate amount of influence on the selection decision.
     3. The unstructured interview—short in duration, casual, and made up of random questions—has been proven to be an ineffective selection device. (ppt 5)
     4. By having interviewers use a standardized set of questions, providing interviewers with a uniform method of recording information, and standardizing the rating of the applicant's qualifications, the variability in results across applicants is reduced and the validity of the interview is greatly enhanced.
     5. Evidence indicates that interviews are most valuable for assessing an applicant's intelligence, level of motivation, and interpersonal skills.

   C. Written Tests (ppt 6)
     1. Typical written tests assess intelligence, aptitude, ability, interests, and integrity.
     2. Tests in intellectual ability, spatial and mechanical ability, perceptual accuracy, and motor ability have shown to be moderately valid predictors.
     3. As ethical problems have increased in organizations, integrity tests have gained popularity.
       a) The evidence is impressive that these tests are powerful in predicting supervisory ratings of job performance and counterproductive behavior on the job.

   D. Performance Simulation Tests (ppt 7)
     1. The logic of performance simulation tests is what better way to find out if an applicant can do the job successfully.
     2. Performance simulation tests have increased in popularity during the past two decades.
     3. Two best-known performance simulation tests are:

        a) Work sampling—hands-on simulations of part or all of the job that must be performed
          (1) Work samples are widely used in the hiring of skills workers.
          (2) Studies consistently demonstrate that work samples yield validities superior to written aptitude and personality tests.
        b) Assessment centers—a more elaborate set of performance simulation tests, specifically designed to evaluate a candidate's managerial potential.
          (1) The evidence on the effectiveness of assessment centers is impressive.

II.   TRAINING AND DELELOPMENT PROGRAMS

A. Competent employees don't remain competent forever—skills deteriorate and become obsolete.

B. Types of Training (ppt 8)
  1. Basic Literacy Skills
    a) Ninety million American adults have limited literacy skills.
    b) Organizations are increasingly having to provide basic reading and math skills for their employees.
  2. Technical Skills
    a) Jobs change as a result of new technologies and improved methods.
    b) Technical training has become increasingly important because of changes in organization design. As organizations flatten their structures, expand their use of teams, and breakdown traditional departmental barriers, employees need to learn a wider variety of tasks.
  3. Interpersonal Skills
    a) Most employees belong to a work unit.
    b) To some degree, their work performance depends on their ability to effectively interact with their co-workers and their boss.
  4. Problem Solving Skills
    a) This would include activities to sharpen employees' logic, reasoning, and problem-defining skills as well as their abilities to assess causation, develop alternatives, analyze alternatives, and selection solutions.
  5. What About Diversity Training?
    a) The centerpiece of most diversity programs is training.
    b) The typical program lasts from half a day to three days and includes role playing exercises, lectures, discussions, and group experiences.
  6. What About Ethics Training?
    a) A recent survey finds that about 75 percent of employees working in the 1,000 largest U.S. corporations receive ethics training.
    b) But the evidence is not clear on whether you can teach ethics.
    c) Critics argue that ethics are based on values, and value systems are fixed at an early age.
    d) Critics also claim that ethics cannot be formally "taught," but must be learned by example.
    e) Supporters of ethics training argue that values can be learned and changed after early childhood.

C. Training Methods
  1. Training methods are most readily classified as formal or informal and on-the-job or off-the-job.
  2. Formal training is planned in advance and has a structured format. (ppt 9)

3. Evidence indicates organizations are increasingly relying on informal training—unstructured, unplanned, and easily adapted to situation and individuals.
4. On-the-job training includes job rotation, apprenticeships, understudy assignments, and formal mentoring programs.
    a) The primary drawback of these training methods is that they often disrupt the workplace.
5. Off-the-job training can include live classroom lectures (the most popular), videotapes, public seminars, self-study programs, internet courses, satellite-beamed television classes, and group activities that use role plays and case studies.
    a) McDonald's Hamburger University example.

D. Career Development (ppt 10)
1. The role of the organization in its employees' careers has gone from paternalism to supporting individuals as they take personal responsibility for their future.
2. The Organization's Responsibilities (ppt 11)
    a) Clearly communicating the organization's goals and future strategies.
    b) Creating growth opportunities
    c) Offering financial assistance
    d) Providing the time for employees to learn
3. The Employee's Responsibilities (ppt 12-13)
    a) Know yourself
    b) Manage your reputation
    c) Build and maintain network contacts
    d) Keep current
    e) Balance your specialist and generalist competencies
    f) Document your achievements
    g) Keep your options open

III. PERFORMANCE APPRAISAL
A. Purposes of Performance Appraisal
1. Management uses appraisals for general personnel decisions.
    a) Promotions, transfers, and terminations
    b) Appraisals identify training and development needs.
2. Used as a criterion against which selection and development programs are validated.
    a) The effectiveness of training and development programs can be determined by using performance appraisals to assess subsequent employee job performance.
3. Appraisals also provide feedback to employees on how the organization views their performance.
4. Appraisals are used as the basis for reward allocations.
    a) Decisions about who gets merit pay increases and other rewards are typically determined by performance appraisals.

B. Performance Appraisal and Motivation (ppt 14-15)
1. The expectancy model of motivation offers the best explanation of what conditions the amount of effort an individual will exert on his or her job.
2. A vital component of this model is performance, specifically the effort-performance and performance-reward linkages.

3. If employees know what is expected of them, how their performance will be measured, and they feel confident that their efforts will result in a satisfactory performance as defined by the criteria by which they are being measured then they will be motivated.

4. They also must feel confident that if they perform as they are being asked, they will receive rewards.

C. What Do We Evaluate?

1. The performance criteria or criterion used to evaluate employee performance will have a major influence on what employees do.

2. Use public employment agency example.

3. Use management consultant specializing in police research example.

4. The three most popular sets of performance appraisal criteria are individual task outcomes, behaviors, and traits. (ppt 16)

   a) Individual task outcomes. If ends count, rather than means, then management should evaluate an employee's task outcomes.

   b) Behaviors. In many cases it's difficult to identify specific outcomes that can be directly attributable to an employee's actions.

      (1) In such instances it is not unusual for management to evaluate the employee's behavior.

   c) Traits. The weakest set of criteria, yet still widely used by organizations.

      (1) Traits include having a good attitude, showing confidence, being dependable and so on.

D. Who Should Do the Evaluating? (ppt 17)

1. By tradition, a manager's authority typically has included appraising subordinates' performance.

2. Others may actually be able to do the job better.

3. Immediate Superior

   a) The employee's immediate boss conducts the majority of all performance evaluations at the lower and middle levels of the organization.

      (1) Many bosses feel unqualified to evaluate the unique contributions of each of their subordinates.

      (2) Others resent being asked to "play God" with their employees' careers.

      (3) Organizations using self-managed teams, telecommuting, and other organizing devices, distance bosses from their employees.

4. Peers

   a) Peer evaluations are one of the most reliable sources of appraisal data.

      (1) Peers are close to the action.

      (2) Using peers as raters results in several independent judgments, whereas a boss can offer only a single evaluation.

      (3) And the average of several ratings is often more reliable than a single evaluation.

   b) On the down side, peer evaluations can suffer from co-workers' unwillingness to evaluate one another and from biases of friendship or animosity.

5. Self-Evaluation

   a) Employees evaluating their own performance is consistent with values such as self-management and empowerment.

   b) Self-evaluations get high marks from employees themselves.

   c) They suffer from overinflated assessment and self-serving bias.

   d) Self-evaluations are often low in agreement with superiors' ratings.
  6. Immediate Subordinates
   a) Immediate subordinates' evaluations can provide accurate and detailed information about a manager's behavior because the evaluators typically have frequent contact with the manager.
   b) The problem—fear of reprisal from bosses given unfavorable evaluations. Respondent anonymity is crucial if these evaluations are to be accurate.
  7. 360-Degree Evaluation
   a) The latest approach to performance evaluation.
   b) Performance feedback comes from the full circle of an employee's daily contacts.
   c) The number of appraisals can be as few as three or as many as twenty-five, with most organizations collecting five to ten per employee.
   d) Its appeal—it fits well with organizations using teams, employee involvement, and quality management programs.

 E. Performance Appraisal Method (ppt 18)
  1. Written Essays
   a) The simplest method of appraisal is to write a narrative describing an employee's strengths, weaknesses, past performance, potential, and suggestions for improvement.
   b) No complex forms or extensive training needed but the results often reflect the ability of the writer.
  2. Critical Incidents
   a) Critical incidents focus the evaluator's attention on those behaviors that are key in making the difference between executing a job effectively or ineffectively.
   b) The appraiser writes down anecdotes that describe what the employee did that was especially effective or ineffective.
   c) The key here is that only specific behaviors are cited.
  3. Graphic Rating Scales
   a) One of the oldest and most popular methods.
   b) A set of performance factors—quantity and quality of work, depth of knowledge, cooperation, loyalty, and so on, are listed.
   c) The evaluator rates each on an incremental scale, typically five points.
   d) They don't provide the depth of information that essays or critical incidents do.
   e) They are less time-consuming to develop and administer.
   f) They also allow for quantitative analysis and comparison.
  4. Behaviorally Anchored Rating Scales
   a) These scales combine major elements from the critical incident and graphic rating scale approaches.
    (1) The employee is rated on the basis of items along a continuum, but the points are examples of actual behavior on the given job rather than general descriptions or traits.
   b) Behaviorally anchored rating scales specify definite, observable, and measurable job behavior.
   c) These behavioral examples are then translated into a set of performance dimensions, each dimension having varying levels of performance.
  5. Multiperson Comparisons
   a) These rankings evaluate one individual's performance against another's.

        b) It is a relative rather than an absolute measuring device.
        c) The three most popular are group order ranking, individual ranking, and paired comparisons.
            (1) The group order ranking requires the evaluator to place employees into a particular classification, such as top one-fifth or second one-fifth.
            (2) The individual ranking approach ranks in order employees from best to worst. This approach allows for no ties.
            (3) The paired comparison approach compares each employee with every other employee and rates each as either the superior or the weaker member of the pair. After all paired comparisons are made, each employee is assigned a summary ranking based on the number of superior scores he or she achieved. This ensures that each employee is compared against every other, but it can become unwieldy when many employees are being compared.
        d) Multiperson comparisons can be combined with one of the other methods to blend the best from both absolute and relative standards.

    F. Suggestions for Improving Performance Appraisals (ppt 19-20)
       1. Evaluators can make leniency, halo, and similarity errors, or use the process for political purposes.
       2. Suggestions
        a) Emphasize behaviors rather than traits.
            (1) Traits have little or no performance relationship.
            (2) Traits such as loyalty, initiative, courage, reliability, and self-expression are intuitively appealing characteristics in employees.
            (3) Another weakness is the judgment of what the trait is.
        b) Document performance behaviors in a diary.
            (1) By keeping a journal of specific critical incidents for each employee, evaluators tend to make more accurate judgments.
            (2) They reduce leniency and halo errors.
         c) Use multiple evaluators.
            (1) As the number of evaluators increases, the probability of attaining accurate information increases.
        d) Evaluate selectively.
            (1) If raters make appraisals on only those dimensions on which they are in a good position to rate, we increase interrater agreement and make the evaluation a more valid process.
            (2) We recommend that appraisers should be as close as possible, in terms of organizational level, to the individual being evaluated.
            (3) The specific application of these concepts would result in having immediate supervisors or co-workers as the major contributors to the appraisal and asking them to evaluate those factors that they are best qualified to judge.
        e) Train evaluators.
            (1) By training evaluators, we can make them more accurate raters.
            (2) Common errors such as halo and leniency have been minimized or eliminated.
            (3) But the effects of training do appear to diminish over time, so regular training refresher sessions may be needed.
        f) Provide employees with due process.
            (1) Three features characterize due process systems:

(a) Individuals are provided with adequate notice of what is expected of them.

(b) All relevant evidence to a proposed violation is aired in a fair hearing so individuals affected can respond.

(c) The final decision is based on the evidence and free from bias.

(2) Where due process has been part of the appraisal system, employees report positive reactions to the appraisal process, perceive the evaluation results as more accurate, and express increased intent to remain with the organization.

G. Don't Forget Performance Feedback. (ppt 21)
   1. Three reasons for reluctance for giving performance feedback:
      a) Managers are often uncomfortable discussing performance weaknesses directly with employees.
      b) Many employees tend to become defensive when their weaknesses are point out.
      c) Employees tend to have an inflated assessment of their own performance.
   2. The solution to the performance feedback problems is not to ignore it, but to train managers in how to conduct constructive feedback session.
      a) The performance review should be designed more as a counseling activity than a judgment process.

H. What About Team Performance Evaluations? (ppt 23)
   1. Performance evaluation concepts have been almost exclusively developed with individual employees in mind.
   2. Four suggestions for a performance appraisal system for teams.
      a) Tie the team results to the organizational goals.
      b) Begin with the team's customers and the work process the team follows to satisfy their needs.
      c) Measure both team and individual performance.
      d) Train the team to create its own measures. This ensures that everyone understands his or her role on the team and helps the team develop into a more cohesive unit

I. Performance Appraisal in a Global Context (ppt 24)
   1. Caution must be used in generalizing across cultures.
   2. To illustrate, consider three elements of culture—a person's relationship to the environment, time orientation, and focus of responsibility.
      a) American and Canadian organizations hold people responsible for their actions because people in these countries believe they can dominate their environment.
      b) In Middle Eastern countries, on the other hand, performance appraisals aren't likely to be widely used, because managers in these countries tend to see people as subjugated to their environment.
      c) Some countries, such as the United States, have a short-term time orientation and conduct annual performance appraisals.
      d) In Japan, however, where people hold a long-term time frame, performance appraisals may occur only at five- or ten-year intervals.
      e) Israel's culture values group activities much more than does the culture of the United States or Canada.

f)   North American managers focus on the individual in performance appraisals, and their counterparts in Israel are likely to emphasize group contributions and performance.

IV. IMPLICATIONS FOR MANAGERS

1.   Managers control the selection process, decisions regarding employee training, and how employees are evaluated. Because these managerial decisions affect the quality of an organization's workforce and the behavior of employees, care needs to be taken to insure that the organization's selection process, training programs, and appraisal system support high employee performance.

2.   An organization's selection practices will determine who gets hired. If properly designed, they will identify competent candidates and accurately match them to the job and the organization.

3.   While employee selection is far from a science, some organizations fail to design their selection systems so as to maximize the likelihood that the right person-job fit will be achieved. Training may be necessary to improve the candidate's skills.

4.   The most obvious effect of training programs on work behavior is directly improving the skills necessary for the employee to successfully complete his or her job.

5.   A major goal of performance appraisal is to assess accurately an individual's performance contribution as a basis for making reward allocation decisions.

SUMMARY (ppt 25-26)

1.   The selection interview is widely used, and also seems to carry a great deal of weight; the results tend to have a disproportionate amount of influence on the selection decision.

2.   Evidence indicates that interviews are most valuable for assessing an applicant's intelligence, level of motivation, and interpersonal skills. The most structured interview appears to be more valid.

3.   Typical written tests assess intelligence, aptitude, ability, interests, and integrity.

4.   Performance simulation tests have increase in popularity during the past two decades, with the two best-known being work sampling and assessment centers.

5.   Training can include everything from teaching employees basic reading skills to advanced courses in executive leadership.

6.   Career planning is something increasingly being done by individual employees rather than by their employers.

7.   Performance appraisals are used for several purposes; general personnel decisions, to pinpoint employee skills and competencies that are currently inadequate, as a criterion against which selection and development programs are validated, to provide feedback to employees, and as the basis for reward allocations.

8.   The expectancy model of motivation offers the best explanation of what conditions the amount of effort an individual will exert on his or her job. A vital component of this model is performance, specifically the effort-performance and performance-reward linkages.

9.   The performance criteria or criterion used to evaluate employee performance will have a major influence on what employees do. The three most popular sets of performance appraisal criteria are-individual task outcomes, behaviors, and traits.

10. Traditionally, a manager's authority typically includes appraising subordinates' performance. The employee's immediate boss conducts about 95 percent of all performance evaluations at the lower and middle levels of the organization. Peer evaluations are one of the most reliable sources of appraisal data. Having employees evaluate their own performance is consistent with values such as self-management and empowerment. Immediate subordinates'

evaluations can provide accurate and detailed information about a manager's behavior because the evaluators typically have frequent contact with the manager.

11. Managers have a variety of performance appraisal systems to choose from. The simplest method of appraisal is written narrative. Critical incidents focus key behaviors. Graphic rating scales is one of the oldest and most popular methods. Behaviorally anchored rating scales combine major elements from the critical incident and graphic rating scale approaches. And finally, multiperson comparisons, a ranking process. The three most popular are group order ranking, individual ranking, and paired comparisons.

12. An employee's evaluation can be distorted for a number of reasons: by a single criterion, through a leniency error, by the tendency to let one trait influence the appraisal, when there is low differentiation, and finally, the forcing of information to match nonperformance criteria.

13. Distortion, problems, and rating errors can be corrected in a number of ways including using multiple criteria, de-emphasizing traits, using measures based on behavior rather than traits, keeping a journal of specific critical incidents for each employee, using multiple evaluators, making appraisals on only those dimensions on which can be evaluated factually, and by training appraisers.

14. Don't forget performance feedback. There seem to be at least three reasons why managers are reluctant to give performance feedback. First, managers are often uncomfortable discussing performance weaknesses directly with employees. Second, many employees tend to become defensive when their weaknesses are point out. Third, employees tend to have an inflated assessment of their own performance.

15. Four suggestions have been offered for designing a system that supports and improves the performance of teams. Tie the team's results to the organization's goals. Begin with the team's customers and the work process the team follows to satisfy their needs. Measure both team and individual performance; Train the team to create its own measures.

16. When conducting performance appraisals in a global context, caution must be used. Managers need to consider three elements of culture—a person's relationship to the environment, time orientation, and focus of responsibility.

DISCUSSION QUESTIONS

1. You are the Human Resources Director for a small company and you have been given the task of outlining the selection devices your company will use in the future. What selection devices would you recommend using?
   Answer – Students' answers should vary depending on what type of organization, and more importantly what type of job or position the candidate is being selected for. However, the answer should include structured interviews, written tests (this can be as detailed as possible), and performance simulation tests.

2. Competent employees don't remain competent forever. Skills deteriorate and become obsolete. That's why organizations must invest in employee training. Describe the four general skill categories most often included in training programs.
   Answer – Basic literacy skills include providing basic reading and math skills for employees. Technical training has become increasingly important today for two reasons—new technology and new structural designs. Most employees belong to a work unit, and to some degree their work performance depends on their ability to effectively interact with their co-workers and their boss, therefore interpersonal skills are included in training. Problem-solving skills training would include activities to sharpen logic, reasoning, problem-defining skills, as well as abilities to assess causation, develop alternatives, analyze alternatives, and selection solutions.

3. As a manager in a small start-up company, you are faced with the task of creating a performance appraisal system for hourly employees. As you design this program how could you use the data it would gather?
    Answer - You can use the appraisals for general personnel decisions—promotions, transfers, and terminations. Second, appraisals identify training and development needs. They also can be used to pinpoint employee skills and competencies that are currently inadequate but can be remedied if appropriate programs are developed. It can be used as a criterion against which selection and development programs are validated. Appraisals also provide feedback to employees on how the organization views their performance. And, they can be used as the basis for reward allocations.

4. What is the organization's responsibility for employee career development
    Answer- Although career development has in recent years shifted to the employee, the organization can provide support by clearly communicating the organization's goals and strategies, creating growth opportunities, providing financial assistance and time for employees to learn new skills. The employee has the responsibility to know their strengths and weaknesses, to manage their reputation, to maintain networks, keep current with both specialist and generalist skills, documenting their achievements, and keeping their options open.

5. How can appraising performance be motivational for employees?
    Answer - The expectancy model of motivation offers the best explanation of what conditions the amount of effort an individual will exert on his or her job. A vital component of this model is performance—specifically the effort-performance and performance-reward linkages. If employees know what is expected of them, how their performance will be measured, and they feel confident that their efforts will result in a satisfactory performance as defined by the criteria by which they are being measured, then they will be motivated.

6. In designing your performance appraisal system, what performance criteria could you use? Why would you use one rather than another?
    Answer - Students' can make an argument for several criteria. They need to cover the following points regardless of the criteria for which they argue. The performance criteria or criterion used to evaluate employee performance will have a major influence on what employees do. The three most popular sets of performance appraisal criteria are individual task outcomes, behaviors, and traits.
    - Individual task outcomes—if ends count, rather than means, then management should evaluate an employee's task outcomes.
    - Behaviors—in many cases, it's difficult to identify specific outcomes that can be directly attributable to an employee's actions.
    - Traits—the weakest set of criteria, yet still widely used by organizations.

7. In this small company we've been discussing, who should do the evaluation? How would you choose who should do the evaluating? Be realistic, this company has four managers and 25 employees.
    Answer - Students probably should choose a traditional approach initially and perhaps argue for movement to peer or 360-degree feedback as the company grows. The big issue is what can realistically be done by very busy people in a small company. By tradition, a manager's authority typically has included appraising subordinates' performance. The employee's immediate boss conducts about 95 percent of all performance evaluations at the lower and middle levels of the organization. Peer evaluations are one of the most reliable sources of appraisal data. Using peers as raters results in several independent judgments, whereas a boss

can offer only a single evaluation. On the downside, peer evaluations can suffer from co-workers' unwillingness to evaluate one another and from biases of friendship or animosity. Having employees evaluate their own performances is consistent with values such as self-management and empowerment. Self-evaluations get high marks from employees themselves. They suffer from overinflated assessment and self-serving bias. Immediate subordinates' evaluations can provide accurate and detailed information about a manager's behavior because the evaluators typically have frequent contact with the manager. The problem—fear of reprisal from bosses given unfavorable evaluations. Respondent anonymity is crucial if these evaluations are to be accurate.

8. In this small company what would be the most effective performance appraisal method?
    Answer - Again, the primary issue is practicality. So, written essays, graphic rating scales, and multiperson comparisons would probably work best. The simplest method of appraisal is to write a narrative describing an employee's strengths, weaknesses, past performance, potential, and suggestions for improvement. No complex forms or extensive training needed but the results often reflect the ability of the writer. Critical incidents focus the evaluator's attention on those behaviors that are key in making the difference between executing a job effectively or ineffectively. Graphic rating scales are one of the oldest and most popular methods. A set of performance factors—quantity and quality of work, depth of knowledge, cooperation, loyalty, and so on., are listed. Behaviorally anchored rating scales combine major elements from the critical incident and graphic rating scale approaches. The employee is rated on the basis of items along a continuum, but the points are examples of actual behavior on the given job rather than general descriptions or traits. Multiperson comparisons evaluate one individual's performance against another's. It is a relative rather than an absolute measuring device. The three most popular are group order ranking, individual ranking, and paired comparisons.

9. What are the potential problems in performance appraisal, and what actions can correct those problems?
    Answer - To the degree that the following factors are prevalent, an employee's evaluation is likely to be distorted. If performance is assessed by a single criterion measure, the result would be a limited evaluation of that job. Some evaluators mark high—a positive leniency error and others low—a negative leniency error. The halo error is the tendency for an evaluator to let the assessment of an individual on one trait influence his or her appraisal of that person on other traits. Similarity error happens when evaluators rate other people by giving special consideration to those qualities that they perceive in themselves. Regardless of whom the appraiser evaluates and what traits are used, all of his or her evaluations seem similar. The final problem error is forcing information to match nonperformance criteria.

    These problems can be overcome by doing several things. 1) The more complex the job, the more criteria that will need to be identified and evaluated. 2) De-emphasize traits. 3) Whenever possible, it is better to use measures based on behavior rather than traits for appraisals. 4) By keeping a journal of specific critical incidents for each employee, evaluators tend to make more accurate judgments. 5) As the number of evaluators increases, the probability of attaining accurate information increases. 6) If raters make appraisals on only those dimensions which they are in a good position to rate, we increase interrater agreement and make the evaluation a more valid process. 7) By training appraisers, we can make them more accurate raters.

10. Why do managers often dislike giving performance reviews?
    Answer - There seem to be at least three reasons why managers are reluctant to give performance feedback. First, managers are often uncomfortable discussing performance weaknesses directly with employees. Second, many employees tend to become defensive when their weaknesses are point out. Third, employees tend to have an inflated assessment of their own performance.

11. If you wanted to use team performance appraisals in your performance appraisal system, what changes would you need to make?
    Answer - Performance evaluation concepts have been almost exclusively developed with individual employees in mind. Here are four suggestions for a performance appraisal system for teams. 1) Tie the team results to the organizational goals. 2) Begin with the team's customers and the work process the team follows to satisfy their needs. 3) Measure both team and individual performance. 4) Train the team to create its own measures. This ensures that everyone understands his or her role on the team and helps the team develop into a more cohesive unit

EXERCISES
A.   Promoting Excellence in Teaching
Students should learn the complexities of creating an administration performance appraisal system. Without referring to the current system used by your college or university, students should design a performance appraisal system for faculty and administrators. This can be done as an individual, team, or class exercise. It is written as a team exercise.
1. Break the class into groups of five.
2. Using this chapter as their outline, they should create a performance evaluation system for either (or both) faculty and administrators.
3. Students should provide a written and oral report outlining their system and justifying it.
4. Their plan should realistically address the following:
    ▪ How will their system motivate faculty [administrators] to be more effective?
    ▪ What will be evaluated? Why?
    ▪ Who will do the evaluating? How often? Why?
    ▪ How will the appraisal be conducted, i.e., what method or methods? (They should create a sample instrument—BARS, essay, and so on.)
    ▪ What would it take to implement such a system?
        ● In terms of people.
        ● In terms of training.
        ● In terms of financial cost.
        ● Changes in reward/compensation structure of your institution.
    ▪ What specific problems would their recommendation create?
    ▪ How would they address the problems?
5. After each student team presents, they should lead the rest of the class in a discussion of how their proposal can be improved and implemented. Especially important is how realistic their proposal is.
6. The discussion should focus on the difficulties of designing a fair and realistic system, not any blunders the students make.

B.   Training Manual: How to Be an Effective College Student

This exercise could be assigned as an individual exercise for outside of class, or it could be used as an in-class small group activity.

Have students think about the skills required to be an effective college student at their institution. Assign them the following:

You are a student ambassador who works in the University Student Affairs Office. In order to help new students get up to speed quicker and be successful at achieving good grades and becoming a contributing and accepted member of the campus (even during their first semester), you and your team have been assigned the duty of developing a training program for new students.

Think about what skills the new student will need, how current skill levels can be assessed, and how additional skills will be provided. Be sure to use the different training methods discussed in your textbook.

Good luck, Ambassadors. The futures of many new college students could very well be at stake.

C.   To Ask, or Not to Ask: Interview Development

Have students, individually outside of class, write down three questions they would ask if they were on the selection team to hire a new faculty member for the College of Business.

During class, break the class into groups of four or five, and have each group develop a structured interview they believe would result in hiring the best candidate for the faculty position. Be sure they identify what skills, knowledge, or ability each question is hoping to assess. They should keep most of the skills that they identify job-related.

D.   The Job Interview as a Selection Device

Based upon the exercise above, actually role-play a job interview. You might have students "sign up" for this and bring a resume to class. Use it to illustrate both how difficult and how important the interview process is. To tie this into the exercise above, re-evaluate the effectiveness of the questions, and also what other selection devices one should use in order to select the best candidate.

Analyzing Your Organization

Have students discuss with those that are responsible for selection the types of tools that they use to make their decisions. Although they most likely use interviews, find out the extent to which they use other devices, such as performance simulation or written tests. Ask about the weight that they put on each selection device.

You can do the same exercise with the performance appraisal process. If you have been through the appraisal, analyze what tools were used, whether the appraisal achieved its purpose, whether it motivated you or not, and finally, whether or not it made you a better employee.

Emphasize the difference between good and bad interviews and evaluations in the context of the chapter items. In other words, what specifically made them good or bad?

CHAPTER 16 - ORGANIZATIONAL CHANGE AND DEVELOPMENT

CHAPTER OBJECTIVES
After reading this chapter, students should be able to:
1. Describe the forces that act as stimulants to change.
2. Define planned change.
3. Summarize Lewin's three-step change model.
4. Explain sources of resistance to change.
5. Describe techniques for overcoming resistance to change.
6. Explain the values underlying most organizational development (OD) efforts.
7. Describe a learning organization.
8. Explain the three key elements in process reengineering.
9. Identify symptoms of work stress.
10. Summarize sources of innovation.

LECTURE OUTLINE
I.   FORCES FOR CHANGE
   A.   Exhibit 16-1 summarizes the six forces for change. (ppt 4)
      1.   Nature of the Workplace.
         a)   Adjustments to a multicultural workforce
         b)   HRM policies and practices have to change in order to attract and keep this more diverse workforce.
         c)   Spending on training to upgrade reading, math, computer, and other skills of employees
      2.   Technology
         a)   The substitution of computer control for direct supervision results in wider spans of control.
         b)   Sophisticated information technology is also making organizations more responsive.
      3.   Economic Shocks
         a)   Oil prices have again significantly increased.
         b)   New dot.com businesses have been created, turned tens of thousands of investors into overnight millionaires, and then crashed.
         c)   The euro has declined 30 percent against other major world currencies.
      4.   Competition
         a)   Competitors are as likely to come from across the ocean as from across town.
         b)   Established organizations need to defend themselves against both traditional competitors who develop new products and services and small, entrepreneurial firms with innovative offerings.
      5.   Social Trends
         a)   In contrast to just ten years ago, people are meeting and sharing information in Internet chat rooms.
         b)   Teenagers are increasingly ornamenting their bodies with piercings and tattoos.
         c)   Many Baby Boomers and Generation Xers are leaving the suburbs and moving to the cities.
      6.   World Politics
         a)   Not even the strongest proponents of globalization could have imagined how world politics would change in recent years.
            (1) The fall of the Berlin Wall and the reunification of Germany

     (2) Iraq's invasion of Kuwait

     (3) The breakup of the Soviet Union

  7. Change agents can be managers or nonmanagers, employees of the organization, or outside consultants. (ppt 6)

   a) For major change efforts, internal management often will hire outside consultants to provide advice and assistance.

   b) Outside consultants usually have an inadequate understanding of the organization's history, culture, operating procedures, and personnel.

   c) Outside consultants also may be prone to initiating more drastic changes—which can be a benefit or a disadvantage—because they do not have to live with the repercussions after the change is implemented.

   d) Internal staff specialists or managers, when acting as change agents, may be more thoughtful (and possibly cautious) because they must live with the consequences of their actions.

II. TWO VIEWS OF CHANGE

 A. Introduction

  1. Simile 1. The organization is like a large ship traveling across the calm Mediterranean Sea to a specific port. Every once in a while, however, a storm will appear, and the crew has to respond. Implementing change in organizations should, therefore, be seen as a response to a break in the status quo and needed only in occasional situations.

  2. Simile 2. The organization is more akin to a forty-foot raft than to a large ship. Rather than sailing a calm sea, this raft must traverse a raging river made up of an uninterrupted flow of permanent white-water rapids. Change is a natural state, and managing change is a continual process.

 B. The "Calm Waters" Simile (ppt 6)

  1. This simile used to dominate the thinking of practicing managers and academics.

   a) Exhibit 16-2, Kurt Lewin's three-step change process, describes it.

    (1) Step 1: Successful change requires unfreezing the status quo.

    (2) Step 2: Changing to a new state.

    (3) Step 3: Refreezing the new change to make it permanent.

    (4) The status quo can be considered an equilibrium state.

  2. Unfreezing can be achieved in one of three ways.

   a) The driving forces, which direct behavior away from the status quo, can be increased.

   b) The restraining forces, which hinder movement from the existing equilibrium, can be decreased.

   c) The two approaches can be combined.

  3. Once unfreezing has been accomplished, the change itself can be implemented.

  4. The new situation needs to be refrozen so it can be sustained over time.

   a) If not done there is a very strong chance the change will be short-lived, and employees will revert to the previous equilibrium state.

   b) The objective of refreezing, then, is to stabilize the new situation by balancing the driving and restraining forces.

  5. Lewin's three-step process treats change as a break in the organization's equilibrium state. (ppt 7)

 C. The "White-Water Rapids" Simile (ppt 8)

  1. This simile is consistent with uncertain and dynamic environments.

2. It is consistent with the trend of an industrial society moving to an information society.
   a) Example of attending a college with variable curriculum.
3. A growing number of managers accept that stability and predictability don't exist.
   a) Nor are disruptions in the status quo only occasional and temporary, followed by a return to calm waters.
   b) Many of today's managers face constant change, bordering on chaos.

D. Putting the Two Views in Perspective
   1. More and more managers face a world of constant and chaotic change.
   2. Few organizations today can treat change as the occasional disturbance in an otherwise peaceful world.
   3. Most competitive advantages last less than eighteen months.

III. RESISTANCE TO CHANGE
   A. Introduction
      1. Organizations and their members resist change.
      2. In a sense, this resistance is positive.
         a) It provides a degree of stability and predictability to behavior.
         b) Resistance to change can also be a source of functional conflict.
         c) The down side to resistance to change is that it hinders adaptation and progress.
      3. Resistance can be overt, implicit, immediate, or deferred.
         a) It is easiest to deal with resistance when it is overt and immediate.
         b) Implicit resistance efforts are subtle—loss of loyalty to the organization, loss of motivation to work, and so on—and hence difficult to recognize.
         c) Deferred actions cloud the link between the source of the resistance and the reaction to it.
            (1) A change may produce what appears to be only a minimal reaction at the time it is initiated but surfaces weeks, months, or even years later.
            (2) Or a single change by itself has little impact. But it becomes the straw that breaks the camel's back.
      4. Sources of resistance are individual and organizational but may overlap.

   B. Individual Resistance (ppt 9)
      1. There are five reasons why individuals may resist change.
         a) Habit. We're creatures of habit relying on habits or programmed responses.
         b) Security. People who have a high need for security are likely to resist change because it threatens their feeling of safety.
         c) Economic factors. The concern that changes will lower one's income. They fear they won't be able to perform the new tasks or routines to their previous standards, especially when pay is closely tied to productivity.
         d) Fear of the unknown. Changes substitute ambiguity and uncertainty for the known.
         e) Selective information processing. Individuals shape their world through their perceptions, and they resist changing it.

   C. Organizational Resistance (ppt 10)
      1. Organizations, by their very nature, are conservative and actively resist change.
      2. There are six major sources of organizational resistance.

224

a) Structural inertia. Organizations have built-in mechanisms to produce stability—the selection process, training, formalization, and so on.

b) Limited focus of change. Organizations are made up of interdependent subsystems. You can't change one without affecting the others. Limited changes in subsystems tend to get nullified by the larger system.

c) Group inertia. Group norms may act as a constraint.

d) Threat to expertise. Changes may threaten the expertise of specialized groups.

e) Threat to established power relationships. Redistribution of decision-making authority can threaten long-established power relationships within the organization.

f) Threat to established resource allocations. Those who control sizable resources often see change as a threat.

D. Overcoming Resistance to Change

1. There are five tactics. (ppt 11)

2. Communication

a) This tactic assumes that the source of resistance lies in misinformation or poor communication.

(1) This approach works provided that the source of resistance is inadequate communication and that mutual trust and credibility characterize management-employee relations.

3. Participation

a) It is difficult for individuals to resist a change decision in which they participated.

(1) If the participants have the expertise to make a meaningful contribution, their involvement can reduce resistance, obtain commitment, and increase the quality of the change decision.

4. Provide Support

a) Change agents can offer a range of supportive efforts to reduce resistance: for instance, showing concern and empathy by practicing active listening, offering employee counseling and therapy, or providing new skills training.

5. Reward Acceptance of Change

a) Rewards are a powerful force in shaping behavior.

b) Change agent should provide attractive rewards that are contingent on acceptance of change.

c) Rewards can range from praise and recognition to pay increases or promotions

6. Create a Learning Organization.

a) Resistance is less in an organization that has been intentionally designed with the capacity to continuously adapt and change.

b) This is called a learning organization and has five basic characteristics.

c) See Exhibit 16-3 for characteristics of a learning organization. (ppt 12)

d) Management can make their firms a learning organization.

(1) Make explicit its commitment to change, innovation, and continuous improvement.

(2) Structure needs to be redesigned to reduce boundaries between people and the increase interdependence.

(3) Culture needs to be reshaped to support continual learning.

IV. MANAGING CHANGE THROUGH ORGANIZATIONAL DEVELOPMENT (OD)

A. Introduction (ppt 13-14)
1. Organizational development refers to systematic, planned change.
2. OD is a term used to encompass a collection of planned-change interventions built on humanistic-democratic values that seek to improve organizational effectiveness and employee well-being.
3. OD paradigm values
   a) Respect for people—Individuals are perceived as being responsible, conscientious, and caring, and should be treated with dignity and respect.
   b) Trust and support—The effective organizations is characterized by trust, authenticity, openness, and a supportive climate.
   c) Power equalization—Effective organizations deemphasize hierarchical authority and control.
   d) Confrontation—Problems shouldn't be swept under the rug. They should be openly confronted.
   e) Participation—The more that people who will be affected by a change are involved in the decisions surrounding that change, the more they will be committed to implementing those decisions.

B. Sensitivity Training
1. Refers to a method of changing behavior through unstructured group interaction.
2. The group members are brought together in a free and open environment in which participants discuss themselves and their interactive processes.
3. The objectives of T-groups are to provide the subjects with increased awareness of their own behavior and how others perceive them, greater sensitivity to the behavior of others, and increased understanding of group processes.
4. Ideally, the result is a better integration between the individual and the organization.
5. Recent years have seen a declining popularity in T-groups.
   a) The intrusive nature of the process because participants have to disclose information about themselves that can threaten self-image.
   b) OD efforts in recent years have moved away from emphasizing individual feelings and focused more on issues related to improving work processes and group performance.

C. Survey Feedback
1. A tool for assessing attitudes held by organizational members, identifying discrepancies among member perceptions, and resolving these differences is the survey feedback approach.
   a) All members in the organization or unit usually complete a questionnaire.
   b) Organizational members may be asked to suggest questions or may be interviewed to determine what issues are relevant.
   c) The data from this questionnaire becomes the springboard for identifying problems and clarifying issues that may be creating difficulties for people.
2. Finally, group discussion in the survey feedback approach should result in members' identifying possible implications of the questionnaire's findings.

D. Process Consultation
1. The purpose of process consultation is for an outside consultant to assist a client, usually a manager, to perceive, understand, and act on process events with which he or she must deal.

a)   These might include workflow, informal relationships among unit members, and formal communication channels.
2.   Process consultation is similar to sensitivity training but is more task-directed than sensitivity training.
3.   The consultant works with the client in jointly diagnosing what processes need improvement.
   a)   Having the client actively participate in both the diagnosis and the development of alternatives enhances understanding of the process and the remedy and reduces resistance to the action plan chosen.
4.   It is important to note that the process consultant need not be an expert in solving the particular problem that is identified.
   a)   If the specific problem uncovered requires technical knowledge outside the client and consultant's expertise, the consultant helps the client locate such an expert and then instructs the client in how to get the most out of this expert resource.

E.   Team Building
   1.   Team building can be applied within groups (intragroup) or between groups (intergroup). Here, we emphasize the intragroup level and leave intergroup development to the next section.
   2.   Intragroup development concerns organizational families (command groups), committees, cross-functional teams, and task groups.
      a)   The activities that form team building can typically include goal setting, development of interpersonal relations among team members, role analysis to clarify each member's role and responsibilities, and team process analysis.
      b)   Basically, team building attempts to use high interaction among group members to increase trust and openness.
   3.   It may be beneficial to begin by having members attempt to define the goals and priorities of the group.
   4.   Next, members can evaluate the group's performance, how effective is it in structuring priorities and achieving the goals.
   5.   Team building can also address the clarification of each member's role in the group.
   6.   Still another team-building activity is to analyze key processes that go on within the team to identify the way work is performed and how these processes might be improved to make the team more effective.

F.   Intergroup Development
   1.   A major area of concern in OD is dysfunctional conflict between groups.
   2.   Intergroup development seeks to change the attitudes, stereotypes, and perceptions that groups have of each other.
   3.   A popular method emphasizes problem solving.
      a)   Members of each group meet independently to develop lists of their perception of themselves, the other group, and how they believe the other group perceives them.
      b)   The groups then share their lists, after which similarities and differences are discussed.
      c)   Differences are clearly articulated, and the groups look for the causes of the disparities.

      4. Once the causes of the difficulty have been identified, the groups can move to the integration phase and work to develop solutions that will improve relations between the groups.

      5. Subgroups, with members from each of the conflicting groups, can now be created for further diagnosis and begin to formulate alternative actions that will improve relations.

G. Appreciative Inquiry (ppt 15)

      1. The traditional OD approach identifies a set of problems, and looks for a solution.

      2. Appreciative inquiring identifies the unique qualities and strengths of the organization, and builds upon them to improve performance.

          a) Argues that problem-solving approaches always asks people to look at failures

      3. Four steps played out in a large-group meeting (ppt 16)

          a) Discovery

          b) Dreaming

          c) Design

          d) Destiny

V. CONTEMPORARY ISSUES IN ORGANIZATIONAL CHANGE

A. Continuous Improvement Processes (ppt 17)

      1. Quality management is seeking the constant attainment of customer satisfaction through the continuous improvement of all organizational processes.

      2. Use 99.9 percent error-free performance examples

          a) The U.S. Post Office would lose 2,000 pieces of mail an hour.

          b) U.S. doctors would perform 500 incorrect surgical procedures each week.

          c) There would be two plane crashes a day at O'Hare Airport in Chicago

      3. Quality management programs seek to achieve continuous process improvements so that variability is constantly reduced increasing the uniformity of the product or service.

          a) This results in lower costs and higher quality.

      4. How will employees be affected?

          a) They will no longer be able to rest on their previous accomplishments and successes.

          b) Increased stress from a work climate that no longer accepts complacency with the status quo.

          c) A race with no finish line can never be won. This situation creates constant tension.

          d) The pressures from an unrelenting search for process improvements can create anxiety and stress in some employees.

          e) The most significant implication for employees is that management will look to them as the prime source for improvement ideas.

          f) Employee involvement programs are part of continuous improvement.

B. Process Reengineering

      1. How you would do things if you could start all over?

          a) It comes from the process of taking apart an electronics product and designing a better version.

          b) As applied to organizations, process reengineering means that management should start with a clean sheet of paper in rethinking and redesigning those processes by which the organization creates value and does work, ridding itself of operations that have become antiquated.

2. Three key elements
   a) An organization's distinctive competencies define what it is that the organization does better than its competition.
      (1) The importance of identifying distinctive competencies is that they guide decisions regarding what activities are crucial to the organization's success.
   b) Assess the core processes that clearly add value to the organization's distinctive competencies.
      (1) These are the processes that transform materials, capital, information, and labor into products and services that the customer values.
      (2) Process value analysis typically uncovers a whole lot of activities that add little or nothing of value and whose only justification is "we've always done it this way."
   c) Reorganize around horizontal processes.
      (1) Use cross-functional and self-managed teams.
      (2) Focus on processes rather than functions.
3. One of the goals of reengineering is to minimize the necessary amount of management.
4. Implications for Employees
   a) Staff support jobs, especially middle managers, have been particularly vulnerable to lost jobs due to process reengineering efforts.
   b) Employees have their jobs changed after process reengineering.
      (1) Require a wider range of skills.
      (2) Include more interaction with customers and suppliers.
      (3) Great challenge.
      (4) Increased responsibilities.
      (5) Higher pay.
   c) The three- to five-year period it takes to implement reengineering is usually tough on employees.

C. Work Stress (ppt 18)
   1. Stress is a dynamic condition in which an individual is confronted with an opportunity, constraint, or demand related to what he or she desires and for which the outcome is perceived to be both uncertain and important.
   2. Stress can be good or bad.
      a) However, stress is more often associated with constraints and demands.
         (1) A constraint prevents you from doing what you desire.
         (2) Demands refer to the possible loss of something desired.
      b) Employees today are increasingly complaining about their stress levels brought on by pressures at work and at home.
   3. Symptoms of Stress (ppt 19)
      a) Stress shows itself in a number of ways that may be subsumed under three general categories: physiological, psychological, and behavioral.
      b) Most of the early concern with stress was directed at physiological symptoms.
         (1) Research led to the conclusion that stress could create changes in metabolism, increase heart and breathing rates, increase blood pressure, bring on headaches, and induce heart attacks.
         (2) Physiological symptoms have the least direct relevance to managers.

        c) Of greater importance are the psychological symptoms.
           (1) Stress can cause dissatisfaction. Job-related stress can cause job-related dissatisfaction.
        d) Behavioral stress symptoms include changes in productivity, absence, and turnover, as well as changes in eating habits, increased smoking or consumption of alcohol, rapid speech, fidgeting, and sleep disorders.

4. Reducing Stress (ppt 20)
    a) Not all stress is dysfunctional, and stress can never be totally eliminated.
    b) In terms of organizational factors
    c) Begin with employee selection.
        (1) Management needs to make sure that an employee's abilities match the requirements of the job.
        (2) Improved organizational communications will keep ambiguity-induced stress to a minimum.
        (3) Similarly, a goal-setting program will clarify job responsibilities and provide clear performance objectives.
        (4) Job redesign is also a way to reduce stress.
    d) Stress that arises from an employee's personal life creates two problems.
        (1) It is difficult for the manager to directly control.
        (2) There are ethical considerations—does the manager have any right to intrude?
        (3) Employee counseling can provide stress relief.
        (4) Offering a time-management program for employees whose personal lives suffer from a lack of planning and organization, which in turn, creates stress.
        (5) Still another approach is organizationally sponsoring physical activity programs.

D. Stimulating Innovation (ppt 21)
    1. W.L. Gore Company Example
        a) A reputation for being able to stimulate innovation over a long period of time.
        b) It's stated objective is that 30 percent of its sales are to come from products less than four years old.
        c) In one recent year alone, 3M launched more than 200 new products.
    2. Characteristics of Innovative Organizations
        a) We group them into structural, cultural, and human resource categories.
    3. Structural Variables
        a) Organic structures positively influence innovation because they facilitate the flexibility, adaptation, and cross-fertilization that make the adoption of innovations easier.
        b) Long tenure in management is associated with innovation.
        c) Innovation is nurtured where there are slack resources.
        d) Interunit communication is high in innovative organizations where there is a high use of committees, task forces, cross-functional, and other mechanisms that facilitate interaction across departmental lines.
    4. Cultural Variables
        a) They encourage experimentation.
        b) They reward both successes and failures. They celebrate mistakes.
        c) Such cultures extinguish risk taking and innovation.
    5. Human Resource Variables

        a)   Innovative organizations actively train and develop their members to keep them current.

        b)   They offer high job security and they encourage individuals to become champions of change.

        c)   Once a new idea is developed, champions of change actively and enthusiastically promote the idea, build support, overcome resistance, and ensure that the innovation is implemented.

6. Summary

        a)   W.L. Gore as a premier product innovator

           (1) It is highly organic.

           (2) Almost everything is done in teams.

           (3) The company encourages its employees to take risks and experiment.

VI.   IMPLICATIONS FOR MANAGERS

1. The need for change encompasses almost all of the concepts within organizational behavior—attitudes, perceptions, teams, leadership, motivation, organizational design, and the like.

2. If environments were perfectly static, if employees' skills and abilities were always up to date and incapable of deteriorating, and if tomorrow was always exactly the same as today, organizational change would have little or no relevance to managers. But the real world is turbulent, requiring organizations and their members to undergo dynamic change if they are to perform at competitive levels.

3. In the past managers could treat change as an occasional disturbance in their otherwise peaceful and predictable world. Such a world no longer exists for most managers. Today's managers are increasingly finding that their world is one of constant and chaotic change. In this world managers must continually act as change agents.

SUMMARY (ppt 22-23)

1. Today's business environment is marked by change, which is driven by primarily by six forces: the changing nature of the workplace, technology, economic shocks, domestic and global competition, new social trends, and world politics.

2. While all businesses face various types of change, we are concerned with change activities that are proactive and purposeful, intentional, and a goal-oriented activity. Planned change seeks to improve the ability of the organization to adapt to changes in its environment.

3. There are two primary views of organizational change; 1) implementing change in organizations is a response to a break in the status quo and needed only in occasional situations, and 2) change is a natural state, and managing change is a continual process.

4. Kurt Lewin proposed a three-step change process to describe the "calm waters" simile of change. 1) Successful change requires unfreezing the status quo. 2) Changing to a new state. 3) Refreezing the new change to make it permanent. The status quo can be considered an equilibrium state. Lewin's three-step process treats change as a break in the organization's equilibrium state.

5. Both experience and research show that organizations and their members resist change. In a sense, resistance is positive. This resistance can be overt, implicit, immediate, or deferred. Sources of resistance are individual and organizational but may overlap. There are five reasons why individuals may resist change and six major sources of organizational resistance.

6. Managers have tactics they can use to overcome resistance to change: communication, participation, provide support, reward acceptance of change, and create a learning organization.

7. Organizational development (OD) is a term used to encompass a collection of change techniques or interventions, from organization-wide changes in structure and systems to psychotherapeutic counseling sessions with groups and individuals, undertaken in response to changes in the external environment that seek to improve organizational effectiveness and employee well-being. Five interventions that change agents might consider using are presented: sensitivity training, survey feedback, process consultation, teaming building, intergroup development, and appreciative inquiry.

8. Continuous improvement is a quality management philosophy that's driven by the constant attainment of customer satisfaction through the continuous improvement of all organizational processes. These programs seek to constantly reduce variability, increasing the uniformity of the product or service.

9. Process reengineering applied to organizations means that management should start with a clean sheet of paper in rethinking and redesigning those processes by which the organization creates value and does work, ridding itself of operations that have become antiquated.

10. Work stress is a dynamic condition in which an individual is confronted with an opportunity, constraint, or demand related to what he or she desires and for which the outcome is perceived to be both uncertain and important. It can be good or bad. Stress shows itself in a number of ways that may be subsumed under three general categories: physiological, psychological, and behavioral.

11. Innovative organizations are characterized by structural, cultural, and human resource innovations. Organic structures positively influence innovation because they facilitate the flexibility, adaptation, and cross-fertilization that make the adoption of innovations easier. Cultural innovation encourages experimentation and rewards both successes and failures. They celebrate mistakes. And, innovative organizations actively train and develop their members to keep them current.

DISCUSSION QUESTIONS

1. You are preparing to address your stockholders at the company's annual meeting. Your topic is "The Changing Business Environment." What changes would you talk about with your stockholders?

   Answer - Note that Exhibit 16-1 summarizes all six. 1) Nature of the workplace—Adjustments to a multicultural workforce. 2) Technology—The substitution of computer control for direct supervision and the growth of sophisticated information technology are also making organizations more responsive. 3) Economic shocks. 4) Competitors are as likely to come from across the ocean as from across town. 5) New social trends. 6) Dramatic changes in world politics—not even the strongest proponents of globalization—could have imagined how world politics would change in recent years.

2. Define planned change.

   Answer - It seeks to improve the ability of the organization to adapt to changes in its environment and it seeks to change the behavior of individuals and groups within the organization. Planned change involves change agents who can be managers or nonmanagers, employees of the organization, or outside consultants.

3. What is a change agent and who might fulfill that role in a planned change?

   Answer - A change agent drives and guides a planned change effort. Change agents can be managers or nonmanagers, employees of the organization, or outside consultants. For major change efforts, internal management often will hire outside consultants to provide advice and assistance. Outside consultants usually have an inadequate understanding of the organization's history, culture, operating procedures, and personnel. Outside consultants also may be prone to initiating more drastic changes—which can be a benefit or a disadvantage—

because consultants do not have to live with the repercussions after the change is implemented. Internal staff specialists or managers, when acting as change agents, may be more thoughtful (and possibly cautious) because they must live with the consequences of their actions.

4. Summarize Lewin's three-step change model.
    Answer - Organizational change is based in two views; that it is a response to a break in the status quo and that it is a natural state, and managing change is a continual process. Lewin's three-step change process relates to the first view of change.
    - Successful change requires unfreezing the status quo.
    - Changing to a new state.
    - Refreezing the new change to make it permanent.

The status quo can be considered an equilibrium state. Lewin's three-step process treats change as a break in the organization's equilibrium state. Unfreezing can be achieved in one of three ways: 1) the driving forces that direct behavior away from the status quo, can be increased, 2) The restraining forces, which hinder movement from the existing equilibrium, can be decreased, or 3) the two approaches can be combined. Once unfreezing has been accomplished, the change itself can be implemented. The new situation needs to be refrozen so it can be sustained over time. If not done there is a very strong chance the change will be short-lived and employees will revert to the previous equilibrium state.

5. Why do individuals and organizations resist planned change efforts?
    Answer - Individuals resist change because of:
    - Habit. We're creatures of habit relying on habits or programmed responses.
    - Security. People who have a high need for security are likely to resist change because it threatens their feeling of safety.
    - Economic factors. The concern that changes will lower one's income. Fear they won't be able to perform the new tasks or routines to their previous standards, especially when pay is closely tied to productivity.
    - Fear of the unknown. Changes substitute ambiguity and uncertainty for the known.
    - Employees in organizations hold the same dislike for uncertainty.
    - Selective information processing. Individuals shape their world through their perceptions and they resist changing it.

While organizations, by their very nature, are conservative and actively resist change, there are six major sources of organizational resistance.
- Structural inertia. Organizations have built-in mechanisms to produce stability—the selection process, training, formalization, and so on.
- Limited focus of change. Organizations are made up of interdependent subsystems. You can't change one without affecting the others. Limited changes in subsystems tend to get nullified by the larger system.
- Group inertia. Group norms may act as a constraint.
- Threat to expertise. Changes may threaten the expertise of specialized groups.
- Threat to established power relationships. Redistribution of decision-making authority can threaten long-established power relationships within the organization.
- Threat to established resource allocations. Those who control sizable resources often see change as a threat.

6. Name five tactics for overcoming resistance to change, why you use each, and any drawbacks to the techniques.

    Answer - 1) Communication—this tactic assumes that the source of resistance lies in misinformation or poor communication. This approach works provided that the source of resistance is inadequate communication and that mutual trust and credibility characterize management-employee relations. However it takes time and effort. 2) Participation—it is difficult for individuals to resist a change decision in which they participated. If the participants have the expertise to make a meaningful contribution, their involvement can reduce resistance, obtain commitment, and increase the quality of the change decision. However, it can result in a poor decision and consume a lot of time. 3) Provide support—when employee fear and anxiety are high, employee counseling and therapy, new skills training, or a short, paid leave of absence may facilitate adjustment. It is expensive, time consuming, and doesn't always work. 4) Reward acceptance of change—rewards are a powerful force in shaping behavior; 5) Create a learning organization—Resistance is less in an organization that has been intentionally designed with the capacity to continuously adapt and change. (See Exhibit 16-3 for characteristics of a learning organization.)

7. What is a learning organization? Why are they the future of organizational change?

    Answer - A learning organization is an organization that has developed the continuous capacity to adapt and change. Most organizations engage in what has been called single-loop learning. When errors are detected, the correction process relies on past routines and present policies. A learning organization uses double-loop learning. When an error is detected, it's corrected in ways that involve the modification of the organization's objectives, policies, and standard routines. Double-loop learning challenges deep-rooted assumptions and norms within an organization. Exhibit 16-3 summarizes the five basic characteristics of a learning organization. Proponents of the learning organization envision it as a remedy for the three fundamental problems—fragmentation, competition, and reactiveness. a) Fragmentation based on specialization creates "walls" and "chimneys" that separate different functions into independent and often warring fiefdoms. b) An overemphasis on competition often undermines collaboration. c) Reactiveness misdirects management's attention to problem solving rather than creation. Think of a learning organization as an ideal to strive toward rather than a realistic description of structured activity. Learning organizations draw on OB concepts.

8. What steps can top management take toward making their companies learning organizations?

    Answer - Three suggestions for creating a learning organization.
    - Establish a strategy. Management needs to make its commitment to change, innovation, and continuous improvement explicit.
    - Redesign the organization's structure. Flattening the structure, eliminating or combining departments, and increasing the use of cross-functional teams reinforces interdependence and reduces boundaries between people.
    - Reshape the organization's culture. Risk-taking, openness, and growth characterize Learning organizations. Management sets the tone for the organization's culture by both what it says (strategy) and what it does (behavior).

9. What are the basic assumptions underlying organizational development (OD) change efforts?

    Answer - Organizational development refers to systematic, planned change. OD is a term used to encompass a collection of change techniques or interventions, from organization-wide changes in structure and systems to psychotherapeutic counseling sessions with groups and individuals, undertaken in response to changes in the external environment that seek to improve organizational effectiveness and employee well-being. It is characterized by:

1. Respect for people—Individuals are perceived as being responsible, conscientious, and caring, and should be treated with dignity and respect.
2. Trust and support—The effective organization is characterized by trust, authenticity, openness, and a supportive climate.
3. Power equalization—An effective organization deemphasizes hierarchical authority and control.
4. Confrontation—problems shouldn't be swept under the rug. They should be openly confronted.
5. Participation—The more that people who will be affected by a change are involved in the decisions surrounding that change, the more they will be committed to implementing those decisions.

10. What are five interventions that change agents might consider using?
Answer - OD has emphasized sensitivity training, survey feedback, process consultation, team building, and intergroup development, and appreciative inquiry.

11. Your company wants to engage in an improvement process. You make high-quality products and control your costs fairly well. The company is well-established in its industry and has managed to keep its workforce fairly "lean." Would you recommend a quality management or a process reengineering approach and why?
Answer - In this case the best solution is quality management, the company needs to improve what it's doing not radically change things. Quality management is a philosophy of management that's driven by the constant attainment of customer satisfaction through the continuous improvement of all organizational processes. Quality management programs seek to achieve continuous process improvements so that variability is constantly reduced increasing the uniformity of the product or service. Process reengineering starts from scratch. There are three key elements. 1) An organization's distinctive competencies define what it is that the organization does better than its competition. 2) Assess the core processes that clearly add value to the organization's distinctive competencies. 3) Reorganize around horizontal processes.

12. Why should managers be sensitive to work stress and how can they reduce it?
Answer - Work stress is a dynamic condition in which an individual is confronted with an opportunity, constraint, or demand related to what he or she desires and for which the outcome is perceived to be both uncertain and important. Stress can be good or bad. Stress shows itself in a number of ways that may be subsumed under three general categories: physiological, psychological, and behavioral. Not all stress is dysfunctional, and stress can never be totally eliminated. Managers can reduce stress by careful employee selection. Management needs to make sure that an employee's abilities match the requirements of the job.

13. What distinguishes an innovative organization from more traditional organizations?
Answer - The characteristics of innovative organizations can be grouped into structural, cultural, and human resource categories.
- Structural variables—organic structures positively influence innovation because they facilitate the flexibility, adaptation, and cross-fertilization that make the adoption of innovations easier.
- Cultural variables—encouraging experimentation, rewarding both successes and failures. They celebrate mistakes. And, such cultures extinguish risk taking and innovation.

- Human resource variables—innovative organizations actively train and develop their members to keep them current. They offer high job security and they encourage individuals to become champions of change.

14. What is Knowledge management (KM), and why is it important for today's organizations? **Answer** – Knowledge management is the process of organizing and distributing an organization's collective wisdom so the right information gets to the right people at the right time. KM is important for three reasons: First, in many organizations intellectual assets are now as important as physical or financial assets. Second, as Baby Boomers begin to leave the workforce, there's an increasing awareness that they represent a wealth of knowledge that will be lost if there are not attempts to capture it. And, third, a well-designed KM system will reduce redundancy and make the organization more efficient.

EXERCISES

A.   Overcoming Resistance

Students will learn that sometimes necessary change is unwanted and resisted and that resistance must be overcome if the organization is to change, grow, and succeed. You can use this as a double exercise. First, to strategize how to overcome resistance. Or, second, and more complex, you can use it to have students think through the whole change process and create alternative courses of action—other change efforts that might help the college/university solve its problem in another way.

1. Propose the following scenario (or one of your own that is more relevant to your situation) to the class:

Situation

Due to massive cutbacks in both federal and state support (or alumni gifts), your college or university must make some significant changes that will affect revenue and cash flow. The institution had anticipated a budget increase this year in order to hire more faculty, reduce class sizes, and improve academic programs. Instead funding was cut.
They are mandating the following:

- All freshmen and sophomores must live on campus in dorms (to increase occupancy).
- There will be Saturday classes (to increase utilization of space).
- All faculty will have their teaching loads increased by one class per semester (to reduce the need for additional faculty).
- All classes must have a minimum of fifteen enrollments or they will be canceled. All introductory courses will be taught as large lecture sections (to reduce the need for faculty and increase the "profit margin" per class).
- Students must pay a $250 per semester parking fee to have a car on campus and a $100 per semester security fee (to pay for parking facilities and campus police).
- All majors with less than 100 students will either be consolidated or eliminated (to focus resources on larger majors).

2. As a class, brainstorm what type of resistance is likely to arise from these changes and from what constituencies.
3. Consolidate the specific examples of resistance into five or six categories.
4. Discuss what strategies might be effective in overcoming each category of resistance.
5. In addition, discuss what other ways the college or university might address the problem.

Tips

1. Students will begin by arguing about the specific changes. Students will want to argue that the changes shouldn't be made or that these are stupid, etc. Help them focus on the fact that as managers they will have to support and implement changes with which they do not agree.

2. Next students will start talking about the kind of resistance and focus on specific acts—protests, demonstrations, angry letters, and so on. Help them think about the constituencies, who have a vested interest in these changes besides students and faculty.
3. Students should begin by going back to the basic problem and assumptions.
   - Basic problem, insufficient money.
   - Assumption, solve the problem by spending less.
4. Then students should think about the particular needs represented by the various "stakeholders."
   - What does the administration need?
   - What does the faculty need?
   - What do students need?
5. Students reference their solutions, alternatives, and overcoming resistance strategies to text content.

B.   Identifying Change Through Current Event Analysis

Articles (not short notes) may be selected from any of the following sources: *Fortune, Business Week, Wall Street Journal, Forbes, Fast Company,* or the World Wide Web. Find a current article on the topic of organizational change.

An entry for each topic assignment consists of five parts: (a) reference citation, (b) brief article summary, (c) reaction, (d) application, and (e) copy of the article.

(a)   Using **APA** style, write the complete reference citation for the article at the top of the first page. This reference citation should be complete enough for someone else to be successful in locating the article.

(b)   The second part of the assignment is to provide a brief summary of the article main points. Give enough detail and information that someone who has not read the article will feel informed about the article content, and be able to evaluate your opinions and analysis in the following sections of the Current Topics Assignment. However, do remember that this is to be a brief summary! Summary sections must be labeled as "Summary," one half page minimum to one page maximum in length, typed or word processed, and double-spaced.

(c)   Once you have read the article, write your reaction to the article, given what you know about the topic. Some issues to include might be: Is the article right? Wrong? Good? Bad? Expected? Unexpected? Innovative? Logical? Unique? Consistent with what you know? Inconsistent? Do you agree? Disagree? Write down your thoughts of the article, given your current state of knowledge. Note: This is NOT simply a review of the article content. You have already included a short review of the article, but I am much more interested in reading your reactions to the article. Reaction sections must be labeled as "Reaction," one half page minimum to one page maximum in length, typed or word processed, and double-spaced.

(d)   The fourth part of each topic assignment, an Application section, should demonstrate the relationship between what you have learned by reading the text and/or coming to class and the content of the article you have selected. Do not simply repeat what you have learned or what you have read; apply what you have learned. Discuss comparisons/contrasts, agreements/disagreements between the article content and the text and/or class discussion. Application sections must be labeled as "Application," ½ page minimum-1 page maximum, "typed" or "word processed," and double-spaced.

(e)   A copy of the article is the fifth part to be included with each topic assignment. Photocopies or originals are acceptable. Photocopies may be reduced in order to get a lengthy article on a single 8-1/2 x 11-inch sheet of paper. Originals should be removed from a periodical **ONLY** with the owner's permission.

Staple the five parts together in the order presented above (a minimum of one-and-a-half word-processed pages-maximum of three word-processed pages) and turn in on the due dates noted.

Note: This page can be photocopied as an instruction sheet for students.

C.   Illustrating Resistance to Change

To start the class, tell students to stand up, and make them sit in a different chair then they normally do. For example, if they normally sit in the back corner, make them move up to the front middle. Do this for every student in the class, but don't tell them why.

Begin the lecture, and when you get to the individual resistances to change section, ask them how they feel about their new seat. In general even small changes can make us uncomfortable, because they disrupt our habits. This helps illustrate how uncomfortable we are when proposed organizational changes really can impact our lives, such as through a reduction in pay.

Analyzing Your Organization

Discuss with your manager the times in which he or she has met resistance to a proposed organizational change. What type of resistances did they encounter? How did they overcome the resistance? What types of change seem to be "hot buttons" with this organization? Have they resisted change when it has come from above?

Related to this, discuss the methods by which your organization tries to improve. Do they have specific quality programs in place? How about OD initiatives? Find out how they work, and how the organization responds to these initiatives. Report your findings to class.

CHAPTER 1 INTRODUCTION TO ORGANIZATIONAL BEHAVIOR

MULTIPLE CHOICE

1.   Managers tend to describe their most troublesome problems as being:
    a. lack of skilled workers.
    b. "people" problems.
    c. overqualified workers.
    d. frequent changes in technology.

Answer: b, difficulty: 1, p. 1

2.   The systematic study of the actions and attitudes that people exhibit within organizations is known as:
    a. human resources.
    b. organizational theory.
    c. organizational behavior.
    d. industrial relations.

Answer: c, difficulty: 1, p. 2

3.   The field of OB seeks to replace intuitive explanations with:
    a. systematic studies.
    b. gut feelings.
    c. inaccurate conclusions.
    d. non-research studies.

Answer: a, difficulty: 2, p. 2

4.   Pat, a manager, is interested in the actions and attitudes of her subordinates at work. Pat's interest is identified most closely with the study of:
    a. prescientific management.
    b. organizational design.
    c. organizational behavior.
    d. organizational theory.

Answer: c, difficulty: 2, p. 2

5.   Three types of behavior that historically proved to be important determinants of employee performance are:
    a. technology, structure, motivation.
    b. work, competitors, decisions.
    c. individuals, groups, organizations.
    d. productivity, absenteeism, turnover.

Answer: d, difficulty: 3, p. 2

6. The discretionary behavior that is not part of an employee's formal job requirements but which nevertheless promotes the effective functioning of the organization is referred to as:
    a. organizational citizenship.
    b. job satisfaction.
    c. job dissatisfaction.
    d. job requirements.

Answer: a, difficulty: 2, p. 2

7. High rates of ____ increase costs and tend to place less experienced people into jobs.
    a. job dissatisfaction
    b. employee turnover
    c. organizational chaos
    d. organizational theory

Answer: b, difficulty: 2, p. 2

8. Examples of organizational citizenship include all of the following EXCEPT:
    a. assisting others on the work team.
    b. volunteering for extra job activities.
    c. making constructive statements about one's work group.
    d. creating unnecessary conflicts.

Answer: d, difficulty: 3, p. 2

9. Organizational behavior is concerned with job satisfaction, which is a(n):
    a. attitude.
    b. behavior.
    c. value.
    d. discipline.

Answer: a, difficulty: 2, p. 2

10. Job satisfaction is a manager's concern for three basic reasons. These reasons include all of the following EXCEPT:
    a. there may be a link between job satisfaction and productivity.
    b. satisfaction is positively related to open office systems.
    c. satisfaction has been found to be negatively related to absenteeism and turnover.
    d. managers have a responsibility to provide employees with satisfying jobs.

Answer: b, difficulty: 3, pp. 2-3

11. A consciously coordinated social unit, composed of two or more people, that functions on a relatively continuous basis to achieve a common goal refers to a(n):
    a. science.
    b. attitude.
    c. job.
    d. organization.

Answer: d, difficulty: 1, p. 2

12. OB encompasses the behavior of people in:
    a. manufacturing and service firms.
    b. military units.
    c. government agencies.
    d. All of the above.

Answer: d, difficulty: 3, p. 3

13. A major influence on organizational behavior has been:
    a. the behavioral disciplines.
    b. the social disciplines.
    c. the physical disciplines.
    d. literature.

Answer: a, difficulty: 2, p. 3

14. Each of the following disciplines has greatly contributed to the study of organizational behavior EXCEPT:
    a. psychology.
    b. sociology.
    c. physiology.
    d. political science.

Answer: c, difficulty: 2, p. 3

15. The contributions of _____ to OB have been mainly at the individual or micro level of analysis.
    a. psychology
    b. sociology
    c. anthropology
    d. political science

Answer: a, difficulty: 3, p. 3

16. The science that seeks to measure, explain, and sometimes change the behavior of humans and other animals is:
    a. psychology.
    b. sociology.
    c. anthropology.
    d. social psychology.

Answer: a, difficulty: 1, p. 3

17. _____ concern themselves with studying and attempting to understand individual behavior.
    a. anthropologists
    b. political scientists
    c. sociologists
    d. psychologists

Answer: d, difficulty: 2, p. 3

18. _____ studies people in relation to their fellow human beings.
    a. Psychology
    b. Sociology
    c. Anthropology
    d. Social psychology

Answer: b, difficulty: 1, p. 3

19. Valuable input from sociologists in the study of OB includes all of the following EXCEPT:
    a. group dynamics.
    b. the use of technology in the virtual office.
    c. work team design.
    d. work-life balance.

Answer: b, difficulty: 3, Exhibit 1-1

20. _____ focuses on the influence of people on one another.
    a. Psychology
    b. Sociology
    c. Anthropology
    d. Social psychology

Answer: d, difficulty: 2, pp. 3-4

21.   Social psychologists have made contributions in all of the following areas EXCEPT:
       a.   measuring, understanding, and changing attitudes.
       b.   communication patterns.
       c.   employee selection techniques.
       d.   group decision processes.

Answer: c, difficulty: 2, Exhibit 1-1

22.   One of the major areas receiving considerable investigation by social psychologists has been:
       a.   change.
       b.   understanding individual motivation.
       c.   understanding how the external environment impacts the organization.
       d.   understanding the impact of the global economy on the organization.

Answer: a, difficulty: 3, p. 4

23.   Contributions from the field of _____ include knowledge about learning, motivation, personality, emotions, and job satisfaction.
       a.   psychology
       b.   sociology
       c.   anthropology
       d.   political science

Answer: a, difficulty: 2, Exhibit 1-1

24.   Contributions from the field of _____ include knowledge about group dynamics, work teams, status, and bureaucracies.
       a.   psychology
       b.   sociology
       c.   anthropology
       d.   political science

Answer: b, difficulty: 2, Exhibit 1-1

25.   Contributions from the field of _____ include knowledge about changing attitudes, understanding communication patterns, and understanding group decision-making processes.
       a.   psychology
       b.   sociology
       c.   anthropology
       d.   political science

Answer: b, difficulty: 2, Exhibit 1-1

26. Contributions from the field of _____ include knowledge about comparative values, cross-cultural analysis, and organizational culture.
    a. psychology
    b. sociology
    c. anthropology
    d. political science

Answer: c, difficulty: 2, Exhibit 1-1

27. Contributions from the field of _____ include knowledge about conflict, intraorganizational politics, and power.
    a. psychology
    b. sociology
    c. anthropology
    d. political science

Answer: d, difficulty: 2, Exhibit 1-1

28. The study of the behavior of individuals and groups within a political environment is:
    a. sociology.
    b. political science.
    c. anthropology.
    d. social psychology.

Answer: b, difficulty: 2, p. 5

29. Specific topics of concern to _____ include structuring of conflict, allocation of power, and how people manipulate power for individual self-interest.
    a. psychologists
    b. sociologists
    c. social psychologists
    d. political scientists

Answer: d, difficulty: 3, p. 5

30. The study of societies to learn about human beings and their activities is called:
    a. psychology.
    b. sociology.
    c. anthropology.
    d. social psychology.

Answer: c, difficulty: 2, p. 5

31. Which of the following is NOT one of the goals of OB?
    a. prediction
    b. cooperation
    c. explanation
    d. control

Answer: b, difficulty: 2, p. 5

32. When we seek answers to *why* an individual or a group of individuals did something, we are pursuing the _____ objective of OB.
    a. explanation
    b. prediction
    c. control
    d. sociological

Answer: a, difficulty: 2, p. 5

33. From a management perspective, the LEAST important of the three goals of OB is:
    a. explanation.
    b. prediction.
    c. control.
    d. sociological.

Answer: a, difficulty: 2, p. 5

34. The goal of _____ focuses on future events.
    a. explanation
    b. prediction
    c. control
    d. intervention

Answer: b, difficulty: 2, p. 5

35. The goal of _____ seeks to determine what outcomes will result from a given action.
    a. explanation
    b. prediction
    c. control
    d. cooptation

Answer: b, difficulty: 2, p. 5

36.   A manager who tries to determine how employees will respond to a new process is engaging in
       a.   explanation
       b.   prediction
       c.   control
       d.   cooptation

Answer: b, difficulty: 3, p. 6

37.   The most controversial goal is using OB knowledge to _____ behavior.
       a.   explain
       b.   predict
       c.   control
       d.   distinguish

Answer: c, difficulty: 1, p. 5

38.   When a manager asks, "What can I do to make Dave put out more effort on his job?" the manager
       is concerned with which of the following OB goals?
       a.   prediction
       b.   cooperation
       c.   explanation
       d.   control

Answer: d, difficulty: 2, p. 5

39.   Which organizational behavior goal is most likely to raise ethical questions?
       a.   prediction
       b.   power
       c.   explanation
       d.   control

Answer: d, difficulty: 2, p. 6

40.   While it is controversial, the _____ objective is frequently seen by managers as the most valuable
       contribution that OB makes toward their effectiveness on the job.
       a.   explain
       b.   predict
       c.   control
       d.   intervene

Answer: c, difficulty: 3, p. 6

41.   Which one of the following is NOT one of the dramatic changes taking place in organizations?
       a.   minimum wage changes
       b.   globalization increasing the need for employees to be more flexible
       c.   diversified work force
       d.   severed loyalty bonds

Answer: a, difficulty: 1, p. 6

42.   What is NOT one of the ways in which the manager's job is changing with globalization?
       a.   increased foreign assignments
       b.   movement of jobs to America to reduce costs
       c.   coping with anti-capitalism backlash
       d.   working with people from different cultures

Answer: b, difficulty: 3, p. 6

43.   Two consequences of _____ are that managers are likely to find themselves in foreign assignments
       and dealing with foreigners within their own country.
       a.   empowerment
       b.   reengineering
       c.   quality management
       d.   globalization

Answer: d, difficulty: 1, pp. 6-7

44,   Capitalistic values are not popular in which of the following places?
       a.   France
       b.   the Middle East
       c.   Scandinavian countries
       d.   All of the above.

Answer: d, difficulty: 2, p. 7

45.   While _____ focuses on differences between people from different countries, _____ addresses
       differences among people within specific countries.
       a.   anticapitalism backlash; workforce diversity
       b.   globalization; workforce diversity
       c.   workforce diversity; globalization
       d.   foreign assignments; globalization

Answer: b, difficulty: 2, p. 7

46. Workforce diversity means:
   a. the workforce is becoming more homogeneous.
   b. the workforce is composed of mostly young people.
   c. the workforce is becoming more heterogeneous in terms of gender, race, and ethnicity.
   d. the workforce demands that everyone be treated exactly the same.

Answer: c, difficulty: 2, p. 7

47. Workforce diversity does NOT include which of the following?
   a. women
   b. the physically disabled
   c. low paying jobs
   d. gays and lesbians

Answer: c, difficulty: 2, p.7

48. Currently, _____ percent of the U.S. labor force are women.
   a. approximately 25
   b. 70
   c. nearly 50
   d. almost 10

Answer: c, difficulty: 3, Exhibit 1-2

49. The melting pot assumption to differences in organizations is being replaced by one that:
   a. assumes people who are different will somehow automatically want to assimilate.
   b. recognizes and values differences.
   c. tolerates differences.
   d. recognizes that employees set aside their differences when they come to work.

Answer: b, difficulty: 2, p. 8

50. The most significant change in the U.S. labor force during the last half of the twentieth century was the rapid:
   a. increase in the number of female workers.
   b. decrease in the number of male workers.
   c. increase in the number of males in managerial jobs.
   d. None of the above.

Answer: a, difficulty: 1, p. 9

51. Which of the following is NOT true concerning changing demographics in the first half of the 21st century?
    a. By 2050, Hispanics will grow from today's 11 percent of the workforce to 24 percent.
    b. Blacks will increase from 12 percent to 14 percent.
    c. Asians will increase from 5 percent to 11 percent.
    d. The 55-and-older age group will decrease from 13 percent to 5 percent.

Answer: d, difficulty: 3, p. 9

52. Workforce diversity has required that managers shift their philosophy in the treatment of their employees. This shift includes all of the following EXCEPT:
    a. providing diversity training to accommodate different needs.
    b. revamping benefits programs.
    c. treating everyone alike.
    d. accommodating the different needs of different employees.

Answer: c, difficulty: 2, p. 9

53. Which of the following is true about workforce diversity?
    a. Management needs to treat everyone alike.
    b. Diversity reduces the potential for higher turnover.
    c. Communication is easier with a diverse workforce.
    d. Diversity can increase creativity and innovation.

Answer: d, difficulty: 2, p. 9

54. Programs being implemented to improve quality and productivity, such as quality management and reengineering, involve:
    a. hiring many new employees.
    b. extensive employee involvement.
    c. increasing employee benefits.
    d. surveying customers.

Answer: b, difficulty: 2, p. 9

55. A philosophy of management that is driven by the constant attainment of customer satisfaction through the continuous improvement of all organizational processes is:
    a. quality management.
    b. process reengineering.
    c. workforce diversity.
    d. reinventing the company.

Answer: a, difficulty: 2, p. 10

56. _____ asks managers to reconsider how work would be done and their organization structured if they were starting over.
a. Quality management
b. Process reengineering
c. Managing diversity
d. Organizational design

Answer: b, difficulty: 1, p. 10

57. Quality management includes all of the following EXCEPT:
a. Intense focus on the customer.
b. Concern for continual improvement.
c. Close supervision of employees.
d. Accurate measurement.

Answer: c, difficulty: 2, Exhibit 1-3

58. Which of the following is not cited as a characteristic of a customer-responsive culture?
a. employees are friendly and courteous
b. employees are willing to do what's necessary to please the customer
c. employees are accessible
d. employees are good communicators

Answer: d, difficulty: 3, p. 11

59. When workers are allowed to operate largely without bosses, it is called:
a. matrix organization.
b. self-managed teams.
c. individualism.
d. neo-organizations.

Answer: b, difficulty: 1, p. 12

60. _____ is putting employees in charge of what they do.
a. Matrix organization
b. Empowering employees
c. Feedback
d. Group dynamics

Answer: b, difficulty: 2, p. 12

61. To effectively empower employees, managers must learn how to give up control and employees must learn:
    a. how to take responsibility for their work and make appropriate decisions.
    b. how to avoid responsibility for their work and make appropriate decisions.
    c. how to take responsibility for only the successes.
    d. how to avoid making decisions that impact them.

Answer: a, difficulty: 3, p. 12

62. Empowerment is changing all of the following EXCEPT:
    a. leadership styles.
    b. power relationships.
    c. the compensation of managers.
    d. the way work is designed.

Answer: c, difficulty: 2, p. 12

63. A networked organization:
    a. allows people to communicate and work together even though they may be thousands of miles apart.
    b. allows people to become independent contractors.
    c. allows people to change employees as the demand for their services change.
    d. All of the above.

Answer: d, difficulty: 2, p. 12

64. _____ in the workforce have been replaced by _____.
    a. Relatively permanent assignments; temporary work groups
    b. Part-time employees; permanent workers
    c. Flexibility; predictability
    d. Skilled labor; unskilled labor

Answer: a, difficulty: 2, p. 13

65. The constant state of flux in organizations is seen in all of the following EXCEPT:
    a. continually reorganizing various divisions.
    b. downsizing operations.
    c. selling off poorly performing businesses.
    d. replacing temporary employees with permanent employees.

Answer: d, difficulty: 3, p. 13

66. Which of the following is NOT a force contributing to the blurring of the lines between employees' work life and personal life?
   a. The creation of global organizations means their world never sleeps.
   b. Organizations are asking employees to put in fewer hours.
   c. Communication technology allows employees to work any time and from any place.
   d. The increase in the number of dual career couples makes it more difficult to fulfill non-work commitments.

Answer: b, difficulty: 3, pp. 13-14

67. Firms have sought to become "lean and mean" by closing factories, moving operations to lower-cost countries, selling off or closing down less profitable businesses, and replacing permanent employees with temporaries. A result of these changes has been:
   a. lower profits.
   b. a decline in employee loyalty.
   c. a less mobile workforce.
   d. a more homogeneous workforce.

Answer: b, difficulty: 1, p. 14

68. Situations in which employees are required to define right and wrong conduct are termed:
   a. ethical dilemmas.
   b. legal problems.
   c. organizational behavior dilemmas.
   d. religious issues.

Answer: a, difficulty: 1, p. 15

69. Which of the following is an example of an ethical dilemma?
   a. an employee's deciding whether to be a "whistle blower"
   b. cost-benefit analysis
   c. bona fide occupational qualification
   d. quality management

Answer: a, difficulty: 2, p. 15

70. In recent years, the line differentiating unethical from ethical behavior:
   a. has become easier to see.
   b. has become more blurred.
   c. has been clarified by laws on ethical behavior.
   d. is only the concern of top management.

Answer: b, difficulty: 2, p. 15

71. Distributing a code of ethics is an attempt to help employees solve:
    a. legal problems.
    b. policy decisions.
    c. ethical dilemmas.
    d. quality decisions.

Answer: c, difficulty: 1, p. 15

72. What are the three levels of analysis in OB presented in your text?
    a. individual, corporate, national
    b. group, organization, national
    c. individual, group, national
    d. individual, group, organization system

Answer: d, difficulty: 2, pp. 15-16 and Exhibit 1-4

73. The foundations of individual behavior include all of the following EXCEPT:
    a. trust.
    b. values.
    c. attitudes.
    d. perceptions.

Answer: a, difficulty: 3, pp. 16

TRUE/FALSE

74. Managers most often describe their most frequent problems as being budgetary problems.

Answer: False, difficulty: 2, p. 1

75. Technical skills are sufficient for succeeding in management.

Answer: False, difficulty: 2, pp. 1-2

76. Organizational behavior is the systematic study of the actions and attitudes that people exhibit within organizations.

Answer: True, difficulty: 1, p. 2

77. Organizational behavior seeks to replace systematic study with intuitive explanations.

Answer: False, difficulty: 2, p. 2

78. Organizational behavior does not seek to attribute cause and effect.

Answer: False, difficulty: 2, p. 2

79. OB systematically studies actions, behaviors, and attitudes.

Answer: True, difficulty: 1, p. 2

80. Organizational citizenship is a part of an employee's formal job requirements.

Answer: False, difficulty: 1, p. 2

81. Managers have a humanistic responsibility to provide their employees with jobs that are challenging, intrinsically rewarding, and satisfying.

Answer: True, difficulty: 2, p. 3

82. An organization is characterized by formal roles that define and shape the behavior of its members.

Answer: True, difficulty: 2, p. 3

83. OB does not encompass the behavior of people in federal government agencies and charitable organizations.

Answer: False, difficulty: 2, p. 3

84. Organizational behavior is applied behavioral science.

Answer: True, difficulty: 2, p. 3

85. The work of psychologists on culture and environment has helped us understand differences in fundamental values, attitudes, and behavior between people in different countries and within organizations.

Answer: False, difficulty: 2, p. 3

86. Today's industrial psychologists are concerned with issues such as workforce diversity, leadership effectiveness, and the impact of the economy on the organization.

Answer: False, difficulty: 3, p. 3

87. Social psychology is an area within psychology, blending concepts from psychology and sociology.

Answer: True, difficulty: 1, p. 3

88. The field of social psychology blends concepts from psychology and anthropology.

Answer: False, difficulty: 2, p. 3

89. Specific topics of concern to social psychologists include structuring of conflict and allocation of power.

Answer: False, difficulty: 2, Exhibit 1-1

90. The field of anthropology helps us understand organizational culture and organizational environment.

Answer: True, difficulty: 2, p. 5

91. Organizational behavior is concerned with developing people skills.

Answer: True, difficulty: 1, p. 5

92. The goals of organizational behavior are to help us explain, predict, and control human behavior.

Answer: True, difficulty: 1, p. 5

93. An attempt to determine what outcomes will result from a given action refers to the OB goal of explanation.

Answer: False, difficulty: 1, p. 5

94. The goal of prediction focuses on determining what outcomes will result from a given action.

Answer: True, difficulty: 1, p. 5

95. The most controversial goal of organizational behavior is using OB knowledge to control behavior.

Answer: True, difficulty: 2, p. 5

96. OB offers technologies that facilitate the control of people.

Answer: True, difficulty: 3, p. 6

97. The control objective is frequently seen by managers as the most valuable contribution that OB makes toward their effectiveness.

Answer: True, difficulty: 2, p. 6

98. The typical employee in today's workforce is younger and more loyal than ever before.

Answer: False, difficulty: 1, p. 6

99.   As the world has become a global village, the manager's job has changed little.

Answer: False, difficulty: 1, p. 6

100.   With increasing globalization, managers are less likely to find themselves in a foreign assignment.

Answer: False, difficulty: 1, p. 6

101.   Even in your own country today, you are going to find yourself working with bosses, peers, and other employees who were born and raised in different cultures.

Answer: True, difficulty: 1, pp. 6-7

102.   Globalization means managers will be forced to deal with different cultures even within their own country.

Answer: True, difficulty: 3, pp. 6-7

103.   Capitalistic values aren't as popular in places like the United States, Australia, and Hong Kong.

Answer: False, difficulty: 2, p. 7

104.   In a global economy, jobs tend to flow to places like China where lower costs provide business firms with a comparative advantage.

Answer: True, difficulty: 2, p. 7

105.   The movement of jobs to places with relatively low labor costs is criticized as undermining the job markets in developed countries.

Answer: True, difficulty: 2, p. 7

106.   While globalization focuses on differences between people from different countries, workforce diversity addresses differences among people within given countries.

Answer: True, difficulty: 3, p. 7

107.   Workforce diversity means that organizations are becoming a more homogeneous group of people.

Answer: False, difficulty: 1, p. 7

108.   The melting pot approach assumes people will somehow automatically want to assimilate.

Answer: True, difficulty: 2, p. 8

109.   Managing workforce diversity includes the notion that managers should treat everyone alike.

Answer: False, difficulty: 2, p. 9

110. The most significant change in the U.S. labor force during the last half of the 20th century was the rapid increase in the number of female workers.

Answer: True, difficulty: 1, p. 9

111. The 55-and-older age group, which currently makes up 13% of the labor force, will increase to 20% in just fifteen years.

Answer: True, difficulty: 2, p. 9

112. Diversity can increase creativity in organizations.

Answer: True, difficulty: 1, p. 9

113. Quality management (QM) is driven by the constant attainment of customer satisfaction through the continuous improvement of all organizational processes.

Answer: True, difficulty: 2, p. 10

114. Reengineering asks managers to reconsider how work would be done if we started over.

Answer: True, difficulty: 2, p. 10

115. Quality management requires that managers take responsibility away from the employees.

Answer: False, difficulty: 1, p. 10

116. Process reengineering requires that managers make incremental changes in basic production processes.

Answer: False, difficulty: 3, p. 10

117. Quality management and process reengineering require extensive employee involvement.

Answer: True, difficulty: 2, p. 10

118. Decision-making is being pushed down to the operating level in organizations.

Answer: True, difficulty: 1, pp. 11-12

119. Self-managed teams represent an example of empowering employees.

Answer: True, difficulty: 2, p. 12

120. Empowered individuals are in charge of *how* they do a job, but are not in charge of *what* they do.

Answer: False, difficulty: 3, p. 12

121. Organizations can foster innovation and change by maintaining flexibility, improving quality, and beating their competition to the marketplace with new products and services.

Answer: True, difficulty: 1, p. 12

122. The manager's job is different in a networked organization, especially when it comes to managing people.

Answer: True, difficulty: 2, p. 12

123. A key challenge for managers today is to stimulate employee creativity and tolerance for change.

Answer: True, difficulty: 1, p. 12

124. Today, managers work in a climate best characterized as temporary.

Answer: True, difficulty: 1, p. 13

125. Work groups are increasingly in a state of flux.

Answer: True, difficulty: 2, p. 13

126. Today's managers and employees must learn to cope with temporariness.

Answer: True, difficulty: 1, p. 13

127. The line between work and nonwork time has become very clear to employees today.

Answer: False, difficulty: 2, p. 13

128. Employees' loyalty to their organizations is on the rise.

Answer: False, difficulty: 1, p. 14

129. An important OB challenge will be for managers to devise ways to motivate workers who feel less committed to their employers, while maintaining their organizations' global competitiveness.

Answer: True, difficulty: 2, p. 14

130. Members of organizations are facing fewer ethical dilemmas today.

Answer: False, difficulty: 2, p. 15

131. When employees wonder if they should follow orders they don't personally agree with, they are facing an ethical dilemma.

Answer: True, difficulty: 2, p. 15

132. Organizations are writing and distributing codes of ethics to guide employees through ethical dilemmas.

Answer: True, difficulty: 3, p. 15

133. Some organizations are using in-house advisors who can be contacted for assistance in dealing with ethical issues.

Answer: True, difficulty: 1, p. 15

134. The behavior of people in groups is a simple extension of their behavior when they are alone.

Answer: False, difficulty: 2, p. 16

ESSAY

135. What does OB systematically study?

OB systematically studies all actions and behaviors. Productivity, absenteeism, turnover, and organizational citizenship are studied as especially important determinants of employee performance. Job satisfaction is a critical attitude studied.

p. 2

136. Discuss some of the many disciplines that have contributed to OB.

Psychology, sociology, social psychology, anthropology, and political science are some of the disciplines that have contributed to organizational behavior. Psychology provides insight into understanding individual behavior. Sociology helps us understand how people relate to others (especially in groups). Social psychology provides assistance in understanding the influence of people on one another and change. The study of societies has been extended with anthropology to understand cultures and environments. Political science provides insight into understanding power and conflict in the organization.

pp. 3-5 and Exhibit 1-1

137. Describe the three goals of organizational behavior.

The three goals of organizational behavior are to help managers explain, predict, and control human behavior. To understand human behavior requires an explanation. This assists in determining causes. Prediction focuses on future events. Prediction determines likely outcomes from given actions. Control focuses on getting others to behave in certain ways.

pp. 5-6

138. How does globalization affect a manager's people skills?

Globalization affects a manager's people skills in at least two ways. First, if you're a manager, you're increasingly likely to find yourself in a foreign assignment. Once there, you'll have to manage a work force that is likely to be very different in needs, aspirations, and attitudes from the ones you were used to dealing with back home. Second, even in your own country, you're going to find yourself working with bosses, peers, and employees who were born and raised in different cultures. To work effectively with these people, you'll need to understand their culture, how it has shaped them, and how to adapt your management style to their differences.

pp. 6-7

139. Discuss the advantages and challenges of managing workforce diversity.

If positively managed, diversity can increase creativity and innovation. It also can improve decision making by providing different perspectives on problems. Managing diversity, however, requires shifting away from the philosophy of treating everyone alike to recognizing differences and responding to those differences. When diversity is not managed properly, there is potential for higher turnover, more difficult communication, and more interpersonal conflicts.

pp. 9

140. Explain the concept of quality management.

Quality management is driven by a constant attainment of customer satisfaction through the continuous improvement of all organizational processes. It requires employees to rethink what they do and become more involved in workplace decisions.

p.10

141. Discuss process reengineering.

Process reengineering requires managers to reconsider how work would be done and their organization structured if they were starting over. It goes beyond making incremental changes in the basic production processes to throw out inefficient processes and introduce new processes.

p. 10

142. What are some of the critical issues facing managers today for which OB offers solutions or insights toward solutions?

OB can offer solutions or insights toward solutions when facing critical issues such as improving quality and productivity, improving people skills, managing work force diversity, responding to globalization, empowering people, stimulating innovation and change, coping with "temporariness," helping employees balance work-life conflicts, addressing declining employee loyalty, and improving ethical behavior.

pp. 10-15

143. How are employees being empowered today?

Managers are putting employees in charge of what they do. Managers are having to learn how to give up control, and employees are having to learn how to take responsibility for their work and make appropriate decisions.

p. 12

144. Discuss the evidence of temporariness in organizations.

The evidence of temporariness is everywhere. Jobs are being continually redesigned; tasks are increasingly being done by flexible teams rather then individuals; companies are relying more on temporary workers; jobs are being subcontracted out to other firms; and pensions are being redesigned to move with people as they change jobs.

p. 13

145. Discuss the forces that have contributed to blurring the lines between an employee's work life and personal life.

A number of forces have contributed to blurring the lines between employees' work life and personal life. First, the creation of global organizations means their world never sleeps. Second, communication technology allows employees to do their work at home, in their car, or on the beach in Tahiti. People can work any time and from any place. Third, organizations are asking employees to put in longer hours. Fourth, fewer families have only a single breadwinner. Today's married employee is typically part of a dual-career couple. This makes it increasingly difficult for married employees to find the time to fulfill commitments to both work and home, spouse, children, parents, and friends.

pp. 13-14

146. How are organizations responding to the problem of ethical behavior?

In response to the problem of ethical behavior, organizations are writing and distributing codes of ethics, offering seminars and workshops, providing in-house advisors, creating protection mechanisms for employees who reveal internal unethical practices, and they are creating ethically healthy climates with a minimal degree of ambiguity about right and wrong behavior.

pp. 14-15

CHAPTER 2 FOUNDATIONS OF INDIVIDUAL BEHAVIOR

MULTIPLE CHOICE

1. The major psychological contributions to OB are subdivided into four concepts. Which of the following is NOT one of those subdivisions?
    a. values
    b. leadership
    c. perception
    d. learning

Answer: b, difficulty: 2, p. 17

2. _____ represent basic convictions that a specific mode of conduct or end-state of existence is personally or socially preferable to an opposite or converse mode of conduct or end-state of existence.
    a. Values
    b. Attitudes
    c. Concerns
    d. Opinions

Answer: a, difficulty: 2, p. 17

3. _____ contain a judgmental element in that they carry an individual's ideas as to what is right, good, or desirable.
    a. Values
    b. Attitudes
    c. Concerns
    d. Opinions

Answer: a, difficulty: 2, p. 17

4. _____ represent(s) a prioritizing by the relative importance an individual assigns to such values as freedom, pleasure, self respect, honesty, obedience, and equality.
    a. Attitudes
    b. Value systems
    c. Opinions
    d. Job satisfaction

Answer: b, difficulty: 2, pp. 17-18

5. The Rokeach Value Survey (RVS) consists of two sets of values: _____ values and _____ values.
    a. individual; organizational
    b. cultural; national
    c. terminal; instrumental
    d. relative; absolute

Answer: c, difficulty: 3, p. 18

6. Goals that a person would like to achieve during his or her lifetime are referred to as:
   a. organizational.
   b. absolute.
   c. instrumental.
   d. terminal.

Answer: d, difficulty: 3, p. 18

7. In the Rokeach Value Survey (RVS), _____ values are desirable end-states of existence.
   a. organizational
   b. absolute
   c. instrumental
   d. terminal

Answer: d, difficulty: 2, p. 18

8. In the Rokeach Value Survey (RVS), _____ values are preferable modes of behavior, or a means of achieving other values.
   a. organizational
   b. absolute
   c. instrumental
   d. terminal

Answer: c, difficulty: 2, p. 18

9. Which of the following is NOT a terminal value?
   a. equality
   b. imaginative
   c. pleasure
   d. social recognition

Answer: b, difficulty: 2, Exhibit 2-1

10. Which of the following is NOT an instrumental value?
    a. capable
    b. cheerful
    c. social recognition
    d. logical

Answer: c, difficulty: 2, Exhibit 2-1

11. Which of the following is an example of a terminal value?
    a. a comfortable life
    b. obedient
    c. helpful
    d. ambitious

Answer: a, difficulty: 2, Exhibit 2-1

12. Which of the following is an instrumental value?
     a. freedom
     b. equality
     c. courageous
     d. salvation

Answer: c, difficulty: 2, Exhibit 2-1

13. One study on RVS values found that _____ ranked equality as their most important primal value.
     a. executives
     b. activists
     c. union members
     d. All of the above.

Answer: b, difficulty: 3, p. 18

14. The segment of the workforce aged 65+ who are hard-working, conservative, and loyal to the organization is termed:
     a. Xers.
     b. boomers.
     c. nexters.
     d. veterans.

Answer: d, difficulty: 2, Exhibit 2-2

15. The _____ in today's workforce are confident, self-reliant, and loyal to both self and relationships.
     a. Xers
     b. boomers
     c. nexters
     d. veterans

Answer: c, difficulty: 2, Exhibit 2-2

16. The loyalty of the _____ segment of today's workforce is to relationships.
     a. Xers
     b. boomers
     c. nexters
     d. veterans

Answer: a, difficulty: 2, Exhibit 2-2

17. Which work group tends to be loyal to their employer and places the greatest importance on a comfortable life and family security?
     a. Xers
     b. boomers
     c. nexters
     d. veterans

Answer: d, difficulty: 2, p. 19

18. Which of the following statements is true of boomers?
    a. They place a great deal of emphasis on achievement and material success.
    b. They believe that ends do not justify the means.
    c. Social recognition ranks low with them.
    d. They were shaped by MTV, AIDS, and computers.

Answer: a, difficulty: 2, p. 19

19. The segment of the workforce that is loyal to their careers is called:
    a. Xers.
    b. boomers.
    c. nexters.
    d. veterans.

Answer: b, difficulty: 2, Exhibit 2-2

20. _____ refers to the category of the workforce whose lives have been shaped by globalization, two-career parents, MTV, AIDS, and computers.
    a. Xers
    b. Boomers
    c. Nexters
    d. Veterans

Answer: a, difficulty: 2, p. 19

21. All of the following are segments of the U.S. workforce EXCEPT:
    a. generation Y.
    b. Xers.
    c. nexters.
    d. boomers.

Answer: a, difficulty: 1, p. 19 and Exhibit 2-2

22. The loyalty of veterans is to _____ while the loyalty of boomers is to _____.
    a. self; careers
    b. organization; career
    c. own values; relationships
    d. self; relationships

Answer: b, difficulty: 3, p. 19 and Exhibit 2-2

23. What is NOT true of Xers?
    a. They have been shaped by globalization, dual career parents, MTV, AIDS, and computers.
    b. They entered the work force from the mid-1960s through the mid-1980s.
    c. They enjoy team-oriented work.
    d. They are willing to trade off salary increases, titles, security, and promotions for increased leisure time and expanded lifestyle options.

Answer: b, difficulty: 3, p. 19

24. Employees in their late 60s are more likely to accept ____ than their coworkers who are 10-15 years younger.
    a. authority
    b. job insecurity
    c. team oriented jobs
    d. None of the above.

Answer: a, difficulty: 3, p. 20

25. Managers consistently report that the most important factor influencing ethical and unethical behavior in their organizations is:
    a. the action of their bosses.
    b. the values reflected by society.
    c. their own self-interest.
    d. All of the above.

Answer: a, difficulty: 3, p. 20

26. Hofstede found that managers and employees vary on _____ value dimensions of national culture.
    a. three
    b. four
    c. five
    d. six

Answer: c, difficulty: 2, p. 21

27. Which one of the following is NOT one of Hofstede's five value dimensions of national culture?
    a. responsibility avoidance
    b. individualism vs. collectivism
    c. power distance
    d. masculinity vs. femininity

Answer: a, difficulty: 2, p. 21

28. Hofstede's _____ dimension of national culture refers to the degree to which people in a country accept that power in institutions and organizations is distributed unequally.
    a. achievement vs. nurturing
    b. long-term vs. short-term orientation
    c. power distance
    d. individualism vs. collectivism

Answer: c, difficulty: 1, p. 21

29.   Hofstede's _____ dimension of national culture refers to the degree to which people prefer structured over unstructured situations.
    a. achievement vs. nurturing
    b. long-term vs. short-term orientation
    c. power distance
    d. uncertainty avoidance

Answer: d, difficulty: 1; p. 21

30.   Hofstede's _____ dimension of national culture refers to the degree to which people in a country prefer to act as individuals rather than as members of a group.
    a. individualism vs. collectivism
    b. power distance
    c. uncertainty avoidance
    d. long-term vs. short-term orientation

Answer: a, difficulty: 1, p. 21

31.   _____ is the equivalent of low individualism.
    a. Achievement
    b. Nurturing
    c. Collectivism
    d. Uncertainty avoidance

Answer: c, difficulty: 2, p. 21

32.   Hofstede's _____ dimension of national culture refers to whether people value thrift and persistence or emphasize respect for tradition and fulfilling social obligations.
    a. achievement vs. nurturing
    b. long-term vs. short-term orientation
    c. power distance
    d. individualism vs. collectivism

Answer: b, difficulty: 1, p. 21

33.   Hofstede's concept of _____ is the degree to which values like assertiveness, the acquisition of money and material goods, and competition prevail.
    a. power distance
    b. femininity vs. masculinity
    c. individualism vs. collectivism
    d. achievement

Answer: d, difficulty: 3, p. 21

34. According to Hofstede, _____ is the degree to which people value relationships, and show sensitivity and concern for the welfare of others.
   a. achievement
   b. individualism
   c. collectivism
   d. nurturing

Answer: d, difficulty: 3, p. 21

35. What nation ranked as the single most individualistic country?
   a. United States
   b. Australia
   c. England
   d. Sweden

Answer: a, difficulty: 2, p. 21

36. Which of the following countries ranked high on Hofstede's dimension of national culture termed long-term orientation?
   a. Russia
   b. France
   c. United States
   d. China

Answer: d, difficulty: 3, p. 21

37. Which of the following is NOT one of the nine dimensions the GLOBE team identified on which national cultures differ?
   a. assertiveness
   b. gender differentiation
   c. reward allocation
   d. human orientation

Answer: c, difficulty: 2, pp. 22-23

38. GLOBE's assertiveness dimension is essentially equivalent to Hofstede's _____ dimension.
   a. Power distance
   b. Achievement
   c. Individualism
   d. Collectivism

Answer: b, difficulty: 2, p. 22

39. GLOBE's human orientation closely approximates Hofstede's _____ dimension.
   a. Nurturing
   b. Achievement
   c. Individualism
   d. Collectivism

Answer: a, difficulty: 2, p. 23

40. The GLOBE dimension that reflect the extent to which a society encourages and rewards individuals for being fair, altruistic, generous, caring, and kind to others is:
   a. humane orientation.
   b. gender differentiation.
   c. power distance.
   d. assertiveness.

Answer: a, difficulty: 1, p. 23

41. The lack of cross-cultural considerations in management and OB research means that not all OB theories and concepts are universally applicable to managing people around the world and:
   a. only studies in the U.S. by American researchers should be considered.
   b. you should take into consideration cultural values when trying to understand the behavior of people in different countries.
   c. no management research is conducted in countries outside the United States.
   d. you don't have to worry about cultures outside the United States.

Answer: b, difficulty: 3, p. 23

42. _____ are evaluative statements concerning objects, people, or events.
   a. Values
   b. Attitudes
   c. Concerns
   d. Issues

Answer: b, difficulty: 1, p. 24

43. _____ reflect how one feels about something.
   a. Values
   b. Attitudes
   c. Concerns
   d. Issues

Answer: b, difficulty: 1, p. 24

44. Organizational behavior focuses on all of the following attitudes EXCEPT:
   a. job satisfaction.
   b. job involvement.
   c. organizational commitment.
   d. profitability.

Answer: d, difficulty: 1, p. 24

45. An indicator of loyalty to, and identification with, the organization is termed:
    a. job loyalty.
    b. job involvement.
    c. organizational commitment.
    d. job satisfaction.

Answer: c, difficulty: 3, p. 24

46.   The job-related attitude that has received the bulk of attention is:
    a. job satisfaction.
    b. job involvement.
    c. organizational commitment.
    d. organizational loyalty.

Answer: a, difficulty: 2, p. 24

47.   The degree to which a person identifies with his/her job and actively participates in it is known as:
    a. job loyalty.
    b. job involvement.
    c. job identification.
    d. job participation.

Answer: b, difficulty: 2, p. 24

48.   _____ refers to a collection of feelings that an individual holds toward his or her job.
    a. Job satisfaction
    b. Job involvement
    c. Job identification
    d. Organizational commitment

Answer: a, difficulty: 2, p. 24

49. A person with a high level of job satisfaction holds:
    a. positive feelings toward the organization.
    b. negative feelings toward the job.
    c. positive feelings toward the job.
    d. negative feelings toward the organization.

Answer: c, difficulty: 2, p. 24

50.   Evidence suggests that important factors conducive to job satisfaction include all of the following EXCEPT:
    a. mentally challenging work.
    b. high pay.
    c. supportive colleagues.
    d. supportive working conditions.

Answer: b, difficulty: 2, p. 24

51. Work can be made mentally challenging by all of the following EXCEPT:
    a. providing an opportunity to use their skills and abilities.
    b. offering a variety of tasks.
    c. avoiding providing feedback on how well they are doing.
    d. offering freedom.

Answer: c, difficulty: 3, p. 24

52. Recent research has indicated that job satisfaction comes down to conceptions of:
    a. fair outcomes.
    b. fair treatment.
    c. fair procedures.
    d. All of the above.

Answer: d, difficulty: 3, p. 24

53. _____ occurs when there are inconsistencies between two or more of a person's attitudes or between a person's behavior and attitudes.
    a. Cognitive dissonance
    b. Job satisfaction
    c. Machiavellianism
    d. Organizational commitment

Answer: a, difficulty: 1, p. 25

54. When there are inconsistencies between attitudes or between behavior and attitudes, individuals will attempt to:
    a. increase their job-related social relationships.
    b. confront their supervisor.
    c. reduce their job involvement.
    d. reduce dissonance.

Answer: d, difficulty: 2, p. 25

55. How individuals react to dissonance is determined by all of the following EXCEPT:
    a. rewards.
    b. work ethic.
    c. degree of perceived influence.
    d. importance of elements creating dissonance.

Answer: b, difficulty: 3, pp. 25-26

56. If attitudes and behavior are inconsistent, individuals will most likely:
    a. discuss their behavior with others to find a solution.
    b. consider why they have a certain attitude.
    c. change either their attitudes and/or behavior.
    d. do nothing.

Answer: c, difficulty: 2, p. 27

57. Attitudes that individuals consider important tend to show
    a. a strong relationship to behavior.
    b. a weak relationship to behavior.
    c. no relationship to behavior.
    d. None of the above.

Answer: a, difficulty: 2, p. 27

58. Perception is a process that involves individuals:
    a. organizing and interpreting their sensory impressions to give meaning to their environment.
    b. examining sensors and activating them to receive stimuli.
    c. receiving inputs and intensifying their symbolic forms.
    d. establishing role episodes and transmitting them to receivers.

Answer: a, difficulty: 2, p. 27

59. Which of the following is NOT a place where factors can reside that operate to shape and sometimes distort perception?
    a. perceiver
    b. content
    c. target
    d. situation

Answer: b, difficulty: 2, p. 28

60. Personal characteristics affecting perception include:
    a. attitudes, expectations, and the target.
    b. the relationship of a target to its background.
    c. attitudes, personality, and past experiences.
    d. the time and location of the situation.

Answer: c, difficulty: 2, p. 28

61. Elements in the environment:
    a. rarely influence perception because perception is internal.
    b. may include the time, location, and light, and can influence perception.
    c. can be controlled by the message receiver.
    d. are the most important elements influencing perception.

Answer: b, difficulty: 3, p. 28

62. All of the following factors influence our perception of whether an individual's behavior is internally or externally caused EXCEPT:
    a. distinctiveness.
    b. complacency.
    c. consensus.
    d. consistency.

Answer: b, difficulty: 2, p. 28

63. Internally caused behaviors are those that are believed to be:
   a. under the personal control of the individual.
   b. the result of outside causes.
   c. behaviors that the person was forced into by the situation.
   d. exaggerated for everyone.

Answer: a, difficulty: 3, p. 28

64. _____ has been proposed to develop explanations of how we judge people differently depending on what meaning we attribute to a given behavior.
   a. Distinctiveness
   b. Attribution theory
   c. Fundamental error
   d. Self-serving bias

Answer: b, difficulty: 2, p. 28

65. Distinctiveness refers to:
   a. similar responses to similar situations.
   b. whether an individual displays different behavior in different situations.
   c. responses that are the same over time.
   d. the distortions we make in judging others' behavior.

Answer: b, difficulty: 2, p. 29

66. The more consistent a behavior, the more the observer is inclined to:
   a. depend on the behavior.
   b. attribute it to external causes.
   c. attribute it to consensus.
   d. attribute it to internal causes.

Answer: d, difficulty: 2, p. 29

67. _____ refers to whether an individual displays different behaviors in different situations.
   a. Consistency
   b. Distinctiveness
   c. Consensus
   d. Attribution

Answer: b, difficulty: 2, p. 29

68. _____ refers to whether a person responds the same way over time.
   a. Consistency
   b. Distinctiveness
   c. Consensus
   d. Attribution

Answer: a, difficulty: 2, p. 29

69.	_____ refers to the fact that individuals tend to attribute their own successes to internal factors such as ability or effort while putting the blame for failure on external factors such as luck.
	a.	Self-serving bias
	b.	Assumed similarity
	c.	Fundamental attribution error
	d.	The halo effect

Answer: a, difficulty: 2, p. 29

70.	_____ refers to the fact that when we judge the behavior of other people, we tend to underestimate the influence of external factors and overestimate the influence of internal or personal factors.
	a.	Self-serving bias
	b.	Assumed similarity
	c.	Fundamental attribution error
	d.	The halo effect

Answer: c, difficulty: 2, p. 29

71.	When we judge someone on the basis of our perception of the group to which he/she belongs, we are using the shortcut called:
	a.	grouping.
	b.	categorizing.
	c.	stereotyping.
	d.	assimilating.

Answer: c, difficulty: 1, p. 30

72.	Individuals use _____ when they cannot assimilate all they observe. They take in data in bits and pieces.
	a.	selectivity
	b.	assumed similarity
	c.	stereotyping
	d.	perception

Answer: a, difficulty: 2, p. 30

73.	_____ results in an individual's perception of others being influenced more by what the observer is like than by what the person being observed is like.
	a.	Selectivity
	b.	Stereotyping
	c.	The halo effect
	d.	Assumed similarity

Answer: d, difficulty: 3, p. 30

74. With selective perception:
   a. we assimilate everything we observe.
   b. we are able to "speed read" others.
   c. we assume others are similar to us.
   d. we avoid shortcuts.

Answer: b, difficulty: 2, p. 30

75. When an interviewer allows a single trait or appearance to override other characteristics in the interviewer's general perception about the individual, _____ is operating.
   a. selectivity
   b. stereotyping
   c. the halo effect
   d. assumed similarity

Answer: c, difficulty: 3, p. 30

76. _____ is a relatively permanent change in behavior that occurs as a result of experience.
   a. Learning
   b. Selectivity
   c. Personality
   d. Consensus

Answer: a, difficulty: 1, p. 30

77. The _____ says that behavior is a function of its consequences.
   a. halo effect
   b. learning curve
   c. Thorndyke effect
   d. law of effect

Answer: d, difficulty: 3, p. 30

78. According to the law of effect, if your boss compliments you on your sales approach:
   a. you're likely to repeat the behavior.
   b. you're unlikely to repeat the behavior.
   c. you're not impacted at all.
   d. you're likely to learn a new sales approach.

Answer: a, difficulty: 3, p. 30

79. Learning that takes place in graduated steps is called:
   a. modeling.
   b. shaping.
   c. reinforcing.
   d. trial and error.

Answer: b, difficulty: 2, p. 31

80. Systematically reinforcing through rewards, each successive step that moves an employee closer to the desired behavior is referred to as:
   a. trial-and-error learning.
   b. stepping.
   c. shaping.
   d. modeling.

Answer: c, difficulty: 2, p. 31

81. A new employee who wants to be successful on her job looks for someone in the organization who is well respected and successful and then tries to imitate that person's behavior. This new employee is using:
   a. trial-and-error learning.
   b. stepping.
   c. shaping.
   d. modeling.

Answer: d, difficulty: 3, p. 31

82. How employees interpret their work environment (perception) will influence all of the following EXCEPT:
   a. what they learn on the job.
   b. their level of motivation.
   c. the employee's attitudes.
   d. their individual work behavior.

Answer: c, difficulty: 3, p. 31

TRUE/FALSE

83. Attitudes represent basic convictions that "a specific mode of conduct or end-state of existence is personally or socially preferable to an opposite or converse mode of conduct or end-state of existence."

Answer: False, difficulty: 2, p. 17

84. The Rokeach Value Survey (RVS) consists of two sets of values: terminal values and instrumental values.

Answer: True, difficulty: 1, p. 18

85. Freedom and equality are examples of instrumental values.

Answer: False, difficulty: 2, Exhibit 2-1

86. Inner harmony is an example of a terminal value.

Answer: True, difficulty: 2, Exhibit 2-1

87.	Happiness and true friendship are examples of terminal values.

Answer: True, difficulty: 2, Exhibit 2-1

88.	Several studies confirm that the RVS values vary among groups.

Answer: True, difficulty: 2, p. 18

89.	The Boomers entered the workforce from the mid-1940s to the late 1950s are hard-working, conservative, and loyal to their careers.

Answer: False, difficulty: 3, Exhibit 2-2

90.	Xers seek job satisfaction and adequate leisure time.

Answer: True, difficulty: 1, p. 19

91.	Veterans are more likely to be conservative and accepting of authority than their Boomer co-workers.

Answer: True, difficulty: 2, p. 19

92.	The loyalty of veterans is to self and the loyalty of Nexters is to their employer.

Answer: False, difficulty: 3, pp. 19-20 and Exhibit 2-2

93.	In search of balance in their lives, Xers are less willing to make personal sacrifices for the sake of their employers than previous generations were.

Answer: True, difficulty: 3, pp. 19-20

94.	The most recent entrants to the workforce are the Nexters.

Answer: True, difficulty: 1, p. 20

95.	We might look forward to an uplifting of ethical standards in business over the next decade or two merely as a result of changing values within the managerial ranks.

Answer: True, difficulty: 3, p. 20

96.	Since Xers' loyalty is to relationships, they are more likely to consider the ethical implications of their actions around them.

Answer: True, difficulty: 2, p. 20

97.	Values rarely differ across cultures.

Answer: False, difficulty: 1, p. 21

98. Perceptual distance is a measure of the extent to which a society accepts unequal distribution of power in organizations.

Answer: False, difficulty: 2, p. 21

99. A society high in uncertainty avoidance is characterized by a decreased level of anxiety among its people.

Answer: False, difficulty: 2, p. 21

100. Individualism is the degree to which people in a country prefer to act as individuals rather than as members of groups.

Answer: True, difficulty: 1, p. 21

101. Hofstede described societies that value the past and present, and emphasized respect for tradition as short-term orientation.

Answer: True, difficulty: 2, p. 21

102. According to Hofstede, the U.S. culture ranked high on individualism, power distance, and uncertainty avoidance.

Answer: False, difficulty: 3, p. 21

103. People in short-term orientation countries look to the future and value thrift and persistence.

Answer: False, difficulty: 2, p. 21

104. According to Hofstede, France and the United States had a long-term orientation.

Answer: False, difficulty: 2, p. 21

105. The GLOBE framework's future orientation is essentially equivalent to Hofstede's long-term/short-term orientation.

Answer: True, difficulty: 2, p. 21

106. Americans rate high on the GLOBE dimensions of future orientation, individualism, and power distance.

Answer: False, difficulty: 2, Exhibit 2-3

107. The United States scores high on the GLOBE dimensions of assertiveness and performance orientation.

Answer: True, difficulty: 2, Exhibit 2-3

108. The GLOBE framework's in-group collectivism focuses on societal institutions as reflected in Hofstede's individualism/collectivism.

Answer: False, difficulty: 3, p. 23

109. The GLOBE dimensions have replaced Hofstede's work.

Answer: False, difficulty: 2, p. 23

110. Most of the concepts that currently make up the knowledge base in the field of organizational behavior have been developed by Americans using American subjects.

Answer: True, difficulty: 1, p. 23

111. All OB theories and concepts are universally applicable to managing people around the world.

Answer: False, difficulty: 2, p. 23

112. Attitudes are evaluative statements concerning objects, people, or events.

Answer: True, difficulty: 1, p. 24

113. Job satisfaction is defined as the degree to which a person identifies with his or her job and actively participates in it.

Answer: False, difficulty: 2, p. 24

114. A person with a high level of job satisfaction holds positive feelings toward the job.

Answer: True, difficulty: 2, p. 24

115. Evidence indicates that the most important factors conducive to job satisfaction are mentally challenging work, equitable pay, supportive working conditions, and supportive colleagues.

Answer: True, difficulty: 3, p. 24

116. Under conditions of very low challenge, most employees will experience pleasure and satisfaction.

Answer: False, difficulty: 2, p. 24

117. Individuals who perceive that promotion decisions are made in a fair and just manner are likely to experience satisfaction from their jobs.

Answer: True, difficulty: 2, p. 24

118.   The happy worker thesis was based on hard evidence.

Answer: False, difficulty: 3, p. 24-25

119.   Current research indicates that satisfaction leads to productivity.

Answer: False, difficulty: 3, p. 25

120.   Satisfaction influences organizational citizenship behavior (OCB) through perceptions of fairness.

Answer: True, difficulty: 3, pp. 25

121.   When you trust your employer, you are more willing to voluntarily engage in behaviors that go beyond your formal job description.

Answer: True, difficulty: 3, p. 25

122.   The theory of cognitive dissonance suggests that people seek to maximize dissonance and the satisfaction that it brings.

Answer: False, difficulty: 1, p. 25

123.   Individuals will be under great tension to reduce dissonance if the issues are of minimal importance and the dissonance is externally imposed and controlled by them.

Answer: False, difficulty: 3, p. 26

124.   Employees often can deal with greater dissonance on their jobs than off their jobs.

Answer: True, difficulty: 2, p. 26

125.   The greater the dissonance, the greater the pressure to reduce the dissonance.

Answer: True, difficulty: 2, p. 26

126.   Recent research has demonstrated that there is very little relationship between attitudes and behavior if moderating contingency variables are considered.

Answer: False, difficulty: 2, p. 27

127.   The more specific the attitude and the more specific behavior, the stronger the link between the two.

Answer: True, difficulty: 3, p. 27

128.   The attitude/behavior relationship is likely to be much stronger if an attitude refers to something with which the individual has direct personal experience.

Answer: True, difficulty: 2, p. 27

129. Different individuals look at the same thing and perceive it in the same way.

Answer: False, difficulty: 2, p. 27

130. Factors that shape and distort perception include the perceiver, the target, and the situation.

Answer: True, difficulty: 3, p. 28

131. The time at which an object or event is seen seldom influences attention.

Answer: False, difficulty: 2, p. 28

132. Attribution theory is used to help explain how we judge people differently depending on what meaning we attribute to a given behavior.

Answer: True, difficulty: 1, p. 28

133. When we observe people, we attempt to develop explanations of why they behave in certain ways.

Answer: True, difficulty: 1, p. 28

134. Externally caused behaviors are those that are believed to be under the personal control of the individual.

Answer: False, difficulty: 2, pp. 28-29

135. Consistency refers to whether an individual displays different behaviors in different situations.

Answer: False, difficulty: 2, p. 29

136. If everyone who is faced with a similar situation responds in the same way, we can say the behavior shows consensus.

Answer: True, difficulty: 2, p. 29

137. According to the self-serving bias, there is a tendency for individuals to attribute their own success to external factors while putting the blame for failure on internal factors.

Answer: False, difficulty: 1, p. 29

138. Selective perception allows us to speed read others.

Answer: True, difficulty: 1, p. 30

139. An example of stereotyping is when an individual's perception of others is influenced more by what the observer is like than by what the person being observed is like.

Answer: False, difficulty: 2, p. 30

140. "Married people are more stable employees than singles" is an example of a stereotype.

Answer: True, difficulty: 1, p. 30

141. When we draw a general impression about an individual based on a single positive or negative characteristic, a halo effect is operating.

Answer: True, difficulty: 1, p. 30

142. Learning is any relatively permanent change in behavior that occurs as a result of experience.

Answer: True, difficulty: 2, p. 30

143. According to the law of effect, behavior that is followed by an unfavorable consequence tends to be repeated; behavior followed by a favorable consequence tends not to be repeated.

Answer: False, difficulty: 2, pp. 30-31

ESSAY

144. Explain Rokeach's Value Survey. Be sure to completely explain terminal and instrumental values and give examples.

The Rokeach Value Survey (RVS) consists of two sets of values, with each set containing 18 individual value items. One set, called terminal values, refers to desirable end-states of existence. These are the goals that a person would like to achieve during his or her lifetime. These include a comfortable life, a sense of accomplishment, a world of peace, a world of beauty, equality, family security, freedom, happiness, inner harmony, pleasure, salvation, social recognition, and true friendship. The other set, called instrumental values, refers to preferable modes of behavior, or means of achieving the terminal values. These include ambitious, capable, cheerful, clean, courageous, helpful, honest, imaginative, logical, loving, obedient, polite, and responsible.

pp 18-19 and Exhibit 2-1

145. What are the four generations in the U.S. workforce? What are the characteristics and loyalties of each group?

The four generations are Veterans, Boomers, Xers, and Nexters. The Veterans entered the workforce in the 1950s and early 1960s. They are hard working, conservative, conforming, and loyal to the organization. The Boomers entered the workforce between 1965 and 1985. They value success and achievement, are ambitious, dislike authority, and are loyal to their career. Xers entered the workforce between 1985 and 2000. They value work-life balance, are team-oriented, dislike rules, and are loyal to relationships. The Nexters entered the workforce since 2000. They are confident, value financial success, are self-reliant, but team-oriented, and are loyal to both themselves and their relationships.

pp. 19-20 and Exhibit 2-2

146. What are the five value dimensions of national culture proposed by Geert Hofstede and how does the U.S. score on each of these dimensions?

The five value dimensions of national culture proposed by Geert Hofstede are power distance, individualism vs. collectivism, quantity of life vs. quality of life, uncertainty avoidance, and long-term vs. short-term orientation. Power distance is the degree to which people in a country accept that power in institutions and organizations is distributed unequally. The U.S. scores low on power distance. Individualism is the degree to which people prefer to act as individuals rather than as members of groups. The U.S. scores high on individualism. Quantity of life is the degree to which values like assertiveness, the acquisition of money and material goods, and competition prevail. Quality of life is the degree to which people value relationships, and show sensitivity and concern for the welfare of others. The U.S. scores high on quantity of life. Uncertainty avoidance is the degree to which people in a country prefer structured over unstructured situations. The U.S. scores low on uncertainty avoidance. People in long-term orientation countries look to the future and value thrift and persistence. Short-term orientated people value the past and present, and emphasize respect for tradition and fulfilling social obligations. The U.S. scores low on long-term orientation (or high on short-term orientation).

p. 21

147. What determines job satisfaction?

The evidence indicates that the most important factors conducive to job satisfaction are mentally challenging work, equitable rewards, supportive working conditions, and supportive colleagues.

p. 24

148. What is the relationship between job satisfaction and productivity?

The introduction of moderating variables has improved the relationship showing that satisfaction does have a positive effect on productivity. Currently, on the basis of a comprehensive review of the evidence, we would conclude that productivity is more likely to lead to satisfaction rather than the other way around.

pp. 24-25

149. Discuss the concept of cognitive dissonance.

Cognitive dissonance occurs when there are inconsistencies between two or more of a person's attitudes or between a person's behavior and attitudes. The theory of cognitive dissonance suggests that people seek to minimize dissonance and the discomfort it causes.

p. 25

150. Explain why different individuals may look at the same thing yet perceive it differently.

Perception is the process by which individuals organize and interpret their sensory impressions in order to give meaning to their environment. Since none of us see reality, we all interpret what we see and call it reality – causing us to look at the same thing yet perceive it differently. The factors that shape and distort perception reside in the perceiver, the object or target being perceived, or in the context of the situation in which the perception is made.

pp. 27-28

151. Explain attribution theory.

When we observe people, we attempt to develop explanations of why they behave in certain ways. Our perceptions and judgment of a person's actions will be significantly influenced by the assumptions we make about the person's internal state. Attribution theory has been proposed to develop explanations of how we judge people differently depending on what meaning we attribute to a given behavior. Basically, we attempt to determine whether it was internally or externally caused.

p. 28

152. Discuss the fundamental attribution error.

The fundamental attribution error suggests that when we make judgments about the behavior of other people, we have a tendency to underestimate the influence of external factors and overestimate the influence of internal or personal factors.

p. 29

153. Explain the self-serving bias.

The self-serving bias suggests that there is a tendency for individuals to attribute their own successes to internal factors such as ability or effort while putting the blame for failure on external factors such as luck.

p. 29

154. Discuss three shortcuts to judging others.

Three shortcuts to judging others include selectivity, assumed similarity, and stereotyping. Selectivity occurs because we cannot assimilate everything we observe. We take in bits and pieces that are selectively chosen depending on the interests, background, experience, and attitudes of the observer. We speed read others. Assumed similarity, or the "like me" effect, results in an individual's perception of others being influenced more by what the observer is like than by what the person being observed is like. When we judge someone on the basis of our perception of the group to which he or she belongs, we are using the shortcut called stereotyping.

pp. 29-30

155.   Explain how the law of effect is used in learning.

The law of effect says that behavior is a function of its consequences. Behavior that is followed by a favorable consequence tends to be repeated; behavior followed by an unfavorable consequence tends not to be repeated.

pp. 30-31

156.   Explain how shaping is used in learning.

When learning takes place in graduated steps, it is shaped. Managers shape employee behavior by systematically reinforcing, through reward, each successive step that moves the employee closer to the desired behavior. "Learning by mistakes" is shaping. We try, we fail, and we try again.

p. 31

CHAPTER 3 PERSONALITY AND EMOTIONS

MULTIPLE CHOICE

1. When we describe people as quiet, passive, loud, aggressive, or loyal, we are categorizing them in terms of:
    a. emotions.
    b. personality traits.
    c. affects.
    d. values.

Answer: b, difficulty: 2, p. 34

2. The combination of psychological traits used to classify a person is known as:
    a. ability.
    b. attitude.
    c. norm.
    d. personality.

Answer: d, difficulty: 1, p. 34

3. A 100-question personality test that asks people how they usually feel or act in particular situations is:
    a. the Big Five Model.
    b. the Myers-Briggs Type Indicator.
    c. the Six-Personality-Types Model.
    d. the Mach Model.

Answer: b, difficulty: 3, p. 35

4. Which of the following is NOT a classification of the Myers-Briggs Type Indicator?
    a. extroverted or introverted
    b. sensing or intuitive
    c. perceiving or judging
    d. pragmatic or sentimental

Answer: d, difficulty: 2, p. 35

5. In the Myers-Briggs Type Indicator, the individual classified as _____ is a visionary, characterized as skeptical, critical, independent, determined, and often stubborn.
    a. ESTJ
    b. INTJ
    c. ENTP
    d. ISFP

Answer: b, difficulty: 3, p. 35

6. In the Myers-Briggs Type Indicator, the individual classified as _____ is a conceptualizer, characterized as innovative, versatile, and attracted to entrepreneurial ideas.
   a. ESTJ
   b. INTJ
   c. ENTP
   d. ISFP

Answer: c, difficulty: 3, p. 35

7. Intuitive thinkers represent about _____ percent of the population.
   a. 5
   b. 15
   c. 25
   d. 50

Answer: a, difficulty: 2, p. 35

8. In the Myers-Briggs Type Indicator, the individual classified as _____ is an organizer, characterized as logical, realistic, and decisive.
   a. ESTJ
   b. INTJ
   c. ENTP
   d. ISFP

Answer: a, difficulty: 3, p. 35

9. A book that profiled 13 contemporary business people who created super successful firms found that all 13 were:
   a. sensing thinkers.
   b. intuitive thinkers.
   c. sensing feelers.
   d. intuitive feelers.

Answer: b, difficulty: 3, p. 35

10. What is the current state of research about the Myers-Briggs Type Indicator?
    a. Research generally supports its validity.
    b. There is no hard evidence that it is a valid measure of personality.
    c. Research overwhelmingly supports the use of the MBTI to match jobs and people.
    d. MBTI has not been taken by a sufficient number of people to draw conclusions.

Answer: b, difficulty: 3, p. 35

11. The Big Five Model of personality uses all of the following basic personality dimensions EXCEPT:
    a. extroversion.
    b. perceptiveness.
    c. conscientiousness.
    d. openness to experience.

Answer: b, difficulty: 3, pp. 35-36

12. The factor in the Big Five Model identified as agreeableness refers to:
    a. an individual's propensity to defer to others.
    b. one's comfort level with relationships.
    c. one's level of reliability.
    d. a person's ability to withstand stress.

Answer: a, difficulty: 1, pp. 35-36

13. The factor in the Big Five Model identified as emotional stability refers to:
    a. an individual's propensity to defer to others.
    b. one's comfort level with relationships.
    c. a measure of reliability.
    d. a person's ability to withstand stress.

Answer: d, difficulty: 1, pp. 35-36

14. The Big Five Model of personality defines _____ as sociable, gregarious, and assertive.
    a. extroversion
    b. agreeableness
    c. conscientiousness
    d. openness to experience

Answer: a, difficulty: 2, pp. 35-36

15. The Big Five Model of personality defines _____ as responsible, dependable, persistent, and organized.
    a. extroversion
    b. agreeableness
    c. conscientiousness
    d. openness to experience

Answer: c, difficulty: 2, p. 36

16. The Big Five Model of personality defines _____ as creative, artistically sensitive, and curious.
    a. extroversion
    b. agreeableness
    c. conscientiousness
    d. openness to experience

Answer: d, difficulty: 2, p. 36

17. According to the Big Five Model of personality, the dimension of _____ addresses an individual's range of interests and fascination with novelty.
    a. extroversion
    b. agreeableness
    c. conscientiousness
    d. openness to experience

Answer: d, difficulty: 2, p. 36

18. The Big Five Model found that _____ predicted job performance for all occupational groups examined in the study.
    a. extroversion
    b. conscientiousness
    c. emotional stability
    d. openness to experience

Answer: b, difficulty: 3, p. 36

19. Research on the Big Five Model found that _____ predicted performance in managerial and sales positions.
    a. agreeableness
    b. emotional stability
    c. openness to experience
    d. extroversion

Answer: d, difficulty: 2, p. 36

20. Research on the Big Five Model found that _____ was important in predicting training proficiency.
    a. agreeableness
    b. emotional stability
    c. openness to experience
    d. extroversion

Answer: c, difficulty: 2, p. 36

21. According to the text, all of the following are key personality attributes in explaining and predicting behavior in organizations EXCEPT:
    a. locus of control.
    b. intelligence.
    c. self-monitoring.
    d. risk propensity.

Answer: b, difficulty: 3, p. 36

22. The belief by an individual as to whether he controls his fate or whether he is a pawn of fate is termed:
    a. locus of control.
    b. authoritarianism.
    c. Machiavellianism.
    d. self-monitoring.

Answer: a, difficulty: 2, p. 36

23. People who believe that they are the masters of their own fate have:
    a. an internal locus of control.
    b. an external locus of control.
    c. a high Mach score.
    d. tough-mindedness.

Answer: a, difficulty: 2, p. 36

24. Evidence shows that employees who rate high in an external locus of control are:
    a. less satisfied with their jobs.
    b. more alienated from the work setting.
    c. less involved in their jobs than internals.
    d. All of the above.

Answer: d, difficulty: 3, pp. 36-37

25. Employees who blame a poor performance evaluation on their boss's prejudice, co-workers, or other external factors are more likely to have:
    a. a high external locus-of-control.
    b. a high internal locus-of-control.
    c. high authoritarianism.
    d. low authoritarianism.

Answer: a, difficulty: 3, pp. 36-37

26. An individual with an external locus of control is:
    a. a chameleon, able to change to fit the situation.
    b. manipulative, maintains emotional distance, and believes that the ends justify the means.
    c. intellectually rigid, judgmental of others, deferential to superiors, and exploitative of those below.
    d. prone to blame a poor performance evaluation on his boss's prejudice, his co-workers, or other events outside his control.

Answer: d, difficulty: 2, pp. 36-37

27.	An individual exhibiting strong Machiavellian tendencies is all of the following EXCEPT:
   a.	manipulative.
   b.	emotionally distant.
   c.	under the impression that the ends justify the means.
   d.	under the impression that the means justify the ends.

Answer: d, difficulty: 2, p. 37

28.	High Machs are _____ to engage in behavior that is ethically questionable than are low Machs.
   a.	more likely
   b.	just as likely
   c.	less likely
   d.	None of the above.

Answer: a, difficulty: 3, p. 37

29.	Which trait is directly related to expectations for success?
   a.	locus of control
   b.	Machiavelliamism
   c.	self-esteem
   d.	Type A personality

Answer: c, difficulty: 2, p.37

30.	People differ in the degree to which they like or dislike themselves. This trait is called:
   a.	locus of control.
   b.	Machiavelliamism.
   c.	self-esteem.
   d.	Type A personality.

Answer: c, difficulty: 2, p. 37

31.	Which of the following statements is true concerning SEs?
   a.	Low SEs are more satisfied with their jobs than are high SEs.
   b.	High SEs are more satisfied with their jobs than are low SEs.
   c.	There is no significant difference in the satisfaction level of high and low SEs.
   d.	In managerial positions, low SEs are more likely to take unpopular stands than are high SEs.

Answer: b, difficulty: 3, p. 37

32. Which of the following is NOT true of people with low self-esteem?
   a. People with low self-esteem are more susceptible to external influences than people with high self-esteem.
   b. Low SEs depend on the receipt of positive evaluations for others.
   c. Low SEs are less likely to seek approval from others.
   d. Low SEs are prone to conform to the beliefs and behaviors of those they respect than are high SEs.

Answer: c, difficulty: 3, p. 37

33. An individual exhibiting strong _____ tendencies is manipulative, maintains emotional distance, and believes that ends can justify means.
   a. Machiavellianism
   b. risk propensity
   c. locus of control
   d. emotional stability

Answer: a, difficulty: 3, p. 37

34. An individual exhibiting strong Machiavellian tendencies is:
   a. a chameleon, able to change to fit the situation.
   b. manipulative, maintains emotional distance, and believes that ends can justify means.
   c. intellectually rigid, judgmental of others, deferential to those above, and exploitative of those below.
   d. prone to blame a poor performance evaluation on his boss's prejudice, his co-workers, or other events outside his control.

Answer: b, difficulty: 2, p. 37

35. People with high _____ believe they possess the ability they need in order to succeed at work.
   a. self-monitoring
   b. Machiavellianism
   c. self-esteem
   d. locus of control

Answer: c, difficulty: 2, p. 37

36. People who are much better than others at adjusting their behavior to changing situations score high in:
   a. Machiavellianism.
   b. authoritarianism.
   c. self-monitoring.
   d. locus of control.

Answer: c, difficulty: 2, p. 37

37. Individuals with a high _____ make more rapid decisions and use less information in making their choices.
   a. Mach score
   b. self-esteem
   c. locus of control
   d. risk propensity

Answer: d, difficulty: 3, p. 37

38. Individuals with a(n) _____ personality are characterized by an incessant struggle to achieve more and more in less and less time.
   a. Type B
   b. Type A
   c. left-brained
   d. right-brained

Answer: b, difficulty: 1, p. 38

39. Which of the following is NOT a characteristic of Type A personalities?
   a. impatient
   b. creative
   c. cope poorly with leisure time
   d. create a life of self-imposed deadlines

Answer: b, difficulty: 2, p. 38

40. Which of the following is NOT true of Type A personality managers?
   a. They demonstrate their competitiveness by working long hours.
   b. They make poor decisions because they make them too fast.
   c. They are always highly creative.
   d. They rely on past experiences when faced with problems.

Answer: c, difficulty: 2, p. 38

41. We expect to find more _____ in cultures where achievement and material success are valued.
   a. authoritarian personalities
   b. low self-monitors
   c. Type A personalities
   d. Type B personalities

Answer: c, difficulty: 1, p. 38

42. It is estimated that about _____ percent of the North American population is Type A.
   a. 10
   b. 25
   c. 50
   d. 75

Answer: c, difficulty: 3, p. 38

43.   The _____ personality type prefers verbal activities where there are opportunities to influence others and attain power.
        a. social
        b. investigative
        c. enterprising
        d. artistic

Answer: c, difficulty: 2, p. 39 and Exhibit 3-1

44.   Which occupation would be best suited for a realistic-personality type?
        a. mechanic
        b. social worker
        c. lawyer
        d. musician

Answer: a, difficulty: 2, p. 39 and Exhibit 3-1

45.   Which occupation would be best suited for a social-personality type?
        a. mechanic
        b. social worker
        c. lawyer
        d. musician

Answer: b, difficulty: 2, p. 39 and Exhibit 3-1

46.   The _____ -personality type is characterized as analytical, original, and curious.
        a. enterprising
        b. conventional
        c. social
        d. investigative

Answer: d difficulty: 2, Exhibit 3-1

47.   Which occupation would be best suited for an artistic-personality type?
        a. mechanic
        b. social worker
        c. lawyer
        d. musician

Answer: d, difficulty: 1, Exhibit 3-1

48.   The personality job-fit theory argues that satisfaction is highest and turnover lowest where:
        a. people's personality and occupation are incongruent.
        b. people with a social personality change occupations frequently.
        c. people's personality and occupation are congruent.
        d. people with an artistic personality hold conventional jobs.

Answer: c, difficulty: 2, pp. 39-40

49. The myth of rationality:
    a. offers a possible explanation for giving emotions little attention within the field of OB
    b. suggests organizations have been essentially designed with the objective of trying to control emotions
    c. suggests a well-run organization successfully eliminates frustration, anger, hate, and similar feelings
    d. All of the above.

Answer: d, difficulty: 3, p. 41

50. _____ is a generic term that covers a broad range of feelings that people experience.
    a. Emotion
    b. Mood
    c. Emotional Labor
    d. Affect

Answer: d, difficulty: 2, p. 41

51. _____ are feelings that tend to be less intense than emotions and they lack a contextual stimulus.
    a. Values
    b. Affect
    c. Emotions
    d. Moods

Answer: d. difficulty: 1, p. 41

52. _____ are intense feelings that are directed at someone or something.
    a. Values
    b. Affect
    c. Emotions
    d. Moods

Answer: c. difficulty: 2, p. 41

53. _____ are reactions to an object while _____ aren't directed at an object.
    a. Emotions; moods
    b. Values; emotions
    c. Moods; values
    d. Moods; emotions

Answer: a, difficulty: 2, p. 41

54. When you show anger toward your colleague, you are showing a/an:
    a. emotion.
    b. value.
    c. affect.
    d. mood.

Answer: a, difficulty: 1, p. 41

55. _____is when an employee expresses organizationally desired emotions during interpersonal transactions.
    a. Emotion
    b. Mood
    c. Emotional Labor
    d. Affect

Answer: c, difficulty: 2, p. 41

56. _____ are organizationally required and considered appropriate for a given job.
    a. Felt emotions
    b. Personality dimensions
    c. Displayed emotions
    d. Universal emotions

Answer: c, difficulty: 2, p. 42

57. _____ are an individual's actual emotions.
    a. Felt emotions
    b. Personality dimensions
    c. Displayed emotions
    d. Universal emotions

Answer: a, difficulty: 2, p. 42

58. Which of the following is NOT an example of displayed emotions?
    a. the ritual look of delight on the face of the first runner-up as the new Miss America is announced
    b. We are expected to act sad at funerals regardless of whether we consider the person's death a loss.
    c. Managers are expected to be serious when giving a negative performance evaluation.
    d. Managers are expected to display their anger when passed over for promotion.

Answer: d, difficulty: 2, p. 42

59. Which of the following is NOT one of the six universal emotions?
    a. happiness
    b. hate
    c. fear
    d. anger

Answer: b, difficulty: 2, p. 42

60. Which of the following is NOT a difference between men and women?
   a. Women show greater emotional expression than men.
   b. Women experience emotions more intensely.
   c. Women display anger more frequently.
   d. Women are better at reading nonverbal cues.

Answer: c, difficulty: 2, p. 43

61. All of the following are possible explanations for emotional differences between men and women EXCEPT:
   a. women are socialized to be nurturing.
   b. women may have more innate ability to read emotions.
   c. women may have a greater need for social approval.
   d. women are biologically better suited to caregiving.

Answer: d, difficulty: 2, p. 43

62. Cultural norms dictate the importance of smiling. Which of the following is NOT true?
   a. In the U.S., employees in service organizations should smile and act friendly when interacting with customers.
   b. In Germany, smiling is viewed as threatening.
   c. In Israel, smiling by supermarket cashiers is seen as a sign of inexperience.
   d. In Moslem cultures, smiling is frequently taken as a sign of sexual attraction.

Answer: b, difficulty: 3, p. 43

63. _____ refers to an assortment of non-cognitive skills, capabilities, and competencies that influence a person's ability to succeed in coping with environmental demands and pressures.
   a. Emotional intelligence
   b. Intelligence quotient
   c. Leadership ability
   d. Self-awareness

Answer: a, difficulty: 2, p. 44

64. _____ is the dimension of emotional intelligence (EI) that refers to the ability to be aware of what you're feeling.
   a. Self-management
   b. Self-motivation
   c. Self-awareness
   d. Empathy

Answer: c, difficulty: 2, p. 44

65.	_____ is the dimension of emotional intelligence (EI) that refers to the ability to manage one's own emotions and impulses.
	a.	Self-management
	b.	Self-motivation
	c.	Self-awareness
	d.	Empathy

Answer: a, difficulty: 2, p. 44

66.	_____ is the dimension of emotional intelligence (EI) that refers to the ability to sense how others are feeling.
	a.	Self-management
	b.	Self-motivation
	c.	Self-awareness
	d.	Empathy

Answer: d, difficulty: 2, p. 44

67.	Which of the following is NOT a dimension of emotional intelligence?
	a.	self-awareness
	b.	self-motivation
	c.	empathy
	d.	sympathy

Answer: d, difficulty: 2, p. 44

68.	In the study examining characteristics of Bell Lab engineers, which of the following characterized high performers?
	a.	emotional intelligence
	b.	academic intelligence
	c.	hard work
	d.	good lab skills

Answer: a, difficulty: 2, p. 44

69.	You can improve your understanding of decision-making by
	a.	considering "the heart" as well as "the head."
	b.	ignoring "the head."
	c.	using only intuitive processes.
	d.	excluding emotions.

Answer: a, difficulty: 2, pp. 44-45

70. Which of the following is true of leadership and emotions?
   a. Effective leaders seldom rely on the expression of feelings to help convey their messages.
   b. Effective leaders almost all rely on the expression of feelings to help convey their messages.
   c. By arousing emotions and linking them to an appealing vision, leaders increase the likelihood that managers and employees alike will accept change.
   d. Leadership and emotions are totally unrelated.

Answer: b, difficulty: 3, p. 45

71. _____ are voluntary actions that violate established norms and threaten the organization, its members, or both.
   a. Negative emotions
   b. Employee deviance
   c. Interpersonal conflict
   d. Emotions

Answer: b, difficulty: 1, p. 46

TRUE/FALSE

72. An employee's personality has a strong influence on his/her behavior about work.

True, difficulty: 1, p. 34

73. An individual's personality is one overall psychological trait that we use to classify that person.

False, difficulty: 1, p. 34

74. Psychologists have studied personality traits extensively, resulting in the identification of two primary personality traits that determine behavior.

False, difficulty: 2, p. 34

75. One of the most widely used frameworks for classifying personalities is called the Myers-Briggs Type Indicator (MBTI).

True, difficulty: 2, p. 35

76. The Big-Four model classifies individuals as extroverted or introverted (E or I), sensing or intuitive (S or N), thinking or feeling (T or F), and perceiving or judging (P or J).

False, difficulty: 1, p. 35

77. According to the MBTI, extroverted individuals are quiet and shy.

False, difficulty: 1, p. 35

78.　　Intuitives are practical and focus on details.

False, difficulty: 2, p. 35

79.　　Judging types want control and prefer their world to be ordered and structured.

True, difficulty: 3, p. 35

80.　　INTJs are visionaries and are characterized as skeptical, critical, independent, determined, and often stubborn.

True, difficulty: 2, p. 35

81.　　The ENTP type is a conceptualizer.

True, difficulty: 2, p. 35

82.　　There is reliable evidence that the Myers-Briggs Type Indicator is a valid measure of personality.

False, difficulty: 2, p. 35

83.　　The five basic personality dimensions of the Big Five Model are: extroversion, agreeableness, conscientiousness, emotional stability, and openness to experience.

True, difficulty: 2, pp. 35-36

84.　　There is reliable evidence that the Big Five model is a valid measure of personality.

True, difficulty: 2, p. 36

85.　　Agreeableness is the dimension that captures one's comfort level with relationships.

False, difficulty: 2, p. 36

86.　　People with positive emotional stability tend to be calm, self-confident, and secure.

True, difficulty: 2, p. 36

87.　　Research on the Big Five has not been able to find any important relationships between those personality dimensions and job performance.

False, difficulty: 2, p. 36

88.　　Extroversion predicted performance in managerial and sales positions.

True, difficulty: 1, p. 36

89.　　Authoritarianism refers to whether people believe they are masters of their own fate.

False, difficulty: 1, p. 36

90. An individual who is manipulative, maintains emotional distance, and believes that ends justify means would rate high on Machiavellianism.

True, difficulty: 2, p. 37

91. High Machs are more likely to engage in behavior that is ethically questionable than are low Machs.

True, difficulty: 2, p. 37

92. Research finds that self-esteem is directly related to expectations for success.

True, difficulty: 2, p. 37

93. Low SEs are more likely to seek approval from others and more prone to conform to the beliefs and behaviors of those they respect than are high SEs.

True, difficulty: 2, p. 37

94. Low self-monitors are sensitive to external cues and can behave differently in different situations.

False, difficulty: 3, p. 37

95. People scoring high in self-monitoring are chameleons – able to change to fit the situation and hide their true selves.

True, difficulty: 2, p. 37

96. Individuals with a high propensity for risk make more rapid decisions and use less information than individuals with low risk propensity.

True, difficulty: 2, p. 37

97. Type A personalities are characterized by an incessant struggle to achieve more and more in less and less time.

True, difficulty: 1, p, 38

98. In managerial positions, Type A's demonstrate their competitiveness by working long hours and, not infrequently, making poor decisions because they make them too fast.

True, difficulty: 3, p. 38

99. There are common personality types for different countries.

False, difficulty: 3, p. 38

100. It is estimated that about 50 percent of the North American population is Type A.

True, difficulty: 3, p. 38

101. Cultures differ in terms of people's relationship to their environment.

True, difficulty: 2, p. 38

102. In cultures like Sweden and France, where materialism is more revered, we would predict a larger proportion of Type A personalities.

False, difficulty: 2, pp. 38-39

103. The most researched personality-job-fit theory is the six-personality-types model in which an employee's satisfaction with and propensity to leave his or her job depends on the degree to which the individual's personality matches his or her occupational environment.

True, difficulty: 3, p. 39

104. The characteristics of the realistic personality are self-confident, ambitious, energetic, and domineering.

False, difficulty: 2, p. 39 and Exhibit 3-1

105. The investigative personality prefers activities involving thinking, organizing, and understanding and is matched with occupations such as economist and mathematician.

True, difficulty: 3, p. 39 and Exhibit 3-1

106. The conventional personality is sociable, friendly, cooperative, and understanding, and is matched with the occupations of lawyer and public relations specialist.

False, difficulty: 3, p. 39 and Exhibit 3-1

107. It is an incongruent situation to put a realistic person in a social job such as counselor.

True, difficulty: 3, p. 39 and Exhibit 3-1

108. People in job environments congruent with their personality type should be more satisfied and less likely to resign voluntarily than people in incongruent jobs.

True, difficulty: 3, p. 40

109. Emotions are an important factor in employee behavior.

True, difficulty: 1, p. 40

110. Emotion is a generic term that covers a broad range of feelings that people experience.

False, difficulty: 2, p. 41

111. Affect is an umbrella concept that encompasses both emotions and moods.

True, difficulty: 2, p. 41

112. Emotional labor is when an employee expresses emotions which the organization wishes to suppress during interpersonal transactions.

False, difficulty: 2, p. 41

113. The concept of emotional labor, originally developed in relation to service jobs, seems relevant to almost every job today.

True, difficulty: 3, pp. 41-42

114. The emotions that are organizationally required and considered appropriate for a given job are termed affect.

False, difficulty: 2, p. 42

115. Felt and displayed emotions are often different.

True, difficulty: 1, p. 42

116. The six universal emotions identified in the research can be conceptualized as existing along a continuum from happiness to disgust.

True, difficulty: 3, p. 42

117. Research has identified six universal emotions: anger, hatred, sadness, happiness, joyfulness, and surprise.

False, difficulty: 1, p. 42

118. Evidence confirms that men and women differ when it comes to emotional reactions and the ability to read others.

True, difficulty: 1, p. 43

119. Men are better at reading nonverbal cues than women.

False, difficulty: 1, p. 43

120. The cultural norm in service organizations to smile and act friendly when interacting with customers applies worldwide.

False, difficulty: 2, p. 43

121. One explanation offered for why men and women differ in their emotional reactions is the different ways they have been socialized.

True, difficulty: 2, p. 43

122. There tends to be high agreement on what emotions mean within cultures, but not between cultures.

True, difficulty: 3, p. 43

123. Intelligence quotient refers to an assortment of non-cognitive skills, capabilities, and competencies that influence a person's ability to succeed in coping with environmental demands and pressures.

False, difficulty: 2, p. 44

124. Emotional intelligence has five dimensions: self-awareness, self-management, self-motivation, empathy, and social skills.

True, difficulty: 3, p. 44

125. Several studies have suggested that EI may play an important role in job performance.

True, difficulty: 1, p. 44

126. People use emotions as well as relational and intuitive processes in making decisions.

True, difficulty: 3, pp. 44-45

127. Effective leaders almost never rely on the expressions of feelings to help convey their messages.

False, difficulty: 2, p. 45

128. The voluntary actions that people often engage in that violate established norms and which threaten the organization, its members, or both are called employee deviance.

True, difficulty: 1, p. 46

129. Employee deviance includes gossiping, sexual harassment, and leaving early.

True, difficulty: 2, p. 46

ESSAY

130. Describe the Myers-Briggs Type Indicator.

The Myers-Briggs Type Indicator (MBTI) is a 100-question personality test that asks people how they usually feel or act in particular situations. On the basis of the answers individuals give, they are classified as extroverted or introverted (E or I), sensing or intuitive (S or N), thinking or feeling (T or F), and perceiving or judging (P or J). These are then combined into sixteen personality types.

p. 35

131.	What are the five basic personality dimensions in the Big Five Model?

The five basic personality dimensions in the Big Five Model are extroversion, agreeableness, conscientiousness, emotional stability, and openness to experience. Extroversion captures one's comfort level with relationships. Agreeableness refers to an individual's propensity to defer to others. Conscientiousness is a measure of reliability. Emotional stability taps a person's ability to withstand stress. Openness to experience addresses an individual's range of interests and fascination with novelty.

pp. 35-36

132.	Define and discuss the personality attribute of locus of control.

Some people believe that they are masters of their own fate. These people believe they control their own destiny. They have an internal locus of control. Other people see themselves as pawns of fate, believing that what happens to them is due to luck or chance. Those who see their life as being controlled by outsider are externals.

pp. 36-37

133.	Define and discuss the personality attribute of Machiavellianism.

An individual exhibiting strong Machiavellian tendencies is manipulative, maintains emotional distance, and believes that ends can justify means. "If it works, use it" is consistent with a high Mach perspective. High Machs are more likely to engage in behavior that is ethically questionable than are low Machs.

p. 37

134.	What is self-esteem and is it related to expectations for success?

Self-esteem is the trait that reflects the degree to which people like or dislike themselves. Research finds that self-esteem is directly related to expectations for success. People with high self-esteem believe that they possess the ability then need in order to succeed at work.

p. 37

135.	Define and discuss the personality attribute of self-monitoring.

High self-monitors are sensitive to external cues and can behave differently in different situations. They're chameleons – able to change to fit the situation and to hide their true selves. Low self-monitors are consistent. They display their true dispositions and attitudes in every situation. High self-monitors tend to be better at playing organizational politics because they're sensitive to cues and can put on different "faces" for different audiences.

p. 37

136. Define and discuss the personality attribute of risk propensity.

People differ in their willingness to take chances. Individuals with a high risk propensity make more rapid decisions and use less information in making their choices than individuals with low risk propensity.

p. 37

137. Define and discuss the personality attribute of the Type A personality.

Type A's are characterized by an incessant struggle to achieve more and more in less and less time. They are impatient, cope poorly with leisure time, and create a life of self-imposed deadlines. In terms of work behavior, Type A's are fast workers.

p. 38

138. Is the prevalence of Type A personalities influenced by the culture in which a person grows up?

The prevalence of Type A personalities will be somewhat influenced by the culture in which a person grows up. There are Type A's in every country, but there will be more in capitalistic countries, where achievement and material success are highly valued. It is estimated that about 50 percent of the North American population is Type A. This shouldn't be surprising since the United States and Canada place a high emphasis on time management and efficiency. Both cultures stress accomplishments and acquisition of money and material goods. In cultures where materialism is less revered, we would predict a smaller proportion of Type A personalities.

pp. 38-39

139. Describe the six-personality-types model. Relate each of the six personality types to an appropriate occupation.

The six personality types are realistic, investigative, social, conventional, enterprising, and artistic. The realistic type is shy, genuine, stable, and practical. An appropriate occupation might be a mechanic, drill press operator, or a farmer. The investigative type is analytical, original, and curious. An appropriate occupation might be a biologist, economist, or a news reporter. The social type is sociable, friendly, and understanding. An appropriate occupation might be a social worker, teacher, or counselor. The conventional type is conforming, efficient, and inflexible. An appropriate occupation would be accountant, corporate manager, or bank teller. The enterprising type is self-confident, ambitious, and domineering. An appropriate occupation would be lawyer, real estate agent, or public relations specialist. The artistic type is imaginative, idealistic, and emotional. An appropriate occupation would be painter, musician, or writer.

pp. 39-40 and Exhibit 3-1

140.   Provide two reasons why until recently, the topic of emotions has been given little or no attention within the field of OB?

The myth of reality suggests that organizations have been essentially designed with the objective of trying to control emotions. It was believed that a well-run organization was one that successfully eliminated frustration, anger, love, hate, joy, grief, and similar feelings. Such emotions were seen as the antithesis of rationality. Researchers tried to create organizations that were emotion-free. The second factor that acted to keep emotions out of OB was the belief that emotions of any kind were disruptive. Emotions were rarely viewed as being constructive or able to stimulate performance-enhancing behaviors.

p. 41

141.   Explain the difference between felt and displayed emotions.

Felt emotions are an individual's actual emotions. Displayed emotions are those that are organizationally required and considered appropriate in a given job. They're not innate; they're learned. Felt and displayed emotions are often different.

p. 42

142.   What are the six universal emotions?

The six universal emotions are anger, fear, sadness, happiness, disgust, and surprise. The emotion continuum places happiness at one end and disgust at the other end.

pp. 42-43

143.   Discuss three possible answers to explain the differences between men and women when it comes to emotions.

One explanation for the differences between men and women is the different ways men and women have been socialized. A second explanation is that women may have more innate ability to read others and present their emotions than do men. Thirdly, women may have a greater need for social approval and thus, a higher propensity to express positive emotions like happiness.

p. 43

144.   What is Emotional Intelligence (EI) and what are the five dimensions?

Emotional intelligence (EI) refers to an assortment of noncognitive skills, capabilities, and competencies that influence a person's ability to succeed in coping with environmental demands and pressures. It is comprised of five dimensions: self-awareness (the ability to be aware of what you're feeling), self-management (the ability to manage one's own emotions and impulses), self-motivation (the ability to persist in the face of setbacks and failures), empathy (the ability to sense how others are feeling), and social skills (the ability to handle the emotions of others).

p. 44

145.   How can emotions be an integral part of leadership?

Effective leaders almost all rely on the expression of feelings to help convey their messages. Corporate executives know that emotional content is critical if employees are to buy into their vision of their company's future and accept change. By arousing emotions and linking them to an appealing vision, leaders increase the likelihood that managers and employees alike will accept changes.

p. 45

CHAPTER 4 BASIC MOTIVATION CONCEPTS

MULTIPLE CHOICE

1.   Motivation is defined as:
        a. high performance.
        b. high job satisfaction.
        c. a willingness to do something.
        d. an external incentive.

Answer: c, difficulty: 1, p. 48

2.   Which of the following is true of motivation?
        a. Motivated people exert a greater effort to perform than those who are not motivated.
        b. Motivation is the willingness to do something.
        c. Motivation is conditioned by the action's ability to satisfy some needs for the individual.
        d. All of the above.

Answer: d, difficulty: 2, p. 48

3.   A physiological or psychological deficiency that makes certain outcomes appear attractive is called a(n):
        a. reward.
        b. hygiene factor.
        c. attitude.
        d. need.

Answer: d, difficulty: 1, p. 48

4.   Motivated employees are in a state of:
        a. tension.
        b. dissatisfaction.
        c. satisfaction.
        d. acceptance.

Answer: a, difficulty: 2, p. 48

5.   Which of the following theories of motivation was NOT developed during the decade of the 1950s?
        a. hierarchy of needs theory
        b. reinforcement theory
        c. Theory X and Theory Y
        d. motivation-hygiene theory

Answer: b, difficulty: 2, p. 48

6. The hierarchy of needs theory was developed by:
    a. Douglas McGregor.
    b. Frederick Herzberg.
    c. Abraham Maslow.
    d. David McClelland.

Answer: c, difficulty: 2, p. 48

7. Maslow's physiological needs include:
    a. hunger, thirst, and shelter.
    b. security and protection from physical and emotional harm.
    c. internal factors, such as self-respect and autonomy.
    d. the drive to become what one is capable of becoming.

Answer: a, difficulty: 1, p. 48

8. Maslow's _____ needs include affective, a sense of belonging, acceptance, and friendship.
    a. physiological
    b. social
    c. esteem
    d. self-actualization

Answer: b, difficulty: 2, p. 48

9. Maslow's _____ needs include security and protection from physical and emotional harm.
    a. physiological
    b. social
    c. esteem
    d. self-actualization

Answer: a, difficulty: 1, p. 48

10. The drive to become what one is capable of becoming is Maslow's _____ need.
    a. physiological
    b. social
    c. esteem
    d. self-actualization

Answer: d, difficulty: 1, p. 49

11. Maslow's _____ needs focus on internal factors that deal with satisfying one's self-respect, autonomy, achievement, and external factors such as status and attention.
    a. safety
    b. social
    c. self-actualization
    d. esteem

Answer: d, difficulty: 2, p. 49

12. Which of the following is NOT one of the needs identified in Maslow's hierarchy of needs theory?
    a. physiological
    b. psychological
    c. social
    d. safety

Answer: b, difficulty: 1, pp. 48-49

13. According to Maslow, lower order needs include:
    a. safety and esteem.
    b. esteem and social.
    c. physiological and safety.
    d. social and esteem.

Answer: c, difficulty: 2, p. 49

14. Maslow's hierarchy of needs is arranged in the following order:
    a. physiological, esteem, safety, social, self-actualization.
    b. physiological, safety, social, esteem, self-actualization.
    c. safety, physiological, esteem, social, self-actualization.
    d. physiological, social, safety, esteem, self-actualization.

Answer: b, difficulty: 2, Exhibit 4-2

15. The hierarchy of needs theory assumes that:
    a. satisfied needs are motivators.
    b. unsatisfied needs are not motivators.
    c. a person advances to the next hierarchical level only when the lower need is at least minimally satisfied.
    d. a person advances to the next hierarchical level only when the individual believes the higher level can be achieved.

Answer: c, difficulty: 3, p. 49

16.   Which of the following provides the best example of a safety need?
        a.   affection
        b.   savings account
        c.   love
        d.   self-respect

Answer: b, difficulty: 2, p. 49

17.   As each of the needs in Maslow's hierarchy becomes substantially satisfied:
        a.   the next need becomes dominant.
        b.   the individual is self-actualized.
        c.   the individual begins to regress back down the pyramid of needs.
        d.   the individual is no longer motivated.

Answer: a, difficulty: 2, p. 49

18.   According to Maslow's hierarchy of needs theory, when does a need stop motivating?
        a.   when it is substantially satisfied
        b.   when an individual is frustrated and drops to a lower-level need
        c.   never because a need is always motivating
        d.   when it is completely satisfied

Answer: a, difficulty: 3, p. 49

19.   Sandy wants to appeal to Donna's esteem needs and has noticed that Donna always wants
        to do her best on all tasks. As Donna's manager, Sandy should:
        a.   assign Donna a team-based project.
        b.   increase Donna's health insurance benefits.
        c.   transfer Donna to another department.
        d.   give Donna an impressive title.

Answer: d, difficulty: 2, p. 49

20.   Which of the following is true concerning Maslow's lower level needs?
        a.   Lower-order needs are predominantly satisfied externally.
        b.   Lower-order needs include physiological and safety needs.
        c.   In times of economic plenty, almost all permanently employed workers will have their
             lower-order needs substantially met.
        d.   All of the above.

Answer: d, difficulty: 3, p. 49

21. Theory X and Theory Y were proposed by:
   a. Abraham Maslow.
   b. Frederick Herzberg.
   c. Douglas McGregor.
   d. David McClelland.

Answer: c, difficulty: 2, p. 50

22. Theory X and Theory Y:
   a. summarize research conducted at Yale up to 1940.
   b. represent what we know about human behavior.
   c. represent basic assumptions about human behavior that can be held by managers.
   d. reflect the views of scientific management and Maslow.

Answer: c, difficulty: 2, p. 50

23. Which of the following statements is an assumption of Theory X?
   a. Employees can view work as being as natural as rest or play.
   b. People will exercise self-control if they are committed to the objective.
   c. Most workers place security above all other factors and seek formal direction whenever possible.
   d. The average person can learn to accept and seek responsibility.

Answer: c, difficulty: 2, p. 50

24. Which of the following statements is an assumption of Theory Y?
   a. Since employees dislike work, they must be coerced and threatened.
   b. Employees will attempt to avoid work.
   c. Employees can view work as being as natural as rest or play.
   d. Employees will avoid responsibility and seek formal direction whenever possible.

Answer: c, difficulty: 2, p. 50

25. Which of the following is NOT an assumption under Theory X?
   a. Employees must be coerced to achieve desired goals.
   b. Employees inherently dislike work and, whenever possible, will attempt to avoid it.
   c. Employees will avoid responsibilities and seek formal direction whenever possible.
   d. The average person can learn to accept, and even seek, responsibility.

Answer: d, difficulty: 2, p. 50

26. Which of the following is NOT an assumption under Theory Y?
     a. Employees can view work as being as natural as rest or play.
     b. The average person can learn to accept, even seek, responsibility.
     c. Employees will avoid responsibilities and seek formal direction whenever possible.
     d. People will exercise self-direction and self-control if they are committed to the objectives.

Answer: c, difficulty: 2, p. 50

27. A manager who is trying to apply Theory Y would:
     a. delegate authority for many decisions.
     b. encourage subordinates to interrupt him/her with their problems.
     c. initiate job specialization.
     d. increase the number of employees who report to him/her.

Answer: a, difficulty: 3, p. 50

28. Theory X assumes that:
     a. Maslow's higher order needs dominate individuals.
     b. Maslow's lover-order needs dominate individuals.
     c. both Maslow's higher-order and lower-order needs dominate individuals.
     d. All of the above.

Answer: b, difficulty: 3, p. 50

29. A manager using Theory Y would maximize an employee's job motivation by avoiding which of the following behaviors?
     a. participation in decision making
     b. creating challenging jobs
     c. developing good group relations
     d. directing employees in everything that they should do

Answer: d, difficulty: 3, p. 50

30. The two-factor theory was developed by:
     a. Abraham Maslow.
     b. Frederick Herzberg.
     c. Douglas McGregor.
     d. David McClelland.

Answer: b, difficulty: 2, p. 50

31. Another name for Herzberg's two-factor theory is:
    a. motivation-hygiene theory.
    b. Theory X and Theory Y.
    c. expectancy theory.
    d. VIE theory.

Answer: a, difficulty: 2, p. 50

32. Herzberg found that:
    a. people gave the same replies regarding when they felt good or bad about their job.
    b. intrinsic factors seem to be related to job dissatisfaction.
    c. extrinsic factors seem to be related to job dissatisfaction.
    d. the opposite of satisfaction is dissatisfaction.

Answer: c, difficulty: 2, pp. 50-51

33. Which of the following factors would be a motivator according to Herzberg?
    a. salary
    b. responsibility
    c. working conditions
    d. supervision

Answer: b, difficulty: 2, pp. 50-51 and Exhibit 4-3

34. Which of the following is considered a hygiene according to Herzberg?
    a. responsibility
    b. achievement
    c. physical working conditions
    d. recognition

Answer: c, difficulty: 2, pp. 50-51 and Exhibit 4-3

35. Which of the following is NOT a motivator according to Herzberg?
    a. recognition
    b. responsibility
    c. achievement
    d. relations with others

Answer: d, difficulty: 2, pp. 50-51 and Exhibit 4-3

36. According to Herzberg, characteristics such as company policy and administration, supervision, and interpersonal relations are known as:
   a. motivation factors.
   b. hygiene factors.
   c. satisfier factors.
   d. achievement factors.

Answer: b, difficulty: 2, pp. 50-51 and Exhibit 4-3

37. Many manufacturing jobs are boring and routine and are carried out in poor working conditions. Herzberg's motivation-hygiene theory predicts that motivation will improve when:
   a. managers focus on both intrinsic and extrinsic factors.
   b. hygiene factors are improved.
   c. technology is brought in to automate jobs.
   d. all dissatisfiers are removed.

Answer: a, difficulty: 3, p. 51

38. Criticisms of the motivation-hygiene theory include all EXCEPT which of the following?
   a. The procedure used is limited by its methodology.
   b. The theory is inconsistent with previous research.
   c. No overall measure of satisfaction is utilized.
   d. Few managers are familiar with its recommendations.

Answer: d, difficulty: 3, pp. 51-52

39. Who developed the Theory of Needs?
   a. Abraham Maslow
   b. David McClelland
   c. Frederick Herzberg
   d. Frederick Taylor

Answer: b, difficulty: 2, p. 52

40. Which of the following was NOT a need proposed by David McClelland's Theory of Needs?
   a. the need for achievement
   b. the need for esteem
   c. the need for power
   d. the need for affiliation

Answer: b, difficulty: 1, p. 52

41. In McClelland's studies, the focus was on three needs called:
    a. achievement, acceptance, and power.
    b. acceptance, affiliation, and power.
    c. affiliation, achievement, and acceptance.
    d. achievement, power, and affiliation.

Answer: d, difficulty: 1, p. 52

42. According to McClelland's Theory of Needs, which of the following is related to a high need for achievement?
    a. desire for warm and friendly relationships
    b. desire to do things more efficiently
    c. desire for low-risk situations
    d. desire for little feedback

Answer: b, difficulty: 1, p. 52

43. Which of the following is NOT true of McClelland's high achievers?
    a. They perform best when they perceive their probability of success as being 0.5.
    b. They differentiate themselves from others by their desire to do things better.
    c. They seek situations in which they can assume personal responsibility for finding solutions to problems.
    d. They strive for influence over others.

Answer: d, difficulty: 2, pp. 52-53

44. McClelland's _____ is the need to make others behave in a way that they would not have otherwise behaved.
    a. need for achievement
    b. need for motivation
    c. need for power
    d. need for affiliation

Answer: c, difficulty: 2, p. 53

45. McClelland's need for _____ is the desire for friendly and close interpersonal relationships.
    a. achievement
    b. motivation
    c. power
    d. affiliation

Answer: d, difficulty: 2, p. 53

46. Which of the following is NOT true of high achievers according to McClelland?
    a. High achievers perform best when they perceive their probability of success as being greater than 90 percent.
    b. High achievers like to set realistic but difficult goals that require stretching themselves a little.
    c. High achievers get no achievement satisfaction from happenstance success.
    d. High achievers dislike a high probability of success because then there is no challenge to their skills.

Answer: a, difficulty: 3, pp. 52-53

47. High achievers perform best when:
    a. they perceive their probability of success as being 0.5.
    b. there is a high probability of success.
    c. there is a low probability of success.
    d. there is no way to estimate their probability of success.

Answer: a, difficulty: 2, p. 53

48. The need for affiliation:
    a. has received the least attention of researchers.
    b. is the need to control others.
    c. has received the most attention of researchers.
    d. All of the above.

Answer: a, difficulty: 2, p. 53

49. A projective test in which subjects respond to a set of pictures was developed to:
    a. determine the presence and strength of McClelland's needs.
    b. identify attractiveness of rewards.
    c. determine the instrumentality of motivator factors.
    d. assess perceptions of equity.

Answer: a, difficulty: 3, p. 53

50. The need isolated by McClelland that has received the least attention by researchers is the need for:
    a. achievement.
    b. equity.
    c. power.
    d. affiliation.

Answer: d, difficulty: 3, p. 53

51. Which of the following is true concerning individuals high in the need for power according to McClelland?
    a. They enjoy being in charge and strive for influence over others.
    b. They strive for friendships.
    c. They prefer cooperative situations rather than competitive ones.
    d. They desire relationships involving a high degree of mutual understanding.

Answer: a, difficulty: 2, p. 53

52. Regarding McClelland's Theory of Needs, all of the following statements are true EXCEPT:
    a. individuals with a high need to achieve prefer situations with personal responsibility.
    b. individuals with a high need to achieve always make good managers.
    c. individuals with a high need to achieve do not necessarily make good sales managers.
    d. individuals with a high need for affiliation do not make good managers.

Answer: b, difficulty: 3, p. 53

53. _____ states that intentions can be a major source of work motivation.
    a. The Theory of Needs
    b. Herzberg's motivation-hygiene theory
    c. Maslow's hierarchy
    d. Goal-setting theory

Answer: d, difficulty: 2, p. 53

54. Which of the following statements is FALSE regarding goal setting?
    a. Higher levels of output result from having specific goals rather than general ones.
    b. As long as difficult goals are perceived as being achievable, higher output levels will result.
    c. Participation in goal setting consistently results in superior performance compared to assigned goals.
    d. Ability and acceptance are important elements in goal setting theory.

Answer: c, difficulty: 3, p. 54

55. Studies testing goal-setting theory have demonstrated the superiority of _____ goals as motivating forces.
    a. easily met
    b. specific and challenging
    c. moderately easy
    d. general and moderate

Answer: b, difficulty: 3, p. 54

56. The counterpoint to goal-setting theory, which is a cognitive approach, is _____, which uses a behaviorist approach.
    a. the theory of needs
    b. the two-factor theory
    c. reinforcement theory
    d. equity theory

Answer: c, difficulty: 3, p. 54

57. Reinforcement theory views behavior as:
    a. a cognitive process.
    b. environmentally caused.
    c. the inner state of the individual.
    d. a function of one's need for power.

Answer: b, difficulty: 2, p. 55

58. Which of the following statements is true concerning reinforcement theory?
    a. It ignores what happens to a person when he or she takes some action.
    b. It is strictly a theory of motivation.
    c. It provides a means of analysis of what controls behavior.
    d. Reinforcement is the single explanation for differences in employee motivation.

Answer: c, difficulty: 3, p. 55

59. The job characteristics model describes jobs in terms of all of the following core job dimensions EXCEPT:
    a. task identity.
    b. employee personality.
    c. autonomy.
    d. feedback.

Answer: b, difficulty: 2, pp. 55-56

60. In terms of the job characteristics model, a factory worker who sprays auto parts eight hours per day exemplifies:
    a. low skill variety.
    b. high skill variety.
    c. low feedback.
    d. high feedback.

Answer: a, difficulty: 1, pp. 55-56

61. Which of the following would be an example of a job characteristic with high task significance?
   a. a body shop worker who spray paints eight hours a day
   b. a nurse who cares for patients in a hospital intensive care unit
   c. a janitor who sweeps hospital floors
   d. a factory worker who assembles engine parts

Answer: b, difficulty: 2, pp. 55-56

62. In the job characteristics model, _____ reflects the degree to which a job requires completion of a whole and identifiable piece of work.
   a. skill variety
   b. task significance
   c. task identity
   d. autonomy

Answer: c, difficulty: 1, pp. 55-56

63. In the job characteristics model, _____ refers to the degree to which the job requires a variety of different activities so the worker can use a number of different skills or talents.
   a. skill variety
   b. task identity
   c. task significance
   d. feedback

Answer: a, difficulty: 2, pp. 55-56

64. In the job characteristics model, _____ is the degree to which a worker's job has a substantial impact on the lives or work of other people.
   a. skill variety
   b. task significance
   c. task identity
   d. autonomy

Answer: b, difficulty: 2, pp. 55-56

65. In the job characteristics model, _____ is the degree to which a job provides substantial freedom, independence, and discretion to an individual in scheduling the work and in determining the procedures to be used in carrying it out.
   a. skill variety
   b. task significance
   c. task identity
   d. autonomy

Answer: d, difficulty: 1, pp. 55-56

66. In the job characteristics model, _____ refers to the degree to which carrying out the work activities required by the job results in the individual's obtaining direct and clear information about the effectiveness of his or her performance.
    a. skill variety
    b. task identity
    c. task significance
    d. feedback

Answer: d, difficulty: 2, pp. 55-56

67. According to the job characteristics model, an electronics factory worker who assembles a modem and then tests it to determine if it operates properly has:
    a. high feedback.
    b. high autonomy.
    c. low task significance.
    d. low task identity.

Answer: a, difficulty: 2, pp. 55-56

68. According to the job characteristics model, all of the following are key psychological states influenced by the core dimensions EXCEPT:
    a. meaningful work.
    b. feeling of personal responsibility.
    c. knowledge of results.
    d. self-actualization.

Answer: d, difficulty: 2, pp. 56-57 and Exhibit 4-4

69. Within the job characteristics model, skill variety, task identity, and task significance lead to the psychological state of:
    a. job satisfaction.
    b. knowledge of results.
    c. personal control.
    d. meaningful work.

Answer: d, difficulty: 3, pp. 56-57 and Exhibit 4-4

70. Within the job characteristics model, feedback leads to the psychological state of:
    a. job satisfaction.
    b. knowledge of results.
    c. personal control.
    d. experienced meaningfulness.

Answer: b, difficulty: 2, pp. 56-57 and Exhibit 4-4

71. Within the job characteristics model, autonomy leads to the psychological state of:
    a. experienced responsibility for outcomes of the work.
    b. experienced meaningfulness of the work.
    c. knowledge of the actual results of the work activities.
    d. low absenteeism and turnover.

Answer: a, difficulty: 3, pp. 56-57 and Exhibit 4-4

72. The personal and work outcomes that result from the critical psychological states in the job characteristics model include all of the following EXCEPT:
    a. high internal work motivation.
    b. high dysfunctional communication.
    c. high satisfaction with the work.
    d. low absenteeism and turnover.

Answer: b, difficulty: 2, pp. 56-57 and Exhibit 4-4

73. The JCM's core dimensions can be combined into a single predictive index called
    a. the autonomy index
    b. the JCM
    c. the motivating potential score
    d. the Myers-Briggs Indicator

Answer: c, difficulty: 3, p. 57

74. The _____ argues that people respond to their jobs as they perceive them rather than to the objective jobs themselves.
    a. social information-processing model
    b. managerial grid
    c. job characteristics model
    d. requisite-task attributes theory

Answer: a, difficulty: 2, p. 57

75. _____ says that employees weigh what they put into a job situation against what they get from it.
    a. Equity theory
    b. Motivation-hygiene theory
    c. Reinforcement theory
    d. Expectancy theory

Answer: a, difficulty: 1, p. 58

76. In equity theory, individuals' behavior is influenced by their perception of the:
    a. cost-benefit equation.
    b. efficiency-effectiveness formula.
    c. attitude-behavior balance.
    d. input-outcome ratio.

Answer: d, difficulty: 2, p. 58

77. The referent that employees choose to compare themselves with in equity theory may include all of the following categories EXCEPT:
    a. other.
    b. system.
    c. supervisor.
    d. self.

Answer: c, difficulty: 2, p. 59

78. Based on equity theory, when employees envision an inequity, they may make all EXCEPT which of the following choices?
    a. Distort their inputs or outcomes
    b. Induce others to change their inputs or outcomes
    c. Choose a different referent
    d. Continue as though they have not recognized the inequity

Answer: d, difficulty: 2, p. 59

79. Janice perceives that she is working harder for lower pay than many of her fellow employees. She is likely to do which of the following?
    a. improve her productivity.
    b. increase the quality of her output.
    c. be absent from work more.
    d. increase her effort.

Answer: c, difficulty: 2, p. 60

80. _____ argue(s) that the strength of a tendency to act in a certain way depends on the strength of an expectation that the act will be followed by a given outcome and on the attractiveness of that outcome to the individual.
    a. Expectancy theory
    b. Motivation-hygiene theory
    c. Theory X and Theory Y
    d. Equity theory

Answer: a, difficulty: 2, p. 60

81. The degree to which an individual believes that working at a particular level will generate a desired outcome is defined by expectancy theory as:
   a. attractiveness.
   b. performance-reward linkage.
   c. effort-performance linkage.
   d. reward-individual goal linkage.

Answer: b, difficulty: 2, p. 60

82. The probability perceived by an individual that exerting a given amount of effort will lead to performance is defined by expectancy theory as:
   a. attractiveness.
   b. performance-reward linkage.
   c. effort-performance linkage.
   d. reward-individual goal linkage.

Answer: c, difficulty: 2, p. 60

83. The importance the individual places on the potential outcome or reward that can be achieved on the job is defined by expectancy theory as:
   a. attractiveness.
   b. performance-reward linkage.
   c. effort-performance linkage.
   d. reward-individual goal linkage.

Answer: a, difficulty: 2, p. 60

84. Most motivation theories developed in the United States have blatant pro-American characteristics such as a strong emphasis on:
   a. individualism.
   b. quality-of-life factors.
   c. collectivism.
   d. power distance.

Answer: a, difficulty: 1, p. 61

85. The _____ need is clearly a motivational concept with a U.S. bias.
   a. social
   b. achievement
   c. physiological
   d. affiliation

Answer: b, difficulty: 1, pp. 61-62

86. Which of the following is NOT true concerning the culture-bound nature of some motivation theories?
   a. Goal-setting theory's recommendations are not likely to increase motivation in countries that are high in uncertainty avoidance.
   b. Goal-setting theory's recommendations are not likely to increase motivation in countries that are extremely high on power distance.
   c. The achievement need is found universally across all countries.
   d. Group work will motivate employees more when the country's culture scores high on the quality-of-life criterion.

Answer: c, difficulty: 3, pp. 61-62

TRUE/FALSE

87. Sometimes individuals of lesser ability can, and do, outperform their more gifted counterparts because of their motivation.

True, difficulty: 1, p. 47

88. An individual's performance at work depends only on ability.

False, difficulty: 1, p. 47

89. A need is a physiological or psychological deficiency that makes certain outcomes appear attractive.

True, difficulty: 1, p. 48

90. A satisfied need creates tension, which stimulates drives within the individual.

False, difficulty: 1, p. 48

91. When we see employees working hard at some activity, we can conclude they are driven by
   a desire to achieve some goal they value.

True, difficulty: 2, p. 48

92. An unsatisfied need creates tension, which stimulates drives within the individual.

True, difficulty: 2, p. 48

93. Motivated employees are in a state of tension.

True, difficulty: 1, p. 48

94.   McGregor's Theory X hypothesized that within every human being there exists a
        hierarchy of needs.

False, difficulty: 2, p. 48

95.   According to Maslow, self-esteem is the drive to become what one is capable of becoming.

False, difficulty: 2, p. 49

96.   Lower-order needs in the hierarchy of needs theory include social, esteem, and self-
        actualization.

False, difficulty: 2, p. 49

97.   Maslow's theory would say that although no need is ever fully gratified, a substantially
        satisfied need no longer motivates.

True, difficulty: 2, p. 49

98.   Higher-order needs are satisfied internally, whereas lower-order needs are predominantly
        satisfied externally.

True, difficulty: 2, p. 49

99.   There is a substantial body of research that validates Maslow's hierarchy of needs theory.

False, difficulty: 2, p. 49

100.   Under Theory X, a manager believes the average person can learn to accept, and even
seek,
        responsibility.

False, difficulty: 2, p. 50

101.   Under Theory Y, a manager believes that employees view work as being as natural as rest
        or play.

True, difficulty: 1, p. 50

102.   Under Theory Y, a manager believes that employees place security above all other factors
        associated with work.

False, difficulty: 2, p. 50

103.   Theory Y assumes that lower-order needs dominate individuals, while Theory X assumes
        higher-order needs dominate.

False, difficulty: 3, p. 50

104. Either Theory X or Theory Y assumptions may be appropriate in a given situation.

True, difficulty: 2, p. 50

105. To motivate people on their jobs, Herzberg suggests emphasizing achievement, recognition, and the work itself.

True, difficulty: 2, pp. 50-51

106. The two-factor theory is unique in that it differentiates the factors that lead to satisfaction from those that lead to dissatisfaction.

True, difficulty: 2, pp. 50-51

107. According to the two-factor theory, salary is characterized as a motivation factor.

False, difficulty: 1, p. 51 and Exhibit 4-3

108. According to Herzberg's two-factor theory, the opposite of "satisfaction" is "dissatisfaction."

False, difficulty: 2, p. 51

109. Much of the initial enthusiasm for vertically expanding jobs to allow workers greater responsibility in planning and controlling their work can probably be attributed to Herzberg's findings and recommendations.

True, difficulty: 3, p. 52

110. The need for achievement (nAch) is considered to be the drive to excel, to achieve in relation to a set of standards.

True, difficulty: 1, p. 52

111. McGregor's Theory of Needs focuses on three major needs: need for achievement, need for respect, and need for affiliation.

False, difficulty: 2, p. 52

112. McClelland's need for power (nPow) is the need to make others behave in a way they would not have behaved otherwise.

True, difficulty: 2, p. 52

113. Low achievers differentiate themselves from others by their desire to do things better.

False, difficulty: 2, pp. 52-53

114.   High achievers perform best when they perceive their probability of success as being 0.5.

True, difficulty: 3, pp. 52-53

115.   Individuals high in the need for power enjoy being in charge and tend to be more concerned with gaining prestige and influence over others than with their effective performance.

True, difficulty: 3, pp. 53

116.   McClelland's need for achievement has received the least attention from researchers.

False, difficulty: 2, p. 53

117.   A high need to achieve is a predictor that a person will be a good manager.

False, difficulty: 2, p. 53

118.   The best managers are high in the need for power and low in their need for affiliation.

True, difficulty: 3, p. 53

119.   To find out if someone is a high achiever, McClelland's administered a 100-item questionnaire.

False, difficulty: 3, p. 53

120.   According to goal-setting theory, intentions can be a major source of work motivation.

True, difficulty: 2, pp. 53-54

121.   Goal-setting theory states that specific goals lead to increased performance and that difficult goals, when accepted, result in higher performance than easy goals.

True, difficulty: 2, pp. 53-54

122.   Specific, hard goals produce a higher level of output than a generalized goal of "do your best."

True, difficulty: 2, p. 54

123.   Self-generated feedback has been shown to be a more powerful motivator than externally generated feedback.

True, difficulty: 3, p. 54

124. Reinforcement theory is a behavioristic approach to motivation.

True, difficulty: 2, p. 55

125. Reinforcement focuses on the inner state of the individual.

False, difficulty: 3, p. 55

126. The job characteristics model confirmed that employees in jobs with more task complexity had higher job satisfaction.

False, difficulty: 3, pp. 55-56

127. Skill variety is the extent to which a job requires a variety of different activities so a worker can use a number of different skills and talents.

True, difficulty: 1, pp. 55-56

128. Task identity is the degree to which a worker's job has a substantial impact on the lives or work of other people.

False, difficulty: 2, pp. 55-56

129. A telephone operator who must handle calls as they come according to a routine, highly specified procedure, has low autonomy.

True, difficulty: 2, pp. 55-56

130. Sweeping hospital floors is an example of a job with high task identity.

False, difficulty: 2, pp. 55-56

131. The extent to which a job offers independence and substantial freedom in scheduling work and determining procedures to use is known as individualism.

False, difficulty: 2, pp. 55-56

132. According to the job characteristics model, job dimensions operate through psychological states in influencing personal and work outcome variables rather than influencing them directly.

True, difficulty: 2, pp. 56-57 and Exhibit 4-4

133. Skill variety, task identity, and task significance combine to create meaningful work.

True, difficulty: 3, pp. 56-57 and Exhibit 4-4

134. Individuals with a high growth need are more likely to experience the psychological states when their jobs are enriched than are their counterparts with a low growth need.

True, difficulty: 3, pp. 56-57

135. The social information-processing model makes it clear that people respond to their jobs as they perceive them rather than to the objective jobs themselves.

True, difficulty: 2, p. 57

136. The social information-processing model holds that managers should give more attention to the actual characteristics of jobs than to employees' perceptions of those jobs.

False, difficulty: 2, p. 57

137. Expectancy theory says that employees weigh their input against their outcome and then compare their input-outcome ratio with the input-outcome ratio of relevant others.

False, difficulty: 2, p. 58

138. Equity theory has concluded that inequities can influence the degree of effort that employees exert.

True, difficulty: 2, p. 58

139. According to equity theory, the "system" category is influenced by such criteria as past jobs or family commitments.

False, difficulty: 3, p. 58

140. In equity theory, there are three referent categories: supervisor, system, and self.

False, difficulty: 2, p. 58

141. Equity theory recognizes that individuals are concerned not only with the absolute amount of rewards they receive but also with the relationship of that amount to what others receive.

True, difficulty: 2, p. 59

142. Equity theory holds that given payment by time, over-rewarded employees will produce less or a poorer quality of output.

False, difficulty: 2, p. 59

143. Equity theory holds that whether one has the desire to produce at any given time depends on one's particular goals and one's perception of the relative worth of performance as a path to the attainment of those goals.

False, difficulty: 3, p. 60

144. The three variables in expectancy theory are attractiveness, performance-reward linkage, and effort-performance linkage.

True, difficulty: 3, p. 60

145. The performance-reward linkage is the probability perceived by the individual that exerting a given amount of effort will lead to performance.

False, difficulty: 2, p. 60

146. According to expectancy theory, whether one has the desire to produce at any given time depends on one's goals and one's perception of the relative worth of performance as a path to the attainment of these goals.

True, difficulty: 2, p. 60

147. The most blatant pro-American characteristic inherent in motivation theories is the emphasis
on individualism.

True, difficulty: 3, p. 61

148. All cultures would tend to satisfy Maslow's hierarchy of needs in the same order.

False, difficulty: 1, p. 61

149. Goal-setting theory is the only motivation theory discussed that does not appear to be culture bound.

False, difficulty: 2, p. 61

150. Goal-setting theory is well adapted to the United States because its key components align reasonably well with U.S. culture.

True, difficulty: 2, p. 61

ESSAY

151.   What is motivation? Describe the motivation process.

Motivation is the willingness to do something and is conditioned by this action's ability to satisfy some need for the individual. An unsatisfied need creates tension, which stimulates drives within the individual. These drives generate a search to find particular goals that, if attained, will satisfy the need and lead to the reduction of tension. Motivated employees are in a state of tension. In order to relieve this tension, they engage in activity. The greater the tension, the more activity will be needed to bring about relief.

p. 48

152.   Discuss Maslow's hierarchy of needs theory.

Maslow proposed the hierarchy of needs theory. Within each human being there exists a hierarchy of five needs: physiological needs, safety needs, social needs, esteem needs, and self-actualization. Physiological needs include hunger, thirst, and shelter. Safety needs include security and protection from physical and emotional harm. Social needs include affection, and a sense of belonging. Esteem needs include self-respect, autonomy, status, and recognition. Self-actualization is the drive to become what one is capable of becoming. As each of these needs becomes substantially satisfied, the next need becomes dominant.

pp. 48-49

153.   Contrast Theory X and Theory Y.

Douglas McGregor proposed two distinct views of human beings: one being negative, labeled Theory X, and the other basically positive, labeled Theory Y.

Under Theory X, four assumptions are held by the manager:
    Employees inherently dislike work, and whenever possible, will attempt to avoid it.
    Since employees dislike work, they must be coerced, controlled and threatened with punishment.
    Employees will avoid responsibilities and seek formal direction whenever possible.
    Most workers place security above all other factors associated with work and will display little ambition.

Under Theory Y, four contrasting assumptions are held by the manager:
    Employees view work as being as natural as rest or play.
    People will exercise self-direction and self-control if they are committed to the objectives.
    The average person can learn to accept, and even seek, responsibility.
    The ability to make innovative decisions is widely dispersed throughout the population and is not necessarily the sole province of those in management positions.

p. 50

154. Discuss Herzberg's two-factor theory.

The two-factor theory (also called motivation-hygiene) was proposed by Herzberg. He concluded that certain characteristics tend to be consistently related to job satisfaction and others to job dissatisfaction. Intrinsic factors, such as advancement and recognition, seem to be related to job satisfaction. Dissatisfied respondents tended to cite extrinsic factors, such as supervision, pay, and working conditions. The opposite of satisfaction is not dissatisfaction. The opposite of satisfaction is no satisfaction and the opposite of dissatisfaction is no dissatisfaction. The factors leading to job satisfaction are separate from those leading to job dissatisfaction. When the hygiene factors (those conditions surrounding the job) are adequate, people will not be dissatisfied; neither will they be satisfied. To motivate people, the motivator factors must be addressed – promotional opportunities, personal growth, and achievement.

pp. 50-51

155. What are the primary criticisms discussed concerning Herzberg's two-factor theory?

The criticisms of the theory include the following:
    The procedure that Herzberg used is limited by its methodology.
    The reliability of Herzberg's methodology is questionable.
    No overall measure of satisfaction was utilized.
    The theory is inconsistent with previous research.
    Herzberg assumed a relationship between satisfaction and productivity, but his research methodology looked only at satisfaction, not at productivity.

pp. 51-52

156. Discuss McClelland's Theory of Needs.

McClelland proposed three needs in the workplace. The need for achievement is the drive to excel, to achieve in relation to a set of standards, to strive to succeed. The need for power is the need to make others behave in a way they would not have behaved otherwise. The need for affiliation is the desire for friendly and close interpersonal relationships.

pp. 52-53

157. Discuss goal-setting theory.

Goal-setting theory states that intentions – expressed as goals – can be a major source of work motivation. Specific goals lead to increased performance and difficult goals, when accepted, result in higher performance than easy goals.

pp. 53-54

158. Contrast reinforcement theory with goal-setting theory.

Goal-setting theory is a cognitive approach proposing that an individual's purposes direct his or her actions. Reinforcement theory is a behavioristic approach which argues that reinforcement conditions behavior. Reinforcement theorists see behavior as environmentally caused; internal cognitive events are not matters for concern. What controls behavior are reinforcers – any consequences that, when immediately following a response, increase the probability that the behavior will be repeated. Reinforcement theory ignores the inner state of the individual and concentrates solely on what happens to a person when he or she takes some action.

p. 55

159. Describe the five core job characteristics of the Job Characteristics Model.

The job characteristics model (JCM) proposes that any job can be described in terms of five core job dimensions: skill variety, task identity, task significance, autonomy, and feedback. Skill variety is the degree to which the job requires a variety of different activities so the worker can use a number of different skills and talent. Task identity is the degree to which the job requires completion of a whole and identifiable piece of work. Task significance is the degree to which the job has a substantial impact on the lives or work of other people. Autonomy is the degree to which the job provides substantial freedom, independence, and discretion to the individual in scheduling the work and in determining the procedures to be used in carrying it out. Feedback is the degree to which carrying out the work activities required by the job results in the individual obtaining direct and clear information about the effectiveness of his or her performance.

pp. 55-56

160. Discuss the choices when employees envision an inequity according to equity theory.

When employees envision an inequity, they may make one or more of five choices. They may distort their own or others' inputs or outcomes. They may behave in a way to induce others to change their inputs or outcomes. They may behave in some way so as to change their own inputs or outcomes. They may choose a different comparison referent. Or they may quit their job.

p. 59

161. Discuss expectancy theory. Include the three variables and the steps inherent in the theory.

Expectancy theory argues that the strength of a tendency to act in a certain way depends on the strength of an expectation that the act will be followed by a given outcome and on the attractiveness of that outcome to the individual. The three variables are attractiveness, performance-reward linkage, and effort-performance linkage. Attractiveness is the importance the individual places on the potential outcome or reward that can be achieved on the job. Performance-reward linkage is the degree to which the individual believes that performing at a particular level will lead to the attainment of a desired outcome. Effort-performance linkage is the probability perceived by the individual that exerting a given amount of effort will lead to performance.

p. 60

162. How are Maslow's hierarchy of needs theory, McClelland's three-needs theory, and goal setting theory culture bound?

Maslow's hierarchy of needs theory argues that people start at the physiological level and then move progressively up the hierarchy in this order: physiological, safety, social, esteem, and self-actualization. This hierarchy aligns with American culture. In other cultures, the order of importance might be different. Countries that score high on quality-of-life characteristics would have social needs on top. The achievement need from McClelland's three-needs theory has a U.S. bias. The view that a high achievement need acts as an internal motivator presupposes a willingness to accept a moderate degree of risk and a concern with performance. While this combination is found in Anglo-American countries, it is relatively absent in countries such as Chile and Portugal. Goal-setting theory is also culture-bound. It is well adapted to the U.S. because its key components align reasonably well with U.S. culture. It assumes that employees will be reasonably independent and performance is considered important by both. Goal-setting theory's recommendations are not likely to increase motivation in countries in which the opposite conditions exist, such as France, Portugal, and Chile.

pp. 61-62

CHAPTER 5 MOTIVATION: FROM CONCEPTS TO APPLICATIONS

MULTIPLE CHOICE

1. The best way for a manager to make goal setting operational is to:
    a. install a management by objectives program.
    b. institute gainsharing.
    c. hire a consultant.
    d. create an ESOP.

Answer: a, difficulty: 2, p. 64

2. _____ emphasize(s) participatively setting goals that are tangible, verifiable, and measurable.
    a. Job sharing
    b. Management by Objectives (MBO)
    c. OB Mod
    d. ESOPs

Answer: b, difficulty: 1, p. 64

3. Management by Objectives was originally proposed by:
    a. Abraham Maslow.
    b. Frederick Herzberg.
    c. Victor Vroom.
    d. Peter Drucker.

Answer: d, difficulty: 1, p. 64

4. _____ operationalize(s) the concept of objectives by devising a process by which objectives cascade down through the organization.
    a. Goal-setting Theory
    b. OB Mod
    c. Management by Objectives (MBO)
    d. Employee Recognition Programs

Answer: c, difficulty: 1, p. 64

5. MBO works from:
    a. the "bottom up."
    b. the "top down."
    c. the "bottom up" as well as from the "top down."
    d. None of the above.

Answer: c, difficulty: 3, p. 64

6. Which of the following statements is NOT true of MBO?
   a. Because lower-unit managers jointly participate in setting their own goals, MBO works from the "bottom up" as well as from the "top down."
   b. For the individual employee, MBO provides specific personal performance objectives.
   c. If all the individuals achieve their goals, then their unit's goals will be attained.
   d. MBO fails to operationalize the concept of objectives.

Answer: d, difficulty: 2, pp. 64-65

7. Which of the following is NOT an ingredient common to MBO programs?
   a. goal specificity
   b. participative decision making
   c. gainsharing
   d. explicit time period

Answer: c, difficulty: 2, pp. 64-65

8. Which of the following is an example of an MBO objective?
   a. to be the best telephone company in the state
   b. to eliminate inefficient units
   c. to raise revenues by three percent
   d. to raise the quality of our product

Answer: c, difficulty: 2, p. 65

9. Which of the following is NOT an appropriate example of an MBO objective?
   a. cut departmental costs by 7%
   b. improve customer service
   c. increase quality by keeping returns to less than 1% of sales
   d. All of the above.

Answer: b, difficulty: 2, p. 65

10. MBO seems to be most compatible with:
    a. goal-setting theory.
    b. motivation-hygiene theory.
    c. gainsharing.
    d. work councils.

Answer: a, difficulty: 3, p. 65

11. The only area of possible disagreement between MBO and goal-setting theory is related to:
   a. feedback.
   b. participation.
   c. pay levels.
   d. grievances.

Answer: b, difficulty: 3, p. 65

12. MBO implies, rather than explicitly states, that:
   a. objectives should not have specific time periods.
   b. goals must be perceived as feasible.
   c. goals are imposed by top management.
   d. feedback is discretionary.

Answer: b, difficulty: 2, p. 65

13. Which of the following is true concerning MBO?
   a. MBO continues to be practiced as a popular technique.
   b. MBO's popularity should not be construed to mean that it always works.
   c. The problems rarely lie with MBO's basic components.
   d. All of the above.

Answer: d, difficulty: 2, pp. 65-66

14. When MBO failed to meet management's expectations, all of the following tend to be the culprits EXCEPT:
   a. unrealistic expectations regarding results.
   b. lack of top-management commitment.
   c. inability or unwillingness by management to allocate rewards based on goal accomplishment.
   d. MBO's basic components.

Answer: d, difficulty: 3, p. 66

15. The classic study at Emery Air Freight represents an application of reinforcement theory to individuals in the work setting known as:
   a. MBO.
   b. OB Mod.
   c. gainsharing.
   d. a variable-pay plan.

Answer: b, difficulty: 2, p. 66

16. _____ represents the application of reinforcement theory to individuals in the work setting.
    a. MBO
    b. An ESOP
    c. OB Mod
    d. A quality circle

Answer: c, difficulty: 2, p. 66

17. In OB Mod, the first step is to identify critical behaviors. Typically, _____ percent of behavior may account for up to _____ percent of each employee's performance.
    a. 20; 75
    b. 10 to 15; 80 to 90
    c. 5 to 10; 70 to 80
    d. 5; 95

Answer: c, difficulty: 3, p. 66

18. The typical OB Mod program follows a five-step problem-solving model. Which of the following is the FIRST step in such a program?
    a. identifying performance-related behaviors
    b. measuring performance-related behaviors
    c. developing and implementing an intervention strategy
    d. evaluating performance improvement

Answer: a, difficulty: 2, pp. 66-68 and Exhibit 5-2

19. Which of the following is NOT one of the steps in the problem-solving model of the typical OB Mod program?
    a. measure the behaviors
    b. identify behavioral contingencies
    c. avoid any intervention strategies
    d. evaluate performance improvement

Answer: c, difficulty: 2, pp. 66-68 and Exhibit 5-2

20. Once the _____ is complete in an OB Mod program, the manager is ready to develop and implement an intervention strategy.
    a. performance improvement evaluation
    b. behavior measurement
    c. identification of performance-related behaviors
    d. functional analysis

Answer: d, difficulty: 3, p. 68

21. Reinforcement theory relies on positive reinforcement, shaping, and recognizing the impact of different schedules of reinforcement on behavior. _____ uses these concepts to change employee behavior.
    a. MBO
    b. An ESOP
    c. OB Mod
    d. A quality circle

Answer: c, difficulty: 2, p. 68

22. All of the following have been successful uses for OB Mod EXCEPT:
    a. improving employee productivity.
    b. creating marketing plans.
    c. reducing tardiness.
    d. reducing accident rates.

Answer: b, difficulty: 2, p. 68

23. The final step in OB Mod is to:
    a. evaluate performance improvement.
    b. measure the behaviors.
    c. identify behavioral contingencies.
    d. identify performance-related behaviors.

Answer: a, difficulty: 1, p. 68

24. OB Mod programs found that, on average, they produced (a) ____% improvement in employee performance.
    a. less than 5
    b. 50
    c. 17
    d. 90

Answer: c, difficulty: 2, p. 68

25. Examples of recognition might include all of the following EXCEPT:
    a. personally congratulating an employee in private for a good job.
    b. sending a handwritten note acknowledging something positive an employee has done.
    c. a write-up in the company magazine.
    d. a regular paycheck.

Answer: d, difficulty: 2, p. 69

26. A survey of 1,500 employees revealed that the most powerful workplace motivator is:
   a. recognition.
   b. pay.
   c. relationship with supervisors.
   d. responsibility.

Answer: a, difficulty: 2, p. 69

27. One of the most attractive features of recognition programs is that they:
   a. are goal oriented.
   b. cost little or no money.
   c. require little managerial time or effort.
   d. rely on negative reinforcement.

Answer: b, difficulty: 2, p. 69

28. In spite of its increased popularity, critics argue that employee recognition programs are highly susceptible to:
   a. budget cuts.
   b. political manipulation by management.
   c. time constraints.
   d. detailed explanations.

Answer: b, difficulty: 2, pp. 69-70

29. _____ is a participative process that uses the entire capacity of employees and is designed to encourage increased commitment to the organization's success.
   a. MBO
   b. OB Mod
   c. Skill-based pay
   d. Employee involvement

Answer: d, difficulty: 2, p. 70

30. Participation is _____ employee involvement.
   a. the same thing as
   b. a broader term than
   c. a more limited term than
   d. unrelated to

Answer: c, difficulty: 2, p. 70

31. Which of the following is a form of employee involvement program?
    a. ESOPs
    b. golden parachutes
    c. BFOQ
    d. EEOC

Answer: a, difficulty: 1, p. 70

32. Which of the following is NOT a form of employee involvement?
    a. participative management
    b. gainsharing
    c. representative participation
    d. employee stock ownership plans

Answer: b, difficulty: 1, p. 70

33. The distinct characteristic common to all participative management programs is:
    a. quality circles.
    b. joint decision making.
    c. MBO.
    d. Maslow's hierarchy.

Answer: b, difficulty: 2, pp. 70-71

34. Which of the following countries has enacted laws that require companies to have elected representatives from their employee groups as members of their boards of directors?
    a. Spain
    b. Sweden
    c. Argentina
    d. Italy

Answer: b, difficulty: 2, p. 71

35. For participative management to work, which conditions must be present?
    a. There must be adequate time to participate.
    b. The issues in which employees get involved must be relevant to them.
    c. Employees must have the ability to participate.
    d. All of the above.

Answer: d, difficulty: 3, p. 71

36. Studies on the participation-performance relationship have found:
    a. participation is no sure means for improving employee performance.
    b. participation almost always improves employee performance.
    c. participation is an ethical imperative for managers.
    d. all employees want to participate in decision making.

Answer: a, difficulty: 2, p. 71

37. Almost every country in Western Europe has some type of legislation requiring companies to practice:
   a. quality circles.
   b. MBO.
   c. representative participation.
   d. employee stock ownership plans.

Answer: c, difficulty: 2, p. 71

38. The goal of representative participation is to:
   a. redistribute power within an organization, putting labor on a more equal footing with the interests of management and stockholders.
   b. allow employees to participate directly in decisions.
   c. ensure improved employee performance.
   d. change the organizational culture.

Answer: a, difficulty: 3, p. 71

39. The two most common forms that representative participation takes are:
   a. works councils and ESOPs
   b. ESOPs and board representatives
   c. works councils and board representatives
   d. None of the above.

Answer: c, difficulty: 2, p. 71

40. _____ link employees with management. They are groups of nominated or elected employees who must be consulted when management makes decisions involving personnel.
   a. Board representatives
   b. Quality circles
   c. Works councils
   d. ESOPs

Answer: c, difficulty: 2, p. 71

41. _____ are employees who sit on a company's board of directors and represent the interests of the firm's employees.
   a. Board representatives
   b. Quality circles
   c. Works councils
   d. ESOPs

Answer: a, difficulty: 1, p. 71

42.   Which of the following is NOT true of representative participation?
        a. Works councils are dominated by management and have little impact on employees or the organization.
        b. There is little evidence that the motivation and satisfaction improvements of the individuals who are doing the representing actually trickle down to the operating employees whom they represent.
        c. The greatest value of representative participation is symbolic.
        d. If one is interested in changing employee attitudes or in improving organizational performance, representative participation would be a great choice.

Answer: d, difficulty: 3, p. 71

43.   The overall influence of representative participation on working employees:
        a. shows increased productivity.
        b. seems to be minimal.
        c. reduces on-the-job injuries.
        d. decreases job satisfaction.

Answer: b, difficulty: 2, p. 71

44.   One type of company-established benefit plan is a(n):
        a. MBO.
        b. ESOP.
        c. BFOQ.
        d. EEOC.

Answer: b, difficulty: 1, pp. 71-72

45.   Which of the following is NOT true about ESOPs?
        a. They increase employee satisfaction.
        b. An employee stock ownership trust is created.
        c. Employees take physical possession of their stock.
        d. They have the potential to increase work motivation.

Answer: c, difficulty: 2, p. 72

46.   Germany, France, the Netherlands, and the Scandinavian countries have firmly established the principle of _____ in Europe.
        a. industrial democracy
        b. gainsharing
        c. ESOPs
        d. profit sharing

Answer: a, difficulty: 2, p. 72

47. Which of the following is inconsistent?
    a. Theory Y with participative management
    b. Theory X with MBO
    c. Two-factor theory with employee involvement programs
    d. Maslow's hierarchy with skill-based plans

Answer: b, difficulty: 3, p. 72

48. Which of the following is NOT an option to redesign jobs to make them more interesting and motivating for employees?
    a. job rotation
    b. job specialization
    c. job enrichment
    d. job enlargement

Answer: b, difficulty: 1, p. 73

49. With job rotation:
    a. there is no major change in the actual skill levels of workers.
    b. management has developed a long-term solution to a short-term problem.
    c. employees are exposed to different jobs so morale and productivity typically increase.
    d. training costs are decreased.

Answer: a, difficulty: 2, p. 73

50. All of the following are drawbacks to job rotation EXCEPT:
    a. it reduces boredom.
    b. many employees may be working jobs in which they have little experience.
    c. it creates disruptions.
    d. supervisors may have to spend more time answering questions of recently rotated employees.

Answer: a, difficulty: 2, p. 73

51. Which of the following is true about job rotation?
    a. Training costs decrease.
    b. Productivity increases.
    c. Supervisors spend less time answering and monitoring newly rotated employees.
    d. Job rotation reduces disruptions.

Answer: c, difficulty: 2, p. 73

52. Increasing the number and variety of tasks that an individual performs is referred to as:
    a. job rotation.
    b. job enlargement.
    c. job enrichment.
    d. job enhancement.

Answer: b, difficulty: 1, p. 74

53. As a result of the _____ redesign technique, an employee might say, "Before I had one lousy job. Now, I have three."
    a. job rotation
    b. job enlargement
    c. job cnrichment
    d. job flexibility

Answer: b, difficulty: 2, p. 74

54. When a mail sorter's job is expanded to include physically delivering the mail to departmcnts or putting postage on outgoing letters, this is called:
    a. job rotation.
    b. job enlargement.
    c. job simplification.
    d. job enrichment.

Answer: b, difficulty: 2, p. 74

55. Expanding jobs vertically refers to:
    a. job rotation.
    b. job enlargement.
    c. job enrichment.
    d. job flexibility.

Answer: a, difficulty: 2, p. 74

56. To enrich the core-job dimension of autonomy, management might:
    a. combine tasks.
    b. form natural work units.
    c. establish client relationships.
    d. open feedback channels.

Answer: c, difficulty: 2, pp. 74-75 and Exhibit 5-3

57. To enrich the core-job dimension of task significance, management might:
    a. combine tasks.
    b. form natural work units.
    c. establish client relationships.
    d. open feedback channels.

Answer: b, difficulty: 3, pp. 74-75 and Exhibit 5-3

58. To enrich the jobs of employees at Bedrock Mining Company, all of the following may be implemented EXCEPT:
    a. increase responsibility.
    b. increase autonomy.
    c. make task significance more meaningful.
    d. make jobs less complex.

Answer: d, difficulty: 2, pp. 74-75 and Exhibit 5-3

59. All of the following have been found to be typical outcomes of job enrichment programs EXCEPT:
    a. employee satisfaction typically increases.
    b. absenteeism generally decreases.
    c. productivity typically increases.
    d. turnover is generally reduced.

Answer: c, difficulty: 3, p. 75

60. _____ is a scheduling option that allows employees some discretion over when they arrive at and leave work.
    a. Flexiplace
    b. Flextime
    c. Job sharing
    d. Telecommuting

Answer: b, difficulty: 1, p. 75

61. The benefits of flextime include all of the following EXCEPT:
    a. reduced absenteeism.
    b. increased productivity.
    c. reduced overtime expense.
    d. decreased autonomy.

Answer: d, difficulty: 2, p. 76

62. _____ allows two or more individuals to split a traditional 40-hour a week job.
    a. Flexiplace
    b. Flextime
    c. Job sharing
    d. Telecommuting

Answer: c, difficulty: 1, p. 76

63. Telecommuting refers to:
    a. those people who choose to talk on the phone while driving.
    b. those employees who do their work at home on a computer linked to their office.
    c. those employees who work out of their cars.
    d. those employees who are frequent fliers.

Answer: b, difficulty: 2, p. 77

64. Which of the following is NOT a form of variable-pay program?
    a. piece-rate plans
    b. minimum wage
    c. bonus
    d. gainsharing

Answer: b, difficulty: 1, p. 79

65. _____ programs turn an organization's fixed labor costs into a variable cost, thereby reducing expenses when performance declines.
    a. ESOP
    b. Variable-pay
    c. Skill-based pay
    d. Base-pay

Answer: b, difficulty: 2, p. 79

66. When pay is tied to performance, earnings recognize _____ rather than being a form of _____.
    a. entitlement, reward
    b. contributions, entitlement
    c. entitlement, bonus
    d. contributions, reward

Answer: b, difficulty: 2, p. 79

67. In a _____ workers are paid a fixed sum for each unit of production completed.
    a. bonus plan
    b. profit-sharing plan
    c. wage-incentive plan
    d. piece-rate plan

Answer: d, difficulty: 1, pp. 79-80

68. Which variable-pay program has been popular as a means for compensating production workers?
    a. profit sharing
    b. bonuses
    c. gainsharing
    d. piece-rate wages

Answer: d, difficulty: 1, pp. 79-80

69. _____ are organization-wide programs that distribute compensation based on some established formula designed around a company's profitability.
    a. Bonus plans
    b. Gainsharing plans
    c. Profit-sharing plans
    d. Piece-rate plans

Answer: c, difficulty: 2, p. 80

70. _____ is a formula-based group incentive plan in which improvements in group productivity determine the amount of money to be allocated among workers.
    a. Profit sharing
    b. A bonus plan
    c. A wage-incentive plan
    d. Gainsharing

Answer: d, difficulty: 2, p. 80

71. By focusing on productivity gains rather than on profits, _____ reward(s) specific behaviors that are less influenced by external factors than profits are.
    a. profit sharing
    b. bonuses
    c. gainsharing
    d. piece-rate wages

Answer: c, difficulty: 2, p. 80

72. Which of the following is NOT true about gainsharing?
    a. Gainsharing has been found to improve productivity.
    b. Grievances dropped among organizations in a study that were using gainsharing.
    c. Lost-time accidents decreased among organizations in a study that were using gainsharing.
    d. Gainsharing has a negative impact on employee attitudes.

Answer: d, difficulty: 2, p. 80

73. Variable pay is compatible with _____ predictions.
    a. expectancy theory
    b. goal-setting theory
    c. motivation-hygiene theory
    d. achievement need

Answer: a, difficulty: 3, pp. 80-81

74. If rewards are allocated completely on nonperformance factors – such as seniority or job title, then employees are likely to:
    a. increase their effort.
    b. reduce their effort.
    c. hold their effort steady.
    d. perceive a strong relationship between their performance and the rewards they receive.

Answer: b, difficulty: 2, pp. 80-81

75. Bonuses, gainsharing, and other variable-reward programs:
    a. are declining in popularity.
    b. avoid the fixed expense of permanent salary boosts.
    c. have not been used for nonmanagerial employees.
    d. do not motivate most employees.

Answer: b, difficulty: 2, p. 81

76. Gainsharing's popularity seems to be narrowly focused among:
    a. small family-owned businesses.
    b. utility firms.
    c. large, unionized manufacturing companies.
    d. medium-sized retail operations.

Answer: c, difficulty: 2, p. 81

77. Rather than having an individual's job title define his or her pay category, _____ sets pay levels on the basis of how many skills employees have or how many jobs they can do.
    a. piece-rate pay
    b. bonus pay
    c. skill-based pay
    d. gainsharing

Answer: c, difficulty: 2, p. 81

78. Skill-based pay is also called:
    a. piece-rate pay.
    b. bonus pay.
    c. competency-based pay.
    d. gainsharing.

Answer: c, difficulty: 2, p. 81

79. Which of the following is an advantage of skill-based pay?
    a. Skill-based pay addresses level of performance.
    b. Skill-based pay encourages the development of a broad range of skills.
    c. Skill-based pay rewards specialists.
    d. Skill-based pay lowers total wage expense.

Answer: b, difficulty: 2, pp. 81-82

80. Which of the following is NOT a benefit to skill-based pay?
    a. It facilitates communication.
    b. It lessens dysfunctional "protection of territory" behavior.
    c. It can help people increase their earnings without a promotion in job title.
    d. It decreases the knowledge of employees.

Answer: d, difficulty: 2, pp. 81-82

81. Skill-based pay plans are consistent with all of the following motivation theories EXCEPT:
    a. Maslow's hierarchy of needs theory.
    b. reinforcement theory.
    c. equity theory.
    d. Herzberg's motivation-hygiene theory.

Answer: d, difficulty: 3, p. 82

82. The overall conclusion of a number of studies investigating skill-based pay is all of the following EXCEPT:
   a. usc of skill-based pay is expanding.
   b. it generally leads to higher employee performance.
   c. use of skill-based pay is declining.
   d. it generally leads to higher employee satisfaction.

Answer: c, difficulty: 2, pp. 82-83

TRUE/FALSE

83. Goal-setting theory lacks research support.

False, difficulty: 2, p. 64

84. Management by Objectives emphasizes joint participation in goal setting.

True, difficulty: 1, p. 64

85. OB Mod's appeal lies in its emphasis on converting overall organizational objectives into specific objectives for organizational units and individual members.

False, difficulty: 2, p. 64

86. MBO operationalizes the concept of objectives by devising a process by which objectives cascade down through the organization.

True, difficulty: 2, p. 64

87. There are four ingredients common to MBO programs: goal specificity, participative decision making, an explicit time period, and performancc fccdback.

True, difficulty: 2, pp. 64-65

88. A good example of an objective in MBO is "to cut departmental costs."

False, difficulty: 3, p. 65

89. The objectives in MBO are unilaterally set by the boss and then assigned to employees.

False, difficulty: 2, p. 65

90. The final ingredient in an MBO program is feedback on performance.

True, difficulty: 1, p. 65

91. The only area of disagreement between MBO and goal-setting theory is related to the issue of compensation.

False, difficulty: 3, p. 65

92. MBO explicitly states that goals must be perceived as feasible.

False, difficulty: 2, p. 65

93. Cultural incompatibilities can be a problem when implementing MBO.

True, difficulty: 2, p. 66

94. OB Mod represents the application of expectancy theory to individuals in the work setting.

False, difficulty: 2, p. 66

95. A now-classic OB Mod study took place 30 years ago with freight packers at UPS.

False, difficulty: 2, p. 66

96. In OB Mod, everything an employee does is equally important in terms of performance outcomes.

False, difficulty: 1, p. 66

97. The five-step problem-solving models in a typical OB Mod program include identifying performance-related behaviors, measuring the behaviors, identifying behavioral contingencies, developing and implementing an intervention strategy, and evaluating performance improvement.

True, difficulty: 1, pp. 66-68 and Exhibit 5-2

98. The first step in OB Mod is to identify those 5 – 10 percent of behaviors that may account for up to 70 – 80 percent of each employee's performance.

True, difficulty: 2, p. 66

99. Reinforcement theory relies on positive reinforcement, shaping, and recognition of the impact of different schedules of reinforcement on behavior.

True, difficulty: 3, p. 68

100. OB Mod programs produced an average of 5 percent improvement in employee performance.

False, difficulty: 3, p. 68

101. Recognition can be a potent motivator.

True, difficulty: 1, p. 68

102. Rewarding behavior with recognition immediately following that behavior is likely to encourage its repetition.

True, difficulty: 1, p. 69

103. Recognition programs typically are an expensive way to motivate employees.

False, difficulty: 2, p. 69

104. Critics of employee recognition programs argue that they are highly susceptible to political manipulation by management.

True, difficulty: 3, pp. 69-70

105. Participation and employee involvement are synonyms.

False, difficulty: 2, p. 70

106. The distinct characteristic common to all participative management programs is their emphasis on the development of employee skills.

False, difficulty: 2, pp. 70-71

107. The laws of Germany, France, Denmark, Sweden, and Austria require companies to have elected representatives from their employee groups as members of their boards of directors.

True, difficulty: 2, p. 71

108. Participative management is appropriate for every organization and every work unit.

False, difficulty: 1, p. 71

109. The use of participation is a sure means for improving employee performance.

False, difficulty: 1, p. 71

110. Representative participation has been called "the most widely legislated form of employee involvement around the world."

True, difficulty: 2, p. 71

111. The goal of representative participation is to redistribute power within an organization, putting labor above the interests of management and stockholders.

False, difficulty: 2, p. 71

112. Board representatives are groups of nominated or elected employees who must be consulted when management makes decisions involving personnel.

False, difficulty: 2, p. 71

113. Evidence suggests that works councils are dominated by management and have little impact on employees or the organization.

True, difficulty: 2, p. 71

114. Employee stock ownership plans (ESOPs) generally increase employee satisfaction.

True, difficulty: 3, pp. 71-72

115. The pressure is on managers to give up their autocratic decision-making style in favor of a more participative, supportive, coaching-like role.

True, difficulty: 2, p. 72

116. Participative management and representative participation were much slower to gain ground in   North American organizations.

True, difficulty: 2, pp. 72-73

117. Job rotation moves an employee to different jobs with similar skill requirements.

True, difficulty: 1, p.73

118. The strengths of job rotation are that it reduces boredom and increases motivation by diversifying the employee's activities.

True, difficulty: 2, p. 73

119. Job enlargement represents the vertical expansion of a job.

False, difficulty: 2, p. 74

120. Job enlargement instills challenge and meaningfulness to a worker's activities.

False, difficulty: 2, p. 74

121. Job enrichment refers to the vertical expansion of jobs.

True, difficulty: 2, p. 74

122. Job enrichment has been shown to increase absenteeism and satisfaction.

False, difficulty: 2, p. 75

123. On the issue of productivity, the evidence on job enrichment is inconclusive.

True, difficulty: 2, p. 75

124. Flextime is short for flexible work hours.

True, difficulty: 1, p. 76

125. Flextime's major drawback is that it is not applicable to every job.

True, difficulty: 1, p. 76

126. Telecommuting refers to employees who do their work at home at least two days a week on a computer linked to their office.

True, difficulty: 1, p. 77

127. Piece-rate plans, wage incentives, profit sharing, bonuses, and gainsharing are all forms of variable-pay programs.

True, difficulty: 1, p. 79

128. Variable pay programs include bonuses and gainsharing.

True, difficulty: 1, p. 79

129. With variable pay, earnings fluctuate with the measure of performance.

True, difficulty: 1, p. 79

130. In wage-incentive plans, workers are paid a fixed sum for each unit of production completed.

False, difficulty: 2, pp. 79-80

131. People who work ballparks selling peanuts and soda pop frequently are paid in piece-rate pay plans.

True, difficulty: 2, pp. 79-80

132. Bonuses are paid exclusively to executives.

False, difficulty: 1, p. 80

133. Gainsharing is a formula-based individual incentive plan.

False, difficulty: 2, p. 80

134. Gainsharing and profit sharing are the same thing.

False, difficulty: 1, p. 80

135. Variable pay is incompatible with expectancy theory predictions.

False, difficulty: 2, p. 80

136. Group and organization-wide incentives reinforce and encourage employees to sublimate personal goals for the best interests of their department or the organization.

True, difficulty: 1, p. 80

137. Variable pay is a concept that is rapidly replacing the annual cost-of-living raise.

True, difficulty: 2, p. 80

138. Skill-based pay sets pay levels on the basis of how many skills employees have or how many jobs they can do.

True, difficulty: 2, p. 81

139. From management's perspective the appeal of skill-based pay plans is the low cost.

False, difficulty: 2, pp. 81-82

140. The downside of skill-based pay is that people can "top out" – learning all the skills the program calls for them to learn.

True, difficulty: 2, p. 82

ESSAY

141. How does the cascading of objectives work in MBO?

The organization's overall objectives are translated into specific objectives for each succeeding level in the organization. But because lower-unit managers jointly participate in setting their own goals, MBO works from the "bottom up" as well as from the "top down." The result is a hierarchy of objectives that links objectives at one level to those at the next level. And for the individual employee, MBO provides specific personal performance objectives. Each person has an identified specific contribution to make so that his or her unit's goals will be attained and the organization's overall objectives will become a reality.

p. 64 and Exhibit 5-1

142.   Identify the ingredients common to MBO programs.

The four ingredients common to MBO programs are goal specificity, participative decision making, an explicit time period, and performance feedback. The objectives in MBO should be concise statements of expected accomplishments. They must reflect tangible objectives that can be measured and evaluated. The objective has a specific time period in which it is to be completed. MBO seeks to give continuous feedback on progress toward goals so that individuals can monitor and correct their own actions.

pp. 64-65

143.   What are the five steps in a typical OB Mod program?

The five steps in a typical OB Mod program include the following: identify performance-related behaviors, measure the behaviors, identify behavioral contingencies, develop and implement an intervention strategy, and evaluate performance improvement. The first step requires that the critical behaviors that have a significant impact on the employee's job performance be identified. The second step requires that the manager develop some baseline performance information. The third step is to perform a functional analysis to identify the behavioral contingencies or consequences of performance. In the next step, the manager is ready to develop and implement an intervention strategy to strengthen desirable performance behaviors and weaken undesirable behaviors. The final step is to evaluate performance improvement.

pp. 66-68 and Exhibit 5-2

144.   Why are employee recognition programs particularly attractive?

Employee recognition provides a relatively low-cost means to stimulate employee performance. Employee recognition programs can take numerous forms. The best ones use multiple sources and recognize both individual and group accomplishments. Examples of recognition might include personally congratulating an employee in private for a good job, sending a handwritten note acknowledging something positive the employee has done, or a write-up in the company magazine. Rewarding a behavior with recognition immediately following that behavior is likely to encourage its repetition.

pp. 69-70

145.   List and explain three examples of employee involvement programs.

Employee involvement is a participative process that uses the entire capacity of employees and is designed to encourage increased commitment to the organization's success. Three examples of employee involvement include participative management, representative participation, and employee stock ownership plans. Participative management uses joint decision making. Employees share a significant degree of decision-making power with their immediate superiors. With representative participation, workers are represented by a small group of employees who actually participate (rather than participate directly in decisions). Employee stock ownership plans are company-established benefit plans in which employees acquire stock as part of their benefits.

pp. 70-72

146.   Explain the differences between job rotation, job enlargement, and job enrichment.

Job rotation is also called cross-training. When an activity is no longer challenging, the employee is rotated to another job, at the same level, that has similar skills requirements. Job enlargement expands jobs horizontally. Increasing the number and variety of tasks that an individual performs results in jobs with more diversity. Although job enlargement attacks the lack of diversity in overspecialized jobs, it does little to instill challenge or meaningfulness to a worker's activities. Job enrichment was introduced to deal with the shortcomings of enlargement. Job enrichment refers to the vertical expansion of jobs. It increases the degree to which the worker controls the planning, execution, and evaluation of his or her work. An enriched job organizes tasks so as to allow the worker to do a complete activity, increases the employee's freedom and independence, increases responsibility, and provides feedback, so an individual will be able to assess and correct his or her own performance.

pp. 73-75

147.   Discuss five suggestions for enriching an employee's job.

There are a number of measures that a manager can take to enrich an employee's job. Combine tasks. Managers should seek to take existing and fractionalized tasks and put them back together to form a new and larger module of work. Create natural work units. The creation of natural work units means that the tasks an employee does form an identifiable and meaningful whole. This measure increases employee "ownership" of the work and improves the likelihood that employees will view their work as meaningful and important rather than as irrelevant and boring. Establish client relationships. The client is the user of the product or service that the employee works on. Wherever possible, managers should try to establish direct relationships between workers and their clients to increase skill variety, autonomy, and feedback for the employee. Expand jobs vertically,. Vertical expansion gives employees responsibilities and control that were formerly reserved to management. It seeks to partially close the gap between the "doing" and the "controlling" aspects of the job. Open feedback channels. Feedback lets employees know not only how well they are performing their jobs but also whether their performance is improving, deteriorating, or remaining at a constant level. Ideally, feedback about performance should be received directly as the employee does the job, rather than from management on an occasional basis.

pp. 74-75

148.	Why are variable-pay programs becoming more appealing to employees and employers?

Variable-pay programs turn part of an organization's fixed labor costs into a variable cost, thereby reducing expenses when performance declines. When pay is tied to performance, earnings recognize contribution rather than being a form of entitlement. Low performers find, over time, that their pay stagnates, and high performers enjoy pay increases commensurate with their contribution.

p. 79

149.	Discuss four of the more widely used of the variable pay programs.

Four of the most widely used of the variable-pay programs are piece-rate wages, bonuses, profit sharing, and gainsharing. In piece-rate plans, workers are paid a fixed sum for each unit of production completed. Bonuses can be paid exclusively to executives or to all employees. They can reflect a percent of annual salary, based on how much the company earns on its cost of invested capital. Profit-sharing plans are organization-wide programs that distribute compensation based on some established formula designed around a company's profitability. These can be cash or stock. Gainsharing is a formula-based group incentive plan. Improvements in group productivity determine the total amount of money that is to be allocated.

pp. 79-80

150.	What are skill-based pay plans?

Skill-based pay is also referred to as competency-based pay. Pay levels are set on the basis of how many skills employees have or how many jobs they can do (rather than having the individual's job title define his or her pay category).

p. 81

CHAPTER 6 INDIVIDUAL DECISION MAKING

MULTIPLE CHOICE

1.   Making choices from among two or more alternatives is termed:
        a. managing.
        b. decision making.
        c. leading.
        d. creative rationalization.

Answer: b, difficulty: 1, p. 84

2.   The manner in which individuals SHOULD behave in order to maximize a certain
        outcome is termed:
        a. rational decision making.
        b. bounded rationality.
        c. creative decision making.
        d. leadership.

Answer: a, difficulty: 2, p. 85

3.   The optimizing decision maker is _____, that is, he or she makes consistent, value-
        maximizing choices within specified constraints.
        a. creative
        b. satisficing
        c. rational
        d. intuitive

Answer: c, difficulty: 2, p. 85

4.   There are six steps in the rational decision-making model. The first step is:
        a. generating alternatives.
        b. weighing the criteria.
        c. computing the optimal decision.
        d. defining the problem.

Answer: d, difficulty: 2, p. 85 and Exhibit 6-1

5.   If you calculate your monthly expenses and find you're spending $50 more than you
        allocated, which of the steps in the rational decision-making model are you addressing?
        a. generating alternatives
        b. weighing the criteria
        c. computing the optimal decision
        d. defining the problem

Answer: d, difficulty: 3, p. 85

6. The step in the rational decision-making model that brings the decision maker's interests, values, and personal preferences into the process is:
    a. identifying the problem.
    b. identifying the decision criteria.
    c. weighing the criteria.
    d. computing the optimal decision.

Answer: b, difficulty: 3, p. 85

7. What is the final step in the rational decision-making model?
    a. identifying the problem
    b. identifying the decision criteria
    c. weighing the criteria
    d. computing the optimal decision

Answer: d, difficulty: 2, p. 86 and Exhibit 6-1

8. Which of the following is NOT an assumption of the rational decision-making model?
    a. The problem is clear and ambiguous.
    b. It's assumed that the specific decision criteria is dynamic and that the weights assigned to them will change over time.
    c. It's assumed that the criteria and alternatives can be ranked and weighted to reflect their importance.
    d. The rational decision maker will choose the alternative that yields the highest perceived value.

Answer: b, difficulty: 2, p. 86

9. All of the following are assumptions of the rational decision-making model EXCEPT:
    a. all options are known.
    b. preferences are constant and clear.
    c. problems are often unclear and ambiguous.
    d. maximum payoff will be chosen.

Answer: c, difficulty: 3, p. 86

10. Which of the following is an assumption of the rational decision-making model?
    a. The problem may be ambiguous.
    b. Specific decision criteria may change over time.
    c. Cost and time constraints can be assessed.
    d. The rational decision maker will choose the alternative that yields the highest perceived value.

Answer: d, difficulty: 2, p. 86

11. The ability to produce novel and useful ideas is called:
    a. synergy.
    b. bounded rationality.
    c. creativity.
    d. satisficing.

Answer: c, difficulty: 1, p. 86

12. Creativity's most obvious value is in helping the decision maker:
    a. identify all viable alternatives.
    b. rank and weigh criteria and alternatives to reflect their importance.
    c. define the problem.
    d. choose the alternative that yields the highest perceived value.

Answer: a, difficulty: 2, p. 86

13. A study of lifetime creativity of 461 men and women found that _____ were exceptionally creative.
    a. half of them
    b. less than 1 percent of them
    c. over 50 percent of them
    d. almost all of them

Answer: b, difficulty: 3, p. 86

14. According to the three-component model of creativity, which of the following is NOT one of the components?
    a. intrinsic task motivation
    b. extrinsic task motivation
    c. creative thinking skills
    d. expertise

Answer: b, difficulty: 2, pp. 87-88

15. Picasso's understanding of art and Einstein's knowledge of physics are examples of _____ being the foundation of all creative work.
    a. expertise
    b. creative thinking skills
    c. analogies
    d. proficiencies

Answer: a, difficulty: 2, p. 87

16. _____ encompass(es) personality characteristics associated with creativity, the ability to use analogies, as well as the talent to see the familiar in a different light.
    a. Expertise
    b. Creative thinking skills
    c. Proficiencies
    d. Independence

Answer: b, difficulty: 2, p. 87

17. ___ is a component of the three-component model of creativity that reflects the desire to work on something because it's interesting or personally challenging.
    a. Expertise
    b. Creative thinking skills
    c. Intrinsic task motivation
    d. Extrinsic task motivation

Answer: c, difficulty: 2, p. 88

18. Which of the following statements is NOT true concerning decision making?
    a. Most decisions in the real world follow the rational model.
    b. Decision-makers generally make limited use of their creativity.
    c. Most significant decisions are made by judgment.
    d. People are usually content to find a reasonable solution to their problem rather then an optimizing one.

Answer: a, difficulty: 3, p. 88

19. What is NOT one of the organizational factors that impedes your creativity?
    a. expected evaluation
    b. surveillance
    c. internal motivators
    d. constrained choice

Answer: c, difficulty: 2, p. 88

20. You have applied to only a few select colleges because of various constraints. Which does NOT describe your decision-making strategy?
    a. bounded rationality
    b. satisficing
    c. choosing an alternative that fits the "good enough" criterion
    d. rational decision making

Answer: d, difficulty: 1, p. 88

21. Looking for a solution that is "good enough" is called:
    a. suboptimizing.
    b. seeking an implicit favorite.
    c. satisficing.
    d. simplifying.

Answer: c, difficulty: 1, p. 88

22. Diane considers alternatives until one arises that sufficiently meets the established criteria. This decision making represents the:
    a. optimizing model.
    b. maximizing model.
    c. satisficing model.
    d. bounded discretion model.

Answer: c, difficulty: 2, p. 88

23. Selecting the first alternative that meets the "good enough" criterion is:
    a. minimizing.
    b. satisficing.
    c. optimizing.
    d. maximizing.

Answer: b, difficulty: 1, p. 88

24. Bounded rationality refers to:
    a. the state of the environment that confines decision boundaries.
    b. rationality that has boundaries for individuals.
    c. decision making as a segmented process in which each segment has a boundary.
    d. individuals who behave rationally within the limits of a simplified model that captures the complexity of the problems.

Answer: d, difficulty: 2, p. 89

25. Decision-makers use simple and limited models, so they typically begin by identifying alternatives that:
    a. are obvious.
    b. are ones with which they are familiar.
    c. are not too far from the status quo.
    d. All of the above.

Answer: d, difficulty: 2, p. 89

26. Which of the following is NOT a bias in decision making?
   a. availability heuristic
   b. information heuristic
   c. representativeness heuristic
   d. escalation of commitment

Answer: b, difficulty: 2, pp. 89-92

27. The _____ bias makes us think we know more than we actually do.
   a. anchoring
   b. overconfidence
   c. confirmation
   d. reliability

Answer: b, difficulty: 3, p. 89

28. Studies have found that, when people say they are 65 to 70 percent confident that they are right, they were actually correct only about _____ percent of the time.
   a. 10
   b. 25
   c. 50
   d. 75

Answer: c, difficulty: 2, p. 90

29. The _____ bias is a tendency to fixate on initial information as a starting point.
   a. anchoring
   b. overconfidence
   c. confirmation
   d. reliability

Answer: a, difficulty: 2, p. 90

30. The _____ bias occurs because our mind appears to give a disproportionate amount of emphasis to the first information it receives.
   a. anchoring
   b. overconfidence
   c. confirmation
   d. reliability

Answer: a, difficulty: 1, p. 90

31.	The _____ bias represents a specific case of selective perception.
	a.	anchoring
	b.	overconfidence
	c.	confirmation
	d.	reliability

Answer: c, difficulty: 2, p. 90

32.	The _____ bias leads us to give too much weight to supporting information and too little to contradictory information.
	a.	anchoring
	b.	overconfidence
	c.	confirmation
	d.	reliability

Answer: c, difficulty: 2, p. 90

33.	Which bias may explain why managers tend to give more weight to recent behaviors during an annual performance appraisal?
	a.	availability bias
	b.	information bias
	c.	representativeness bias
	d.	escalation of commitment

Answer: a, difficulty: 1, p. 91

34.	The tendency for people to base their judgments on information that is readily available to them is:
	a.	the availability bias.
	b.	the representative bias.
	c.	the rationality bias.
	d.	poor judgment.

Answer: a, difficulty: 1, p. 91

35.	When decision makers assess the likelihood of an occurrence by trying to match it with a preexisting category, it is called:
	a.	availability bias.
	b.	representative bias.
	c.	rationality bias.
	d.	bounded rationality.

Answer: b, difficulty: 2, p. 91

36.   When we overstate the risk in flying and understate the risk in driving due to the increased media attention to air accidents as compared to car accidents, which bias are we experiencing?
        a. availability bias
        b. representative bias
        c. escalation of commitment
        d. error in judgment

Answer: a, difficulty: 2, p. 91

37.   When a manager predicts the performance of a new product by relating it to a previous product's success, he is suffering from a(n):
        a. availability bias.
        b. representative bias.
        c. escalation of commitment.
        d. error in judgment.

Answer: b, difficulty: 2, p. 91

38.   If a manager predicts that a current job applicant won't be a good employee because the company hired three graduates from the same university who turned out to be poor performers, which bias is the manager using?
        a. availability bias
        b. representative bias
        c. escalation of commitment
        d. error in judgment

Answer: b, difficulty: 3, p. 91

39.   _____ is an increased commitment to a previous decision in spite of negative information.
        a. The availability bias
        b. The representative bias
        c. Escalation of commitment
        d. Bounded rationality

Answer: c, difficulty: 1, p. 91

40.   You have worked at your job for eight years and have decided that you are unhappy with the career you have chosen. Your spouse suggests a career change but you refuse because you have too much invested to change. You are suffering from:
        a. the availability bias.
        b. the representative bias.
        c. escalation of commitment.
        d. bounded rationality.

Answer: c, difficulty: 2, p. 91

41. Which bias is demonstrated by the statement that we "throw good money after bad"?
    a. availability bias
    b. representative bias
    c. escalation of commitment
    d. bounded rationality

Answer: c, difficulty: 2, p. 91

42. The _____ bias occurs when we try to create meaning out of random events.
    a. confirmation
    b. hindsight
    c. randomness
    d. anchoring

Answer: c, difficulty: 1, p. 92

43. When decision-makers become controlled by their superstitions, they are impaired by the _____ bias.
    a. confirmation
    b. hindsight
    c. randomness
    d. anchoring

Answer: c, difficulty: 3, p. 92

44. The _____ bias is the tendency for us to believe falsely that we'd have accurately predicted the outcome of an event, after that outcome is actually known.
    a. confirmation
    b. hindsight
    c. randomness
    d. anchoring

Answer: b, difficulty: 2, p. 92

45. Which bias reduces our ability to learn from the past?
    a. confirmation
    b. hindsight
    c. randomness
    d. anchoring

Answer: b, difficulty: 2, p. 92

46.   _____ is an unconscious process created out of distilled experience.
        a. Rational decision making
        b. Bounded rationality
        c. Satisficing
        d. Intuitive decision making

Answer: d, difficulty: 1, p. 93

47.   When experience allows an expert to recognize a situation and draw upon previously
        learned information associated with that situation to quickly arrive at a decision choice, the
        expert is engaging in:
        a. rational decision making.
        b. bounded rationality.
        c. satisficing.
        d. intuitive decision making.

Answer: d, difficulty: 2, p. 93

48.   Which statement is true of the relationship between intuitive decision making and rational
        analysis?
        a. The two always operate independently of each other.
        b. The two are mutually exclusive.
        c. The two complement each other.
        d. One is clearly superior to the other.

Answer: c, difficulty: 2, p. 93

49.   You have been a manager in your department for seven years and are able to make good
        decisions more quickly than the newer managers. You are drawing upon previously
        learned information and are engaging in:
        a. bounded rationality.
        b. satisficing.
        c. intuitive decision making.
        d. rational decision making.

Answer: c, difficulty: 2, p. 93

50.   Which is NOT a condition when people are most likely to use intuitive decision-making?
        a. when a high level of uncertainty exists
        b. when facts are limited
        c. when analytical data is of the most use
        d. when time is limited and there is pressure to come up with the right decision.

Answer: c, difficulty: 3, p. 93

51. The decision-style model makes the assumption that people differ along what two dimensions?
    a. thinking; tolerance for ambiguity
    b. commitment; thinking
    c. people; task
    d. consistency; commitment

Answer: a, difficulty: 3, p. 94 and Exhibit 6-3

52. Which is NOT one of the four styles of decision making?
    a. directive
    b. analytical
    c. contradictory
    d. behavioral

Answer: c, difficulty: 1, p. 94 and Exhibit 6-3

53. The decision-style model states that people using the directive style have:
    a. greater tolerance for ambiguity and ability to copy with new situations.
    b. low tolerance for ambiguity and seek rationality.
    c. a long-range focus and are good at finding creative solutions to problems.
    d. the ability to work well with others and seek to avoid conflict.

Answer: b, difficulty: 2, p. 94

54. The decision-style model states that people using the analytic style have:
    a. a greater tolerance for ambiguity and an ability to copy with new situations.
    b. low tolerance for ambiguity than directive decision makers.
    c. a long-range focus and are good at finding creative solutions to problems.
    d. the ability to work well with others and seek to avoid conflict.

Answer: a, difficulty: 2, p. 95

55. The decision-style model states that people using the conceptual style have:
    a. a greater tolerance for ambiguity and an ability to copy with new situations.
    b. low tolerance for ambiguity and seek rationality.
    c. a long-range focus and are good at finding creative solutions to problems.
    d. the ability to work well with others and seek to avoid conflict.

Answer: c, difficulty: 2, p. 95

56. The _____decision-making style characterizes decision makers who work well with others.
   a. directive
   b. analytical
   c. conceptual
   d. behavioral

Answer: d, difficulty: 2, p. 95

57. The decision-style model states that people using the behavioral style have:
   a. a greater tolerance for ambiguity and an ability to copy with new situations.
   b. low tolerance for ambiguity and seek rationality.
   c. a long-range focus and are good at finding creative solutions to problems.
   d. the ability to work well with others and seek to avoid conflict.

Answer: d, difficulty: 2, p. 95

58. Which of the following is NOT true of rumination?
   a. The evidence indicates that women analyze decisions more than men.
   b. In terms of decision-making, rumination means not thinking much about problems.
   c. Women, in general, are more likely to engage in rumination.
   d. Rumination tendencies appear to be moderated by age.

Answer: b, difficulty: 3, p. 95

59. Moral development is relevant because many decisions have a(n) _____ dimension.
   a. ethical
   b. judgmental
   c. logical
   d. constraint

Answer: a, difficulty: 1, p. 96

60. The stages of moral development include all of the following EXCEPT:
   a. preconventional.
   b. conventional.
   c. postconventional.
   d. principled.

Answer: c, difficulty: 2, p. 96 and Exhibit 6-4

61.   The preconventional stage of moral development is the level in which:
    a.   individuals respond to notions of right or wrong only when personal consequences are involved.
    b.   the moral value resides in maintaining the conventional order and the expectations of others.
    c.   individuals make a clear effort to define moral principles apart from the authority of the groups to which they belong.
    d.   individuals do not respond to notions of right or wrong.

Answer: a, difficulty: 2, p. 96

62.   The conventional stage of moral development is the level in which:
    a.   individuals respond to notions of right or wrong only when personal consequences are involved.
    b.   the moral value resides in maintaining the conventional order and the expectations of others.
    c.   individuals make a clear effort to define moral principles apart from the authority of the groups to which they belong.
    d.   individuals do not respond to notions of right or wrong.

Answer: b, difficulty: 2, p. 96

63.   The principled level of moral development is the level in which:
    a.   individuals respond to notions of right or wrong only when personal consequences are involved.
    b.   the moral value resides in maintaining the conventional order and the expectations of others.
    c.   individuals make a clear effort to define moral principles apart from the authority of the groups to which they belong.
    d.   individuals do not respond to notions of right or wrong.

Answer: c, difficulty: 2, p. 96

64.   All of the following are conclusions drawn from research on the stages of moral development EXCEPT:
    a.   people proceed through the six stages in a lock-step fashion.
    b.   there is no guarantee of continued development.
    c.   most adults are at stage six.
    d.   the higher the stage a manager reaches, the more he/she will be predisposed to make ethical decision.

Answer: c, difficulty: 3, pp. 96-97

65. Which of the following is NOT an <u>organizationally</u> imposed constraint on decision makers?
   a. performance evaluation
   b. reward systems
   c. cultural differences
   d. historical precedents

Answer: c, difficulty: 3, p. 97

66. Which of the following is NOT one of the three criteria that individuals can use in making ethical choices?
   a. utilitarianism
   b. policy
   c. rights
   d. justice

Answer: b, difficulty: 2, p. 99

67. The goal of the decision criteria known as _____ is to provide the greatest good for the greatest number.
   a. utilitarianism
   b. policy
   c. rights
   d. justice

Answer: a, difficulty: 2, p. 99

68. Which decision criterion tends to dominate business decision-making?
   a. utilitarianism
   b. policy
   c. rights
   d. justice

Answer: a, difficulty: 2, p. 99

69. The decision criterion which focuses on _____ calls on individuals to make decisions consistent with fundamental liberties and privileges as set forth in documents like the Bill of Rights.
   a. utilitarianism
   b. policy
   c. rights
   d. justice

Answer: c, difficulty: 2, p. 99

70. Union members typically favor the decision criterion which focuses on:
    a. utilitarianism.
    b. policy.
    c. rights.
    d. justice.

Answer: d, difficulty: 3, p. 99

71. Making ethical decisions by focusing on _____ promotes efficiency and productivity, but may result in ignoring rights of those with minority representation.
    a. utilitarianism
    b. policy
    c. rights
    d. justice

Answer: a, difficulty: 2, p. 99

72. The use of _____ as a criterion protects individuals from injury and is consistent with freedom and privacy, but it can create an overly legalistic workplace that hinders productivity and efficiency.
    a. utilitarianism
    b. policy
    c. rights
    d. justice

Answer: c, difficulty: 2, p. 99

73. A focus on _____ as a decision criterion protects the interests of the underrepresented and less powerful, but it can encourage a sense of entitlement.
    a. utilitarianism
    b. policy
    c. rights
    d. justice

Answer: d, difficulty: 2, p. 99

74. Suggestions for managers to improve their decision making include all of the following EXCEPT:
    a. analyze the situation.
    b. be aware of biases.
    c. combine rational analysis with intuition.
    d. recognize that your specific decision style is appropriate for every job.

Answer: d, difficulty: 3, p. 100

TRUE/FALSE

75.   The making of decisions is the sole province of managers.

False, difficulty: 1, p. 84

76.   The optimizing decision maker uses bounded rationality.

False, difficulty: 2, p. 85

77.   The rational decision-making model begins with defining the problem.

True, difficulty: 2, p. 85 and Exhibit 6-1

78.   Since the decision criteria identified are all equal in importance, there is no need for the decision-maker to weight the identified criteria.

False, difficulty: 3, p. 85

79.   When generating possible alternatives in the rational decision-making model, it is possible to appraise them at this step.

False, difficulty: 2, p. 86

80.   In the final step of the rational decision-making model, each alternative is evaluated against the weighted criteria and the alternative with the highest total score is selected.

True, difficulty: 2, p. 86

81.   The rational decision-making model assumes the problem is clear and unambiguous.

True, difficulty: 1, p. 86

82.   The rational decision-making model assumes cost and time constraints are known.

False, difficulty: 3, p. 86

83.   The rational decision-making model assumes the rational decision-maker will choose the alternative that yields the highest perceived value.

True, difficulty: 1, p. 86

84.   Creativity is the ability to produce novel and useful ideas.

True, difficulty: 2, p. 86

85.   Creativity's most obvious value is in helping the decision maker identify all viable alternatives.

True, difficulty: 2, p. 86

86.   People are equal in their inherent creativity.

False, difficulty: 2, p. 86

87.   A study of lifetime creativity found that over 50% of the respondents were exceptionally creative.

False, difficulty: 3, p. 86

88.   The effective use of analogies allows decision makers to apply an idea from one context to another.

True, difficulty: 1, p. 87

89.   One of the most famous examples in which analogy resulted in a creative breakthrough was Alexander Graham Bell's observation that it might be possible to take concepts that operate in the ear and apply them to his "talking box."

True, difficulty: 2, p. 87

90.   When decision makers are faced with a simple problem having few alternative courses of action, and when the cost of searching out and evaluating alternatives is low, the rational model provides a fairly accurate description of the decision-making process.

True, difficulty: 3, p. 88

91.   Most decisions in the real world don't follow the rational model.

True, difficulty: 2, p. 88

92.   Decision makers generally make extensive use of their creativity.

False, difficulty: 1, p. 88

93.   The capacity of the human mind for formulating and solving complex problems is far too small to meet the requirements for full rationality.

True, difficulty: 1, p. 89

94.   Optimizing is seeking solutions that are satisfactory and sufficient.

False, difficulty: 2, p. 89

95.   People satisfice when they seek solutions that are satisfactory and sufficient.

True, difficulty: 2, p. 89

96.   In bounded rationality the order in which alternatives are considered is of no importance in determining which alternative is selected.

False, difficulty: 2, p. 89

97.   The overconfidence bias is a tendency to fixate on initial information as a starting point.

False, difficulty: 1, pp. 89-90

98.   Those individuals whose intellectual and interpersonal abilities are weakest are among those likely to overestimate their performance and ability.

True, difficulty: 1, p. 90

99.   The anchoring bias occurs because our mind appears to give a disproportionate amount of emphasis to the first information it receives.

True, difficulty: 1, p. 90

100.   Any time a negotiation takes place, so does anchoring.

True, difficulty: 3, p. 90

101.   According to the confirmation bias, we seek out information that contradicts our past judgments.

False, difficulty: 2, p. 90

102.   The availability bias is increased commitment to a previous decision in spite of negative information.

False, difficulty: 1, p. 91

103.   When managers use a representative bias, they are assessing the likelihood of an occurrence by trying to match it with a preexisting category.

True, difficulty: 2, p. 91

104.   A friend of yours has been dating the same woman for five years. Although the relationship isn't going well, he decides to marry the woman because he has "a lot invested in the relationship." This is an example of escalation of commitment.

True, difficulty: 1, p. 91

105. Individuals escalate commitment to a failing course of action when they view themselves as responsible for the failure.

True, difficulty: 1, p. 91

106. Effective managers are those who are able to differentiate between situations in which persistence will pay off and situations where it won't.

True, difficulty: 2, p. 92

107. Decision-making is rarely impaired by the randomness bias.

False, difficulty: 2, p. 92

108. The hindsight bias reduces our ability to learn from the past.

True, difficulty: 2, p. 92

109. Managers regularly use their intuition, and doing so may actually help improve decision making.

True, difficulty: 1, p. 93

110. Using intuition always hinders decision making.

False, difficulty: 2, p. 93

111. Intuitive decision-making is an unconscious process created out of distilled experience.

True, difficulty: 1, p. 93

112. The intuitive decision-maker can make decisions rapidly with what appears to be very limited information.

True, difficulty: 2, p. 93

113. Since rational analysis still continues to be more socially desirable, intuitive ability is often disguised or hidden.

True, difficulty: 3, p. 93

114. The foundation of the decision-style model is that people differ along two dimensions: thinking and commitment.

False, difficulty: 2, p. 94

115.   The four styles of decision making identified by the decision-style model are directive, analytic, conceptual, and behavior.

True, difficulty: 3, p. 94 and Exhibit 6-3

116.   People using the directive style have high tolerance for ambiguity and focus on the long run.

False, difficulty: 2, p. 94

117.   Using the decision-style model, business students tend to score highest in the analytic style.

True, difficulty: 2, p. 95

118.   Overall, the evidence indicates that men analyze decisions more than women.

False, difficulty: 2, p. 95

119.   An understanding of the concept of moral development can help a manager see how different people impose ethical standards on their decisions.

True, difficulty: 1, p. 96

120.   The preconventional level of moral development is the level at which individuals are living up to what is expected by people close to them.

False, difficulty: 2, p. 96

121.   Research on the stages of moral development suggests that people skip steps as they move up the development ladder.

False, difficulty: 3, p. 96

122.   Because problem-solving managers believe that they can and should change situations to their benefit, American managers might identify a problem long before their Thai or Indonesian counterparts would choose to recognize it as such.

True, difficulty: 3, p. 99

123.   Individuals using the utilitarianism criterion for ethical decision making focus on enforcing rules fairly and impartially.

False, difficulty: 2, p. 99

124.   The goal of utilitarianism is to provide the greatest good for the greatest number.

True, difficulty: 1, p. 99

125. A focus on the use of rights as an ethical decision-making criterion protects the interests of the underrepresented and less powerful.

False, difficulty: 2, p. 99

126. A focus on utilitarianism in ethical decision making promotes efficiency and productivity.

True, difficulty: 2, p. 99

127. Union members typically favor the ethical decision-making criterion known as rights.

False, difficulty: 3, p. 99

128. Decision makers, particularly in for-profit organizations, tend to feel safe and comfortable when they use utilitarianism as a decision-making criterion.

True, difficulty: 2, p. 99

ESSAY

129. What are the six steps of the rational decision-making model?

The six steps in the rational decision-making model are as follows:
1. define the problem
2. identify decision criteria
3. weight the criteria
4. generate alternatives
5. rate each alternative on each criterion
6. compute the optimal decision

pp. 85-86 and Exhibit 6-1

130. What are the assumptions of the rational decision-making model?

There are six assumptions of the rational decision-making model. The first is the assumption that the problem is clear and unambiguous. The second is that the decision maker can identify all the relevant criteria and can list all the viable alternatives. The third assumption is that the criteria and alternatives can be ranked and weighted to reflect their importance. Rationality assumes that the criteria and alternatives can be ranked and weighted to reflect their importance. The fourth assumption is that the specific decision criteria are constant and that the weights assigned to them are stable over time. The rational decision maker can obtain full information about criteria and alternatives because it's assumed that there are no time or cost constraints. The final assumption is that the rational decision maker will choose the alternative that yields the highest perceived value.

p. 86

131.	Discuss the three-component model of creativity.

The three-component model of creativity proposes that individual creativity essentially requires expertise, creative thinking skills, and intrinsic task motivation. The higher the level of each, the higher the creativity is. The potential for creativity is enhanced when individuals have abilities, knowledge, proficiencies, and similar expertise in their fields of endeavor. Creative thinking skills encompass personality characteristics associated with creativity, the ability to use analogies, as well as the talent to see the familiar in a different light. Intrinsic task motivation is the desire to work on something because it's interesting, involving, exciting, satisfying, or personally challenging. This component turns creativity potential into actual creative ideas.

pp. 87-88

132.	Explain the concept of bounded rationality.

Because the capacity of the human mind for formulating and solving complex problems is far too small to meet the requirements for full rationality, individuals operate within the confines of bounded rationality. They construct simplified models that extract the essential features from problems without capturing all of their complexity. Individuals can then behave rationally within the limits of the simple model.

pp. 88-89

133.	Discuss the overconfidence, anchoring, and confirmation biases.

The overconfidence bias makes us think we know more than we actually do. From an organizational standpoint, one of the more interesting findings related to overconfidence is that those individuals whose intellectual and interpersonal abilities are weakest are most likely to overestimate their performance and ability. The anchoring bias is a tendency to fixate on initial information as a starting point. Once set, we then fail to adequately adjust for subsequent information. The anchoring bias occurs because our mind appears to give a disproportionate amount of emphasis to the first information it receives. So initial impressions, ideas, prices, and estimates carry undue weight relative to information received later. The confirmation bias represents a specific case of selective perception. We seek out information that reaffirms our pasts choices, and we discount information that contradicts past judgments. We also tend to accept information at face value that confirms our preconceived views, while being critical and skeptical of information that challenges these views. Therefore, the information we gather is typically biased toward supporting views we already hold.

pp. 89-90

134.	Explain the role of the availability bias in performance appraisals.

The availability bias is the tendency for people to base their judgments on information that is readily available to them. The availability bias can explain why managers, when doing annual performance appraisals, tend to give more weight to recent behaviors of an employee than those behaviors of six to nine months ago.

p. 91

135.   What is an escalation of commitment?

Escalation of commitment is an increased commitment to a previous decision in spite of negative information. Individuals escalate commitment to a failing course of action when they view themselves as responsible for the failure. That is, they "throw good money after bad."

pp. 91-92

136.   What is the hindsight bias and what explains it?

The hindsight bias is the tendency for us to believe falsely that we'd have accurately predicted the outcome of an event, after that outcome is actually known. We apparently aren't very good at recalling the way an uncertain event appeared to us before we find out the actual results of that event. On the other hand, we seem to be fairly well adept at reconstructing the past by overestimating what we knew beforehand based upon what we learned later. So the hindsight seems to be a result of both selective memory and our ability to reconstruct earlier predictions.

p. 92

137.   Explain intuitive decision making and its relationship to rational analysis.

Intuitive decision making is an unconscious process created out of distilled experience. Managers regularly use intuition, and doing so may help improve decision making. It doesn't necessarily operate independently of rational analysis; the two may complement each other.

p. 93

138.   Discuss the four approaches to making decisions identified in the decision styles model.

The four decision-making styles are directive, analytic, conceptual, and behavioral. People using the directive style have low tolerance for ambiguity and seek rationality. They are efficient and logical. The analytic type has a greater tolerance for ambiguity than do directive decision makers. They desire more information and consider more alternatives than do directives. Individuals with a conceptual style tend to be very broad in their outlook and consider many alternatives. Their focus is long range, and they are good at finding creative solutions to problems. Those with a behavioral style work well with others. They avoid conflict and seek acceptance.

pp. 94-95 and Exhibit 6-3

139.   List and describe the stages of moral development.

The three levels of moral development are preconventional, conventional, and principled. The six stages are as follows:

1. Sticking to rules to avoid physical punishment.
2. Following rules only when it's in your immediate interest.
3. Living up to what is expected by people close to you.
4. Maintaining conventional order by fulfilling obligations to which you have agreed.
5. Valuing rights of others, and upholding nonrelative values and rights regardless of the majority's opinion.
6. Following self-chosen ethical principles even if they violate the law.

pp. 96-97 and Exhibit 6-4

140. How does the organization constrain decision makers?

The organization constrains decision makers with performance evaluations, reward systems, formal regulations, historical precedents, and time constraints. Managers are strongly influenced in their decision making by the criteria by which they are evaluated. The organization's reward system influences decision makers by suggesting to them what choices are preferable in terms of personal payoff. By programming decisions, organizations are able to get individuals to achieve high levels of performance without paying for the years of experience that would be necessary in the absence of regulations. And in so doing, they limit the decision maker's choices. Decisions made in the past are ghosts that continually haunt current choices. Choices made today are largely a result of choices made over the years. Organizations also impose deadlines on decisions. Almost all important decisions come with explicit deadlines. These conditions create time pressures on decision makers and often make it difficult, if not impossible, to gather all the information they might like before having to make a final choice.

pp. 97-98

141. What are the three different criteria that individuals can use in making ethical choices? What are the advantages or disadvantages of each?

The three criteria used in making ethical choices are utilitarianism, justice, and rights. The goal of utilitarianism is the greatest good for the greatest number. The focus on rights calls on individuals to make decisions consistent with fundamental liberties and privileges as set forth in documents such as the Bill of Rights. This means respecting the basic rights of individuals. A third criterion is to focus on justice. This requires individuals to impose and enforce rules fairly and impartially so there is an equitable distribution of benefits and costs. Union members tend to favor this view.

p. 99

CHAPTER 7 FOUNDATIONS OF GROUP BEHAVIOR

MULTIPLE CHOICE

1.   Two or more individuals, interacting and interdependent, who come together to achieve particular objectives, are a(n):
    a. organization.
    b. group.
    c. structure.
    d. role.

Answer: b, difficulty: 1, p. 101

2.   _____ groups are defined by the organization's structure, with designated work assignments.
    a. Formal
    b. Informal
    c. Impromptu
    d. Hawthorne

Answer: a, difficulty: 1, pp. 101-102

3.   In _____ groups, the behaviors one should engage in are stipulated by and directed toward organizational goals.
    a. informal
    b. formal
    c. power
    d. emergent

Answer: b, difficulty: 2, p. 102

4.   _____ groups are alliances that are neither structured nor organizationally determined and they form naturally as responses to the need for social contact.
    a. Informal
    b. Formal
    c. Command
    d. Task

Answer: a, difficulty: 2, p. 102

5.   _____ groups are determined by the organizational chart and are composed of the subordinates who report directly to a given manager.
    a. Security
    b. Special interest
    c. Command
    d. Friendship

Answer: c, difficulty: 1, p. 102

6. An example of a command group is:
   a. an elementary school principal and her twelve teachers.
   b. a college committee composed of adviser, registrar, dean of students, and director of security.
   c. employees who band together to support a peer who has been fired.
   d. a college fraternity.

Answer: a, difficulty: 2, p. 102

7. The manager of a department store wants to develop a program to prevent shoplifting. Therefore, the manager forms a group consisting of the security director and managers from shipping, women's clothing, men's clothing, and gifts. This group is called a _____ group.
   a. special interest
   b. functional
   c. task
   d. friendship

Answer: c, difficulty: 2, p. 102

8. _____ groups are organizationally determined and represent persons working together to complete a job. The group's boundaries are not limited to its immediate hierarchical superior.
   a. Task
   b. Command
   c. Friendship
   d. Special interest

Answer: a, difficulty: 2, p. 102

9. Employees who affiliate in order to attain a specific objective with which each is concerned form a(n) _____ group.
   a. command
   b. task
   c. interest
   d. friendship

Answer: c, difficulty: 2, p. 102

10. Alumni of the University of South Carolina have formed a group to share information. This is an example of a(n):
    a. command group.
    b. friendship group.
    c. task group.
    d. formal group.

Answer: b, difficulty: 1, p. 102

11. Employees of Arnold Trucking Co. have banded together to seek better group insurance. This is an example of a(n) _____ group.
   a. command
   b. task
   c. interest
   d. friendship

Answer: c, difficulty: 2, p. 102

12. Informal groups satisfy members':
   a. self-actualization needs.
   b. physiological needs.
   c. safety needs.
   d. social needs.

Answer: d, difficulty: 1, p. 102

13. Groups that develop because the individual members have one or more common characteristics are termed:
   a. command groups.
   b. task groups.
   c. interest groups.
   d. friendship groups.

Answer: d, difficulty: 1, p. 102

14. The most popular reasons for joining a group include all of the following EXCEPT:
   a. security.
   b. status.
   c. power.
   d. money.

Answer: d, difficulty: 3, Exhibit 7-1

15. A set of expected behavior patterns attributed to someone in a particular position describes a:
   a. role.
   b. structure.
   c. status hierarchy.
   d. norm.

Answer: a, difficulty: 2, p. 103

16. The concept of _____ can help us understand why Glenn's behavior at a family reunion is different from his behavior during a meeting at work.
    a. roles
    b. status
    c. norms
    d. structure

Answer: a, difficulty: 2, p. 103

17. Which of the following statements is NOT correct concerning roles?
    a. People play multiple roles.
    b. People have difficulty shifting roles even when they recognize that the situation demands it.
    c. People learn roles from stimuli around them.
    d. People often experience role conflict.

Answer: b, difficulty: 2, p. 103

18. The _____ set(s) out mutual expectations – what management expects from workers, and vice versa.
    a. management contract
    b. psychological contract
    c. norms
    d. rituals

Answer: b, difficulty: 2, pp. 103-104

19. Acceptable standards of behavior shared by group members are known as:
    a. sanctions.
    b. norms.
    c. roles.
    d. goals.

Answer: b, difficulty: 1, p. 104

20. Managers tend to be most concerned with:
    a. performance-related norms.
    b. dress norms.
    c. friendship norms.
    d. All of the above.

Answer: a, difficulty: 2, p. 104

21.	_____ help(s) explain why golfers don't speak while their partners are putting and why students raise their hands before asking questions in class.
	a.	Norms
	b.	Status symbols
	c.	Referent power
	d.	Roles

Answer: a, difficulty: 2, p. 104

22.	Which of the following is INCORRECT regarding the Hawthorne studies?
	a.	The original research examined the relation between the physical environment and productivity.
	b.	Dr. Frederick Herzberg was the primary researcher.
	c.	Group performance was influenced by its status of being a "special" group.
	d.	Norms have a significant place in determining individual work behavior.

Answer: b, difficulty: 2, pp. 105-106

23.	The Hawthorne studies began as:
	a.	experiments on peer pressure.
	b.	illumination experiments.
	c.	experiments on motivation.
	d.	experiments on role conflict.

Answer: b, difficulty: 3, p. 105

24.	What was NOT one of the experiments conducted as part of the Hawthorne studies?
	a.	illumination experiment
	b.	relay assembly test room test
	c.	research assistant experiment
	d.	bank wiring observation room experiment

Answer: c, difficulty: 2, pp. 105-106

25.	The Hawthorne bank wiring observation room studies were introduced to ascertain:
	a.	the effect of sophisticated wage incentive plans.
	b.	the change in behavior when being observed.
	c.	the optimum illumination level.
	d.	the relation between physical environment and productivity.

Answer: a, difficulty: 3, p. 106

26.   How did the bank wiring group of the Hawthorne studies enforce their norms on the job?
        a. sarcasm
        b. name-calling
        c. physical punches
        d. All of the above.

Answer: d, difficulty: 2, p. 106

27.   One of the main contributions to understanding behavior from the Hawthorne studies was that:
        a. special attention does not affect productivity.
        b. productivity decreases if workers don't receive special attention.
        c. management pressure has a stronger influence on worker productivity than pressure from group members.
        d. norms have a significant place in determining individual work behavior.

Answer: d, difficulty: 2, p. 106

28.   The MAJOR contribution of the Asch study was to demonstrate the impact of:
        a. group norms pressing us toward conformity.
        b. seating arrangements.
        c. the Hawthorne effect.
        d. status on group performance.

Answer: a, difficulty: 2, pp. 106-107

29.   Conformity was demonstrated in the studies undertaken by:
        a. Frederick Herzberg.
        b. Abraham Maslow.
        c. Solomon Asch.
        d. David McClelland.

Answer: c, difficulty: 1, p. 106

30.   Which of the following is NOT true of the Asch experiments?
        a. There are group norms that press us toward conformity.
        b. We desire to be one of the group.
        c. We strive to be visibly different.
        d. When an individual's opinion of objective data differs significantly from that of others in the group, he or she feels no pressure to align his or her opinion to conform with those of the others.

Answer: c, difficulty: 1, pp. 106-107

31. Asch found that:
   a. individuals would give answers they knew were wrong in order to be consistent with other group members.
   b. conformity is only of importance in times of crisis.
   c. group members ostracize those who do not agree.
   d. the Hawthorne effect is unimportant in small groups.

Answer: a, difficulty: 2, p. 107

32. _____ refers to a position or rank given to groups or group members.
   a. Role
   b. Status
   c. Position
   d. Identity

Answer: b, difficulty: 1, p. 107

33. Which of the following statements is true concerning status and group interaction?
   a. Low status people interrupt others more often.
   b. High status people tend to be more assertive.
   c. High status members tend to be less active participants in group discussions.
   d. Status differences don't inhibit creativity in groups.

Answer: b, difficulty: 3, p. 108

34. Which of the following is NOT one of the sources of status?
   a. the power a person wields over others
   b. a person's ability to contribute to a group's goals
   c. the person's lack of control over resources
   d. an individual's personal characteristics

Answer: c, difficulty: 2, p. 107-108

35. Which of the following statements is NOT true concerning status?
   a. High-status members of groups often are given more freedom to deviate from norms than are other group members.
   b. High-status people are also better able to resist conformity pressure than their lower-status peers.
   c. An individual who is highly valued by a group but who doesn't much need or care about social rewards the group provides is particularly able to pay minimal attention to conformity norms.
   d. Informal status is always less important than formal status.

Answer: d, difficulty: 2, p. 108

36. Which of the following is NOT an example of status incongruence?
    a. a more desirable office location being held by a lower-ranking individual
    b. paid country club membership being provided by the company for division managers but not for vice presidents
    c. top sales agents earn five times more than senior corporate executives
    d. All of the above.

Answer: d, difficulty: 3, p. 109

37. Examples of status determinants include all of the following EXCEPT:
    a. personal income.
    b. growth rate of the company.
    c. size of budget.
    d. amount of conflict.

Answer: d, difficulty: 1, p. 109

38. The degree to which members of a group are attracted to each other and are motivated to stay in the group is:
    a. synergy.
    b. cohesiveness.
    c. norms.
    d. roles.

Answer: b, difficulty: 2, p. 109

39. Which of the following statements is true regarding cohesiveness?
    a. Highly cohesive groups are generally less effective than less cohesive ones.
    b. Cohesiveness influences productivity but productivity has no influence on cohesiveness.
    c. Camaraderie increases tension.
    d. If cohesiveness is high and performance norms are low, productivity will be low.

Answer: d, difficulty: 3, p. 110

40. Managers can encourage group cohesiveness by:
    a. making the group larger.
    b. limiting competition with other groups.
    c. rewarding individuals rather than the group.
    d. physically isolating the group.

Answer: d, difficulty: 3, p. 110

41. Which is NOT a tactic to encourage group cohesiveness?
    a. Make the group smaller.
    b. Encourage disagreement with group goals.
    c. Physically isolate the group.
    d. Increase the time members spend together.

Answer: b, difficulty: 2, p. 110

42. Which of the following is NOT true about the relationship between alignment of group and organizational goals and cohesiveness?
    a. High cohesiveness and high alignment result in a strong increase in productivity.
    b. High cohesiveness and low alignment result in a decrease in productivity.
    c. Low cohesiveness and high alignment do not have a significant effect on productivity.
    d. Low cohesiveness and low alignment do not have a significant effect on productivity.

Answer: c, difficulty: 3, Exhibit 7-3

43. Which of the following statements is true about group size?
    a. Smaller groups are faster at completing tasks than larger ones.
    b. Larger groups get lower marks for problem solving.
    c. Groups of approximately three members are the most effective for taking action.
    d. Small groups are good for gaining diverse input.

Answer: a, difficulty: 2, p. 110

44. Although John, Jim, and Dave each exert 100 percent effort when they work individually, each only exerts 20 percent when they work together in a group. This is an example of:
    a. group norming.
    b. social facilitation.
    c. group affiliation.
    d. social loafing.

Answer: d, difficulty: 2, p. 111

45. The tendency for individuals to expend less effort when working collectively than when working individually is known as:
    a. group norming.
    b. social facilitation.
    c. group affiliation.
    d. social loafing.

Answer: d, difficulty: 1, p. 111

46. Max Ringelmann compared the results of individual and group performance on a rope-pulling task to demonstrate:
   a. social facilitation.
   b. social loafing.
   c. cohesiveness.
   d. group norming.

Answer: b, difficulty: 3, p. 111

47. All of the following cause social loafing EXCEPT:
   a. a belief that others in the group are not carrying their fair share.
   b. dispersion of responsibility.
   c. individuals think their contribution cannot be measured.
   d. the relationship between an individual's input and the group's output is very clear.

Answer: d, difficulty: 2, p. 111

48. When a group is _____ in terms of gender, personalities, opinions, abilities, skills, and perspectives, there is an increased probability that the group will have the characteristics to complete its tasks effectively.
   a. diverse
   b. homogeneous
   c. unrelated
   d. socially similar

Answer: a, difficulty: 2, p. 111

49. Which of the following statements is true of heterogeneous groups?
   a. Heterogeneous groups perform more effectively than do those that are homogeneous.
   b. Homogenous groups perform more effectively than do those that are heterogeneous.
   c. Diversity promotes conformity.
   d. Diversity ultimately stifles improved decision making.

Answer: a, difficulty: 2, p. 111

50. Group demography is:
   a. the degree to which members of a group share a common demographic attribute.
   b. the degree to which members of a group share a common geographic origin.
   c. the degree to which members of a group share decision-making techniques.
   d. the degree to which members of a group speak the same language.

Answer: a, difficulty: 1, p. 112

51. Individuals who hold a common attribute are defined as:
   a. a group
   b. a team
   c. cohorts
   d. None of the above.

Answer: c, difficulty: 1, p. 112

52. Which of the following is true about group decision making?
   a. Groups generate less complete information and knowledge.
   b. Groups offer decreased diversity of views.
   c. Groups generate higher-quality decisions.
   d. Groups lead to decreased acceptance of a solution.

Answer: c, difficulty: 1, p. 113

53. Which of the following is NOT true about group decision making?
   a. Groups generate higher-quality decisions.
   b. Groups generate faster decisions.
   c. Groups lead to increased acceptance of a solution.
   d. Groups offer increased diversity of views.

Answer: b, difficulty: 2, p. 113

54. Individuals are preferred over groups for decision making when all of the following occur EXCEPT:
   a. the decision is relatively unimportant.
   b. the decision doesn't require subordinate commitment to its success.
   c. the subordinates will be committed to the outcome even if they aren't consulted.
   d. the decision is important.

Answer: d, difficulty: 3, p. 113

55. In terms of effectiveness, groups are superior since:
   a. they generate more alternatives.
   b. are more creative.
   c. produce higher-quality decisions than do individuals.
   d. All of the above.

Answer: d, difficulty: 2, p. 113

56.   _____ is the phenomenon that occurs when group members become so enamored of seeking concurrence that the norm for consensus overrides the realistic appraisal of alternative courses of action.
        a.   Groupthink
        b.   Norming
        c.   Social facilitation
        d.   Social loafing

Answer: a, difficulty: 2, p. 113

57.   Which is NOT one of the characteristics of groupthink?
        a.   Group members solicit resistance to the assumptions they've made.
        b.   Members pressure any doubters to support the alternative favored by the majority.
        c.   Doubters keep silent about misgivings.
        d.   The group interprets members' silence as a "yes" vote for the majority.

Answer: a, difficulty: 1, p. 114

58.   Which of the following is NOT present when groupthink occurs?
        a.   incomplete assessment of the problem
        b.   poor information search
        c.   thorough development of alternatives
        d.   failure to reappraise initially rejected alternatives

Answer: c, difficulty: 2, p. 114

59.   The unpreparedness at Pearl Harbor in 1941, the Bay of Pigs fiasco in the early 1960s, and the launch of the space shuttle *Challenger* disaster are all examples of:
        a.   groupshift.
        b.   groupthink.
        c.   social norming.
        d.   brainstorming.

Answer: b, difficulty: 2, p. 114

60.   Which of the following is NOT one of the variables that seem to influence when groupthink is likely to surface?
        a.   the group's cohesiveness
        b.   the group's insulation from outsiders
        c.   aggressive member participation
        d.   time pressures

Answer: c, difficulty: 3, p. 114

61. To avoid groupthink, managers should do all of the following EXCEPT:
    a. strive for an open leadership style
    b. discourage member participation
    c. downplay time constraints
    d. avoid allowing the group to detach itself from external sources

Answer: b, difficulty: 3, p. 114

62. A special case of groupthink in which the decision of the group reflects the dominant decision- making norm that develops during the group's discussion is termed:
    a. socialization.
    b. norming.
    c. groupshift.
    d. nominal grouping.

Answer: c, difficulty: 1, p. 115

63. Which of the following has been offered as an explanation for groupshift?
    a. The discussion creates familiarization among the members.
    b. The group diffuses responsibility.
    c. Even if the decision fails, no one member can be held wholly responsible.
    d. All of the above.

Answer: d, difficulty: 2, p. 115

64. Which of the following have been proposed as ways to reduce problems inherent in the traditional interacting group?
    a. brainstorming
    b. nominal-group technique
    c. electronic meetings
    d. All of the above.

Answer: d, difficulty: 1, p. 115

65. A nonjudgmental process for generating ideas in which members "free-wheel" as many alternatives as they can is termed:
    a. brainstorming.
    b. groupshift.
    c. nominal-group technique.
    d. electronic meetings.

Answer: a, difficulty: 1, p. 115

66. Which group decision making technique is meant to overcome pressures for conformity in the interacting group that retard the development of creative alternatives?
   a. brainstorming
   b. nominal-group
   c. electronic-meeting
   d. consensus

Answer: a, difficulty: 2, p. 115

67. The _____ method of idea generation restricts discussion or interpersonal communication during the decision-making process.
   a. brainstorming
   b. nominal-group
   c. electronic-meeting
   d. consensus

Answer: b, difficulty: 2, pp. 115-116

68. Which of the following is the first step in the nominal group technique?
   a. Each member presents one idea to the group.
   b. Discussion begins immediately.
   c. Before any discussion, each member independently writes down his or her ideas on the problem.
   d. Evaluation begins immediately.

Answer: c, difficulty: 2, p. 116

69. No discussion takes place until all ideas have been recorded in which decision making technique?
   a. brainstorming
   b. nominal-group
   c. electronic-meeting
   d. consensus

Answer: b, difficulty: 2, p. 116

70. A recent approach to group decision making, which blends the nominal-group technique with sophisticated computer technology, is the:
   a. electronic brainstorm.
   b. computer meeting.
   c. electronic meeting.
   d. comp-group.

Answer: c, difficulty: 2, p. 116

71.   Which is NOT an advantage of electronic meetings?
       a.   anonymity
       b.   simplicity
       c.   honesty
       d.   speed

Answer: b, difficulty: 1, p. 116

72.   The early evidence indicates that electronic meetings:
       a.   achieve most of their proposed benefits.
       b.   actually led to increased group effectiveness.
       c.   required more time to complete tasks.
       d.   resulted in increased member satisfaction when compared to face-to-face groups.

Answer: c, difficulty: 3, p. 116

73.   _____ control group behavior by establishing standards of right and wrong.
       a.   Norms
       b.   Social skills
       c.   Roles
       d.   Ranks

Answer: a, difficulty: 2, p. 117

74.   If a manager does not provide a means to identify individual efforts within the work
       group, _____ may lead to decreased productivity.
       a.   synergy
       b.   social facilitation
       c.   the Hawthorne effect
       d.   social loafing

Answer: d, difficulty: 2, p. 117

75.   Social loafing is consistent with:
       a.   individualistic cultures.
       b.   collectivist cultures.
       c.   Chinese culture.
       d.   Israeli culture.

Answer: a, difficulty: 2, p. 117

TRUE/FALSE

76.   A team is defined as two or more individuals, interacting and independent, who come
       together to achieve particular objectives.

False, difficulty: 2, p. 101

77.   Informal groups are alliances that are neither structured nor organizationally determined.

True, difficulty: 1, p. 102

78.   The friendship group is determined by the organizational chart.

False, difficulty: 1, p. 102

79.   The command group is composed of the subordinates who report directly to a given manager.

True, difficulty: 1, p. 102

80.   Task groups occur when employees band together to seek increased fringe benefits.

False, difficulty: 2, p. 102

81.   The command group is determined by the organizational chart.

True, difficulty: 1, p. 102

82.   A task group's boundaries are limited to its immediate hierarchical superior.

False, difficulty: 2, p. 102

83.   Employees who band together to seek improved benefits are an interest group.

True, difficulty: 2, p. 102

84.   Friendship groups develop because the individual members have one or more common characteristics.

True, difficulty: 1, p. 102

85.   Informal groups provide a very important function by satisfying their members' social needs.

True, difficulty: 2, p. 102

86.   There is one overarching reason why individuals join groups.

False, difficulty: 1, p. 102

87.   Different groups provide different benefits to their members.

True, difficulty: 1, p. 102

88.   Different groups impose different role requirements on people.

True, difficulty: 2, p. 103

89.   We are all required to play a number of roles, and our behavior varies with the role we are playing.

True, difficulty: 1, p. 103

90.   The psychological contract between employees and their employer is a written agreement of expectations.

False, difficulty: 2, p. 103

91.   One of the reasons people join groups is that there is power in numbers.

True, difficulty: 1, Exhibit 7-1

92.   People often experience role conflict when compliance with one role requirement is at odds with another.

True, difficulty: 1, p. 103

93.   When employees fail to live up to expectations of the psychological contract, the result is usually some form of disciplinary action that may include termination.

True, difficulty: 2, p. 104

94.   People learn roles from stimuli around them – including movies and television.

True, difficulty: 2, p. 104

95.   Many current police officers learned their roles from reading Joseph Wambaugh novels.

True, difficulty: 3, p. 104

96.   People do NOT have the ability to shift roles rapidly when they recognize that the situation and its demands require major changes.

False, difficulty: 2, p. 104

97.   Norms are a set of expected behavior patterns that are attributed to occupying a given position in a social unit.

False, difficulty: 1, p. 104

98.   Each group will establish its own set of norms.

True, difficulty: 1, p. 104

99.   Groups exert pressure on members to bring members' behavior into conformity with a group's standards.

True, difficulty: 2, p. 105

100.   The Hawthorne researchers' initial findings confirmed their anticipated results.

False, difficulty: 2, pp. 105-106

101.   The Hawthorne researchers began by examining the relationship between the physical environment and productivity.

True, difficulty: 1, p. 105

102.   The Hawthorne researchers concluded that illumination intensity was a major influence that affected an employee's productivity.

False, difficulty: 2, pp. 105-106

103.   The second set of experiments in the Hawthorne studies focused on the bank wiring group.

False, difficulty: 1, pp. 105-106

104.   Solomon Asch demonstrated the importance of group influence in his studies.

True, difficulty: 2, p. 106

105.   The results of the Asch study suggested that there are group norms that press us toward conformity.

True, difficulty: 1, p. 107

106.   The results obtained by Asch demonstrated that subjects conformed in about 10 percent of the trials.

False, difficulty: 2, p. 107

107.   Anything can have status value if group members evaluate it as status-conferring.

True, difficulty: 2, p. 108

108. High status members of groups often are given more freedom to deviate from norms than are other group members.

True, difficulty: 3, p. 108

109. Lower status people tend to be more assertive.

False, difficulty: 2, p. 108

110. The importance of status does not vary between cultures.

False, difficulty: 2, p. 109

111. There has been no evidence that cohesiveness is positively related to productivity.

False, difficulty: 2, pp. 109-110

112. If cohesiveness is low and performance norms are low, productivity will be high.

False, difficulty: 3, p. 110

113. To encourage group cohesiveness, a manager should make the group smaller and encourage disagreement with group goals.

False, difficulty: 2, p. 110

114. Small groups are better for problem solving.

False, difficulty: 1, p. 110

115. Groups of approximately 15 members tend to be more effective for taking actions.

False, difficulty: 3, p. 110

116. A sense of team spurs individual effort and enhances the group's overall production.

False, difficulty: 3, p. 111

117. Increases in group size are inversely related to individual performance.

True, difficulty: 2, p. 111

118. Evidence generally supports the conclusion that homogeneous groups perform more effectively than do those that are heterogeneous.

False, difficulty: 2, p. 111

119. Diversity promotes conflict, which stimulates creativity, which leads to improved decision making.

True, difficulty: 2, p. 111

120. Racial and national diversity within groups enhances group performance in the short term.

False, difficulty: 3, pp. 111-112

121. Group demography is the degree to which members of a group share a common geographic location.

False, difficulty: 2, p. 112

122. When a decision is needed quickly, groups have the advantage over individuals.

False, difficulty: 2, p. 113

123. Groups consistently generate lower-quality decisions than do individuals.

False, difficulty: 1, p. 113

124. Groups generate more complete information and knowledge than individuals.

True, difficulty: 2, p. 113

125. Individual decision making is preferred when the decision is relatively unimportant and doesn't require subordinate commitment to its success.

True, difficulty: 3, p. 113

126. Individuals are more efficient than groups.

True, difficulty: 3, p. 113

127. Groupthink describes a deterioration in an individual's mental efficiency, reality testing, and moral judgment as a result of group pressures.

True, difficulty: 3, p. 113

128. The disaster of the space shuttle *Challenger* is a result of the nominal-group technique.

False, difficulty: 2, p. 114

129. All groups seem equally vulnerable to groupthink.

False, difficulty: 1, p. 114

130.   Groupthink is influenced by the group's cohesiveness.

True, difficulty: 1, p. 114

131.   More often, groupshift is toward greater caution.

False, difficulty: 3, p. 114

132.   Groupshift can be viewed as a special case of groupthink.

True, difficulty: 2, p. 115

133.   The most common form of group decision making is now the electronic meeting.

False, difficulty: 1, p. 115

134.   Brainstorming utilizes an idea-generation process that specifically encourages any and all alternatives while withholding any criticism of those alternatives.

True, difficulty: 2, p. 115

135.   The brainstorming technique restricts discussion or interpersonal communication during the decision-making process.

False, difficulty: 1, p. 115

136.   The chief advantage of the nominal group technique is that it permits the group to meet formally but does not restrict independent thinking.

True, difficulty: 3, p. 116

137.   The major advantages of electronic meetings are anonymity, honesty, and speed.

True, difficulty: 2, p. 116

138.   Norms control group behavior by establishing standards of right or wrong.

True, difficulty: 2, p. 117

139.   In studies with employees from China and Israel, the employees showed the same propensity as Americans to engage in social loafing.

False, difficulty: 2, p. 117

140.   To increase the performance of work groups, a manager should try to choose individuals as members who can bring a diverse perspective to problems and issues.

True, difficulty: 2, p. 117

ESSAY

141.   Explain the differences between a command group, a task group, an interest group, and a friendship group.

A command group is determined by the organizational chart. It is composed of the subordinates who report directly to a given manager. A task group is organizationally determined and represents persons working together to complete a job. It can cross command relationships. An interest group is comprised of people who affiliate to attain a specific objective with which each is concerned. Friendship groups develop because the individual members have one or more common characteristics.

p. 102

142.   Explain five different reasons why people join groups.

People join groups for security, status, self-esteem, affiliation, and power. By joining a group, individuals can reduce the insecurity of "standing alone." Inclusion in a group that is viewed as important by others provides recognition and status for its members. Groups can also provide people with feelings of self-worth. Groups can fulfill social needs since people enjoy the regular interaction that comes with group membership. There is power in numbers. What cannot be achieved individually often becomes possible through group action.

p. 102 and Exhibit 7-1

143.   Explain the importance of roles and role conflict to group productivity.

A role is the set of expected behavior patterns that is attributed to occupying a given position in a social unit. People are all required to play a number of roles, and their behavior varies with the role they are playing. Different groups impose different role requirements. People play multiple roles. These roles are learned from the stimuli around them. People have the ability to shift roles rapidly when they recognize that their situation and its demands clearly require major changes. People often experience role conflict when compliance with one role requirement is at odds with another.

p. 103

144.   What are norms? With which norms are managers most concerned?

Norms are acceptable standards of behavior within a group that are shared by the group's members. Managers tend to be most concerned with performance-related norms. These norms are extremely powerful in affecting an individual employee's performance.

p. 104

145.   Explain the importance of the Hawthorne Studies.

The Hawthorne studies were conducted at the Western Electric Company's Hawthorne Works in Chicago between 1924 and 1932. Overseen by Elton Mayo, the studies concluded that a worker's behavior and sentiments were closely related, that group influences were significant in affecting individual behavior, that group standards were highly effective in establishing individual worker output, and that money was less a factor in determining worker output than were group standards, sentiments, and security. The studies were critical in explaining group behavior – particularly the significant place that norms have in determining individual work behavior.

pp. 105-106

146.   Explain the findings of the Asch studies.

Solomon Asch researched conformity. He found that subjects gave answers to questions concerning the length of lines that they knew were wrong but that were consistent with the replies of other group members. The results suggested that there are group norms that press us toward conformity. People desire to be one of the group and avoid being visibly different. When an individual's opinion of objective data differs significantly from that of others in the group, he or she feels extensive pressure to align his or her opinion to conform with those of the others.

pp. 106-107

147.   What determines status?

According to status characteristics theory, differences in status characteristics create status hierarchies within groups. Moreover, status tends to be driven from one of three sources: the power a person wields over others; a person's ability to contribute to a group's goals; and an individual's personal characteristics.

pp. 107-108

148.   What is the relationship between cohesiveness and productivity?

Cohesiveness is the degree to which members are attracted to each other and are motivated to stay in the group. Studies consistently show that the relationship of cohesiveness and productivity depends on the performance-related norms established by the group. The more cohesive the group, the more its members will follow its goals. If performance-related norms are high, a cohesive group will be more productive than a less cohesive group. If cohesiveness is high and performance norms are low, productivity will be low. If cohesiveness is low and performance norms are high, productivity increases, but less than in the high cohesiveness-high norms situation. Where cohesiveness and performance-related norms are both low, there will be no significant effect on productivity.

pp. 110-111

149.   What can a manager do to encourage group cohesiveness?

To encourage group cohesiveness, a manager can make the group smaller. The manager might also encourage agreement with group goals or increase the time members spend together. The manager might increase the status of the group and the perceived difficulty of attaining membership in the group. Competition with other groups may be stimulated or the manager might give rewards to the group rather than to members. Finally, the manager could physically isolate the group to encourage group cohesiveness.

p. 111

150.   Explain how the size of a group affects the group's overall behavior.

The size of a group affects the group's overall behavior in several ways. Smaller groups are faster at completing tasks than larger ones. Large groups are better at problem solving than smaller groups. Large groups are good for gaining diverse input. So if the goal of the group is fact-finding, larger groups should be more effective. Smaller groups, however, are better at doing something productive with that input. Increases in group size are inversely related to individual performance.

pp. 111-112

151.   Explain social loafing and why it is important for managers.

Social loafing was researched by Max Ringelmann in a rope-pulling task. Groups of three people exerted a force only two-and-a-half times the average individual performance. Increases in group size are inversely related to individual performance. More may be better in the sense that the total productivity of a group of four is greater than that of two or three people, but the individual productivity of each group member declines. This social loafing may be due to a belief that others in the group are not carrying their fair share. Because the results of the group cannot be attributed to any single person, the relationship between an individual's input and the group's output is clouded. There will be a reduction in efficiency when individuals think that their contribution cannot be measured.

p. 112

152.   What are the advantages and disadvantages of both individual and group decision making?

When a decision is needed quickly, individuals have the advantage. Individual decisions have clear accountability. Accountability is more ambiguous with group decisions. Individual decisions also tend to convey consistent values. Groups generate more complete information and knowledge. Groups also bring heterogeneity to the decision process. They offer increased diversity of views, so more approaches and alternatives can be considered. Groups generate higher-quality decisions and lead to increased acceptance of a solution.

p. 113

153.   Describe the symptoms of a group showing groupthink.

The four characteristics of a group showing groupthink are as follows:
a. Group members rationalize any resistance to the assumptions they've made.
b. Members pressure any doubters to support the alternative favored by the majority.
c. To give the appearance of group consensus, doubters keep silent about misgivings and even minimize to themselves the importance of their doubts.
d. The group interprets members' silence as a "yes" vote for the majority.

p. 114

154.   Describe groupshift.

Groupshift is a special case of groupthink. The decision of the group reflects the dominant decision-making norm that develops during the group's discussion. Managers must recognize that group decisions exaggerate the initial position of the individual members, that the shift has shown more often to be toward greater risk, and that whether a group will shift toward greater risk or caution is a function of the members' prediscussion inclinations.

pp. 114-115

155.   List and explain three different group decision-making techniques.

Three different group decision-making techniques include brainstorming, the nominal group technique, and electronic meetings. Brainstorming is meant to overcome pressures for conformity in the interacting group that retard the development of creative alternatives. The technique encourages any and all alternatives, while withholding any criticism of those alternatives. The nominal group technique restricts discussion or interpersonal communication during the decision-making process. Group members are all physically present, but the members are required to operate independently. Members begin by independently writing down their ideas on the problem. Then each member presents one idea to the group, taking turns until all ideas are presented. Next, the group discusses the ideas for clarity and evaluates them. Finally, the members silently and independently rank the ideas. The final decision is determined by the idea with the highest aggregate ranking. Electronic meetings use sophisticated computer technology. Up to fifty people sit around a horseshoe-shaped table, empty except for a series of computer terminals. Issues are presented to participants and they type their responses onto their computer screen. Individual comments are displayed on a projection screen in the room.

pp. 115-116

CHAPTER 8 UNDERSTANDING WORK TEAMS

MULTIPLE CHOICE

1.   _____ are increasingly becoming the primary means for organizing work in contemporary business firms.
   a.   Bureaucracies
   b.   Teams
   c.   Quality circles
   d.   Work groups

Answer: b, difficulty: 2, p. 120

2.   It has been reported that approximately _____ percent of Fortune 500 companies now have half of their employees on teams.
   a.   10
   b.   30
   c.   50
   d.   80

Answer: d, difficulty: 2, p. 120

3.   Evidence suggests that teams typically outperform individuals when:
   a.   tasks are programmed.
   b.   speed is required.
   c.   a crisis situation exists.
   d.   tasks require multiple skills, judgment, and experience.

Answer: d, difficulty: 2, p. 120

4.   Teams have all of the following benefits EXCEPT:
   a.   more flexibility.
   b.   capability to quickly assemble, deploy, refocus, and disband.
   c.   easier to manage.
   d.   better utilization of employee talents.

Answer: c, difficulty: 2, p. 120

5.   A _____ is a group whose members interact primarily to share information and to make decisions to help one another perform within each one's area of responsibility.
   a.   work team
   b.   work group
   c.   committee
   d.   quality circle

Answer: b, difficulty: 2, p. 121 and Exhibit 8-1

6.	The difference between a work group and a work team is:
	a.	compatibility.
	b.	popularity.
	c.	ability.
	d.	positive synergy.

Answer: d, difficulty: 2, p. 121

7.	A _____ generates positive synergy through coordinated effort.
	a.	work group
	b.	work team
	c.	consortium
	d.	group

Answer: b, difficulty: 2, p. 121

8.	Which is a characteristic of work teams?
	a.	goal of shared information
	b.	individual and mutual accountability
	c.	random and varied skills
	d.	neutral (sometimes negative) synergy

Answer: b, difficulty: 2, p. 121 and Exhibit 8-1

9.	All of the following are characteristics of work teams EXCEPT:
	a.	a goal of collective performance.
	b.	neutral or negative synergy.
	c.	individual and mutual accountability.
	d.	complementary skills.

Answer: b, difficulty: 1, p. 121 and Exhibit 8-1

10.	Which of the following is characteristic of work groups (not work teams)?
	a.	a goal of collective performance
	b.	neutral or negative synergy
	c.	individual and mutual accountability
	d.	complementary skills

Answer: b, difficulty: 1, pp. 121-122 and Exhibit 8-1

11.	Which of the following is a characteristic found in work teams but not in work groups?
	a.	individual accountability
	b.	goal of sharing information
	c.	random and varied skills
	d.	positive synergy

Answer: d, difficulty: 2, p. 121 and Exhibit 8-1

12. Which of the following is NOT one of the three most common forms of teams likely to be found in an organization?
    a. problem-solving teams
    b. self-managed teams
    c. goal-driven teams
    d. cross-functional teams

Answer: c, difficulty: 2, p. 121

13. Five to twelve hourly employees from the same department who meet a few hours each week to discuss ways of improving quality, efficiency, and the work environment are called a:
    a. self-managed team.
    b. cross-functional team.
    c. task force.
    d. problem-solving team.

Answer: d, difficulty: 2, p. 122

14. One of the most widely practiced applications of problem-solving teams in the 1980s was the:
    a. task force.
    b. quality circle.
    c. synergy circle.
    d. committee.

Answer: b, difficulty: 1, p. 122

15. A work team of eight to ten employees and supervisors who have a shared area of responsibility and meet regularly to discuss their quality problems, investigate causes of the problems, and recommend solutions is called a:
    a. task force.
    b. quality circle.
    c. synergy circle.
    d. committee.

Answer: b, difficulty: 2, p. 122

16. A problem-solving team today might seek out ways to do all of the following EXCEPT:
    a. improve quality.
    b. eliminate scrap.
    c. generally cut costs.
    d. hire employees.

Answer: d, difficulty: 2, p. 122

17. _____ go farther than problem solving in getting employees involved in work-related decisions and processes.
    a. Self-managed work teams
    b. Quality teams
    c. Task forces
    d. Teams

Answer: a, difficulty: 2, p. 122

18. _____ are generally composed of ten to fifteen people who take on the responsibilities of their former supervisors.
    a. Self-managed work teams
    b. Quality circles
    c. Task forces
    d. Committees

Answer: a, difficulty: 1, p. 122

19. Typically, the responsibility of self-managed work teams includes all of the following EXCEPT:
    a. determination of compensation.
    b. collective control over the pace of work.
    c. determination of work assignments.
    d. planning and scheduling of work.

Answer: a, difficulty: 1, p. 122

20. Which of the following is a logical result of instituting self-managed work teams?
    a. Morale will decline.
    b. Supervisors will determine work assignments.
    c. Supervisors will select new employees.
    d. Supervisory positions will take on decreased importance.

Answer: d, difficulty: 2, p. 122

21. The benefits of the team approach at Eaton-Aeroquip include all of the following EXCEPT:
    a. response time to customer concerns improved 99 percent.
    b. productivity and manufacturing output increased by more than 50 percent.
    c. absenteeism decreased by 75 percent.
    d. accident rates dropped by more than half.

Answer: c, difficulty: 2, p. 123

22. One drawback to self-managed teams may be:
    a. higher absenteeism.
    b. lower morale.
    c. lower effectiveness.
    d. increased need for supervisory personnel.

Answer: a, difficulty: 2, p. 123

23. All of the following are true about self-managed teams EXCEPT:
    a. they tend to report higher levels of job satisfaction.
    b. they increase the need for supervisors.
    c. they have higher absenteeism.
    d. they have higher turnover.

Answer: b, difficulty: 3, p. 123

24. _____ teams are made up of employees from about the same hierarchical level, but from different work areas, who come together to accomplish a task.
    a. Self-managed work
    b. Problem-solving
    c. Cross-functional
    d. Quality circle

Answer: c, difficulty: 2, p. 123

25. Cross-functional teams include all of the following EXCEPT:
    a. horizontal, boundary-spanning groups.
    b. committees.
    c. quality circles.
    d. task forces.

Answer: c, difficulty: 2, p. 123

26. Committees composed of members from across departmental lines are an example of:
    a. self-managed teams.
    b. virtual teams.
    c. cross-functional teams.
    d. problem-solving teams.

Answer: c, difficulty: 2, p. 123

27. Which of the following is NOT true about cross-functional teams?
    a. They are difficult to manage.
    b. They allow people from diverse areas to work together.
    c. They are horizontal, boundary-spanning groups.
    d. It takes little time to build trust and teamwork.

Answer: a, difficulty: 2, pp. 123-124

28. A task force is a:
    a. form of problem-solving team.
    b. form of self-managed work team.
    c. temporary cross-functional team.
    d. permanent cross-functional team.

Answer: c, difficulty: 3, p. 123

29. When IBM's senior management pulled together 21 employees from among its 100,000 information technology staff to come up with recommendations on how the company could speed up and bring products to market faster, which type of team were they using?
    a. cross-functional team
    b. functional team
    c. departmental team
    d. technology team

Answer: a, difficulty: 1, p. 123

30. When Harley-Davidson brings together employees from design, manufacturing, and purchasing to manage each line of its motorcycles, the company is using _____ teams.
    a. cross-functional
    b. virtual
    c. quality focused
    d. linear

Answer: a, difficulty: 2, p. 124

31. _____ teams use computer technology to tie together physically dispersed members in order to achieve a common goal.
    a. Virtual
    b. Self-managed
    c. Cross-functional
    d. Problem-solving

Answer: a, difficulty: 2, p. 124

32. Which of the following is NOT a primary factor that differentiates virtual teams from face-to-face teams?
    a. absence of paraverbal and nonverbal cues
    b. diversity of team members
    c. limited social context
    d. ability to overcome time and space constraints

Answer: b, difficulty: 2, p. 124

33. Voice tone, inflection, and voice volume are examples of _____ cues.
    a. verbal
    b. nonverbal
    c. paraverbal
    d. virtual

Answer: c, difficulty: 2, p. 124

34. Virtual teams tend to be:
    a. more satisfied.
    b. more task oriented.
    c. less task oriented.
    d. better able to communicate.

Answer: b, difficulty: 2, p. 124

35. Which of the following statements is NOT true of virtual teams?
    a. Virtual teams exchange less social-emotional information.
    b. Virtual team members report more satisfaction with the group interaction process than do face-to-face teams.
    c. Virtual teams cannot duplicate the normal give-and-take of face-to-face discussion.
    d. Virtual teams have the ability to overcome time and space constraints.

Answer: b, difficulty: 2, p. 124

36. Which of the following is NOT a contextual factor that is related to team performance?
    a. abilities of members
    b. the presence of adequate resources
    c. effective leadership
    d. a performance evaluation and reward system that reflects team contributors

Answer: a, difficulty: 1, p. 126

37. The support that effective work groups must receive from the organization includes which of the following?
    a. timely information
    b. encouragement
    c. adequate staffing
    d. All of the above.

Answer: d, difficulty: 2, p. 126

38. Which of the following is NOT one of the key components making up effective teams?
    a. contextual influences
    b. team's composition
    c. product success
    d. work design

Answer: c, difficulty: 2, p. 126

39. Team leadership for effective teams can be provided:
    a. directly by management.
    b. by the team members themselves.
    c. Both a and b.
    d. None of the above.

Answer: c, difficulty: 2, p. 126

40. Which of the following is NOT true of effective teams?
    a. Members of effective teams trust each other.
    b. Interpersonal trust among team members facilitates competition.
    c. Team members are more likely to take risks and expose vulnerabilities when they believe
       they can trust others on their team.
    d. Trust in leadership allows the team to be willing to accept and commit to their leader's
       goals and decisions.

Answer: b, difficulty: 3, pp. 126-127

41. Group-based rewards include:
    a. gainsharing.
    b. cost of living adjustments.
    c. fixed hourly wages.
    d. individual merit raises.

Answer: a, difficulty: 1, p. 127

42. Which of the following statements is true concerning the personality of team members?
    a. The variance in team members' personality characteristics may be more important
       than the mean.
    b. Mixing both conscientious and not-so-conscientious members raises team
       performance.
    c. A single member who lacks a minimal level of a characteristic will not negatively
       affect the whole team's performance.
    d. The dimensions in the Big Five personality model have not been shown to be relevant
       to team effectiveness.

Answer: a, difficulty: 3, p. 127

43. The three skill sets a team requires to perform effectively include which of the following?
   a. technical expertise
   b. computer expertise
   c. cultural awareness
   d. political skills

Answer: a, difficulty: 1, p. 127

44. Which of the following is NOT a type of skill listed by your text as necessary for effective teams?
   a. cultural awareness
   b. interpersonal skills
   c. technical expertise
   d. problem-solving and decision-making skills

Answer: a, difficulty: 2, p. 127

45. The person who can identify problems, generate alternatives, evaluate those alternatives, and make competent choices is valuable to a team because this person has:
   a. technical expertise.
   b. empathy.
   c. problem-solving and decision-making skills.
   d. interpersonal skills.

Answer: c, difficulty: 2, p. 127

46. People with good listening, feedback, and conflict resolution skills are valuable to a team because they possess:
   a. technical expertise.
   b. synergy.
   c. problem-solving and decision-making skills.
   d. interpersonal skills.

Answer: d, difficulty: 2, p. 127

47. Which of the following statements is NOT true concerning the allocation of team roles?
   a. Successful work teams have selected people to play their different roles based on their skills and preferences.
   b. On many teams, individuals will play multiple roles.
   c. Successful work teams need people to fill only about half of the nine potential team roles.
   d. By matching individual preferences with team role demands, managers increase the likelihood that the team members will work well together.

Answer: c, difficulty: 2, p. 128

48.   A diverse team:
       a.   may be more conflict-laden.
       b.   more expedient.
       c.   is less creative.
       d.   leads to poorer decision-making.

Answer: a, difficulty: 2, p. 128

49.   Margerison and McCann identified nine team roles that people prefer to play. Creator-innovators:
       a.   have strong analytical skills.
       b.   are imaginative and good at initiating ideas or concepts.
       c.   like to set up operating procedures.
       d.   focus on insisting that deadlines and commitments are kept.

Answer: b, difficulty: 1, p. 128 and Exhibit 8-4

50.   Margerison and McCann identified nine team roles that people prefer to play. Explorer-promoters:
       a.   are imaginative and good at initiating ideas or concepts.
       b.   have strong analytical skills.
       c.   like to take new ideas and "champion" their cause.
       d.   try to understand all views.

Answer: c, difficulty: 2, p. 128 and Exhibit 8-4

51.   The person in the role of _____ analyzes decision options.
       a.   assessor-developer
       b.   explorer-promoter
       c.   creator-innovator
       d.   concluder-producer

Answer: a, difficulty: 2, Exhibit 8-4

52.   One stream of research has identified nine potential team roles that people prefer to play. The role of the upholder-maintainer is to:
       a.   take new ideas and "champion" their cause.
       b.   try to understand all views.
       c.   examine details and make sure inaccuracies are avoided.
       d.   fights the team's battles with outsiders.

Answer: d, difficulty: 2, Exhibit 8-4

53. One stream of research has identified nine potential team roles that people prefer to play. The role of the linker is to:
     a. take new ideas and "champion" their cause.
     b. coordinate and integrate.
     c. examine details and make sure inaccuracies are avoided.
     d. defend and fight the team's battles with outsiders while strongly supporting internal team members.

Answer: b, difficulty: 2, Exhibit 8-4

54. Which one of the following is NOT one of the nine potential team roles that people prefer to play?
     a. critiquer
     b. creator-innovator
     c. concluder-producer
     d. linker

Answer: a, difficulty: 1, Exhibit 8-4

55. The person in the role of _____ is focused on providing direction and follow-through.
     a. concluder-producer
     b. upholder-maintainer
     c. reporter-adviser
     d. linker

Answer: a, difficulty: 2, Exhibit 8-4

56. As work teams become larger than ten or twelve people:
     a. they become overly committed.
     b. they can't develop cohesiveness.
     c. they use more nonverbal communication.
     d. they develop mutual accountability.

Answer: b, difficulty: 2, p. 128

57. When teams have excess members:
     a. cohesiveness declines.
     b. mutual accountability declines.
     c. social loafing increases.
     d. All of the above.

Answer: d, difficulty: 1, p. 128

58.	Generally speaking, the most effective teams have fewer than _____ members.
	a.	20
	b.	10
	c.	7
	d.	5

Answer: b, difficulty: 2, p. 128

59.	When selecting team members which of the following should be considered?
	a.	abilities
	b.	personalities
	c.	individual preferences
	d.	All of the above.

Answer: d, difficulty: 3, p. 129

60.	Which of the following is a process variable related to team effectiveness?
	a.	adequate resources
	b.	effective leadership
	c.	establishment of specific team goals
	d.	a performance evaluation and reward system that reflects team contributions

Answer: c, difficulty: 2, p. 129

61.	A team has a meaningful purpose, broader than specific goals, that provides direction for members. This is termed a(n):
	a.	mission statement.
	b.	vision.
	c.	superordinate goal.
	d.	gainsharing.

Answer: b, difficulty: 1, p. 129

62.	Which of the following is true about effective teams?
	a.	Members put a tremendous amount of time and effort into discussing, shaping, and agreeing upon a purpose that belongs to them both collectively and individually.
	b.	Because goals define the team's end targets, little leadership or structure is necessary.
	c.	High-performing teams hold only themselves accountable.
	d.	The team should only be evaluated using group-based appraisals.

Answer: a, difficulty: 2, p. 129

63.   Team goals should be:
        a. challenging.
        b. specific.
        c. measurable.
        d. All of the above.

Answer: d, difficulty: 1, p. 130

64.   Teams that believe they can succeed possess:
        a. over-rated goals.
        b. team efficacy.
        c. misguided perceptions about their future.
        d. little motivation.

Answer: b. difficulty: 1, p. 130

65.   To increase team efficacy, management could:
        a. help the team achieve small successes.
        b. help reduce the team's collective belief about future success.
        c. reduce training for individual team members.
        d. reduce conflict among team members.

Answer: a, difficulty: 3, p. 130

66.   Effective teams have confidence in themselves and believe they can succeed. This is
        called:
        a. social loafing.
        b. team efficacy.
        c. gainsharing.
        d. collectivism.

Answer: b, difficulty: 1, p. 130

67.   When individuals engage in _____, they are coasting on the group's efforts because their
        individual contributions can't be identified.
        a. positive synergistic behavior
        b. social facilitation
        c. social loafing
        d. gainsharing

Answer: c, difficulty: 2, p. 130

68. Teams fit well in countries that score high on:
    a. individualism.
    b. power distance.
    c. masculinity.
    d. collectivism.

Answer: d, difficulty: 1, p. 131

69. The challenge of creating team players is greatest when:
    a. national culture is highly individualistic.
    b. national culture stresses consensus.
    c. national culture stresses collectivist values.
    d. forming a new organization.

Answer: a, difficulty: 2, p. 131

70. Management will find it easiest to create effective work teams when:
    a. national culture is highly individualistic.
    b. teams are being introduced into an established organization.
    c. there is a climate of competitiveness.
    d. creating a new organization.

Answer: d, difficulty: 2, pp. 131-132

71. Creating team players would be easiest in:
    a. the United States.
    b. Canada.
    c. Japan.
    d. Australia.

Answer: c, difficulty: 2, pp. 131-132

72. Primary options managers have for trying to turn individuals into team players include all of the following EXCEPT:
    a. selection.
    b. training.
    c. top-down policy making.
    d. using teams as their initial form for structuring work.

Answer: c, difficulty: 2, pp. 131-132

73. Primary options for managers trying to turn individuals into team players include:
    a. a competitive reward system.
    b. a system that rewards individual accomplishments.
    c. a system of top-down policy making.
    d. a system that rewards training new colleagues and mentoring.

Answer: d, difficulty: 2, pp. 131-132

74. When managers are faced with job candidates that don't have team skills, which of the following is NOT an option for them?
   a. The candidates can undergo training to make them into team players.
   b. Place the candidate in a unit within the organization that doesn't have teams.
   c. Don't hire the candidate.
   d. Redesign the unit so that team skills are not necessary.

Answer: d, difficulty: 3, p. 132

75. To turn individuals into team players, the reward system needs to be reworked to encourage _____ efforts rather than _____ ones.
   a. competitive; cooperative
   b. cooperative; competitive
   c. cooperative; performance
   d. performance; seniority

Answer: b, difficulty: 2, pp. 132

76. Which of the following is NOT a characteristic of high-performing teams?
   a. They tend to be small.
   b. They have a commitment to a common purpose.
   c. They sublimate personal interests for the common good.
   d. They thrive on competition.

Answer: d, difficulty: 2, pp. 134-35

TRUE/FALSE

77. Individuals typically outperform teams when the tasks require multiple skills, judgment, and experience.

False, difficulty: 1, p. 120

78. Teams facilitate employee participation in operating decisions.

True, difficulty: 1, p. 120

79. One explanation for the popularity of teams is that they are an effective means for management to democratize their organizations and increase employee motivation.

True, difficulty: 2, p. 120

80. Work groups have no need or opportunity to engage in collective work that requires joint effort.

True, difficulty: 2, p. 121

81. A work group has positive synergy while a work team does not.

False, difficulty: 2, p. 121

82. The positive synergy of a work team creates an overall level of performance that is greater than the sum of the inputs.

True, difficulty: 2, p. 121

83. The extensive use of teams creates the POTENTIAL for an organization to generate greater output with no increase in inputs.

True, difficulty: 2, p. 121

84. Work groups have individual and mutual accountability.

False, difficulty: 3, Exhibit 8-1

85. Work groups have random and varied skills while work teams have complementary skills.

True, difficulty: 2, Exhibit 8-1

86. One of the most widely practiced applications of self-managed teams during the 1980s was quality circles.

False, difficulty: 2, p. 122

87. Quality circles are work teams that meet regularly to discuss their quality problems, investigate causes of problems, and recommend solutions.

True, difficulty: 2, p. 122

88. The deficiency in problem-solving teams led to experimentations with truly autonomous teams that could not only solve problems but could also implement solutions and take full responsibility for outcomes.

True, difficulty: 2, p. 122

89. In self-managed work teams, supervisory positions take on decreased importance and may even be eliminated.

True, difficulty: 2, p. 122

90. Employees on self-managed work teams seem to have lower absenteeism and turnover rates than do employees working in traditional work structures.

False, difficulty: 3, p. 123

91. Cross-functional teams are from different hierarchical levels.

False, difficulty: 2, p. 123

92. When Harley-Davidson brings together employees from design, manufacturing, and purchasing to manage each line of its motorcycles, the company is using cross-functional teams.

True, difficulty: 1, pp. 123-124

93. A task force is really nothing other than a temporary cross-functional team.

True, difficulty: 1, p. 123

94. Committees and task forces are examples of self-managed work teams.

False, difficulty: 2, p. 123

95. Virtual teams allow people to collaborate online.

True, difficulty: 1, p. 124

96. Virtual teams use paraverbal cues to communicate.

False, difficulty: 2, p. 124

97. Virtual teams tend to be more task oriented.

True, difficulty: 2, p. 124

98. Cross-functional teams often suffer from less social rapport and less direct interaction among members.

False, difficulty: 2, p. 124

99. Virtual teams report greater job satisfaction than face-to-face teams.

False, difficulty: 2, p. 124

100. Cross-functional teams are very difficult to manage – especially in their early stages of development.

False, difficulty: 2, p. 124

101. Process variables reflect those things that go on in the team that influences effectiveness.

True, difficulty: 1, p. 126

102. Teams don't need the support from management if they are going to succeed in achieving their goals.

False, difficulty: 1, p. 126

103. Leadership is always needed.

False, difficulty: 2, p. 126

104. Trust is the foundation of leadership.

True, difficulty: 1, pp. 126-127

105. Teams that rate higher in mean levels of extroversion, agreeableness, conscientiousness, and emotional stability tend to receive higher managerial ratings for team performance.

True, difficulty: 3, p. 127

106. No team can achieve its performance potential without developing all three types of skills: technical, problem-solving, and decision-making.

True, difficulty: 3, p. 127

107. By matching individual preferences with team role demands, managers increase the likelihood that the team members will work well together.

True, difficulty: 2, p. 128

108. Homogeneous teams are more likely to have diverse abilities and information and should be more effective.

False, difficulty: 3, p. 128

109. Homogeneous teams perform more effectively than do those that are heterogeneous.

False, difficulty: 2, p. 128

110. High-performing teams properly match people to various roles.

True, difficulty: 1, p. 128

111. Assessor-organizers are imaginative and good at initiating ideas or concepts.

False, difficulty: 2, Exhibit 8-4

112. The role of the thruster-organizer is to provide structure.

True, difficulty: 2, Exhibit 8-4

113.	Linkers are coordinators and integrators.

True, difficulty: 2, Exhibit 8-4

114.	Newly formed culturally diverse teams under-perform newly formed culturally homogeneous teams.

True, difficulty: 3, p. 128

115.	In designing effective teams, managers should try to keep them under six.

False, difficulty: 2, p. 128

116.	There is a pervasive tendency for managers to err on the side of making teams too large.

True, difficulty: 2, p. 128

117.	Effective teams need to work together and take collective responsibility to complete significant tasks.

True, difficulty: 1, p. 129

118.	There is a pervasive tendency for managers to err on the side of making teams too small.

False, difficulty: 2, p. 128

119.	The best work teams tend to be very small (under 4 or 5).

False, difficulty: 1, p. 129

120.	Given the option, many employees will select themselves out of team participation.

True, difficulty: 1, p. 129

121.	Successful teams translate their respective common purposes into specific, measurable, and realistic performance goals.

True, difficulty: 1, p. 130

122.	Teams that have been successful raise their beliefs about future success which, in turn, motivates them to work harder.

True, difficulty: 2, p. 130

123.	Conflict on a team isn't necessarily bad.

True, difficulty: 2, p. 130

124.   Social loafing is when an individual coasts on the group's effort because his individual contributions can't be identified.

True, difficulty: 2, p. 130

125.   High performing teams undermine social loafing by holding themselves accountable at both the individual and team levels.

True, difficulty: 2, p. 130

126.   Many people are not inherently "team players."

True, difficulty: 1, p. 130

127.   Teams fit well in cultures that score high on power distance.

False, difficulty: 2, p. 131

128.   The challenge for management is less demanding when teams are introduced where employees have strong collectivist values or in existing organizations where teams have never been used.

False, difficulty: 2, pp. 131-132

129.   Some people already possess the interpersonal skills to be effective team players.

True, difficulty: 1, p. 131

130.   A large proportion of people raised on the importance of individual accomplishment can be trained to become team players.

True, difficulty: 2, p. 132

131.   All employees can be trained to be team players.

False, difficulty: 3, p. 132

132.   The reward system needs to be reworked to encourage cooperative efforts rather than competitive ones.

True, difficulty: 2, p. 132

133.   Three conditions favor teams: the work is complex and can be done better by more than one person; the work has a common purpose or set of goals that are more than the aggregate of individual goals; and there is interdependence between tasks.

True, difficulty: 3, pp. 134-135

134.   Why have teams become so popular?

Teams typically outperform individuals when the tasks done require multiple skills, judgment, and experience. As organizations have restructured themselves to compete more effectively and efficiently, they have turned to teams as a way to better utilize employee talents. Teams are more flexible and responsive to changing events than are traditional departments or other forms of permanent groupings. Teams have the capability to quickly assemble, deploy, refocus, and disband. Teams also facilitate employee participation in operating decisions. Teams, then, are an effective means for management to democratize their organizations and increase employee motivation.

p. 120

135.   What is the difference between a work group and a work team?

Work groups have neutral synergy, individual accountability, random skills, and a goal of shared information. Work teams have positive synergy, individual and mutual accountability, complementary skills, and a goal of collective performance. A work group is a group that interacts primarily to share information and to make decisions to help one another perform within each member's area of responsibility. Their performance is a summation of all the group members' individual contributions. A work team generates positive synergy through coordinated effort. Their individual efforts result in a level of performance that is greater than the sum of those individual inputs.

pp. 120-121 and Exhibit 8-1

136.   List the four most common forms of teams.

The four most common forms of teams are problem-solving teams, self-managed work teams, cross-functional teams, and virtual teams. In problem-solving teams, members share ideas or offer suggestions on how work processes and methods can be improved. These teams are typically composed of five to twelve hourly employees from the same department who meet for a few hours each week to discuss ways of improving quality, efficiency, and the work environment. Self-managed work teams are generally composed of 10 to 15 people who take on the responsibilities of their former supervisors. These responsibilities include collective control over the pace of work, determination of work assignments, organization of breaks, and collective choice of inspection procedures. Some even select their own members and have the members evaluate each other's performance. Cross-functional teams are made up of employees from about the same hierarchical level, but from different work areas, who come together to accomplish a task. Virtual teams use computer technology to tie together physically disperse members in order to achieve a common goal. They allow people to collaborate online, regardless of whether they're only a room apart or geographically separated by continents.

pp. 121-124 and Exhibit 8-2

137.	What are the three primary factors that differentiate virtual teams from face-to-face teams?

The three primary factors that differentiate virtual teams from face-to-face teams are: (1) the absence of paraverbal and nonverbal cues, (2) limited social context, and (3) the ability to overcome time and space constraints. Virtual teams often suffer from less social rapport and less direct interaction among members. Virtual team members report less satisfaction with the group interaction process than do face-to-face teams. And virtual teams are able to do their work even if members are thousands of miles apart and separated by a dozen or more time zones. They allow people to work together who might otherwise never be able to collaborate.

p. 124

138.	Discuss the four categories of key components making up effective teams.

The key components making up effective teams are the resources and other contextual influences that make teams effective; the team's composition; work design; and process variables reflecting those things that go on in the team that influences effectiveness.

pp. 125-126 and Exhibit 8-3

139.	What are the four contextual factors related to team performance?

The four contextual factors that appear to be most significantly related to team performance are the presence of adequate resources, effective leadership, a climate of trust, and a performance evaluation and reward system that reflects team contribution.

pp. 126-127

140.	What are the three different types of skills a team requires to perform effectively?

The three different types of skills a team requires to perform effectively are technical expertise, problem-solving and decision-making skills, and interpersonal skills. The problem-solving and decision-making skills are needed to identify problems, generate alternatives, evaluate those alternatives, and make competent choices. Teams also need people with good listening, feedback, conflict resolution, and other interpersonal skills. No team can achieve its performance potential without developing all three types of skills.

p. 127

141.	List at least five of the nine potential team roles that people play and describe them.

The nine potential team roles are as follows:
Creator-innovator: This team member initiates creative ideas.
Explorer-promoter: This team member champions ideas after they're initiated.
Assessor-developer: This team member analyzes decision options.
Thruster-organizer: This team member provides structure.
Concluder-producer: This team member provides direction and follow-through.
Controller-inspector: This team member checks for details.

Upholder-maintainer: This team member fights external battles.

Reporter-adviser: This team member seeks full information.

Linker: This team member coordinates and integrates.

p. 128 and Exhibit 8-4

142.   Discuss work design as a key component of effective teams.

Work design includes variables like freedom and autonomy, the opportunity to utilize different skills and talents, the ability to complete a whole and identifiable task or product, and working on a task or project that has a substantial impact on others. These characteristics enhance member motivation and increase team effectiveness. They motivate because they increase members' sense of responsibility and ownership over the work and because they make the work more interesting to perform.

p. 129

143.   Why is conflict on a team not necessarily bad?

Conflict on a team is not necessarily bad. Teams that are completely void of conflict are likely to become apathetic and stagnant. Conflict can actually improve team effectiveness. But not all conflict. Relationship conflicts are almost always dysfunctional. On teams performing non-routine activities, disagreement among members about task content is not detrimental. In fact, it's often beneficial because it lessens the likelihood of groupthink. Task conflicts stimulate discussion, promote critical assessment of problems and options, and can lead to better team decisions.

pp. 130-131

144.   When is the challenge of creating team players the greatest?

The challenge of creating team players is the greatest where the national culture is highly individualistic and the teams are being introduced into an established organization that has historically valued individual achievement.

p. 131

145.   What are options for managers who are trying to turn individuals into team players?

The options for managers who are trying to turn individuals into team players are selection, training, and rewards. When hiring team members, managers should take care to ensure that candidates can fulfill their team roles as well as having the technical skills required to fill the job. A large proportion of people raised on the importance of individual accomplishment can be trained to become team players. Training specialists conduct exercises that allow employees to experience the satisfaction that teamwork can provide. The reward system needs to be reworked to encourage cooperative efforts rather than competitive ones.

pp. 131-132

146.   Discuss why teams aren't always the answer.

Three tests have been suggested to see if a team fits the situation. First, can the work be done better by more than one person? A good indicator is the complexity of the work and the need for different perspectives. Simple tasks that don't require diverse input are probably better left to individuals. Second, does the work create a common purpose or set of goals for the people in the group that is more than the aggregate of individual goals? The final test to assess whether teams fit the situation is: Are the members of the group interdependent? Teams make sense when there is interdependence between tasks; when the success of the whole depends on the success of each one and the success of each one depends on the success of the others.

pp. 134-135

Chapter 9 Communication

MULTIPLE CHOICE

1. The most frequently cited source of interpersonal conflict is poor:
    a. academic preparation.
    b. communication.
    c. attitude.
    d. training.

Answer: b, difficulty: 1, p.136

2. Communication must include:
    a. transference and conveyance.
    b. feedback and understanding of meaning.
    c. transference and understanding of meaning.
    d. transference and feedback.

Answer: c, difficulty: 2, p. 136

3. Perfect communication, if it were possible, would exist when:
    a. a oneness of mind and soul exists between the sender and receiver.
    b. a thought is transmitted so the mental picture perceived by the receiver is exactly the same as that envisioned by the sender.
    c. no channel is needed.
    d. senders rely on the message transmitted rather than on feedback.

Answer: b, difficulty: 3, p. 136

4. Which is NOT one of the four major functions of communication within a group?
    a. leadership
    b. control
    c. motivation
    d. information

Answer: a, difficulty: 3, p. 137

5. Communication fosters _____ by clarifying for employees what is to be done, how well they are doing, and what can be done to improve performance if it's subpar.
    a. control
    b. information
    c. motivation
    d. emotional expression

Answer: c, difficulty: 2, p. 137

6.   When employees are required to first communicate job-related grievance to their immediate boss or follow the job description, communication is performing which function?
      a. motivation
      b. control
      c. emotional expression
      d. information

Answer: b, difficulty: 3, p. 137

7.   Communication provides the _____ that individuals and groups need to make decisions by transmitting the data to identify and evaluate choices.
      a. control
      b. information
      c. motivation
      d. emotional expression

Answer: b, difficulty: 2, p. 137

8.   The activity by which a message is converted to a symbolic form by the sender is known as:
      a. decoding.
      b. mental formation.
      c. articulation.
      d. encoding.

Answer: d, difficulty: 1, pp. 137-138

9.   The activity when the receiver retranslates the message initiated by the sender is:
      a. decoding.
      b. mental formation.
      c. articulation.
      d. encoding.

Answer: a, difficulty: 1, p. 138

10.   The _____ is the object to whom a message is directed.
      a. receiver
      b. decoder
      c. interpreter
      d. translator

Answer: a, difficulty: 1, p. 138

11. Which of the following is NOT a part of the communication process?
    a. sender
    b. receiver
    c. feedback
    d. understanding

Answer: d, difficulty: 1, pp. 137-139 and Exhibit 9-1

12. John did not decipher what Allen said. John is said to have failed to _____ the message.
    a. understand
    b. receive
    c. interpret
    d. decode

Answer: d, difficulty: 2, p. 138

13. The _____ is the medium through which the message travels.
    a. receiver
    b. source
    c. channel
    d. decoder

Answer: c, difficulty: 1, p. 138

14. The communication model is composed of the following elements:
    a. levels, encoding, channel, message, decoding, receiver, feedback.
    b. message, source, encoding, channel, receiver, decoding, noise.
    c. sender, encoding, message, channel, decoding, receiver, feedback.
    d. message, links, source, channel, receiver, decoding, feedback.

Answer: c, difficulty: 3, pp. 137-138 and Exhibit 9-1

15. _____ is the check on how successful we have been in transferring our messages as originally intended.
    a. Feedback
    b. Decoding
    c. Source
    d. Channel

Answer: a, difficulty: 2, p. 138

16. Formal channels of communication traditionally follow:
    a. the authority chain.
    b. the path of least resistance.
    c. the most efficient channel.
    d. personal or social chains.

Answer: a, difficulty: 1, p. 138

17. Communication that flows from one level of a group or organization to a lower level is a _____ communication.
    a. downward
    b. upward
    c. lateral
    d. feedback

Answer: a, difficulty: 1, p. 138

18. Examples of downward communication include all of the following EXCEPT:
    a. management sends letters to employees' homes to advise them of the organization's new sick leave policy.
    b. an e-mail from a team leader to the team members reminds them of an upcoming deadline.
    c. a manager provides job instructions to subordinates.
    d. a manager tells his boss about the problem employee.

Answer: d, difficulty: 2, p. 138

19. Communication that is used to provide feedback to higher-ups, inform them of progress toward goals, and relay current problems is:
    a. downward.
    b. upward.
    c. lateral.
    d. feedback.

Answer: b, difficulty: 2, p. 139

20. Examples of upward communication include all of the following EXCEPT:
    a. suggestion boxes.
    b. employee attitude surveys.
    c. feedback to subordinates on their performance.
    d. grievance procedures.

Answer: c, difficulty: 2, p. 139

21. Communication that takes place among members of the same work group, among members of work groups at the same level, or among managers at the same level is termed:
    a. downward.
    b. upward.
    c. lateral.
    d. feedback.

Answer: c, difficulty: 2, p. 139

22.	Which of the following is NOT true about horizontal (or lateral) communication?
	a.	Horizontal communications are often necessary to save time and facilitate coordination.
	b.	Lateral communications can be good or bad.
	c.	Strict adherence to the formal vertical structures facilitates the efficient and accurate transfer of information.
	d.	Horizontal communication can create dysfunctional conflicts.

Answer: c, difficulty: 3, p. 139

23.	Which of the following is NOT one of the three basic communication methods?
	a.	visual
	b.	oral
	c.	written
	d.	nonverbal

Answer: a, difficulty: 2, p. 139

24.	Barbara used the chief method of communicating when she communicated with Jean. Barbara communicated using:
	a.	a memo.
	b.	nonverbal communication.
	c.	oral communication.
	d.	a fax machine.

Answer: c, difficulty: 2, p. 139

25.	All of the following are popular forms of oral communication EXCEPT:
	a.	speeches.
	b.	e-mail.
	c.	group discussions.
	d.	grapevine.

Answer: b, difficulty: 1, p. 139

26.	The advantages of oral communication are:
	a.	clarity and speed.
	b.	speed and feedback.
	c.	feedback and clarity.
	d.	interpretation and speed.

Answer: b, difficulty: 2, pp. 139-140

27. The major disadvantage of oral communication surfacing whenever the message has to be passed through a number of people is:
   a. speed.
   b. distortion.
   c. slow feedback.
   d. tangibility.

Answer: b, difficulty: 2, p. 140

28. Memos, letters, e-mail, faxes, and notices placed on bulletin boards are examples of:
   a. oral communication.
   b. written communication.
   c. visual communication.
   d. nonverbal communication.

Answer: b, difficulty: 1, p. 140

29. Advantages of written communication include all BUT which of the following?
   a. There is a record of the communication.
   b. The message can be stored indefinitely.
   c. It has a built-in feedback mechanism.
   d. It is more thought-out and logical.

Answer: c, difficulty: 2, p. 140

30. The major disadvantage of written communication is:
   a. lack of feedback.
   b. distortion.
   c. tangibility.
   d. verifiability.

Answer: a, difficulty: 2, p. 140

31. Nonverbal communication is best described as:
   a. body movements.
   b. facial expressions.
   c. intonation.
   d. All of the above.

Answer: d, difficulty: 2, pp. 140-141

32. Body language adds to and often complicates:
   a. oral communication.
   b. written communication.
   c. visual communication.
   d. configuration science.

Answer: a, difficulty: 2, p. 141

33. Which of the following statements is true about the ways individuals space themselves in terms of physical distance?
    a. Americans tend to stand very close to someone when talking.
    b. Europeans stand further away from one another in businesslike situations than Americans.
    c. What is considered proper spacing is largely dependent on cultural norms.
    d. If someone stands closer to you than is considered appropriate, it may mean displeasure with what you are saying.

Answer: c, difficulty: 2, p. 141

34. All of the following are formal organizational networks EXCEPT:
    a. chain.
    b. circle.
    c. wheel.
    d. all-channel.

Answer: b, difficulty: 1, p. 142

35. The _____ small-group communication network relies on a central figure to act as the central conduit for the group's communication.
    a. wheel
    b. chain
    c. all-channel
    d. grapevine

Answer: a, difficulty: 2, p. 142

36. When a problem-solving task force is created in which all group members are free to contribute to resolving the problem, and no one person takes a leadership role, this is an example of the _____ communication network.
    a. chain
    b. wheel
    c. all-channel
    d. grapevine

Answer: c, difficulty: 1, p. 142

37. The _____ form of small-group network rigidly follows the formal chain of command.
    a. chain
    b. wheel
    c. all-channel
    d. grapevine

Answer: a, difficulty: 1, p. 142

38. To facilitate the emergence of a leader, the _____ network is best.
    a. chain
    b. wheel
    c. all-channel
    d. grapevine

Answer: b, difficulty: 2, p. 142

39. If member satisfaction is important, the _____ network is best.
    a. chain
    b. wheel
    c. all-channel
    d. grapevine

Answer: c, difficulty: 2, p. 142

40. If accuracy is most important, the _____ network is best.
    a. chain
    b. wheel
    c. all-channel
    d. grapevine

Answer: a, difficulty: 2, p. 142

41. Grapevines can be described as:
    a. communication systems that management controls in order to maintain internal communication.
    b. informal networks that flourish alongside the formal networks.
    c. communication networks that begin in the lower levels of the organization and flourish at the management levels.
    d. informal networks that should be eliminated by management.

Answer: b, difficulty: 2, pp. 142-143

42. Which of the following is NOT one of the main characteristics of the grapevine?
    a. It is not controlled by management.
    b. It is perceived by most employees as being more believable and reliable than formal communiques issued by top management.
    c. It is largely used to serve the self-interests of those people within it.
    d. It is largely used to serve the self-interests of management.

Answer: d, difficulty: 2, p. 143

43. Evidence suggests that the accuracy of the grapevine:
    a. is very poor.
    b. depends on whether the information flows upward or downward.
    c. may be as high as 75 percent.
    d. depends on the size of the organization.

Answer: c, difficulty: 2, p. 143

44. About _____ percent of the information carried through the grapevine is accurate.
    a. 10
    b. 25
    c. 50
    d. 75

Answer: d, difficulty: 2, p. 143

45. Rumors and an active grapevine are fostered under a number of conditions that include all of the following EXCEPT:
    a. important situations.
    b. ambiguous situations.
    c. situations that arouse anxiety.
    d. more female employees.

Answer: d, difficulty: 3, pp. 143-144

46. While the grapevine has been found to be an important source of information, _____ of executives were found to act as liaison individuals who passed the information on to more than one other party.
    a. roughly half
    b. over 90 percent
    c. two-thirds
    d. only ten percent

Answer: d, difficulty: 3, p. 144

47. Computer-aided technologies include all of the following EXCEPT:
    a. electronic mail
    b. extranet links
    c. videoconferencing
    d. newspapers

Answer: c, difficulty: 1, p. 144

48. _____ is computer-aided technology that uses the Internet to transmit and receive computer-generated text and documents.
    a. E-mail
    b. Intranet
    c. Teleconferencing
    d. Videoconferencing

Answer: a, difficulty: 1, p. 144

49. While the communication belief is that people are swamped with e-mails, a recent study found ____ percent of employees with e-mail access report receiving more than 50 messages a day.
   a. 6
   b. 15
   c. 30
   d. 50

Answer: a, difficulty: 1, p. 144

50. The benefits of e-mail include which of the following:
   a. They can be quickly written, edited, and stored.
   b. They can be read at the convenience of the recipient.
   c. The cost of sending formal e-mail messages to employees is a fraction of what it would cost to print, duplicate, and distribute a comparable letter or brochure.
   d. All of the above.

Answer: d, difficulty: 2, p. 144

51. The drawbacks of e-mail include all of the following EXCEPT:
   a. e-mail is not the ideal means to convey information like layoffs that might involve emotional responses.
   b. the remote nature of e-mail fuels "conflict spirals."
   c. e-mail tends to be filled with emotional content.
   d. e-mail tends to be cold and impersonal.

Answer: c, difficulty: 2, pp. 144-145

52. "Real-time" e-mail is known as:
   a. instant messaging.
   b. teleconferencing.
   c. face-to-face communication.
   d. extranet links.

Answer: a, difficulty: 1, p. 145

53. Which of the following is NOT an advantage instant messaging offers over e-mail?
   a. There's no delay.
   b. There's no in-box clutter of messages.
   c. There's no lack of emotional content.
   d. There's no uncertainty as to whether the message was received.

Answer: c. difficulty: 2, p. 145

54. _____ are private, organization-wide information networks that look and act like a website but to which only people in an organization have access.
   a. Extranets
   b. Intranets
   c. Internets
   d. E-mails

Answer: b, difficulty: 1, p. 146

55. A/n _____ allows GM employees to send electronic messages and documents to its steel and rubber suppliers as well as to communicate with its dealers.
   a. Extranet
   b. Intranet
   c. Internet
   d. E-mail

Answer: a, difficulty: 3, p. 146

56. The computer-aided communication technology that permits employees in an organization to have meetings with people at different locations is known as:
   a. e-mail.
   b. intranet.
   c. videoconferencing.
   d. video games.

Answer: c, difficulty: 1, p. 146

57. ____ is a process of organizing and distributing an organization's collective wisdom so the right information gets to the right people at the right time.
   a. The grapevine
   b. The rumor mill
   c. Knowledge management
   d. None of the above.

Answer: c, difficulty: 2, p. 147

58. Which of the following is NOT one of the reasons that knowledge management is increasingly important today?
   a. Intellectual assets are now as important in organizations as physical or financial assets.
   b. As baby boomers begin to leave the workforce, there's an increasing awareness that they represent a wealth of knowledge that will be lost if there are no attempts to capture it.
   c. A knowledge system prohibits employees from accessing what previous employees have learned.
   d. A well-designed knowledge system will reduce redundancy and make the organization more efficient.

Answer: c, difficulty: 3, pp. 147-148

59. Which of the following is NOT a barrier to effective communication?
   a. filtering
   b. selective perception
   c. gender style
   d. technology

Answer: d, difficulty: 1, pp. 148-150

60. Tom manipulates information before he tells the boss so that the information won't sound negative to his boss. This is an example of:
   a. selective perception.
   b. filtering.
   c. male communication style.
   d. status barrier.

Answer: b, difficulty: 1, p. 148

61. _____ refers to a sender's purposely manipulating information so it will be seen more favorably by the receiver.
   a. Selective perception
   b. Filtering
   c. Male communication style
   d. Status barrier

Answer: b, difficulty: 1, p. 148

62. When a receiver sees and hears things based on his or her own needs, experience, and other personal characteristics, this is known as:
   a. selective perception.
   b. filtering.
   c. male communication style.
   d. status barrier.

Answer: a, difficulty: 1, p. 149

63. When the information we have to work with exceeds our processing capacity, the result is:
   a. processor overload.
   b. selective perception.
   c. information overload.
   d. filtering.

Answer: c, difficulty: 1, p. 149

64. Research shows that men speak and hear a language of _____, and women speak and hear a language of connection and intimacy.
   a. negotiation
   b. support and teamwork
   c. emotion and closeness
   d. status and independence

Answer: d, difficulty: 1, p. 149

65. Research shows that men use talk to _____ whereas women use it to _____.
   a. ask help; ask for solutions
   b. maintain status; negotiate closeness
   c. create alliances; follow the chain of command
   d. create relationships; maintain status

Answer: b, difficulty: 3, p. 149

66. When faced with _____ we are most prone to disregard our rational and objective thinking processes and substitute emotional judgments.
   a. language differences
   b. gender differences
   c. emotions
   d. cultural differences

Answer: c, difficulty: 2, p. 149

67. When communicating with people from a different culture, all BUT which of the following will improve the communication process?
   a. Assume differences until similarity is proven.
   b. Emphasize description rather than interpretation or evaluation.
   c. Practice empathy.
   d. Assume similarity until differences are shown.

Answer: d, difficulty: 2, p. 150

68. Which of the following will improve communication when dealing with people from a different culture?
   a. Emphasize interpretation rather than description.
   b. Practice sympathy.
   c. Treat your interpretations as a working hypothesis.
   d. Assume similarity until differences are proven.

Answer: c, difficulty: 3, pp. 151-152

69. Suggestions for making communication more effective include all of the following EXCEPT:
    a. show emotions.
    b. use feedback.
    c. simplify language.
    d. listen actively.

Answer: a, difficulty: 2, pp. 152-155

70. Which of the following is a suggestion to help managers be more effective in providing feedback to others?
    a. Focus on general behaviors.
    b. Keep feedback personal.
    c. Keep feedback goal oriented.
    d. Direct negative feedback toward behavior that is not controllable by the recipient.

Answer: c, difficulty: 2, Exhibit 9-6

71. Understanding is improved by:
    a. simplifying the language used.
    b. using jargon.
    c. using the same language for all receivers.
    d. always repeating the communication twice.

Answer: a, difficulty: 2, p. 154

72. Which of the following is correct regarding active listening?
    a. Listening is usually more satisfying than talking.
    b. Listening is enhanced when the receiver develops empathy with the sender.
    c. Empathy makes it more difficult to understand the actual content of the message.
    d. An empathetic listener judges the message's content as quickly as possible.

Answer: b, difficulty: 2, pp. 154-155 and Exhibit 9-7

73. Which of the following suggestions is helpful for one who wishes to become a more effective active listener?
    a. Make eye contact.
    b. Avoid distracting actions or gestures.
    c. Ask questions.
    d. All of the above.

Answer: b, difficulty: 1, Exhibit 9-7

74. The average person speaks at a rate of about 150 words per minute whereas we have the capacity to listen at _____ per minute.
    a. only 100 words
    b. 200 words
    c. over 1,000 words
    d. approximately 3,000 words

Answer: c, difficulty: 2, p. 155

TRUE/FALSE

75. We spend nearly 70 percent of our waking hours communicating.

True, difficulty: 3, p. 136

76. Communication must include both the transference and understanding of meaning.

True, difficulty: 1, p. 136

77. Perfect communication is achievable with a practiced communicator and an active listener.

False, difficulty: 2, p. 136

78. When work groups tease a member who produces too much (and makes the rest of the group look bad), they are formally communicating with and controlling the member's behavior.

False, difficulty: 2, p. 137

79. Communication provides an avenue for expression of emotions and fulfillment of social needs.

True, difficulty: 2, p. 137

80. Of the four functions of communication, the most important function is to provide an avenue for expression of emotions.

False, difficulty: 1, p. 137

81. Decoding is the final link in the communication process.

False, difficulty: 2, p. 137

82. When we gesture, the movements of our arms and the expressions on our faces are the message.

True, difficulty: 1, p. 138

83. Formal channels of communication are spontaneous and emerge as a response to individual choices.

False, difficulty: 3, p. 138

84. Feedback is the check on how successful we have been in transferring our messages as originally intended.

True, difficulty: 1, p. 138

85. Downward communication is used to provide feedback to higher-ups.

False, difficulty: 1, p. 138

86. Downward communication must be oral or face-to-face contact.

False, difficulty: 2, p. 138

87. Some organizational examples of downward communication are performance reports prepared by lower management for review by middle and top management, suggestion boxes, and grievance procedures.

False, difficulty: 2, p. 138

88. The FedEx program where all its employees annually complete climate surveys and reviews of management is an example of upward communication.

True, difficulty: 3, p. 139

89. Strict adherence to the formal vertical structure for all communications can impede the efficient and accurate transfer of communication.

True, difficulty: 2, p. 139

90. Three basic methods of interpersonal communication are oral, written, and nonverbal communication.

True, difficulty: 2, p. 139

91. The advantages of oral communication are speed and feedback.

True, difficulty: 2, pp. 139-140

92. The major disadvantage of oral communication surfaces in organizations or whenever the message has to be passed through a number of people creating a greater potential for distortion.

True, difficulty: 2, p. 140

93. Any device that is transmitted via written records or symbols is oral communication.

False, difficulty: 1, p. 140

94. You are usually more careful with the written word than the oral word.

True, difficulty: 2, p. 140

95. The advantages of written communication are speed and feedback.

False, difficulty: 2, p. 140

96. The disadvantages of written messages are that they are time-consuming and lack feedback.

True, difficulty: 2, p. 140

97. Written communication has a built-in feedback mechanism.

False, difficulty: 2, p. 140

98. Every time we verbally give a message to someone, we also import a nonverbal message.

True, difficulty: 1, p. 140

99. Actions really do speak louder than words.

True, difficulty: 1, p. 141

100. Nonverbal communication includes body movements, the intonations we give to words, facial expressions, and the physical distance between the sender and receiver.

True, difficulty: 2, p. 141

101. No body movement is accidental.

True, difficulty: 3, p. 141

102. We are more likely to display body movements if we feel we are higher status than another.

True, difficulty: 2, p. 141

103. What is considered proper spacing is largely dependent on cultural norms.

True, difficulty: 2, p. 141

104. The all-channel communication network follows the formal chain of command.

False, difficulty: 2, p. 142

105. When all group members actively communicate with each other, they are structured in a wheel network.

False, difficulty: 2, p. 142

106. The all-channel network is most often characterized in practice by self-managed teams, in which all group members are free to contribute.

True, difficulty: 3, p. 142

107. The wheel type of small-group network is the most effective if you are concerned with having high member satisfaction.

False, difficulty: 2, p. 142

108. The all-channel network is best for allowing leaders to emerge.

False, difficulty: 3, p. 142

109. If member satisfaction is important, the all-channel network is best.

True, difficulty: 3, p. 142

110. The informal communication system is called the grapevine.

True, difficulty: 1, p. 142

111. The grapevine is perceived by most employees as being more believable and reliable than formal communication issued by top management.

True, difficulty: 2, p. 143

112. Evidence indicates that about 75 percent of what flows along the grapevine is accurate.

True, difficulty: 2, p. 143

113. Rumors emerge as a response to situations that are important to us, where there is ambiguity, and under conditions that arouse anxiety.

True, difficulty: 2, pp. 143-144

114. A rumor will persist either until the wants and expectations creating the uncertainty underlying the rumor are fulfilled or until the anxiety is reduced.

True, difficulty: 2, p. 144

115. The grapevine acts as both a filter and feedback mechanism, picking up the issues that employees consider relevant.

True, difficulty: 2, p. 144

116.	A disadvantage of e-mail is lack of emotional content.

True, difficulty: 1, p. 144

117.	IM is expected to replace e-mail.

False, difficulty: 3, p. 145

118.	The latest wrinkle in intranets is using high-speed wireless Internet access for telephone calls within an organization.

True, difficulty: 2, p. 145

119.	Videoconferencing technology allows employees to conduct interactive meetings without the necessity of everyone physically being in the same location.

True, difficulty: 2, p. 146

120.	When done properly, knowledge management provides an organization with both a competitive advantage and improved organizational performance because it makes its employees smarter.

True, difficulty: 2, p. 147

121.	More knowledge means better knowledge.

False, difficulty: 3, p. 148

122.	The major determinant of filtering is the number of levels in an organization's structure.

False, difficulty: 3, p. 148

123.	Filtering and selective perception are barriers to effective communication.

True, difficulty: 1, pp. 148-149

124.	When individual's experience information overload, they tend to select out, pass over, or forget information.

True, difficulty: 2, p. 149

125.	Men use talk to emphasize status, while women use it to create connection.

True, difficulty: 2, p. 149

126.	The existence of vertical levels within organizations simplifies language problems.

False, difficulty: 2, p. 150

127. Senders tend to assume that the words and terms they use mean the same to the receiver as they do to them.

True, difficulty: 1, p. 150

128. In cross-cultural communication, one should assume similarity until differences are proven.

False, difficulty: 3, p. 151

129. Cross-cultural communication is enhanced when the sender develops empathy with the listener.

True, difficulty: 3, p. 151

130. When you use a single channel to convey a message, you improve the likelihood of clarity.

False, difficulty: 2, p. 152

131. Feedback is enhanced by focusing on specific behaviors.

True, difficulty: 2, Exhibit 9-6

132. Listening is a passive search for meaning, whereas hearing is active.

False, difficulty: 1, p. 154

133. Listening is more tiring than talking and demands intellectual effort.

True, difficulty: 2, p. 154

ESSAY

134. Discuss the four major functions communication serves within a group or organization.

Communication acts to control member behavior. For example, when employees are required to comply with company policies, communication is performing a control function. Communication also fosters motivation by clarifying for employees what is to be done, how well they are doing, and what can be done to improve performance if it is not acceptable. Communication also provides an avenue for expression of emotions and fulfillment of social needs. For many employees, their work group is a primary source for social interaction. Fourth, communication provides the information that individuals and groups need to make decisions by transmitting the data to identify and evaluate choices.

p. 137

135. Discuss the components of the communication process.

The communication process is comprised of the communication source, encoding, the message, the channel, decoding, the receiver, and feedback. The sender initiates a message by encoding a thought. The message is the actual physical product from the source encoding. The channel is the medium through which the message travels. It is selected by the source. They may be formal or informal. The receiver is the object to whom the message is directed. But before the message can be received, the symbols in it must be translated into a form that can be understood by the receiver. This step is the decoding. Noise represents communication barriers that distort the clarity of the message. The final link in the communication process is a feedback loop. Feedback is the check on how successful we have been in transferring our messages as originally intended.

pp. 137-138 and Exhibit 9-1

136. Discuss the three different directions of communication.

Communication can flow downward, upward, or vertically in the organization. Downward communication flows from one level of a group or organization to a lower level. It is used by groups or managers to assign goals, provide job instructions, inform employees of policies and procedures, point out problems that need attention, and offer feedback about performance. Upward communication flows to a higher level in the group or organization. It's used to provide feedback to higher-ups, inform them of progress toward goals, and relay current problems. Upward communication keeps managers aware of how employees feel about their jobs, co-workers, and the organization in general. When communication takes place among members of the same work group, among members of work groups on the same level, among managers at the same level, or among any horizontally equivalent personnel, we describe it as lateral communication. This horizontal communication often is necessary to save time and facilitate coordination.

pp. 138-139

137. Discuss the three basic methods of interpersonal communication.

The three basic methods in interpersonal communication are oral, written, and nonverbal. The chief means of conveying message is oral communication. Speeches, formal one-on-one and group discussions, and the informal rumor mill or grapevine are popular forms of oral communication. The advantages of oral communication are speed and feedback. Written communications include memos, letters, electronic mail, fax transmissions, organizational periodicals, notices placed on bulletin boards, or any other device that is transmitted via written words or symbols. Written communications are tangible and verifiable. On the downside, they are time-consuming and do not have a built-in feedback mechanism. Nonverbal communication includes body movements, the intonations or emphasis we give to words, facial expressions, and the physical distance between the sender and receiver. Every body movement has a meaning and no movement is accidental. Body language adds to, and often complicates, verbal communication.

pp. 139-141

138. Describe the three common types of small-group networks and list their advantages and disadvantages.

The three common types of small-group networks are the chain, wheel, and all-channel. The chain rigidly follows the formal chain of command. The wheel relies on a central figure to act as the conduit for all the group's communication. The all-channel network permits all group members to actively communicate with each other. This is often used in self-managed team, in which all group members are free to contribute and no one person takes on a leadership role. The chain is moderate in speed, yet highly accurate. The wheel is the fastest, but provides the least member satisfaction. And the all-channel is fast and provides the highest member satisfaction.

p. 142 and Exhibit 9-2

139.   What are the three main characteristics of the grapevine?

There are three main characteristics of the grapevine. First, it is not controlled by management. Second, it is perceived by most employees as being more believable and reliable than formal communications issued by top management. Third, it is largely used to serve the self-interests of those people within it.

pp. 142-144

140.   Discuss four computer-aided technologies enhancing communication.

Four computer-aided technologies enhancing communication are e-mail, instant messaging, intranet and extranet links, and videoconferencing. E-mail uses the Internet to transmit and receive computer-generated text and documents. Its messages can be quickly written, edited, and stored. They can be distributed to one person or thousands with a click of a mouse. They also can be read at the convenience of the recipient. The cost of sending formal e-mail messages to employees is a fraction of what it would cost to print, duplicate, and distribute a comparable letter or brochure. E-mail is, however, lacking in emotional content and tends to be cold and impersonal. It is difficult to distinguish important e-mails from junk mail and irrelevant messages. Intranets are private, organization-wide information networks that look and act like a Web site but to which only people in the organization have access. Instant messaging (IM) is essentially real-time e-mail. Organizations are also creating extranet links that connect internal employees with selected suppliers, customers, and strategic partners. Videoconferencing is an extension of intranet or extranet systems. It permits employees in an organization to have meetings with people at different locations. Live audio and video images of members allow them to see, hear, and talk with each other. The technology enables employees to conduct interactive meetings without the necessity of all physically being in the same location.

pp. 144-146

141.   What are the advantages IM provides over e-mail?

IM provides several advantages over e-mail. There's no delay, no in-box clutter of messages, and no uncertainty as to whether the message was received. Managers also find that IM is an excellent means for monitoring employees' physical presence at their work stations.

p. 145

142.   What is knowledge management and why is it increasing in importance?

Knowledge management (KM) is a process of organizing and distributing an organization's collective wisdom so the right information gets to the right people at the right time. When done properly, KM provides an organization with both a competitive edge and improved organizational performance because it makes its employees smarter. Knowledge management is increasingly important for three reasons. First, in many organizations, intellectual assets are now as important as physical or financial assets. Second, as baby boomers begin to leave the workforce, there's an increasing awareness that they represent a wealth of knowledge that will be lost if there are no attempts to capture it. And third, a well-designed KM system will reduce redundancy and make the organization more efficient.

pp. 147-148

143. Discuss filtering, selective perception, information overload, and gender styles as barriers to effective communication.

Four barriers to communication include filtering, selective perception, information overload, and gender styles. Filtering refers to a sender's purposely manipulating information so it will be seen more favorably by the receiver. The more vertical levels in the organization's hierarchy, the more opportunities there are for filtering. Selective perception occurs when the receiver sees and hears things in a selective way, based on his or her needs, motivations, experience, background, and other personal characteristics. The receiver also projects his or her interests and expectations into communications as he or she decodes them. Individuals have a limited capacity for processing data. When the information we have to work with exceeds our processing capacity, the result is information overload. When this occurs, people tend to select out, ignore, pass over, forget information, or put off further processing. Men and women use oral communication for different reasons. As a result, gender becomes a barrier to communication. Men use talk to emphasize status, whereas women use it to create connection.

pp. 148-149

144. What are the differences in the ways that men and women communicate?

Men use talk to emphasize status, whereas women use it to create connection. Men speak and hear a language of status and independence, and women speak and hear a language of connection and intimacy. For many men, conversations are primarily a means to preserve independence and maintain status in a hierarchical social order. For many women, conversations are negotiations for closeness in which people try to seek and give confirmation and support.

p. 149

145. When communicating with people from a different culture, what can you do to reduce misinterpretations?

When communicating with people from a different culture, the following may be helpful:
Assume differences until similarity is proved.
Emphasize description rather than interpretation or evaluation.
Practice empathy.
Treat your interpretation as a working hypothesis.

pp. 151-152

146. What suggestions can you give for managers who wish to be more effective in providing feedback?

For managers who wish to be more effective in providing feedback, the following suggestions can be given:
1. Focus on specific behaviors. Feedback should be specific rather than general.
2. Keep feedback impersonal. Feedback should be job related.
3. Keep feedback goal oriented. Make sure feedback is directed toward the recipient's goals.
4. Make feedback well timed. Feedback is more meaningful when there is a short interval between the behavior and the feedback.
5. Ensure understanding. Managers should consider having the recipient rephrase the content of the feedback to see whether it fully captures the intended meaning.
6. Direct negative feedback toward behavior that is controllable by the recipient. There's little value in reminding a person of a shortcoming over which he or she has no control.

Exhibit 9-6

147. How can one improve active listening skills?

One can improve active listening skills with the following:
1. Make eye contact.
2. Exhibit affirmative head nods and appropriate facial expressions.
3. Avoid distracting actions or gestures.
4. Ask questions.
5. Paraphrase.
6. Avoid interrupting the speaker.
7. Don't overtalk.

Exhibit 9-7

Chapter 10 Leadership and Creating Trust

MULTIPLE CHOICE

1. Which of the following is true about leadership?
    a. *Leader* and *manager* are similar terms.
    b. Leadership is the ability to influence a group to achieve goals.
    c. When the organization provides its managers with certain rights, they are assured of leading effectively.
    d. Leadership has to be granted by the organization.

Answer: b, difficulty: 2, pp. 156-157

2. _____ is the ability to influence that arises outside of the formal structure of an organization.
    a. Nonsanctioned leadership
    b. Formal leadership
    c. Illegitimate leadership
    d. Legitimate leadership

Answer: a, difficulty: 1, p. 157

3. _____ theories of leadership searched for characteristics that would differentiate leaders from nonleaders.
    a. Behavioral
    b. Path-goal
    c. Trait
    d. Bipolar

Answer: c, difficulty: 2, p. 157

4. Which of the following traits was found to be consistently associated with leadership according to the trait approach?
    a. judgment
    b. tact
    c. intelligence
    d. adaptability

Answer: c, difficulty: 3, p. 157

5. Comprehensive reviews of the leadership literature, when organized around the Big Five, has found that _____ is the most important trait of effective leaders.
    a. extroversion
    b. self-confidence
    c. emotional stability
    d. agreeableness

Answer: a, difficulty: 3, p. 157

6. The failure of early trait studies led researchers to examine:
    a. contingency theories of leadership.
    b. behavioral theories of leadership.
    c. Path-Goal theory.
    d. supportive theories of leadership.

Answer: b, difficulty: 2, p. 158

7. Which of the following statements is true concerning the differences between trait and behavioral theories of leadership?
    a. If trait theories were valid, then leaders were basically born.
    b. If there were specific behaviors that identified leaders, then we could teach leadership.
    c. If trait research had been successful it would have provided a basis for selecting the right person to assume a formal position that required leadership.
    d. All of the above.

Answer: d, difficulty: 3, p. 158

8. The extent to which a leader is likely to define and structure his or her role and those of subordinates in the search for goal attainment is referred to by the Ohio State studies as:
    a. employee orientation.
    b. initiating structure.
    c. cooperation.
    d. consideration.

Answer: b, difficulty: 2, p. 158

9. According to the Ohio State studies, the extent to which a leader has job relationships characterized by mutual trust, respect for subordinates' ideas, and regard for their feelings is known as:
    a. employee orientation.
    b. initiating structure.
    c. cooperation.
    d. consideration.

Answer: d, difficulty: 2, p. 159

10. The leader who is high in consideration is characterized by all of the following EXCEPT:
    a. shows concern for followers' comfort.
    b. helps subordinates with personal problems.
    c. treats all subordinates as equal.
    d. emphasizes the meeting of deadlines.

Answer: d, difficulty: 2, p. 159

11. The Ohio State studies suggested those leader _____ in consideration and ___ in initiating structure generally resulted in positive outcomes.
    a. low; high
    b. high; low
    c. high; high
    d. low; low

Answer: c, difficulty: 3, p. 159

12. According to the University of Michigan studies, a leader who emphasizes the technical or task aspects of the job is:
    a. production oriented.
    b. employee oriented.
    c. task structured.
    d. people centered.

Answer: a, difficulty: 2, p. 159

13. The two dimensions of leadership behavior identified by the University of Michigan studies are:
    a. initiating structure and consideration.
    b. concern for people and concern for production.
    c. employee oriented and production oriented.
    d. relational and job.

Answer: c, difficulty: 3, p. 159

14. According to the University of Michigan studies, a leader who emphasizes interpersonal relations is:
    a. production oriented.
    b. people centered.
    c. task structured.
    d. employee oriented.

Answer: d, difficulty: 3, p. 159

15. Which of the following statements is NOT true of the University of Michigan studies?
    a. They were conducted 10 years before the Ohio State studies.
    b. They identified two dimensions of leadership behavior.
    c. Leaders who were employee-oriented were described as emphasizing interpersonal relations.
    d. The production-oriented leaders tended to emphasize the technical or task aspects of the job.

Answer: a, difficulty: 2, p. 159

16. Which is NOT true of the conclusions arrived at by the University of Michigan researchers?
    a. The leaders who were employee oriented in their behavior were strongly favored.
    b. The leaders who were production oriented in their behavior were strongly favored.
    c. Employee-oriented leaders were associated with higher group productivity and higher job satisfaction.
    d. Production-oriented leaders tended to be associated with low group productivity and low worker satisfaction.

Answer: b, difficulty: 3, p. 159

17. Blake and Mouton developed the:
    a. managerial grid.
    b. University of Michigan studies.
    c. path-goal theory.
    d. least-preferred coworker theory.

Answer: a, difficulty: 2, p. 159

18. The two dimensions of leadership on the managerial grid are:
    a. initiating structure and consideration.
    b. concern for people and concern for production.
    c. employee oriented and production oriented.
    d. relational and job.

Answer: b, difficulty: 2, p. 159

19. Blake and Mouton developed a two-dimensional view of leadership style that identifies various leadership positions as to their "concern for people" and their "concern for production." This theory is called the:
    a. path-goal theory.
    b. managerial grid.
    c. two-factor theory.
    d. contingency model.

Answer: b, difficulty: 1, pp. 159-160

20. Which management style in the managerial grid reflects impoverished management?
    a. 1,9 management
    b. 9,1 management
    c. 9,9 management
    d. 1,1 management

Answer: d, difficulty: 1, p. 160 and Exhibit 10-1

21. Which management style in the managerial grid reflects team management?
    a. 1,9 management
    b. 9,1 management
    c. 9,9 management
    d. 1,1 management

Answer: c, difficulty: 1, p. 160 and Exhibit 10-1

22. What was missing from the behavioral theories of leadership?
    a. an examination of leader's behaviors
    b. consideration of the situational factors that influence success or failure
    c. concern for people
    d. concern for completing the task at hand

Answer: b, difficulty: 1, p. 160

23. Which of the following statements is true concerning contingency leadership theories?
    a. Researchers found that predicting leadership success was more complex than isolating a few traits or preferable behaviors.
    b. The failure to obtain consistent results led to a new focus on situational influences.
    c. The relationship between leadership style and effectiveness suggested that style x would be appropriate under condition a, whereas style y would be more suitable for condition b, and style z for condition c.
    d. All of the above.

Answer: d, difficulty: 2, p. 161

24. Sandy isn't sure whether there is one type of leadership best in all situations. She thinks that group performance is a function of the leader's style and relevant situational factors. Sandy believes in what leadership approach?
    a. behavioral
    b. trait
    c. contingency
    d. grid

Answer: c, difficulty: 2, p. 161

25. Which of the following is NOT a contingency approach to leadership theory?
    a. Fiedler's LPC model
    b. path-goal theory
    c. managerial grid
    d. leader-participation model

Answer: c, difficulty: 2, p. 161

26. The first comprehensive contingency model for leadership was developed by:
    a. Blake and Mouton.
    b. Fred Fiedler.
    c. Abraham Maslow.
    d. Robert House.

Answer: b, difficulty: 2, p. 161

27. _____ proposes that effective group performance depends on the proper match between a leader's style of interacting with his or her subordinates and the degree to which the situation gives control and influence to the leader.
    a. House
    b. Blake
    c. Fiedler
    d. Herzberg

Answer: c, difficulty: 2, p. 161

28. The _____, developed by Fiedler, measures whether a person is task oriented or relationship oriented.
    a. least-preferred coworker questionnaire
    b. path-goal scale
    c. managerial grid
    d. leader-participation survey

Answer: a, difficulty: 2, p. 161

29. Tom is accepted by his staff who trust and respect him. What aspect of Fiedler's situational favorableness does this represent?
    a. leader-member relations
    b. task structure
    c. position power
    d. charismatic leadership

Answer: a, difficulty: 2, pp. 161-162

30. Chris's employees perceive that he is able to give rewards or punishments at will. What aspect of Fiedler's situational favorableness does this describe?
    a. leader-member relations
    b. task structure
    c. position power
    d. initiating structure

Answer: c, difficulty: 3, pp. 161-162

31.   According to Fiedler, the situational factors reflecting the degree of confidence and trust that subordinates have in their leader is:
    a.   leader-member relations.
    b.   task structure.
    c.   position power.
    d.   the least preferred co-worker.

Answer: a, difficulty: 3, pp. 161-162

32.   In Fiedler's model, what are the three situational factors or contingency dimensions that must be assessed?
    a.   initiating structure, consideration, position power
    b.   task structure, position power, leader-member relations
    c.   initiating structure, leader-member relations, consideration
    d.   task structure, consideration, position power

Answer: b, difficulty: 2, pp. 161-162

33.   The leadership theory that views leaders as being inflexible in their ability to change their basic style is the:
    a.   Ohio State studies.
    b.   path-goal theory.
    c.   Fiedler's model.
    d.   leader-participation model.

Answer: c, difficulty: 2, p. 162

34.   What is the leadership model that stated that the two ways to improve leadership effectiveness were (a) to choose the leader whose style best fits the situation, or (b) to change the situation to fit the leader?
    a.   Ohio State studies
    b.   path-goal theory
    c.   Fiedler's model
    d.   leader-participation model

Answer: c, difficulty: 2, pp. 162-163

35.   According to Fiedler's model, Lucy feels she is in a highly favorable leadership situation. She enjoys good leader-follower relations, the task is highly structured, and she has strong position power. According to Fiedler, it would be best if Lucy were what type of leader?
    a.   relationship-oriented leader
    b.   task-oriented leader
    c.   delegating leader
    d.   organization leader

Answer: b, difficulty: 3, pp. 162-163

36. _____ theory argues that leaders establish a special relationship with a small group of their followers.
    a. Leader-member exchange
    b. Path-goal
    c. Leader-participation
    d. Charismatic leadership

Answer: a, difficulty: 1, p. 163

37. Which is NOT characteristic of out-group members according to LMX theory?
    a. They get less of the leader's time.
    b. They get fewer of the preferred rewards that the leader controls.
    c. They have leader-follower relations based on formal authority interactions.
    d. They are more likely to receive special privileges.

Answer: d, difficulty: 1, p. 163

38. LMX theory has confirmed all of the following EXCEPT:
    a. followers with in-group status have lower turnover intentions.
    b. leaders do not differentiate among followers.
    c. the disparities among followers are far from random.
    d. followers with in-group status have higher performance ratings.

Answer: b, difficulty: 2, p. 163

39. _____ developed the path-goal theory.
    a. Herzberg
    b. House
    c. Fiedler
    d. Blake and Mouton

Answer: b, difficulty: 1, p. 163

40. Which is NOT one of the leadership behaviors developed by House in path-goal theory?
    a. directive
    b. supportive
    c. team-oriented
    d. achievement-oriented

Answer: c, difficulty: 2, p. 164

41. Which dimension of House's path-goal theory closely parallels the Ohio State studies' initiating structure?
    a. directive
    b. supportive
    c. team oriented
    d. achievement oriented

Answer: a, difficulty: 2, p. 164

42. In contrast to Fiedler's view of a leader's behavior, House assumes that leaders are:
    a. inflexible.
    b. flexible.
    c. always participative.
    d. None of the above.

Answer: b, difficulty: 3, p. 164

43. Neil's managerial philosophy is based on two ideas - reward people for effective performance and clarify the way for employees trying to accomplish their work goals. Which leadership theory most closely resembles Neil's philosophy?
    a. Fiedler's model
    b. leader-participation model
    c. path-goal theory
    d. charismatic leadership

Answer: c, difficulty: 3, p. 164

44. The _____ leader is friendly and shows concern for the needs of subordinates.
    a. directive
    b. supportive
    c. participative
    d. achievement-oriented

Answer: b, difficulty: 2, p. 164

45. According to the path-goal theory, a leader's behavior is acceptable to the degree that it is viewed as:
    a. an immediate source of satisfaction or as a means of future satisfaction.
    b. equitable.
    c. providing coaching, guidance, support, and rewards.
    d. quantifiable.

Answer: a, difficulty: 2, p. 164

46. The path-goal theory proposes two classes of contingency variables. They are:
    a. task and people.
    b. initiating structure and initiating consideration.
    c. concern for people and concern for production.
    d. environment and subordinate.

Answer: d, difficulty: 2, pp. 164-165

47. Dixie sets challenging goals and expects her subordinates to perform at their highest level. Dixie is a(n) _____ leader.
    a. directive
    b. supportive
    c. participative
    d. achievement-oriented

Answer: d, difficulty: 2, p. 164

48. Dixie consults with subordinates and uses their suggestions before making a decision. Dixie is a(n) _____ leader.
    a. directive
    b. supportive
    c. participative
    d. achievement-oriented

Answer: c, difficulty: 2, p. 164

49. The contingency variable in the path-goal theory that deals with locus of control, experience, and perceived ability is termed:
    a. environment.
    b. subordinate.
    c. task.
    d. concern for people.

Answer: b, difficulty: 2, pp. 164-165 and Exhibit 10-3

50. Which of the following is NOT a hypothesis that has evolved out of path-goal theory?
    a. Subordinates with an internal locus of control will be more satisfied with a directive style.
    b. Directive leadership leads to greater satisfaction when tasks are ambiguous.
    c. Supportive leadership results in high employee performance and satisfaction when subordinates are performing structured tasks.
    d. Directive leadership will lead to higher employee satisfaction when there is substantive conflict within a work group.

Answer: a, difficulty: 3, p. 165

51. Which of the following is NOT one of the contingency variables in the revised Leader-Participation Model?
    a. Importance of the decision.
    b. How well structured the problem is.
    c. Whether subordinates genuinely like the leader.
    d. Whether subordinates buy into the organizational goals.

Answer: c, difficulty: 3, Exhibit 10-4

52. The model that uses a decision tree incorporating seven contingencies and five alternative leadership styles is the:
    a. path-goal theory.
    b. managerial grid.
    c. leader-participation model.
    d. Ohio State studies.

Answer: c, difficulty: 2, p. 165

53. The type of leader who inspires followers to transcend their own self-interests for the good of the organization and who is capable of having a profound effect on followers is a:
    a. transcendental leader.
    b. transformational leader.
    c. transactional leader.
    d. supportive leader.

Answer: b, difficulty: 1, p. 166

54. Which of the following would be considered a transformational leader?
    a. Franklin D. Roosevelt
    b. Steven Jobs
    c. Rudy Gulliani
    d. All of the above.

Answer: d, difficulty: 3, p. 166

55. The type of leader who guides or motivates followers in the direction of established goals by clarifying role and task requirements is a:
    a. transcendental leader.
    b. transformational leader.
    c. transactional leader.
    d. supportive leader.

Answer: c, difficulty: 2, p. 166

56. Which of the following is NOT an attribute of charismatic leaders?
    a. self-confidence
    b. ordinary behavior
    c. a vision
    d. image as a change agent

Answer: b, difficulty: 1, pp. 166-167 and Exhibit 10-5

57. Charismatic leaders are more likely to surface in all the following EXCEPT:
    a. politics.
    b. religion.
    c. a mature company maintaining its success.
    d. a business firm in its infancy.

Answer: c, difficulty: 3, pp. 167-168

58. Charisma has more direct relevance to explaining the success and failure of managers at which organizational level?
   a. top levels
   b. middle levels
   c. lower levels
   d. all levels

Answer: a, difficulty: 2, p. 168

59. Recent studies have indicated that ___ is the best predictor of who will emerge as a leader.
   a. IQ
   b. emotional intelligence
   c. loyalty
   d. social interaction

Answer: b, difficulty: 3, p. 169

60. Leadership effectiveness needs to address the _____ that a leader uses in trying to achieve goals as well as the content of those goals.
   a. speed
   b. means
   c. efficiency
   d. technology

Answer: b, difficulty: 2, p. 169

61. All of the following statements concerning cross-cultural leadership are true EXCEPT:
   a. Leaders need to adjust their style to the unique cultural aspects of a country.
   b. A leader's choice of a style is constrained by the cultural conditions that his or her followers have come to expect.
   c. Korean leaders are expected to be paternalistic toward employees.
   d. All of the above.

Answer: d, difficulty: 3, p. 170

62. A situation in which leadership may NOT be important is when:
   a. employees are inexperienced.
   b. jobs are ambiguous.
   c. employees lack professionalism.
   d. organizations have explicit formalized procedures.

Answer: d, difficulty: 2, pp. 170-171

63. Which of the following is NOT included in the five dimensions that underlie the concept of trust?
   a. integrity
   b. competence
   c. resourcefulness
   d. openness

Answer: c, difficulty: 2, p. 171 and Exhibit 10-6

64. _____ is the dimension of trust that can be defined as reliability, predictability, and good judgment in handling situations.
   a. Integrity
   b. Competence
   c. Loyalty
   d. Consistency

Answer: d, difficulty: 2, pp. 171-172

65. Which dimension of trust encompasses an individual's technical and interpersonal knowledge and skills?
   a. integrity
   b. competence
   c. loyalty
   d. consistency

Answer: b, difficulty: 2, pp. 171-172

66. Honesty and truthfulness are embodied in the definition of which dimension of the concept of trust?
   a. integrity
   b. loyalty
   c. openness
   d. consistency

Answer: a, difficulty: 1, pp. 171-172

67. _____ is the dimension of trust that can be defined as willingness to protect and save face for a person.
   a. Integrity
   b. Loyalty
   c. Openness
   d. Consistency

Answer: b, difficulty: 1, pp. 171-172

68. Which characteristic consistently ranks at the top of most people's list of characteristics they admire in their leaders?
   a. intelligence
   b. competence
   c. honesty
   d. loyalty

Answer: c, difficulty: 2, pp. 171-172

69. Which of the following is NOT one of the three types of trust in organizational relationships?
   a. deterrence-based
   b. position-based
   c. knowledge-based
   d. identification-based

Answer: b, difficulty: 2, p. 173

70. The most fragile relationships are contained in _____ trust, which will work only to the degree that punishment is possible, consequences are clear, and the punishment is actually imposed if the trust is violated.
   a. deterrence-based
   b. position-based
   c. knowledge-based
   d. identification-based

Answer: a, difficulty: 2, p. 173

71. When you trust your new boss even though there is little experience to base that trust on, the relationship is an example of _____ trust.
   a. deterrence-based
   b. position-based
   c. knowledge-based
   d. identification-based

Answer: a, difficulty: 2, p. 173

72. Trust that is based on the behavioral predictability that comes from a history of interaction is termed:
   a. deterrence-based.
   b. position-based.
   c. knowledge-based.
   d. identification-based.

Answer: c, difficulty: 2, pp. 173-174

73. In an organizational context, most manager-employee relationships are:
    a. deterrence-based.
    b. position-based.
    c. knowledge-based.
    d. identification-based.

Answer: c, difficulty: 3, pp. 173-174

74. The highest level of trust is _____ which is achieved when there is an emotional connection between the parties.
    a. deterrence-based
    b. position-based
    c. knowledge-based
    d. identification-based

Answer: d, difficulty: 2, p. 174

75. A long-term, happily married couple is an example of _____ trust.
    a. deterrence-based
    b. position-based
    c. knowledge-based
    d. identification-based

Answer: d, difficulty: 2, p. 174

76. Which of the following is suggested as a way to build trust among team members?
    a. Speak your feelings.
    b. Be fair.
    c. Demonstrate competence.
    d. All of the above.

Answer: d, difficulty: 1, pp. 174-175

TRUE/FALSE

77. Leadership is the organization-granted authority to influence a group toward the achievement of goals.

False, difficulty: 2, p. 156

78. Leaders can emerge from within a group as well as being formally appointed.

True, difficulty: 1, p. 157

79. The theory that some people have specific characteristics necessary for leadership whereas others do not is called implicit personality theory.

False, difficulty: 2, p. 157

80. Research efforts at isolating leadership traits resulted in a number of dead ends.

True, difficulty: 1, p. 157

81. Traits can predict leadership.

True, difficulty: 2, p. 158

82. The difference between trait and behavioral theories is that trait theories rely on the belief that leaders are born whereas behavioral theories rely on the belief that leaders can be taught.

True, difficulty: 2, p. 158

83. In the Ohio State leadership studies, the leadership behavior dimensions of consideration and initiating structure are independent of one another.

True, difficulty: 2, pp. 158-159

84. Consideration refers to the extent to which a leader is likely to define and structure his or her role and those of subordinates in the search for goal attainment.

False, difficulty: 2, pp. 158-159

85. Leaders high in initiating structure and consideration tended to achieve high subordinate performance and satisfaction more frequently than those who rated low either on initiating structure, consideration, or both.

True, difficulty: 3, p. 159

86. According to the University of Michigan studies, the ideal combination for managers is high employee orientation and high production orientation.

False, difficulty: 3, p. 159

87. Blake and Mouton developed the managerial grid, which assesses a leader's "concern for people" and "concern for production."

True, difficulty: 2, p. 159

88. Blake and Mouton concluded that managers perform best under a 1,1 style.

False, difficulty: 1, p. 160

89. Missing from behavioral theories of leadership was consideration of the situational factors that influence success or failure.

True, difficulty: 2, p. 160

90. Examples of contingency theories are the path-goal theory and the managerial grid.

False, difficulty: 2, p. 161

91. There was very little success in behavioral leadership theories in identifying consistent relationships between patterns of leadership behavior and group performance.

True, difficulty: 2, p. 161

92. In Fiedler's leadership model, the questionnaire of contrasting adjectives used to determine a person's basic style is called the Leader Behavior Description Questionnaire.

False, difficulty: 2, p. 161

93. The LPC questionnaire asks respondents to think of all the co-workers they have ever had and to describe the one person they least enjoyed working with by rating that person on a scale of 1 to 8 for each of the 16 sets of contrasting adjectives.

True, difficulty: 2, p. 161

94. Fiedler viewed an individual's leadership style as fixed.

True, difficulty: 1, p. 161

95. According to Fiedler, if a situation requires a task-oriented leader and the person in that leadership position is relationship-oriented, either the situation has to be modified or the leader replaced if optimum effectiveness is to be achieved.

True, difficulty: 2, p. 162

96. According to Fiedler's model, high LPC leaders are more effective than low LPC leaders in extremely favorable and unfavorable situations.

False, difficulty: 3, pp. 162-163

97. There is considerable evidence to support at least substantial parts of Fiedler's model of leadership.

True, difficulty: 2, p. 163

98. The logic underlying LPC is well understood.

False, difficulty: 3, p. 163

99. LMX Theory proposes that the leader implicitly categorizes the follower as an "in" or "out" and that relationship changes frequently over time.

False, difficulty: 2, p. 163

100.	Path-goal theory extracts key elements from the Ohio State leadership research.

True, difficulty: 3, p. 163

101.	The leadership model that integrates the expectancy model of motivation with the Ohio State leadership research is the leader-participation model.

False, difficulty: 2, p. 163

102.	The term path-goal is derived from the belief that effective leaders classify the path to help their followers get from where they are to the achievement of their work goals and make the journey along the path easier by reducing roadblocks and pitfalls.

True, difficulty: 3, p. 164

103.	The path-goal theory suggests that a single leader may use all four styles of leadership behavior in different situations.

True, difficulty: 2, p. 164

104.	According to path-goal theory, a leader's behavior is motivational to subordinates to the degree that it is viewed by them as an immediate source of satisfaction or as a means of future satisfaction.

False, difficulty: 3, p. 164

105.	Directive leadership is likely to be redundant among subordinates with high ability or with considerable experience.

True, difficulty: 3, p. 164

106.	Subordinates with an internal locus of control will be most satisfied with a directive style.

False, difficulty: 3, p. 165

107.	Vroom and Yetton developed a leader-participation model that related leadership behavior and participation in decision making.

True, difficulty: 1, p. 165

108.	Vroom and Jago have developed a comprehensive program to guide managers through all the decision branches in the revised model.

True, difficulty: 2, p. 165

109.	Transformational leaders guide or motivate their followers in the direction of established goals by clarifying roles and task requirements.

False, difficulty: 2, p. 166

110. By the force of his personal abilities, Rudy Giuliani is considered a transformational leader.

True, difficulty: 3, p. 166

111. Examples of transactional leaders are Jesse Jackson and Franklin D. Roosevelt.

False, difficulty: 2, p. 166

112. The five personal characteristics of the charismatic leader include having a vision, willing to take risks to achieve that vision, sensitivity to environmental constraints and follower needs, and exhibiting behaviors that are out of the ordinary.

True, difficulty: 3, Exhibit 10-5

113. There is a growing body of evidence indicating that charisma may not be generalizable; that is, its effectiveness may be situational.

True, difficulty: 3, p. 167

114. Charisma probably has more direct relevance to explaining the success and failure of first line supervisors than chief executives.

False, difficulty: 3, p. 168

115. EI is the best indicator of who will emerge as a leader.

True, difficulty: 1, p. 169

116. Leaders must adapt their style to different national cultures.

True, difficulty: 1, p. 170

117. Certain individual, job, and organizational variables can act as substitutes for leadership.

True, difficulty: 2, p. 170

118. Charismatic leaders often perform poorly after a crisis subsides and ordinary conditions return.

True, difficulty: 3, p. 171

119. Most of us find it hard, if not impossible, to trust someone immediately if we don't know anything about them.

True, difficulty: 1, p. 171

120. Loyalty and competence are two of the dimensions that underlie the concept of trust.

True, difficulty: 2, p. 171

121. Competence is reliability, predictability, and good judgment in handling situations.

False, difficulty: 2, p. 172

122. When followers trust a leader, they are willing to be vulnerable to the leader's actions.

True, difficulty: 2, p. 172

123. There are three types of trust in organizational relationships: deterrence-based, position-based, and knowledge-based.

False, difficulty: 2, p. 173

124. One violation or inconsistency can destroy deterrence-based trust.

True, difficulty: 2, p. 173

125. Most new relationships begin on a base of knowledge.

False, difficulty: 2, p. 173

126. Most organizational relationships are rooted in knowledge-based trust.

True, difficulty: 2, pp. 173-174

127. At the knowledge-based trust level, trust is not necessarily broken by inconsistent behavior.

True, difficulty: 2, pp. 173-174

128. The highest level of trust is knowledge-based trust.

False, difficulty: 2, pp. 173-174

129. Identification-based trust is the type of trust that managers ideally seek in teams.

True, difficulty: 2, p. 174

130. Mistrust comes as much from what people don't know as from what they do know.

True, difficulty: 2, p. 174

131. In building trust, it is important to give credit where it's due.

True, difficulty: 1, p. 174

ESSAY

132. Define leadership.

Leadership is the ability to influence a group toward the achievement of goals. The source of this influence may be formal or informal. Not all leaders are managers and not all managers are leaders. Just because an organization provides its managers with certain rights is no assurance that they will be able to lead effectively. Leaders can emerge from within a group as well as being formally appointed.

pp. 156-157

133. Discuss the failings of trait theories and the move to behavioral theories of leadership.

The primary failing of trait theories is that they ignore situational factors. Possessing the appropriate traits only makes it more likely that an individual will be an effective leader. He or she still has to take the right actions. And the right actions in one situation are not necessarily right for a different situation. The inability to strike gold in the trait mines led researchers to look at the behaviors that specific leaders exhibited.

p. 158

134. Discuss Blake and Mouton's managerial grid.

Blake and Mouton developed the managerial grid based on the styles of concern for people and concern for production. The grid has nine possible positions along each axis, creating eighty-one different positions in which the leader's style may fall. The grid does not show results produced but rather the dominating factors in a leader's thinking in regard to getting results. They concluded that managers perform best under a 9,9 style. The 9,1 style was called task-oriented and the 1,9 was called country-club type.

pp. 159-160

135. Explain Fiedler's contingency model.

Fred Fiedler's leadership model proposes that effective group performance depends on the proper match between the leader's style of interacting with his or her subordinates and the degree to which the situation gives control and influence to the leader. He used the least-preferred co-worker (LPC) questionnaire to determine if leaders are task-oriented or relationship-oriented. After an individual's basic leadership style has been assessed through the LPC, it is necessary to match the leader with the situation. The three situational factors are leader-member relations, task structure, and position power. Fiedler concluded that task-oriented leaders tend to perform better in situations that were very favorable to them and in situations that were very unfavorable. If there is not a match between the situation and leader's style, either the situation has to be modified or the leader replaced if optimum effectiveness is to be achieved.

pp. 161-163

136. Contrast in-group and out-group members according to LMX theory.

The leader-member exchange (LMX) theory argues that leaders establish a special relationship with a small group of their followers. These individuals make up the leader's in-group. These are the people that the leader trusts, get a disproportionate amount of the leader's time, and are more likely to receive special privileges. Other followers fall into the out-group. They get less of the leader's time, fewer of the preferred rewards that the leader controls, and have leader-follower relations based on formal authority interactions.

p. 163

137. List examples of some hypotheses that have resulted from path-goal theory.

Some hypotheses that have evolved out of path-goal theory are as follows:
1. Directive leadership leads to greater satisfaction when tasks are ambiguous or stressful than when they are highly structured and well laid out.
2. Supportive leadership results in high employee performance and satisfaction when subordinates are performing structured tasks.
3. Directive leadership is likely to be redundant among subordinates with high ability or with considerable experience.
4. The clearer and more bureaucratic the formal authority relationships, the more leaders should exhibit supportive behavior and deemphasize directive behavior.
5. Directive leadership will lead to higher employee satisfaction when there is substantive conflict within a work group.
6. Subordinates with an internal locus of control will be most satisfied with a participative style.
7. Subordinates with an external locus of control will be most satisfied with a directive style.
8. Achievement-oriented leadership will increase subordinates' expectations that effort will lead to high performance when tasks are ambiguously structured.

p. 165

138. Explain how the Vroom-Yetton leader-participation model relates leadership behavior and participation in decision making.

Recognizing that task structures have varying demands for routine and nonroutine activities, Vroom and Yetton argued that leader behavior must adjust to reflect the task structure. Their model provided a sequential set of rules that should be followed in determining the form and amount of participation in decision making as determined by different types of situations. The model was a decision tree incorporating seven contingencies and five alternative leadership styles.

pp. 165-166

139. Explain the difference between transactional and transformational (charismatic) leadership.

Transactional leaders guide or motivate their followers in the direction of established goals by clarifying role and task requirements. The type of leader who inspires followers to transcend their own self-interests for the good of the organization and who is capable of having a profound and extraordinary effect on his or her followers is the transformational

having a profound and extraordinary effect on his or her followers is the transformational (or charismatic) leader. Examples of transformational leaders are Jesse Jackson, Winston Churchill, Franklin D. Roosevelt, and Rudy Giuliani. By the force of their personal abilities they transform their followers by raising the sense of the importance and value of their tasks. "I'd walk through fire if my boss asked me" is the kind of support that charismatic leaders inspire.

p. 166

140. What characteristics differentiate charismatic leaders from non-charismatic ones?

Charismatic leaders possess five attributes. Charismatic leaders have self-confidence. They have complete confidence in their judgment and ability. They also have a vision. They have an idealized goal that proposes a future better than the status quo. Charismatic leaders have a strong conviction in that vision and demonstrate extraordinary behavior. They engage in behavior that is perceived as novel, unconventional, and counter to norms. And charismatic leaders have an image as a change agent. They are perceived as agents of radical change rather than as caretakers of the status quo.

Exhibit 10-5

141. Explain the relationship between EI and leadership effectiveness.

Without EI, a person can have outstanding training, a highly analytical mind, a long-term vision, and an endless supply of terrific ideas, but still not make a great leader. The evidence indicates that the higher the rank of a person considered to be a star performer, the more that EI capabilities surface as the reason for his of her effectiveness. EI has shown to be positively related to job performance at all levels. But it appears to be especially relevant in jobs that demand a high degree of social interaction. And of course, that's what leadership is all about. EI is an essential element in leadership effectiveness.

p. 169

142. Explain how cross-cultural leadership is consistent with contingency leadership.

National culture affects leadership style by way of the follower. A leader's choice of a style is constrained by the cultural conditions that his or her followers have come to expect. Consistent with the contingency approach, leaders need to adjust their style to the unique aspects of a country.

p. 170

143. What are the five dimensions underlying trust?

The key dimensions that underlie the concept of trust are integrity, competence, consistency, loyalty, and openness. Integrity refers to honesty and truthfulness. This seems to be the most critical when someone assesses another person's trustworthiness. Competence encompasses an individual's technical and interpersonal knowledge and skills. You need to believe that the person has the skills and abilities to carry out what he or she says they will do. Consistency relates to an individual's reliability, predictability, and good judgment in handling situations. Loyalty is the willingness to protect and save face for

481

another person. Trust requires that you can depend on someone not to act opportunistically. Openness is the degree to which you can rely on the person to give you the full truth.

pp. 171-172

144. What are the three types of trust found in organizational relationships?

The three types of trust found in organizational relationships are deterrence-based, knowledge-based, and identification-based. The most fragile relationships are contained in deterrence-based trust. One violation or inconsistency can destroy the relationship. This form of trust is based on fear of reprisal if the trust is violated. Individuals who are in this type of relationship do what they say because they fear the consequences from not following through on their obligations. Most new relationships begin on a base of deterrence. Most organizational relationships are rooted in knowledge-based trust. Trust is based on the behavioral predictability that comes from a history of interaction. It exists when you have adequate information about someone to understand them well enough to be able to accurately predict their likely behavior. This trust relies on information rather then deterrence. Most manager-employee relationships are knowledge-based. The highest level of trust is achieved when there is an emotional connection between the parties. It allows one party to act as an agent for the other and substitute for that person in interpersonal transactions. This is called identification-based trust. Trust exists because the parties understand each other's intentions and appreciate the other's wants and desires. This mutual understanding is developed to the point that each can effectively act for the other.

pp. 173-174

145. What can a manager do in order to build trust?

Managers can build trusting relationships in a number of ways. They must practice openness. Mistrust comes as much from what people don't know as from what they do know. People must be kept informed. Managers must be fair. Before making any decisions or taking actions, managers should consider how others will perceive them in terms of objectivity and fairness. They must also speak their feelings. Managers who convey only hard facts come across as cold and distant. Sharing feelings allows others to see the managers as real and human. It is important for managers to tell the truth. If integrity is critical to trust, managers must be perceived as people who tell the truth. Since people want predictability, managers must show consistency. They should take the time to think about their values and beliefs. They must fulfill their promises since trust requires that people believe that managers are dependable. Managers must also maintain confidences. People trust those who are discreet. Finally, they must demonstrate competence. They must develop the admiration and respect of others by demonstrating technical and professional ability with particular attention to communication, negotiating, and interpersonal skills.

pp. 174-175

Chapter 11 Power and Politics

MULTIPLE CHOICE

1. _____ refers to a capacity that A has to influence the behavior of B so that B does something he or she would not otherwise do.
   a. Power
   b. Politics
   c. Dependence
   d. Persuasion

Answer: a, difficulty: 1, p. 176

2. The definition of power implies all of the following EXCEPT:
   a. a *potential* that need not be actualized to be effective.
   b. a *political* environment.
   c. a *dependence* relationship.
   d. individuals have some *discretion* over their own behavior.

Answer: b, difficulty: 2, p. 176

3. The MOST important aspect of power is that it is a function of:
   a. discretion.
   b. dependence.
   c. persuasion.
   d. potential.

Answer: b, difficulty: 2, p. 177

4. One major difference between leadership and power is that:
   a. leadership is organizationally granted.
   b. power does not require goal compatibility.
   c. power requires independence.
   d. research on leadership tends to focus on tactics for gaining compliance.

Answer: b, difficulty: 2, p. 177

5. Leadership research, for the most part, emphasizes:
   a. characteristics of followers.
   b. traits.
   c. style.
   d. behaviors.

Answer: c, difficulty: 3, p. 177

6. The sources of power are divided into two general groupings:
   a. formal and position.
   b. formal and informal.
   c. formal and personal.
   d. informal and personal.

Answer: c, difficulty: 1, p. 177

7. _____ power is based on an individual's position in an organization.
   a. Referent
   b. Expert
   c. Personal
   d. Formal

Answer: d, difficulty: 2, p. 177

8. Which of the following is NOT a source of formal power?
   a. coercive
   b. reward
   c. expert
   d. legitimate

Answer: c, difficulty: 2, p. 177

9. Identify the base of power in the following situation: A person can make things difficult for other people, and you want to avoid getting him or her angry.
   a. coercive power
   b. reward power
   c. legitimate power
   d. referent power

Answer: a, difficulty: 2, pp. 177-178

10. Which power base is dependent on fear?
    a. coercive power
    b. reward power
    c. legitimate power
    d. referent power

Answer: a, difficulty: 2, pp. 177-178

11. Which of the following is a power base?
    a. opportunity
    b. reward
    c. personality
    d. experience

Answer: b, difficulty: 2, pp. 177-178

12. Which of the following bases of power obtains compliance through threats and punishment?
    a. normative
    b. coercive
    c. calculative
    d. compliance

Answer: b, difficulty: 2, pp. 177-178

13. When a bank robber points a gun at the branch manager, his base of power is:
    a. reward.
    b. legitimate.
    c. coercive.
    d. referent.

Answer: c, difficulty: 2, pp. 177-178

14. Allen has the power to dismiss, suspend, or demote Becky. Since Becky values her job, Allen has _____ power.
    a. reward
    b. referent
    c. expert
    d. coercive

Answer: d, difficulty: 2, pp. 177-178

15. The opposite of coercive power is _____ power.
    a. legitimate
    b. expert
    c. reward
    d. referent

Answer: c, difficulty: 2, p. 178

16. Identify the base of power in the following situation: A person has the right, considering his or her position and your job responsibilities, to expect you to comply with reasonable requests.
    a. coercive power
    b. reward power
    c. legitimate power
    d. expert power

Answer: c, difficulty: 1, p. 178

17. Departments that possess information that is critical to a company's performance in times of high uncertainty demonstrate _____ power.
   a. coercive
   b. reward
   c. information
   d. personal

Answer: c, difficulty: 1, p. 178

18. The most frequent access to power is based on one's structural position. This is called _____ power.
   a. legitimate
   b. expert
   c. reward
   d. referent

Answer: a, difficulty: 1, p. 178

19. Which of the following is NOT a source of personal power?
   a. expert
   b. referent
   c. charismatic
   d. coercive

Answer: d, difficulty: 1, p. 179

20. Identify the base of power in the following situation: A person has the experience and knowledge to earn your respect and you defer to his or her judgment in some matters.
   a. coercive power
   b. reward power
   c. legitimate power
   d. expert power

Answer: d, difficulty: 2, p. 179

21. _____ is influence wielded as a result of expertise, special skill, or knowledge.
   a. Coercive power
   b. Reward power
   c. Legitimate power
   d. Expert power

Answer: d, difficulty: 1, p. 179

22. Which power base has become one of the most powerful sources of influence as the world has become more technologically oriented?
   a. legitimate
   b. expert
   c. reward
   d. referent

Answer: b, difficulty: 3, p. 179

23. Which of the following sources of power is due to controlling specialized information?
    a. expert
    b. opportunity
    c. position
    d. knowledge

Answer: a, difficulty: 2, p. 179

24. Identify the base of power in the following situation: You like a person and enjoy doing things for him or her.
    a. coercive power
    b. reward power
    c. legitimate power
    d. referent power

Answer: d, difficulty: 2, p. 179

25. The base of power of a person who has desirable resources or personal traits is:
    a. expert.
    b. referent.
    c. coercive.
    d. reward.

Answer: b, difficulty: 2, p. 179

26. _____ power develops out of admiration of another and a desire to be like that power.
    a. Referent
    b. Expert
    c. Reward
    d. Coercive

Answer: a, difficulty: 1, p. 179

27. Which power base is really an extension of referent power stemming from an individual's personality and interpersonal style?
    a. expert
    b. charismatic
    c. reward
    d. coercive

Answer: b, difficulty: 2, p. 179

28. _____ explains why celebrities are paid millions of dollars to endorse products in commercials.
    a. Coercive power
    b. Reward power
    c. Legitimate power
    d. Referent power

Answer: d, difficulty: 2, p. 179

29. Dependency is inversely proportional to:
    a. sources of power.
    b. financial resources.
    c. bases of power.
    d. alternative sources of supply.

Answer: d, difficulty: 2, p. 179

30. Dependency is decreased when the resource you control is:
    a. important.
    b. scarce.
    c. highly substitutable.
    d. desirable.

Answer: c, difficulty: 2, p. 180

31. ABC Corporation needs a large supply of widgets in order to keep its production line going. ABC uses many suppliers of widgets in order to:
    a. decrease its dependency.
    b. increase its dependency.
    c. negotiate prices.
    d. create a monopoly.

Answer: a, difficulty: 2, p. 180

32. Dependency is increased when the resource you control is _____ and scarce.
    a. expensive
    b. important
    c. substitutable
    d. prestigious

Answer: b, difficulty: 2, p. 180

33. Low-ranking members in an organization who have important knowledge not available to high-ranking members can gain power over the high-ranking members through the factor known as:
    a. substitutability.
    b. goal compatibility.
    c. scarcity.
    d. negotiation.

Answer: c, difficulty: 2, p. 180

34. A resource needs to be perceived as _____ to create dependency.
    a. scarce
    b. plentiful
    c. accountable
    d. substitutable

Answer: a, difficulty: 2, p. 180

35. Which one of the following is FALSE regarding coalitions and power?
    a. Coalitions often seek to maximize their size.
    b. Coalitions are often created where there is a great deal of resource interdependence.
    c. The less routine the task of a group, the greater the likelihood coalitions will form.
    d. Coalitions seek a broad constituency to support their objectives.

Answer: c, difficulty: 2, p. 181

36. More coalitions will likely be created if there is a great deal of _____ and resource interdependence.
    a. management
    b. cooperation
    c. structure
    d. task

Answer: d, difficulty: 3, p. 182

37. The more routine the task of a group, the higher the probability:
    a. that coalitions will form.
    b. of group cohesiveness.
    c. that unions will be rejected.
    d. of sexual harassment.

Answer: a, difficulty: 2, p. 182

38. _____ is defined as unwelcome activity of a sexual nature that affects an individual's employment.
    a. Sexual discrimination
    b. Sexual behavior
    c. Sexual harassment
    d. Sexual atmosphere

Answer: c, difficulty: 1, p. 182

39. Which of the following statements is FALSE regarding sexual harassment?
    a. Individuals in high-status roles believe at times that sexually harassing female subordinates is an extension of their right to make demands on lower-status individuals.
    b. Sexual harassment by bosses typically creates the greatest difficulty for those being harassed.
    c. Coworkers don't have position power, so they typically do not sexually harass peers.
    d. Sexual harassment is about power.

Answer: c, difficulty: 3, p. 182

40. Most studies confirm that the concept of _____ is central to understanding sexual harassment.
    a. equity
    b. power
    c. politics
    d. coalitions

Answer: b, difficulty: 1, p. 182

41. _____ are the most frequent perpetrators of sexual harassment in organizations.
    a. Union bosses
    b. Vice presidents
    c. Coworkers
    d. Subordinates

Answer: c, difficulty: 2, p. 183

42. When employees in organizations convert their power into action, they are engaged in _____.
    a. politics
    b. influence
    c. cooperation
    d. manipulation

Answer: a, difficulty: 2, p. 183

43. _____ is those activities that are not required as part of one's formal role in an organization but that influence, or attempt to influence, the distribution of advantages and disadvantages within the organization.
    a. Legitimate power
    b. Sexual harassment
    c. Decision making
    d. Political behavior

Answer: d, difficulty: 2, p. 184

44. Which of the following is NOT a form of political behavior?
    a. calling on customers
    b. withholding key information from decision makers
    c. spreading rumors
    d. lobbying for a particular decision

Answer: a, difficulty: 2, p. 184

45. A(n) _____ perspective can lead one to believe that employees will always behave in ways consistent with the interests of the organization.
    a. political
    b. nonconformist
    c. nonpolitical
    d. cconomic

Answer: c, difficulty: 2, p. 184

46. An individual most likely to engage in political behavior would have all of the following EXCEPT:
    a. a high self-monitoring score.
    b. a low Mach score.
    c. a high need for power.
    d. an internal locus of control.

Answer: b, difficulty: 2, p. 184

47. Political activity is probably more a function of _____ than of _____.
    a. individual differences; organizational culture
    b. organizational structure; organizational culture
    c. national culture; organizational culture
    d. organizational characteristics; individual differences

Answer: d, difficulty: 2, p. 185

48. In which environment would organizational politics most likely occur?
    a. when organizations use objective criteria in appraising performance
    b. when decisions are made autocratically within an organization
    c. when there is role ambiguity
    d. when there is a high level of trust throughout an organization

Answer: c, difficulty: 3, p. 185

49. The less _____ there is within the organization, the higher the level of political behavior.
    a. knowledge
    b. ambiguity
    c. risk-taking
    d. trust

Answer: d, difficulty: 2, p. 185

50. Certain cultures promote politics. Which of the following is NOT a characteristic of a culture that promotes politics?
    a. low trust
    b. autocratic decision making
    c. zero-sum reward allocation practices
    d. role ambiguity

Answer: b, difficulty: 2, p. 186

51. _____ have consistently been found to be one of the most political actions in organization.
   a. Lack of resources
   b. Promotion decisions
   c. Performance appraisals
   d. All of the above.

Answer: b, difficulty: 2, p. 185

52. The _____ approach to reward allocation treats the reward "pie" as fixed so that any gain one person achieves has to come at the expense of another.
   a. zero-sum
   b. synergistic
   c. arbitration
   d. expanded-purse

Answer: a, difficulty: 2, p. 185

53. Politicking by top management:
   a. gives permission to those lower in the organization to play politics.
   b. implies such behavior is acceptable.
   c. supports the behavior.
   d. All of the above.

Answer: d, difficulty: 2, p. 186

54. There is a greater likelihood that an employee can get away with politicking in the practice of performance evaluation when which of the following are present?
   a. The more that organizations use subjective criteria in the appraisal.
   b. The more that organizations emphasize a single outcome measure
   c. The more that organizations allow significant time to pass between the time of an action and its appraisal.
   d. All of the above.

Answer: d, difficulty: 2, p. 185-6

55. Which of the following is NOT true concerning organizational politics?
   a. There is very strong evidence indicating that perceptions of organizational politics are negatively related to job satisfaction.
   b. The perception of politics tends to increase stress.
   c. The perception of politics tends to increase job anxiety.
   d. Perceived organizational politics leads to increased performance levels.

Answer: d, difficulty: 3, p. 186-7

56. When people perceive politics as a threat rather than as an opportunity, they often respond with:
   a. gifts.
   b. sabotage.
   c. defensive behaviors.
   d. increased politicking.

Answer: c, difficulty: 2, p. 187

57. Which of the following is NOT an example of a defensive behavior?
   a. underperforming
   b. playing safe
   c. misrepresenting
   d. prevention

Answer: a, difficulty: 3, Exhibit 11-2

58. The process by which individuals attempt to control the impression others form of them is called:
   a. impression management.
   b. politicking.
   c. political behavior.
   d. haloing.

Answer: a, difficulty: 1, p. 189

59. Which of the following is NOT an example of an impression-management technique?
   a. acclaiming
   b. self-descriptions
   c. accounts
   d. mirroring

Answer: d, difficulty: 2, pp. 189

60. The impression-management technique that uses excuses, justifications, or other explanations of a predicament-creating event aimed at minimizing the apparent severity of the predicament is _____.
   a. acclaiming
   b. self-descriptions
   c. accounts
   d. mirroring

Answer: c, difficulty: 2, pp. 189

61. A person's explanation of favorable events in order to maximize the desirable implications for that person is an example of:
    a. flattery.
    b. acclaiming.
    c. favors.
    d. mirroring.

Answer: b, difficulty: 2, pp. 189

62. Admitting responsibility for an undesirable event and simultaneously seeking to get a pardon for the action is termed:
    a. conformity.
    b. accounts.
    c. apologies.
    d. favors.

Answer: c, difficulty: 2, pp. 189

63. When the manager says to the boss, "You're absolutely right on your reorganization plan for the western regional office. I couldn't agree with you more," this is an example of the _____ impression management technique.
    a. conformity
    b. accounts
    c. apologies
    d. favors

Answer: a, difficulty: 2, pp. 189

64. When a salesperson says to a peer, "The sales in our division have nearly tripled since I was hired," this is an example of the _____ impression management technique.
    a. conformity
    b. acclaiming
    c. apologies
    d. favors

Answer: b, difficulty: 2, pp. 189

65. When a new sales trainee says to a peer, "You handled that client's complaint so tactfully! I could never have handled that as well as you did," this is an example of the _____ impression management technique.
    a. conformity
    b. acclaiming
    c. flattery
    d. favors

Answer: c, difficulty: 2, pp. 189

66. All of the following are questions used to guide ethical actions EXCEPT:
   a. Is the political action motivated by self-serving interests rather than the organization's goals?
   b. Does the political action respect the rights of the individuals affected?
   c. Is the political activity fair and equitable?
   d. All of the above are used as ethical guidelines.

Answer: d, difficulty: 2, p. 191 and Exhibit 11-3

67. Which of the following statements is true concerning power?
   a. If you want to get things done in a group or organization, it helps to have power.
   b. While you seek to maximize other's dependence on you, you will also be seeking to maximize your dependence on others.
   c. By assessing behavior in a political framework, you can still not predict the actions of others.
   d. As a manager you want to minimize your power.

Answer: a, difficulty: 2, p. 191

68. Which of the following statements is NOT true concerning power?
   a. If you want to get things done in a group or organization, it helps to have power.
   b. As a manager, you will want to increase others' dependence on you.
   c. As a manager, you will want to minimize your power.
   d. As a manager, you will seek to minimize your dependence on others.

Answer: c, difficulty: 2, p. 191

69. What is the value of assessing behavior in a political framework?
   a. You can better predict the actions of others.
   b. You can use this information to formulate political strategies that will gain advantage for you.
   c. You can use this information to formulate political strategies that will gain advantage for your work unit.
   d. All of the above.

Answer: d, difficulty: 3, p. 191

TRUE/FALSE

70. Power determines what goals a group will pursue and how the group's resources will be distributed among its members.

True, difficulty: 1, p. 176

71. Power is a function of dependence.

True, difficulty: 1, p. 176

72.   One can have power but not impose it.

True, difficulty: 2, p. 176

73.   Leaders use power as a way to attain group goals, and power is a means for facilitating their achievement.

True, difficulty: 2, p. 177

74.   Power requires goal compatibility whereas leadership does not.

False, difficulty: 2, p. 177

75.   Formal power is based on an individual's position in an organization.

True, difficulty: 2, p. 177

76.   Referent power is dependent on fear.

False, difficulty: 2, pp. 177-178

77.   Coercive and reward power are actually counterparts.

True, difficulty: 2, pp. 177-178

78.   If A can assign B work activities that B finds unpleasant or treat B in a manner that B finds embarrassing, A possesses coercive power over B.

True, difficulty: 2, p. 178

79.   One who can distribute rewards that others view as valuable will have power over those others.

True, difficulty: 1, p. 178

80.   In formal groups and organizations, the most frequent access to power is one's knowledge and expertise.

False, difficulty: 1, p. 178

81.   Positions of authority include coercive and reward powers.

True, difficulty: 2, p. 178

82.   Legitimate power is actually narrower than the power to coerce and reward.

False, difficulty: 2, p. 178

83. Expert power includes acceptance by members in an organization by the authority of a position.

False, difficulty: 3, p. 178

84. You must have a formal position on an organization to have power.

False, difficulty: 1, p. 178

85. Personal power comes from an individual's unique characteristics.

True, difficulty: 1, p. 178

86. Patients follow their physician's advice because the physician has legitimate power.

False, difficulty: 2, p. 179

87. Subordinates may have more expert power than their superiors.

True, difficulty: 2, p. 179

88. Personal power comes from access to and control over information.

False, difficulty: 2, p. 179

89. People in an organization who have data or knowledge that others need can make those others dependent on them.

True, difficulty: 2, p. 179

90. If I like, respect, and admire you, you can exercise referent power over me.

True, difficulty: 2, p. 179

91. Referent power is really an extension of charismatic power.

False, difficulty: 2, p. 179

92. Charismatic power seems from an individual's personality and interpersonal style.

True, difficulty: 2, p. 179

93. Referent power explains why celebrities are paid millions of dollars to endorse products in commercials.

True, difficulty: 1, p. 179

94. Dependency is directly related to alternative sources of supply.

False, difficulty: 2, p. 179

95. Financial independence reduces the power others have over us.

True, difficulty: 2, pp. 179-180

96. The more one can expand his or her options, the more power can be placed in the hands of others.

True, difficulty: 1, p. 180

97. Dependency is increased when the resource one controls is important and scarce.

True, difficulty: 1, p. 180

98. If nobody wants what you've got, it's not going to create dependency.

True, difficulty: 2, p. 180

99. A resource needs to be perceived as scarce to create dependency.

True, difficulty: 2, p. 180

100. The more that a resource has no viable substitutes, the less power that control over that resource provides.

False, difficulty: 3, p. 181

101. Efforts are often made to form a coalition of two or more "outs" who, by joining together, can each better themselves at the expense of those outside the coalition.

True, difficulty: 3, p. 181

102. Coalitions in organizations often seek to maximize their size.

True, difficulty: 1, p. 181

103. More coalitions will likely be created where there is a great deal of task and resource interdependence.

True, difficulty: 3, p. 182

104. The more routine the task of a group or the work of individual jobs, the less the likelihood that coalitions will form.

False, difficulty: 2, p. 182

105. There is a clear agreement as to what specifically constitutes sexual harassment.

False, difficulty: 2, p. 182

106. The problems today are likely to surface around the more subtle forms of sexual harassment.

True, difficulty: 2, p. 182

107. The concept of power is central to understanding sexual harassment.

True, difficulty: 1, p. 182

108. Women in positions of power can be subjected to sexual harassment from males who occupy less powerful positions.

True, difficulty: 2, p. 183

109. Bosses are the most frequent perpetrators of sexual harassment in organizations.

False, difficulty: 3, p. 183

110. Political behavior is within one's formal role requirements on the job.

False, difficulty: 2, p. 184

111. When employees in organizations convert their power into action, they are engaged in politics.

True, difficulty: 2, p. 184

112. Whistle-blowing is a form of political behavior.

True, difficulty: 3, p. 184

113. A political view can explain much of what may seem to be irrational behavior in organizations.

True, difficulty: 2, p. 184

114. Individual characteristics have not been identified as a factor associated with political behavior.

False, difficulty: 2, p. 184

115. Political activity is probably more a function of individual differences than of an organization's culture.

False, difficulty: 2, p. 185

116. Certain organizational cultures actually promote politics.

True, difficulty: 1, p. 185

117. High trust should suppress the level of political behavior.

True, difficulty: 2, p. 185

118. The greater the role ambiguity, the more one can engage in political activity with little chance of its being visible.

True, difficulty: 2, p. 185

119. A zero-sum approach to reward allocations encourages politicking of employees.

True, difficulty: 2, p. 185

120. A general move in North America has been to make organizations more autocratic.

False, difficulty: 1, p. 186

121. "Politicking" by top management, in a sense, gives permission to those lower in the organization to play politics by implying that such behavior is acceptable.

True, difficulty: 2, p. 186

122. For most people - who have modest political skills or are unwilling to play the politics game – outcomes tend to be predominantly negative.

True, difficulty: 3, p. 186

123. When people perceive politics as a threat rather than as an opportunity, they often respond with defensive behaviors.

True, difficulty: 2, p. 187

124. The process by which individuals attempt to control the impressions they form of others is called impression management.

False, difficulty: 3, p. 189

125. Evidence demonstrates that impression-management techniques seem to work.

True, difficulty: 2, p. 191

126. The effective manager accepts the political nature of organizations.

True, difficulty: 2, p. 191

ESSAY

127. Define power and discuss the definition's three implications.

Power refers to the capacity that A has to influence the behavior of B so that B does something he or she would not otherwise do. This definition implies (1) a potential that need not be actualized to be effective, (2) a dependence relationship, and (3) that B has some discretion over his or her own behavior.

p. 176

128. Discuss the differences between leadership and power.

Leaders use power as a way to attain group goals, and power is a means for facilitating their achievement. Power does not require goal compatibility, merely dependence. Leadership requires some congruence between the goals of the leader and those being led. Leadership research seeks answers to questions such as how supportive the leaders should be and how much decision making should be shared with subordinates. The research on power has tended to encompass a broader area and focus on tactics for gaining compliance. It has gone beyond the individual as exerciser because power can be used by groups as well as individuals to control other individuals or groups.

p. 177

129. Describe the seven bases of power.

Seven bases, or sources, of power have been proposed: coercive, reward, legitimate, expert, referent, information, and charismatic. The coercive power base is dependent on fear. One reacts to this power out of fear of the negative results that might occur if one failed to comply. This is the most used power base. The opposite of coercive power is reward power. People comply with the wishes or directives of another because doing so produces positive benefits; therefore, one who can distribute rewards that others view as valuable will have power over them. In formal groups and organizations, the most frequent access to one or more of the power bases is one's structural position. This is called legitimate power. It represents the power a person receives as a result of his or her position in the formal hierarchy of the firm. Expert power is influence wielded as a result of expertise, special skill, or knowledge. This has become one of the most powerful sources of influence as the world has become more technologically oriented. Referent power is identification with a person who has desirable resources or personal traits. If I admire and identify with you, you can exercise power over me because I want to please you. This develops out of admiration. Information power comes from access to and control over information. People in an organization who have data or knowledge that others need can make those others dependent on them. Charismatic power is really an extension of referent power stemming from an individual's personality and interpersonal style.

pp. 177-179

130. Explain the general dependency postulate.

The general postulate is: the greater B's dependency on A, the greater power A has over B. When you possess anything that others require but that you alone control, you make them

501

dependent on you and, therefore, you gain power over them. Dependency, then, is inversely proportional to the alternative sources of supply.

pp. 179-180

131. Explain how dependency is increased.

Dependency is increased when the resource you control is important and scarce. To create dependency, you must control things that are perceived as important. If nobody wants what you've got, it's not going to create dependency. If something is plentiful, possession of it will not increase your power. A resource needs to be perceived as scarce to create dependency.

pp. 180-181

132. What predictions can be made about the formation of coalitions?

Several predictions can be made about the formation of coalitions. First, coalitions in organizations often seek to maximize their size. Second, more coalitions will likely be created when there is a great deal of task and resource interdependence. In contrast, there will be less interdependence among subunits and less coalition formation activity where subunits are largely self-contained or resources are abundant. Third, coalition formation will be influenced by the actual tasks that workers perform. The more routine the task of a group, or the work of individual jobs, the greater the likelihood that coalitions will form.

pp. 181-182

133. Define and explain sexual harassment.

Sexual harassment is defined as unwelcome advances, requests for sexual favors, and other verbal or physical conduct, whether overt or subtle, of a sexual nature. The problems today are likely to surface around the more subtle forms of sexual harassment Ä such as unwanted looks or comments; sexual artifacts (like nude calendars); or misinterpretation of where the line between "being friendly" ends and harassment begins. The concept of power is central to understanding sexual harassment. It's about one individual's controlling or threatening another. It's wrong and it's illegal.

pp. 182-183

134. What is political behavior? Provide some examples of political behavior.

Political behavior is defined as those activities that are not required as part of one's formal role in the organization, but that influence, or attempt to influence, the distribution of advantages and disadvantages within the organization. Political behaviors may include withholding key information from decision makers, whistle-blowing, filing of grievances, spreading rumors, leaking confidential information about organizational activities to the media, or exchanging favors with others in the organization for mutual benefit.

pp. 183-184

135. What organizational factors contribute to political behavior?

Some organizational factors that contribute to political behavior include low trust, role ambiguity, unclear performance evaluation systems, zero-sum reward allocation practices, democratic decision making, high pressures for performance, and self-serving senior managers. These conditions create opportunities for political activities to be nurtured. The less trust there is within the organization, the higher the level of political behavior. The greater the role ambiguity, the more one can engage in political activity with little chance of its being visible. The more that organizations use subjective criteria in the appraisal, emphasize a single outcome measure, or allow significant time to pass between an action and its appraisal, the greater the likelihood an employee can get away with politicking. The more an organization's culture emphasizes the zero-sum or win-lose approach to reward allocation, the more employees will be motivated to engage in politicking. The moves toward democracy in organization is not necessarily embraced by all managers. Sharing power with others rubs some the wrong way. The result is that managers may use the required teams, committees, and group meetings in a superficial way as arenas for maneuvering and manipulating. The more pressure that employees feel to perform well, the more likely they are to engage in politicking. Finally, when employees see the people on top engaging in political behavior, a climate is created that supports politicking.

pp. 185-186

136. Discuss the relationship between the perception of organizational politics and individual outcomes.

There is strong evidence indicating that perceptions of organizational politics are negatively related to job satisfaction. The perception of politics also tends to increase job anxiety and stress. There is preliminary evidence suggesting that politics leads to self-reported declines in employee performance. Perceived organizational politics appears to have a demotivating effect on individuals, thus leading to decreased performance levels.

p. 187 and Exhibit 11-1

137. What are defensive behaviors?

When people perceive politics as a threat rather than as an opportunity, they often respond with defensive behaviors. These are reactive and protective behaviors to avoid action, blame, or change. These behaviors are often associated with negative feelings toward the job and work environment.

p. 187-8

138. Explain four impression management techniques.

There are seven impression management techniques. Self-descriptions are statements made by a person that describe such personal characteristics as traits, abilities, feelings, opinions, and personal lives. Conformity is agreeing with someone else's opinion in order to gain his or her approval. Excuses, justifications, or other explanations of a predicament-creating event aimed at minimizing the apparent severity of the situation are accounts. Apologies refer to admitting responsibility for an undesirable event and simultaneously seeking to get a pardon for the action. Acclaiming is an explanation of favorable events by someone in order to maximize the desirable implications for the person. Flatter is complimenting others about their virtues in an effort to make oneself appear perceptive and likable. Favors include doing something nice for someone to gain that person's approval.

pp. 188

139. What questions should be considered to differentiate ethical from unethical politicking?

To differentiate ethical from unethical politicking, three questions should be considered. The first question addresses self-interest versus organizational goals. Ethical actions are consistent with the organization's goals. The second question concerns the rights of other parties. The third question is related to whether the political activity conforms to standards of equity and justice.

p. 191 and Exhibit 11-3

Chapter 12 CONFLICT AND NEGOTIATION

MULTIPLE CHOICE

1. Which of the following is FALSE regarding conflict?
    a. The definition of conflict is purposely narrow.
    b. Conflict must be perceived by the parties involved.
    c. Conflict can exist when the parties' goals are incompatible.
    d. If no one is aware of a conflict, it is generally agreed that no conflict exists.

Answer: a, difficulty: 2, pp. 193-194

2. The traditional view of conflict argues that conflict:
    a. cannot be avoided.
    b. is good for a group.
    c. indicates a malfunctioning within the group.
    d. increases performance at times.

Answer: c, difficulty: 1, p. 194

3. The _____ view of conflict uses the term synonymously with terms such as violence, destruction, and irrationality in order to reinforce its negative connotation.
    a. traditional
    b. human relations
    c. interactionist
    d. rational

Answer: a, difficulty: 1, p. 194

4. The traditional view of conflict argued that conflict was a dysfunctional outcome resulting from:
    a. poor communication.
    b. a lack of openness and trust between people.
    c. the failure of mangers to be responsive to the needs and aspirations of their employees.
    d. All of the above.

Answer: d, difficulty: 2, p. 194

5. Which view of conflict rationalized its existence?
    a. traditional
    b. human relations
    c. interactionist
    d. rational

Answer: b, difficulty: 1, p. 194

6. The human relations view of conflict advocates:
    a. open communication to resolve conflict.
    b. group therapy to resolve conflict.
    c. encouraging conflict.
    d. acceptance of conflict.

Answer: d, difficulty: 2, pp. 194-195

7. Which of the following is NOT one of the schools of thought on conflict?
    a. traditional
    b. human relations
    c. interactionist
    d. rational

Answer: d, difficulty: 2, pp. 194-195

8. According to the interactionist view of conflict:
    a. conflict is always a negative force in determining group performance.
    b. conflict may benefit a group's performance.
    c. conflict is evident in all groups.
    d. some conflict may be inevitable.

Answer: b, difficulty: 3, p. 195

9. The _____ view encourages conflict.
    a. traditional
    b. human relations
    c. interactionist
    d. rational

Answer: c, difficulty: 2, p. 195

10. Whereas the _____ approach accepted conflict, the _____ approach encourages conflict.
    a. interactionist, human relations
    b. human relations, interactionist
    c. rational, human relations
    d. rational, traditional

Answer: b, difficulty: 3, p. 195

11. The major contribution of the interactionist approach is encouraging group leaders to:
    a. eliminate conflict.
    b. maintain an on-going minimal level of conflict.
    c. avoid conflict.
    d. None of the above.

Answer: b, difficulty: 3, p. 195

12. What differentiates functional from dysfunctional conflict?
    a. overall morale
    b. turnover rates
    c. group performance
    d. type of conflict

Answer: d, difficulty: 2, p. 195

13. Which is NOT one of the types of conflict?
    a. task
    b. performance
    c. relationship
    d. process

Answer: b, difficulty: 1, p. 195

14. Conflict is dysfunctional when it:
    a. serves organizational interests.
    b. hinders group performance.
    c. results in hurt feelings.
    d. serves organizational and self-interests.

Answer: b, difficulty: 2, p. 195

15. _____ conflict relates to the content and goals of the work.
    a. Task
    b. Performance,
    c. Relationship
    d. Process

Answer: a, difficulty: 3, p. 195

16. _____ conflict focuses on interpersonal relationships.
    a. Task
    b. Performance
    c. Relationship
    d. Process

Answer: c, difficulty: 1, p. 195

17. _____ conflict relates to how the work gets done.
    a. Task
    b. Performance
    c. Relationship
    d. Process

Answer: d, difficulty: 2, p. 195

18. Which conflicts are almost always dysfunctional?
    a. task
    b. performance
    c. relationship
    d. process

Answer: c, difficulty: 2, p. 195

19. The order of the four stages of the conflict process is:
    a. cognition and personalization, behavior, potential opposition, and outcomes.
    b. potential opposition, behavior, cognition and personalization, and outcomes.
    c. potential opposition, cognition and personalization, behavior, and outcomes.
    d. behavior, potential opposition, cognition and personalization, and outcomes.

Answer: c, difficulty: 2, p. 195 and Exhibit 12-1

20. The first stage of the conflict process is the:
    a. cognition and personalization stage.
    b. behavior stage.
    c. potential opposition stage.
    d. outcomes stage.

Answer: c, difficulty: 1, pp. 195-196 and Exh. 12-1

21. Which of the following is NOT a potential antecedent condition to conflict?
    a. communication
    b. structure
    c. personal variables
    d. nonroutine activities

Answer: d, difficulty: 2, Exhibit 12-1

22. Which of the following is NOT a potential antecedent condition to conflict?
    a. semantic difficulties
    b. insufficient exchange of information
    c. degree of structure
    d. noise in the communication process

Answer: c, difficulty: 3, Exhibit 12-1

23. Eric is angry at his boss because he received unclear information that led to a serious error. Eric's conflict is the result of the following antecedent condition:
    a. communication factors.
    b. structural conditions.
    c. personal variables.
    d. dogmatic personalities.

Answer: a, difficulty: 2, p. 196

24. Poor communication in organizations:
    a. is the source of all conflict.
    b. is rarely the source of any conflict.
    c. enhances collaboration.
    d. stimulates misunderstanding.

Answer: d, difficulty: 3, p. 196

25. The potential for conflict increases:
    a. when too little communication takes place.
    b. when too much communication takes place.
    c. when too little or too much communication takes place.
    d. when "noise" is removed.

Answer: c, difficulty: 2, p. 196

26. Conflict that results from reward systems that are limited in the amounts available is likely a result of:
    a. communication factors.
    b. structural conditions.
    c. personal variables.
    d. "noise."

Answer: b, difficulty: 2, p. 197

27. Research confirms that participation and conflict are:
    a. positively correlated.
    b. counterproductive.
    c. negatively correlated.
    d. always coexisting.

Answer: a, difficulty: 3, p. 197

28. Which of the following traits is most likely to be possessed by conflict-prone individuals?
    a. highly democratic
    b. high esteem
    c. highly authoritarian
    d. open-minded

Answer: c, difficulty: 2, p. 197

29. Don and Ed are always having conflicts over what is most important. These conflicts probably result from:
    a. communication factors.
    b. structural conditions.
    c. personal variables.
    d. semantic difficulties.

Answer: c, difficulty: 2, p. 197

30. The stage of conflict when individuals become emotionally involved is the:
   a. cognition and personalization stage.
   b. behavior stage.
   c. potential opposition stage.
   d. outcomes stage.

Answer: a, difficulty: 3, p. 197

31. Attributes of the behavior stage of the conflict process include all of the following EXCEPT:
   a. most conflict-handling behaviors are initiated.
   b. member engages in action that frustrates the attainment of another's goals.
   c. conflict is out in the open.
   d. individuals become emotionally involved.

Answer: d, difficulty: 3, p. 198

32. Which of the following is NOT a conflict-handling approach typically available?
   a. communication
   b. competition
   c. collaboration
   d. compromise

Answer: a, difficulty: 2, pp. 198-199

33. Which of the following conflict-handling approaches includes a win-lose struggle?
   a. compromise
   b. competition
   c. collaboration
   d. avoidance

Answer: b, difficulty: 2, pp. 198-199

34. Which of the following conflict-handling approaches includes a win-win approach?
   a. compromise
   b. competition
   c. collaboration
   d. avoidance

Answer: c, difficulty: 2, pp. 198-199

35. When a party recognizes that a conflict exists but reacts by withdrawing from or suppressing the conflict, it is termed:
   a. compromise.
   b. competition.
   c. collaboration.
   d. avoidance.

Answer: d, difficulty: 1, pp. 198-199

36. Which conflict management style attempts to truly satisfy the concerns of both sides through honest discussion?
   a. compromise
   b. competition
   c. collaboration
   d. avoidance

Answer: c, difficulty: 2, pp. 198-199

37. When a manager seeks to appease their opponents and may be willing to place their opponents' interests above their own, which style of conflict management is being used?
   a. competition
   b. avoidance
   c. accommodation
   d. collaboration

Answer: c, difficulty: 3, pp. 198-199

38. In which conflict management style is one party likely willing to be self-sacrificing?
   a. accommodation
   b. competition
   c. compromise
   d. avoidance

Answer: a, difficulty: 2, pp. 198-199

39. Which conflict management style requires that each party give up something?
   a. competition
   b. collaboration
   c. accommodation
   d. compromise

Answer: d, difficulty: 2, pp. 198-199

40. In negotiations between unions and management, _____ is required in order to reach a settlement and agree upon a labor contract.
   a. competition
   b. collaboration
   c. accommodation
   d. compromise

Answer: d, difficulty: 3, pp. 198-199

41. If the cultural climate of a country is low on uncertainty avoidance and high on achievement, it tends to create individuals who favor such conflict-handling techniques as:
   a. accommodation and compromise.
   b. avoidance and accommodation.
   c. competition and collaboration.
   d. compromise and collaboration.

Answer: c, difficulty: 3, p. 199

42. Scandinavian countries, which tend to rate high on nurturing, emphasize the conflict handling techniques of:
    a. compromise or competition.
    b. collaboration or compromise.
    c. avoidance or compromise.
    d. avoidance or accommodation.

Answer: d, difficulty: 3, p. 199

43. Conflict is _____ when it improves the quality of decisions, stimulates creativity and innovation, and fosters an environment of self-evaluation and improvement.
    a. dysfunctional
    b. constructive
    c. destructive
    d. distributive

Answer: b, difficulty: 1, p. 199

44. All of the following are results of conflict EXCEPT:
    a. better decisions.
    b. more creative ideas.
    c. lower quality solutions to problems.
    d. increased probability that the group will respond to change.

Answer: c, difficulty: 2, p. 199-200

45. Conflict is an antidote for:
    a. compromise.
    b. groupthink.
    c. integrative bargaining.
    d. zero-sum resource allocation.

Answer: b, difficulty: 2, p. 200

46. Yahoo! and General Motors are both examples of companies that suffered because of:
    a. too much conflict.
    b. too little conflict.
    c. being top heavy in management.
    d. too lean.

Answer: b, difficulty: 2, p. 200

47. Groups that are _____ tend to produce higher-quality solutions to a variety of problems.
    a. homogeneous
    b. dysfunctional
    c. heterogeneous
    d. of a zero-sum mentality

Answer: c, difficulty: 2, pp. 200-201

48. Heteregeneity among group and organization members can:
    a. increase creativity.
    b. improve the quality of decisions.
    c. facilitate change by enhancing member flexibility.
    d. All of the above.

Answer: d, difficulty: 3, p. 201

49. Which of the following is NOT a consequence of dysfunctional conflict?
    a. reduces group effectiveness
    b. enhances communication
    c. reduces group cohesiveness
    d. threatens group's survival

Answer: b, difficulty: 2, p. 201

50. One common ingredient in organization that successfully create functional conflict is that they:
    a. reward dissent and reward conflict avoiders.
    b. reward dissent and punish conflict avoiders.
    c. punish dissent and punish conflict avoiders.
    d. reward tirades and sarcasm.

Answer: b, difficulty: 3, p. 202

51. _____ is a process in which two or more parties exchange goods or services and attempt to agree on the exchange rate for them.
    a. Conflict
    b. Cognition
    c. Zero-sum bargaining
    d. Negotiation

Answer: d, difficulty: 1, p. 202

52. Which two terms are used interchangeably?
    a. negotiation and bargaining
    b. negotiation and compromise
    c. bargaining and conflict
    d. conflict and compromise

Answer: a, difficulty: 2, p. 202

53. The negotiation strategy that operates under zero-sum conditions is known as:
    a. zero-sum negotiation.
    b. unethical bargaining.
    c. distributive bargaining.
    d. integrative bargaining.

Answer: c, difficulty: 1, pp. 202-203

54. Which of the following is NOT true about distributive bargaining?
   a. Labor-management wage negotiations are an example.
   b. There is a win-lose motivation.
   c. Groups are opposed to each other.
   d. Win-win solutions can be created.

Answer: d, difficulty: 3, p. 203

55. The _____ is found between the resistance points in distributive bargaining.
   a. persuasive point
   b. integrative bargaining point
   c. settlement range
   d. divisive point

Answer: c, difficulty: 2, p. 203

56. _____ is negotiating over who gets what share of a fixed pie.
   a. The winner's curve
   b. Escalation of commitment
   c. Distributive bargaining
   d. Integrative bargaining

Answer: c, difficulty: 2, p. 203

57. The point below which negotiating parties would break off negotiations rather than accept a less favorable settlement is the:
   a. target point.
   b. refusal point.
   c. negative point.
   d. resistance point.

Answer: d, difficulty: 2, p. 203

58. In distributive bargaining, the _____ defines what each negotiator would like to receive.
   a. target point
   b. refusal point
   c. negative point
   d. resistance point

Answer: a, difficulty: 2, p. 203

59. In distributive bargaining, the _____ is the area where the aspiration ranges of the two negotiators overlap.
   a. target point
   b. resistance range
   c. confidence area
   d. settlement range

Answer: d, difficulty: 2, pp. 203-204

60. Which of the following is NOT a condition necessary for integrative bargaining to succeed in organizations?
   a. Parties must be open with information and candid about their concerns.
   b. Parties must be sensitive to the others' needs.
   c. Parties must trust one another.
   d. Parties must be rigid and inflexible.

Answer: d, difficulty: 2, p. 204

61. Which of the following is true about integrative bargaining?
   a. Distributive bargaining is preferable to integrative bargaining.
   b. It builds long-term relationships.
   c. Primary motivation is I win, you lose.
   d. Openness and trust are not necessary.

Answer: b, difficulty: 2, p. 204

62. Which bargaining strategy is preferable for use in intraorganizational behavior?
   a. positive negotiation
   b. integrative bargaining
   c. equal bargaining
   d. distributive bargaining

Answer: b, difficulty: 2, p. 204

63. When people continue a previously selected course of action beyond what rational analysis would recommend, they are illustrating which one of the following biases?
   a. overconfidence
   b. availability of information
   c. irrational escalation of commitment
   d. anchoring

Answer: c, difficulty: 1, p. 205

64. When bargainers assume that their gain must come at the expense of the other party, they are experiencing which decision-making bias?
   a. overconfidence
   b. the mythical fixed pie
   c. the winner's curse
   d. framing negotiation

Answer: b, difficulty: 2, p. 205

65. _____ is the decision-making bias where people tend to be overly affected by the way information is presented to them.
   a. Anchoring and adjustments
   b. Overconfidence
   c. Framing negotiations
   d. Availability of information

Answer: c, difficulty: 2, p. 205

66. The regret one often feels after closing a negotiation is referred to as:
    a. framing negotiations.
    b. the winner's curse.
    c. depression.
    d. mythical fixed pie.

Answer: b, difficulty: 2, p. 205

67. Overall assessments of the personality-negotiation relationship find that:
    a. extroverts make better negotiators.
    b. Type A personalities make ineffective negotiators.
    c. personality traits have no significant effect on either the bargaining process or negotiation outcomes.
    d. certain Myers-Briggs types are associated with more effective negotiations.

Answer: c, difficulty: 3, p. 206

68. Managerial women demonstrate _____ confidence in anticipation of negotiating and are _____ satisfied with their performance after the process is complete.
    a. more; more
    b. more; less
    c. less; more
    d. less; less

Answer: d, difficulty: 3, p. 206

69. Which of the following statements concerning cultural styles is NOT true?
    a. The Chinese tend to draw out negotiations.
    b. The French like conflict.
    c. The Japanese negotiate to develop a relationship and a commitment to work together.
    d. Americans are known for patience in negotiations.

Answer: d, difficulty: 1, pp. 206-207

70. Which of the following findings about negotiating style is true?
    a. North Americans try to persuade by relying on facts and appealing to logic.
    b. North Americans treat deadlines as unimportant.
    c. Arabs try to persuade by appealing to logic.
    d. Russians make concessions easily.

Answer: a, difficulty: 2, p. 207

71. Which of the following is NOT a lesson for managers regarding negotiating?
    a. Emphasize win-lose solutions.
    b. Begin with a positive overture.
    c. Research your opponent
    d. Pay little attention to initial offers.

Answer: a, difficulty: 3, pp. 208-209

TRUE/FALSE

72. If no one is aware of a conflict, it is generally agreed that no conflict exists.

True, difficulty: 1, p. 193

73. The traditional view of conflict argued that conflict was a natural occurrence in all groups and organizations.

False, difficulty: 2, p. 194

74. The traditional view and the human relations view of conflict argue that conflict should be avoided.

False, difficulty: 1, p. 194

75. The interactionist view of conflict argues that some conflict is absolutely necessary for a group to perform effectively.

True, difficulty: 2, p. 194

76. The early approach to conflict assumed that conflict was bad and was to be avoided.

True, difficulty: 2, p. 194

77. A lack of organizational conflict can lead to a lack of creativity.

True, difficulty: 2, p. 195

78. The human relations approach accepted conflict, while the interactionist approach encouraged conflict.

True, difficulty: 3, p. 195

79. Whether a conflict is good or bad depends on the type of conflict.

True, difficulty: 2, p. 195

80. The interactionist view proposes that all conflicts are good.

False, difficulty: 2, p. 195

81. Conflict stimulation is part of the human relations view of conflict.

False, difficulty: 2, p. 195

82. Dysfunctional conflict hinders group performance.

True, difficulty: 1, p. 195

83. In an appraisal of the functional or dysfunctional impacts of conflict on group behavior, we assess whether individual group members perceive the conflict as good or bad.

False, difficulty: 3, p. 195

84. Relationship conflicts are almost always dysfunctional.

True, difficulty: 3, p. 195

85. Process conflict relates to how the work gets done.

True, difficulty: 2, p. 195

86. Task conflict focuses on interpersonal relationships.

False, difficulty: 1, p. 195

87. For process conflict to be productive it must be kept low.

True, difficulty: 3, p. 195

88. The first stage of the conflict process is cognition.

False, difficulty: 2, pp. 195-196 and Exhibit 12-1

89. Poor communication is the source of all conflict.

False, difficulty: 2, p. 196

90. The potential for conflict increases when either too little or too much communication takes place.

True, difficulty: 2, p. 196

91. The larger the number of people in a group, the greater the potential for conflict.

True, difficulty: 3, p. 197

92. Tenure and conflict have been found to be inversely related.

True, difficulty: 2, p. 197

93. The potential for conflict tends to be greatest where group members are younger and where turnover is high.

True, difficulty: 3, p. 197

94. Participation and conflict are highly correlated.

True, difficulty: 3, p. 197

95. The most important personal variables in creation of opportunities for conflict are individual value systems and individual idiosyncrasies and differences.

True, difficulty: 3, p. 197

96. The second stage of the conflict process when individuals become emotionally involved is termed *behavior*.

False, difficulty: 2, p. 197

97. The potential for opposition becomes realized in the second stage of the conflict process.

True, difficulty: 2, p. 197

98. If a conflict is perceived it is personalized.

False, difficulty: 3, p. 197

99. Stage IV of the conflict process is when most conflict-handling behaviors are initiated.

False, difficulty: 2, p. 198

100. Competition is a win-win approach to conflict.

False, difficulty: 1, p. 198

101. Accommodation occurs when the parties to a conflict each desire to fully satisfy the concern of all parties.

False, difficulty: 2, p. 198

102. When one party is willing to be self-sacrificing, accommodation is occurring.

True, difficulty: 2, p. 198

103. Avoidance occurs when a party recognizes that a conflict exists but reacts by withdrawing from or suppressing the conflict.

True, difficulty: 2, p. 198

104. The distinguishing characteristic of accommodation is the requirement that each party give up something.

False, difficulty: 2, p. 198

105. National culture appears to be unrelated to conflict-handling behavior.

False, difficulty: 1, p. 199

106. The cultural climate of low uncertainty avoidance and high achievement tends to create individuals who favor competition and collaboration.

True, difficulty: 3, p. 199

107. The interplay between overt conflict behavior and conflict-handling behavior has consequences.

True, difficulty: 2, p. 199

108. Conflict is constructive when it improves the quality of decisions.

True, difficulty: 1, p. 199

109. Conflict exacerbates groupthink.

False, difficulty: 2, p. 200

110. Conflict challenges the status quo and therefore is dysfunctional.

False, difficulty: 2, p. 200

111. General Motors is an example of a company that suffered from too much conflict.

False, difficulty: 3, p. 200

112. Yahoo! provides an example of a company that was too insulated and void of functional conflict.

True, difficulty: 2, p. 200

113. Conflict can be positively related to productivity.

True, difficulty: 2, p. 200

114. Researchers have found that groups composed of members with different interests tend to produce higher quality solutions to a variety of problems than do homogeneous groups.

True, difficulty: 3, p. 200

115. The increasing cultural diversity of the workforce should provide benefits to organizations.

True, difficulty: 1, p. 200

116. A dysfunctional consequence of conflict can be retarding of communication.

True, difficulty: 2, p. 201

117. Organizations that don't encourage and support dissent may find their survival threatened.

True, difficulty: 2, p. 201

118. The Walt Disney Company purposely encourages disruptive meetings to create friction.

True, difficulty: 3, p. 202

119. Two general approaches to negotiation are distributive bargaining and integrative bargaining.

True, difficulty: 1, p. 202

120. Framing negotiations is the process in which two or more parties exchange goods or services and attempt to agree on the exchange rate for them.

False, difficulty: 2, p. 202

121. When negotiating the price of a car, you are probably using a distributive bargaining strategy.

True, difficulty: 2, pp. 202-203

122. The essence of distributive bargaining is negotiating over who gets what share of a fixed pie.

True, difficulty: 1, p. 203

123. Integrative bargaining operates under a win-lose assumption.

False, difficulty: 2, p. 203

124. Integrative bargaining is the strategy most used in today's intraorganizational problem-solving behavior.

False, difficulty: 3, p. 204

125. Irrational escalation of commitment is a decision-making bias that can blind us.

True, difficulty: 1, p. 205

126. When people tend to continue a previously selected course of action beyond what rational analysis would recommend, they are experiencing the mythical fixed pie.

False, difficulty: 2, p. 205

127. Effective negotiators don't give much weight to their opponent's initial offer too early in the negotiation.

True, difficulty: 3, p. 205

128. When negotiators rely too much on readily available information while ignoring more relevant data, they are being blinded by the availability of information.

True, difficulty: 2, p. 205

129. You can reduce the winner's curse by gaining as much information as possible and putting yourself in your opponent's shoes.

True, difficulty: 3, p. 205

<u>ESSAY</u>

130. How is conflict defined?

Conflict is a process that begins when one party perceives that another party has negatively affected, or is about to negatively affect, something that the first party cares about.

p. 193

131. What are the assumptions of the traditional, human relations, and interactionist views of conflict?

The traditional view of conflict argues that conflict must be avoided and that it indicates a malfunction within the group. The human relations view argues that conflict is a natural and inevitable outcome in any group. It need not be evil, but rather has the potential to be a positive force in determining group performance. The interactionist view argues not only that conflict can be a positive force in a group, but explicitly argues that some conflict is absolutely necessary for a group to perform effectively.

pp. 194-195

132. Explain the difference between functional and dysfunctional conflict.

Functional conflict is constructive. These are the conflicts that support the goals of the group and improve its performance. The dysfunctional conflicts are destructive. They are the conflicts that hinder group performance.

p. 195

133. What are the three types of conflict?

The three types of conflict are task, relationship, and process. Task conflict relates to the content and goals of the work. Relationship conflict focuses on interpersonal relationships. Process conflict relates to how the work gets done. Relationship conflicts are almost always dysfunctional. Low levels of process conflict and low-to-moderate levels of task conflict are functional. For process conflict to be productive, it must be kept low. A low-to-moderate level of task conflict consistently demonstrates a positive effect on group performance because it stimulates discussion of ideas that help groups perform better.

p. 195

134. What are the stages in the conflict process?

The four stages in the conflict process are potential opposition, cognition and personalization, behavior, and outcomes. The first step is the presence of conditions that create opportunities for conflict to arise. Stage I is cognition and personalization. If the conditions in stage I generate frustration, then the potential for opposition becomes realized in the second stage. The antecedent conditions can lead to conflict only when one or more of the parties are affected by, and cognizant of, the conflict. Stage II occurs when a member engages in action that frustrates the attainment of another's goals or prevents the furthering of the other's interests. This action must be intended; there must be a known effort to frustrate another. At this juncture, the conflict is out in the open. The interplay between the overt conflict behavior and conflict-handling behaviors results in consequences. It may be either functional or dysfunctional.

pp. 195-201 and Exhibit 12-1

135. What are the three general categories of potential opposition in the conflict process?

The three general categories are communication, structure, and personal variables. The communicative source represents those opposing forces that arise from semantic difficulties, misunderstandings, and noise in the communication channels. Too much information as well as too little can lay the foundation for conflict. Structure includes variables such as size, degree of routinization, specialization, and standardization in the tasks assigned to group members; heterogeneity of the group; leadership styles; reward systems; and the degree of dependence between groups. The larger the group and the more specialized its activities, the greater the likelihood of conflict. The most important personal variables are individual value systems and individual idiosyncrasies and differences.

pp. 195-197

136. What are the five conflict-handling approaches?

The five conflict-handling behaviors are competition, collaboration, avoidance, accommodation, and compromise. When one party seeks to achieve certain goals or to further personal interests, regardless of the impact on the parties to the conflict, he or she competes and dominates. In these win-lose struggles, each party will use his or her own power base in order to resolve a victory in his or her favor. When each of the parties in conflict desires to satisfy fully the concern of all parties, we have cooperation and the search for a mutually beneficial outcome. In collaboration, the behavior of the parties is aimed at solving the problem and at clarifying the differences rather than accommodating various points of view. A party may recognize that a conflict exists but react by withdrawing from or suppressing the conflict. Indifference or the desire to evade overt demonstration of a disagreement can result in withdrawal. When the parties seek to appease their opponents, they may be willing to place their opponent's interests above their own. In order to maintain the relationship, one party is willing to be self-sacrificing. This behavior is accommodation. In compromising, there is no clear winner or loser. Rather, there is a rationing of the object of the conflict, or, where the object is not divisible, one rewards the other by yielding something of substitute value. The distinguishing characteristic of compromise, therefore, is the requirement that each party give up something.

pp. 198-199

137. Discuss the impact of national culture on conflict behavior.

Your approach to handling conflict will, to some degree, be influenced by your cultural roots. People in countries low in uncertainty avoidance feel secure and relatively free from threats of uncertainty. Their organizations, therefore, tend to be rather open and flexible. Countries ranked high in achievement emphasize assertiveness. The cultural climate of low, uncertainty avoidance and high achievement tends to shape a society that is open, direct, and competitive. It would also tend to create individuals who favor such conflict-handling behaviors as competition and collaboration. Uncertainty avoidance and achievement/nurturing rankings would be fairly good predictors of which conflict styles are preferred in different countries.

p. 199

138. How might conflict increase group performance?

Conflict is constructive when it improves the quality of decisions, stimulates creativity and innovation, encourages interest and curiosity among group members, provides the medium through which problems can be aired and tensions released, and fosters an environment of self-evaluation and improvement.

pp. 199-201

139. Discuss the destructive consequences of conflict on a group or organization's performance.

Destructive consequences of conflict on a group include uncontrolled opposition breeds discontent; reduction of group effectiveness; retardation of communication; reduction of group cohesiveness; subordination of group goals to the primacy of infighting among members; and a halt on group functioning that threatens the group's survival.

p. 201

140. Contrast distributive and integrative bargaining.

Distributive bargaining operates under zero-sum conditions. The available amount of resources to be divided is fixed, the primary motivations are I win, you lose, the primary interests are opposed to each other, and the focus of relationships is short term. Integrative bargaining operates under the assumption that one or more settlements exist that can create a win-win solution. The available amount of resources to be divided is variable, the primary motivation is I win, you win, the primary interests are convergent or congruent with each other, and the focus of relationships is long term.

pp. 202-204 and Exh 12-2

141. List and define the decision-making biases that hinder effective negotiation.

The decision-making biases that hinder effective negotiation are as follows:
1. Irrational escalation of commitment. People tend to continue a previously selected course of action beyond what rational analysis would recommend.
2. The mythical fixed pie. Bargainers assume that their gain must come at the expense of the other party.

3. Anchoring and adjustments. People often have a tendency to anchor their judgments on irrelevant information, such as an initial offer.

4. Framing negotiations. People tend to be overly affected by the way information is presented to them.

5. Availability of information. Negotiators of ten rely too much on readily available information while ignoring more relevant data.

6. The winner's curse. People often tend to act in a negotiation as if their opponent is inactive and ignore the valuable information that can be learned by thinking about the other side's decisions. You can reduce this by gaining as much information as possible and putting yourself in your opponent's shoes.

7. Overconfidence. When people hold certain beliefs and expectations, they tend to ignore information that contradicts them. The result is that negotiators tend to be overconfident.

pp. 205-206

142. How can you improve your effectiveness at negotiating?

You can improve your effectiveness at negotiating with several recommendations. Research your opponent. Acquire as much information as you can about your opponent's interests and goals. Begin with a positive overture. Concessions tend to be reciprocated and lead to agreements. Address the problem, not personalities. Concentrate on the negotiation issues, not on the personal characteristics of your opponent. Pay little attention to initial offers. Treat initial offers as merely a point of departure. Emphasize win-win solutions. If conditions are supportive, look for an integrative solution. Create an open and trusting climate. Skilled negotiators are good listeners, ask questions, focus their arguments directly, are not defensive, and have learned to avoid words and phrases that can irritate an opponent. That is, they are good at creating the open and trusting climate necessary for reaching an integrative settlement.

p. 209

Chapter 13 Foundations of Organization Structure

MULTIPLE CHOICE

1.   _____ defines how job tasks are formally divided, grouped, and coordinated.
   a.   An organization's structure
   b.   Work specialization
   c.   Formalization
   d.   Span of control

Answer: a, difficulty: 1, p. 211

2.   Which one of the following is NOT one of the six key elements that managers need to address when they design their organization's structure?
   a.   work specialization
   b.   employee attitudes
   c.   departmentalization
   d.   formalization

Answer: b, difficulty: 2, p. 211

3.   _____ answers the question, "To what degree are tasks subdivided into separate jobs?"
   a.   Departmentalization
   b.   Work specialization
   c.   Span of control
   d.   Chain of command

Answer: b, difficulty: 2, p. 211 and Exhibit 13-1

4.   _____ answers the question, "To whom do individuals and groups report?"
   a.   Departmentalization
   b.   Work specialization
   c.   Span of control
   d.   Chain of command

Answer: d, difficulty: 2, Exhibit 13-1

5.   _____ answers the question, "How many individuals can a manager efficiently and effectively direct?"
   a.   Departmentalization
   b.   Work specialization
   c.   Span of control
   d.   Chain of command

Answer: c, difficulty: 2, Exhibit 13-1

6. _____ answers the question, "On what basis will jobs be grouped together?"
   a. Departmentalization
   b. Work specialization
   c. Span of control
   d. Chain of command

Answer: a, difficulty: 2, Exhibit 13-1

7. _____ answers the question, "Where does decision-making authority lie?"
   a. Departmentalization
   b. Work specialization
   c. Span of control
   d. Chain of command

Answer: d, difficulty: 2, Exhibit 13-1

8. Chain of command provides the answer to the question:
   a. "To what degree are tasks subdivided into separate jobs?"
   b. "Where does decision-making authority lie?"
   c. "On what basis will jobs be grouped together?"
   d. "To whom do individuals and groups report?"

Answer: d, difficulty: 1, p. Exhibit 13-1

9. The essence of _____ is that, rather than an entire job being done by one individual, it is broken down into steps, each step being completed by a separate individual.
   a. departmentalization
   b. work specialization
   c. chain of command
   d. centralization

Answer: b, difficulty: 2, p. 211

10. Ford's assembly line was an example of:
    a. departmentalization.
    b. work specialization.
    c. chain of command.
    d. centralization.

Answer: b, difficulty: 3, p. 211

11. Work specialization is synonymous with:
    a. division of labor.
    b. formalization.
    c. departmentalization.
    d. centralization.

Answer: a, difficulty: 1, p. 211

12. All of the following are human diseconomies from specialization EXCEPT:
    a. boredom.
    b. increased absenteeism.
    c. increased productivity.
    d. high turnover.

Answer: c, difficulty: 2, pp. 212-213

13. Which of the following companies has had success by broadening the scope of jobs and reducing specialization?
    a. General Motors
    b. Chrysler
    c. Saturn
    d. Ford Motor Company

Answer: c, difficulty: 2, p. 213

14. The basis on which jobs are grouped together is called:
    a. span of control.
    b. functionalization.
    c. specialization.
    d. departmentalization.

Answer: d, difficulty: 2, p. 213

15. A newspaper staff could be departmentalized by function in each of the following ways EXCEPT:
    a. photographers, writers, and editors.
    b. news, advertising, and production.
    c. city edition, weekend edition, and out-of-state edition.
    d. operations, finance, and marketing.

Answer: c, difficulty: 3, p. 213

16. Functional departmentalization seeks to achieve economies of scale by:
    a. grouping products together.
    b. placing people with common skills and orientations into common units.
    c. grouping services together.
    d. grouping customer types together.

Answer: b, difficulty: 2, p. 213

17. Procter and Gamble recently reorganized using _____ departmentalization.
    a. functional
    b. product
    c. geographic
    d. process

Answer: b, difficulty: 2, p. 213

18. To group a sales function by western, southern, Midwestern and eastern regions reflects
_____ departmentalization.
a. functional
b. product
c. geographic
d. process

Answer: c, difficulty: 2, p. 213

19. _____ departmentalization offers a basis for the homogeneous categorizing of activities
because of the requirement for different skills.
a. Customer
b. Process
c. Geographical
d. Product

Answer: b, difficulty: 2, pp. 213-214

20. At an Alcoa aluminum tubing plant in upstate New York, production is organized into five
departments: casting, pressing, tubing, finishing, and inspecting, packing, and shipping.
This is an example of _____ departmentalization.
a. functional
b. process
c. product
d. geographic

Answer: b, difficulty: 2, pp. 213-214

21. The office supply firm that has three separate departments Ä one to service retail clients,
one wholesale clients, and one government clients Ä is practicing _____
departmentalization.
a. functional
b. customer
c. product
d. geographic

Answer: b, difficulty: 2, p. 214

22. The trend across organizations of all sizes today is:
a. rigid, functional departmentalization is being complemented by teams that cross over
departmental lines.
b. rigid, geographic departmentalization is being complemented by teams that cross over
departmental lines.
c. rigid, process departmentalization is being complemented by teams that cross over
departmental lines.
d. rigid, product departmentalization is being complemented by teams that cross over
departmental lines.

Answer: a, difficulty: 3, p. 214

23.   _____ is the unbroken line of authority that extends from the top of the organization to the lowest echelon and clarifies who reports to whom.
    a. Unity of command
    b. Span of control
    c. Chain of command
    d. Centralized management

Answer: c, difficulty: 1, p. 214

24.   The rights inherent in a managerial position to give orders and expect them to be obeyed refers to:
    a. coercive power.
    b. legitimacy.
    c. span of control.
    d. authority.

Answer: d, difficulty: 2, p. 214

25.   The unity of command principle specifies that:
    a. all organizations should have an organization chart.
    b. managers should supervise a small number of subordinates.
    c. line and staff positions should be clearly documented.
    d. each employee should report to only one superior.

Answer: d, difficulty: 1, p. 214

26.   Which concepts have substantially less relevance today because of advancements in computer technology and the trend toward empowering employees?
    a. chain of command
    b. authority
    c. unity of command
    d. All of the above.

Answer: d, difficulty: 3, p. 214

27.   Suzanne argues that she can supervise forty employees effectively. Suzanne believes she can have a large:
    a. span of control.
    b. chain of command.
    c. unity of command.
    d. division of labor.

Answer: a, difficulty: 1, p. 215

28.   The number of subordinates a manager can efficiently and effectively direct is termed the:
    a. span of control.
    b. chain of command.
    c. unity of command.
    d. division of labor.

Answer: a, difficulty: 1, p. 215

29. Which of the following is NOT a drawback of a small span of control?
    a. It is expensive.
    b. It makes vertical communication more difficult.
    c. It isolates upper management.
    d. It encourages employee autonomy.

Answer: d, difficulty: 2, p. 216

30. _____ refers to the degree to which decision making is concentrated at a single point in the organization.
    a. Decentralization
    b. Centralization
    c. Span of control
    d. Authority

Answer: b, difficulty: 2, p. 216

31. The more lower-level personnel provide input or are actually given discretion to make decisions, the more _____ there is.
    a. decentralization
    b. centralization
    c. span of control
    d. authority

Answer: a, difficulty: 2, p. 216

32. With _____, action can be taken more quickly to solve problems and employees are less likely to feel alienated from those who make the decisions that affect their work lives.
    a. departmentalization
    b. decentralization
    c. centralization
    d. bureaucracy

Answer: b, difficulty: 2, p. 216

33. The degree to which jobs within the organization are standardized refers to:
    a. centralization.
    b. job variation.
    c. formalization.
    d. routineness.

Answer: c, difficulty: 1, p. 216

34. All of the following are characteristics of high formalization EXCEPT:
    a. explicit job descriptions.
    b. many organization rules.
    c. clearly defined procedures.
    d. high employee discretion.

Answer: d, difficulty: 2, pp. 216-217

35. Which of the following is NOT one of the three most common organizational designs?
   a. simple structure
   b. complex structure
   c. bureaucracy
   d. matrix structure

Answer: b, difficulty: 1, p. 217

36. A _____ has a low degree of departmentalization, wide spans of control, and little formalization.
   a. bureaucracy
   b. matrix structure
   c. simple structure
   d. technological organization

Answer: c, difficulty: 2, p. 217

37. Which is the preferred structure in time of temporary crisis since it centralizes control?
   a. bureaucracy
   b. matrix structure
   c. simple structure
   d. technological organization

Answer: c, difficulty: 3, p. 217

38. Which of the following is NOT a strength of a simple structure?
   a. It's fast.
   b. It's flexible.
   c. Accountability is clear.
   d. It is difficult to establish in large organizations.

Answer: d, difficulty: 2, p. 217

39. One major weakness of the simple structure is that:
   a. it is difficult to maintain in anything other than small organizations.
   b. it is seldom risky.
   c. its low formalization tends to create a lack of information at the top.
   d. it is dependent on many people.

Answer: a, difficulty: 3, p. 217

40. A _____ is characterized by highly routine operating tasks achieved through specialization and very formalized rules and regulations.
   a. simple structure
   b. matrix structure
   c. bureaucracy
   d. functional department

Answer: c, difficulty: 2, p. 218

41. The primary strength of the bureaucracy lies in its:
    a. flexibility.
    b. ability to perform standardized activities in a highly efficient manner.
    c. simplicity.
    d. putting like specialists together.

Answer: b, difficulty: 2, p. 218

42. Which of the following is NOT a weakness of bureaucracies?
    a. displays an obsessive concern with rules
    b. achieves economies of scale
    c. creates subunit conflicts
    d. has difficulty responding rapidly to change

Answer: b, difficulty: 2, p. 218

43. The popularity of the bureaucracy peaked in:
    a. the 1970s and 1980s.
    b. the 1990s.
    c. the 1950s and 1960s.
    d. the 1920s.

Answer: c, difficulty: 2, p. 218

44. Putting like specialties together in functional departments results in:
    a. economies of scale.
    b. minimum duplication of personnel and equipment.
    c. employees who have the opportunity to talk "the same language" among their peers.
    d. All of the above.

Answer: d, difficulty: 3, p. 219

45. A _____ combines two forms of departmentalization - functional and product.
    a. matrix structure
    b. bureaucracy
    c. simple structure
    d. complex structure

Answer: a, difficulty: 2, p. 219

46. A matrix structure combines:
    a. functional and simple structures.
    b. functional and product structures.
    c. simple and product structures.
    d. organic and mechanistic structures.

Answer: b, difficulty: 2, p. 219

47. The strength of functional departmentalization lies in its:
    a. flexibility.
    b. ability to perform standardized activities in a highly efficient manner.
    c. simplicity.
    d. putting like specialists together.

Answer: d, difficulty: 2, p. 219

48. The strength of the matrix lies in its:
    a. flexibility.
    b. ability to facilitate coordination when the organization has multiple complex and interdependent activities.
    c. simplicity.
    d. putting like specialists together.

Answer: b, difficulty: 2, p. 220

49. Which of the following is a disadvantage of the matrix organization?
    a. encourages power struggles
    b. allocates specialists inefficiently
    c. hinders coordination
    d. makes communication difficult

Answer: a, difficulty: 2, p. 220

50. The _____ structure has a dual chain of command.
    a. simple
    b. bureaucracy
    c. complex
    d. matrix

Answer: d, difficulty: 1, p. 220

51. Which is NOT one of the three new structural designs?
    a. team structure
    b. virtual organization
    c. bureaucracy
    d. boundaryless organization

Answer: c, difficulty: 1, p. 220

52. A _____ breaks down departmental barriers and decentralizes decision making to the level of the work team.
    a. virtual organization
    b. boundaryless organization
    c. simple structure
    d. team structure

Answer: d, difficulty: 2, p. 220

53. To achieve the efficiency of standardization while gaining flexibility, among larger organizations, the team structure can complement what is typically a _____.
    a. team structure
    b. virtual organization
    c. bureaucracy
    d. boundaryless organization

Answer: c, difficulty: 3, p. 221

54. A _____ outsources major business functions.
    a. virtual organization
    b. boundaryless organization
    c. simple structure
    d. team structure

Answer: a, difficulty: 2, p. 221

55. The _____ is also called the network or modular organization.
    a. boundaryless organization
    b. team structure
    c. virtual organization
    d. bureaucracy

Answer: c, difficulty: 2, p. 221

56. When large organizations use the virtual structure, they frequently use it to outsource which function?
    a. accounting
    b. human resources
    c. manufacturing
    d. information technology

Answer: c, difficulty: 2, p. 221

57. The major advantage of the virtual organization is:
    a. control.
    b. routinization of tasks.
    c. flexibility.
    d. narrow spans of control.

Answer: c, difficulty: 2, p. 222

58. The primary drawback of the _____ is that it reduces management's control over key parts of its business.
    a. virtual organization
    b. boundaryless organization
    c. simple structure
    d. team structure

Answer: a, difficulty: 2, p. 222

59. A _____ attempts to eliminate vertical and horizontal boundaries while breaking down external barriers.
   a. virtual organization
   b. simple structure
   c. team structure
   d. boundaryless organization

Answer: d, difficulty: 1, p. 222

60. Who coined the term *boundaryless organization*?
   a. Henry Ford
   b. Jack Welch
   c. Peter Drucker
   d. Bill Gates

Answer: b, difficulty: 1, p. 222

61. Characteristics of the boundaryless organization include all of the following EXCEPT:
   a. cross-hierarchical teams.
   b. flatter hierarchy.
   c. it looks more like a silo than a pyramid.
   d. chain of command.

Answer: d, difficulty: 3, p. 223

62. What is the one common technological thread that makes the boundaryless organization possible?
   a. telephones
   b. networked computers
   c. videoconferencing technology
   d. None of the above.

Answer: b, difficulty: 2, p. 223

63. Firms characterized by high formalization and a limited information network are:
   a. organic.
   b. structural.
   c. mechanistic.
   d. contextual.

Answer: c, difficulty: 2, p. 224

64. All of the following are characteristics of the organic structure EXCEPT:
   a. flat.
   b. comprehensive information network.
   c. high participation in decisions.
   d. high formalization.

Answer: d, difficulty: 2, p. 224 and Exhibit 13-6

65. A mechanistic structure has all of the following characteristics EXCEPT:
   a. low horizontal differentiation.
   b. fixed duties.
   c. high formalization.
   d. centralized decision authority.

Answer: a, difficulty: 3, p. 224 and Exhibit 13-6

66. Which of the following is a characteristic of a mechanistic structure?
   a. low horizontal differentiation
   b. low formalization
   c. centralized decision authority
   d. informal communication

Answer: c, difficulty: 2, p. 224 and Exhibit 13-6

67. Organizations following a(n) _____ strategy try to capitalize on the best of two strategies Ä they seek to minimize risk and to maximize opportunity for profit.
   a. organic
   b. mechanistic
   c. imitation
   d. technology

Answer: c, difficulty: 2, p. 225

68. The _____ strategy focuses on the degree to which the organization introduces major new products or services.
   a. imitation
   b. innovation
   c. cost minimization
   d. maximization

Answer: b, difficulty: 1, p. 225

69. An organization pursuing the _____ strategy tightly controls costs, refrains from incurring unnecessary innovation or marketing expenses, and cuts prices in selling a basic product.
   a. imitation
   b. innovation
   c. cost minimization
   d. maximization

Answer: c, difficulty: 3, p. 225

70. All of the following impact an organization's structure EXCEPT:
   a. technology.
   b. industry.
   c. organization size.
   d. environmental uncertainty.

Answer: b, difficulty: 2, pp. 225-226

71. An increase in organization size tends to result in:
    a. less departmentalization.
    b. more rules and regulations.
    c. fewer vertical levels.
    d. more specialization.

Answer: d, difficulty: 2, p. 225

72. _____ refers to how an organization transfers its inputs into outputs.
    a. Technology
    b. Strategy
    c. Integration
    d. Formalization

Answer: a, difficulty: 1, p. 225

73. Which of the following is NOT true about the relationship between organizational structure and employee behavior?
    a. Work specialization contributes to higher employee productivity.
    b. Work specialization contributes to reduced job satisfaction.
    c. People today are more tolerant of overly specialized jobs than were their parents.
    d. There is no evidence to support a relationship between span of control and employee performance.

Answer: c, difficulty: 2, pp. 226-227

TRUE/FALSE

74. Departmentalization defines how job tasks are formally divided, grouped, and coordinated.

False, difficulty: 3, p. 211

75. Departmentalization answers the question, "To what degree are tasks subdivided into separate jobs?"

False, difficulty: 2, Exhibit 13-1

76. Formalization answers the question, "To what degree will there be rules and regulations to direct employees and managers?"

True, difficulty: 2, Exhibit 13-1

77. Work specialization refers to a job that is broken down into a number of steps where each step is completed by a separate individual.

True, difficulty: 1, p. 211

78. Chain of command answers the question "To whom do individuals and groups report?"

True, difficulty: 2, Exhibit 13-1

79. The classical theorists viewed division of labor as an unending source of increased productivity.

True, difficulty: 2, p. 212

80. By the 1960s the point had been reached in some jobs at which the human diseconomies from specialization more than offset the economic advantage.

True, difficulty: 3, p. 212

81. Most managers today see work specialization as obsolete.

False, difficulty: 2, p. 213

82. Departmentalization is the basis on which jobs are grouped together.

True, difficulty: 2, p. 213

83. One of the most popular ways to group activities is by location of suppliers.

False, difficulty: 2, p. 213

84. The strength of product departmentalization is putting similar specialists together.

False, difficulty: 2, p. 213

85. The major advantage to product grouping is increased accountability for product performance.

True, difficulty: 2, p. 213

86. Grouping the sales activities in an office supply firm into service retail, wholesale, and government customers is an example of functional departmentalization.

False, difficulty: 2, p. 214

87. The assumption underlying customer departmentalization is that customers in each department have a common set of problems and needs that can best be met by having specialists for each.

True, difficulty: 2, p. 214

88. Unity of command is an unbroken line of authority that extends from the top of the organization to the lowest echelon.

False, difficulty: 1, p. 214

89. Functional departmentalization is being complemented today by teams that cross over traditional departmental lines.

True, difficulty: 2, p. 214

90. Authority refers to the rights inherent in a managerial position to give orders and expect the orders to be obeyed.

True, difficulty: 2, p. 214

91. If the unity of command is broken, a subordinate might have to cope with conflicting demands or priorities from several superiors.

True, difficulty: 2, p. 214

92. The concepts of chain of command, authority, and unity of command have more relevance today than before the invention of computer technology.

False, difficulty: 2, p. 214

93. All things being equal, the wider or larger the span, the more efficient the organization.

True, difficulty: 1, p. 215

94. At some point, wider spans reduce effectiveness.

True, difficulty: 3, p. 215

95. Small spans of control encourage overly tight supervision and discourage employee autonomy.

True, difficulty: 1, p. 216

96. The trend in recent years has been toward narrower spans of control.

False, difficulty: 2, p. 216

97. Managers can handle a wider span of control when employees know their jobs inside and out or can turn to their co-workers when they have questions.

True, difficulty: 3, p. 216

98. Formalization is the degree to which decision making is concentrated at a single point in the organization.

False, difficulty: 2, p. 216

99. The concept of centralization includes only formal authority.

True, difficulty: 3, p. 216

100. The more that lower-level personnel provide input or are actually given the discretion to make decisions, the more centralization there is.

False, difficulty: 2, p. 216

101. Consistent with recent management efforts to make organizations more flexible and responsive, there has been a marked trend toward decentralizing decision making.

True, difficulty: 2, p. 216

102. Centralization refers to the degree to which jobs within the organization are standardized.

False, difficulty: 2, p. 216

103. If a job is highly formalized, then the job incumbent has a minimum amount of discretion over what is to be done, when it is to be done, and how he or she should do it.

True, difficulty: 2, p. 216

104. An individual's discretion on the job is inversely related to the amount of behavior in that job that is preprogrammed by the organization.

True, difficulty: 2, p. 217

105. The degree of formalization can vary widely among organizations, but not within organizations.

False, difficulty: 3, p. 217

106. The simple structure has a low degree of departmentalization, wide spans of control, and little formalization.

True, difficulty: 1, p. 217

107. The strength of the simple structure is that it is fast, flexible, inexpensive to maintain, and has clear accountability.

True, difficulty: 2, p. 217

108. One major weakness of the simple structure is that it is difficult to maintain in anything other than small organizations.

True, difficulty: 2, p. 217

109. The simple structure is risky since everything depends on one person.

True, difficulty: 3, p. 218

110. The key concept underlying the matrix organization is standardization.

False, difficulty: 1, pp. 219

111. One of the major weaknesses of the bureaucracy is that specialization creates subunit conflicts.

True, difficulty: 2, p. 218

112. Bureaucracy combines two forms of departmentalization Ä functional and product.

False, difficulty: 1, pp. 218-219

113. The peak of bureaucracy's popularity was in the 1990s.

False, difficulty: 2, p. 218

114. Bureaucracy is out of fashion today largely because it has difficulty responding rapidly to change.

True, difficulty: 2, p. 218

115. The most obvious structural characteristic of the matrix is that it breaks the unity-of-command concept.

True, difficulty: 2, p. 219

116. The strength of the simple structure is its ability to facilitate coordination when the organization has multiple complex and interdependent activities.

False, difficulty: 2, p. 220

117. The primary characteristics of the team structure are that it breaks down departmental barriers and centralizes decision-making.

False, difficulty: 2, p. 220

118. The boundaryless organization outsources its major business functions.

False, difficulty: 2, p. 221

119. The prototype of the bureaucracy is today's movie-making organizations.

False, difficulty: 2, p. 221

120. The virtual organization is on a quest for maximum flexibility.

True, difficulty: 1, p. 221

121. The virtual organization outsources many functions to concentrate on what it does best; for most US firms that means focusing on design or marketing.

True, difficulty: 3, pp. 221-222

122. The primary drawback to the virtual organization is that it reduces management's control over key parts of its business.

True, difficulty: 2, p. 222

123. By removing vertical boundaries, management flattens the hierarchy.

True, difficulty: 3, p. 223

124. The way to reduce horizontal boundaries is to replace functional departments with cross-functional teams.

True, difficulty: 2, p. 223

125. Globalization, strategic alliances, customer-organization linkages, and telecommuting are all examples of practices that reduce external boundaries.

True, difficulty: 1, p. 223

126. A mechanistic structure is characterized by fixed duties, formalized communication channels, and centralized decision authority.

True, difficulty: 2, p. 224 and Exhibit 13-6

127. Structure should follow strategy.

True, difficulty: 2, p. 224

128. Wal-Mart could best be described as pursuing the cost-minimization strategy.

True, difficulty: 2, p. 225

129. The innovation strategy characterizes IBM and Caterpillar.

False, difficulty: 3, p. 225

130. Technology using routine tasks is associated with taller and more departmentalized structures.

True, difficulty: 2, p. 226

131. The more dynamic and uncertain the environment, the greater the need for flexibility.

True, difficulty: 2, p. 226

132. There is fairly strong evidence linking centralization and job satisfaction.

True, difficulty: 3, pp. 226-227

133. An organization's internal structure contributes to explaining and predicting employee behavior.

True, difficulty: 3, p. 228

ESSAY

134. What are the six questions that managers need to answer in designing the proper organization structure?

The six key elements that managers need to address when they design their organization's structure are work specialization, departmentalization, chain of command, span of control, centralization and decentralization, and formalization. Work specialization answers the question to what degree task are subdivided into separate jobs. Departmentalization answers the question on what basis jobs will be grouped together. Chain of command answers the question to whom individuals and groups report. Span of control answers the question of how many individuals a manager can effectively and efficiently direct. Centralization and decentralization answer the question where the decision-making authority lies. Formalization answers the question to what degree there will be rules and regulations to direct employees and managers.

Exhibit 13-1

135. Explain work specialization.

Work specialization is also referred to as division of labor. It describes the degree to which tasks in the organization are subdivided into separate jobs. The essence of work specialization is that, rather than an entire job being done by one individual, it is broken down into steps, each step being completed by separate individuals. In essence, individuals specialize in doing part of an activity rather than the entire activity.

pp. 211-213

136. Discuss four departmentalization choices.

The basis by which jobs are grouped together is called departmentalization. One of the popular ways to group activities is by functions performed. Functional departmentalization seeks to achieve economies of scale by placing people with common skills and orientations into common units. Tasks can also be departmentalized by the type of product the organization produces. The major advantage of this type of grouping is increased accountability for product performance, since all activities related to a specific product are under the direction of a single manager. Another way to departmentalize is on the basis of geography or territory. Because each process requires different skills, this method offers a basis for the homogeneous categorizing of activities. A final category of departmentalization is to use the particular type of customer the organization seeks to reach. The assumption underlying customer departmentalization is that customers in each department have a set of problems and needs that can best be met by having specialists for each.

pp. 213-214

137. Explain the relevance of chain of command, authority, and unity of command in today's environment.

The concepts of chain of command, authority, and unity of command have substantially less relevance today because of advancements in computer technology and the trend toward empowering employees. A low-level employee today can access information in seconds that, 20 years ago, was available only to top managers. Networked computers increasingly allow employees anywhere in an organization to communicate with anyone else without going through formal channels. Moreover, the concepts of authority and maintaining the chain of command are increasingly less relevant as operating employees are being empowered to make decisions that previously were reserved for management. With the popularity of self-managed and cross-functional teams and the creation of new structural designs that include multiple bosses, the unity-of-command concept takes on less relevance.

pp. 214-215

138. Discuss span of control and today's trends.

Span of control answers the question of how many subordinates a manager can efficiently and effectively direct. All things being equal, the wider or larger the span, the more efficient the organization. By keeping the span of control to five or six employees, a manager can maintain close control. But small spans have three major drawbacks. First, they are expensive because they add levels of management. Second, they make vertical communication in the organization more complex. The added levels of hierarchy slow down decision making, and tend to isolate upper management. Third, small spans of control encourage overly tight supervision and discourage employee autonomy. The trend in recent years has been toward larger spans of control. Wide spans are consistent with recent efforts by companies to reduce costs, cut overhead, speed up decision making, increase flexibility, get closer to customers, and empower employees. However, to ensure that performance doesn't suffer because of these wider spans, organizations have been investing heavily in employee training. Managers recognize that they can handle a wider span when employees know their jobs inside and out or can turn to their co-workers when they have questions.

pp. 215-216

139. Discuss centralization versus decentralization.

The term centralization refers to the degree to which decision making is concentrated at a single point in the organization. Typically, it's said that if top management makes the organization's key decisions with little or no input from lower-level personnel, then the organization is centralized. In contrast, the more that lower-level personnel provide input or are actually given the discretion to make decisions, the more decentralization there is.

p. 216

140. Explain the characteristics of the simple structure, bureaucracy, and the matrix structure.

The simple structure is not elaborate. It is a flat organization with a low degree of departmentalization, wide spans of control, and little formalization. It usually has only two or three vertical levels, a loose body of employees, and one individual in whom the decision-making authority is centralized. The bureaucracy is characterized by highly routine operating tasks achieved through specialization, very formalized rules and regulations, tasks that are grouped into functional departments, centralized authority, narrow spans of control, and decision making that follows the chain of command. The matrix structure combines two forms of departmentalization Ä functional and product. It breaks the unity-of-command concept since employees have two bosses.

pp. 217-220

141. What are the strengths and weaknesses of the matrix?

The strength of the matrix lies in its ability to facilitate coordination when the organization has multiple complex and interdependent activities. The direct and frequent contact between different specialties in the matrix can make for better communication and more flexibility. Information permeates the organization and more quickly reaches those people who need to take account of it. Further, the matrix reduces bureaupathologies. The dual lines of authority reduce tendencies of departmental members to become so busy protecting their little worlds that the organization's overall goals become secondary. The matrix also facilitates the efficient allocation of specialists. The matrix achieves the advantages of economies of scale by providing the organization with both the best resources and an effective way of ensuring their efficient deployment. The major drawbacks of the matrix lie in the confusion it creates, its propensity to foster power struggles, and the stress it places on individuals. Reporting to more than one boss introduces role conflict, and unclear expectations introduce role ambiguity. The comfort of bureaucracy's predictability is replaced by insecurity and stress.

p. 220

142. Discuss the team structure.

The primary characteristics of the team structure are that it breaks down departmental barriers and decentralizes decision making to the level of the work team. In smaller organizations, the team structure can define the entire organization. More often, particularly among larger organizations, the team structure complements what is typically a bureaucracy.

pp. 220-221

143. What is the virtual organization?

The virtual organization is a small, core organization that outsources major business functions. It is highly centralized, with little or no departmentalization. The virtual organizations have created networks of relationships that allow them to contract out manufacturing, distribution, marketing, or any other business function that management feels can be done better or cheaper by others. The major advantage to the virtual organization is its flexibility. The primary drawback to this structure is that it reduces management's control over key parts of its business.

pp. 221-222

144. What is a boundaryless organization?

The boundaryless organization seeks to eliminate the chain of command, have limitless spans of control, and replace departments with empowered teams. By removing vertical boundaries, management flattens the hierarchy. Status and rank are minimized. And the organization looks more like a silo than a pyramid. Functional departments create horizontal boundaries. The way to reduce these barriers is to replace functional departments with cross-functional teams and to organize activities around processes. The boundaryless organization also breaks down barriers to external constituencies and barriers created by geography. Networked computers allow people to communicate across intraorganizational and interorganizational boundaries.

pp. 222-223

145. What are the differences in mechanistic and organic structures?

The mechanistic structure has extensive departmentalization, high formalization, a limited information network (mostly downward communication), and little participation by low-level members in decision making. The organic structure is flat, uses cross-hierarchical and cross-functional teams, has low formalization, possesses a comprehensive information network (using lateral and upward communication as well as downward), and involves high participation in decision making.

Exhibit 13-6

146. What are the three most common strategies pursued by organizations?

The three most common strategies pursued by organizations are innovation, cost minimization, and imitation. An innovation strategy does not mean a strategy merely for simple or cosmetic changes from previous offerings but rather one for meaningful and unique innovations. An organization that is pursuing a cost-minimization strategy tightly controls costs, refrains from incurring unnecessary innovations or marketing expenses, and cuts prices in selling a basic product. Organizations following an imitation strategy try to capitalize on the best of both of the previous strategies. They seek to minimize risk and maximize opportunity for profit. Their strategy is to move into new products or new markets only after viability has been proved by innovators. They take the successful ideas of innovators and copy them. They essentially follow their smaller and more innovative competitors with superior products, but only after their competitors have demonstrated that the market is there.

p. 225

147. How do organization size, technology, and environmental uncertainty impact organizational structure?

An organization's size affects its structure. Size affects structure at a decreasing rate. The impact of size becomes less important as an organization expands. Once an organization has around 2,000 employees, it's already fairly mechanistic. An additional 500 employees will not have much impact. But adding 500 employees to an organization that has only 300 members is likely to result in a shift toward a more mechanistic structure. Organization structures adapt to their technology. Routine tasks are associated with taller and more departmentalized structures. The relationship between technology and formalization is strong. Routineness is associated with the presence of rule manuals, job descriptions, and other formalized documentation. Static environments create significantly less uncertainty for managers than do dynamic ones. Since uncertainty is a threat to an organization's effectiveness, management will try to minimize it. One way to reduce environmental uncertainty is through adjustments in the structure. The more dynamic and uncertain the environment, the greater the need for flexibility. In stable and predictable environments, the mechanistic form will be the structure of choice.

p. 226

Chapter 14 Organizational Culture

<u>MULTIPLE CHOICE</u>

1. The term _____ can be used to describe a systems variable in organizations that, although hard to define or describe precisely, nevertheless exists, and that employees generally describe in common terms.
    a. organizational strategy
    b. organizational culture
    c. organization design
    d. organizational hierarchy

Answer: b, difficulty: 1, p. 230

2. Organizational _____ refers to a system of shared meaning held by members that distinguishes their organization from other organizations.
    a. culture
    b. strategy
    c. development
    d. design

Answer: a, difficulty: 1, p. 230

3. All of the following are characteristics of an organization's culture EXCEPT:
    a. innovation and risk taking.
    b. attention to detail.
    c. aggressiveness.
    d. differentiation.

Answer: d, difficulty: 2, p. 230

4. The characteristic of organizational culture that describes the degree to which management focuses on results rather than on techniques and processes is termed:
    a. stability.
    b. people orientation.
    c. outcome orientation.
    d. aggressiveness.

Answer: c, difficulty: 2, p. 230

5. The characteristic of organizational culture that addresses the degree to which organizational activities emphasize maintaining the status quo in contrast to growth is termed:
    a. innovation and risk taking.
    b. people orientation.
    c. stability.
    d. aggressiveness.

Answer: c, difficulty: 2, p. 230

6. The characteristic of organizational culture that addresses the degree to which employees are expected to exhibit precision, analysis, and attention to detail is termed:
   a. attention to detail.
   b. people orientation.
   c. stability.
   d. aggressiveness.

Answer: a, difficulty: 2, p. 230

7. The characteristic of organizational culture that addresses the degree to which people are aggressive and competitive rather than easygoing is termed:
   a. innovation and risk taking.
   b. people orientation.
   c. stability.
   d. aggressiveness.

Answer: d, difficulty: 2, p. 230

8. The characteristic of organizational culture that addresses the degree to which work activities are organized around teams rather than individuals is termed:
   a. outcome orientation.
   b. team orientation.
   c. people orientation.
   d. synergy orientation.

Answer: b, difficulty: 1, p. 230

9. Research on organizational culture has sought to measure:
   a. how employees see their organization.
   b. how employees try to change their organization.
   c. how management indoctrinates employees.
   d. whether employees like the characteristics of their organization.

Answer: a, difficulty: 2, p. 230

10. The term _____ is an evaluative term, whereas _____ is a descriptive term.
    a. job design; organizational strategy
    b. organizational strategy; job design
    c. job satisfaction; organizational culture
    d. organizational culture; job satisfaction

Answer: c, difficulty: 2, p. 230

11. The dominant culture in an organization is:
    a. the sum of the subcultures.
    b. synonymous with the organization's culture.
    c. the culture of the industry leader.
    d. the degree of sharedness.

Answer: b, difficulty: 2, p. 231

12. A dominant culture:
    a. expresses the core values that are shared by a majority of the organization's members.
    b. is the micro view of culture.
    c. is likely to be defined by department designations.
    d. differs throughout the organization.

Answer: a, difficulty: 2, p. 231

13. Subcultures are MOST likely to be defined by:
    a. departmental designations.
    b. the dominant culture.
    c. the structure.
    d. the degree of sharedness.

Answer: a, difficulty: 2, p. 231

14. A _____ is characterized by an organization's core values being both intensely held and widely shared.
    a. subculture
    b. strategy
    c. strong culture
    d. division of labor

Answer: c, difficulty: 1, p. 231

15. A strong culture will have the GREATEST impact on:
    a. productivity.
    b. satisfaction.
    c. absenteeism.
    d. behavior.

Answer: d, difficulty: 3, p. 231

16. One specific result of a strong culture should be:
    a. low employee cohesiveness.
    b. low employee satisfaction.
    c. low productivity.
    d. low employee turnover.

Answer: d, difficulty: 2, p. 231

17. Which one of the following terms is NOT part of the definition of a strong culture?
    a. core values
    b. highly structured values
    c. widely shared values
    d. intensely held values

Answer: b, difficulty: 2, p. 231

18. A weak culture is characterized by:
   a. vagueness
   b. ambiguity
   c. inconsistencies
   d. All of the above.

Answer: d, difficulty: 1, p. 231

19. Culture performs all of the following functions EXCEPT:
   a. enhances commitment to one's individual self-interests.
   b. defines boundaries.
   c. conveys members' identity.
   d. enhances social system stability.

Answer: a, difficulty: 2, p. 232

20. All of the following statements are true of the benefits of culture EXCEPT:
   a. culture enhances organizational commitment.
   b. culture increases the consistency of employee behavior.
   c. culture decreases the predictability of employee behavior.
   d. culture reduces ambiguity.

Answer: c, difficulty: 2, p. 232

21. Organizational _____ creates the rules of the game.
   a. leadership
   b. culture
   c. selection process
   d. management

Answer: b, difficulty: 2, p. 232

22. Culture is a liability when:
   a. management is incompetent.
   b. it increases behavioral consistency.
   c. the organization's environment is dynamic.
   d. it increases ambiguity.

Answer: c, difficulty: 2, p. 232

23. Which of the following is NOT true about organizational culture?
   a. It reduces ambiguity.
   b. It is a liability when shared values do not agree with those that will further the organization's effectiveness.
   c. It decreases the consistency of employee behavior.
   d. It enhances organizational commitment.

Answer: c, difficulty: 1, pp. 232-233

24. The founders of an organization lay the foundation for the creation of the organization's:
    a. board members.
    b. founders.
    c. employees.
    d. local community.

Answer: b, difficulty: 1, p. 233

25. Which is NOT true of founders regarding their impact in establishing culture?
    a. The founders have a vision of what the organization should be.
    b. The founders are unconstrained by previous customs of doing things.
    c. The founders have biases on how to get the idea fulfilled.
    d. The founder's influence is largely only symbolic.

Answer: d, difficulty: 2, p. 233

26. Organizational culture is strongly influenced by the organization's founder. Which of the following is NOT a match between founder and organization?
    a. Jim Johnson; Federal Express
    b. Bill Gates; Microsoft
    c. Herb Kelleher; Southwest Airlines
    d. Mary Kay; Mary Kay Cosmetics

Answer: a, difficulty: 2, p. 233

27. Which of the following is NOT listed by your text as a force in sustaining culture?
    a. selection practices
    b. vacation practices
    c. actions of top management
    d. socialization methods

Answer: b, difficulty: 2, p. 233

28. The EXPLICIT goal of the selection process is:
    a. to identify and hire individuals who have the knowledge, skills, and abilities to perform the jobs within an organization successfully.
    b. to spread the organization's culture.
    c. to make a profit.
    d. to socialize new employees.

Answer: a, difficulty: 2, p. 233

29. Which of the following is true about the selection process?
    a. It socializes new employees.
    b. It establishes norms.
    c. It gives applicants information about the organization so they can self-select themselves out of the applicant pool if they perceive a conflict between their values and those of the organization.
    d. It is when employees work out problems discovered during the encounter stage.

Answer: c, difficulty: 2, pp. 233-234

30. Which company uses teams of employees in the selection process to ensure that candidates who can't deal with the level of uncertainty, flexibility, and teamwork of their plants are selected out?
   a. Sony
   b. IBM
   c. Gore
   d. Microsoft

Answer: c, difficulty: 3, p. 234

31. The actions of top management have an impact on an organization's culture because senior executives establish:
   a. norms.
   b. jargon.
   c. management perks.
   d. subcultures.

Answer: a, difficulty: 2, p. 234

32. The process by which employees adapt to an organization's culture is called:
   a. indoctrination.
   b. orientation.
   c. socialization.
   d. confirmation.

Answer: c, difficulty: 2, p. 234

33. Marines going through boot camp and new Disneyland employees watching films about their jobs are both examples of the _____ process.
   a. indoctrination
   b. orientation
   c. socialization
   d. confirmation

Answer: c, difficulty: 2, p. 234

34. Which is the most critical socialization stage?
   a. metamorphosis
   b. time of entry
   c. selection
   d. termination

Answer: b, difficulty: 2, p. 234

35. The _____ stage of socialization occurs before an employee joins an organization so that he or she arrives with an established set of values, attitudes, and expectations.
    a. interviewing
    b. prearrival
    c. encounter
    d. metamorphosis

Answer: b, difficulty: 2, p. 235

36. Which of the following statements concerning socialization is NOT true?
    a. The most critical socialization stage is the time of entry into the organization.
    b. Employees who fail to learn the essential or pivotal role behaviors risk being labeled nonconformists.
    c. The organization will be socializing every employee explicitly throughout his or her career.
    d. Socialization is made up of three stages.

Answer: c, difficulty: 3, p. 235

37. Which of the following is NOT one of the stages of socialization?
    a. interviewing
    b. prearrival
    c. encounter
    d. metamorphosis

Answer: a, difficulty: 2, p. 235 and Exhibit 14-1

38. An example of the prearrival stage of socialization is:
    a. a training program.
    b. a business school.
    c. an orientation program.
    d. job rotation.

Answer: b, difficulty: 2, p. 235

39. In the _____ stage of socialization, employees compare their expectations to the organization's reality.
    a. metamorphosis
    b. encounter
    c. prearrival
    d. investiture

Answer: b, difficulty: 2, pp. 235-236

40. If expectations prove to have been more or less accurate, _____ merely provides a reaffirmation of the perceptions gained earlier.
   a. the prearrival stage
   b. the encounter stage
   c. metamorphosis
   d. the reentry phase

Answer: b, difficulty: 2, pp. 235-236

41. When new members to a group have internalized the norms of the organization, and they understand and accept these norms, _____ is complete.
   a. the prearrival stage
   b. the encounter stage
   c. metamorphosis
   d. the reentry phase

Answer: c, difficulty: 2, p. 236

42. _____ socialization confirms and supports a newcomer's qualities and qualifications when he or she joins an organization.
   a. Individual
   b. Collective
   c. Divestiture
   d. Investiture

Answer: d, difficulty: 2, Exhibit 14-2

43. _____ socialization is characterized by the use of role models who train and encourage a newcomer.
   a. Serial
   b. Random
   c. Collective
   d. Variable

Answer: a, difficulty: 2, Exhibit 14-2

44. _____ socialization tries to strip away certain characteristics of the recruit.
   a. Divestiture
   b. Random
   c. Individual
   d. Investiture

Answer: a, difficulty: 2, Exhibit 14-2

45. The typical promotion system, in which one is NOT advanced to the next stage until he or she is "ready" is an example of a _____ entry socialization option.
    a. collective
    b. random
    c. divestiture
    d. serial

Answer: b, difficulty: 1, Exhibit 14-2

46. A(n) _____ option for the metamorphosis stage of socialization establishes probationary periods and standardizes the stages of transition.
    a. informal
    b. serial
    c. investiture
    d. fixed

Answer: d, difficulty: 2, Exhibit 14-2

47. The stage of socialization when a new member works out the problems discovered during the encounter stage is termed the _____ stage.
    a. prearrival
    b. secondary
    c. metamorphosis
    d. divestiture

Answer: c, difficulty: 2, p. 236

48. Which of the following is a way in which culture is transmitted to employees?
    a. stories
    b. rituals
    c. material symbols
    d. All of the above.

Answer: d, difficulty: 1, p. 237

49. _____ contain a narrative of events about an organization's founders, top management, and key decisions affecting the organization's future course.
    a. Rituals
    b. Stories
    c. Material symbols
    d. Languages

Answer: b, difficulty: 2, p. 237

50. _____ are repetitive sequences of activities that express and reinforce the key values of an organization, what goals are most important, and which people are important and which expendable.
    a. Rituals
    b. Stories
    c. Material symbols
    d. Languages

Answer: a, difficulty: 1, p. 238

51. When faculty undergo a lengthy process in their quest for tenure, this is an example of:
    a. symbolic acceptance.
    b. prearrival socialization.
    c. a ritual.
    d. jargon.

Answer: c, difficulty: 2, p. 238

52. Wal-Mart's company chant is an example of a:
    a. symbolic acceptance.
    b. prearrival socialization.
    c. ritual.
    d. jargon.

Answer: c, difficulty: 3, p. 238

53. Mary Kay Cosmetics' annual award meeting is an example of a corporate:
    a. symbol.
    b. role.
    c. training program.
    d. ritual.

Answer: d, difficulty: 1, p. 238

54. All of the following are examples of material symbols EXCEPT:
    a. top executives' unlimited use of the company jet.
    b. a swimming pool for employees' use.
    c. an annual award meeting.
    d. different types of cars for different executives.

Answer: c, difficulty: 2, p. 238

55. Elegant furnishings, executive perks, and reserved parking spaces are examples of:
    a. rituals.
    b. stories.
    c. material symbols.
    d. languages.

Answer: c, difficulty: 1, p. 238

56. Material symbols convey:
    a. who is important.
    b. the degree of egalitarianism desired by top management.
    c. the kinds of behavior that are appropriate.
    d. All of the above.

Answer: d, difficulty: 2, p. 238

57. _____ are used as a way to identify members of a culture or subculture.
    a. Rituals
    b. Stories
    c. Material symbols
    d. Languages

Answer: d, difficulty: 2, p. 238

58. Forces operating to maintain a given culture include all of the following EXCEPT:
    a. written statements about the organization's mission.
    b. the design of physical spaces and buildings.
    c. the organization's language.
    d. the dominant leadership style.

Answer: c, difficulty: 2, p. 239

59. Cultures in younger organizations are:
    a. deeply ingrained.
    b. seldom reflective of their founders' personal values.
    c. less entrenched.
    d. hard to communicate.

Answer: c, difficulty: 2, p. 239

60. Cultural change is most likely to take place when:
    a. a dramatic crisis exists or is created.
    b. leadership is stable.
    c. culture is strong.
    d. the organization is mature and large.

Answer: a, difficulty: 2, pp. 239-240

61. All of the following are favorable conditions for culture change EXCEPT:
    a. a dramatic crisis exists.
    b. leadership is stable.
    c. the organization is young and small.
    d. the culture is weak.

Answer: b, difficulty: 2, pp. 239-240

62. An organization most likely to shape high ethical standards:
   a. is low in risk tolerance.
   b. is high in aggressiveness.
   c. focuses on means as well as outcomes.
   d. discourages innovation.

Answer: c, difficulty: 3, p. 240

63. Managers in an organizational culture most likely to shape high ethical standards display all of the following characteristics EXCEPT:
   a. supported for taking risks and innovating.
   b. are discouraged from engaging in unbridled competition.
   c. will pay attention to how goals are achieved as well as what goals are achieved.
   d. supported for avoiding mistakes at all costs.

Answer: d, difficulty: 3, pp. 240-241

64. _____ recognizes that people have an inner life that nourishes and is nourished by meaningful work that takes place in the context of community.
   a. Community service
   b. Workplace spirituality
   c. Religion
   d. Social responsibility

Answer: b, difficulty: 2, p. 243

65. Which of the following is NOT a reason for the growing interest in spirituality?
   a. Aging, baby-boomers, reaching mid-life, are looking for something in their life.
   b. The desire to integrate personal life with one's professional life.
   c. In times of economic prosperity, some people have the luxury to engage in a search to reach their full potential.
   d. Formalized religion has worked for many and they want to bring this religion to the workplace.

Answer: d, difficulty: 3, Exhibit 14-4

66. Spiritual organizations are concerned with helping people develop and reach their full potential. This is analogous to Maslow's description of :
   a. self-esteem.
   b. self-actualization.
   c. social.
   d. security.

Answer: b, difficulty: 2, p. 243

67. Ben & Jerry's commitment to socially responsible behavior is an example of which characteristic of spiritual organizations?
   a. toleration of employee expression
   b. employee empowerment
   c. focus on individual development
   d. strong sense of purpose

Answer: d, difficulty: 2, p. 244

68. Which is NOT one of the five cultural characteristics that tend to be evident in spiritual organizations?
   a. strong sense of purpose
   b. trust and openness
   c. stifling of employee expression
   d. focus on individual development

Answer: c, difficulty: 2, p. 244

69. Which of the following is NOT true of spirituality in organizations?
   a. Profits and compatibility are not compatible.
   b. Companies introducing spiritually-based techniques improved productivity
   c. Organizations that provide their employees with opportunities for spiritual development outperformed those that didn't.
   d. Spirituality in organizations has been found to be positively related to creativity.

Answer: a, difficulty: 2, pp. 244-245

70. What conclusion has research reached concerning national cultural and organizational culture?
   a. National culture influences the behavior of people at work.
   b. Organizational culture influences the behavior of people at work.
   c. Organizational culture does have a great influence on the behavior of people at work, but national culture has even more.
   d. None of the above.

Answer: c, difficulty: 3, p. 245

71. The dilemma that management faces when it wants to support differences between employees but also wants those employees to accept the organization's core culture is termed:
   a. information overload.
   b. paralysis of analysis.
   c. the paradox of diversity.
   d. culture shock.

Answer: c, difficulty: 2, pp. 245-246

72.   Organizational culture refers to a system of shared meaning held by members that distinguishes their organization from other organizations.

True, difficulty: 1, p. 230

73.   The characteristic that addresses the degree to which organizational activities emphasize maintaining the status quo is termed outcome orientation.

False, difficulty: 2, p. 230

74.   The degree to which organizational activities emphasize maintaining the status quo in contrast to growth is called stability.

True, difficulty: 1, p. 230

75.   Organizational culture can be viewed as a set of key characteristics that the organization values.

True, difficulty: 2, p. 230

76.   Organizational culture is a descriptive term.

True, difficulty: 1, p. 230

77.   Organizational culture and job satisfaction are synonymous.

False, difficulty: 2, p. 230

78.   Most large organizations have a dominant culture and numerous sets of subcultures.

True, difficulty: 1, p. 231

79.   An organization's subculture expresses the core values that are shared by the majority of the organization's members.

False, difficulty: 2, p. 231

80.   Subcultures tend to develop in large organizations to reflect common problems, situations, or experiences that members face.

True, difficulty: 2, p. 231

81.   A specific result of a strong culture is low employee turnover.

True, difficulty: 2, p. 231

82. It is the shared meaning aspect of culture that makes it such a potent device for guiding and shaping behavior.

True, difficulty: 1, p. 232

83. The stronger an organization's culture, the more management needs to be concerned with developing formal rules and regulations to guide employee behavior.

False, difficulty: 2, p. 232

84. Culture is the social glue that helps hold the organization together by providing appropriate standards for what employees should say and do.

True, difficulty: 2, p. 232

85. Culture enhances social system stability.

True, difficulty: 1, p. 232

86. Culture decreases organizational commitment and the consistency of employee behavior.

False, difficulty: 1, p. 232

87. Culture by definition is elusive, intangible, implicit, and taken for granted.

True, difficulty: 1, p. 232

88. It is a coincidence that employees at Disney theme parks appear to be almost universally attractive, clean, and wholesome with bright smiles.

False, difficulty: 1, p. 232

89. Culture can be a liability when an organization's environment is dynamic.

True, difficulty: 2, p. 232

90. Once established, an organization's culture quickly fades away.

False, difficulty: 1, p. 233

91. Consistency of behavior is an asset to an organization in a dynamic environment.

False, difficulty: 3, p. 233

92. The founders of an organization traditionally have little impact in establishing the early culture.

False, difficulty: 1, p. 233

93. Once culture is in place, practices within the organization act to maintain it by exposing employees to a set of similar experiences.

True, difficulty: 2, p. 233

94. Many of an organization's HR practices reinforce its culture.

True, difficulty: 2, p. 233

95. The final decision about who is hired will be significantly influenced by the decision makers' judgment of how well the candidates will fit into the organization.

True, difficulty: 2, pp. 233-234

96. Through what they say and how they behave, senior executives establish norms that filter down through the organization.

True, difficulty: 1, p. 234

97. Ritualization is the process of adapting new employees to an organization's culture.

True, difficulty: 1, p. 234

98. Old employees are potentially the most likely to disturb the beliefs and customs that are in place.

False, difficulty: 2, p. 234

99. The most critical socialization stage is at the time of entry into the organization.

True, difficulty: 1, p. 234

100. The organization socializes every employee, though maybe no explicitly, throughout his or her career in the organization.

True, difficulty: 1, p. 235

101. The metamorphosis stage of socialization encompasses all the learning that occurs before a new member joins the organization.

False, difficulty: 1, p. 235

102. One major purpose of a business school is to socialize its students into the attitudes and behaviors that business firms want.

True, difficulty: 2, p. 235

103. Entry into the organization begins the prearrival stage of socialization.

False, difficulty: 2, p. 235

104. The encounter stage of socialization is when employee attitudes and behaviors are changed.

False, difficulty: 2, pp. 235-236

105. Military boot camp is an example of collective socialization.

True, difficulty: 2, Exhibit 14-2

106. Serial socialization is characterized by the use of role models who train and encourage a newcomer.

True, difficulty: 3, Exhibit 14-2

107. Investiture socialization tries to strip away certain characteristics of a recruit.

False, difficulty: 2, Exhibit 14-2

108. A fixed schedule of socialization establishes standardized stages of transition.

True, difficulty: 2, Exhibit 14-2

109. Metamorphosis is complete when new members have become comfortable with the organization and their job.

True, difficulty: 1, p. 236

110. The original culture of an organization is derived from the founder's philosophy.

True, difficulty: 1, p. 237

111. Rituals are repetitive sequences of activities that express and reinforce the key values of the organization, important goals, and which people are important.

True, difficulty: 1, p. 238

112. Language acts as a common denominator that unites members of a culture or subculture.

True, difficulty: 2, p. 238

113. One of the better-known rituals is Wal-Mart's company chant.

True, difficulty: 2, p. 238

114. The layout of corporate headquarters is an example of a material symbol.

True, difficulty: 2, p. 238

115. Because an organization's culture is made up of relatively stable characteristics, it is difficult to change.

True, difficulty: 3, p. 239

116. A dramatic crisis will probably deter an organization from cultural change until the status quo is reestablished.

False, difficulty: 2, p. 239

117. It's easier for management to communicate new values when the organization is small.

True, difficulty: 3, p. 239

118. Organizational culture is more likely to change if the culture is strong than if it is weak.

False, difficulty: 1, p. 240

119. Cultural change is a lengthy process – often taking years.

True, difficulty: 2, p. 240

120. Under the most favorable conditions, cultural changes have to be measured in years, not weeks or months.

True, difficulty: 2, p. 240

121. An organizational culture most likely to shape high ethical standards is high in risk tolerance, low-to-moderate in aggressiveness, and focuses on means as well as outcomes.

True, difficulty: 3, p. 240

122. Johnson & Johnson has a strong culture that has long stressed corporate obligations to customers, employees, the community, and shareholders.

True, difficulty: 3, p. 240

123. A weak organizational culture will exert more influence on employees than a strong one.

False, difficulty: 1, p. 240

124. An organization's code of ethics should state the organization's primary values and the ethical rules that employees are expected to follow.

True, difficulty: 1, p. 240

125. Many organizations today are trying very hard to be like French retailers who create a customer-responsive culture that recognizes this is the path to customer loyalty and long-term profitability.

False, difficulty: 2, p. 241

126. Customer-responsive cultures hire service-oriented employees with good listening skills and the willingness to go beyond the constraints of their job descriptions to do what is necessary to please the customer.

True, difficulty: 1, p. 241

127. Studies have shown that friendliness, enthusiasm, and attentiveness in service employees have no significant effect on customers' perceptions of service quality.

False, difficulty: 2, p. 242

128. Workplace spirituality is about organized religious practices.

False, difficulty: 2, p. 243

129. Spiritual organizations recognize the worth and value of people.

True, difficulty: 1, p. 244

130. Managers in spiritually-based organizations are seldom comfortable delegating authority.

False, difficulty: 2, p. 244

131. A recent research study found companies that introduced spiritually-based techniques improved productivity and significantly reduced turnover.

True, difficulty: 3, p. 245

132. Research indicates that organizational culture has a stronger impact than national culture on employees.

False, difficulty: 2, p. 245

133. When an organization is well established, so is its dominant culture.

True, difficulty: 2, p. 246

ESSAY

134. What is organizational culture and what are the primary characteristics that capture the essence of organizational culture?

Organizational culture refers to a system of shared meaning held by members that distinguishes the organization from other organizations. This system of shared meaning is a set of key characteristics the organization values. Innovation and risk taking is the degree to which employees are encouraged to be innovative and take risks. Attention to detail is the degree to which employees are expected to exhibit precision, analysis, and attention to detail. Outcome orientation is the degree to which management focuses on results or outcomes rather than on the technique and process used to achieve those outcomes. People orientation is the degree to which management decisions take into consideration the effect of outcomes on people within the organization. Team orientation is the degree to which work activities are organized around teams rather than individuals. Aggressiveness is the degree to which people are aggressive and competitive rather than easygoing. Stability is the degree to which organizational activities emphasize maintaining the status quo in contrast to growth.

p. 230

135. Explain the difference between a dominant culture and a subculture.

A dominant culture expresses the core values that are shared by a majority of the organization's members. When we talk about an organization's culture, we are referring to its dominant culture. It is this macro view of culture that gives an organization its distinct personality. Subcultures tend to develop in large organizations to reflect common problems, situations, or experiences that members face. These subcultures are likely to be defined by department designations and geographical separation.

p. 231

136. What are the differences between strong and weak cultures?

A strong culture is characterized by the organization's core values being both intensely held and widely shared. The more members that accept the core values and the greater their commitment to those values, the stronger the culture is. A strong culture will have a greater influence on the behavior of its members because the high degree of sharedness and intensity creates an internal climate of high behavioral control. One result of a strong culture should be low employee turnover. A strong culture demonstrates high agreement among members about what the organization stands for. Such unanimity of purpose builds cohesiveness, loyalty, and organizational commitment. These qualities lessen employees' propensity to leave the organization.

p. 231

137. What are the functions that culture performs within an organization?

Culture performs several functions within an organization. First, it has a boundary-defining role; that is, it creates distinctions between one organization and others. Second, it conveys a sense of identity for organization members. Third, culture facilitates the generation of commitment to something larger than one's individual self-interest. Fourth, it enhances social system stability. Culture is the glue that helps hold the organization together by providing appropriate standards for what employees should say and do. Finally, culture serves as a sense-making and control mechanism that guides and shapes the attitudes and behavior of employees.

p. 232

138. When can culture be a liability?

Culture is a liability when the shared values do not agree with those that will further the organization's effectiveness. This situation is most likely to occur when the organization's environment is dynamic. When the environment is undergoing rapid change, the organization's entrenched culture may no longer be appropriate. Consistency of behavior is an asset to an organization in a stable environment. It may, however, burden the organization and hinder its ability to respond to changes in the environment.

pp. 232-233

139. What is the role of founders in creating culture?

The founders of an organization traditionally have a major impact in establishing the early culture. They have a vision of what the organization should be. They are unconstrained by previous customs of doing things or ideologies. The small size that typically characterizes any new organization further facilitates the founders' imposing their vision on all organizational members. Because the founders have the original idea, they also typically have biases on how to get the idea fulfilled. The organizations' culture results from the interaction between the founders' biases and assumptions and what the original members learn subsequently from their own experiences.

p. 233

140. What are the three forces that play a particularly important part in sustaining a culture?

Three forces that play an important part in sustaining culture are selection practices, the actions of top management, and socialization methods. The explicit goal of the selection process is to identify and hire individuals who have the knowledge, skills, and abilities to perform the jobs within the organization successfully. But, typically, more than one candidate will meet any given job's requirements. The final decision about who is hired will be significantly influenced by the decision maker's judgment of how well the candidates will fit into the organization. The selection process sustains an organization's culture by selecting out those individuals who might attack or undermine its core values. The actions of top management also have a major impact on an organization's culture. Through what they say and how they behave, senior executives establish norms that filter down through the organization as to whether risk taking is desirable, how much freedom managers should give their subordinates, what is appropriate dress, what actions will pay off in terms of pay raises, promotions, and other rewards, and the like. No matter how good a job the organization does in recruiting and selection, new employees are not fully indoctrinated in the organization's culture. Because they are least familiar with the organization's culture, new employees are potentially the most likely to disturb the beliefs and customs that are in place. The organization will, therefore, want to help new employees adapt to its culture. This adaptation process is called socialization.

pp. 233-235

141. Explain the three stages of the socialization process.

Socialization can be conceptualized as a process made up of three stages: prearrival, encounter, and metamorphosis. The first stage encompasses all the learning that occurs before a new member joins the organization. In the second stage, the new employee sees what the organization is really like and confronts the likelihood that expectations and reality may diverge. In the third stage, the relatively long-lasting changes take place. The new employee masters the skills required for his or her job, successfully performs his or her new roles, and makes the adjustments to his or her work group's values and norms.

This three-stage process has an impact on the new employee's work productivity, commitment to the organization's objectives, and his or her decision to stay with the organization.

pp. 235-236 and Exhibit 14-1

142. Explain the various entry socialization options.

There are a number of entry socialization options. The more a new employee is segregated from the ongoing work setting and differentiated in some way to make explicit his or her newcomer's role, the more formal socialization is. Informal socialization puts the new employee directly into his or her job, with little or no special attention. New members can be socialized individually. New members can also be grouped together and processed through an identical set of experiences. The time schedule in which newcomers make the transition from outsider to insider can be fixed or variable. A fixed schedule establishes standardized stages of transition. Variable schedules give no advanced notice of their transition timetable. Serial socialization is characterized by the use of role models who train and encourage the newcomer. In random socialization, role models are deliberately withheld. The new employee is left on his or her own to figure things out. Investiture socialization assumes that the newcomer's qualities and qualifications are the necessary ingredients for job success, so those qualities and qualifications are confirmed and supported. Divestiture socialization tries to strip away certain characteristics of the recruit.

Exhibit 14-2

143. What are some of the ways that employees learn culture?

Culture is transmitted to employees with stories, rituals, material symbols, and language. Stories contain a narrative of events about the organization's founders, rule breaking, rags-to-riches successes, reductions in the work force, relocation of employees, reactions to past mistakes, and organizational coping. These stories anchor the present in the past and provide explanations and legitimacy for current practices. Rituals are repetitive sequences of activities that express and reinforce the key values of the organization, what goals are most important, which people are important and which are expendable. Material symbols convey messages to new employees. Messages can also be conveyed by material symbols bestowed on executives. These material symbols convey to employees who is important, the degree of egalitarianism desired by top management, and the kinds of behavior that are appropriate. Many organizations and units within organizations use language as a way to identify members of a culture or subculture. By learning this language, members attest to their acceptance of the culture and, in so doing, help to preserve it.

pp. 237-239

144. What organizational conditions are favorable for cultural change?

Cultural change is most likely to take place when most or all of the following four conditions exist: a dramatic crisis exists or is created, turnover in leadership, young and small organizations, and weak culture. A dramatic crisis exists or is created with the shock that undermines the status quo and calls into question the relevance of the current culture. New top leadership, which can provide an alternative set of key values, is usually needed to make cultural change work. They are more likely to be perceived as capable of responding to the crisis. Bringing in a new CEO from outside the organization is likely to increase the chances that new cultural values will be introduced. An outside CEO, in contrast to promoting someone from within the organization, also conveys a message to employees that change is in the wind. Cultural change is more likely to take if the organization is both young and small. Cultures in younger organizations are less entrenched. And it's easier for management to communicate its new values when the organization is small. The more widely held a culture is and the higher the agreement among members on its values, the more difficult it will be to change. Conversely, weak cultures are more amenable to change than strong ones.

pp. 239-240

145. What can management do to create a more ethical culture?

An organizational culture most likely to shape high ethical standards is one that is high in risk tolerance, low-to-moderate in aggressiveness, and focuses on means as well as outcomes. Managers in such a culture are supported for taking risks and innovating, are discouraged from engaging in unbridled competition, and will pay attention to how goals are achieved as well as what goals are achieved. Management should also consider the following: Be a visible role model. Employees look up to top-management behavior as a benchmark for defining appropriate behavior. Communicate ethical expectations. Ethical ambiguities can be minimized by creating and disseminating an organizational code of ethics. Provide ethical training. Use training programs to reinforce the organization's standards of conduct to clarify what practices are and are not permissible. Visibly reward ethical acts and punish unethical ones. Performance appraisals of managers should include a point-by-point evaluation of how his or her decisions measured against the organization's code of ethics. Provide protective mechanisms. Formal mechanisms must be provided so employees can discuss ethical dilemmas and report unethical behavior without fear of reprimand.

pp. 240-241

146. Discuss the key variables that shape customer-responsive cultures?

The variables that routinely are evident in customer-responsive cultures are as follows: they hire employees who are outgoing and friendly, have low formalization, have widespread use of empowerment, good listening skills, and role clarity.

p. 241

147. What are the reasons for the growing interest in spirituality?

There are a number of reasons for the growing interest in spirituality. It is a counterbalance to the pressures and stress of a turbulent pace of life. Contemporary lifestyles underscore the lack of community many people feel and increase the need for involvement and connection. Aging baby-boomers are looking for something in their life. Formalized religion hasn't worked for many people and they look for anchors to replace lack of faith and to fill a growing feeling of emptiness. Job demands have made the workplace dominant in many people's lives yet they continue to question the meaning of work.

The desire to integrate personal life values with one's professional life. In times of economic prosperity, more people have the luxury to engage in a search to reach their full potential.

Exhibit 14-4

148. What are the characteristics of a spiritual organization?

A spiritual organization has five cultural characteristics. They have strong sense of purpose. Spiritual organizations build their cultures around a meaningful purpose. They focus on individual development. Spiritual organizations recognize the worth and value of people. Spiritual organizations are also characterized by mutual trust, honesty, and openness. The high-trust climate in spiritual organizations, when combined with the desire to promote employee learning and growth, leads to management empowering employees to make most work-related decisions. Managers in spiritually-based organizations are comfortable delegating authority to individual employees and teams. They trust their employees to make thoughtful and conscientious decisions. The final characteristic is that they don't stifle employee emotions. They allow people to be themselves.

pp. 243-244

149. What is the paradox of diversity?

Socializing new employees who, because of race, gender, ethnic, or other differences, are not like the majority of the organization's members creates what we call the paradox of diversity. Management wants new employees to accept the organization's core cultural values. Otherwise, these employees are unlikely to fit in or be accepted. But at the same time, management wants to openly acknowledge and demonstrate support for the differences that these employees bring to the workplace.

pp. 245-246

Chapter 15 HUMAN RESOURCE POLICIES AND PRACTICES

MULTIPLE CHOICE

1. According to the text, which of the following is NOT an important selection device?
    a. application forms
    b. employment tests
    c. newspaper advertisements
    d. background checks

Answer: c, difficulty: 1, p. 247

2. Employee interviews traditionally have not been part of the selection process in:
    a. South Korea.
    b. Japan.
    c. Asian countries.
    d. All of the above.

Answer: d, difficulty: 2, p. 248

3. Which of the following statements is NOT true concerning interviews?
    a. Most people have landed a full-time job without any interviews.
    b. The interview continues to be the selection device most frequently used.
    c. Even companies in Asian countries have begun to rely on employee interviews.
    d. In many Asian countries, selection decisions traditionally did not include interviews.

Answer: a, difficulty: 2, p. 248

4. Interviewing biases include all of the following EXCEPT:
    a. favoring applicants who share their attitudes.
    b. giving unduly high weight to negative information.
    c. allowing the order in which applicants are interviewed to influence evaluation.
    d. leniency.

Answer: d, difficulty: 2, p. 248

5. _____ are most valuable for assessing an applicant's intelligence, level of motivation, and interpersonal skills.
    a. Application forms
    b. Employee tests
    c. Background checks
    d. Interviews

Answer: d, difficulty: 2, p. 248

6.	By having interviewers use a standardized set of questions:
	a. the variability in results across applicants is increased.
	b. the validity of the interview as a selection device is greatly enhanced.
	c. the validity of the interview as a selection device is greatly reduced.
	d. None of the above.

Answer: b, difficulty: 3, p. 248

7.	Written tests suffered a decline in use between the late 1960s and the mid-1980s since they
	were characterized as:
	a. ineffective.
	b. discriminating.
	c. unreliable.
	d. too time consuming.

Answer: b, difficulty: 2, p. 249

8.	Integrity tests measure factors such as:
	a.	dependability.
	b.	carefulness.
	c.	honesty.
	d.	All of the above.

Answer: d, difficulty: 3, p. 249

9.	As ethical problems have increased in organizations, _____ tests have gained
	popularity.
	a.	intelligence
	b.	aptitude
	c.	integrity
	d.	interest

Answer: c, difficulty: 2, p. 249

10.	Today, more than ____ percent of all U.S. organizations use some type of employment
	test.
	a. 10
	b. 25
	c. 60
	d. 90

Answer: c, difficulty: 2, p. 249

11.	The logic of the _____ is that the best way to find out if an applicant can do a job
	successfully is to have him or her do it.
	a.	performance simulation test
	b.	interview
	c.	integrity test
	d.	personality test

Answer: a, difficulty: 2, p. 249

12. _____ more easily meet the requirement of job relatedness than do most written tests.
    a. Performance simulation tests
    b. Interviews
    c. Integrity tests
    d. Personality tests

Answer: a, difficulty: 3, p. 249

13. _____ are hands-on simulations of part or all of the job that must be performed by applicants.
    a. Assessment centers
    b. Work sampling tests
    c. Integrity tests
    d. Interviews

Answer: b, difficulty: 1, p. 249

14. A more elaborate set of performance simulation tests, specifically designed to evaluate a candidate's managerial potential is the:
    a. assessment center.
    b. work sampling test.
    c. integrity test.
    d. interview.

Answer: a, difficulty: 1, p. 250

15. Most workplace demands require:
    a. a college degree.
    b. a fourth-grade reading level.
    c. a tenth- or eleventh-grade reading level.
    d. a high school diploma.

Answer: c, difficulty: 2, p. 250

16. Most training is directed at upgrading and improving an employee's:
    a. interpersonal skills.
    b. problem-solving skills.
    c. critical thinking skills.
    d. technical skills.

Answer: d, difficulty: 2, p. 251

17. _____ training has become increasingly important because of new technology and new structural designs.
    a. Interpersonal skills
    b. Problem-solving skills
    c. Critical thinking skills
    d. Technical skills

Answer: d, difficulty: 2, p. 251

18. Learning how to be a better listener, how to communicate ideas more clearly, and how to be a more effective team player are included in _____ training.
   a. interpersonal skills
   b. problem solving skills
   c. critical thinking skills
   d. technical skills

Answer: a, difficulty: 2, p. 251

19. Activities to sharpen employees' logic and reasoning and abilities to assess causation, develop alternatives, analyze alternatives, and select solutions might be included in:
   a. interpersonal skills.
   b. problem-solving skills.
   c. critical thinking skills.
   d. technical skills.

Answer: b, difficulty: 2, p. 251

20. Participants learn to value individual difference, increase their cross-cultural understanding, and confront stereotypes in:
   a. interpersonal skills training.
   b. problem-solving skills training.
   c. diversity training.
   d. technical skills training.

Answer: c, difficulty: 2, p. 251

21. A recent survey found that about _____ percent of employees working in the 1000 largest U.S. corporations received ethics training.
   a. 25
   b. 50
   c. 75
   d. 100

Answer: c, difficulty: 1, p. 252

22. Which of the following is true concerning the teaching of ethics?
   a. Critics claim that ethics cannot be formally taught, but must be learned by example.
   b. The evidence is not really clear on whether you can teach ethics.
   c. Supporters of ethics training argue that ethics training would be effective because it helps employees to recognize ethical dilemmas, become more aware of the ethical issues underlying their actions, and reaffirms an organization's expectations that members will act ethically.
   d. All of the above.

Answer: d, difficulty: 3, p. 252

23. Historically, training meant:
    a. formal training.
    b. informal training.
    c. on-the-job training.
    d. off-the-job training.

Answer: a, difficulty: 3, p. 252

24. Unstructured, unplanned training that is easily adapted to situations and individuals is:
    a. formal training.
    b. informal training.
    c. on-the-job training.
    d. off-the-job training.

Answer: b, difficulty: 2, p. 252

25. One of the most famous _____ programs is the two-week course offered at McDonald's Hamburger University.
    a. formal training
    b. informal training
    c. on-the-job training
    d. off-the-job training

Answer: d, difficulty: 3, p. 252

26. Job rotation, apprenticeships, understudy assignments, and formal mentoring programs are examples of:
    a. on-the-job training.
    b. off-the job training.
    c. performance appraisal approaches.
    d. None of the above.

Answer: a, difficulty: 2, p. 252

27. It has become the _____ responsibility to keep employee skills, abilities, and knowledge current and to prepare for tomorrow's new tasks.
    a. human resource departments'
    b. immediate managers'
    c. entire organizations'
    d. employees'

Answer: d, difficulty: 3, p. 253

28. The organization's responsibilities to its employees for career development include all of the following EXCEPT:
    a. offering financial assistance.
    b. clearly communicating the organization's goals and future strategies.
    c. maintaining network contacts.
    d. providing the time for employees to learn.

Answer: c, difficulty: 3, p. 253

29. In managing their own careers, which of the following should employees do?
    a. know their strengths and weaknesses
    b. manage their reputation
    c. build and maintain network contacts
    d. All of the above.

Answer: d, difficulty: 2, p. 254

30. The three most popular sets of criteria for evaluating performance include all of the following EXCEPT:
    a. critical incidents.
    b. individual task outcomes.
    c. behaviors.
    d. traits.

Answer: a, difficulty: 2, p. 255

31. If ends rather than means count, then management should evaluate:
    a. individual task outcomes.
    b. behaviors.
    c. individual traits.
    d. critical incidents.

Answer: a, difficulty: 2, p. 255

32. A plant manager is judged by cost per unit of production. This is an example of evaluation based on:
    a. critical incidents.
    b. individual task outcomes.
    c. behaviors.
    d. traits.

Answer: b, difficulty: 2, p. 255

33. A salesman's performance evaluation is based upon the average number of clients he calls on per day. This is an example of evaluation based on:
    a. critical incidents.
    b. individual task outcomes.
    c. behaviors.
    d. traits.

Answer: c, difficulty: 2, p. 255

34. An example of appraising behaviors might involve measuring which of the following?
    a. promptness in submitting monthly reports
    b. the number of monthly reports submitted
    c. sales volume of a sales person
    d. the number of new accounts established by a salesperson

Answer: a, difficulty: 3, p. 255

35. When employees are evaluated on criteria such as "a good attitude" and being "dependable," evaluation is based on:
    a. critical incidents.
    b. individual task outcomes.
    c. behaviors.
    d. traits.

Answer: d, difficulty: 2, pp. 255-256

36. The weakest set of criteria is:
    a. individual task outcomes.
    b. behaviors.
    c. individual traits.
    d. critical incidents.

Answer: c, difficulty: 2, pp. 255-256

37. By tradition, performance evaluations are typically done by:
    a. peers.
    b. immediate supervisor.
    c. immediate subordinates.
    d. 360-degree evaluation.

Answer: b, difficulty: 1, p. 256

38. One of the most reliable sources of appraisal data is:
    a. peers.
    b. immediate supervisor.
    c. self-evaluation.
    d. immediate subordinates.

Answer: a, difficulty: 2, p. 256

39. Which of the following is NOT true about evaluation by immediate subordinates?
    a. Immediate subordinates' evaluations can be accurate.
    b. Subordinates may fear reprisal for unfavorable appraisals.
    c. Immediate subordinates typically have frequent contact with the manager.
    d. Responses should be signed in order to evaluate honesty.

Answer: d, difficulty: 2, pp. 256-257

40. The performance feedback from the full circle of daily contacts that an employee might have is called:
    a. continuous feedback.
    b. circular evaluation.
    c. 360-degree evaluation.
    d. team-based evaluation.

Answer: c, difficulty: 2, p. 257

41. 360-degree appraisals fit well into organizations that introduced:
    a. teams.
    b. employee involvement.
    c. quality management programs.
    d. All of the above.

Answer: d, difficulty: 2, p. 257

42. Which of the following groups would likely be included in a 360-degree performance appraisal?
    a. self
    b. subordinates
    c. peers
    d. All of the above.

Answer: d, difficulty: 2, p. 257 and Exhibit 15-1

43. The simplest method of appraising performance is to use:
    a. critical incidents.
    b. written essays.
    c. graphic rating scales.
    d. behaviorally anchored rating scales.

Answer: b, difficulty: 1, p. 258

44. The performance appraisal method that requires no complex forms or extensive training to complete is the _____ method.
    a. multiperson comparison
    b. behaviorally anchored rating scale
    c. critical incidents
    d. written essays

Answer: d, difficulty: 2, p. 258

45. _____ focus an evaluator's attention on those behaviors that are key in making the difference between executing a job effectively or ineffectively.
    a. Job tasks
    b. Critical incidents
    c. Job anchors
    d. Task rankings

Answer: b, difficulty: 2, p. 258

46. Graphic rating scales are popular because:
    a. they are less time consuming to develop and administer.
    b. they are relative rather than absolute measuring devices.
    c. they specify definite, observable, and measurable job behavior.
    d. they provide greater depth of information.

Answer: a, difficulty: 2, p. 258

47. The performance appraisal method that combines major elements from the critical incident and graphic rating scale approaches is the:
    a. behaviorally anchored rating scale.
    b. individual ranking method.
    c. multiperson comparison method.
    d. paired comparison method.

Answer: a, difficulty: 2, p. 258

48. The performance appraisal method that uses a set of performance factors rated on an incremental scale is the:
    a. critical incidents method.
    b. graphic rating-scale method.
    c. behaviorally anchored rating-scale method.
    d. individual ranking method.

Answer: b, difficulty: 2, p. 258

49. The performance appraisal method specifying definite, observable, and measurable job behaviors by asking participants to give specific illustrations of effective and ineffective behavior regarding each performance dimension is the:
    a. critical incidents method.
    b. graphic rating-scale method.
    c. behaviorally anchored rating-scale method.
    d. individual ranking method.

Answer: c, difficulty: 2, p. 258

50. _____ are relative rather than absolute measuring devices.
    a. Graphic rating scales
    b. Multiperson comparisons
    c. Behaviorally anchored rating scales
    d. Critical incidents

Answer: b, difficulty: 2, p. 258

51. Multiperson comparisons include:
    a. behaviorally anchored rating scales.
    b. group order ranking.
    c. graphic rating scales.
    d. critical incidents.

Answer: b, difficulty: 2, pp. 258-259

52. The _____ method of evaluating performance requires the evaluator to place employees into a specific classification, such as the top one-fifth.
    a. individual ranking
    b. group order-ranking
    c. paired comparison
    d. critical comparison

Answer: b, difficulty: 2, p. 259

53. The _____ method of evaluating performance rank orders employees from best to worst.
    a. individual ranking
    b. group order-ranking
    c. paired comparison
    d. critical comparison

Answer: a, difficulty: 2, p. 259

54. One way for universities to deal with the problem of grade inflation is to combine _____ with one of the other methods of performance evaluation.
    a. multiperson comparisons
    b. group order-ranking
    c. individual ranking
    d. critical comparison

Answer: a, difficulty: 3, p. 259

55. All of the following are potential problems in conducting a performance appraisal EXCEPT:
    a. leniency error.
    b. halo error.
    c. behavioral error.
    d. similarity error.

Answer: c, difficulty: 2, p. 259

56. An evaluator who understates the performance of employees on many dimensions is guilty of which one of the following errors?
    a. leniency
    b. single criterion
    c. halo
    d. similarity error

Answer: a, difficulty: 3, p. 259

57. When the assessment of an individual on one trait influences our evaluation of that person on other traits, a _____ error is committed.
    a. similarity
    b. halo
    c. forcing-information-to-match-nonperformance-criteria
    d. leniency

Answer: b, difficulty: 2, p. 259

58. The similarity error involves:
    a. perceiving the universe as more similar than it really is.
    b. formally evaluating a person after a decision is made on how the individual has been performing.
    c. a bias of the evaluator by unconsciously favoring people who have qualities and traits similar to themselves.
    d. giving different evaluations for identical job performance.

Answer: c, difficulty: 2, p. 259

59. In the past, Jack has tended to be trustworthy and loyal. His supervisor has become biased and rates him high on many desirable attributes. This is an example of _____ error.
    a. leniency
    b. halo
    c. low differentiation
    d. similarity

Answer: b, difficulty: 1, p. 259

60. Sandra, who supervises six employees, is very aggressive. She tends to positively evaluate employees who are aggressive and negatively evaluate those who are not. Sandra suffers from _____ error.
    a. leniency
    b. halo
    c. low differentiation
    d. similarity

Answer: d, difficulty: 1, p. 259

61. When an evaluator's ability to appraise objectively and accurately is impeded by the evaluator's tendency to understate performance, this is called a _____ error.
    a. negative leniency
    b. positive leniency
    c. halo effect
    d. similarity

Answer: a, difficulty: 2, p. 259

62. The text identified a number of errors that may be encountered during performance appraisals. All of the following are ways to overcome these problems EXCEPT:
   a. emphasize traits.
   b. emphasize behaviors.
   c. appraise selectively.
   d. use multiple evaluators.

Answer: a, difficulty: 2, pp. 259-261

63. Which of the following is true about the relationship between traits and performance?
   a. Loyal employees are more productive.
   b. Rating traits is a valid way to appraise performance.
   c. There is no evidence that certain traits will predict job performance in a large cross-section of jobs.
   d. There is strong agreement among evaluators when judging traits.

Answer: c, difficulty: 2, pp. 259-260

64. _____ tend to reduce leniency and halo errors because they encourage focus on performance-related behaviors rather than on traits.
   a. Multiple evaluators
   b. Multiple criteria
   c. Diaries
   d. The 360-degree evaluations

Answer: c, difficulty: 2, p. 260

65. The logic of _____ is used in athletic competitions in such sports as diving and gymnastics, with the highest and lowest scores being dropped and the final performance appraisal made up from the cumulative scores of those remaining.
   a. using multiple evaluations
   b. using performance behaviors in a diary
   c. evaluating selectively
   d. graphic rating scales

Answer: a, difficulty: 3, p. 260

66. Generally, in terms of organizational level, it is best if appraisers are _____ to the individual being evaluated.
   a. above
   b. as close as possible
   c. below
   d. unrelated

Answer: b, difficulty: 2, p. 260

67. Which of the following is true about training appraisers?
   a. There is little effect on halo errors.
   b. The halo error is minimized but the leniency effect is not affected.
   c. The effects of training diminish over time.
   d. Effective training of appraisers must be a lengthy process to be successful.

Answer: c, difficulty: 2, pp. 260-261

68. Which is NOT a characteristic of due process?
   a. Individuals are provided with adequate notice of what is expected of them.
   b. All relevant evidence to a proposed violation is aired in a fair hearing so individuals affected can respond.
   c. Employees provide little input into the process.
   d. The final decision is based on the evidence and free from bias.

Answer: c, difficulty: 3, p. 261

69. Which is NOT a reason managers are reluctant to give performance feedback?
   a. Managers want to redirect blame to someone else.
   b. Managers are often uncomfortable discussing performance weakness directly with employees.
   c. Many employees tend to become defensive when their weaknesses are pointed out.
   d. Employees tend to have an inflated assessment of their own performance.

Answer: a, difficulty: 2, p. 261

70. Performance evaluation concepts have been developed almost exclusively with _____ in mind.
   a. individual employees
   b. teams
   c. motivation
   d. culture

Answer: a, difficulty: 1, p. 262

71. Which of the following is NOT a suggestion offered by the text for designing a system that supports and improves the performance of a team?
   a. Tie the team's results to the organization's goals.
   b. Begin with the team's customers and the work process that the team follows to satisfy customers' needs.
   c. Measure only team performance.
   d. Train the team to create its own measures.

Answer: c, difficulty: 1, p. 262

72. Which of the following is true about performance appraisal in a global context?
    a. In Middle Eastern countries, performance appraisals aren't likely to be widely used because managers tend to see people as subjugated to their environment.
    b. North American managers focus on team-performance appraisals.
    c. Japanese managers typically prepare annual performance appraisals.
    d. Israel's culture values individual activities more than does the culture of Canada.

Answer: a, difficulty: 2, p. 262

73. Care needs to be taken to ensure that the organization's selection process, training programs, and appraisal system support:
    a. high employee performance.
    b. high social satisfaction.
    c. low budgets.
    d. group contributions.

Answer: a, difficulty: 2, p. 263

74. The use of the proper _____ will increase the probability that the right person will be chosen to fill a slot in the organization.
    a. training programs
    b. appraisal systems
    c. selection devices
    d. managers

Answer: c, difficulty: 1, p. 263

75. A major goal of performance appraisal is to assess accurately an individual's performance contribution as a basis for making _____ decisions.
    a. reward allocation
    b. termination
    c. replacement
    d. transfer

Answer: a, difficulty: 2, p. 263

TRUE/FALSE

76. In South Korea, Japan, and many other Asian countries, employee interviews traditionally have not been part of the selection process.

True, difficulty: 2, p. 248

77. Of all the selection devices that organizations use to differentiate job candidates, the interview continues to be the one most frequently used.

True, difficulty: 1, p. 248

78. The interview results tend to have a disproportionate amount of influence on the selection decision.

True, difficulty: 2, p. 248

79. The unstructured interview has been proven to be a highly effective selection device.

False, difficulty: 2, p. 248

80. Evidence indicates that interviews are most valuable for assessing an applicant's intelligence, level of motivation, and interpersonal skills.

True, difficulty: 2, p. 248

81. Intelligence tests have proven to be particularly good predictors for jobs that require cognitive complexity.

True, difficulty: 2, p. 249

82. Japanese auto makers, when staffing plants in the United States, have relied heavily on written tests to predict candidates that will be high performers.

True, difficulty: 3, p. 249

83. Integrity tests have increased in popularity since they more easily meet the requirement of job relatedness than do most written tests.

False, difficulty: 3, p. 249

84. Work samples are suited to routine jobs, whereas assessment centers are relevant for the selection of managerial personnel.

True, difficulty: 3, p. 249

85. Work sampling tests are hands-on simulations of part or all of the job that must be performed by applicants.

True, difficulty: 1, p. 249

86. Studies almost consistently demonstrate that personality tests yield validities superior to written aptitude and work sample experiments.

False, difficulty: 3, p. 250

87. Organizations increasingly have to provide basic reading and math skills for their employees.

True, difficulty: 2, p. 250

88. About 20 percent of Americans between the ages of 21 and 25 can't read at even an eighth-grade level.

True, difficulty: 3, p. 250

89. Most training is directed at upgrading and improving an employee's interpersonal skills.

False, difficulty: 2, p. 251

90. Technical training has become increasingly important because of changes in organization design.

True, difficulty: 1, p. 251

91. Since most employees belong to a work unit, to some degree, their work performance depends on their ability to effectively interact with their co-workers and their boss.

True, difficulty: 1, p. 251

92. The centerpiece of most diversity programs is training.

True, difficulty: 2, p. 251

93. The evidence is not clear on whether you can teach ethics.

True, difficulty: 2, p. 252

94. Critics argue that ethics must be learned by example.

True, difficulty: 2, p. 252

95. Recent evidence indicates that organizations are increasingly relying on informal training for teaching skills and keeping employees current.

True, difficulty: 2, p. 252

96. Off-the-job training includes job rotation, apprenticeships, understudy assignments, and formal mentoring programs.

False, difficulty: 2, p. 252

97. On-the-job training programs seldom disrupt the workplace.

False, difficulty: 1, p. 252

98. The most popular off-the-job type of training is live classroom lectures.

False, difficulty: 2, p. 252

99. The organization's responsibility to employees for their career development is to build self-reliance and to help employees maintain their marketability through continual learning.

True, difficulty: 1, p. 253

100. The organization should offer tuition reimbursement to help employees keep current.

True, difficulty: 2, p. 253

101. Today's employees should manage their own careers like entrepreneurs managing a small business.

True, difficulty: 3, p. 253

102. The criteria that management choose to evaluate when appraising employee performance will have a major influence on what employees do.

True, difficulty: 2, p. 255

103. The three most popular sets of criteria for performance evaluation are individual task outcomes, behaviors, and traits.

True, difficulty: 2, p. 255

104. If ends rather than means count, then management should evaluate an employee's behavior.

False, difficulty: 2, p. 255

105. The weakest set of criteria for performance evaluation is behaviors.

False, difficulty: 2, p. 255

106. Others may actually be able to do a better job of evaluating an employee's performance than the immediate superior.

True, difficulty: 2, p. 256

107. The vast majority of all performance appraisals around the lower and middle levels of the organization are conducted by the employee's immediate boss.

True, difficulty: 1, p. 256

108. One of the most reliable sources of appraisal data is peer evaluation.

True, difficulty: 2, p. 256

109. Self-evaluations usually agree with superiors' ratings.

False, difficulty: 1, p. 256

110. Self-evaluations are better suited for developmental uses than evaluative purposes.

True, difficulty: 3, p. 256

111. Subordinate evaluations can provide accurate and detailed information about a manager's behavior because the evaluators typically have frequent contact with the manager.

True, difficulty: 2, p. 256

112. The 360-degree appraisal provides performance feedback from the full circle of daily contacts that an employee might have.

True, difficulty: 1, p. 257

113. About 1/5 of employers are now using 360-degree appraisals.

True, difficulty: 2, p. 257

114. In written essay performance appraisals, the appraiser writes down anecdotes that describe what the employee did that was especially effective or ineffective.

False, difficulty: 3, p. 258

115. Behaviorally anchored rating scales use a list of performance factors, such as quantity and quality of work, depth of knowledge, and cooperation, which are related by the evaluator on incremental scales.

False, difficulty: 3, p. 258

116. Graphic rating scales provide a greater depth of information than critical incidents.

False, difficulty: 2, p. 258

117. The group order ranking is often used in recommending students to graduate schools.

True, difficulty: 2, p. 259

118. The individual ranking approach rates employees from best to worst.

True, difficulty: 1, p. 259

119. The performance appraisal approach that rates employees from best to worst is the group order-ranking method.

False, difficulty: 2, p. 259

120. When evaluators bias their evaluations by unconsciously favoring people who have qualities and traits similar to themselves, they are making a negative leniency error.

False, difficulty: 2, p. 259

121. The halo error is the tendency for an evaluator to let the assessment of an individual on one trait influence his or her appraisal of that person on other traits.

True, difficulty: 1, p. 259

122. Some evaluators see the appraisal process as a political opportunity to overtly reward or punish employees they like or dislike.

True, difficulty: 2, p. 259

123. Traits such as loyalty and initiative may be prized by managers, but there is no evidence to support the belief that certain traits will be adequate synonyms for performance in a large cross section of jobs.

True, difficulty: 3, p. 259

124. Whenever possible, it is better to use performance measures based on traits rather than behaviors for appraisals.

False, difficulty: 2, pp. 259-260

125. As the number of evaluators increases, the probability of attaining more accurate information increases.

True, difficulty: 1, p. 260

126. In general, appraisers should be as close as possible, in terms of organizational level, to the individual being evaluated.

True, difficulty: 2, p. 260

127. The effects of training appraisers to reduce halo and leniency errors tend to diminish over time.

True, difficulty: 2, pp. 260-261

128. The concept of due process can be applied to appraisals to increase the perception that employees are treated fairly.

True, difficulty: 3, p. 261

129. For many managers, few activities are more unpleasant than providing performance feedback to employees.

True, difficulty: 2, p. 261

130. In team performance evaluations, both team and individual performance should be measured.

True, difficulty: 2, p. 262

131. In team performance appraisals, the team should not create its own measures.

False, difficulty: 3, p. 262

132. In Israel, where culture values individual activities, the focus is on individual performance evaluations.

False, difficulty: 2, p. 262

133. Yearly performance evaluations are the norm in Japan.

False, difficulty: 1, p. 262

134. A major goal of performance appraisal is to assess accurately an individual's performance contribution as a basis for making reward allocation decisions.

True, difficulty: 2, p. 263

ESSAY

135. Discuss the role of interviews as a selection device.

The interview is one of the more important selection devices. Of all the selection devices that organizations use to differentiate job candidates, the interview continues to be the one most frequently used. It also carries a great deal of weight. The results tend to have a disproportionate amount of influence on the selection decision. The unstructured interview has proven to be an ineffective selection device. The data gathered from such interviews are typically biased and often unrelated to future job performance. Without structure, a number of biases can distort results. The evidence indicates that interviews are most valuable for assessing an applicant's intelligence, level of motivation, and interpersonal skills. When these qualities are related to job performance, the validity of the interview as a selection device is increased.

p. 248

136. What are integrity tests? What factors do they measure?

As ethical problems have increased in organizations, integrity tests have gained popularity. Integrity tests are paper-and-pencil tests that measure factors such as dependability, carefulness, responsibility, and honesty.

p. 249

137. Explain the use of performance simulation tests and discuss two types.

Performance simulation tests are increasing in popularity. These tests more easily meet the requirements of job relatedness than do most written tests. The logic of performance simulation tests is that there is no better way to find out if an applicant can do a job successfully than having him or her do it. The two best known performance simulation tests are work sampling and assessment centers. The former is suited to routine jobs and the latter is relevant for selection of managerial personnel. Work sampling tests are hands-on simulations of part or all of the job that must be performed by applicants. A more elaborate set of performance simulation tests, specifically designed to evaluate a candidate's managerial potential, is administered in assessment centers. In assessment centers, line executives, supervisors, and/or trained psychologists evaluate candidates as they go through one to several days of exercises that simulate real problems that they would confront on the job.

pp. 249-250

138. What are the four general skill categories of training discussed in the text?

Four general skill categories of training discussed in the text are basic literacy, technical, interpersonal, and problem-solving skills. Organizations are increasingly having to provide basic reading and math skills for their employees. Most training is directed at upgrading and improving an employee's technical skills. Jobs change as a result of new technologies and improved methods. Employees' work performance depends on their ability to effectively interact with their co-workers and their boss. Since managers, as well as many employees who perform nonroutine tasks, have to solve problems on their job, problem-solving skills training is being offered. Problem-solving training has become a basic part of almost every organizational effort to introduce self-managed teams or implement quality management programs.

pp. 250-251

139. What is the intent of diversity training?

The centerpiece of most diversity programs is training. Diversity training programs are generally intended to provide a vehicle for increasing awareness and examining stereotypes. Participants learn to value individual differences, increase their cross-cultural understanding, and confront stereotypes.

pp. 251-252

140. Discuss the two views of teaching ethics.

Evidence is not clear on whether you can teach ethics. Critics argue that ethics are based on values, and value systems are fixed at an early age. By the time employers hire people, their ethical values have already been established. The critics also claim that ethics cannot be formally "taught," but must be learned by example. Supporters of ethics training argue that values can be learned and changed after early childhood. And even if they couldn't, ethics training would be effective because it helps employees to recognize ethical dilemmas, become more aware of the ethical issues underlying their actions, and reaffirms an organization's expectations that members will act ethically.

p. 252

141. What is the difference between formal and informal training?

Historically, training meant formal training. It's planned in advance and has a structured format. However, recent evidence indicates that organizations are increasingly relying on informal training – unstructured, unplanned, and easily adapted to situations and individuals – for teaching skills and keeping employees current. In reality, most informal training is nothing other than employees helping each other out. They share information and solve work-related problems with one another.

p. 252

142. Discuss the difference between on-the-job and off-the-job training. Provide examples of each.

On-the-job training includes job rotation, apprenticeships, understudy assignments, and formal mentoring programs. The primary drawback of these on-the-job training methods is that they often disrupt the workplace. So organizations invest in off-the-job training. The most popular is live classroom lectures. It also includes videotapes, public seminars, self-study programs, Internet course, satellite-beamed television classes, and group activities that use role plays and case studies.

pp. 252-253

143. What are the organization's responsibilities in regards to employees' career development?

The organization's responsibility is to build employee self-reliance and to help employees maintain their marketability through continual learning. The organization's support includes clearly communicating the organization's goals and future strategies, creating growth opportunities, offering financial assistance, and providing the time for employees to learn.

p. 253

144. What are the employee's responsibilities in regards to career development?

Today's employees should manage their own careers like entrepreneurs managing a small business. They should think of themselves as self-employed, even if employed in a large organization. The employee's responsibilities include knowing themselves; managing their reputation; building and maintaining network contacts; keeping current; balancing their specialist and generalist competencies; documenting their achievements; and keeping their options open.

pp. 253-254

145. What are the purposes of performance appraisal?

Performance appraisals provide two important links when addressing motivation Ä the effort-performance link and the performance-reward link. People have to know what is expected of them. They need to know how their performance will be measured. Further, they must feel confident that if they exert an effort within their capabilities, it will result in a satisfactory performance as defined by the criteria by which they are being measured. Finally, they must feel confident that if they perform as they are being asked, they will achieve the rewards they value. If the objectives that employees are seeking are unclear, if the criteria for measuring those objectives are vague, and if the employees lack confidence that their efforts will lead to a satisfactory appraisal of their performance, or believe there will be an unsatisfactory payoff by the organization when their performance objectives are achieved, we can expect individuals to work considerably below their potential. Hence, performance appraisal plays an important role in influencing an employee's motivation.

pp. 254-255

146. What are the three most popular sets of criteria in performance appraisal?

The three most popular sets of criteria in performance appraisal are individual task outcomes, behaviors, and traits. If ends count, rather than means, then management should evaluate an employee's task outcomes. In many cases, it's difficult to identify specific outcomes that can be directly attributable to an employee's actions. This is particularly true of employees in staff positions and individuals whose work assignments are intrinsically part of a team effort. The weakest set of criteria, yet one that is still widely used by organizations, is individual traits. They are furthest removed from the actual performance of the job itself.

pp. 255-256

147. Who is involved in evaluating performance appraisals in organizations today?

Performance appraisals are being conducted by a variety of people in organizations today. While traditionally, the immediate boss performed the appraisal, it is recognized today that others may actually be able to do the job better. The vast majority of all performance appraisals at the lower and middle levels of the organization are conducted by the employee's immediate boss. Peer evaluations are one of the most reliable sources of appraisal data since they are close to the action. Having employees evaluate their own performance is consistent with values such as self-management and empowerment. Another source is an employee's immediate subordinates. These evaluations can provide accurate and detailed information about a manager's behavior because the evaluators typically have frequent contact with the manager.

pp. 256-257

148. Explain the advantages and disadvantages of peer evaluation.

Peer evaluations are one of the most reliable sources of appraisal data. Peers are close to the action. Using peers as raters results in several independent judgments, whereas a boss can offer only a single evaluation. And the average of several ratings is often more reliable than a single evaluation. One the down side, peer evaluations can suffer from co-workers' unwillingness to evaluate one another and from biases of friendship or animosity.

p. 256

149. Explain the appeal of the 360-degree evaluation.

The 360-degree appraisal is a comprehensive approach. It provides for performance feedback from the full circle of daily contacts that an employee might have. The number of appraisals can be as few as three or four or as many as 25. The 360-degree appraisal fits well into organizations that have introduced teams, employee involvement, and quality management programs. By relying on feedback from co-workers, customers, and subordinates, these organizations are hoping to give everyone more of a sense of participation in the review process and to gain more accurate readings on employee performance.

p. 257

150. What are the two most popular multiperson comparisons?

The two most popular multiperson comparisons are group order ranking and individual ranking. The group order ranking requires the evaluator to place employees into a particular classification. This method is often used in recommending students to graduate schools. The individual ranking approach rank orders employees from best to worst. The result is a clear ordering of employees, from the highest performer down to the lowest.

pp. 258-259

151. What are some of the potential problems in performance evaluations?

The performance appraisal process is a potential minefield of problems. Evaluators can make leniency, halo, and similarity errors, or use the process for political purposes. They can unconsciously inflate evaluations (positive leniency), understate performance (negative leniency), or allow the assessment of one characteristic to unduly influence the assessment of other characteristics (the halo error). Some appraisers bias their evaluations by unconsciously favoring people who have qualities and traits similar to themselves (the similarity error). And some evaluators see the appraisal process as a political opportunity to overtly reward or punish employees they like or dislike. While there are no protections that will guarantee accurate performance appraisals, the following suggestions can significantly help to make the process more objective and fair.

p. 259

152. Discuss some suggestions for improving performance appraisal.

Suggestions for improving performance appraisals include the following: emphasize behaviors rather than traits, document performance behaviors in a diary, use multiple evaluators, evaluate selectively, train evaluators, and provide employees with due process. Many traits often considered to be related to good performance may, in fact, have little or no performance relationship. Traits suffer from weak interrater agreement. Diaries help evaluators to better organize information in their memory. By keeping a diary of specific critical incidents for each employee, appraisals tend to be more accurate and less prone to rating errors. As the number of evaluators increases, the probability of attaining more accurate information increases. Appraisers should evaluate in only those areas in which they have some expertise. If you can't find good evaluators, the alternative is to make good evaluators. There is substantial evidence that training evaluators can make them more accurate raters. Due process increases the perception that employees are treated fairly. Three features characterize due process systems: individuals are provided with adequate notice of what is expected of them; all relevant evidence to a proposed violation is aired in a fair hearing so individuals affected can respond; and the final decision is based on the evidence and free from bias.

pp. 259-261

153. Offer some suggestions for evaluating the performance of teams.

There are four suggestions that have been offered for designing a system that supports and improves the performance of teams. Tie the teams' results to the organization's goals. It's important to find measurements that apply to important goals that the team is supposed to accomplish. Begin with the team's customers and the work process that the team follows to satisfy their needs. The final product the customer receives can be evaluated in terms of the customer's requirements. The transactions between teams can be evaluated on the basis of delivery and quality. And the process steps can be evaluated on the basis of waste and cycle time. Measure both team and individual performance. Define the roles of each team member in terms of accomplishments that support the team's work process. Then assess each member's contribution and the team's overall performance. Train the team to create its own measures. Having the team define its objectives and those of each member ensures that everyone understands his or her role on the team and helps the team develop into a more cohesive unit.

p. 262

Chapter 16 ORGANIZATIONAL CHANGE AND DEVELOPMENT

MULTIPLE CHOICE

1. Which of the following is NOT true about the changing nature of the workforce?
    a. more cultural diversity
    b. decrease in professionals
    c. many new entrants with inadequate skills
    d. increase in professionals

Answer: b, difficulty: 1, p. 265

2. Changes in oil prices and the rise and fall of dot.com stocks are examples of:
    a. the changing nature of the workforce.
    b. changing technology.
    c. changing competition.
    d. economic shocks.

Answer: d, difficulty: 2, p. 265

3. Changing social trends include all of the following EXCEPT:
    a. Internet chat rooms.
    b. the retirement of Baby Boomers.
    c. global competitors.
    d. increased interest in urban living.

Answer: c, difficulty: 1, Exhibit 16-1

4. Which of the following is NOT a force for change?
    a. technology
    b. economic shocks
    c. world politics
    d. employee behavior

Answer: d, difficulty: 1, Exhibit 16-1

5. _____ are responsible for managing change activities in organizations.
    a. Change agents
    b. Governmental agencies
    c. Only top executives
    d. Driving forces

Answer: a, difficulty: 2, p. 266

6. Change agents include all BUT which of the following?
    a. managers
    b. employees
    c. outside consultants
    d. All of the above.

Answer: d, difficulty: 1, p. 266

7. Which of the following is NOT true about using outside consultants as change agents?
    a. They offer an objective perspective.
    b. They are prone to initiate more drastic changes.
    c. They are at a disadvantage because they have inadequate knowledge of the organization's history and culture.
    d. They may be more cautious because they must live with the consequences of their actions.

Answer: d, difficulty: 2, p. 266

8. Disadvantages of using outside consultants as change agents include all of the following EXCEPT:
    a. outside consultants have inadequate understanding of the organization's history.
    b. outside consultants are prone to initiating more drastic changes.
    c. outside consultants are more cautious since they must live with the consequences.
    d. outside consultants have an inadequate understanding of the organization's personnel.

Answer: c, difficulty: 3, p. 266

9. Which of the following describes the step in Kurt Lewin's three-step process in which an employee makes the new change permanent?
    a. unfreezing
    b. refreezing
    c. changing
    d. implementation

Answer: b, difficulty: 2, p. 267

10. Kurt Lewin's three-step description of the change process best illustrates:
    a. the calm waters simile.
    b. the white-water rapids simile.
    c. Both (a) and (b).
    d. None of the above.

Answer: a, difficulty: 2, p. 267

11. The three-step description of the change process was developed by:
    a. Lewin.
    b. Herzberg.
    c. House.
    d. McClelland.

Answer: a, difficulty: 2, p. 267

12. The correct order of the steps in the change process is:
    a. change, unfreeze, refreeze.
    b. unfreeze, refreeze, change.
    c. unfreeze, change, refreeze.
    d. refreeze, change, unfreeze.

Answer: c, difficulty: 1, Exhibit 16-2

13. Moving from equilibrium to refreezing can be achieved by all of the following EXCEPT:
    a. the driving forces.
    b. the restraining forces.
    c. combined driving and restraining forces.
    d. white-water forces.

Answer: d, difficulty: 2, p. 267

14. The "white-water rapids" simile is consistent with:
    a. static environments.
    b. predictability.
    c. dynamic environments.
    d. stability.

Answer: c, difficulty: 1, p. 268

15. Which of the following statements is NOT true concerning change?
    a. Few organizations today can treat change as the occasional disturbance in an otherwise peaceful world.
    b. Too much is changing too fast for any organization or its managers to be complacent.
    c. Today's adage is "If it ain't broke, don't fix it."
    d. Calm waters no longer describe the kind of seas that managers have to negotiate.

Answer: c, difficulty: 2, p. 268

16. Which of the following illustrates how resistance is positive?
    a. Resistance provides a degree of stability and predictability to behavior.
    b. Resistance to change can be a source of functional conflict.
    c. Without resistance, organizations would take on characteristics of chaotic randomness.
    d. All of the above.

Answer: d, difficulty: 2, p. 269

17. Resistance to change may surface _____.
    a. overtly
    b. immediately
    c. implicitly
    d. All of the above.

Answer: d, difficulty: 2, p. 269

18. Subtle implicit resistance efforts include all of the following EXCEPT:
    a. loss of loyalty to the organization.
    b. increased motivation to work.
    c. increased errors or mistakes.
    d. increased absenteeism due to "sickness."

Answer: b, difficulty: 3, p. 269

19. It is easiest for management to deal with resistance when it is:
    a. overt and deferred.
    b. overt and immediate.
    c. implicit and immediate.
    d. implicit and deferred.

Answer: b, difficulty: 3, p. 269

20. _____ is the tendency to respond in our accustomed ways.
    a. Habit
    b. Security
    c. Economic factors
    d. Selective information processing

Answer: a, difficulty: 2, p. 269

21. Which of the following is NOT a reason why individuals resist change?
    a. habit
    b. fear of the unknown
    c. structural inertia
    d. selective information processing

Answer: c, difficulty: 2, pp. 269-270

22. All of the following are reasons individuals resist change EXCEPT:
    a. economic factors.
    b. security.
    c. limited focus of change.
    d. selective information processing.

Answer: c, difficulty: 2, pp. 269-270

23. Tom opposes the proposed reorganization at his firm because he fears he won't be able to meet his new quota and his pay is tied to meeting his quota. Tom's basis for resisting the change is:
    a. economic.
    b. habit.
    c. fear of the unknown.
    d. security.

Answer: a, difficulty: 1, p. 270

24. Employees resist change with _____, by hearing what they want to hear and ignoring information in order to keep their perceptions intact.
    a. structural inertia
    b. cooptation
    c. selective information processing
    d. organizational development

Answer: c, difficulty: 2, p. 270

25. Organizations have built-in mechanisms to produce stability called:
    a. group inertia.
    b. structural inertia.
    c. organizational charts.
    d. power structures.

Answer: b, difficulty: 2, p. 270

26. Because organizations are made up of interdependent subsystems, it's impossible to change one without affecting the others. This is an example of:
    a. a limited focus of change.
    b. group inertia.
    c. structural inertia.
    d. a threat to established resource allocations.

Answer: a, difficulty: 2, p. 270

27. Which of the following is NOT a source of organizational resistance to change?
    a. structural inertia
    b. limited focus of change
    c. selective information processing
    d. threat to expertise

Answer: c, difficulty: 2, pp. 270-271

28. Which of the following is NOT true about organizational resistance to change?
    a. Organizations have built-in mechanisms to produce stability.
    b. Changes in organizational patterns may threaten the expertise of specialized groups.
    c. Groups in the organization that control sizable resources usually embrace change.
    d. Any redistribution of decision-making authority can threaten existing power relationships.

Answer: c, difficulty: 2, pp. 270-271

29. Which of the following is an organizational barrier to change?
    a. limited focus of change
    b. fear of the unknown
    c. economic insecurity
    d. habit

Answer: a, difficulty: 2, pp. 270-271

30. The recent move to outsource many human resource activities has been resisted by many human resource departments as:
    a. a limited focus of change.
    b. a threat to expertise.
    c. a threat to established power relationships.
    d. an example of structural inertia.

Answer: b, difficulty: 3, p. 271

31. Introduction of participative decision-making or autonomous work teams are examples of changes that are seen as
    a. a limited focus of change.
    b. a threat to expertise.
    c. a threat to established power relationships.
    d. an example of structural inertia.

Answer: c, difficulty: 3, p. 271

32. The introduction of participative decision making or autonomous work teams are examples of changes that are often seen as:
    a. threats to established power relationships.
    b. a limited focus of change.
    c. group inertia.
    d. threat to expertise.

Answer: a, difficulty: 3, p. 271

33. Which of the following is a tactic to overcome organizational resistance to change?
    a. communication
    b. participation
    c. rewarding acceptance of change
    d. All of the above.

Answer: d, difficulty: 2, pp. 271-272

34. Training employees in new skills is an example of the _____ tactic for overcoming resistance to change.
    a. communication
    b. participation
    c. providing support
    d. reward acceptance of change

Answer: c, difficulty: 2, pp. 271-272

35. The organization that has been intentionally designed with the capacity to continuously adapt and change is called a(n):
   a. adaptive organization.
   b. learning organization.
   c. change agent.
   d. innovative organization.

Answer: b, difficulty: 1, p. 272

36. All of the following may be used as strategies to create a learning organization EXCEPT:
   a. making the commitment to change implicit.
   b. making the commitment to change part of the vision.
   c. redesigning structure to reduce boundaries between people.
   d. reshaping culture to support continual learning.

Answer: a, difficulty: 3, p. 272

37. Which of the following is NOT a characteristic of a learning organization?
   a. shared vision
   b. open communication
   c. heightened self-interest and fragmented departmental interests
   d. people discarding old ways of thinking and standard routines

Answer: c, difficulty: 1, Exhibit 16-3

38. _____ is a term used to encompass a collection of change techniques undertaken in response to change in the external environment, that seek to improve organizational effectiveness and employee well-being.
   a. Organizational development
   b. Organizational design
   c. Organization chart
   d. Planned change

Answer: a, difficulty: 2, p. 273

39. Which is NOT an underlying value in most OD efforts?
   a. respect for people
   b. trust and support
   c. hierarchical authority
   d. confrontation

Answer: c, difficulty: 2, p. 273

40. The OD paradigm values:
   a. human and organizational growth.
   b. collaborative and participative processes.
   c. a spirit of inquiry.
   d. All of the above.

Answer: d, difficulty: 3, p. 273

41. Which is NOT true of most OD efforts?
    a. Problems should be swept under the rug.
    b. Effective organizations deemphasize hierarchical authority and control.
    c. People should be treated with dignity and respect.
    d. The effective and healthy organization is characterized by a climate of trust and support.

Answer: a, difficulty: 2, p. 273

42. OD change agents hold which of the following in low esteem?
    a. collaboration
    b. participative process
    c. power
    d. spirit of inquiry

Answer: c, difficulty: 2, p. 273

43. _____ refers to a method of changing behavior through unstructured group interaction.
    a. Sensitivity training
    b. A quality-of-worklife program
    c. Survey feedback
    d. Process consultation

Answer: a, difficulty: 2, p. 273

44. Which of the following is NOT synonymous with sensitivity training?
    a. laboratory training
    b. encounter groups
    c. T-groups
    d. None of the above.

Answer: d, difficulty: 2, p. 273

45. The objectives of the T-groups are to provide the subjects with:
    a. increased awareness of their own behavior and how others perceive them
    b. greater sensitivity to the behavior of others.
    c. increased understanding of group processes
    d. All of the above.

Answer: d, difficulty: 3, p. 273

46. Questionnaires are an essential part of:
    a. sensitivity training.
    b. survey feedback.
    c. process consultation.
    d. intergroup development.

Answer: b, difficulty: 1, p. 274

47. The questionnaire in survey feedback typically asks organizational members about topics including all of the following EXCEPT:
    a. decision-making practices.
    b. communication effectiveness.
    c. satisfaction with the organization.
    d. what new customer markets to consider.

Answer: d, difficulty: 2, p. 274

48. _____ occurs when a manager uses an outsider to help provide insight into what is going on.
    a. Insensitivity training.
    b. Team building.
    c. Process consultation.
    d. Intergroup development.

Answer: c, difficulty: 2, p. 274

49. Which of the following is NOT true of process consultation?
    a. Process consultation is less task directed than sensitivity training.
    b. Consultants in process consultation do not solve the organization's problems.
    c. The process consultant need not be an expert in solving the particular problem that is identified.
    d. Process consultation assumes that organizational effectiveness can be improved by dealing with interpersonal problems and in its emphasis on involvement.

Answer: a, difficulty: 3, pp. 274-275

50. Team-building activities typically include all of the following EXCEPT:
    a. individual development.
    b. goal setting.
    c. role analysis.
    d. team-process analysis.

Answer: a, difficulty: 1, p. 275

51. _____ utilizes high interaction group activities to increase trust and openness among team members.
    a. Sensitivity analysis
    b. Team building
    c. Intergroup development
    d. Process consultation

Answer: b, difficulty: 2, p. 275

52. When using _____ to facilitate change, members compile and compare lists of their perceptions of others, how they think others perceive them, and how they perceive themselves.
   a. sensitivity analysis
   b. team building
   c. intergroup development
   d. process consultation

Answer: c, difficulty: 3, p. 276

53. _____ is an OD approach that accentuates the positive. Rather than looking for problems to fix, this approach seeks to identify the unique qualities and special strengths of an organization, which can then be built on to improve performance.
   a. Team building
   b. Intergroup development
   c. Appreciative inquiry
   d. Process consultation

Answer: c, difficulty: 3, p. 276

54. Which of the following is NOT one of the three key elements of process reengineering?
   a. identifying key elements of the organization's culture
   b. identifying an organization's distinctive competencies
   c. assessing core processes
   d. reorganizing horizontally by process

Answer: a, difficulty: 3, p. 278

55. Process reengineering requires management to reorganize around horizontal processes. This means doing all but which of the following?
   a. using cross-functional teams
   b. using self-managed teams
   c. adding middle-management levels
   d. focuses on processes rather than functions

Answer: c, difficulty: 3, p. 278

56. _____ is a dynamic condition in which an individual is confronted with an opportunity, constraint, or demand related to what he or she desires and for which the outcome is perceived to be both uncertain and important.
   a. Conflict
   b. Stress
   c. Empowerment
   d. Role overload

Answer: b, difficulty: 1, p. 279

57. Which of the following statements is NOT true concerning stress?
   a. Stress is not necessarily bad in and of itself.
   b. Employees today are increasingly complaining about higher stress levels brought on by pressures at work and home.
   c. Managers are ignoring stress since it doesn't affect the bottom line.
   d. Stress shows itself in a number of ways.

Answer: c, difficulty: 2, p. 279

58. Stress can cause all of the following EXCEPT:
   a. lower job satisfaction.
   b. increased tension.
   c. less accidents.
   d. increased boredom.

Answer: c, difficulty: 2, p. 279

59. Symptoms of stress can be:
   a. physiological.
   b. psychological.
   c. behavioral.
   d. All of the above.

Answer: d, difficulty: 1, pp. 279-280

60. Job stress is estimated to cost U.S. industry between:
   a. $100 and $200 million.
   b. $300 and $400 million.
   c. $700 and $800 million.
   d. $200 and $300 billion.

Answer: d, difficulty: 3, p. 280

61. Physical activity programs to reduce stress include:
   a. teaching relaxation techniques.
   b. re-designing jobs.
   c. improving organizational communication.
   d. better matching employee abilities with jobs.

Answer: a, difficulty: 1, p. 280

62. Which of the following is a conclusion of the finding on the structure-innovation relationship?
   a. Organic structures positively influence innovation.
   b. Long tenure in management is associated with low innovation.
   c. Innovation is nurtured where there is a shortage of resources.
   d. Interunit communication is low in innovative organizations.

Answer: d, difficulty: 2, p. 281

63. Which of the following is NOT true about innovative organizations?
    a. They tend to have similar cultures.
    b. They reward successes and punish failures.
    c. They celebrate mistakes.
    d. They encourage experimentation.

Answer: b, difficulty: 3, p. 281

TRUE/FALSE

64. Technology has little impact on jobs and organizations.

False, difficulty: 1, p. 265

65. We live in an age of discontinuity.

True, difficulty: 1, p. 265

66. Economic shocks include the rise and fall of dot.com stocks and the rapid escalation of home prices during a weak economy.

True, difficulty: 2, Exhibit 16-1.

67. In today's global economy, competitors are as likely to come from across the ocean as from across the street.

True, difficulty: 2, p. 266

68. Social trends remain static.

False, difficulty: 1, p. 266

69. Change agents can be managers, non-managers, employees of the organization or outside consultants.

True, difficulty: 2, p. 266

70. Outside consultants are prone to initiating drastic changes.

True, difficulty: 2, p. 266

71. Internal staff specialists, when acting as change agents, might be more cautious because they have to live with the consequences of their actions.

True, difficulty: 2, p. 266

72. For major change efforts, internal management rarely will hire the services of outside consultants.

False, difficulty: 3, p. 266

73. Until very recently, the white-water rapids simile dominated the thinking of practicing managers and academics.

False, difficulty: 2, p. 267

74. Lewin's three-step process for describing the change process is most similar to the white-water rapids simile of change.

False, difficulty: 2, p. 267

75. According to Lewin's description of the change process, *driving forces* direct behavior away from the status quo.

True, difficulty: 2, p. 267

76. According to Lewin's description of the change process, restraining forces direct behavior away from the status quo.

False, difficulty: 2, p. 267

77. Once unfreezing has been accomplished, the change itself can be implemented.

True, difficulty: 2, p. 267

78. Unless unfreezing occurs in the change process, there is a very strong chance the change will be short-lived and employees will revert to the previous equilibrium state.

False, difficulty: 3, p. 267

79. Lewin's three-step process treats change as a break in the organization's equilibrium state.

True, difficulty: 2, p. 268

80. Few organizations today can treat change as the occasional disturbance in an otherwise peaceful world.

True, difficulty: 2, p. 268

81. The old adage "If it ain't broke, don't fix it" has been replaced by "If it ain't broke, you just haven't looked hard enough. Fix it anyway."

True, difficulty: 2, p. 268

82. One of the most well documented findings from studies of individual and organizational behavior is that organizations and their members resist change.

True, difficulty: 3, p. 269

83. Resistance to change can also be a source of functional conflict.

True, difficulty: 2, p. 269

84.   In change situations, deferred actions make the link between the source of the resistance and the reaction to it easier to understand.

False, difficulty: 2, p. 269

85.   The greater challenge is managing resistance that is implicit or deferred.

True, difficulty: 2, p. 269

86.   When we are confronted with change, the tendency to respond in our accustomed ways becomes a source of resistance.

True, difficulty: 3, p. 269

87.   Habit, security, and structural inertia are all sources of individual resistance to change.

False, difficulty: 1, pp. 269-270

88.   People who have a high need for security are likely to resist change because it threatens their feeling of safety.

True, difficulty: 3, p. 270

89.   In general, people love the unknown.

False, difficulty: 1, p. 270

90.   Individuals selectively process information in order to keep their perceptions intact.

True, difficulty: 2, p. 270

91.   Organizations, by their nature, are conservative and actively resist change.

True, difficulty: 1, p. 270

92.   *Group inertia* is the term used to describe an organization's built-in mechanism to produce stability.

False, difficulty: 2, p. 270

93.   Since organizations are made up of interdependent subsystems, you can't change one without affecting the others.

True, difficulty: 3, p. 270

94.   Changes in organizational patterns may threaten the expertise of specialized groups.

True, difficulty: 2, p. 271

95.   Those groups in the organization that control sizable resources often see change as a threat.

True, difficulty: 3, p. 271

96.   Those who most benefit from the current allocation of resources are often threatened by changes that may affect future allocations.

True, difficulty: 2, p. 271

97.   People who participate in making a decision are typically more strongly committed to the final outcome than those who aren't involved.

True, difficulty: 2, p. 271

98.   Change agents should provide employees with attractive rewards that are contingent on acceptance of change.

True, difficulty: 2, p. 272

99.   Some examples of learning organizations would include FedEx, the U.S. Army, and Wal-Mart.

True, difficulty: 2, p. 272

100. A learning organization has developed the continuous capacity to adapt and change.

True, difficulty: 1, p. 272

101. To create learning organizations, management needs to create a climate that brings paradoxes and differences out into the open.

True, difficulty: 3, p. 272

102. OD is a term used to encompass a collection of planned change interventions built on humanistic-democratic values that seek to improve organizational effectiveness and employee well-being.

True, difficulty: 1, p. 273

103. Concepts such as power, authority, control, conflict, and coercion are held in relatively low esteem among OD change agents.

True, difficulty: 2, p. 273

104. The more that people who will be affected by a change are involved in the decisions surrounding that change, the more they will be committed to implementing those decisions.

True, difficulty: 2, p. 273

105. Another name for T-groups is sensitivity training.

True, difficulty: 2, p. 273

106. Sensitivity training describes a process by which an organization responds to employee needs by developing mechanisms to allow employees to share fully in making the decisions that delineate their lives at work.

False, difficulty: 2, p. 273

107. A tool for assessing attitudes held by organizational members, identifying discrepancies among perceptions, and solving these differences is process consultation.

False, difficulty: 2, p. 274

108. The purpose of process consultation is to assist a client through an outside consultant to perceive, understand, and act on process events with which the client must deal.

True, difficulty: 2, p. 274

109. Process consultation is more task directed than sensitivity training.

True, difficulty: 3, pp. 274-275

110. In process consultation, consultants solve an organization's problems.

False, difficulty: 2, p. 275

111. The emphasis in process consultation is on joint diagnosis because the client develops a skill at analyzing processes within his or her unit that can be continually called on long after the consultant is gone.

True, difficulty: 3, p. 275

112. The process consultant need not be an expert in solving the particular problem that is identified.

True, difficulty: 3, p. 275

113. Team building can be applied within groups or at the intergroup level where activities are interdependent.

True, difficulty: 2, p. 275

114. Intergroup development seeks to change the attitudes, stereotypes, and perceptions that groups have of each other.

True, difficulty: 2, p. 276

115. Appreciative inquiry looks for problems to fix.

False, difficulty: 2, p. 276

116. AI proponents claim it makes more sense to refine and enhance what the organization is already doing well.

True, difficulty: 2, p. 277

117. The three key elements of process reengineering are identifying an organization's distinctive competencies, assessing core processes, and reorganizing horizontally by process.

True, difficulty: 3, p. 278

118. Employee stress is an increasing problem in organizations.

True, difficulty: 1, p. 279

119. Stress is always a negative condition.

False, difficulty: 1, p. 279

120. Most of the early concern with stress was directed at physiological symptoms, primarily because the topic was researched by specialists in the health and medical sciences.

True, difficulty: 3, p. 279

121. Job dissatisfaction is the simplest and most obvious psychological effect of stress.

True, difficulty: 2, p. 280

122. Some of the physiological symptoms of stress are tension, anxiety, irritability, boredom, and procrastination.

False, difficulty: 1, p. 280

123. Realistically, stress can be totally eliminated from a person's life if it is managed well.

False, difficulty: 2, p. 280

124. Improved organizational communication will keep ambiguity-induced stress to a minimum.

True, difficulty: 2, p. 280

125. Human resource variables have been the most studied potential source of innovation.

False, difficulty: 3, p. 281

126. Long tenure in management is associated with innovation.

True, difficulty: 2, p. 281

127. Innovative organizations actively train and develop their members to keep them current.

True, difficulty: 1, p. 281

ESSAY

128. What are some of the forces for change?

There are six forces that act as stimulants for change: the nature of the work force, technology, economic shocks, competition, social trends, and world politics.

Exhibit 16-1

129. Who is responsible for managing change activities in organizations?

Change agents are responsible for managing change activities. These change agents can be managers or nonmanagers, employees of the organization, or outside consultants.

p. 266

130. Summarize Lewin's three-step change model.

Lewin's three-step change model requires unfreezing the status quo, changing to a new state, and refreezing the new change to make it permanent. Unfreezing is accomplished by increasing driving forces that direct behavior away from the status quo, decreasing restraining forces which hinder movement from the existing equilibrium, or both. Once unfreezing is accomplished, the change itself can be implemented. The new situation then needs to be refrozen so it can be sustained over time.

p. 267 and Exhibit 16-2

131. What are some of the individual sources of resistance to change?

Five reasons that individuals may resist change include habit, security, economic factors, fear of the unknown, and selective information processing. When we are confronted with change, we tend to respond in our accustomed ways (habit) and this becomes a source of resistance. People who have high need for security are likely to resist change because it threatens their feeling of safety. Changes in job tasks or established work routines can arouse economic fears if people are concerned they won't be able to perform the new tasks or routines to their previous standards, especially when pay is closely tied to productivity. Changes substitute ambiguity and uncertainty for the unknown. And people generally don't like the unknown. Individuals shape their world through their perceptions. Once they have created this world, they resist changing it. So individuals are guilty of selectively processing information in order to keep their perceptions intact. They hear what they want to hear. They ignore information that challenges the world they've created.

pp. 269-270

132. What are some of the sources of organizational resistance to change?

There are six major sources of organizational resistance to change: structural inertia, limited focus of change, group inertia, threat to expertise, threat to established power relationships, and threat to established resource allocations. Organizations have built-in mechanisms to produce stability. The people who are hired into an organization are chosen for fit; they are then shaped and directed to behave in certain ways. When an organization is confronted with change, this structural inertia acts as a counterbalance to sustain stability. Organizations are made up of interdependent subsystems. You can't change one without affecting the others. So limited changes in subsystems tend to get nullified by the larger system. Even if individuals want to change their behavior, group norms act as a constraint. Changes in organizational patterns may threaten the expertise of specialized groups. Any redistribution of decision-making authority can threaten long-established power relationships within the organization. Those groups in the organization that control sizable resources often see change as a threat. They tend to be content with the status quo.

pp. 270-271

133. List some techniques for overcoming resistance to change.

Some techniques for overcoming resistance to change include communication, participation, providing support, and rewarding acceptance of change. Resistance can be reduced through communicating with employees to help them see the logic of change. People who participate in the decision-making process are typically more strongly committed to the final outcome than those who are not. Change agents can offer a range of supportive efforts to reduce resistance such as showing concern and empathy by practicing active listening, offering employee counseling and therapy, or providing new skills training. Change agents should provide employees with attractive rewards that are contingent on acceptance of change. These rewards can range from praise and recognition to pay increases or promotions.

p. 271-272

134. What is a learning organization and what are its characteristics?

An organization that has been intentionally designed with the capacity to continuously adapt and change is a learning organization. There is a shared vision. People discard their old ways of thinking and the standard routines they use for solving problems or doing their jobs. Members think of all organizational processes, activities, functions, and interactions with the environment as part of a system of interrelationships. People openly communicate with each other without fear of criticism or punishment. People sublimate their personal self-interest and fragmented departmental interests to work together to achieve the organization's shared vision.

p. 272 and Exhibit 16-3

135. What are the underlying values in most OD efforts?

There are five underlying values in most OD efforts. Respect for people: Individuals are perceived as being responsible, conscientious, and caring. They should be treated with dignity and respect. Trust and support: The effective and healthy organization is characterized by trust, authenticity, openness, and a supportive climate. Power equalization: Effective organizations deemphasize hierarchical authority and control. Confrontation: Problems shouldn't be swept under the rug. They should be openly confronted. Participation: The more that people who will be affected by a change are involved in the decisions surrounding that change, the more they will be committed to implementing those decisions.

p. 273

136. Discuss six OD interventions that change agents might consider using.

Six OD interventions that change agents might consider using are sensitivity training, survey feedback, process consultation, team building, intergroup development, and appreciative inquiry. In sensitivity training, members are brought together in a free and open environment in which participants discuss themselves and their interactive processes, loosely directed by a professional behavioral scientist. Survey feedback is used to assess attitudes held by organizational members, identifying discrepancies among member perceptions, and solving these differences. Process consultation uses an outside consultant to assist a client, usually a manager, to perceive, understand, and act upon process events with which he or she must deal. The consultant works with the client in jointly diagnosing what processes need improvement. Team building utilizes high-interaction group activities to increase trust and openness among team members. Intergroup development seeks to change the attitudes, stereotypes, and perceptions that groups have of each other. Appreciative inquiry accentuates the positive. Rather than looking for problems to fix, this approach seeks to identify the unique qualities and special strengths of an organization, which can then be built on to improve performance.

pp. 273-277

137. What are the key elements of process reengineering?

The three elements of process reengineering are identifying an organization's distinctive competencies, assessing core processes, and reorganizing horizontally by process. An organization's distinctive competencies define what it is that he organization does better than its competition. Identifying competencies is important because it guides decisions regarding what activities are crucial to the organization's success. Management also needs to assess the core processes that clearly add value to the organization's distinctive competencies. These are the processes that transform materials, capital, information, and labor into products and services that the customer values. Reorganizing around horizontal processes means using cross-functional and self-managed teams. It means focusing on processes rather than functions. It also means cutting out unnecessary levels of middle management.

p. 278

138. What is stress and what are the symptoms of work stress?

Stress is a dynamic condition in which an individual is confronted with an opportunity, constraint, or demand related to what he or she desires and for which the outcomes are perceived to be both uncertain and important. Stress is not necessarily bad in and of itself. Some symptoms of work stress include high blood pressure, ulcers, irritability, difficulty in making routine decisions, loss of appetite, and accident proneness.

pp. 279-280

139. Discuss some organizational factors that can lower stress levels.

Any attempt to lower stress levels has to begin with employee selection. Management needs to make sure that an employee's abilities match the requirements of the job. An objective job preview during the selection process will lessen stress by reducing ambiguity. Improved organizational communications will keep ambiguity-induced stress to a minimum. Similarly, a goal-setting program will clarify job responsibilities and provide clear performance objectives. Job redesign is also a way to reduce stress. If stress can be traced directly to boredom or work overload, jobs should be redesigned to increase challenge or reduce the workload. Redesigns that increase opportunities for employees to participate in decisions and to gain social support have also been found to lessen stress.

p. 280

140. Discuss four structural variables of innovative organizations.

Organic organizations positively influence innovation. Because they're lower in vertical differentiation, formalization, and centralization, organic organizations facilitate the flexibility, adaptation, and cross-fertilization that make the adoption of innovations easier. Long tenure in management is associated with innovation. Managerial tenure apparently provides legitimacy and knowledge of how to accomplish tasks and obtain desired outcomes. Innovation is nurtured where there are slack resources. Having an abundance of resources allows an organization to afford to purchase innovations, bear the cost of instituting innovations, and absorb failures. Interunit communication is high in innovative organizations. These organizations are high users of committees, task forces, cross-functional, and other mechanisms that facilitate across departmental lines.

p. 281

Chapter 1 Organizational Culture: American Apparel

Learning Objectives
The purpose of this video is to help you:
1. Understand the role ethical leadership plays in forming organizational culture.
2. Identify how organizations go green.
3. Discuss the power of social impact management to create lasting change.

Synopsis
The self styled renegade of the garment industry, 35 year old Montreal native Dov Charney, is founder and CEO of American Apparel <www.american apparel.net>; the largest T-shirt manufacturer in the U.S. Mr. Charney is a champion of worker's rights and environmentalism, who energetically courts the media. His unique brand of workplace ethics combined with a long-term sustainable business mode enabled the company to double sales for three years running, from $20 million in 2001 to an estimated $80 million in 2003.[1] Entirely housed in a seven story building in downtown L.A., American Apparel doesn't outsource, pays its predominantly Latino workers an average of $12.50 per hour, provides an on site masseuse, health benefits, paid vacation, internship programs, and English classes. Its T-shirts are sweatshop-free, hip, sexy and available online and at the company's three retail stores in L.A., New York, and Montreal. Proud of its recycling of one million lbs. of scrap material per year, American Apparel is currently moving toward offering a 100% organic, domestically sourced T-shirt. Dov Charney's future goals include opening stores and manufacturing plants in the developing world with China and India as the preferred locations.

Discussion Questions
1. *For analysis:* From a business perspective, what are the advantages and disadvantages to American Apparel of having a vocal and visible, corporate executive like Dov Charney?

    Among the advantages is his ability to serve as an ethical leader. The media attention helps maintain the company's high profile in the industry. His progressive stance against offshore manufacturing and his high level of socioeconomic commitment instill pride in his labor force and serve as an example for other businesses. Among the disadvantages are that the global business community may view him as an outsider and a grandstander. His identity is one with the company's identity which may not serve American Apparel well in the long term (i.e. Martha Stewart). In time his outspoken manner and total control may cause some employees to leave the company and eventually erode the high morale that exists now. Student answers will vary.

2. *For analysis:* What are some of the factors that make the organizational culture at American Apparel strong?

    Shared values, support teams, employee appreciation, educational opportunities, workplace opportunities, health care, work environment, a diverse management team,

---

[1] www.americanapparel.net/presscenter/articles/20031201industry.html

Dov Charney's open door policy, his ubiquitous presence, energy and passion for his company all contribute to American Apparel's strong organizational culture. Students may want to discuss Mr. Charney's use of the word "propaganda" in the video clip, and his wink at the camera meant to convey his awareness that all of these factors are smart moves that work to protect the business.

3. *For application:* In addition to recycling and using 10% organic cotton to produce its T-shirts, what other steps should American Apparel work toward as it continues to go green?

Students may make any number of suggestions for American Apparel as it adopts a more activist (dark green) approach toward environmentalism. Highly sensitive to its use of natural resources, eventually American Apparel might operate a green factory or lead a movement in the garment industry to eliminate waste, or donate a percentage of profits to green causes.

4. *For application:* What changes, if any, would you suggest that American Apparel make to its business model, if it were preparing to make an Initial Public Offering in the near future? Explain.

Suggestions for change may include presenting a more polished image to investors; promoting his belief in social impact management via strategic and operational plans for the future, rather than rhetoric, and changing some of the language in his mission statement(i.e. "hyper capitalist-socialist business fusion").Many students may feel the "vertically integrated" business model is excellent, emphasizing high quality, quick turn, social responsibility and a positive work environment along with sustainability and a global perspective. Students may want to discuss why and how private ownership serves Dov Charney's purposes as an entrepreneur.

5. *For debate:* "Kids today are more liberal and I think they are going to become more and more political," Dov Charney recently told Chris Jones of the Las Vegas Review-Journal.[2] Do you agree that his political stance will continue to draw target customers from "Generation X and Generation Y?"

Students who agree may argue that there is no doubt that young people are Dov Charney's target market. American Apparel does not sell to Wal-Mart and other high volume, low cost department stores, not only because it allows the company to determine its own margins, but because Mr. Charney believes that unlike the Boomers, youth rejects mass market values, and they're idealism will shape the future. Students who disagree may feel that youth are largely materialistic and choose to buy his T-shirts because they are" hip", not out of political and environmentalist convictions.

---

[2] http://www.reviewjournal.comlvrj_home/2002/Aug-27-Tue-2002/business/19497715.html

Online Exploration

Browse American Apparel's sexy website<www.american apparel.net>.Did you notice the New York, L.A., Montreal (the locations of American Apparel's three retail stores) times neatly positioned along the border or were you mesmerized by the "bathing beauty" video story floating by on your screen? Does it make you want to run out and buy yourself a sweatshop free T? Read the FAQ's for both consumers and wholesalers. Read the company's mission statement and browse any of the options available to you including the online store offerings, streaming videos and press center articles. What makes this mission statement unique? Who is the web site designed to appeal to? Do you think it is effective? Explain your response.

The Website is geared to a young college crowd and the hip wholesalers who serve them. It is designed to appeal to idealistic young people who want to demonstrate social awareness while looking and feeling good in their basic T's. It showcases Dov Charney's larger than life personality, the company's passion for ethical business practices and clearly answers key questions for both wholesalers and consumers. The mission statement is unique in its espousal of an activist political viewpoint; in its translation selections to global customers in French, German, Italian and Spanish and in its bold faced lettering. Student responses will vary across ethnic, generational, political and economic boundaries. Note that the opening of the mission statement is addressed to the business community. Some students may consider it to be a rallying cry against outsourcing. The plethora of media may strike some people as overkill. They may suggest the site be edited and streamlined to maximize effectiveness.

Chapter 2 NIDEK

Note: For anecdotal material on the topic of global Japanese corporations and American business people see James Brooks, Learning to Avoid a Deal-Killing Faux Pas in Japan, The New York Times, Sept. 17, 2002, pp. C10

1. Do you think a firm grasp of organizational behavior might have helped David Yeh to avoid high turnover rates among his sales people? If so, explain how. If not, explain why not. You may want to include an intuitive guess at his people skills in your answer.

OB concepts may have helped David Yeh to gain a deeper understanding of American culture and how it has shaped his employees. Most importantly he might have been able to better adapt his management style to prevent this situation from escalating. Additionally, stronger people skills might have helped him to predict this behavior and saved Nidek the cost of high turnover among sales team members in both financial and human terms. Some students may argue that David Yeh could not have foreseen the use of such aggressive tactics by his competitors.

2. Do you agree with David Yeh's assessment that salesmanship is an innate personality trait? Why or why not? Which individual level variables, i.e. biographical characteristics, abilities, values, attitudes and personality type, would you look for in a potential sales person for Nidek, U.S.A.? Explain how your criteria would ensure satisfied employees and organizational productivity.

Opinions may vary as to whether salesmanship is a natural talent or an acquired skill. Regardless, students might look for the following variables when filling a sales position at Nidek, U.S.A.: A background in science or engineering would be desirable for in-depth understanding of surgical and dermatological equipment; excellent communication skills would indicate an ability to deal effectively with doctors, suppliers, and fellow sales people. Someone who is ethical, ambitious, extroverted, and open to new ideas and learning would do well at Nidek where sound business principles and innovation go hand in hand.

3. What could management at Nidek USA do *now* in order to forestall the problems of a 2006 labor shortage?

By implementing sophisticated recruitment and retention strategies now, Nidek might be able to minimize the effects of the impending labor shortage. Hypothetical strategies would include use of in-house training and development programs to groom employees for assignments abroad; design of highly motivating jobs to attract the largest talent pool possible; and modification of hiring practices in each branch to reflect culture-based norms. Finally, a concerted effort should be made to continue to build Nidek's reputation not only as a leader in its field, but as a great place to work, as well.

4. What work/life conflicts might employees at Nidek, U.S.A. encounter as a result of both the company's Japanese roots and the company's global presence? Explain.

Judging from the video, the dominant culture among management at Nidek is Japanese. It is based on a tradition of employee loyalty and dedication to work. Employees in America may experience difficulty in balancing a lifestyle that is predicated on leisure and family time with high corporate expectations at work. For those married to a working spouse and juggling parental responsibilities, the demands may be quite stressful. Additional sources of conflict would stem from the travel requirements that often accompany jobs in global companies like Nidek. The need to consult with colleagues or customers around the world, across time zones, may force employees to work at all hours, interfering with a harmonious home life.

Chapter 2

Doc Martens

1. *Howard Johnstone talks about company benefit plans as a means of motivating employees, but he does not mention any ways in which the work itself might satisfy employees. What general aspects of their work would most people at Dr. Martens find motivating? If you gave different answers for factory works than for management, explain why.* Managers might be motivated by status, pay, and opportunities for advancement. Production workers might be motivated by benefits and the potential for job security created by a tight job market.

2. *Do you agree with Howard Johnstone that younger people have different attitudes toward work than older people? Why or why not? How might that observation be related to his statement that "people are motivated by different things at different points in their career"?* Motivating factors do change based on career stage and personal circumstances, of which age is only one. Workers with family responsibilities may be more motivated by stability and security or by family benefits like flexible hours and job sharing, while single workers or those without dependents may look for rapid advancement, high pay or bonuses, or opportunities for creativity.

3. *Use what you've learned from the text to assess the problem of absenteeism at Dr. Martens.* Workers in standardized, repetitive jobs, like the line workers at Dr. Martens or any manufacturing firm, are likely to pose special challenges in motivation. High pay can help, but equally important when the job itself can't be redesigned are selecting workers more carefully and providing clean and attractive surroundings, ample work breaks and opportunities to socialize with colleagues, and empathetic supervisors.
   What are some of the decision criteria used in hiring at Dr. Martens? (Some are mentioned in the film; you can infer others.) What are some of the external limitations on the choices its managers can make in hiring? If these were removed, how do you think the hiring decision would change? Management looks for people who fit in with its culture, who relate easily to others and work well in a team. Dr. Martens also looks for people with some minimal technical skills and a certain amount of ambition. Limitations on hiring choices include the difficulty of finding people with the right technical skills (since many factories have moved overseas), and workers' higher expectations in a tight labor market. If employees were more plentiful, obviously the firm's choices would be wider.

Praendex Incorporated

Case Overview

Dinah Daniels is President & Chairman of Massachusetts-based Praendex Incorporated, owners of the Predictive Index (PI), a personality survey created in 1955. The survey is based on psychological and sociological studies done by Ms. Daniel's father and takes just minutes to complete. The PI survey gives hiring managers insight into potential new employees and allows them to better understand current employees to assess whether they are in the jobs best suited to their personality traits. The deceptively simple form consists of a two-sided work sheet with 86 adjectives on each side. On the first side people are asked to check off any words they feel describe how others expect them to act. On the second side, they are asked to select adjectives they believe pertain to them. The results uncover things like how independent an individual is, what their pace of activity is, and how they are going to interact with other people. PI gives managers a tool for maximizing performance excellence, productivity, and job satisfaction. Satisfied clients span 77 countries and vary from small businesses to large conglomerates.

Questions for Discussion:

1. In the video Michael Roberts, Senior Lecturer Harvard Business School/Praendex Board of Directors, states that the Predictive Index gives managers and employees ' a comfortable means of discussing the sensitive issue of personality in a neutral way rather than in a critical way.' Do you agree with this statement? Explain.

Yes. The survey is designed as a learning tool, and because it is based entirely on their own responses; people are less likely to feel criticized than in a performance appraisal. The PI is geared to uncover qualities like interpersonal strengths, communication style, honesty, and ability to thrive in certain work environments. Therefore, both the manager and the employee can focus on specific work related behaviors rather than on character;

making open, constructive discussion possible. (Having a chart—or any piece of paper—to refer to probably helps too!)

2. Praendex Incorporated is advertising opportunities for talented consultants. The position requires a strong self starter. The job description includes the following: "As a Predictive Index Consultant you would sell and deliver the PI management techniques and methods to business executives and managers in your area. The freedom is there to set your own schedules and to have a great deal of control over the growth of your client base. You would have a chance to greatly impact the effectiveness and culture of a company.[1] Using John Holland's Typology of Personality and Sample Occupations (Exhibit 8-3), assess whether you would be a good candidate for this job.

Student responses should include their type and personality characteristics based on John Holland's theory and their evaluations of whether or not they would be good candidates for this position. Depending on the cohesiveness of the class, it might be interesting to see whether students agree with the self-perceptions of their classmates.

3. In your opinion, would the Predictive Index be a good indicator of a person's Emotional intelligence? Explain.

Yes. Since the PI is concerned with revealing underlying attitudes and capabilities an assessing how effectively people can work with others and deal with the specific requirements of an organizational culture, it would be a good EI indicator.

4. You are interested in applying for a position that is about to open up in your department. Your supervisor is aware of your aspirations and you have been working extra hard to make a good impression. The company has just invested in Praendex's Predictive Index and will begin the program before the job is officially posted. Now you will be required to fill out the survey, along with everyone else who is eligible for this internal opening. How does this make you feel? Discuss the possibilities and the conflicts this presents.

---

[1] Ibid.

Student answers will vary. Some students may choose to use the five personality traits delineated in the text: locus of control, Machiavellianism, self esteem, self monitoring, and risk propensity as a basis for their response. Others may base their answers on the Big Five Model.: extroversion, agreeableness, conscientiousness, emotional stability, and openness to experience. Depending on attitude and personality, some people will see the introduction of the PI survey as a threat to their "in" on competition for the job. Others may view it as an opportunity to prove that they are the best person for that particular job, or to find out about alternative, perhaps even better, opportunities for themselves.

Chapters 4 and 5

Motivation: Ernst & Young

Learning Objectives
The purpose of this video is to help you:
1. Understand motivation as a need-satisfying process.
2. Identify the challenges managers face in motivating large, diverse groups of employees.
3. Discuss how Human Resource strategies affect employee motivation and career planning.

Synopsis
Ernst & Young, the third-largest U.S. accounting firm, increased its employee retention rate by 5% as a result of an HR initiative to put "People First." By creating a feedback-rich culture, building great resumes for its 160,000 people in New York City and around the world, and giving them time and freedom to pursue personal goals; Ernst & Young has reaped the benefits of a highly motivated workforce. The company uses mandatory goal setting, provides people with learning opportunities in areas of interest, and measures HR processes using an employee survey to evaluate the workplace environment. While conceding that everyone is somewhat motivated by money, Jim Freer, Americas Vice Chair of People believes that the way a person is treated is the determining factor in a person's level of performance. "People don't leave organizations." he says, "They leave managers."

Discussion Questions
1. *For analysis:* How might the jobs characteristics model be useful to managers at Ernst & Young?
   Given the global reach of Human Resources at Ernst & Young, the job characteristics model (JCM) might be extremely useful as a guideline for designing and redesigning jobs in its offices around the world to align with employee needs and organizational goals. The JCM would be well suited to this firm which actively recruits talented, creative thinkers who want to make a difference in people's lives and be challenged in their jobs. Student answers may include motivation, performance, satisfaction, growth need, job enrichment, and the importance of client focus and feedback.

2. *For analysis:* Recently Ernst & Young was barred from accepting any new audit clients in the United States for six months after an SEC administrative judge called "Ernst & Young "reckless," "highly unreasonable" and "negligent" in forming a business relationship with an audit client, PeopleSoft.[1] As an undergraduate intern at the firm, how might this affect your career plans? Explain.
   Student responses will vary. If the internship was created to accommodate anticipated business, the internship may be withdrawn or postponed until a later date. Some students may feel betrayed by this breach of trust on the company's part and no

---

[1] www.theithacajournal.com/news/stories/20040419/localnews/255401.html

longer wish to consider pursuing a career there; some students may see it as a welcome "reality check" and go ahead with their plans with a more pragmatic view of the workplace; others may not be fazed at all and consider it a lack of judgment on the part of specific employees rather than a reflection on the company as a whole.

3. *For application:* In light of the damage to the firm's public image as a result of the six-month ban on new business, what steps would you take as a manager to maintain employee motivation at Ernst & Young?

Honest communication on the part of management is critical when the company is facing an unforeseen constraint on its operations and a blow to its respected position. At a time when the entire industry is laboring under the cloud of scandal, managers must make every effort to boost morale, to be a model of integrity, and to insure employees, prospective employees and clients that they do have a future with the company. Managers can take on support roles or coaching roles if employees need help dealing with worried clients. Students will have additional ideas.

4. *For application:* How would you suggest that diversity initiative managers at Ernst & Young create an inclusive environment that will motivate employees from diverse cultural backgrounds to excel?

Student answers may include matching personalities to jobs, implementing a thorough orientation process for both current employees and the new hires who will be working together, ongoing skills training programs, support programs, clarifying goals, and setting aside time for individual counseling, and evaluation; as well as, using measurement tools such as feedback surveys to assess whether the initiative is working.

5. *For debate:* According to Richard Whiteley, author of "Love the Work You're With," by discovering your purpose in life you can increase your job satisfaction. Would you agree that Ernst & Young's "People First" initiative supports this viewpoint? Explain why you feel the HR initiative either supports or contradicts Richard Whiteley's premise.

Students who argue that the initiative supports this viewpoint may say that it emphasizes respect for the whole person including family, community and personal commitments. It grants employees freedom to engage in outside interests so that when they are at work they are 100% focused on work. People do feel valued as a result of this freedom and tend to work even harder to please clients and achieve organizational goals. Students who argue that the initiative contradicts this premise, may say that the initiative allows people to separate work and personal time so that they can gain satisfaction form pursuits outside of work and perform well for the company because they are able to satisfy their needs outside of the workplace. Students may cite examples of employees in the video clip to support their arguments.

Online Exploration
Browse Ernst & Young's home page www.ey.com. Read the newsletter. What topics does it cover? Do you feel the communication is open and honest? What purposes does the newsletter serve? Now click on the resource link for careers and read the Six Core

Values, the Overview, the Message from the Chairman, and the Views on Key Issues. Does the company's self- presentation ring true? Do you think the company was significantly hurt by the recent SEC ruling against it? Would the fact that Ernst & Young has been recognized as a top learning organization in the United States influence your decision to seek a career there? Would you seek a position in one of the firm's foreign offices?

Student answers will vary. The newsletter is a forum for self promotion to employees, clients and even competitors. It attempts to deal with all major company events including the recent SEC ruling on its relationship with PeopleSoft. The six core values reflect the values espoused in the video clip, putting "People First." Although the SEC ruling has caused Ernst & Young to sell most of their consulting businesses and for some former partners to separate themselves from the firm, it is not likely the company will suffer a severe economic setback, according to an article appearing in The New York Times on pages C1 and C2April, 19, 2004. The fact that Ernst & Young is a learning organization may appeal to many students who wish to build resumes and careers in the United States. The offices in other countries may operate somewhat differently and students wishing to work abroad would need to inquire further.

Chapters 4 and 5

Starbucks

1. *How does management at Starbucks exemplify the core OB topics of motivation, leadership, communication, learning, and attitude development?* Management at Starbucks appears to motivate in part by building trust among employees and giving them a voice in the firm. Generous benefits are also motivating. Leadership is most evident in Howard Schultz's ability to convey his vision to others and make it a reality. Communication appears to work both ways since employees are encouraged to participate in the many decisions. Starbuck' commitment to diversity is one aspect of attitude development in that it encourages a wide variety of ways of thinking. Learning is suggested in the statement that the firm cannot "embrace the status quo."

2. *Cite some evidence from the video that indicates to you whether or not Starbucks managers accept that behavior in the workplace is directed toward a goal that the individuals believes is in his or her best interest.* Behar speaks of employees having financial and/or emotional ownership of the organizations to which they belong. This suggests that by offering employees a share of this type of "ownership," Starbucks hopes to align its employees' interest with the firm's.

   Howard Behar has said that one distinctive thing about Starbucks is its "diversity of thought," which comes from hiring a wide diversity of people. What do you think are some of the motivations for Starbucks' commitment to diversity in hiring? What advantages does the company gain from this value? Like other firms Starbucks can gain in creativity and innovation by hiring a diversity of employees.

Chapter 6:
AMY'S ICE CREAMS SERVES UP TEXAS-SIZED EXPANSION
Analysis

1. Why would Amy Miller choose to form a corporation rather than a partnership when starting her business with a partner?

With a partnership, Miller and her partner(s) would still be financially accountable for any business mistakes and any outstanding debts. The partnership might also suffer if Miller and her partner(s) had disagreements. Forming a corporation solves the problem of personal liability, because the corporation becomes responsible for debts and mistakes. It also allows Miller and her partner(s) to gain liquidity by selling their shares, something they can't do with a partnership. Finally, the corporation would survive even if Miller had disagreements with her partner(s).

2. What are the tax implications of making Amy's Ice Creams a corporation rather than a partnership?

If Amy's Ice Creams were a partnership, the profits (or losses) would belong to the owners—split in any way designated by the partnership agreement. Profits would be categorized as income for the owners and would therefore be taxed at personal rates. If the company were a corporation, profits (or losses) would belong to the corporation and would be taxed at corporate rates. Once profits are distributed as dividends to shareholders, however, they are taxed at personal rates.

3. If Amy's Ice Creams agreed to be acquired by Procter & Gamble, would this combination be considered a horizontal merger, vertical merger, or conglomerate merger?

Because Procter & Gamble makes so many different and unrelated products, its acquisition of Amy's Ice Cream would be considered a conglomerate merger. A horizontal merger would consist of the combination of competing companies performing the same function; a vertical merger would occur when one firm involved in a particular part of the industry acquires or joins with another firm involved in different part of the same industry.

4. If Amy's Ice Creams went public, under what circumstances might top management decide to take the company private later on?

Management might want to take Amy's Ice Creams private if it felt public scrutiny of decisions and results was interfering with its ability to operate the company or if it felt the company was at risk for a hostile takeover.

5. How do techniques such as the paper bag job application help Amy Miller manage her growing ice cream empire?

Because Miller cannot personally oversee all aspects of her growing business, she needs to find talented and entrepreneurial employees capable of handling specific business decisions and tasks on their own. The paper bag job application is one of several techniques she and her managers use to determine whether a job candidate has the ability and potential to become a productive employee.

Application

Students were asked to suggest the kinds of people they think Amy Miller should invite to serve on her board of directors. Students may offer various responses to this question. In general, Miller should invite experts from different fields—such as finance, marketing, retailing, and so on—so she can leverage their expertise and experience to build her business.

Decision

Students were asked how Amy Miller might evaluate the advantages and disadvantages of agreeing to be acquired by Unilever. In addition to analyzing the price Unilever is willing to pay, Miller should think about whether she and her business are a good fit with the Unilever culture, whether the merger will provide resources to help Miller achieve her long-term goals for Amy's Ice Creams, and how the merger will affect the market perception of Amy's Ice Creams as well as its competitive position. Students may suggest additional areas to be evaluated.

Communication

Students were asked to draft a letter outlining five or more questions they would ask before investing in Amy's Ice Cream.

Sample questions students may include in their letter are: (1) What are your long-term goals for Amy's Ice Creams, and how do you plan to reach those goals? (2) What was the financial performance of Amy's Ice Creams for the past three to five years? (3) How much debt has the company incurred and how will it pay this debt off? (4) Is Amy's Ice Creams paying dividends and if so, how often and how much? (5) What major expenditures are you planning for the coming year or two, and how will these be financed? Students may have additional questions.

Integration

Students were asked whether Amy's Ice Creams should use a strategic alliance or joint venture to open new stores in Mexico.

Students who argue in favor of a strategic alliance may say that this approach allows Amy's Ice Creams to form a partnership and work toward its own goals while the other partner works toward its own goals, which should be complementary. In this way, the companies will share ideas, resources, technologies, costs, risks, and profits without being bound together by a formal company structure.

Students who argue in favor of a joint venture may say that creating an entirely new business entity with a separate legal existence from its parents offers legal protection in case the new venture falters. They may also say that it allows management of the joint venture to operate in the best interests of the new business under the guidance of the parents, which may eliminate some disagreements.

Ethics

Students were asked whether it would be ethical for Amy Miller to share certain proprietary information about the business with some shareholders but not with others.

No, Miller should not share proprietary business information with selected shareholders, as all are part owners and entitled to know what is happening with their investments. Students may identify certain sensitive information (such as information about potential liabilities or lawsuits) that Miller would conceivably want to keep quiet if these were pending problems, but all investors should be informed about these matters.

Debate

Students were asked to debate whether Amy's Ice Creams should go public or remain privately held.

Some arguments students may cite for remaining private are: the company retains all the advantages of the corporate form of ownership but doesn't have to explain its decisions and performance to anyone other than the shareholders; owners retain full control over operations and decisions; owners are protected from unwanted takeovers. Some arguments for going public include: gaining a ready supply of capital and increased liquidity; enjoying enhanced visibility that can give sales a boost and help the company recruit talented managers and employees; reveal the market value of the company; gain the flexibility to use such stock to acquire other companies.

Teamwork

Students were asked to team up and brainstorm a list of five or more questions that Amy Miller would want to ask before acquiring a two-store ice cream parlor chain in Dallas.

Students may suggest a range of areas to be covered by Miller's questions. Some sample questions include: (1) What was the financial performance of your chain for the past three to five years? (2) How much debt has your company incurred and how is it paying this debt off? (3) What are the sales and expenses associated with each of your stores? (4) What are the basic values and beliefs of your corporate culture? (5) What is your tax situation and are all your obligations current? (6) What are the strengths and weaknesses of your workforce?

Online Research

Students were asked to research trends in U.S. ice cream consumption. Specific questions included:

What are the implications for the future growth of Amy's Ice Creams? How are these trends likely to affect shareholders who have invested in Amy's Ice Creams?

Students may want to check the company's Web site at *http://www.amysicecream.com/* to see if it has any links to sources of information about consumption trends. Search sites such as *http://www.google.com* may help students locate suitable sources, as well. If ice cream consumption is going up, the trend may point to higher sales for Amy's Ice Creams and, in turn, better returns for shareholders. If consumption is dropping, the trend may indicate slower or no growth for Amy's Ice Creams, which means lower returns for shareholders.

players, trainers, coaches, and manager. The executives are acutely aware of status and less adept at subjugating their own vision to a team effort. However they must deal with the same issues of setting clear goals, employing members with relevant skills, building a foundation of trust and good communication.

3. *For application:* What suggestions would you have for Bristol-Myers-Squibb and Pepsi to improve the long-term effectiveness of team building exercises? Do you feel these are worthwhile investments for top corporate executives? Explain.

Bristol-Myers-Squibb might want to include front-line supervisors and office staff in these exercises, rather than limiting the experience to top tier personnel who may be too removed from operations to implement them on a factory floor or at a weekly marketing meeting. Maybe covering the event in a company newsletter or hiring a consultant to lead teams through role playing on site following this session would be of value. It could be argued that the investment in time and capital is not justifiable, as it seems to require too little serious effort from its participants. Students will have many additional ideas to contribute.

4. *For application:* As a dotcom manager, how would you go about assembling a work team for a long-term project? What insights from the WNBA might you use to accomplish your task?

Starting with the external conditions imposed by the dotcom, students might want to begin by recruiting one or two employees whose work and personalities are complementary and then add people who have the skill sets needed to accomplish the chosen project. The WNBA video clip stressed the importance of establishing a managerial strategy before building a team, communicating clearly to each person what role he or she is expected to play and what the goals of the team are. The manager of a work team also needs to be aware of the strengths, weaknesses, and different levels of experience existing on his or her team. The selected people must be able to trust and respect one another, to share information openly and to get along for the duration of the project.

5. **For debate:** Point guard, Debbie Black sees a strong correlation between professional sports and the business world. Do you agree with her view that the best way to handle conflict is "to let it roll off you?" Please address your response to this issue as it applies to business and to professional sports.

Some students may wish to argue that while her view may work on the basketball court, when everyone is concentrating on working toward a win; off the court and in the office it may be better to air differences in the open so they can be resolved or used for constructive purposes. Some students may feel that letting relationship conflicts "roll off" may avoid the dysfunction that follows intense argument in both sports and business. Other students may wish to argue that there are times in any professional capacity when people should keep their emotions and their egos in check and learn not to place blame or bear grudges in order to accomplish a goal or a task.

Online exploration

Browse the home page of The Connecticut Sunwww.wnba.com/sun/. After you have seen the WBNA home page, go to The Connecticut Sun pages and explore the team history where you can read about the logo that features a fiery orange sunburst, a WNBA basketball and a blue ribbon with four white semicircular domes which is a modern interpretation of an ancient Mohegan symbol and represents the four corners of the earth under a sky dome. Then read the latest news, any player chats that might interest you and go to the ticket holder's pages and also view the mini plans and the community relations items. Decide who they are communicating with and whether there is anything else they might do to make this site a more effective tool. Would you say this young team is using the website to its maximum potential? Explain.

Student opinions will vary with website design knowledge and level of interest in sports sites. Many students may feel the WNBA has provided the team with an appropriate format, excellent for showing fan appreciation and getting fan feedback as well as selling tickets and displaying social responsibility by supporting well chosen causes like "Read to Achieve," and "Jr. NBA & Jr. NBA Keys to Success." Sports fans and students with graphic arts knowledge might feel there is room for improvement and offer suggestions to make the site more user friendly, more appealing to young people and more inspiring to girls considering a career in the world of professional athletics. Some people might feel that the Mohegan Sun arena and its state of the art resort hotel facilities should be more prominently featured as an attraction to new fans and a source of pride for the team.

Chapters 7 and 8

IQ SOLUTIONS

1. According to Human Resource Manager, Connie Holland, the firm's mission is to make a real difference in people's quality of life. Based on your knowledge of work values and organizational culture, assess whether Nexters would be a good fit for IQ Solutions.

   Nexters grew up with technology and see the Internet as a powerful tool for social change. They are comfortable with diversity and eager to make a difference in the world through meaningful work. Still young, they would be likely to find the training and tuition reimbursement programs attractive. Nexters would also have a lot to offer to a team oriented, public service company like IQ Solutions.

2. As a manager at IQ Solutions, which of the following motivation programs would you choose: Management by Objectives (MBO), Employee Recognition Programs, or Employee Involvement Programs? Why?

   All three motivation techniques are valid options. Employee Recognition Programs are efficacious and relatively easy to implement. Without a great deal of paperwork or added expense such programs interject personal attention and appreciation for a job well done into the office routine. Recognition can be expressed in a variety of ways; tailored to the needs of a diverse staff. These include handwritten notes, e-mails, and cash rewards.

3. Do you think that Flow and Intrinsic Motivation are operative at IQ Solutions? Why or why not? Consider the variety of positions that exist at IQ Solutions in the managerial, technical, and creative realm, when devising your answer.

   Yes. Enormous talent and energy are required to succeed in any type of minority outreach. Aside from money and deadlines, the desire to disseminate health care information to those who need it most is a motivating factor. For example, one or more members of the creative, marketing and technical team responsible for the Game Plan Steroids commercial may have experienced flow. It is likely that IQ Solutions employees achieve intrinsic motivation through feelings of choice, competence, meaningfulness and progress in their work.

4. IQ Solutions offers training and financial assistance to employees in order to help them grow with the firm. What more could be done to further maximize motivation of this diverse workforce?

The company should be ready to design flexible work schedules to meet varied needs. Variable Pay Programs, Skill-Based Pay Plans, and Flexible Benefits are all instrumental in motivating employees. Physical work settings that accommodate individual and team needs are also important to fostering innovation and increased productivity.

Chapter 9

Communication: Second City Communications

Learning Objectives
The purpose of this video is to help you:
1. Understand the functions of interpersonal communication in the workplace.
2. Identify the ways to overcome barriers to effective communication.
3. Discuss the importance of active listening both socially and professionally.

Synopsis
Now the world's greatest comedy theatre, Chicago's Second City Improv<www.secondcity.com>, is bringing much more than its famous brand of humor to corporate giants like Coca-Cola, Motorola, and Microsoft. With over 40 years of experience in corporate services, Second City's teachers give business professionals the communication skills they never learned in school: like taking risks and thinking on their feet. Business Communications Training is Second City's fastest growing practice, fueled by the demands of over 200 Fortune 500 companies for solutions. Workshops are tailored to client's needs including: improved listening and presentation skills, collaborative leadership and team skills, interview skills, breaking down barriers to successful communication, and the uses of humor to convey important messages. The next time you sit back and watch Saturday Night Live, ask yourself how a lesson in the art of improvisation might give your career and your social life a boost.

Discussion Questions
1. *For analysis:* How do the exercises featured in this video clip address the contrasting needs of the trial lawyer, the divorce lawyer, and the media buyer?
All of the exercises address the seven elements of the communication process. Each of these students is learning about their own skills and attitudes as they encode messages and receive messages. However they are facing different barriers to communication. For example students may include any of the following in their responses: the trial lawyer needs to improve his skills in watching and using nonverbal cues; the divorce lawyer needs to accurately assess feedback that may be colored by extreme emotions; the media buyer needs to gain confidence.

2. *For analysis:* Would ABC's talkative guest Kay Jarman, the 47 year old award winning salesperson, be a good candidate for Second City's training workshop?
All the exercises featured in the workshop including the "and that's all " exercise alluded to, would help Kay to "dialogue" rather than to "monologue", to focus on others rather than on herself and to listen. However, some students may feel that her pronounced lack of self awareness may be a liability in the social context of a group workshop; making her a better candidate for private coaching.

3. *For application:* What other workshops might Tom Yorton want to offer companies in response to our current economic and political climate?

Suggestions might include workshops to raise the level of communication skills among employees who must face constant security threats (travel industry), or participate in the rebuilding of a company after an unforeseeable disaster (such as 9/11) or an unplanned corporate crisis (such as that suffered by Martha Stewart Living Omnimedia as a result of Martha Stewarts indictment; or who face the challenge of a corporate merger; or who will be managing or working with diverse populations. Students will have additional ideas.

4. *For application:* How might the" yes and rule of improvisation" be used to train customer service representatives at an L.L. Bean or a Dell computer call center? Without physical cues, such as facial expression and body language, is the "yes and rule" still effective?

Today customer service requires representatives to have all pertinent information available and that they are able to respond quickly and effectively to customer needs; regardless of the channel of communication. The yes and rule of improvisation would work well as a training tool in both cases; even without nonverbal cues. Some students may feel that diversity and language differences may be a stumbling block in the case of Dell, where much of the call center business is outsourced to India.

5. *For debate:* According to President and Managing Director, Second City Communications, Tom Yorton: "You have to be willing to fail to be able to get the results you want....to connect with an audience." Do you agree that this is as true in business as it is in comedy? Support your chosen position.

Students who agree may follow an entrepreneurial path, where risk taking is necessary in order to succeed; or they may believe that adversity can be a valuable teacher; or that in order to make business connections we must constantly risk failure. Other students may argue that avoiding failure can be a successful business strategy, as well.

Online Exploration

Enjoy Second City Communication's website www.secondcity.com. If you are a loyal fan, you might want to check out the book titles offered, and read more about the group's history. Now explore Second City's Corporate Services: scan their client roster, read the testimonials, and then select a case study you find compelling. If you are currently employed, which workshop would be most beneficial to you and to your work team? Explain. If you are currently a student, how might you and your fellow business students benefit from a Second City workshop? Which workshop would you most like to participate in? Explain how you think it might help you in terms of your social life, your career planning, and your interviewing skills.

Student responses will differ, depending on the variety of professions and the age groups represented in each class. If students are serving in internships, they may have specific challenges in downward, upward, lateral, and diagonal communication. Regardless of current career status, there is no one who cannot benefit from practicing public speaking and learning to listen actively. Students who belong to on or off campus organizations may want to hone leadership skills in order to gain more prominence or to boost self-confidence.

Chapter 9

Allaboutself.com

This segment presents a scenario with two options from which students can select. This segment explores pertinent topics in the text and flow sequentially from one to the other. Although only two options are featured in the segment, the situations suggest additional choices, and students should be encouraged to explore all possibilities. The segment is intended as a starting point for discussion of critical issues and concepts.

Segment: Communicating (length: 7:32). Supportive communication is a critical management skill. Its eight characteristics are that it is problem oriented, congruent, descriptive, validating, specific, conjunctive, owned, and marked by supportive listening. The goal of supportive communication is to deliver the message accurately but also to foster and enhance the relationship between the parties who are communicating. Organizations that nurture supportive communication enjoy higher productivity, faster problem solving, higher-quality output, and fewer conflicts.

Coaching and counseling are among the types of employee communication that managers report finding the most difficult to do well. In coaching situations, managers offer advice and information or set standards for subordinates. The focus is on helping the employee to improve his or her ability to do the job. When counseling, managers address problems that stem from attitudes, personality clashes, defensiveness, or other emotionally charged factors. Here the focus is on helping the employee recognize that an attitude problem exists. Managers should be sure they know which type of communication is appropriate for the situation.

In this video segment, Mia must handle a problem with *allaboutself.com's* receptionist, Sarah, whose mediocre performance and disappointing attitude call out for management intervention. Mia can take one of two courses here: she can take Mike's word for it and assume Sarah is at fault, or she can approach Sarah with an open mind and find out why her performance isn't as expected.

Teaching Notes for Discussion Questions.

1. Should Mia follow Mike's advice or take another approach?
   Mike's advice (that Mia tell Sarah to "shape up or ship out") offers equally harsh alternatives that would do little to promote supportive communication between Mia and Sarah. Mia should not take his advice; she should first get Sarah's side of the story and try to find out why her attendance is poor, using all the listening skills at her command.

2. What approach should Mia use in confronting Sarah? What should she say?
   Students' specific ideas will vary, but they should recognize that letting Sarah talk about her feelings and her approach to the job, and finding out why she is not performing up to expectations without creating a hostile confrontation, is an important component of a successful interaction between the two.

3. Is this a coaching problem or a counseling problem? Why?
   This is a coaching situation because (in addition to finding out why Sarah isn't doing well) Mia should be trying to advise her employee about her future with the company and set standards for her job performance, as well as giving her information about how to deal with some of the problems that have arisen within her job.

4. Option 1: What principles of supportive communication are illustrated and/or violated by Mia?

641

Mia's communication violates the principles of being problem oriented (it becomes person oriented), of being validating (she doesn't invite Sarah to present her own ideas about how to do things better), of being conjunctive (Mia gets her own points across without heeding Sarah's), and of being specific (Mia falls back on generalizations).

Option 2: What is right, and wrong, with the way Mia handled this scenario with Sarah in terms of supportive communication?
Mia's communication is problem oriented (she focuses on how to reduce the amount of work Sarah has to handle for others), descriptive (she suggests better ways of handling overbearing colleagues), validating (she adjusts her solution to include Sarah's suggestions), specific (Mia avoids generalizing about Sarah's work), conjunctive (she accepts Sarah's input), and supportive (Mia invites Sarah's input).

5. Option 1 only: What response types are most frequently used by Mia, and by Sarah?
    Both rely on closed, especially deflecting, responses.

6. What is your prediction about the likely outcome of this scenario? Why?
    In scenario 1, the situation will likely not improve and Sarah may even quit her job. In scenario 2, Sarah's attendance and performance are likely to improve and other employees may stop taking advantage of her position, allowing her to feel more positive about the work and the opportunities it may offer her.

7. How might you have handled this scenario differently with Sarah?
    Students' answers will vary. For option 1, they should recognize the errors listed in Question 4. For option 2, there may be few ways to improve on the way Mia handled the situation.

Chapter 10

BusNow: Sytel: A CEO Who Makes Things Happen

"When you hire Sytel, you get the entire company including the CEO," says Jeannette Lee White. White founded Sytel in 1987 after becoming frustrated with the sluggish bureaucracy that bogged down her analytic work at government and nonprofit organizations "Everything was just so slow-paced...I knew that it could be done better and that there was a big market for what I wanted to do." [1] By 1991 she had maxed out 16 credit cards to keep Sytel going. She felt it was more important to protect the company than to protect her own credit rating.

Today this small, agile e-Business solutions firm with a staff of 275 is in a much better position with annual revenues of $40 million in 2002[2]. Sytel's partner list includes industry giants Dell, Compaq, and Oracle. White attributes the company's success to an effective set of internal checks and balances, a short term focus, and the ability to draw top talent who can deliver *fast*.

White is a hands-on leader. She came to America from South Korea as a shy 12 year old girl who wanted to become a nun. But years of helping out at her father's Maryland convenience store helped her develop her outgoing personality and a capacity for hard work. She understands that clients like the U.S. Air force and National Institutes of Health work in an unforgiving environment where there is no allowance for errors. Sytel's history of meeting customer demands with a blend of creativity, accuracy and speed have earned it accolades in both the government and the private sector. Sytel has made the Inc. 500 list several times. In 2,000 White won a national entrepreneur award from Working Woman magazine One of her proudest accomplishments, she feels, is the Web portal designed to help the Air Force improve its mission performance, and to

---

[1] Ellen McCarthy, *Master of Change and Challenge,* washingtonpost.com
[2] www.washingtonpost.com/

provide employees with access to information in just seconds, a task that used to take days or weeks.

In the late 1990's Sytel took 2 years off, but the company's growth slowed down and she reclaimed her position as CEO. Experience has taught her to delegate the technical work to the IT people and concentrate on the big picture. With her eye on the future, Jeannette Lee White is planning to lead Sytel into the wireless technology market and through the changes that lie beyond.

QUESTIONS

1. Would you say Jeannette Lee White has succeeded in creating a culture of trust at Sytel? Explain why or why not.

2. Your text describes e-business leaders as sprinters and leaders in traditional businesses as long-distance runners. Using this analogy, how would you characterize Jeannette Lee White?

3. Which of the cutting-edge approaches to leadership best describes Jeannette Lee White? Explain.

4. As a woman competing in a male dominated sector, do you think Jeannette Lee White's leadership is in any way affected by the gender differences discussed in your text? Support your opinion.

Kinetics U.S.A.
A CEO Who Believes That People Come First

David Melnick, Founder and CEO, Kinetics U.S.A. knows that at the heart of his company's success lies the collective passion of his employees. His Florida-based firm is solidly anchored in the belief that each person needs to feel that they are truly" making a difference." "People need to know that they are not just a 'cog' in the machinery that can be easily replaced," he explains.

Talking to his employees is proof positive that Mr. Melnick's personal blend of integrity and frankness has made Kinetics U.S.A. the dominant provider of self-service terminals for the airline industry. This small organization of 42 dedicated employees counts Continental, Northwest, Alaska, American Trans Air, Delta, American West and Aero Mexico among its clients.[1] In 1988, with his mother-in-law's vote of confidence and the capital to back it up, David Melnick set out to prove that self-service check-in terminals were the wave of the future. Today his company designs and manufactures the hardware and software for airport kiosks throughout the country.

Kinetics U.S.A. enables carriers to embrace what Mr. Melnick calls the "Age of the Consumer." "What consumers want," he says," is control of their own time." People have grown accustomed to the convenience of e-commerce. "Consumers want to make their own reservations and choose their own seats." Kinetics U.S.A.'s latest self- service machines allow travel agents like Orbitz to view all of a customer's ticket arrangements on screen and make any necessary changes electronically. Soon the software will allow consumers to apply unused e-tickets towards future e-tickets or to credit their charge accounts. According to Mr. Melnick, it won't even be necessary to take out your wallet to complete a transaction. The latest machines will become part of a "trusted traveler" program helping frequent flyers and employees to move faster through airport

---

[1] www.kiosk.com/

security. To enroll, members will have their identities certified by the government. A fingerprint will be stored in a database, enabling a passenger to simply touch the monitor for "instant recognition." [2]

Everyone, from the production technicians responsible for putting on logo stickers to the engineers designing the software, is excited to be a part of bringing this innovative technology to the public. No one on the team feels left out of the process, thanks to a job enrichment program that allows employees to learn various jobs within the company. "Although a person may start out soldering all day," says Kerry Myers, Director of Production and Field Services," ultimately they will be testing units, doing final assembly, trouble-shooting, and going out in the field to gauge customer response to the machines. At Kinetics U.S.A., "the moon is the limit in terms of career advancement, "he affirms.

The group benefits from Mr. Melnick's policy of giving employees a surprise day off, or a vacation package, or a day of roller coaster riding to let off steam. A massage therapist visits the facility once a week, and when frustrations are running high, a spirited game of foosball always helps.

But "fun" is only part of the picture. Mr. Melnick believes in "brutal honesty." He encourages all employees to speak out. "People have categorical permission (without regard to the organizational command structure) to call someone else an idiot as long as they have the facts to back that statement up," he asserts.

Under Mr. Melnick's leadership, the staff has become close. After the terrorist attacks of September 11th, they found themselves confronted by a crisis in the travel industry. Facing an uncertain future, Mr. Melnick brought everyone together for a prayer vigil. He was open about corporate finances and job cuts. "He did everything in his power to keep the business in tact," says, Pat George, Field Services Coordinator. "He comforted us". The war in Iraq has once again disrupted air travel, and along with it, Kinetics U.S.A.'s prospective plans.

---

[2] Ibid.

As you listen to Mr. Melnick's forthright observations about his workforce and hear his staff's testament to his leadership, it might be useful to bear in mind the following statement made by the founders of *Fast Company* magazine:" It has always been true that leaders not only have to make decisions, but, even more important they also have to make sense of a complex, confusing, fast-changing world…They generate confidence and build momentum. In other words, leaders do the hard work that creates the conditions for growth."[3]

QUESTIONS

1. Which of the following leader behaviors does David Melnick exhibit: transactional, transformational, or the Level 5 Leadership Style? Explain.

2. David Melnick has shared some of his methods for motivating employees. What are some additional "rewards" you would suggest he use in order to keep morale and production high during stressful times

3. Discuss how informal communications are fostered at Kinetics U.S.A.

4. What leadership style would you use to pull the company through the latest crisis in the aviation industry: the war in Iraq? Choose a style that reflects your own qualities and beliefs. Remember, you do not have to be like David Melnick to be an effective leader.

---

[3] *Fast Company,* April 2003, p. 12

 **Video Guide**

Kinetics U.S.A.

Case Overview

Mr. Melnick's personal blend of integrity and frankness has made Kinetics U.S.A. the dominant provider of self-service terminals for the airline industry. This small organization of 42 dedicated employees counts Continental, Northwest , Alaska, American Trans Air, Delta, American West and Aero Mexico among its clients.[4] In 1988, with his mother-in-law's vote of confidence and the capital to back it up, David Melnick set out to prove that self service check-in terminals were the wave of the future. Today his company designs and manufactures the hardware and software for airport kiosks throughout the country.

Everyone at the Florida-based firm, from the production technicians responsible for putting on logo stickers to the engineers designing the software, benefits from a job enrichment program. The program allows employees to learn various jobs within the company. Mr. Melnick has a policy of giving employees a surprise day off, or a vacation package, or a day of roller coaster riding to let off steam. But "fun" is only part of the picture. Mr. Melnick believes in "brutal honesty." All employees have categorical permission to speak out on any issues they may have at any time.

Facing an uncertain future, after the terrorist attacks of September 11th, Mr. Melnick brought everyone together for a prayer vigil. He was open about corporate finances and job cuts. He did everything in his power to keep the business in tact. The challenge ahead lies in weathering the disruption caused by the war in Iraq.

Questions for Discussion:

---

[4] www.kiosk.com/

1. Which of the following leader behaviors does David Melnick exhibit: transactional, transformational, or the Level 5 Leadership Style? Explain.

Class opinion may be divided. He can be seen as a transformational leader. In the eyes of his employees he is charismatic, inspirational, considerate, and stimulating. He clearly displays the following transformational behaviors: articulates a clear and appealing vision, explains how to attain that vision, acts confident and optimistic, expresses confidence in followers, provides opportunities for early successes, celebrates successes, leads by example and empowers his workers. It could also be argued, however, that he displays Level 5 leadership, based on the personal humility and professional will he demonstrates in the video. Differences in perception may vary according to age and work experience.

2. David Melnick has shared some of his methods for motivating employees. What are some additional "rewards" you would suggest he use in order to keep morale and production high during stressful times?

Job enrichment , massages, roller coaster rides, vacations, and foosball are keeping employees at Kinetics U.S.A. motivated right now, but given the fluctuations inherent today's economy, some people might prefer more "individualized" rewards. College or in-house educational programs would serve as an excellent reinforcement for job enrichment. Bonuses, skill based pay, and merit raises might mean more to employees in the long run than the "fun" perks already in place.

3. Discuss how informal communications are fostered at Kinetics U.S.A.

A small staff of 42 makes informal communications much easier than in a larger corporation. However, it is David Melnick's honest, open leadership style that sets the tone for free flowing communication among everyone in the company. He encourages "brutal honesty," and asks everyone to voice any issues they might have without fear of reprisal. Regardless of professional status, every employee's opinion is given equal weight. At Kinetics U.SA., workers have many opportunities to gather and talk informally; including at the foosball table and at the amusement park. There is a great deal of teaching and learning going on as people are given the opportunity to better themselves. One has the feeling that information is being exchanged intensely at all times; both in the field and in the office. David Melnick and his employees clearly know one another well. David Melnick's excellent listening skills and this ability to convey to people what he expects of them, have contributed to the closeness of this group. As a result they are united in their belief in themselves, in one another, and in their product.

4. What leadership style would you use to pull the company through the latest crisis in the aviation industry: the war in Iraq? Choose a style that reflects your own qualities and beliefs. Remember, you do not have to be like David Melnick to be an effective leader.

Students may refer to any of the leader behaviors or situational leadership theories presented in Chapter 10 of the text. However, answers should be indicative of an honest and accurate self appraisal.

Chapter 11

Bertelsman
RECRUITMENT AND PLACEMENT

TEACHING NOTES FOR DISCUSSION QUESTIONS

1.   Do you agree with Cheryl Brie that Sylvie Aronson is "looking to place blame" on the HR department? If you do agree, how would you have reacted to Sylvie's accusations? If you do not agree with Cheryl Brie, explain why you feel Sylvie is justified in her view of the HR department's role in this instance.

Regardless of whether students agree or disagree, their answers should stress that hiring the right person for the job is a partnership between HR and line management. There should have been more of an ongoing dialogue between HR and the Music Placement Department.

2.   Describe the steps that Bertelsman BMG would need to take in order to rewrite the job specifications for this opening. Why might this be useful to you as an HR manager? If you feel it would not be useful, explain why.

If one takes the view that HR failed to recruit according to the department's criteria, it might be worth asking Sylvie and her supervisors to fine tune the job specifications. This would entail analyzing and listing the human traits and experience needed to do this job well. Some students might feel that the real issue here is that Sylvie wants to find a way to get the new employee out of her department, without taking responsibility for the error in judgment made in hiring him. In this case, a new job specification would not be helpful.

3.   Do you think running an ad in Rolling Stone Magazines was a wise choice for drawing outside candidate to fill the position that Sylvie had open in her department? What are some other sources they could have used to attract qualified people? When considering alternatives, remember that you have a limited budget.

Students who are particularly knowledgeable about the music industry might have some interesting ideas to consider. While Rolling Stone Magazine was certainly an appropriate source, The Village Voice, Spin, internal job posting, employee referrals, networking, and on-line ads might have drawn a better pool of applicants.

4. *What type of an interview do you feel would be best suited to this dynamic Music Placement department? Why?*

Students may choose to use an unstructured interview, a structured interview, a situational interview, a job-related interview, or a panel interview. The goal of the interview should be to evaluate whether the applicant's past experience and personality are a fit for BMG. It sounds like this department needs a self-motivated go-getter with fresh ideas and lots of contacts in the business. It would probably be a good idea to do a thorough reference check for this position.

5. *Paul Fiolek's conversation revealed a great deal about the formal structure of Bertelsman BMG's HR department. Bertelsman is a giant in the music and entertainment industry. Analyze how this might have both a positive and a negative influence on hiring practices.*

Bertelsman has a formal HR structure, with well-defined areas of responsibility for recruiting, selection and placement. In theory, this stratified arrangement works well to eliminate the risk of error, but only if communication is effective. Clearly the very complex needs of managing HR in a company that is growing in many directions at once may make it impossible for HR to maintain a close relationship with each department manager. This lack of contact may have a negative impact on the efficacy of the hiring process.

6.   **OPTIONAL**

Taking into account, the comments you have just heard on SPOTLIGHT and the information in your text, how do you think online recruiting might impact on your own job search after graduation?

Students' answers will differ according to their own job search experiences and aspirations. They should mention that the downside of limiting themselves to on-line searching is that companies are often flooded with resumes. It is easier to differentiate yourself from the crowd in person than on-line.

Chapter 12

Corporate Coaching International

1. *What techniques of effective group behavior does Frankel use herself, and which does she advocate for the group? How will participants try to change their behavior as a result?* Lois Frankel uses good communication skills and good listening skills. She acts as a facilitator, of course, and she is careful to treat everyone in the group in the same way regardless of their position in the organization. She advocates the same techniques for the group as well as constructive (functional) conflict and problem solving, leadership, group maintenance and mutual encouragement, gate-keeping, and the establishment of clear roles. Her hope for changed behavior, as she expresses it herself, is that the group will learn how to create an action plan for future tasks.

2. *Do you think the group's body language conveys the same message as their words? If not, point out inconsistencies.* Allowing for their occasional self-consciousness, the members of the group seem generally consistent in their spoken language and body language.

3. *Is there a group leader (not Lois Frankel)? Who is it, and what is the basis of his or her leadership?* Various members play leadership roles at different points in the session. Sometimes these are formal, such as when individuals act as facilitators or recorders for discussions, and sometimes they are informal, such as when individuals direct group discussion by being particularly vocal or emphatic.

4. *Can you discern any conflict within the group? What kind of conflict do you think it is—task, relationship, process? Do you think it can be turned into functional conflict? If so, how?* Most of the conflict within the group appears to be task conflict. Some of this is apparent in group discussions and some is generated by the nature of the group assignments members are given, such as the desert survival and boat-drawing exercises. There are some references to process or perhaps relationship conflicts in the past that appear to have been resolved. The type of task conflict shown in the video appears to be capable of being turned into functional conflict as the group completes its assignments.

Chapter 13

SAS Institute

1. *How would you characterize SAS Institute's span of control and its degree of centralization? How do you think these aspects of its organizational structure help account for its employee-friendly environment?* SAS has a wide span of control and a low degree of centralization. These give employees much greater access to management and to the decision-making process, both of which would tend to make employees satisfied who are comfortable with a high degree of independence and accountability.

2. *What can you conclude about the physical design of SAS's work spaces? How do they balance the needs for privacy and interaction? Do you think the physical environment of SAS contributes to its employees' productivity? Why or why not?* Employees' privacy is enhanced by their having individual offices and the freedom to light and decorate their own spaces. The resulting quiet, freedom from interruptions, and sense of ownership contribute to productivity and creativity. The prevailing sense of camaraderie helps employees interact.

3. *Contrast SAS Institute's 35-hour workweek with some of the work schedule options employed at other firms, such as flextime, compressed workwee, job sharing, and telecommuting. Why do you think SAS chose a traditional work schedule for the vast majority of its employees? How do you think the expansion of other options would change its culture?* Maintaining a standard workweek ensures that employees can consult and collaborate with each other easily during real time and reinforces the company's expressed value of "sanity" and the importance of having a "whole life" in which everyone is free to go home at 5 PM. Employees in turn are willing to put in extra hours when needed, because overtime is not the norm. The addition of other work-hour options might change the culture, perhaps by reducing camaraderie or accountability or by encouraging people to put in longer but less productive hours. Undue stress on the *appearance* of hard work, in the form of routinely long days, and a decrease in the quality of employees' home lives might also result from such a change in policy and culture.

4. *Managers at SAS not only oversee the work; they also do it. How do you think this management style influences the firm's distinctive culture? Do you think it makes for effective controls? Why or why not?* Managers who work as well as manage contribute to the we're-all-in-this-together culture at SAS and reflect another practical aspect of the firm's wide spans of control. The practice can make for effective controls in that thc managers truly know and understand the work they are controlling; if, however, they are working under their own performance deadlines and pressure, they might be less able to successfully control others.

   How do you think SAS's management prevents employees from taking advantage of the freedom it gives them? One reason is that employees are selected partly on the basis of whether they are comfortable with freedom and its accompanying responsibility. Another is that the level of accountability is very high. As expressed in the video, an employee who is out sick for several days, even for months, merits the care and concern of his or her manager and colleagues. An employee who is out sick for several Mondays in a row will simply be fired.

CHAPTER 14

CATERING TO SERIOUS USERS - PATAGONIA

Learning Objectives

The purpose of this video is to help you

1. recognize the ethical challenges facing many businesses today
2. understand the ways in which firms can act responsibly
3. grasp the relationship between ethics and quality

Background Information

Yvon Chouinard founded Patagonia over 20 years ago, making climbing gear by hand for his friends. Today the company makes clothing for a wide variety of activities with a focus on function, durability, and innovation. Its rigorously field-tested products are available worldwide, and it has offices in North America, Europe, and Japan, with headquarters in Ventura, California where it all began. In addition to its commitment to customers, "serious users who rely on the product in extreme conditions," the firm is also responsible to its employees, providing a family-friendly workplace, and to the environment, donating millions of dollars to grass-roots environmentalist groups in the United States and abroad.

The Video

The video segment describes the founding of Patagonia and its commitment to high-quality products. It also details the company's recent struggle to maintain financial success without the runaway growth that its managers believe would be damaging to the natural environment. You will see how the firm balances slow growth with its efforts to reduce the impact its business processes have on the environment.

Discussion Questions

1. In what ways does Patagonia demonstrate its ethical commitment to its employees?

   The firm has a relaxed corporate culture and worker-friendly policies such as on-site day care and cafeterias that serve organic food. It has also developed a socially responsible culture that employees can relate to.

2. What is the relationship between ethics and quality?

   At Patagonia, good design, rigorous field testing, and the responsible use of natural resources result in reliable products that demonstrate a responsible commitment to customers and to the environment in which those customers live.

3. How would you reconcile Patagonia's highly developed sense of social responsibility with its decision to lay off 20 percent of its workforce?

   Patagonia chose what it considered the alternative least harmful to the natural environment in order to slow growth that it saw as unnecessarily wasteful of resources.

Follow-up Assignment

Choose a company in the service sector that claims it is socially responsible. What are some of the ways in which this firm treats its employees, its customers, its investors, and the environment that prove (or disprove) the company's stated ethical objectives?

For Further Exploration

Visit the website of Patagonia (www.patagonia.com) and explore the page called "About Us." Of special interest are the articles under "Selected Essays," in which various writers and employees—and founder Yvon Chouinard—talk about the company's history and philosophy. Read Chouinard's essay ("Patagonia: The Next 100 Years") and scan two or three of the others. Do all the articles express a consistent viewpoint about the company's mission? Put that philosophy in your own words. Do you think it is a sustainable business strategy? Why or why not?

Chapter 15

Managing the Human Side of the Business: Park Place Entertainment

Learning Objectives

The purpose of this video is to help you:

1. Recognize how human resource management contributes to organizational performance.
2. Understand how and why HR managers make plans and decisions about staffing.
3. Identify some of the ways in which HR managers handle staff evaluation and development.

Synopsis

Park Place Entertainment owns and operates many resorts and casinos around the world. Its human resources department is responsible for hiring, training, and managing a diverse group of more than 52,000 employees. HR managers have created specific job descriptions for each position, instituted training programs for employee and management development, and established incentive programs to reward good performance. Park Place's 360-degree evaluation method allows supervisors to get performance feedback from the employees they supervise. Because its customers come from many countries and speak many languages, the company seeks out employees from diverse backgrounds, varying the recruitment process for different properties in different areas.

Discussion Questions

1. *For analysis:* What are the advantages and disadvantages of centralizing the recruiting process at a company such as Park Place Entertainment?

Students should be able to cite a number of advantages and disadvantages. For example, centralization would enable the company to manage recruiting activities such as advertising open jobs and screening résumés in an efficient manner, avoiding duplication of resources and actions in different locations. Another advantage is the ability to consider candidates for jobs at more than one property in the area, rather than going through the selection process one property at a time. A disadvantage is that centralization is likely to make recruiting more time-consuming because each property will have to submit its open positions to headquarters and then wait for résumés to be screened. A second disadvantage is that each property's managers will see only the résumés that have been screened and forwarded for a particular open position; therefore, they will not know whether any of the other applicants are qualified for other jobs.

2. *For analysis:* Why did Park Place begin the restructuring of its HR department by standardizing training for supervisors?

According to the video, Park Place realized that good supervisor training was the key to avoiding major employee problems. Properly trained supervisors are better equipped to manage their employees and provide the guidance and knowledge needed to support good performance.

3. *For application:* What steps might Park Place's HR executives take to reduce turnover among the employees at particular resorts?

Students may offer a variety of suggestions. For example, they may suggest more emphasis on promotion from within and employee development programs that groom employees for more responsible jobs within the firm. They may also suggest offering special recognition or incentives to encourage employee retention and periodic internal surveys to learn about issues that contribute to turnover. Ask students to consider the probable roots of high turnover when they respond to this question.

4. *For application:* How might Park Place encourage its employees to refer friends as candidates for open positions?

This is an opportunity for students to be creative. Two sample ideas are (1) offering a cash bonus to employees who refer friends who are subsequently hired and remain on the job for at least three months and (2) inviting employees to bring friends to internal job fairs where they can learn about open positions while enjoying a taste of the resort's or casino's hospitality.

5. *For debate:* Rather than hiring employees when business booms and then laying some off when business falls off, should Park Place temporarily rehire some of its retired supervisors and employees during peak periods? Support your chosen position.

Students who agree with the idea of rehiring retirees may say that those employees and supervisors are already trained and familiar with the company and its customers. Thus, they can be more productive more quickly than new hires. Also, retirees may be willing to work for brief periods as temporary help. Students who disagree may say that the company may have insufficient retirees to handle the work during peak periods. They may also note that because these temporary workers are retired, they may be less flexible about the hours or positions they are willing to work, and they may require a different approach to management and motivation compared to the regular workforce.

Online Exploration

Visit the Park Place Entertainment website at <www.ballys.com> and browse the home page to see the locations and names of the company's resorts and casinos. Then follow the company information link to look at career opportunities and company benefits. What kinds of jobs are being featured on the website? Why would Park Place arrange jobs by region? How does the firm make it convenient for applicants to submit résumés online? Why would Park Place put so much emphasis on Internet recruiting?

The jobs featured on Park Place's website change from time to time, but often include security staff, cashiers, and other positions that are needed for all shifts and all locations. Park Place arranges jobs by region knowing that many applicants will seek out jobs in their local area or in an area where they would like to relocate. The company invites applicants to submit their résumés online, expediting the application process. Park Place emphasizes Internet recruiting because of its low cost and broad geographic reach. Students may suggest other reasons, as well.

CHAPTER 15

CHANNELING HUMAN RESOURCES: SHOWTIME

Learning Objectives

The purpose of this video is to help you

1. identify the many ways in which human resource managers can actively develop employees
2. appreciate the role of mentoring in employee development
3. understand how a performance appraisal system can be designed and administered

Background Information

Showtime Networks Inc. (SNI) is a wholly owned subsidiary of Viacom Inc., a giant media conglomerate, and operates the premium television networks Showtime, The Movie Channel (TMC), Flix, and Showtime Event Television. It also operates the premium network Sundance Channel, a joint venture with Robert Redford and PolyGram Filmed Entertainment. One of the biggest challenges at SNI, as anywhere, is attracting, retaining, and motivating a committed workforce. Demographic changes, work and family issues, and increasing diversities of age, race, and lifestyle call forth the dedication and creativity of its human resource staff.

The Video

This segment introduces various Showtime executives who discuss the company's human resource policies and challenges. The firm is a leader in creating a broad training and career development program that serves many different kinds of employee needs. It also uses a performance appraisal system that employees have helped design and has a formal program for encouraging mentoring.

Discussion Questions

1. Among the organizational changes recently made at Showtime are the combining of the legal and the human resource departments, and the appointment of one particular human resource manager to each SNI division. Comment on the advantages or disadvantages of these changes.

   The advantage of having the legal department so closely aligned with HRM is the opportunity for specialists in each area to use each others' expertise in resolving employee questions or problems correctly. A possible disadvantage is that it might take longer to reach a conclusion if more people are involved. The advantages of dedicating one specific HRM manager to each division are the chance for the HRM person to become more familiar with the HRM issues specific to that department and for the employees to have a single place to go for answers. One possible disadvantage is the chance for a bottleneck to occur when one person is responsible for too many employees.

2. How good a job do you think Showtime is doing of offering its employees chances to develop and improve their skills? Can you suggest additional programs it could undertake to achieve this goal?

   It appears the company is doing a good job of offering course and programs that allow employees to grow. Suggestions for additional options will vary.

3. Do you think the performance appraisal system at Showtime is an effective one? Why or why not?

The system appears to offer plenty of feedback at frequent intervals and to use employees' input in establishing their individual goals.

Follow-up Assignment

Consider a small business such as a restaurant or consulting firm. What particular human resource challenges does this firm face in acknowledging diversity and planning career development programs? Sketch a plan for overcoming these obstacles, making your recommendations as specific as you can. Include the benefits the business will enjoy from diversity and career development.

For Further Exploration

Visit the website of the Occupational Safety and Health Administration (www.osha.gov) and use the "News Room" or the search function to research the current status of OSHA initiatives on either indoor air pollution, asbestos removal, or workplace violence. Where does OSHA stand on this issue, and what action, if any, is it planning in the future?

Chapter 16

Organizational Change
Video summary

Change is one of the challenges every manager can count on facing, as the employees and managers of Student Advantage attest in this video segment. Acquisition has been one of Student Advantage's most successful growth strategies, and the company's managers recognize the potential for corporate cultures to collide instead of meshing in the course of this kind of change. They discuss several strategies they have used to avoid conflict between cultures and other aspects of change that, for this firm, has so far been mostly top down.

Teaching notes for discussion questions

1. Do you think Student Advantage's reliance on teamwork would help managers' efforts to implement change within the firm? Why or why not? What can a company do to ensure that teams promote needed change instead of resisting?

   Students' opinions may vary but it seems likely that teamwork would be an asset to change in this firm because employees are motivated to achieve group goals. Lowering group resistance to change requires ensuring that group norms are not unnecessarily threatened, that cohesiveness does not lead to groupthink, and that groups are not permitted to fall back on escalation of commitment when change is called for.

2. Can you recall any instance in which you witnessed or experienced conflict during a period of change in an organization? What do you think was the reason for the conflict, and how was it resolved?

   Responses will vary according to the situation. Students' experiences might point up the differences between evolutionary and revolution change, or between top-down and bottom-up change.

3. What are some of the potential sources of external change for a firm like Student Advantage? How can an organization be forewarned about these kinds of changes?

   External change can come from any factor of the external environment including economic, political, legal, competitive, demographic, social, and ethical forces. An organization is best forewarned by maintaining a constant watch on the forces most likely to affect its operation.

4. How does a service firm like Student Advantage control quality during periods of change? What elements of total quality management (TQM) apply to service firms?

   The principles of TQM apply equally to manufacturing and service firms and focus on taking continuous incremental steps toward higher performance, with all the organization's functions cooperating to improve quality. Students should mention at least several specific TQM principles such as creating constancy of purpose toward improvement, replacing reliance on inspection with programs to build quality in from the beginning, minimizing total cost, elevating training and leadership, eliminating fear and barriers to communication, decentralizing decision making, and empowering workers by placing management in the role of facilitator rather than supervisor.

5. Why would a firm's managers resist certain changes imposed from outside the organization? List as many sources of such change as you can and the reasons you think an on organization would oppose them.

An organization might resist political and legal changes it felt would be detrimental to its business, such as surcharges, use taxes, tariffs, quotas, embargoes, pollution controls, hiring quotas, safety regulations, antitrust laws, price ceilings and other kinds of restrictions. It might also resist changes that appear to be illegal or unethical, such as price fixing schemes, the payment of bribes, or the user of insider information for financial gain. Firms have also resisted unionization, minimum wages, and various work-life benefits such as family leave. Students will undoubtedly suggest additional examples.